MW01702157

Spreadsheet Modeling & Decision Analysis

FOURTH EDITION

A Practical Introduction to Management Science

Cliff T. Ragsdale

Virginia Polytechnic Institute
and State University

THOMSON
SOUTH-WESTERN

Australia · Canada · Mexico · Singapore · Spain · United Kingdom · United States

THOMSON
SOUTH-WESTERN

Spreadsheet Modeling & Decision Analysis: A Practical Introduction to Management Science, 4e
Cliff T. Ragsdale

Editor-in-Chief:
George Werthman

Senior Acquisitions Editor:
Charles McCormick, Jr.

Senior Developmental Editor:
Alice Denny

Marketing Manager:
Larry Qualls

Production Editor:
Chris Hudson

Manufacturing Coordinator:
Diane Lohman

Media Developmental Editor:
Christine Wittmer

Media Production Editor:
Amy Wilson

Compositor:
settingPace

Printer:
R.R. Donnelley
Willard, Ohio

Design Project Manager
Chris Miller

Internal Design:
Carolyn Deacy Design
San Francisco

Cover Design:
Chris Miller

Cover Photography:
Getty Images

Printed in the United States of America
3 4 5 06 05

For more information contact South-Western, 5191 Natorp Boulevard, Mason, Ohio 45040.
Or you can visit our Internet site at: http://www.swlearning.com

Library of Congress Control Number:
2003103568

ISBN: 0-324-18399-2
0-324-18400-X (text only)
0-324-18401-8 (student CD)
0-324-20253-9 (Microsoft Project CD)
0-324-20305-5 (International Student Edition)
0-324-20408-6 (ISE text only)

Preface

Spreadsheets are now one of the most popular and ubiquitous software packages on the planet. Every day, millions of business people use spreadsheet programs to build models of the decision problems they face as a regular part of their work activities. As a result, employers look for experience and ability with spreadsheets in the people they recruit. Perhaps this is part of the reason why the *Chronicle of Higher Education* recently listed Microsoft® Office as the #1 selling software product in university bookstores in September of 2002.

Spreadsheets have also become the standard vehicle for introducing undergraduate and graduate students in business and engineering to the concepts and tools covered in the introductory Management Science/Operations Research (MS/OR) course. This simultaneously develops students' skills with a standard tool of today's business world and opens their eyes to how a variety of MS/OR techniques can be used in this modeling environment. Spreadsheets also capture students' interest and add a new relevance to MS/OR as they see how it can be applied with popular commercial software being used in the business world.

Spreadsheet Modeling & Decision Analysis provides an introduction to the most commonly used MS/OR techniques and shows how these tools can be implemented using Microsoft® Excel. Prior experience with Excel is certainly helpful, but is not a requirement for using this text. In general, a student familiar with computers and the spreadsheet concepts presented in most introductory computer courses should have no trouble using this text. Step-by-step instructions and screen shots are provided for each example, and software tips are included throughout the text as needed.

WHAT'S NEW IN THE FOURTH EDITION?

The primary message we received from reviewers for the new edition of this book was clear: Don't mess up a good thing. As a result, our work on the fourth edition of *Spreadsheet Modeling & Decision Analysis* could be characterized as a "tune-up" rather than a "major overhaul." In general, we have tried to take what worked well in the past and make it better. Specific changes include:

- New coverage of anchoring and framing effects in decision making (Chapter 1).
- Expanded discussion of generalized network flow models (Chapter 5).
- New Premium Solver for Education v5.0 including the "alldifferent" option for variable cells (Chapter 8).
- New spreadsheets for time series analysis showing how forecasts are calculated (Chapter 11).
- An innovative, simplified technique for implementing project management networks (Chapter 14) that automatically adjust to changes in precedence relationships and activity times.
- New coverage of Microsoft® Project 2002 (Chapter 14).
- New coverage of radar charts for multiple criteria decision problems (Chapter 15).
- Numerous new cases and end-of-chapter problems throughout.

INNOVATIVE FEATURES

Aside from its strong spreadsheet orientation, the fourth edition of *Spreadsheet Modeling & Decision Analysis* contains a number of other unique features that distinguish it from traditional MS/OR texts.

- Algebraic formulations and spreadsheets are used side-by-side to help develop conceptual thinking skills.
- Step-by-step instructions and numerous annotated screen shots make examples easy to follow and understand.
- Emphasis is placed on model formulation and interpretation rather than algorithms.
- Realistic examples motivate the discussion of each topic.
- Solutions to example problems are analyzed from a managerial perspective.
- Spreadsheet files for all the examples are provided on a CD bundled with the text.
- A unique and accessible chapter covering discriminant analysis is provided (Chapter 10).
- Sections entitled "The World of Management Science" show how each topic has been applied in a real company.
- Excel add-ins and templates are provided to support: decision trees, sensitivity analysis, discriminant analysis, queuing, forecasting, simulation, and project management.

ORGANIZATION

The table of contents for *Spreadsheet Modeling & Decision Analysis* is laid out in a fairly traditional format, but topics may be covered in a variety of ways. The text begins with an overview of MS/OR in chapter 1. After completing chapter 1, a quick refresher on spreadsheet fundamentals (entering and copying formulas, basic formatting and editing, etc.) is always a good idea. Suggestions for the Excel review may be found at the textbook's website, http://ragsdale.swlearning.com.

- Chapters 2 through 8 cover various topics in deterministic modeling techniques: linear programming, sensitivity analysis, networks, integer programming, goal programming and multiple objective optimization, and nonlinear and evolutionary programming.
- Chapters 9 through 11 cover predictive modeling and forecasting techniques: regression analysis, discriminant analysis, and time series analysis.
- Chapters 12 and 13 cover stochastic modeling techniques: simulation (using Crystal Ball) and queuing theory. Updated coverage of simulation using the inherent capabilities of Excel alone, or with the @Risk add-in is available on the textbook's website.
- Chapters 14 and 15 cover project management and decision theory, respectively.

Following chapter 1, an instructor could cover the material on optimization, forecasting, or simulation depending on his or her personal preferences. The chapters on queuing and project management make general references to simulation and, therefore, should follow the discussion of that topic.

ANCILLARY MATERIALS

New copies of the textbook include two CD-ROMs. One CD includes Premium Solver™ for Education v5.0, a 140-day version of Crystal Ball® Professional 2000.5.2, several other add-ins, and data files for examples, cases, and problems within the text. The other CD provides a 120-day Trial Edition of Microsoft® Project 2002.

Several excellent ancillaries for the instructor accompany the new edition of *Spreadsheet Modeling & Decision Analysis.* Instructors who adopt the text for their classes may call the Thomson Learning Academic Resource Center at 1-800-423-0563 to request the Instructor's Resource CD-ROM (ISBN: 0-324-18402-6). Included in this convenient format are:

- **Instructor's Manual.** The Instructor's Manual, prepared by Cliff Ragsdale, contains solutions to all the text problems and cases.
- **Test Bank.** The Test Bank, prepared by Raymond Hill of Wright State University, includes multiple choice, true/false, and short answer problems for each text chapter. It also includes small projects that may be assigned as take-home assignments. The Test Bank is included as Word files and also comes in ExamView™ software format that allows instructors to use or modify the questions as well as create original questions.
- **PowerPoint Presentation Slides.** PowerPoint presentations, prepared by Cliff Ragsdale, provide ready-made lecture material for each chapter in the book.

ACKNOWLEDGMENTS

I would like to thank the following reviewers who made important contributions to the development of this fourth edition:

David W. Ashley, University of Missouri–Kansas City
James J. Cochran, Louisiana Tech University
Charles H. Davis IV, Southwest Texas State University
Deborah Hanson, University of Great Falls
Raymond R Hill, Air Force Institute of Technology
Richard A. Lewallen, Lincoln Memorial University
Bruce Murphy, Mercyhurst College
Steven Nahmias, Santa Clara University
Alan Olinsky, Bryant College
Susan W. Palocsay, James Madison University
Javier Pena, Carnegie Mellon University
Gary Reeves, University of South Carolina
Octavio Richetta, University of Massachusetts, Boston
Bryan Schurle, Kansas State University
Peter Shenkin, CUNY–John Jay College of Criminal Justice
Andrew W. Shogan, University of California, Berkeley
Pete Soule, Park University
Peter Wibawa Sutanto, Prairie View A&M University
Bijan Vasigh, Embry-Riddle University
Jack Yurkiewicz, Pace University

David Ashley also provided many of the summary articles found in "The World of Management Science" feature throughout the text and created the queuing template used in chapter 14. Mike Middleton, University of San Francisco, once again provided the TreePlan decision tree add-in found in chapter 16. Jack Yurkiewicz, Pace University, contributed several of the cases found throughout the text.

I would like to extend a special word of thanks to Rasmus Rasmussen of Molde College in Norway and Steven Sacks at the University of Connecticut for continuing to provide many valuable comments and suggestions about this book. I also extend my gratitude to Decisioneering, Inc. (http://www.crystalball.com) for providing the Crystal Ball software that accompanies this book and to Dan Fylstra and the crew at Frontline Systems (http://www.solver.com) for bringing the power of optimization to the world of spreadsheets. I also thank the wonderful SMDA team at South-Western College Publishing: Charles McCormick, Senior Acquisitions Editor; Alice Denny, Senior Developmental Editor; Larry Qualls, Marketing Manager; and Chris Hudson, Production Editor.

Once again, I would like to thank my dear wife, Kathy, for her continued patience, support, encouragement, and love throughout this project. This book is dedicated to our sons, Thomas, Patrick, and Daniel. I am still so glad that God let me be your daddy.

FINAL THOUGHTS

I hope you enjoy the spreadsheet approach to teaching MS/OR as much as I do and that you find this book to be very interesting and helpful. If you find creative ways to use the techniques in this book and/or need help applying them, please let me hear from you. Also, any comments, questions, suggestions, or constructive criticism you have concerning this text are always welcome.

Cliff T. Ragsdale
email: crags@vt.edu

Brief Contents

1 Introduction to Modeling and Decision Analysis 1

2 Introduction to Optimization and Linear Programming 17

3 Modeling and Solving LP Problems in a Spreadsheet 45

4 Sensitivity Analysis and the Simplex Method 143

5 Network Modeling 185

6 Integer Linear Programming 244

7 Goal Programming and Multiple Objective Optimization 313

8 Nonlinear Programming and Evolutionary Optimization 354

9 Regression Analysis 429

10 Discriminant Analysis 485

11 Time Series Forecasting 515

12 Introduction to Simulation Using Crystal Ball 595

13 Queuing Theory 668

14 Project Management 703

15 Decision Analysis 754

Index 833

Contents

1. Introduction to Modeling and Decision Analysis 1

Introduction 1

The Modeling Approach to Decision Making 2

Characteristics and Benefits of Modeling 4

Mathematical Models 5

Categories of Mathematical Models 7

The Problem-Solving Process 8

Anchoring and Framing Effects 11

Good Decisions vs. Good Outcomes 12

Summary 13

References 13

The World of Management Science 14

Questions and Problems 16

2. Introduction to Optimization and Linear Programming 17

Introduction 17

Applications of Mathematical Optimization 18

Characteristics of Optimization Problems 18

Expressing Optimization Problems Mathematically 19
Decisions 19 Constraints 20 Objective 20

Mathematical Programming Techniques 21

An Example LP Problem 21

Formulating LP Models 22
Steps in Formulating an LP Model 22

Summary of the LP Model for the Example Problem 23

The General Form of an LP Model 24

Solving LP Problems: An Intuitive Approach 25

Solving LP Problems: A Graphical Approach 26
Plotting the First Constraint 26 Plotting the Second Constraint 27 Plotting the Third Constraint 29 The Feasible Region 30 Plotting the Objective Function 30 Finding the Optimal Solution Using Level Curves 32 Finding the Optimal Solution by Enumerating the Corner Points 33 Summary of Graphical Solution to LP Problems 33

Special Conditions in LP Models 34
Alternate Optimal Solutions 35 Redundant Constraints 35 Unbounded Solutions 37 Infeasibility 39

Summary 40

References 40

Questions and Problems 41

3. Modeling and Solving LP Problems in a Spreadsheet 45

Introduction 45

Spreadsheet Solvers 46

Solving LP Problems in a Spreadsheet 46

The Steps in Implementing an LP Model in a Spreadsheet 47

A Spreadsheet Model for the Blue Ridge Hot Tubs Problem 48
Organizing the Data 48 Representing the Decision Variables 49 Representing the Objective Function 49 Representing the Constraints 50 Representing the Bounds on the Decision Variables 51

How Solver Views the Model 52

Using Solver 54
Defining the Set (or Target) Cell 56 Defining the Variable Cells 57 Defining the Constraint Cells 58 Defining the Nonnegativity Conditions 59 Reviewing the Model 60 Options 60 Solving the Model 60

Goals and Guidelines for Spreadsheet Design 62

Make vs. Buy Decisions 64
Defining the Decision Variables 65 Defining the Objective Function 65 Defining the Constraints 66 Implementing the Model 66 Solving the Model 68 Analyzing the Solution 68

An Investment Problem 69
Defining the Decision Variables 70 Defining the Objective Function 71 Defining the Constraints 71 Implementing the Model 71 Solving the Model 73 Analyzing the Solution 74

A Transportation Problem 74
Defining the Decision Variables 75 Defining the Objective Function 76 Defining the Constraints 76 Implementing the Model 77 Heuristic Solution for the Model 79 Solving the Model 80 Analyzing the Solution 80

A Blending Problem 81
Defining the Decision Variables 82 Defining the Objective Function 82 Defining the Constraints 82 Some Observations About Constraints, Reporting, and Scaling 83 Rescaling the Model 84 Implementing the Model 85 Solving the Model 87 Analyzing the Solution 87

A Production and Inventory Planning Problem 88
Defining the Decision Variables 89 Defining the Objective Function 89 Defining the Constraints 90 Implementing the Model 91 Solving the Model 93 Analyzing the Solution 93

A Multiperiod Cash Flow Problem 94
Defining the Decision Variables 95 Defining the Objective Function 96 Defining the Constraints 96 Implementing the Model 98 Solving the Model 101 Analyzing the Solution 102 Modifying the Taco-Viva Problem to Account for Risk (Optional) 102 Implementing the Risk Constraints 104 Solving the Model 106 Analyzing the Solution 107

Data Envelopment Analysis 107
Defining the Decision Variables 108 Defining the Objective 108 Defining the Constraints 108 Implementing the Model 109 Solving the Model 111 Analyzing the Solution 116

Summary 118

References 118

The World of Management Science 118

Questions and Problems 119

Cases 137

4. Sensitivity Analysis and the Simplex Method 143

Introduction 143

The Purpose of Sensitivity Analysis 143

Approaches to Sensitivity Analysis 144

An Example Problem 145

The Answer Report 146

The Sensitivity Report 147
Changes in the Objective Function Coefficients 147 A Note About Constancy 149 Alternate Optimal Solutions 150 Changes in the RHS Values 150 Shadow Prices for Nonbinding Constraints 151 A Note About Shadow Prices 151 Shadow Prices and the Value of Additional Resources 152 Other Uses of Shadow Prices 154 The Meaning of the Reduced Costs 154 Analyzing Changes in Constraint Coefficients 157 Simultaneous Changes in Objective Function Coefficients 158 A Warning About Degeneracy 159

The Limits Report 159

The Sensitivity Assistant Add-In (Optional) 160
Creating Spider Tables and Plots 161 Creating a Solver Table 164 Comments 167

The Simplex Method (Optional) 167
Creating Equality Constraints Using Slack Variables 167 Basic Feasible Solutions 168 Finding the Best Solution 170

Summary 171

References 171

The World of Management Science 172

Questions and Problems 173

Cases 181

5. Network Modeling 185

Introduction 185

The Transshipment Problem 185
Characteristics of Network Flow Problems 186 The Decision Variables for Network Flow Problems 187 The Objective Function for Network Flow Problems 188 The Constraints for Network Flow Problems 188 Implementing the Model in a Spreadsheet 190 Analyzing the Solution 191

The Shortest Path Problem 192
An LP Model for the Example Problem 194 The Spreadsheet Model and Solution 195 Network Flow Models and Integer Solutions 197

The Equipment Replacement Problem 197
The Spreadsheet Model and Solution 199

Transportation/Assignment Problems 201

Generalized Network Flow Problems 203
Formulating an LP Model for the Recycling Problem 204 Implementing the Model 205 Analyzing the Solution 207 Generalized Network Flow Problems and Feasibility 209

Maximal Flow Problems 210
An Example of a Maximal Flow Problem 211 The Spreadsheet Model and Solution 212

Special Modeling Considerations 215

Minimal Spanning Tree Problems 218
An Algorithm for the Minimal Spanning Tree Problem 219 Solving the Example Problem 219

Summary 220

References 221

The World of Management Science 221

Questions and Problems 222

Cases 236

6. Integer Linear Programming 244

Introduction 244

Integrality Conditions 244

Relaxation 245

Solving the Relaxed Problem 246

Bounds 248

Rounding 249

Stopping Rules 251

Solving ILP Problems Using Solver 253

Other ILP Problems 255

An Employee Scheduling Problem 257
Defining the Decision Variables 258 Defining the Objective Function 258 Defining the Constraints 258 A Note About the Constraints 259 Implementing the Model 260 Solving the Model 260 Analyzing the Solution 261

Binary Variables 262

A Capital Budgeting Problem 262
Defining the Decision Variables 263 Defining the Objective Function 263 Defining the Constraints 264 Setting Up the Binary Variables 264 Implementing the Model 264 Solving the Model 265 Comparing the Optimal Solution to a Heuristic Solution 266

Binary Variables and Logical Conditions 268

The Fixed-Charge Problem 268
Defining the Decision Variables 269 Defining the Objective Function 270 Defining the Constraints 270 Determining Values for "Big M" 271 Implementing the Model 271 Solving the Model 273 Analyzing the Solution 274

Minimum Order/Purchase Size 276

Quantity Discounts 276
Formulating the Model 277 The Missing Constraints 277

A Contract Award Problem 278
Formulating the Model: The Objective Function and Transportation Constraints 279 Implementing the Transportation Constraints 279 Formulating the Model: The Side Constraints 280 Implementing the Side Constraints 281 Solving the Model 283 Analyzing the Solution 283

The Branch-and-Bound Algorithm (Optional) 284
Branching 285 Bounding 287 Branching Again 288 Bounding Again 288 Summary of B&B Example 289

Summary 290

References 292

The World of Management Science 292

Questions and Problems 293

Cases 306

7. Goal Programming and Multiple Objective Optimization 313

Introduction 313

Goal Programming 314

A Goal Programming Example 314
Defining the Decision Variables 315 Defining the Goals 315 Defining the Goal Constraints 315 Defining the Hard Constraints 316 GP Objective Functions 317 Defining the Objective 318 Implementing the Model 319 Solving the Model 321 Analyzing the Solution 321 Revising the Model 321 Trade-offs: The Nature of GP 322

Comments About Goal Programming 324

Multiple Objective Optimization 325

An MOLP Example 326
Defining the Decision Variables 326 Defining the Objectives 327 Defining the Constraints 327 Implementing the Model 327 Determining Target Values for the Objectives 328 Summarizing the Target Solutions 331 Determining a GP Objective 332 The MINIMAX Objective 333 Implementing the Revised Model 334 Solving the Model 335

Comments on MOLP 337

Summary 338

References 339

The World of Management Science 339

Questions and Problems 340

Cases 351

8. Nonlinear Programming and Evolutionary Optimization 354

Introduction 354

The Nature of NLP Problems 355

Solution Strategies for NLP Problems 356

Local vs. Global Optimal Solutions 357

Economic Order Quantity Models 360
Implementing the Model 362 Solving the Model 363 Analyzing the Solution 363 Comments on the EOQ Model 365

Location Problems 365
Defining the Decision Variables 367 Defining the Objective 367 Defining the Constraints 367 Implementing the Model 368 Solving the Model and Analyzing the Solution 368 Another Solution to the Problem 370 Some Comments About the Solution to Location Problems 371

Nonlinear Network Flow Problem 371
Defining the Decision Variables 372 Defining the Objective 373 Defining the Constraints 373 Implementing the Model 374 Solving the Model and Analyzing the Solution 374

Project Selection Problems 376
Defining the Decision Variables 378 Defining the Objective Function 378 Defining the Constraints 378 Implementing the Model 379 Solving the Model 381

Optimizing Existing Financial Spreadsheet Models 382
Implementing the Model 383 Optimizing the Spreadsheet Model 384 Analyzing the Solution 384 Comments on Optimizing Existing Spreadsheets 385

The Portfolio Selection Problem 386
Defining the Decision Variables 387 Defining the Objective 388 Defining the Constraints 388 Implementing the Model 389 Analyzing the Solution 391 Handling Conflicting Objectives in Portfolio Problems 392

Sensitivity Analysis 394
Lagrange Multipliers 397 Reduced Gradients 397

Solver Options for Solving NLPs 398

Evolutionary Algorithms 399

Beating the Market 401
A Spreadsheet Model for the Problem 401 Solving the Model 401 Analyzing the Solution 402

The Traveling Salesperson Problem 403
A Spreadsheet Model for the Problem 404 Solving the Model 406 Analyzing the Solution 407

Summary 408

References 408

The World of Management Science 409

Questions and Problems 409

Cases 424

9. Regression Analysis 429

Introduction 429

An Example 429

Regression Models 432

Simple Linear Regression Analysis 433

Defining "Best Fit" 434

Solving the Problem Using Solver 435

Solving the Problem Using the Regression Tool 437

Evaluating the Fit 439

The R^2 Statistic 442

Making Predictions 444
The Standard Error 444 Prediction Intervals for New Values of Y 444 Confidence Intervals for Mean Values of Y 447 A Note About Extrapolation 447

Statistical Tests for Population Parameters 448
Analysis of Variance 448 Assumptions for the Statistical Tests 449 A Note About Statistical Tests 451

Introduction to Multiple Regression 451

A Multiple Regression Example 453

Selecting the Model 453
Models with One Independent Variable 455 Models with Two Independent Variables 456 Inflating R^2 458 The Adjusted-R^2 Statistic 458 The Best Model with Two Independent Variables 459 Multicollinearity 459 The Model with Three Independent Variables 460

Making Predictions 461

Binary Independent Variables 462

Statistical Tests for the Population Parameters 463

Polynomial Regression 463
Expressing Nonlinear Relationships Using Linear Models 465 Summary of Nonlinear Regression 468

Summary 469

References 470

The World of Management Science 470

Questions and Problems 471

Cases 482

10. Discriminant Analysis 485

Introduction 485

The Two-Group DA Problem 486
Group Locations and Centroids 487 Calculating Discriminant Scores 489 The Classification Rule 491 Refining the Cutoff Value 493 Classification Accuracy 494 Classifying New Employees 495

The *k*-Group DA Problem 497
Multiple Discriminant Analysis 498 Distance Measures 500 MDA Classification 502

Summary 504

References 505

The World of Management Science 505

Questions and Problems 506

Cases 511

11. Time Series Forecasting 515

Introduction 515

Time Series Methods 516

Measuring Accuracy 517

Stationary Models 517

Moving Averages 518
Forecasting with the Moving Average Model 521

Weighted Moving Averages 522
Forecasting with the Weighted Moving Average Model 524

Exponential Smoothing 525
Forecasting with the Exponential Smoothing Model 528

Seasonality 529

Stationary Data with Additive Seasonal Effects 529
Forecasting with the Model 534

Stationary Data with Multiplicative Seasonal Effects 534
Forecasting with the Model 537

Trend Models 538
An Example 538

Double Moving Average 539
Forecasting with the Model 541

Double Exponential Smoothing (Holt's Method) 542
Forecasting with Holt's Method 544

Holt-Winter's Method for Additive Seasonal Effects 545
Forecasting with Holt-Winter's Additive Method 549

Holt-Winter's Method for Multiplicative Seasonal Effects 550
Forecasting with Holt-Winter's Multiplicative Method 554

Modeling Time Series Trends Using Regression 554

Linear Trend Model 554
Forecasting with the Linear Trend Model 555

Quadratic Trend Model 558
Forecasting with the Quadratic Trend Model 559

Modeling Seasonality with Regression Models 560

Adjusting Trend Predictions with Seasonal Indices 561
Computing Seasonal Indices 562 Forecasting with Seasonal Indices 563 Refining the Seasonal Indices 564

Seasonal Regression Models 566
The Seasonal Model 567 Forecasting with the Seasonal Regression Model 570

Crystal Ball Predictor 571
Using CB Predictor 571

Combining Forecasts 576

Summary 577

References 577

The World of Management Science 578

Questions and Problems 579

Cases 589

12. Introduction to Simulation Using Crystal Ball 595

Introduction 595

Random Variables and Risk 596

Why Analyze Risk? 596

Methods of Risk Analysis 597
Best-Case/Worst-Case Analysis 597 What-If Analysis 598 Simulation 599

A Corporate Health Insurance Example 599
A Critique of the Base Case Model 601

Spreadsheet Simulation Using Crystal Ball 602
Starting Crystal Ball 602

Random Number Generators 603
Discrete vs. Continuous Random Variables 606

Preparing the Model for Simulation 607
Alternate RNG Entry 609

Running the Simulation 610
Selecting the Output Cells to Track 610 Selecting the Number of Iterations 611 Determining the Sample Size 612 Running the Simulation 612

Data Analysis 613
The Best Case and the Worst Case 613 Viewing the Distribution of the Output Cells 614 Viewing the Cumulative Distribution of the Output Cells 615 Obtaining Other Cumulative Probabilities 616

Incorporating Graphs and Statistics into a Spreadsheet 617

The Uncertainty of Sampling 618
Constructing a Confidence Interval for the True Population Mean 618 Constructing a Confidence Interval for a Population Proportion 620 Sample Sizes and Confidence Interval Widths 621

The Benefits of Simulation 621

Additional Uses of Simulation 621

A Reservation Management Example 622
Implementing the Model 623 Using the Decision Table Tool 625

An Inventory Control Example 629
Creating the RNGs 630 Implementing the Model 631 Replicating the Model 634 Optimizing the Model 634 Comment on Using OptQuest 637

A Project Selection Example 638
A Spreadsheet Model 639 Solving the Problem with OptQuest 640 Considering Other Solutions 642

Summary 646

References 646

The World of Management Science 647

Questions and Problems 647

Cases 660

13. Queuing Theory 668

Introduction 668

The Purpose of Queuing Models 669

Queuing System Configurations 670

Characteristics of Queuing Systems 671
Arrival Rate 671 Service Rate 673

Kendall Notation 675

Queuing Models 675

The M/M/s Model 677
An Example 677 The Current Situation 677 Adding a Server 678 Economic Analysis 680

The M/M/s Model with Finite Queue Length 680
The Current Situation 681 Adding a Server 682

The M/M/s Model with Finite Population 682
An Example 684 The Current Situation 684 Adding Servers 686

The M/G/1 Model 686
The Current Situation 689 Adding the Automated Dispensing Device 689

The M/D/1 Model 690

Simulating Queues and the Steady-State Assumption 692

Summary 693

References 693

The World of Management Science 694

Questions and Problems 695

Cases 701

14. Project Management 703

Introduction 703

An Example 704

Creating the Project Network 704
A Note on Start and Finish Points 706

CPM: An Overview 707

The Forward Pass 708

The Backward Pass 711

Determining the Critical Path 713
A Note on Slack 714

Project Management Using Spreadsheets 715

Project Crashing 721
An LP Approach to Crashing 722 Determining the Earliest Crash Completion Time 723 Implementing the Model 725 Solving the Model 726 Determining a Least Costly Crash Schedule 727 Crashing as an MOLP 727

Certainty vs. Uncertainty 729

PERT: An Overview 730
The Problems with PERT 731 Implications 733

Simulating Project Networks 733
An Example 733 Generating Random Activity Times 733 Implementing the Model 735 Running the Simulation 735 Analyzing the Results 737

Microsoft Project 738

Summary 741

References 742

The World of Management Science 742

Questions and Problems 743

Cases 751

15. Decision Analysis 754

Introduction 754

Good Decisions vs. Good Outcomes 755

Characteristics of Decision Problems 755

An Example 756

The Payoff Matrix 757
Decision Alternatives 757 States of Nature 757 The Payoff Values 758

Decision Rules 759

Nonprobabilistic Methods 760
The Maximax Decision Rule 760 The Maximin Decision Rule 761 The Minimax Regret Decision Rule 761

Probabilistic Methods 764
Expected Monetary Value 765 Expected Regret 766 Sensitivity Analysis 768

The Expected Value of Perfect Information 770

Decision Trees 771
Rolling Back a Decision Tree 773

Using TreePlan 775
Adding Branches 775 Adding Event Nodes 776 Adding the Cash Flows 780 Determining the Payoffs and EMVs 782 Other Features 782

Multistage Decision Problems 784
A Multistage Decision Tree 785

Analyzing Risk in a Decision Tree 786
Risk Profiles 788 Strategy Tables 789

Using Sample Information in Decision Making 791
Conditional Probabilities 793 The Expected Value of Sample Information 793

Computing Conditional Probabilities 794
Bayes's Theorem 796

Utility Theory 797
Utility Functions 798 Constructing Utility Functions 799 Using Utilities to Make Decisions 801 The Exponential Utility Function 802 Incorporating Utilities in TreePlan 803

Multicriteria Decision Making 805

The Multicriteria Scoring Model 806

The Analytic Hierarchy Process 809
Pairwise Comparisons 809 Normalizing the Comparisons 810 Consistency 811 Obtaining Scores for the Remaining Criteria 814 Obtaining Criterion Weights 814 Implementing the Scoring Model 817

Summary 817

References 817

The World of Management Science 818

Questions and Problems 819

Cases 830

Index 833

Chapter 1

Introduction to Modeling and Decision Analysis

1.0 INTRODUCTION

This book is titled *Spreadsheet Modeling & Decision Analysis: A Practical Introduction to Management Science,* so let's begin by discussing exactly what this title means. By the very nature of life, all of us must continually make decisions that we hope will solve problems and lead to increased opportunities for ourselves or the organizations for which we work. But making good decisions is rarely an easy task. The problems faced by decision makers in today's competitive, fast-paced business environment are often extremely complex and can be addressed by numerous possible courses of action. Evaluating these alternatives and choosing the best course of action represents the essence of decision analysis.

During the past decade, millions of business people discovered that one of the most effective ways to analyze and evaluate decision alternatives involves using electronic spreadsheets to build computer models of the decision problems they face. A **computer model** is a set of mathematical relationships and logical assumptions implemented in a computer as a representation of some real-world decision problem or phenomenon. Today, electronic spreadsheets provide the most convenient and useful way for business people to implement and analyze computer models. Indeed, most business people would probably rate the electronic spreadsheet as their most important analytical tool apart from their brain! Using a **spreadsheet model** (a computer model implemented via a spreadsheet), a business person can analyze decision alternatives before having to choose a specific plan for implementation.

This book introduces you to a variety of techniques from the field of management science that can be applied in spreadsheet models to assist in the decision-analysis process. For our purposes, we will define **management science** as a field of study that uses computers, statistics, and mathematics to solve business problems. It involves applying the methods and tools of science to management and decision making. Management science is also sometimes referred to as operations research or decision science. See Figure 1.1 for a summary of how management science has been applied successfully in a number of real-world situations.

In the not too distant past, management science was a highly specialized field that generally could be practiced only by those who had access to mainframe computers and who possessed an advanced knowledge of mathematics and computer programming languages. However, the proliferation of powerful personal computers (PCs) and the development of easy-to-use electronic spreadsheets have made the tools of management science far more practical and available to a much larger audience. Virtually everyone who uses a spreadsheet today for model building and decision making is a practitioner of management science—whether they realize it or not.

1.1 THE MODELING APPROACH TO DECISION MAKING

The idea of using models in problem solving and decision analysis is really not new, and is certainly not tied to the use of computers. At some point, all of us have used a modeling approach to make a decision. For example, if you have ever moved into a dormitory, apartment, or house, you undoubtedly faced a decision about how to arrange the furniture in your new dwelling. There were probably a number of different arrangements to consider. One arrangement might give you the most open space but require that you build a loft. Another might give you less space but allow you to avoid the hassle and expense of building a loft. To analyze these different arrangements and make a decision, you did not build the loft. You more likely built a **mental model** of the two arrangements, picturing what each looked like in your mind's eye. Thus, a simple mental model is sometimes all that is required to analyze a problem and make a decision.

For more complex decision problems, a mental model might be impossible or insufficient and other types of models might be required. For example, a set of drawings or blueprints for a house or building provides a **visual model** of the real-world structure. These drawings help illustrate how the various parts of the structure will fit together when it is completed. A road map is another type of visual model because it assists a driver in analyzing the various routes from one location to another.

You have probably also seen car commercials on television showing automotive engineers using **physical,** or **scale, models** to study the aerodynamics of various car designs in order to find the shape that creates the least wind resistance and maximizes fuel economy. Similarly, aeronautical engineers use scale models of airplanes to study the flight characteristics of various fuselage and wing designs. And civil engineers might use scale models of buildings and bridges to study the strengths of different construction techniques.

FIGURE 1.1
Examples of successful management science applications

Home Runs in Management Science

Over the past decade, scores of operations research and management science projects saved companies millions of dollars. Each year, the Institute For Operations Research and the Management Sciences (INFORMS) sponsors the Franz Edelman Awards competition to recognize some of the most outstanding OR/MS projects during the past year. Here are some of the "home runs" from the 2000 and 2001 Edelman Awards (described *Interfaces,* vol. 31, no. 1, January-February, 2001 and *Interfaces,* vol. 32, no. 1, January-February, 2002).

- **Merrill Lynch** employs nearly 16,000 Financial Advisors (FAs) who provide financial advice to over 5 million customers. Traditionally, payment for these services was based on commissions from trades. Merrill Lynch recognized that this pricing mechanism was not tied directly to its core competence, namely the individual financial advice delivered by the FAs. Because of increased competition from electronic trading firms that do not provide financial advice, Merrill Lynch's Management Science Group developed a model to design product features and pricing options to better reflect the customer value provided by its FAs. This work led Merrill Lynch to launch the Integrated Choice service, which allows clients to choose the level of advice they receive and to pay accordingly. **Benefits:** Integrated Choice has yielded additional annual revenues of $80 million and net assets of $22 billion.
- **Jan de Wit Co.** is Brazil's largest lily farmer, planting about 3.5 million bulbs and producing 420,000 pots and 220,000 bundles of lilies each year in 50 varieties. Deciding what to plant, when to plant, and when to harvest is a difficult optimization problem—complicated by the fact that Jan de Wit must also decide how to sell its crop, either in advance through contracts at a known price or in an auction at spot market prices. To solve this planning problem, Jan de Wit developed a Linear Programming-based decision support system. **Benefits:** Linear Programming increased revenues by 26 percent and the contribution margin by 32 percent in 2000.
- **NBC,** with the help of management science analysts at its parent company (GE), implemented an optimization model to generate commercial sales plans. Every spring, major television networks determine their program schedules for the next season. In a two- to three-week period in May, the networks sell most of their time slots for commercials. Major advertisers give a network a set of requirements, including its advertising budget, the desired audience demographics, and preferred shows and time slots. The network must then design a commercial sales plan for the entire year that best meets the clients' requirements. **Benefits:** NBC's optimization model led to increased revenues of $50 million per year by generating sales plans that result in better timing and pricing of commercials.

FIGURE 1.1
(continued)

- **Samsung Electronics** is the leading manufacturer of dynamic random access memory (DRAM) devices in the world. The manufacturing process for these devices in complex, starting with as many as 400 process steps through a semiconductor fabrication facility that can cost between $2 and $3 billion to build. Samsung must optimize the flow of work through its fabrication facilities to get high equipment utilization and throughput with the least amount of work-in-process inventory. Samsung developed a comprehensive planning and scheduling system, based on a new paradigm that controls the work in process (WIP) to achieve a target output schedule. Samsung implemented this system in all its fabrication sites and cut its manufacturing cycle times by over one half. **Benefits:** Samsung estimates $1 billion in additional revenue from this reduction in cycle times.

Another common type of model is a **mathematical model,** which uses mathematical relationships to describe or represent an object or decision problem. Throughout this book, we will study how various mathematical models can be implemented and analyzed on computers using spreadsheet software. But before we move to an in-depth discussion of spreadsheet models, let's look at some of the more general characteristics and benefits of modeling.

1.2 CHARACTERISTICS AND BENEFITS OF MODELING

Although this book focuses on mathematical models implemented in computers via spreadsheets, the examples of nonmathematical models given earlier are worth discussing a bit more because they help illustrate a number of important characteristics and benefits of modeling in general. First, the models mentioned earlier are usually simplified versions of the object or decision problem they represent. To study the aerodynamics of a car design, we do not need to build the entire car complete with engine and stereo. Such components have little or no effect on aerodynamics. So, although a model is often a simplified representation of reality, the model is useful as long as it is valid. A **valid** model is one that accurately represents the relevant characteristics of the object or decision problem being studied.

Second, it is often less expensive to analyze decision problems using a model. This is especially easy to understand with respect to scale models of big-ticket items such as cars and planes. Besides the lower financial cost of building a model, the analysis of a model can help avoid costly mistakes that might result from poor decision making. For example, it is far less costly to discover a flawed wing design using a scale model of an aircraft than after the crash of a fully loaded jet liner.

Frank Brock, former executive vice president of the Brock Candy Company, related the following story about blueprints his company prepared for a new production facility. After months of careful design work, he proudly showed the plans to several of his production workers. When he asked for their comments, one worker responded, "It's a fine looking building Mr. Brock, but that sugar valve looks like it's about twenty feet away from the steam valve." "What's wrong with that?" asked Brock. "Well, nothing," said the worker, "except that I have to have my hands on both valves at the same time!"[1] Needless to say, it was far less expensive to discover and correct this "little" problem using a visual model before pouring the concrete and laying the pipes as originally planned.

Third, models often deliver needed information on a more timely basis. Again, it is relatively easy to see that scale models of cars or airplanes can be created and analyzed more quickly than their real-world counterparts. Timeliness is also an issue when vital data will not become available until some later point in time. In these cases, we might create a model to help predict the missing data to assist in current decision making.

Fourth, models are frequently helpful in examining things that would be impossible to do in reality. For example, human models (crash dummies) are used in crash tests to see what might happen to an actual person if a car hits a brick wall at a high speed. Likewise, models of DNA can be used to visualize how molecules fit together. Both of these are difficult, if not impossible, to do without the use of models.

Finally, and probably most importantly, models allow us to gain insight and understanding about the object or decision problem under investigation. The ultimate purpose of using models is to improve decision making. As you will see, the process of building a model can shed important light and understanding on a problem. In some cases, a decision might be made while building the model as a previously misunderstood element of the problem is discovered or eliminated. In other cases, a careful analysis of a completed model might be required to "get a handle" on a problem and gain the insights needed to make a decision. In any event, it is the insight gained from the modeling process that ultimately leads to better decision making.

1.3 MATHEMATICAL MODELS

As mentioned earlier, the modeling techniques in this book differ quite a bit from scale models of cars and planes or visual models of production plants. The models we will build use mathematics to describe a decision problem. We use the term "mathematics" in its broadest sense, encompassing not only the most familiar elements of math, such as algebra, but also the related topic of logic.

Now, let's consider a simple example of a mathematical model:

$$\text{PROFIT} = \text{REVENUE} - \text{EXPENSES} \qquad \textbf{1.1}$$

Equation 1.1 describes a simple relationship between revenue, expenses, and profit. It is a mathematical relationship that describes the operation of determining profit—or a mathematical model of profit. Of course, not all models are this simple, but taken piece by piece, the models we will discuss are not much more complex than this one.

1 Colson, Charles and Jack Eckerd, *Why America Doesn't Work* (Denver, CO: Word Publishing, 1991), 146–147.

Frequently, mathematical models describe functional relationships. For example, the mathematical model in equation 1.1 describes a functional relationship between revenue, expenses, and profit. Using the symbols of mathematics, this functional relationship is represented as:

$$\text{PROFIT} = f(\text{REVENUE} - \text{EXPENSES}) \qquad \mathbf{1.2}$$

In words, the previous expression means "profit is a function of revenue and expenses." We could also say that profit *depends* on (or is *dependent* on) revenue and expenses. Thus, the term PROFIT in equation 1.2 represents a **dependent** variable, whereas REVENUE and EXPENSES are **independent** variables. Frequently, compact symbols (such as A, B, and C) are used to represent variables in an equation like 1.2. For instance, if we let Y, X_1, and X_2 represent PROFIT, REVENUE, and EXPENSES, respectively, we could rewrite equation 1.2 as follows:

$$Y = f(X_1, X_2) \qquad \mathbf{1.3}$$

The notation $f(\cdot)$ represents the function that defines the relationship between the dependent variable Y and the independent variables X_1 and X_2. In the case of determining PROFIT from REVENUE and EXPENSES, the mathematical form of the function $f(\cdot)$ is quite simple because we know that $f(X_1, X_2) = X_1 - X_2$. However, in many other situations we will model, the form of $f(\cdot)$ is quite complex and might involve many independent variables. But regardless of the complexity of $f(\cdot)$ or the number of independent variables involved, many of the decision problems encountered in business can be represented by models that assume the general form,

$$Y = f(X_1, X_2, \ldots, X_k) \qquad \mathbf{1.4}$$

In equation 1.4, the dependent variable Y represents some bottom-line performance measure of the problem we are modeling. The terms $X_1, X_2, \ldots, X_k$ represent the different independent variables that play some role or have some impact in determining the value of Y. Again, $f(\cdot)$ is the function (possibly quite complex) that specifies or describes the relationship between the dependent and independent variables.

The relationship expressed in equation 1.4 is very similar to what occurs in most spreadsheet models. Consider a simple spreadsheet model to calculate the monthly payment for a car loan, as shown in Figure 1.2.

The spreadsheet in Figure 1.2 contains a variety of **input** cells (for example, purchase price, down payment, trade-in, term of loan, annual interest rate) that correspond conceptually to the independent variables $X_1, X_2, \ldots, X_k$ in equation 1.4. Similarly, a variety of mathematical operations are performed using these input cells in a manner analogous to the function $f(\cdot)$ in equation 1.4. The results of these mathematical operations determine the value of some **output** cell in the spreadsheet (for example, monthly payment) that corresponds to the dependent variable Y in equation 1.4. Thus, there is a direct correspondence between equation 1.4 and the spreadsheet in Figure 1.2. This type of correspondence exists for most of the spreadsheet models in this book.

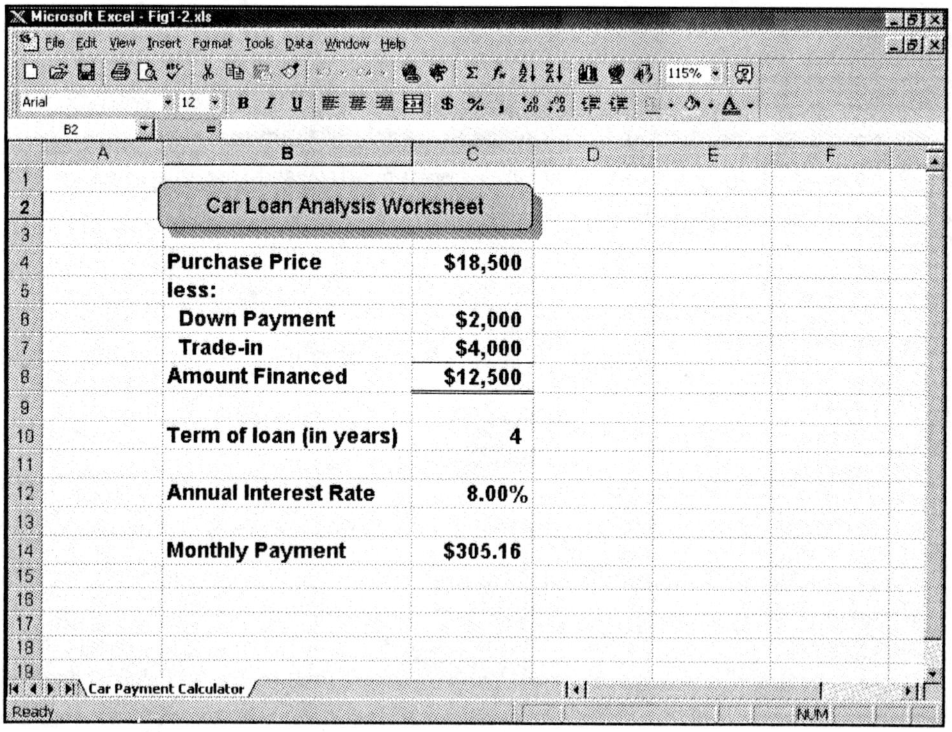

FIGURE 1.2
Example of a simple spreadsheet model

1.4 CATEGORIES OF MATHEMATICAL MODELS

Not only does equation 1.4 describe the major elements of mathematical or spreadsheet models, but it also provides a convenient means for comparing and contrasting the three categories of modeling techniques presented in this book—Prescriptive Models, Predictive Models, and Descriptive Models. Figure 1.3 summarizes the characteristics and techniques associated with each of these categories.

In some situations, a manager might face a decision problem involving a very precise, well-defined functional relationship $f(\cdot)$ between the independent variables $X_1, X_2, \ldots, X_k$ and the dependent variable Y. If the values for the independent variables are under the decision maker's control, the decision problem in these types of situations boils down to determining the values of the independent variables $X_1, X_2, \ldots, X_k$ that produce the best possible value for the dependent variable Y. These types of models are called **Prescriptive Models** because their solutions tell the decision maker what actions to take. For example, you might be interested in determining how a given sum of money should be allocated to different investments (represented by the independent variables) in order to maximize the return on a portfolio without exceeding a certain level of risk.

A second category of decision problems is one in which the objective is to predict or estimate what value the dependent variable Y will take on when the independent variables $X_1, X_2, \ldots, X_k$ take on specific values. If the function $f(\cdot)$ relating the dependent and independent variables is known, this is a very simple task—simply enter the specified values for $X_1, X_2, \ldots, X_k$ into the function $f(\cdot)$ and compute Y. In some cases, however, the functional form of $f(\cdot)$ might be unknown and must be estimated in order for the decision maker to make predictions about the

FIGURE 1.3
Categories and characteristics of management science modeling techniques

	Model Characteristics		
Category	**Form of $f(\cdot)$**	**Values of Independent Variables**	**Management Science Techniques**
Prescriptive Models	known, well-defined	known or under decision-maker's control	Linear Programming, Networks, Integer Programming, CPM, Goal Programming, EOQ, Nonlinear Programming
Predictive Models	unknown, ill-defined	known or under decision-maker's control	Regression Analysis, Time Series Analysis, Discriminant Analysis
Descriptive Models	known, well-defined	unknown or uncertain	Simulation, Queuing, PERT, Inventory Models

dependent variable Y. These types of models are called **Predictive Models.** For example, a real estate appraiser might know that the value of a commercial property (Y) is influenced by its total square footage (X_1) and age (X_2), among other things. However, the functional relationship $f(\cdot)$ that relates these variables to one another might be unknown. By analyzing the relationship between the selling price, total square footage, and age of other commercial properties, the appraiser might be able to identify a function $f(\cdot)$ that relates these two variables in a reasonably accurate manner.

The third category of models you are likely to encounter in the business world is called **Descriptive Models.** In these situations, a manager might face a decision problem that has a very precise, well-defined functional relationship $f(\cdot)$ between the independent variables $X_1, X_2, \ldots, X_k$ and the dependent variable Y. However, there might be great uncertainty as to the exact values that will be assumed by one or more of the independent variables $X_1, X_2, \ldots, X_k$. In these types of problems, the objective is to describe the outcome or behavior of a given operation or system. For example, suppose a company is building a new manufacturing facility and has several choices about the type of machines to put in the new plant, as well as various options for arranging the machines. Management might be interested in studying how the various plant configurations would affect on-time shipments of orders (Y), given the uncertain number of orders that might be received (X_1) and the uncertain due dates (X_2) that might be required by these orders.

1.5 THE PROBLEM-SOLVING PROCESS

Throughout our discussion, we have said that the ultimate goal in building models is to assist managers in making decisions that solve problems. The modeling techniques we will study represent a small but important part of the total problem-solving process. To become an effective modeler, it is important to understand how modeling fits into the entire problem-solving process.

Because a model can be used to represent a decision problem or phenomenon, we might be able to create a visual model of the phenomenon that occurs when people solve problems—what we call the problem-solving process. Although a variety of models could be equally valid, the one in Figure 1.4 summarizes the key elements of the problem-solving process and is sufficient for our purposes.

The first step of the problem-solving process, identifying the problem, is also the most important. If we do not identify the correct problem, all the work that follows will amount to nothing more than wasted effort, time, and money. Unfortunately, identifying the problem to solve is often not as easy as it seems. We know that a problem exists when there is a gap or disparity between the present situation and some desired state of affairs. However, we usually are not faced with a neat, well-defined problem. Instead, we often find ourselves facing a "mess"![2] Identifying the real problem involves gathering a lot of information and talking with many people to increase our understanding of the mess. We must then sift through all this information and try to identify the root problem or problems causing the mess. Thus, identifying the real problem (and not just the symptoms of the problem) requires insight, some imagination, time, and a good bit of detective work.

The end result of the problem-identification step is a well-defined statement of the problem. Simply defining a problem well will often make it much easier to solve. Having identified the problem, we turn our attention to creating or formulating a model of the problem. Depending on the nature of the problem, we might use a mental model, a visual model, a scale model, or a mathematical model. Although this book focuses on mathematical models, this does not mean that mathematical models are always applicable or best. In most situations, the best model is the simplest model that accurately reflects the relevant characteristic or essence of the problem being studied.

We will discuss several different management science modeling techniques in this book. It is important that you not develop too strong a preference for any one technique. Some people have a tendency to want to formulate every problem they face as a model that can be solved by their favorite management science technique. This simply will not work.

As indicated in Figure 1.3, there are fundamental differences in the types of problems a manager might face. Sometimes, the values of the independent variables affecting a problem are under the manager's control; sometimes they are not. Sometimes, the form of the functional relationship $f(\cdot)$ relating the dependent and independent variables is well-defined, and sometimes it is not. These fundamental characteristics of the problem should guide your selection of an appropriate management science modeling technique. Your goal at the model-formulation stage is to select a modeling technique that fits your problem, rather than trying to fit your problem into the required format of a preselected modeling technique.

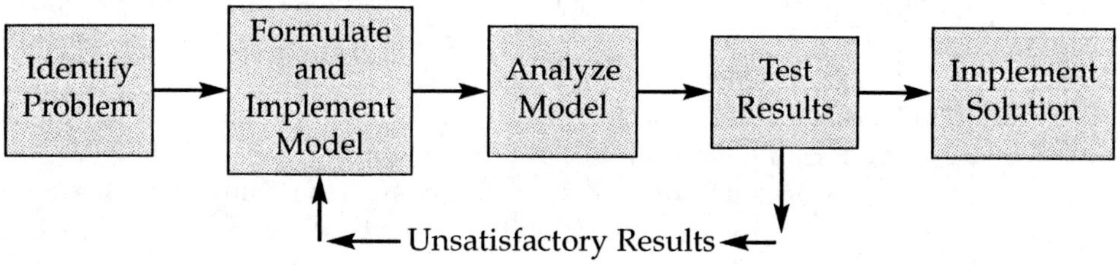

FIGURE 1.4
A visual model of the problem-solving process

2 This characterization is borrowed from Chapter 5, James R. Evans, *Creative Thinking in the Decision and Management Sciences* (Cincinnati, OH: South-Western, 1991), 89–115.

After you select an appropriate representation or formulation of your problem, the next step is to implement this formulation as a spreadsheet model. We will not dwell on the implementation process now because that is the focus of the remainder of this book. After you verify that your spreadsheet model has been implemented accurately, the next step in the problem-solving process is to use the model to analyze the problem it represents. The main focus of this step is to generate and evaluate alternatives that might lead to a solution of the problem. This often involves playing out a number of scenarios or asking several "What if?" questions. Spreadsheets are particularly helpful in analyzing mathematical models in this manner. In a well-designed spreadsheet model, it should be fairly simple to change some of the assumptions in the model to see what might happen in different situations. As we proceed, we will highlight some techniques for designing spreadsheet models that facilitate this type of "what if" analysis. "What if" analysis is also very appropriate and useful when working with nonmathematical models.

The end result of analyzing a model does not always provide a solution to the actual problem being studied. As we analyze a model by asking various "What if?" questions, it is important to test the feasibility and quality of each potential solution. The blueprints Frank Brock showed to his production employees represented the end result of his analysis of the problem he faced. He wisely tested the feasibility and quality of this alternative before implementing it, and discovered an important flaw in his plans. Thus, the testing process can give important new insights into the nature of a problem. The testing process is also important because it provides the opportunity to double check the validity of the model. At times, we might discover an alternative that appears to be too good to be true. This could lead us to find that some important assumption has been left out of the model. Testing the results of the model against known results (and simple common sense) helps ensure the structural integrity and validity of the model. After analyzing the model, we might discover that we need to go back and modify the model.

The last step of the problem-solving process, implementation, is often the most difficult. By their very nature, solutions to problems involve people and change. For better or for worse, most people resist change. However, there are ways to minimize the seemingly inevitable resistance to change. For example, it is wise, if possible, to involve anyone who will be affected by the decision in all steps of the problem-solving process. This not only helps develop a sense of ownership and understanding of the ultimate solution, but it also can be the source of important information throughout the problem-solving process. As the Brock Candy story illustrates, even if it is impossible to include those affected by the solution in all steps, their input should be solicited and considered before a solution is accepted for implementation. Resistance to change and new systems can also be eased by creating flexible, user-friendly interfaces for the mathematical models that are often developed in the problem-solving process.

Throughout this book, we focus mostly on the model formulation, implementation, analysis, and testing steps of the problem-solving process, summarized in Figure 1.4. Again, this does not imply that these steps are more important than the others. If we do not identify the correct problem, the best we can hope for from our modeling effort is "the right answer to the wrong question," which does not solve the real problem. Similarly, even if we do identify the problem correctly and design a model that leads to a perfect solution, if we cannot implement the solution, then we still have not solved the problem. Developing the interpersonal and investigative skills required to work with people in defining the problem and implementing the solution are as important as the mathematical modeling skills you will develop by working through this book.

1.6 ANCHORING AND FRAMING EFFECTS

At this point, some of you reading this book are probably thinking it is better to rely on subjective judgement and intuition rather than models when making decisions. Indeed, most nontrivial decision problems involve some issues that are difficult or impossible to structure and analyze in the form of a mathematical model. These unstructurable aspects of a decision problem may require the use of judgement and intuition. However, it is important to realize that human cognition is often flawed and can lead to incorrect judgements and irrational decisions. Errors in human judgement often arise because of what psychologists term **anchoring** and **framing** effects associated with decision problems.

Anchoring effects arise when a seemingly trivial factor serves as a starting point (or anchor) for estimations in a decision-making problem. Decision makers adjust their estimates from this anchor but nevertheless remain too close to the anchor and usually under-adjust. In a classic psychological study on this issue, one group of subjects was asked to individually estimate the value of $1\times2\times3\times4\times5\times6\times7\times8$ (without using a calculator). Another group of subjects were each asked to estimate the value of $8\times7\times6\times5\times4\times3\times2\times1$. The researchers hypothesized that the first number presented (or perhaps the product of the first three or four numbers) would serve as a mental anchor. The results supported the hypothesis. The median estimate of subjects shown the numbers in ascending sequence ($1\times2\times3\ldots$) was 512, whereas the median estimate of subjects shown the sequence in descending order ($8\times7\times6\ldots$) was 2,250. Of course, the order of multiplication for these numbers is irrelevant and the product of both series is the same: 40,320.

Framing effects refer to how a decision maker views or perceives the alternatives in a decision problem—often involving a win/loss perspective. The way a problem is framed often influences the choices made by a decision maker and can lead to irrational behavior. For example, suppose you have just been given $1,000 but must choose one of the following alternatives: (A_1) Receive an additional $500 with certainty, or ($B_1$) Flip a fair coin and receive an additional $1,000 if heads occurs or $0 additional is tails occurs. Here, alternative A_1 is a "sure win" and is the alternative most people prefer. Now suppose you have been given $2,000 and must choose one of the following alternatives: (A_2) Give back $500 immediately, or ($B_2$) Flip a fair coin and give back $0 if heads occurs or $1,000 if tails occurs. When the problem is framed this way, alternative A_2 is a "sure loss" and many people who previously preferred alternative A_1 now opt for alternative B_2 (because it holds a chance of avoiding a loss). However, Figure 1.5 shows a single decision tree for these two scenarios making it clear that, in both cases, the "A" alternative guarantees a total payoff of $1,500, whereas the "B" alternative offers a 50% chance of a $2,000 total payoff and a 50% chance of a $1,000 total payoff. (Decision trees will be covered in greater detail in a later chapter.) A purely rational decision maker should focus on the consequences of his or her choices and consistently select the same alternative, regardless of how the problem is framed.

FIGURE 1.5
An example of a decision tree for framing effects

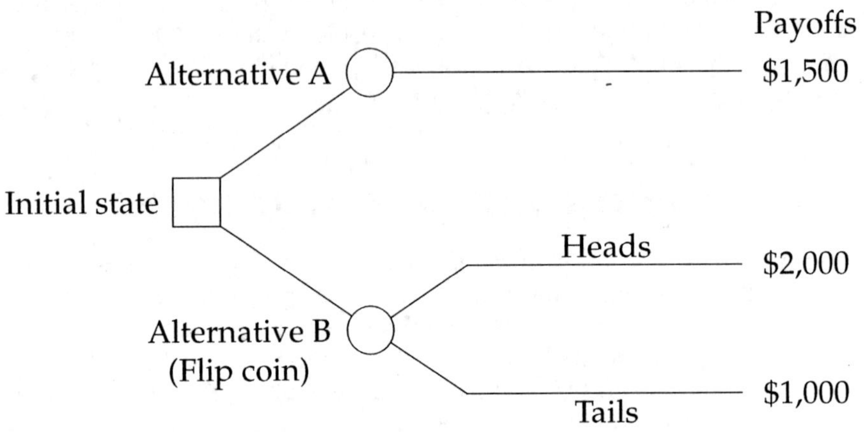

Whether we want to admit it or not, we are all prone to make errors in estimation due to anchoring effects and may exhibit irrationality in decision making due to framing effects. As a result, it is best to use computer models to do what they are best at (*i.e.*, modeling structurable portions of a decision problem) and let the human brain do what it is best at (*i.e.*, dealing with the unstructurable portion of a decision problem).

1.7 GOOD DECISIONS VS. GOOD OUTCOMES

The goal of the modeling approach to problem solving is to help individuals make good decisions. But good decisions do not always result in good outcomes. For example, suppose the weather report on the evening news predicts a warm, dry, sunny day tomorrow. When you get up and look out the window tomorrow morning, suppose there is not a cloud in sight. If you decide to leave your umbrella at home and subsequently get soaked in an unexpected afternoon thundershower, did you make a bad decision? Certainly not. Unforeseeable circumstances beyond your control caused you to experience a bad outcome, but it would be unfair to say that you made a bad decision. Good decisions sometimes result in bad outcomes. See Figure 1.6 for the story of another good decision having a bad outcome.

The modeling techniques presented in this book can help you make good decisions, but cannot guarantee that good outcomes will always occur as a result of those decisions. Even when a good decision is made, luck often plays a role in determining whether a good or bad outcome occurs. However, using a structured, modeling approach to decision making should produce good outcomes more frequently than making decisions in a more haphazard manner.

Andre-Francois Raffray thought he had a great deal in 1965 when he agreed to pay a 90-year-old woman named Jeanne Calment $500 a month until she died to acquire her grand apartment in Arles, northwest of Marseilles in the south of France—a town Vincent Van Gogh once roamed. Buying apartments "for life" is common in France. The elderly owner gets to enjoy a monthly income from the buyer who gambles on getting a real estate bargain—betting the owner doesn't live too long. Upon the owner's death, the buyer inherits the apartment regardless of how much was paid. But in December of 1995, Raffray died at age 77, having paid more than $180,000 for an apartment he never got to live in.

On the same day, Calment, then the world's oldest living person at 120, dined on foie gras, duck thighs, cheese, and chocolate cake at her nursing home near the sought-after apartment. And she does not need to worry about losing her $500 monthly income. Although the amount Raffray already paid is twice the apartment's current market value, his widow is obligated to keep sending the monthly check to Calment. If Calment also outlives her, then the Raffray children will have to pay. "In life, one sometimes makes bad deals," said Calment of the outcome of Raffray's decision. (Source: *The Savannah Morning News*, 12/29/95.)

FIGURE 1.6
A good decision with a bad outcome

1.8 SUMMARY

This book introduces you to a variety of techniques from the field of management science that can be applied in spreadsheet models to assist in decision analysis and problem solving. This chapter discussed how spreadsheet models of decision problems can be used to analyze the consequences of possible courses of action before a particular alternative is selected for implementation. It described how models of decision problems differ in a number of important characteristics and how you should select a modeling technique that is most appropriate for the type of problem being faced. Finally, it discussed how spreadsheet modeling and analysis fit into the problem-solving process.

1.9 REFERENCES

Forgione, G. "Corporate MS Activities: An Update." *Interfaces*, vol. 13, no. 1, 1983.
Grayson, C. "Management Science and Business Practice." *Harvard Business Review*, vol. 51, 1973.
Hall, R. "What's So Scientific about MS/OR?" *Interfaces*, vol. 15, 1985.
Hastie, R. and R.M. Dawes. *Rational Choice in an Uncertain World*, Sage Publications, 2001.
Schrage, M. *Serious Play*, Harvard Business School Press, 2000.
Sonntag, C. and Grossman, T. "End-User Modeling Improves R&D Management at AgrEvo Canada, Inc." *Interfaces*, vol. 29, no. 5, 1999.
Wysoki, R. "OR/MS Implementation Research: A Bibliography." *Interfaces*, vol. 9, no. 2, 1979.

THE WORLD OF MANAGEMENT SCIENCE

Business Analysts Trained in Management Science Can Be a Secret Weapon in a CIO's Quest for Bottom-Line Results

Efficiency nuts. These are the people you see at cocktail parties explaining how the host could disperse that crowd around the popular shrimp dip if he would divide it into three bowls and place them around the room. As she draws the improved traffic flow on a paper napkin, you notice that her favorite word is "optimize"—a tell-tale sign she has studied the field of "operations research" or "management science" (also known as OR/MS).

OR/MS professionals are driven to solve logistics problems. This trait may not make them the most popular people at parties but is exactly what today's information systems (IS) departments need to deliver more business value. Experts say smart IS executives will learn to exploit the talents of these mathematical wizards in their quest to boost a company's bottom line.

According to Ron J. Ponder, chief information officer (CIO) at Sprint Corp. in Kansas City, Mo., and former CIO at Federal Express Corp., "If IS departments had more participation from operations research analysts, they would be building much better, richer IS solutions." As someone who has a Ph.D. in operations research and who built the renowned package-tracking systems at Federal Express, Ponder is a true believer in OR/MS. Ponder and others say analysts trained in OR/MS can turn ordinary information systems into money-saving, decision-support systems and are ideally suited to be members of the business process reengineering team. "I've always had an operations research department reporting to me, and it's been invaluable. Now I'm building one at Sprint," says Ponder.

The Beginnings

OR/MS got its start in World War II, when the military had to make important decisions about allocating scarce resources to various military operations. One of the first business applications for computers in the 1950s was to solve operations research problems for the petroleum industry. A technique called linear programming was used to figure out how to blend gasoline for the right flash point, viscosity, and octane in the most economical way. Since then, OR/MS has spread throughout business and government, from designing efficient drive-thru window operations for Burger King Corp. to creating ultrasophisticated computerized stock trading systems.

A classic OR/MS example is the crew scheduling problem faced by all major airlines. How do you plan the itineraries of 8,000 pilots and 17,000 flight attendants when there is an astronomical number of combinations of planes, crews, and cities? The OR/MS analysts at United Airlines came up with a scheduling system called Paragon that attempts to minimize the amount of paid time that crews spend waiting for flights. Their model factors in constraints such as union rules and Federal Aviation Administration regulations and is projected to save the airline at least $1 million a year.

OR/MS and IS

Somewhere in the 1970s, the OR/MS and IS disciplines went in separate directions. "The IS profession has had less and less contact with the operations research folks...and IS lost a powerful intellectual driver," says Peter G. W. Keen, executive director of the International Center for Information Technologies in Washington, D.C. However, many feel that now is an ideal time for the two disciplines to rebuild some bridges.

Today's OR/MS professionals are involved in a variety of IS-related fields, including inventory management, electronic data interchange, computer-integrated manufacturing, network management, and practical applications of artificial intelligence. Furthermore, each side needs something the other side has: OR/MS analysts need corporate data to plug into their models, and the IS folks need to plug the OR/MS models into their strategic information systems. At the same time, CIOs need intelligent applications that enhance the bottom line and make them heroes with the chief executive officer.

OR/MS analysts can develop a model of how a business process works now and simulate how it could work more efficiently in the future. Therefore, it makes sense to have an OR/MS analyst on the interdisciplinary team that tackles business process reengineering projects. In essence, OR/MS professionals add more value to the IS infrastructure by building "tools that really help decision makers analyze complex situations," says Andrew B. Whinston, director of the Center for Information Systems Management at the University of Texas at Austin.

Although IS departments typically believe their job is done if they deliver accurate and timely information, Thomas M. Cook, president of American Airlines Decision Technologies, Inc. says that adding OR/MS skills to the team can produce intelligent systems that actually recommend solutions to business problems. One of the big success stories at Cook's operations research shop is a "yield management" system that decides how much to overbook and how to set prices for each seat so that a plane is filled up and profits are maximized. The yield management system deals with more than 250 decision variables and accounts for a significant amount of American Airlines' revenue.

Where to Start

So how can the CIO start down the road toward collaboration with OR/MS analysts? If the company already has a group of OR/MS professionals, the IS department can draw on their expertise as internal consultants. Otherwise, the CIO can simply hire a few OR/MS wizards, throw a problem at them, and see what happens. The payback may come surprisingly fast. As one former OR/MS professional put it: "If I couldn't save my employer the equivalent of my own salary in the first month of the year, then I wouldn't feel like I was doing my job."

Adapted from: Mitch Betts. "Efficiency Einsteins." *ComputerWorld*, March 22, 1993, p. 64.

QUESTIONS AND PROBLEMS

1. What is meant by the term decision analysis?
2. Define the term computer model.
3. What is the difference between a spreadsheet model and a computer model?
4. Define the term management science.
5. What is the relationship between management science and spreadsheet modeling?
6. What kinds of spreadsheet applications would not be considered management science?
7. In what ways do spreadsheet models facilitate the decision-making process?
8. What are the benefits of using a modeling approach to decision making?
9. What is a dependent variable?
10. What is an independent variable?
11. Can a model have more than one dependent variable?
12. Can a decision problem have more than one dependent variable?
13. In what ways are prescriptive models different from descriptive models?
14. In what ways are prescriptive models different from predictive models?
15. In what ways are descriptive models different from predictive models?
16. How would you define the words description, prediction, and prescription? Carefully consider what is unique about the meaning of each word.
17. Identify one or more mental models you have used. Can any of them be expressed mathematically? If so, identify the dependent and independent variables in your model.
18. Consider the spreadsheet model shown in Figure 1.2. Is this model descriptive, predictive, or prescriptive in nature, or does it not fall into any of these categories?
19. What are the steps in the problem-solving process?
20. Which step in the problem-solving process do you think is most important? Why?
21. Must a model accurately represent every detail of a decision situation to be useful? Why or why not?
22. If you were presented with several different models of a given decision problem, which would you be most inclined to use? Why?
23. Describe an example in which business or political organizations may use anchoring effects to influence decision making.
24. Describe an example in which business or political organizations may use framing effects to influence decision making.
25. Suppose sharks have been spotted along the beach where you are vacationing with a friend. You and your friend have been informed of the shark sightings and are aware of the damage a shark attack can inflict on human flesh. You both decide (individually) to go swimming anyway. You are promptly attacked by a shark while your friend has a nice time bodysurfing in the waves. Did you make a good or bad decision? Did your friend make a good or bad decision? Explain your answer.
26. Describe an example in which a well-known business, political, or military leader made a good decision that resulted in a bad outcome, or a bad decision that resulted in a good outcome.

Chapter 2

Introduction to Optimization and Linear Programming

2.0 INTRODUCTION

Our world is filled with limited resources. The amount of oil we can pump out of the earth is limited. The amount of land available for garbage dumps and hazardous waste is limited and, in many areas, diminishing rapidly. On a more personal level, each of us has a limited amount of time in which to accomplish or enjoy the activities we schedule each day. Most of us have a limited amount of money to spend while pursuing these activities. Businesses also have limited resources. A manufacturing organization employs a limited number of workers. A restaurant has a limited amount of space available for seating.

Deciding how best to use the limited resources available to an individual or a business is a universal problem. In today's competitive business environment, it is increasingly important to make sure that a company's limited resources are used in the most efficient manner possible. Typically, this involves determining how to allocate the resources in such a way as to maximize profits or minimize costs. **Mathematical programming** (MP) is a field of management science that finds the optimal, or most efficient, way of using limited resources to achieve the objectives of an individual or a business. For this reason, mathematical programming is often referred to as **optimization.**

2.1 APPLICATIONS OF MATHEMATICAL OPTIMIZATION

To help you understand the purpose of optimization and the types of problems for which it can be used, let's consider several examples of decision-making situations in which MP techniques have been applied.

Determining Product Mix. Most manufacturing companies can make a variety of products. However, each product usually requires different amounts of raw materials and labor. Similarly, the amount of profit generated by the products varies. The manager of such a company must decide how many of each product to produce in order to maximize profits or to satisfy demand at minimum cost.

Manufacturing. Printed circuit boards, like those used in most computers, often have hundreds or thousands of holes drilled in them to accommodate the different electrical components that must be plugged into them. To manufacture these boards, a computer-controlled drilling machine must be programmed to drill in a given location, then move the drill bit to the next location and drill again. This process is repeated hundreds or thousands of times to complete all the holes on a circuit board. Manufacturers of these boards would benefit from determining the drilling order that minimizes the total distance the drill bit must be moved.

Routing and Logistics. Many retail companies have warehouses around the country that are responsible for keeping stores supplied with merchandise to sell. The amount of merchandise available at the warehouses and the amount needed at each store tends to fluctuate, as does the cost of shipping or delivering merchandise from the warehouses to the retail locations. Large amounts of money can be saved by determining the least costly method of transferring merchandise from the warehouses to the stores.

Financial Planning. The federal government requires individuals to begin withdrawing money from individual retirement accounts (IRAs) and other tax-sheltered retirement programs no later than age 70.5. There are various rules that must be followed to avoid paying penalty taxes on these withdrawals. Most individuals want to withdraw their money in a manner that minimizes the amount of taxes they must pay while still obeying the tax laws.

2.2 CHARACTERISTICS OF OPTIMIZATION PROBLEMS

These examples represent just a few areas in which MP has been used successfully. We will consider many other examples throughout this book. However, these examples give you some idea of the issues involved in optimization. For instance, each example involves one or more *decisions* that must be made: How many of each product should be produced? Which hole should be drilled next? How much of each product should be shipped from each warehouse to the various retail locations? How much money should an individual withdraw each year from various retirement accounts?

Also, in each example, restrictions, or *constraints*, are likely to be placed on the alternatives available to the decision maker. In the first example, when determining the number of products to manufacture, a production manager is probably faced with a limited amount of raw materials and a limited amount of labor. In the second example, the drill should never return to a position where a hole has already been drilled. In the third example, there is a physical limitation on the amount of merchandise a truck can carry from one warehouse to the stores on its route. In the fourth example, laws determine the minimum and maximum amounts that can be withdrawn from retirement accounts without incurring a penalty. Many other constraints can also be identified for these examples. Indeed, it is not unusual for real-world optimization problems to have hundreds or thousands of constraints.

A final common element in each of the examples is the existence of some goal or *objective* that the decision maker considers when deciding which course of action is best. In the first example, the production manager can decide to produce several different product mixes given the available resources, but the manager will probably choose the mix of products that maximizes profits. In the second example, a large number of possible drilling patterns can be used, but the ideal pattern will probably involve moving the drill bit the shortest total distance. In the third example, there are numerous ways merchandise can be shipped from the warehouses to supply the stores, but the company will probably want to identify the routing that minimizes the total transportation cost. Finally, in the fourth example, individuals can withdraw money from their retirement accounts in many ways without violating the tax laws, but they probably want to find the method that minimizes their tax liability.

2.3 EXPRESSING OPTIMIZATION PROBLEMS MATHEMATICALLY

From the preceding discussion, we know that optimization problems involve three elements: decisions, constraints, and an objective. If we intend to build a mathematical model of an optimization problem, we will need mathematical terms or symbols to represent each of these three elements.

2.3.1 Decisions

The decisions in an optimization problem are often represented in a mathematical model by the symbols $X_1, X_2, \ldots, X_n$. We will refer to $X_1, X_2, \ldots, X_n$ as the **decision variables** (or simply the variables) in the model. These variables might represent the quantities of different products the production manager can choose to produce. They might represent the amount of different pieces of merchandise to ship from a warehouse to a certain store. They might represent the amount of money to be withdrawn from different retirement accounts.

The exact symbols used to represent the decision variables are not particularly important. You could use $Z_1, Z_2, \ldots, Z_n$ or symbols like Dog, Cat, and Monkey to represent the decision variables in the model. The choice of which symbols to use is largely a matter of personal preference and might vary from one problem to the next.

2.3.2 Constraints

The constraints in an optimization problem can be represented in a mathematical model in a number of ways. Three general ways of expressing the possible constraint relationships in an optimization problem are:

A less than or equal to constraint:	$f(X_1, X_2, \ldots, X_n) \leq b$
A greater than or equal to constraint:	$f(X_1, X_2, \ldots, X_n) \geq b$
An equal to constraint:	$f(X_1, X_2, \ldots, X_n) = b$

In each case, the **constraint** is some function of the decision variables that must be less than or equal to, greater than or equal to, or equal to some specific value (represented above by the letter b). We will refer to $f(X_1, X_2, \ldots, X_n)$ as the left-hand-side (LHS) of the constraint and to b as the right-hand-side (RHS) value of the constraint.

For example, we might use a less than or equal to constraint to ensure that the total labor used in producing a given number of products does not exceed the amount of available labor. We might use a greater than or equal to constraint to ensure that the total amount of money withdrawn from a person's retirement accounts is at least the minimum amount required by the IRS. You can use any number of these constraints to represent a given optimization problem depending on the requirements of the situation.

2.3.3 Objective

The objective in an optimization problem is represented mathematically by an objective function in the general format:

$$\text{MAX (or MIN):} \quad f(X_1, X_2, \ldots, X_n)$$

The **objective function** identifies some function of the decision variables that the decision maker wants to either MAXimize or MINimize. In our earlier examples, this function might be used to describe the total profit associated with a product mix, the total distance the drill bit must be moved, the total cost of transporting merchandise, or a retiree's total tax liability.

The mathematical formulation of an optimization problem can be described in the general format:

$$\text{MAX (or MIN):} \quad f_0(X_1, X_2, \ldots, X_n) \qquad 2.1$$

$$\text{Subject to:} \quad f_1(X_1, X_2, \ldots, X_n) \leq b_1 \qquad 2.2$$

$$\vdots$$

$$f_k(X_1, X_2, \ldots, X_n) \geq b_k \qquad 2.3$$

$$\vdots$$

$$f_m(X_1, X_2, \ldots, X_n) = b_m \qquad 2.4$$

This representation identifies the objective function (equation 2.1) that will be maximized (or minimized) and the constraints that must be satisfied (equations 2.2 through 2.4). Subscripts added to the f and b in each equation emphasize that the functions describing the objective and constraints can all be different. The goal in optimization is to find the values of the decision variables that maximize (or minimize) the objective function without violating any of the constraints.

2.4 MATHEMATICAL PROGRAMMING TECHNIQUES

Our general representation of an MP model is just that—general. There are many kinds of functions you can use to represent the objective function and the constraints in an MP model. Of course, you should always use functions that accurately describe the objective and constraints of the problem you are trying to solve. Sometimes, the functions in a model are linear in nature (that is, form straight lines or flat surfaces); other times, they are nonlinear (that is, form curved lines or curved surfaces). Sometimes, the optimal values of the decision variables in a model must take on integer values (whole numbers); other times, the decision variables can assume fractional values.

Given the diversity of MP problems that can be encountered, many techniques have been developed to solve different types of MP problems. In the next several chapters, we will look at these MP techniques and develop an understanding of how they differ and when each should be used. We will begin by examining a technique called **linear programming** (LP), which involves creating and solving optimization problems with linear objective functions and linear constraints. LP is a very powerful tool that can be applied in many business situations. It also forms a basis for several other techniques discussed later and is, therefore, a good starting point for our investigation into the field of optimization.

2.5 AN EXAMPLE LP PROBLEM

We will begin our study of LP by considering a simple example. You should not interpret this to mean that LP cannot solve more complex or realistic problems. LP has been used to solve extremely complicated problems, saving companies millions of dollars. However, jumping directly into one of these complicated problems would be like starting a marathon without ever having gone out for a jog—you would get winded and could be left behind very quickly. So we'll start with something simple.

> Blue Ridge Hot Tubs manufactures and sells two models of hot tubs: the Aqua-Spa and the Hydro-Lux. Howie Jones, the owner and manager of the company, needs to decide how many of each type of hot tub to produce during his next production cycle. Howie buys prefabricated fiberglass hot tub shells from a local supplier and adds the pump and tubing to the shells to create his hot tubs. (This supplier has the capacity to deliver as many hot tub shells as Howie needs.) Howie installs the same type of pump into both hot tubs. He will have only 200 pumps available during his next production cycle. From a manufacturing standpoint, the main difference between the two models of hot tubs is the amount of tubing and labor required. Each Aqua-Spa requires 9 hours of labor and 12 feet of tubing. Each Hydro-Lux requires 6 hours of labor and 16 feet of tubing. Howie expects to have 1,566 production labor hours and 2,880 feet of tubing available during the next production cycle. Howie earns a profit of $350 on each Aqua-Spa he sells and $300 on each Hydro-Lux he sells. He is confident that he can sell all the hot tubs he produces. The question is, how many Aqua-Spas and Hydro-Luxes should Howie produce if he wants to maximize his profits during the next production cycle?

2.6 FORMULATING LP MODELS

The process of taking a practical problem—such as determining how many Aqua-Spas and Hydro-Luxes Howie should produce—and expressing it algebraically in the form of an LP model is known as **formulating** the model. Throughout the next several chapters, you will see that formulating an LP model is as much an art as a science.

2.6.1 Steps in Formulating an LP Model

There are some general steps you can follow to help make sure your formulation of a particular problem is accurate. We will walk through these steps using the hot tub example.

1. **Understand the problem.** This step appears to be so obvious that it hardly seems worth mentioning. However, many people have a tendency to jump into a problem and start writing the objective function and constraints before they really understand the problem. If you do not fully understand the problem you face, it is unlikely that your formulation of the problem will be correct.

   The problem in our example is fairly easy to understand: How many Aqua-Spas and Hydro-Luxes should Howie produce to maximize his profit, while using no more than 200 pumps, 1,566 labor hours, and 2,880 feet of tubing?

2. **Identify the decision variables.** After you are sure you understand the problem, you need to identify the decision variables. That is, what are the fundamental decisions that must be made in order to solve the problem? The answers to this question often will help you identify appropriate decision variables for your model. Identifying the decision variables means determining what the symbols $X_1, X_2, \ldots, X_n$ represent in your model.

   In our example, the fundamental decision Howie faces is this: How many Aqua-Spas and Hydro-Luxes should be produced? In this problem, we will let X_1 represent the number of Aqua-Spas to produce and X_2 represent the number of Hydro-Luxes to produce.

3. **State the objective function as a linear combination of the decision variables.** After determining the decision variables you will use, the next step is to create the objective function for the model. This function expresses the mathematical relationship between the decision variables in the model to be maximized or minimized.

   In our example, Howie earns a profit of \$350 on each Aqua-Spa (X_1) he sells and \$300 on each Hydro-Lux (X_2) he sells. Thus, Howie's objective of maximizing the profit he earns is stated mathematically as:

   $$\text{MAX:} \quad 350X_1 + 300X_2$$

   For whatever values might be assigned to X_1 and X_2, the previous function calculates the associated total profit that Howie would earn. Obviously, Howie wants to maximize this value.

4. **State the constraints as linear combinations of the decision variables.** As mentioned earlier, there are usually some limitations on the values that can be

assumed by the decision variables in an LP model. These restrictions must be identified and stated in the form of constraints.

In our example, Howie faces three major constraints. Because only 200 pumps are available and each hot tub requires one pump, Howie cannot produce more than a total of 200 hot tubs. This restriction is stated mathematically as:

$$1X_1 + 1X_2 \leq 200$$

This constraint indicates that each unit of X_1 produced (that is, each Aqua-Spa built) will use one of the 200 pumps available—as will each unit of X_2 produced (that is, each Hydro-Lux built). The total number of pumps used (represented by $1X_1 + 1X_2$) must be less than or equal to 200.

Another restriction Howie faces is that he has only 1,566 labor hours available during the next production cycle. Because each Aqua-Spa he builds (each unit of X_1) requires 9 labor hours and each Hydro-Lux (each unit of X_2) requires 6 labor hours, the constraint on the number of labor hours is stated as:

$$9X_1 + 6X_2 \leq 1{,}566$$

The total number of labor hours used (represented by $9X_1 + 6X_2$) must be less than or equal to the total labor hours available, which is 1,566.

The final constraint specifies that only 2,880 feet of tubing is available for the next production cycle. Each Aqua-Spa produced (each unit of X_1) requires 12 feet of tubing, and each Hydro-Lux produced (each unit of X_2) requires 16 feet of tubing. The following constraint is necessary to ensure that Howie's production plan does not use more tubing than is available:

$$12X_1 + 16X_2 \leq 2{,}880$$

The total number of feet of tubing used (represented by $12X_1 + 16X_2$) must be less than or equal to the total number of feet of tubing available, which is 2,880.

5. **Identify any upper or lower bounds on the decision variables.** Often, simple upper or lower bounds apply to the decision variables. You can view upper and lower bounds as additional constraints in the problem.

   In our example, there are simple lower bounds of zero on the variables X_1 and X_2 because it is impossible to produce a negative number of hot tubs. Therefore, the following two constraints also apply to this problem:

$$X_1 \geq 0$$
$$X_2 \geq 0$$

   Constraints like these are often referred to as nonnegativity conditions and are quite common in LP problems.

2.7 SUMMARY OF THE LP MODEL FOR THE EXAMPLE PROBLEM

The complete LP model for Howie's decision problem can be stated as:

$$\begin{array}{llr}
\text{MAX:} & 350X_1 + 300X_2 & \quad 2.5 \\
\text{Subject to:} & 1X_1 + 1X_2 \leq 200 & \quad 2.6 \\
 & 9X_1 + 6X_2 \leq 1{,}566 & \quad 2.7 \\
 & 12X_1 + 16X_2 \leq 2{,}880 & \quad 2.8 \\
 & 1X_1 \geq 0 & \quad 2.9 \\
 & 1X_2 \geq 0 & \quad 2.10
\end{array}$$

In this model, the decision variables X_1 and X_2 represent the number of Aqua-Spas and Hydro-Luxes to produce, respectively. Our goal is to determine the values for X_1 and X_2 that maximize the objective in equation 2.5 while simultaneously satisfying all the constraints in equations 2.6 through 2.10.

2.8 THE GENERAL FORM OF AN LP MODEL

The technique of linear programming is so-named because the MP problems to which it applies are linear in nature. That is, it must be possible to express all the functions in an LP model as some weighted sum (or linear combination) of the decision variables. So, an LP model takes on the general form:

$$\begin{array}{llr}
\text{MAX (or MIN):} & c_1X_1 + c_2X_2 + \ldots + c_nX_n & \quad 2.11 \\
\text{Subject to:} & a_{11}X_1 + a_{12}X_2 + \ldots + a_{1n}X_n \leq b_1 & \quad 2.12 \\
 & \vdots & \\
 & a_{k1}X_1 + a_{k2}X_2 + \ldots + a_{kn}X_n \geq b_k & \quad 2.13 \\
 & \vdots & \\
 & a_{m1}X_1 + a_{m2}X_2 + \ldots + a_{mn}X_n = b_m & \quad 2.14
\end{array}$$

Up to this point, we have suggested that the constraints in an LP model represent some type of limited resource. Although this is frequently the case, in later chapters you will see examples of LP models in which the constraints represent things other than limited resources. The important point here is that *any* problem that can be formulated in the above fashion is an LP problem.

The symbols $c_1, c_2, \ldots, c_n$ in equation 2.11 are called **objective function coefficients** and might represent the marginal profits (or costs) associated with the decision variables $X_1, X_2, \ldots, X_n$, respectively. The symbol a_{ij} found throughout equations 2.12 through 2.14 represents the numeric coefficient in the ith constraint for variable X_j. The objective function and constraints of an LP problem represent different weighted sums of the decision variables. The b_i symbols in the constraints, once again, represent values that the corresponding linear combination of the decision variables must be less than or equal to, greater than or equal to, or equal to.

You should now see a direct connection between the LP model we formulated for Blue Ridge Hot Tubs in equations 2.5 through 2.10 and the general definition of an LP model given in equations 2.11 through 2.14. In particular, note that the various symbols used in equations 2.11 through 2.14 to represent numeric constants (that is, the c_j, a_{ij}, and b_i) were replaced by actual numeric values in equations 2.5 through 2.10. Also, note that our formulation of the LP model for Blue Ridge Hot Tubs did not require the use of equal to constraints. Different problems require different types of constraints, and you should use whatever types of constraints are necessary for the problem at hand.

2.9 SOLVING LP PROBLEMS: AN INTUITIVE APPROACH

After an LP model has been formulated, our interest naturally turns to solving it. But before we actually solve our example problem for Blue Ridge Hot Tubs, what do you think is the optimal solution to the problem? Just by looking at the model, what values for X_1 and X_2 do you think would give Howie the largest profit?

Following one line of reasoning, it might seem that Howie should produce as many units of X_1 (Aqua-Spas) as possible because each of these generates a profit of \$350, whereas each unit of X_2 (Hydro-Luxes) generates a profit of only \$300. But what is the maximum number of Aqua-Spas that Howie could produce?

Howie can produce the maximum number of units of X_1 by making no units of X_2 and devoting all his resources to the production of X_1. Suppose we let $X_2 = 0$ in the model in equations 2.5 through 2.10 to indicate that no Hydro-Luxes will be produced. What then is the largest possible value of X_1? If $X_2 = 0$, then the inequality in equation 2.6 tells us:

$$X_1 \leq 200 \qquad \textbf{2.15}$$

So we know that X_1 cannot be any greater than 200 if $X_2 = 0$. However, we also have to consider the constraints in equations 2.7 and 2.8. If $X_2 = 0$, then the inequality in equation 2.7 reduces to:

$$9X_1 \leq 1{,}566 \qquad \textbf{2.16}$$

If we divide both sides of this inequality by 9, we find that the previous constraint is equivalent to:

$$X_1 \leq 174 \qquad \textbf{2.17}$$

Now consider the constraint in equation 2.8. If $X_2 = 0$, then the inequality in equation 2.8 reduces to:

$$12X_1 \leq 2{,}880 \qquad \textbf{2.18}$$

Again, if we divide both sides of this inequality by 12, we find that the previous constraint is equivalent to:

$$X_1 \leq 240 \qquad \textbf{2.19}$$

So, if $X_2 = 0$, the three constraints in our model imposing upper limits on the value of X_1 reduce to the values shown in equations 2.15, 2.17, and 2.19. The most restrictive of these constraints is equation 2.17. Therefore, the maximum number of units of X_1 that can be produced is 174. In other words, 174 is the largest value X_1 can take on and still satisfy all the constraints in the model.

If Howie builds 174 units of X_1 (Aqua-Spas) and 0 units of X_2 (Hydro-Luxes), he will have used all of the labor that is available for production ($9X_1 = 1{,}566$ if $X_1 = 174$). However, he will have 26 pumps remaining ($200 - X_1 = 26$ if $X_1 = 174$) and 792 feet of tubing remaining ($2{,}880 - 12X_1 = 792$ if $X_1 = 174$). Also, notice that the objective function value (or total profit) associated with this solution is:

$$\$350X_1 + \$300X_2 = \$350 \times 174 + \$300 \times 0 = \$60{,}900$$

From this analysis, we see that the solution $X_1 = 174$, $X_2 = 0$ is a *feasible solution* to the problem because it satisfies all the constraints of the model. But is it the *optimal solution?* In other words, is there any other possible set of values for X_1 and X_2 that also satisfies all the constraints *and* results in a higher objective function value? As you will see, the intuitive approach to solving LP problems that we have taken here cannot be trusted because there actually is a *better* solution to Howie's problem.

2.10 SOLVING LP PROBLEMS: A GRAPHICAL APPROACH

The constraints of an LP model define the set of feasible solutions—or the **feasible region**—for the problem. The difficulty in LP is determining which point or points in the feasible region correspond to the best possible value of the objective function. For simple problems with only two decision variables, it is fairly easy to sketch the feasible region for the LP model and locate the optimal feasible point graphically. Because the graphical approach can be used only if there are two decision variables, it has limited practical use. However, it is an extremely good way to develop a basic understanding of the strategy involved in solving LP problems. Therefore, we will use the graphical approach to solve the simple problem faced by Blue Ridge Hot Tubs. chapter 3 shows how to solve this and other LP problems using a spreadsheet.

To solve an LP problem graphically, you first must plot the constraints for the problem and identify its feasible region. This is done by plotting the *boundary lines* of the constraints and identifying the points that will satisfy all the constraints. So, how do we do this for our example problem (repeated below)?

MAX:	$350X_1 + 300X_2$	**2.20**
Subject to:	$1X_1 + 1X_2 \leq 200$	**2.21**
	$9X_1 + 6X_2 \leq 1{,}566$	**2.22**
	$12X_1 + 16X_2 \leq 2{,}880$	**2.23**
	$1X_1 \geq 0$	**2.24**
	$1X_2 \geq 0$	**2.25**

2.10.1 Plotting the First Constraint

The boundary of the first constraint in our model, which specifies that no more than 200 pumps can be used, is represented by the straight line defined by the equation:

$$X_1 + X_2 = 200 \qquad \textbf{2.26}$$

If we can find any two points on this line, the entire line can be plotted easily by drawing a straight line through these points. If $X_2 = 0$, we can see from equation 2.26 that $X_1 = 200$. Thus, the point $(X_1, X_2) = (200, 0)$ must fall on this line. If we let $X_1 = 0$, from equation 2.26, it is easy to see that $X_2 = 200$. So, the point $(X_1, X_2) = (0, 200)$ must also fall on this line. These two points are plotted on the graph in Figure 2.1 and connected to form the straight line representing equation 2.26.

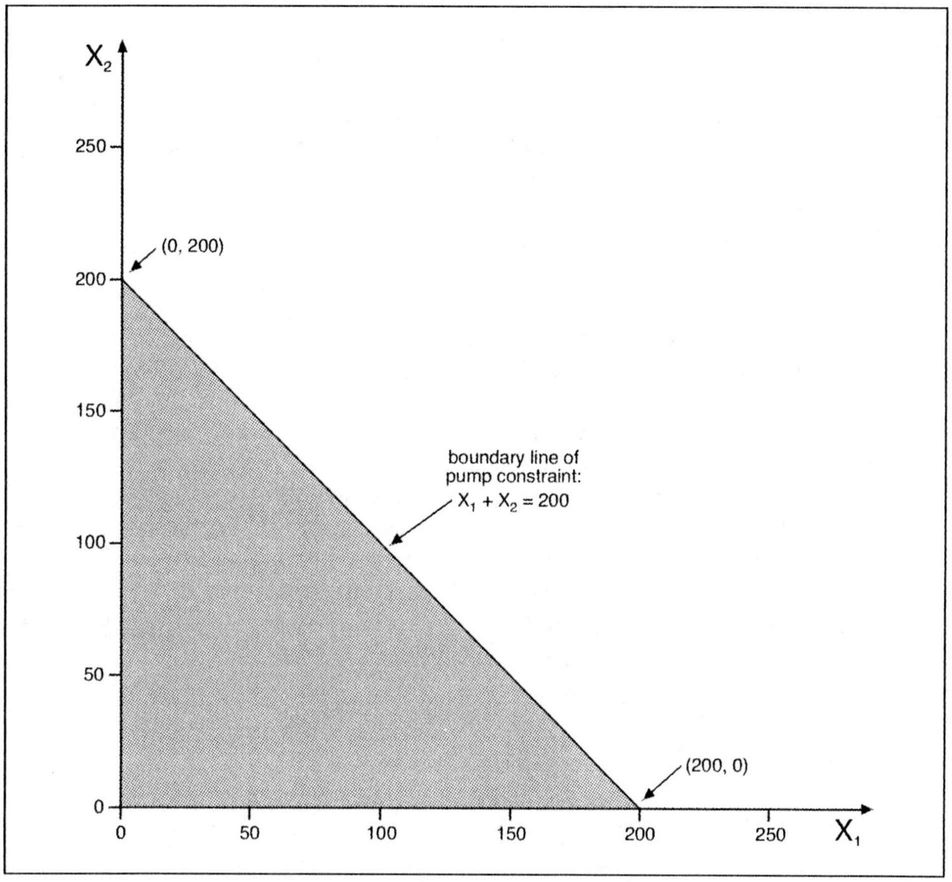

FIGURE 2.1
Graphical representation of the pump constraint

Note that the graph of the line associated with equation 2.26 actually extends beyond the X_1 and X_2 axes shown in Figure 2.1. However, we can disregard the points beyond these axes because the values assumed by X_1 and X_2 cannot be negative (because we also have the constraints given by $X_1 \geq 0$ and $X_2 \geq 0$).

The line connecting the points (0, 200) and (200, 0) in Figure 2.1 identifies the points (X_1, X_2) that satisfy the equality $X_1 + X_2 = 200$. But recall that the first constraint in the LP model is the inequality $X_1 + X_2 \leq 200$. Thus, after plotting the boundary line of a constraint, we must determine which area on the graph corresponds to feasible solutions for the original constraint. This can be done easily by picking an arbitrary point on either side of the boundary line and checking whether it satisfies the original constraint. For example, if we test the point (X_1, X_2) = (0, 0), we see that this point satisfies the first constraint. Therefore, the area of the graph on the same side of the boundary line as the point (0, 0) corresponds to the feasible solutions of our first constraint. This area of feasible solutions is shaded in Figure 2.1.

2.10.2 Plotting the Second Constraint

Some of the feasible solutions to one constraint in an LP model usually will not satisfy one or more of the other constraints in the model. For example, the point

$(X_1, X_2) = (200, 0)$ satisfies the first constraint in our model, but it does not satisfy the second constraint, which requires that no more than 1,566 labor hours be used (because $9 \times 200 + 6 \times 0 = 1{,}800$). So, what values for X_1 and X_2 will simultaneously satisfy both of these constraints? To answer this question, we need to plot the second constraint on the graph as well. This is done in the same manner as before—by locating two points on the boundary line of the constraint and connecting these points with a straight line.

The boundary line for the second constraint in our model is given by:

$$9X_1 + 6X_2 = 1{,}566 \quad \textbf{2.27}$$

If $X_1 = 0$ in equation 2.27, then $X_2 = 1{,}566/6 = 261$. So, the point (0, 261) must fall on the line defined by equation 2.27. Similarly, if $X_2 = 0$ in equation 2.27, then $X_1 = 1{,}566/9 = 174$. So, the point (174, 0) must also fall on this line. These two points are plotted on the graph and connected with a straight line representing equation 2.27, as shown in Figure 2.2.

The line drawn in Figure 2.2 representing equation 2.27 is the boundary line for our second constraint. To determine the area on the graph that corresponds to feasible solutions to the second constraint, we again need to test a point on either side of this line to see if it is feasible. The point $(X_1, X_2) = (0, 0)$ satisfies $9X_1 + 6X_2 \leq 1{,}566$. Therefore, all points on the same side of the boundary line satisfy this constraint.

FIGURE 2.2
Graphical representation of the pump and labor constraints

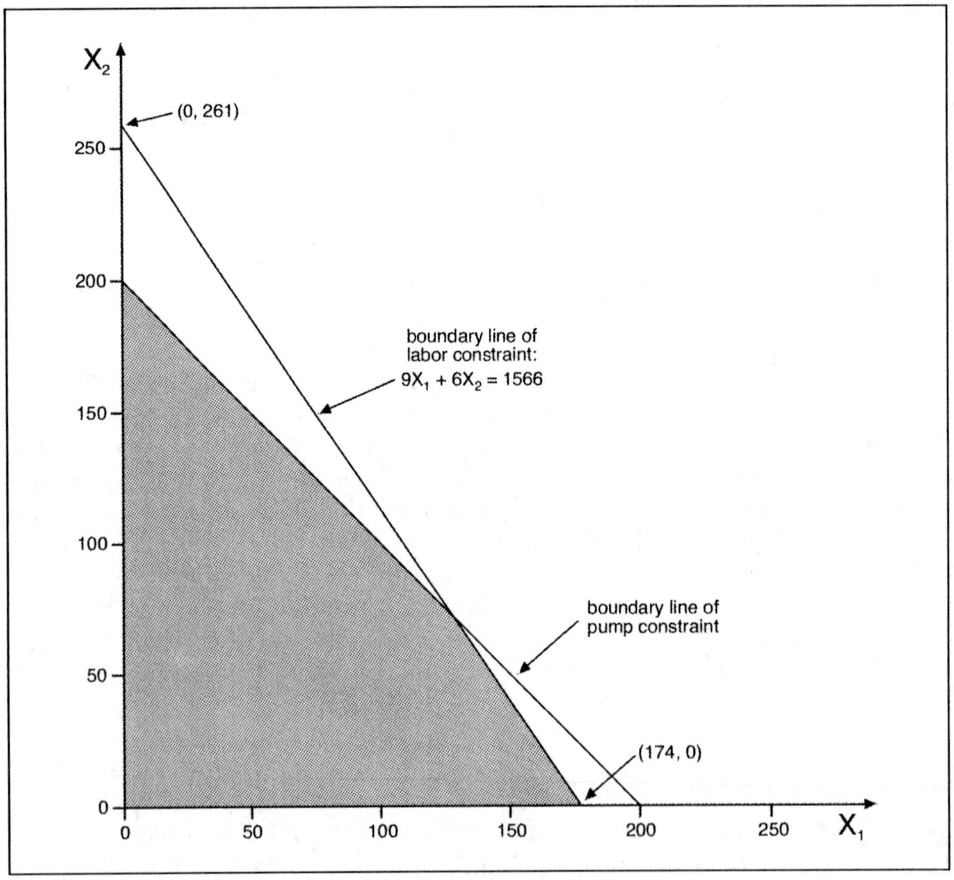

2.10.3 Plotting the Third Constraint

To find the set of values for X_1 and X_2 that satisfies all the constraints in the model we need to plot the third constraint. This constraint requires that no more than 2,880 feet of tubing be used in producing the hot tubs. Again, we will find two points on the graph that fall on the boundary line for this constraint and connect them with a straight line.

The boundary line for the third constraint in our model is:

$$12X_1 + 16X_2 = 2{,}880 \qquad \textbf{2.28}$$

If $X_1 = 0$ in equation 2.28, then $X_2 = 2{,}880/16 = 180$. So the point (0, 180) must fall on the line defined by equation 2.28. Similarly, if $X_2 = 0$ in equation 2.28, then $X_1 = 2{,}880/12 = 240$. So the point (240, 0) must also fall on this line. These two points are plotted on the graph and connected with a straight line representing equation 2.28, as shown in Figure 2.3.

Again, the line drawn in Figure 2.3 representing equation 2.28 is the boundary line for our third constraint. To determine the area on the graph that corresponds to feasible solutions to this constraint, we need to test a point on either side of this line to see if it is feasible. The point $(X_1, X_2) = (0, 0)$ satisfies $12X_1 + 16X_2 \leq 2{,}880$. Therefore, all points on the same side of the boundary line satisfy this constraint.

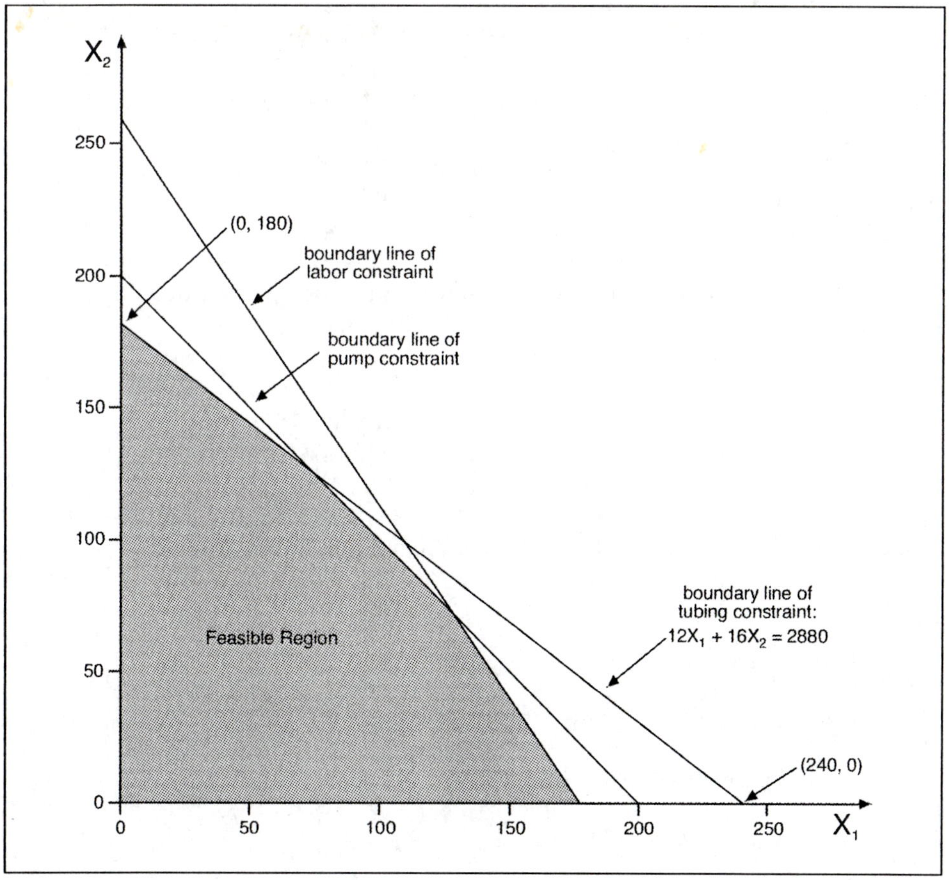

FIGURE 2.3
Graphical representation of the feasible region

2.10.4 The Feasible Region

It is now easy to see which points satisfy all the constraints in our model. These points correspond to the shaded area in Figure 2.3, labeled "Feasible Region." The **feasible region** is the set of points or values that the decision variables can assume and simultaneously satisfy all the constraints in the problem. Take a moment now to carefully compare the graphs in Figures 2.1, 2.2, and 2.3. In particular, notice that when we added the second constraint in Figure 2.2, some of the feasible solutions associated with the first constraint were eliminated because these solutions did not satisfy the second constraint. Similarly, when we added the third constraint in Figure 2.3, another portion of the feasible solutions for the first constraint was eliminated.

2.10.5 Plotting the Objective Function

Now that we have isolated the set of feasible solutions to our LP problem, we need to determine which of these solutions is best. That is, we must determine which point in the feasible region will maximize the value of the objective function in our model. At first glance, it might seem that trying to locate this point is like searching for a needle in a haystack. After all, as shown by the shaded region in Figure 2.3, there are an *infinite* number of feasible solutions to this problem. Fortunately, we can easily eliminate most of the feasible solutions in an LP problem from consideration. It can be shown that if an LP problem has an optimal solution with a finite objective function value, this solution will always occur at a point in the feasible region where two or more of the boundary lines of the constraints intersect. These points of intersection are sometimes called **corner points** or **extreme points** of the feasible region.

To see why the finite optimal solution to an LP problem occurs at an extreme point of the feasible region, consider the relationship between the objective function and the feasible region of our example LP model. Suppose we are interested in finding the values of X_1 and X_2 associated with a given level of profit, such as \$35,000. Then, mathematically, we are interested in finding the points (X_1, X_2) for which our objective function equals \$35,000, or where:

$$\$350X_1 + \$300X_2 = \$35{,}000 \qquad \textbf{2.29}$$

This equation defines a straight line, which we can plot on our graph. Specifically, if $X_1 = 0$ then, from equation 2.29, $X_2 = 116.67$. Similarly, if $X_2 = 0$ in equation 2.29, then $X_1 = 100$. So, the points $(X_1, X_2) = (0, 116.67)$ and $(X_1, X_2) = (100, 0)$ both fall on the line defining a profit level of \$35,000. (Note that all the points on this line produce a profit level of \$35,000.) This line is shown in Figure 2.4.

Now, suppose we are interested in finding the values of X_1 and X_2 that produce some higher level of profit, such as \$52,500. Then, mathematically, we are interested in finding the points (X_1, X_2) for which our objective function equals \$52,500, or where:

$$\$350X_1 + \$300X_2 = \$52{,}500 \qquad \textbf{2.30}$$

This equation also defines a straight line, which we could plot on our graph. If we do this, we'll find that the points $(X_1, X_2) = (0, 175)$ and $(X_1, X_2) = (150, 0)$ both fall on this line, as shown in Figure 2.5.

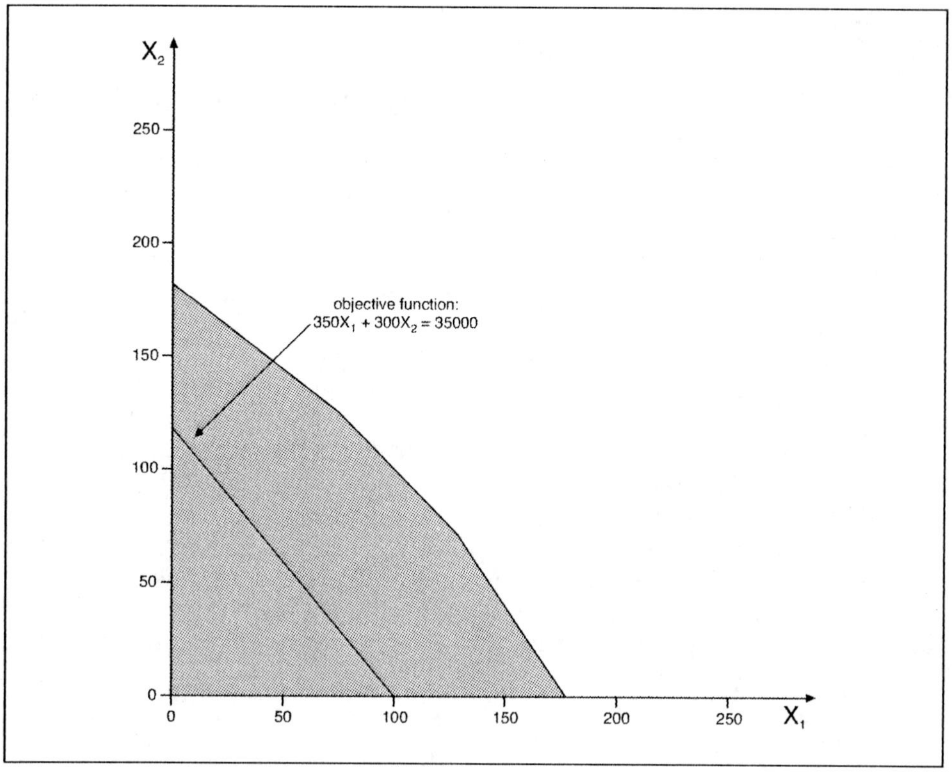

FIGURE 2.4
Graph showing values of X_1 and X_2 that produce an objective function value of $35,000

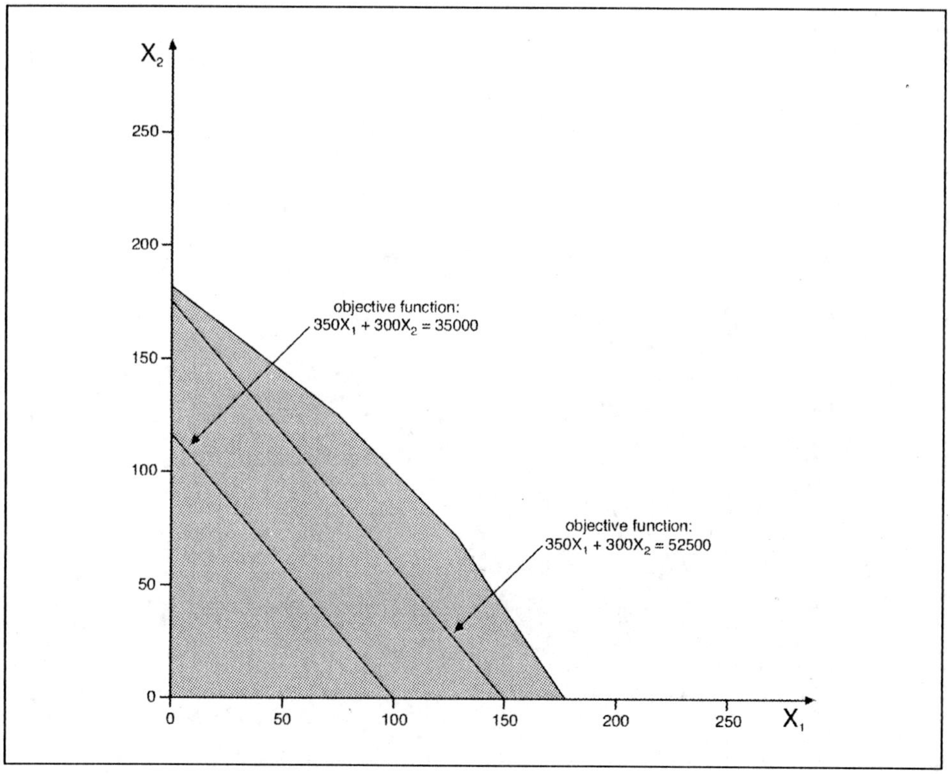

FIGURE 2.5
Parallel level curves for two different objective function values

2.10.6 Finding the Optimal Solution Using Level Curves

The lines in Figure 2.5 representing the two objective function values are sometimes referred to as **level curves** because they represent different levels or values of the objective. Note that the two level curves in Figure 2.5 are *parallel* to one another. If we repeat this process of drawing lines associated with larger and larger values of our objective function, we will continue to observe a series of parallel lines shifting away from the origin—that is, away from the point (0, 0). The very last level curve we can draw that still intersects the feasible region will determine the maximum profit we can achieve. This point of intersection, shown in Figure 2.6, represents the optimal feasible solution to the problem.

As shown in Figure 2.6, the optimal solution to our example problem occurs at the point where the largest possible level curve intersects the feasible region at a single point. This is the feasible point that produces the largest profit for Blue Ridge Hot Tubs. But how do we figure out exactly what point this is and how much profit it provides?

If you compare Figure 2.6 to Figure 2.3, you see that the optimal solution occurs where the boundary lines of the pump and labor constraints intersect (or are equal). Thus, the optimal solution is defined by the point (X_1, X_2) that simultaneously satisfies equations 2.26 and 2.27, which are repeated on the next page:

FIGURE 2.6
Graph showing optimal solution where the level curve is tangent to the feasible region

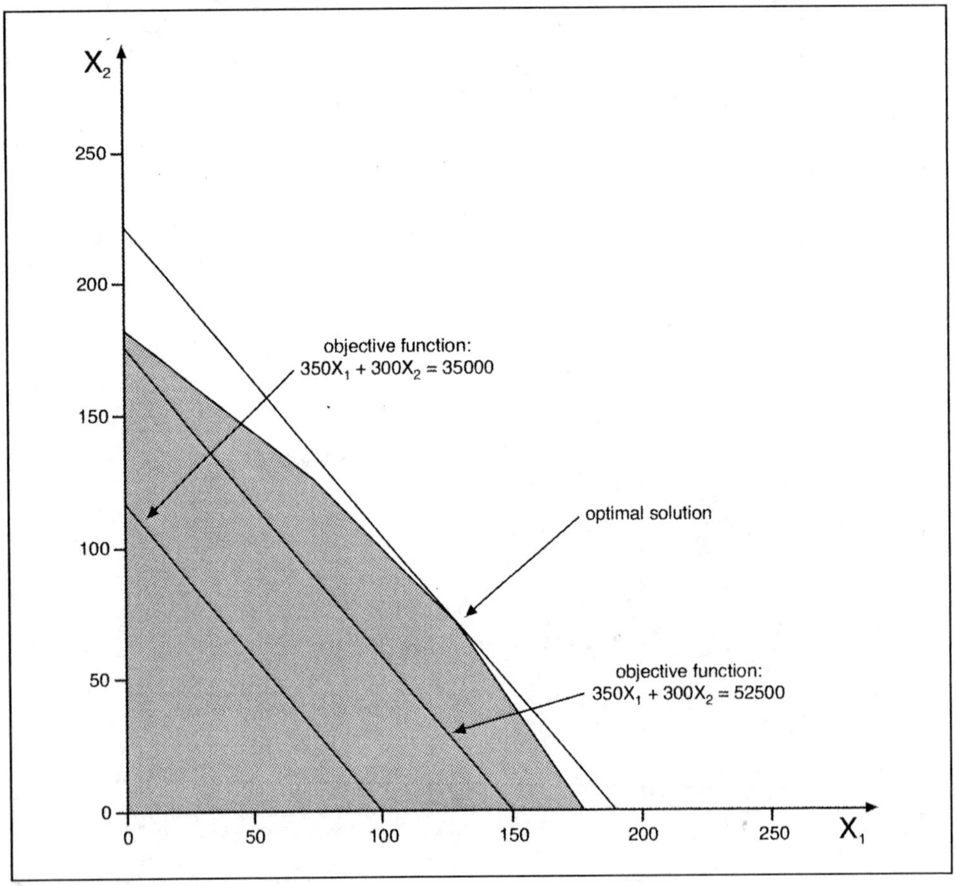

$$X_1 + X_2 = 200$$
$$9X_1 + 6X_2 = 1{,}566$$

From the first equation, we easily conclude that $X_2 = 200 - X_1$. If we substitute this definition of X_2 into the second equation, we obtain:

$$9X_1 + 6(200 - X_1) = 1{,}566$$

Using simple algebra, we can solve this equation to find that $X_1 = 122$. And because $X_2 = 200 - X_1$, we can conclude that $X_2 = 78$. Therefore, we have determined that the optimal solution to our example problem occurs at the point $(X_1, X_2) = (122, 78)$. This point satisfies all the constraints in our model and corresponds to the point in Figure 2.6 identified as the optimal solution.

The total profit associated with this solution is found by substituting the optimal values of $X_1 = 122$ and $X_2 = 78$ into the objective function. Thus, Blue Ridge Hot Tubs can realize a profit of \$66,100 if it produces 122 Aqua-Spas and 78 Hydro-Luxes ($\$350 \times 122 + \$300 \times 78 = \$66{,}100$). Any other production plan results in a lower total profit. In particular, note that the solution we found earlier using the intuitive approach (which produced a total profit of \$60,900) is inferior to the optimal solution identified here.

2.10.7 Finding the Optimal Solution by Enumerating the Corner Points

Earlier, we indicated that if an LP problem has a finite optimal solution, this solution will always occur at some corner point of the feasible region. So, another way of solving an LP problem is to identify all the corner points, or extreme points, of the feasible region and calculate the value of the objective function at each of these points. The corner point with the largest objective function value is the optimal solution to the problem.

This approach is illustrated in Figure 2.7, where the X_1 and X_2 coordinates for each of the extreme points are identified along with the associated objective function values. As expected, this analysis also indicates that the point $(X_1, X_2) = (122, 78)$ is optimal.

Enumerating the corner points to identify the optimal solution is often more difficult than the level curve approach because it requires that you identify the coordinates for *all* the extreme points of the feasible region. If there are many intersecting constraints, the number of extreme points can become rather large, making this procedure very tedious. Also, a special condition exists for which this procedure will not work. This condition, known as an unbounded solution, is described shortly.

2.10.8 Summary of Graphical Solution to LP Problems

To summarize this section, a two-variable LP problem is solved graphically by performing these steps:

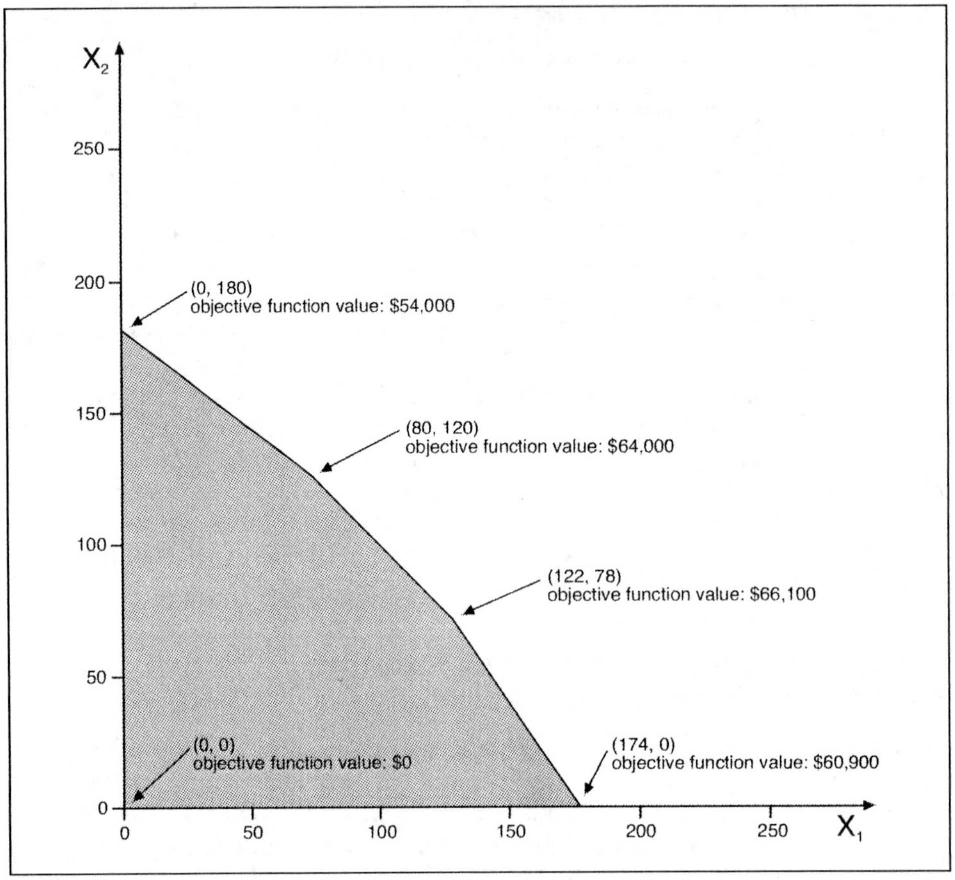

FIGURE 2.7
Objective function values at each extreme point of the feasible region

1. Plot the boundary line of each constraint in the model.
2. Identify the feasible region, that is, the set of points on the graph that simultaneously satisfies all the constraints.
3. Locate the optimal solution by one of the following methods:
   a. Plot one or more level curves for the objective function and determine the direction in which parallel shifts in this line produce improved objective function values. Shift the level curve in a parallel manner in the improving direction until it intersects the feasible region at a single point. Then find the coordinates for this point. This is the optimal solution.
   b. Identify the coordinates of all the extreme points of the feasible region and calculate the objective function values associated with each point. If the feasible region is bounded, the point with the best objective function value is the optimal solution.

2.11 SPECIAL CONDITIONS IN LP MODELS

Several special conditions can arise in LP modeling: *alternate optimal solutions, redundant constraints, unbounded solutions,* and *infeasibility.* The first two conditions do not prevent you from solving an LP model and are not really problems—they are just anomalies that sometimes occur. On the other hand, the last two conditions represent real problems that prevent us from solving an LP model.

2.11.1 Alternate Optimal Solutions

Some LP models can actually have more than one optimal solution, or **alternate optimal solutions.** That is, there can be more than one feasible point that maximizes (or minimizes) the value of the objective function.

For example, suppose Howie can increase the price of Aqua-Spas to the point at which each unit sold generates a profit of $450 rather than $350. The revised LP model for this problem is:

$$
\begin{array}{llrcrcr}
\text{MAX:} & & 450X_1 & + & 300X_2 & & \\
\text{Subject to:} & & 1X_1 & + & 1X_2 & \leq & 200 \\
& & 9X_1 & + & 6X_2 & \leq & 1{,}566 \\
& & 12X_1 & + & 16X_2 & \leq & 2{,}880 \\
& & 1X_1 & & & \geq & 0 \\
& & & & 1X_2 & \geq & 0
\end{array}
$$

Because none of the constraints changed, the feasible region for this model is the same as for the earlier example. The only difference in this model is the objective function. Therefore, the level curves for the objective function are different from what we observed earlier. Several level curves for this model are plotted with its feasible region in Figure 2.8.

Notice that the final level curve in Figure 2.8 intersects the feasible region along an *edge* of the feasible region rather than at a single point. All the points on the line segment joining the corner point at (122, 78) to the corner point at (174, 0) produce the same optimal objective function value of $78,300 for this problem. Thus, all these points are alternate optimal solutions to the problem. If we used a computer to solve this problem, it would identify only one of the corner points of this edge as the optimal solution.

The fact that alternate optimal solutions sometimes occur is really not a problem because this anomaly does not prevent us from finding an optimal solution to the problem. In fact, in chapter 7, "Goal Programming and Multiple Objective Optimization," you will see that alternate optimal solutions are sometimes very desirable.

2.11.2 Redundant Constraints

Redundant constraints present another special condition that sometimes occurs in an LP model. A **redundant constraint** is a constraint that plays no role in determining the feasible region of the problem. For example, in the hot tub example, suppose that 225 hot tub pumps are available instead of 200. The earlier LP model can be modified as follows to reflect this change:

$$
\begin{array}{llrcrcr}
\text{MAX:} & & 350X_1 & + & 300X_2 & & \\
\text{Subject to:} & & 1X_1 & + & 1X_2 & \leq & 225 \\
& & 9X_1 & + & 6X_2 & \leq & 1{,}566 \\
& & 12X_1 & + & 16X_2 & \leq & 2{,}880 \\
& & 1X_1 & & & \geq & 0 \\
& & & & 1X_2 & \geq & 0
\end{array}
$$

FIGURE 2.8
Example of an LP problem with an infinite number of alternate optimal solutions

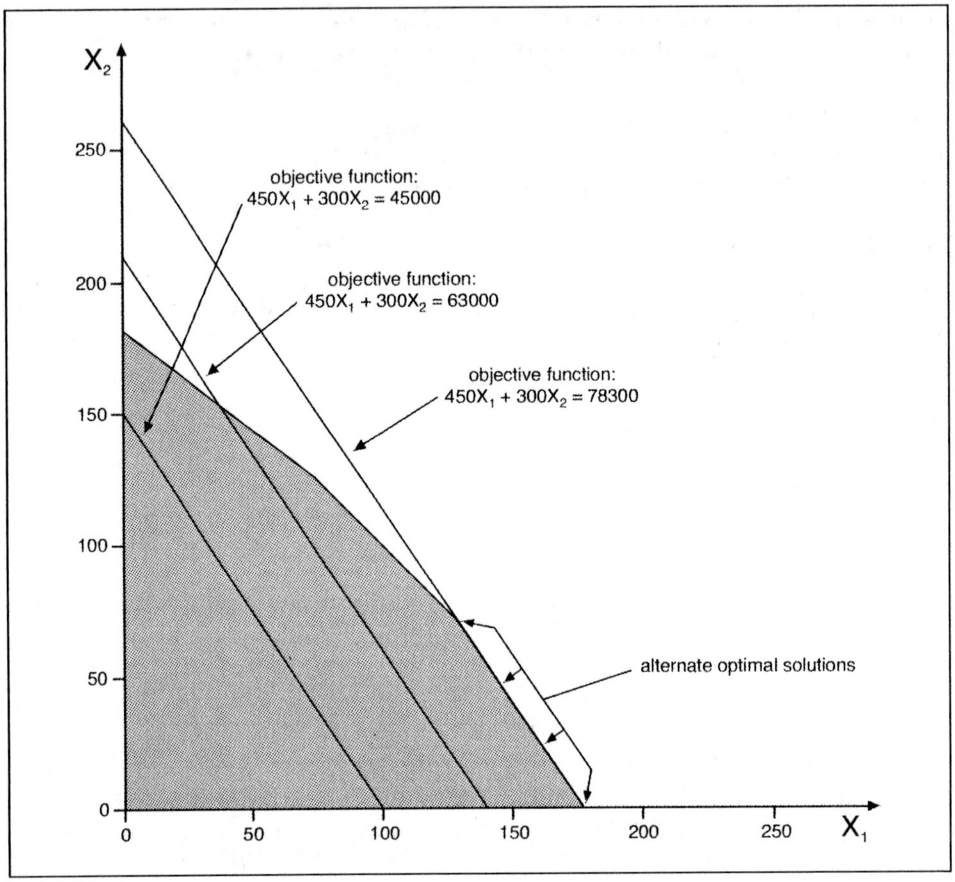

This model is identical to the original model we formulated for this problem *except* for the new upper limit on the first constraint (representing the number of pumps that can be used). The constraints and feasible region for this revised model are shown in Figure 2.9.

Notice that the pump constraint in this model no longer plays any role in defining the feasible region of the problem. That is, as long as the tubing constraint and labor constraints are satisfied (which is always the case for any feasible solution), then the pump constraint will also be satisfied. Therefore, we can remove the pump constraint from the model without changing the feasible region of the problem—the constraint is simply redundant.

The fact that the pump constraint does not play a role in defining the feasible region in Figure 2.9 implies that there will always be an excess number of pumps available. Because none of the feasible solutions identified in Figure 2.9 fall on the boundary line of the pump constraint, this constraint will always be satisfied as a strict inequality ($1X_1 + 1X_2 < 225$) and never as a strict equality ($1X_1 + 1X_2 = 225$).

Again, redundant constraints are not really a problem. They do not prevent us (or the computer) from finding the optimal solution to an LP problem. However, they do represent "excess baggage" for the computer; so if you know that a constraint is redundant, eliminating it saves the computer this excess work. On the other hand, if the model you are working with will be modified and used

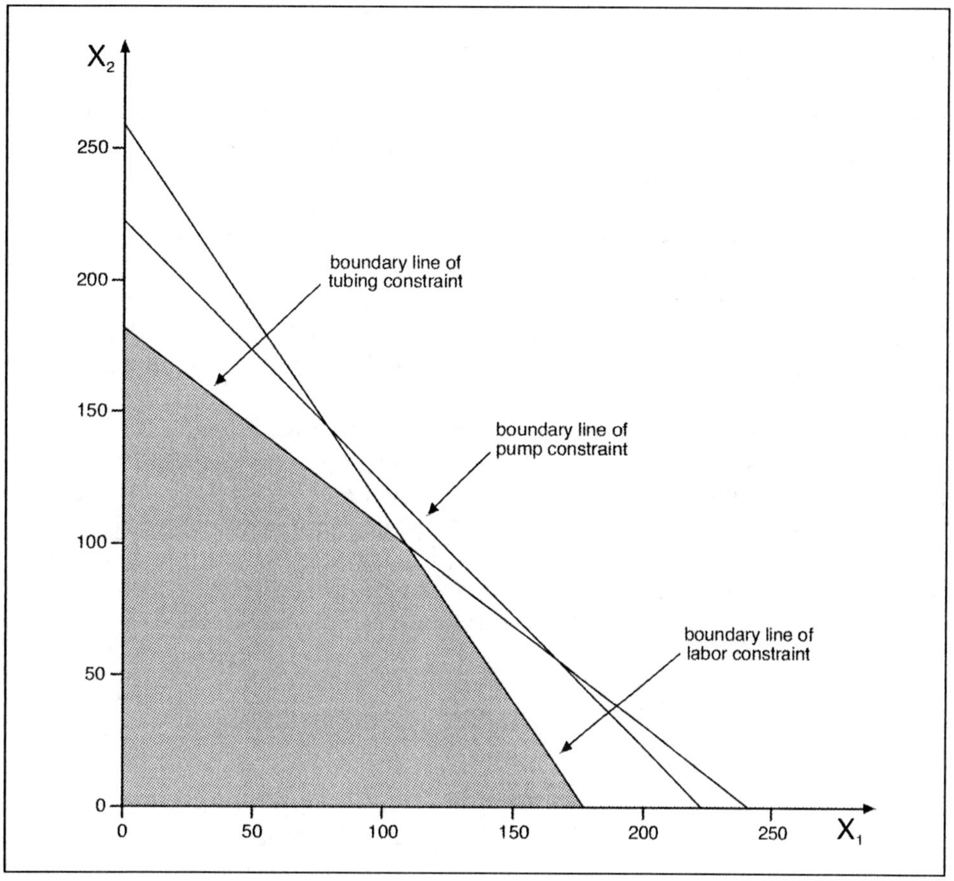

FIGURE 2.9
Example of a redundant constraint

repeatedly, it might be best to leave any redundant constraints in the model because they might not be redundant in the future. For example, from Figure 2.3, we know that if the availability of pumps is returned to 200, then the pump constraint again plays an important role in defining the feasible region (and optimal solution) of the problem.

2.11.3 Unbounded Solutions

When attempting to solve some LP problems, you might encounter situations in which the objective function can be made infinitely large (in the case of a maximization problem) or infinitely small (in the case of a minimization problem). As an example, consider this LP problem:

$$\begin{array}{ll} \text{MAX:} & X_1 + X_2 \\ \text{Subject to:} & X_1 + X_2 \geq 400 \\ & -X_1 + 2X_2 \leq 400 \\ & X_1 \geq 0 \\ & X_2 \geq 0 \end{array}$$

The feasible region and some level curves for this problem are shown in Figure 2.10. From this graph, you can see that as the level curves shift farther and farther away from the origin, the objective function increases. Because the feasible region is not bounded in this direction, you can continue shifting the level curve by an infinite amount and make the objective function infinitely large.

Although it is not unusual to encounter an **unbounded** solution when solving an LP model, such a solution indicates that there is something wrong with the formulation—for example, one or more constraints were omitted from the formulation, or a less than constraint was erroneously entered as a greater than constraint.

While describing how to find the optimal solution to an LP model by enumerating corner points, we noted that this procedure will not always work if the feasible region for the problem is unbounded. Figure 2.10 provides an example of such a situation. The only extreme points for the feasible region in Figure 2.10 occur at the points (400, 0) and ($133.\bar{3}$, $266.\bar{6}$). The objective function value at both of these points (and at any point on the line segment joining them) is 400. By enumerating the extreme points for this problem, we might erroneously conclude that alternate optimal solutions to this problem exist that produce an optimal objective function value of 400. This is true if the problem involved *minimizing* the objective function. However, the goal here is to *maximize* the objective function value, which, as we have seen, can be done without limit. So, when trying to solve an LP

FIGURE 2.10
Example of an LP problem with an unbounded solution

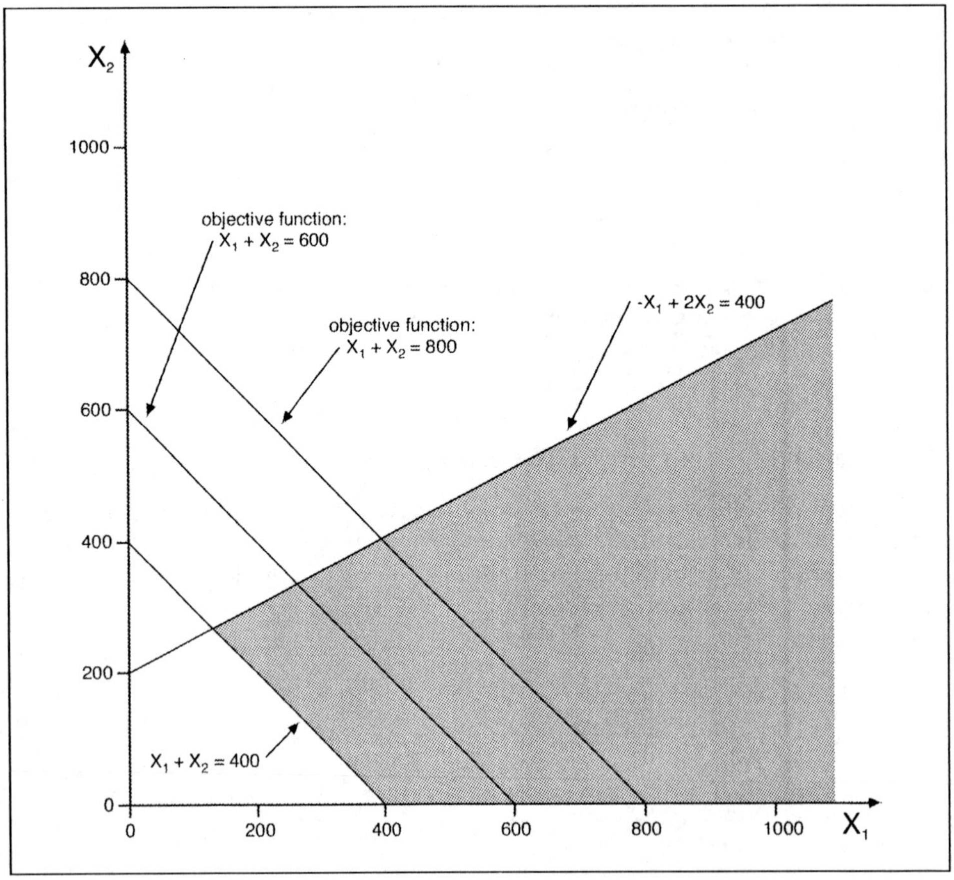

problem by enumerating the extreme points of an unbounded feasible region, you must also check whether or not the objective function is unbounded.

2.11.4 Infeasibility

An LP problem is **infeasible** if there is no way to simultaneously satisfy all the constraints in the problem. As an example, consider the LP model:

$$\begin{array}{lrl} \text{MAX:} & X_1 + X_2 & \\ \text{Subject to:} & X_1 + X_2 & \leq 150 \\ & X_1 + X_2 & \geq 200 \\ & X_1 & \geq 0 \\ & X_2 & \geq 0 \end{array}$$

The feasible solutions for the first two constraints in this model are shown in Figure 2.11. Notice that the feasible solutions to the first constraint fall on the left side of its boundary line, whereas the feasible solutions to the second constraint fall on the right side of its boundary line. Therefore, no possible values for X_1 and X_2 exist that simultaneously satisfy both constraints in the model. In such a case, there are no feasible solutions to the problem.

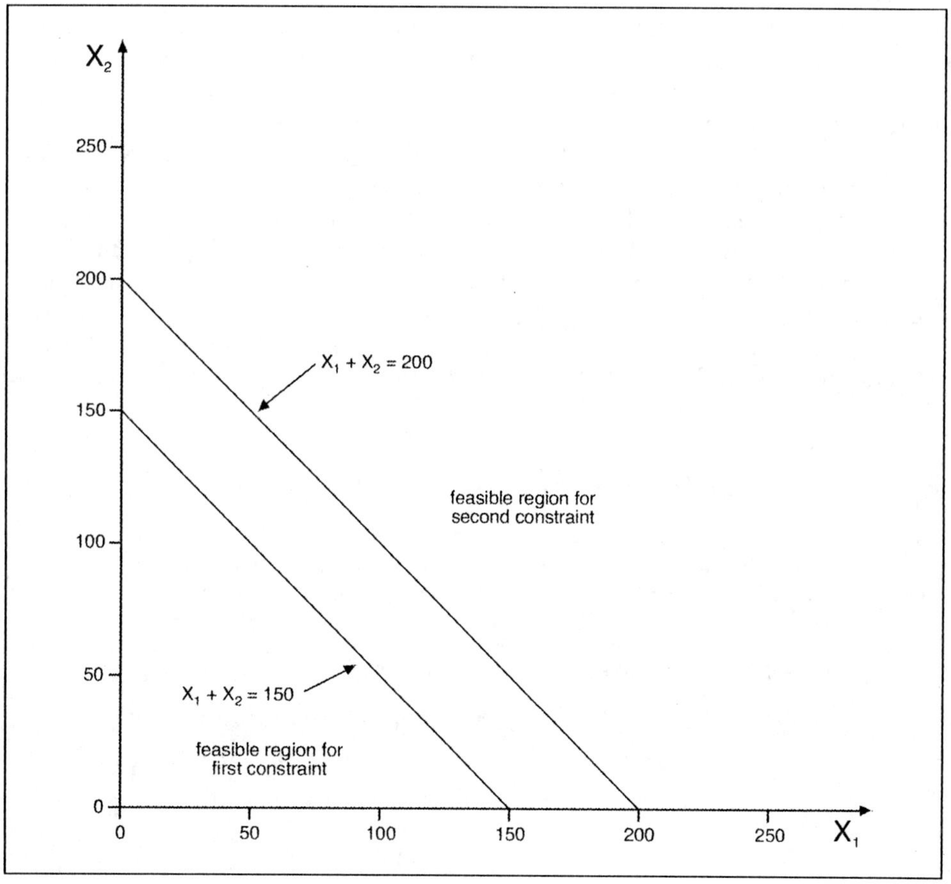

FIGURE 2.11
Example of an LP problem with no feasible solution

Infeasibility can occur in LP problems, perhaps due to an error in the formulation of the model—such as unintentionally making a less than or equal to constraint a greater than or equal to constraint. Or there just might not be a way to satisfy all the constraints in the model. In this case, constraints will have to be eliminated or loosened in order to obtain a feasible region (and feasible solution) for the problem.

Loosening constraints involves increasing the upper limits (or reducing the lower limits) to expand the range of feasible solutions. For example, if we loosen the first constraint in the previous model by changing the upper limit from 150 to 250, there is a feasible region for the problem. Of course, loosening constraints should not be done arbitrarily. In a real model, the value 150 would represent some actual characteristic of the decision problem (such as the number of pumps available to make hot tubs). We obviously cannot change this value to 250 unless it is appropriate to do so—that is, unless we know another 100 pumps can be obtained.

2.12 SUMMARY

This chapter provided an introduction to an area of management science known as mathematical programming (MP), or optimization. Optimization covers a broad range of problems that share a common goal—determining the values for the decision variables in a problem that will maximize (or minimize) some objective function while satisfying various constraints. Constraints impose restrictions on the values that can be assumed by the decision variables and define the set of feasible options (or the feasible region) for the problem.

Linear programming (LP) problems represent a special category of MP problems in which the objective function and all the constraints can be expressed as linear combinations of the decision variables. Simple, two-variable LP problems can be solved graphically by identifying the feasible region and plotting level curves for the objective function. An optimal solution to an LP problem always occurs at a corner point of its feasible region (unless the objective function is unbounded).

Some anomalies can occur in optimization problems; these include alternate optimal solutions, redundant constraints, unbounded solutions, and infeasibility.

2.13 REFERENCES

Bazaraa, M. and J. Jarvis. *Linear Programming and Network Flows.* New York: Wiley, 1990.

Dantzig, G. *Linear Programming and Extensions.* Princeton, NJ: Princeton University Press, 1963.

Eppen, G., F. Gould, and C. Schmidt, *Introduction to Management Science.* Englewood Cliffs, NJ: Prentice Hall, 1993.

Shogan, A. *Management Science.* Englewood Cliffs, NJ: Prentice Hall, 1988.

Winston, W. *Operations Research: Applications and Algorithms.* Belmont, CA: Duxbury Press, 1997.

QUESTIONS AND PROBLEMS

1. An LP model can have more than one optimal solution. Is it possible for an LP model to have exactly two optimal solutions? Why or why not?
2. In the solution to the Blue Ridge Hot Tubs problem, the optimal values for X_1 and X_2 turned out to be integers (whole numbers). Is this a general property of the solutions to LP problems? In other words, will the solution to an LP problem always consist of integers? Why or why not?
3. To determine the feasible region associated with less than or equal to constraints or greater than or equal to constraints, we graphed these constraints as if they were equal to constraints. Why is this possible?
4. Are the following objective functions for an LP model equivalent? That is, if they are both used, one at a time, to solve a problem with exactly the same constraints, will the optimal values for X_1 and X_2 be the same in both cases? Why or why not?

$$\begin{aligned} &\text{MAX:} && 2X_1 + 3X_2 \\ &\text{MIN:} && -2X_1 - 3X_2 \end{aligned}$$

5. Which of the following constraints are not linear or cannot be included as a constraint in a linear programming problem?

   a. $2X_1 + X_2 - 3X_3 \geq 50$

   b. $2X_1 + \sqrt{X_2} \geq 60$

   c. $4X_1 - \frac{1}{3}X_2 = 75$

   d. $\dfrac{3X_1 + 2X_2 - 3X_3}{X_1 + X_2 + X_3} \leq 0.9$

   e. $3X_1^2 + 7X_2 \leq 45$

6. Solve the following LP problem graphically by enumerating the corner points.

$$\begin{aligned} &\text{MAX:} && 3X_1 + 4X_2 \\ &\text{Subject to:} && X_1 \leq 12 \\ & && X_2 \leq 10 \\ & && 4X_1 + 6X_2 \leq 72 \\ & && X_1, X_2 \geq 0 \end{aligned}$$

7. Solve the following LP problem graphically using level curves.

$$\begin{aligned} &\text{MIN:} && 2X_1 + 3X_2 \\ &\text{Subject to:} && 2X_1 + 1X_2 \geq 3 \\ & && 4X_1 + 5X_2 \geq 20 \\ & && 2X_1 + 8X_2 \geq 16 \\ & && 5X_1 + 6X_2 \leq 60 \\ & && X_1, X_2 \geq 0 \end{aligned}$$

8. Solve the following LP problem graphically using level curves.

$$\begin{aligned} \text{MAX:}\quad & 2X_1 + 5X_2 \\ \text{Subject to:}\quad & 6X_1 + 5X_2 \leq 60 \\ & 2X_1 + 3X_2 \leq 24 \\ & 3X_1 + 6X_2 \leq 48 \\ & X_1, X_2 \geq 0 \end{aligned}$$

9. Solve the following LP problem graphically by enumerating the corner points.

$$\begin{aligned} \text{MIN:}\quad & 5X_1 + 20X_2 \\ \text{Subject to:}\quad & X_1 + X_2 \geq 12 \\ & 2X_1 + 5X_2 \geq 40 \\ & X_1 + X_2 \leq 15 \\ & X_1, X_2 \geq 0 \end{aligned}$$

10. Consider the following LP problem.

$$\begin{aligned} \text{MAX:}\quad & 3X_1 + 2X_2 \\ \text{Subject to:}\quad & 3X_1 + 3X_2 \leq 300 \\ & 6X_1 + 3X_2 \leq 480 \\ & 3X_1 + 3X_2 \leq 480 \\ & X_1, X_2 \geq 0 \end{aligned}$$

a. Sketch the feasible region for this model.
b. What is the optimal solution?
c. Identify any redundant constraints in this model.

11. Solve the following LP problem graphically by enumerating the corner points.

$$\begin{aligned} \text{MAX:}\quad & 10X_1 + 12X_2 \\ \text{Subject to:}\quad & 8X_1 + 6X_2 \leq 98 \\ & 6X_1 + 8X_2 \leq 98 \\ & X_1 + X_2 \geq 14 \\ & X_1, X_2 \geq 0 \end{aligned}$$

12. Solve the following LP problem using level curves.

$$\begin{aligned} \text{MAX:}\quad & 4X_1 + 5X_2 \\ \text{Subject to:}\quad & 2X_1 + 3X_2 \leq 120 \\ & 4X_1 + 3X_2 \leq 140 \\ & X_1 + X_2 \geq 80 \\ & X_1, X_2 \geq 0 \end{aligned}$$

13. The marketing manager for Mountain Mist soda needs to decide how many TV spots and magazine ads to run during the next quarter. Each TV spot costs \$5,000 and is expected to increase sales by 300,000 cans. Each magazine ad costs \$2,000 and is expected to increase sales by 500,000 cans. A total of \$100,000 may be spent on TV and magazine ads; however, Mountain Mist

wants to spend no more than $70,000 on TV spots and no more than $50,000 on magazine ads. Mountain Mist earns a profit of $0.05 on each can it sells.

a. Formulate an LP model for this problem.
b. Sketch the feasible region for this model.
c. Find the optimal solution to the problem using level curves.

14. The Electrotech Corporation manufactures two industrial-sized electrical devices: generators and alternators. Both of these products require wiring and testing during the assembly process. Each generator requires 2 hours of wiring and 1 hour of testing and can be sold for a $250 profit. Each alternator requires 3 hours of wiring and 2 hours of testing and can be sold for a $150 profit. There are 260 hours of wiring time and 140 hours of testing time available in the next production period and Electrotech wants to maximize profit.
    a. Formulate an LP model for this problem.
    b. Sketch the feasible region for this problem.
    c. Determine the optimal solution to this problem using level curves.
15. Refer to Question 14. Suppose that Electrotech's management decides that they need to make at least 20 generators and at least 20 alternators.
    a. Reformulate your LP model to account for this change.
    b. Sketch the feasible region for this problem.
    c. Determine the optimal solution to this problem by enumerating the corner points.
16. Refer to Question 15. Suppose that Electrotech can acquire additional wiring time at a very favorable cost. Should it do so? Why or why not?
17. Bill's Grill is a popular college restaurant that is famous for its hamburgers. The owner of the restaurant, Bill, mixes fresh ground beef and pork with a secret ingredient to make delicious quarter-pound hamburgers that are advertised as having no more than 25% fat. Bill can buy beef containing 80% meat and 20% fat at $0.85 per pound. He can buy pork containing 70% meat and 30% fat at $0.65 per pound. Bill wants to determine the minimum cost way to blend the beef and pork to make hamburgers that have no more than 25% fat.
    a. Formulate an LP model for this problem. (*Hint:* The decision variables for this problem represent the percentage of beef and the percentage of pork to combine.)
    b. Sketch the feasible region for this problem.
    c. Determine the optimal solution to this problem by enumerating the corner points.
18. The Springer Dog Food Company makes dry dog food from two ingredients. The two ingredients (A and B) provide different amounts of protein and vitamins. Ingredient A provides 16 units of protein and 4 units of vitamins per pound. Ingredient B provides 8 units of protein and 8 units of vitamins per pound. Ingredients A and B cost $0.50 and $0.20 per pound, respectively. The company wants its dog food to contain at least 12 units of protein and 6 units of vitamins per pound and be as inexpensive as possible.
    a. Formulate an LP model for this problem.
    b. Sketch the feasible region for this model.
    c. Find the optimal solution to the problem by enumerating the corner points.
19. Refer to Question 18. How will the optimal solution change if the company requires only 5 units of vitamins per pound rather than 6?

20. GeoTherm Mining Company owns two mines that each produce three different grades of coal: high, medium, and low. During each hour of operation, mine 1 produces 6 tons of high-grade coal, 2 tons of medium-grade coal, and 4 tons of low-grade coal. Mine 2 produces 2 tons of high-grade coal, 2 tons of medium-grade coal, and 8 tons of low-grade coal per hour of operation. It costs \$200 per hour to operate mine 1 and \$160 per hour to operate mine 2. To fulfill its contractual obligations to a local powerplant, GeoTherm has to supply at least 12 tons of high-grade coal, 8 tons of medium-grade coal, and 24 tons of low-grade coal per day. How many hours per day should each mine be operated in order for GeoTherm to supply the powerplant in the least costly way?
    a. Formulate an LP model for this problem.
    b. Sketch the feasible region for this model.
    c. Find the optimal solution to the problem using level curves.
21. A farmer in Georgia has a 100-acre farm on which to plant watermelons and cantaloupes. Every acre planted with watermelons requires 50 gallons of water per day and must be prepared for planting with 20 pounds of fertilizer. Every acre planted with cantaloupes requires 75 gallons of water per day and must be prepared for planting with 15 pounds of fertilizer. The farmer estimates that it will take 2 hours of labor to harvest each acre planted with watermelons and 2.5 hours to harvest each acre planted with cantaloupes. He believes that watermelons will sell for about \$3 each, and cantaloupes will sell for about \$1 each. Every acre planted with watermelons is expected to yield 90 salable units. Every acre planted with cantaloupes is expected to yield 300 salable units. The farmer can pump about 6,000 gallons of water per day for irrigation purposes from a shallow well. He can buy as much fertilizer as he needs at a cost of \$10 per 50-pound bag. Finally, the farmer can hire laborers to harvest the fields at a rate of \$5 per hour. If the farmer sells all the watermelons and cantaloupes he produces, how many acres of each crop should the farmer plant in order to maximize profits?
    a. Formulate an LP model for this problem.
    b. Sketch the feasible region for this model.
    c. Find the optimal solution to the problem using level curves.
22. PC-Express is a computer retail store that sells two kinds of microcomputers: desktops and laptops. The company earns \$600 on each desktop computer it sells and \$900 on each laptop. The microcomputers PC-Express sells are actually manufactured by another company. This manufacturer has a special order to fill for another customer and cannot ship more than 80 desktop computers and 75 laptops to PC-Express next month. The employees at PC-Express must spend about 2 hours installing software and checking each desktop computer they sell. They spend roughly 3 hours to complete this process for laptop computers. They expect to have about 300 hours available for this purpose during the next month. The store's management is fairly certain that they can sell all the computers they order, but are unsure how many desktops and laptops they should order to maximize profits.
    a. Formulate an LP model for this problem.
    b. Sketch the feasible region for this model.
    c. Find the optimal solution to the problem by enumerating the corner points.

Chapter 3

Modeling and Solving LP Problems in a Spreadsheet

3.0 INTRODUCTION

Chapter 2 discussed how to formulate linear programming (LP) problems and how to solve simple, two-variable LP problems graphically. As you might expect, very few real-world LP problems involve only two decision variables. So, the graphical solution approach is of limited value in solving LP problems. However, the discussion of two-variable problems provides a basis for understanding the issues involved in all LP problems and the general strategies for solving them.

For example, every solvable LP problem has a feasible region, and an optimal solution to the problem can be found at some extreme point of this region (assuming the problem is not unbounded). This is true of all LP problems regardless of the number of decision variables. Although it is fairly easy to graph the feasible region for a two-variable LP problem, it is difficult to visualize or graph the feasible region of an LP problem with three variables because such a graph is three-dimensional. If there are more than three variables, it is virtually impossible to visualize or graph the feasible region for an LP problem because such a graph involves more than three dimensions.

Fortunately, several mathematical techniques exist to solve LP problems involving almost any number of variables without visualizing or graphing their feasible regions. These techniques are now built into spreadsheet packages in a way that makes solving LP problems a fairly simple task. So, using the appropriate computer software, you can solve almost any LP problem easily. The main challenge is ensuring that you formulate the LP problem correctly and communicate this formulation to the computer accurately. This chapter shows you how to do this using spreadsheets.

3.1 SPREADSHEET SOLVERS

The importance of LP (and optimization in general) is underscored by the fact that Excel, Quattro Pro, and Lotus 1-2-3 all come with built-in spreadsheet optimization tools called **solvers.** This book uses Excel to illustrate how spreadsheet solvers can solve optimization problems. However, the same concepts and techniques presented here apply to other spreadsheet packages, although certain details of implementation may differ.

You can also solve optimization problems without using a spreadsheet by using a specialized mathematical programming package. A partial list of these packages includes: LINDO, MPSX, CPLEX, and MathPro. Typically, these packages are used by researchers and businesses interested in solving extremely large problems that do not fit conveniently in a spreadsheet.

The Spreadsheet Solver Company

Frontline Systems, Inc. created the solvers in Microsoft Excel, Lotus 1-2-3, and Corel Quattro Pro. Frontline markets enhanced versions of these spreadsheet solvers that offer greater capacity, faster speed, and several ease-of-use features. You can find out more about Frontline Systems and their products by visiting their Web site at http://www.solver.com.

3.2 SOLVING LP PROBLEMS IN A SPREADSHEET

We will demonstrate the mechanics of using the Solver in Excel by solving the problem faced by Howie Jones, described in chapter 2. Recall that Howie owns and operates Blue Ridge Hot Tubs, a company that sells two models of hot tubs: the Aqua-Spa and the Hydro-Lux. Howie purchases prefabricated fiberglass hot tub shells and installs a common water pump and the appropriate amount of tubing into each hot tub. Every Aqua-Spa requires 9 hours of labor and 12 feet of tubing; every Hydro-Lux requires 6 hours of labor and 16 feet of tubing. Demand for these products is such that each Aqua-Spa produced can be sold to generate a profit of $350, and each Hydro-Lux produced can be sold to generate a profit of $300. The company expects to have 200 pumps, 1,566 hours of labor, and 2,880 feet of tubing available during the next production cycle. The problem is to determine the optimal number of Aqua-Spas and Hydro-Luxes to produce in order to maximize profits.

Chapter 2 developed the following LP formulation for the problem Howie faces. In this model, X_1 represents the number of Aqua-Spas to be produced, and X_2 represents the number of Hydro-Luxes to be produced.

MAX:	$350X_1 + 300X_2$	} profit
Subject to:	$1X_1 + 1X_2 \leq 200$	} pump constraint
	$9X_1 + 6X_2 \leq 1{,}566$	} labor constraint
	$12X_1 + 16X_2 \leq 2{,}880$	} tubing constraint
	$1X_1 \geq 0$	} simple lower bound
	$1X_2 \geq 0$	} simple lower bound

So, how do you solve this problem in a spreadsheet? First, you must implement, or build, this model in the spreadsheet.

3.3 THE STEPS IN IMPLEMENTING AN LP MODEL IN A SPREADSHEET

The following four steps summarize what must be done to implement any LP problem in a spreadsheet.

1. **Organize the data for the model on the spreadsheet.** The data for the model consist of the coefficients in the objective function, the various coefficients in the constraints, and the right-hand-side (RHS) values for the constraints. There is usually more than one way to organize the data for a particular problem on a spreadsheet, but you should keep in mind some general guidelines. First, the goal is to organize the data so their purpose and meaning are as clear as possible. Think of your spreadsheet as a management report that needs to communicate clearly the important factors of the problem being solved. To this end, you should spend some time organizing the data for the problem in your mind's eye—visualizing how the data can be laid out logically—before you start typing values in the spreadsheet. Descriptive labels should be placed in the spreadsheet to clearly identify the various data elements. Often, row and column structures of the data in the model can be used in the spreadsheet to facilitate model implementation. (Note that some or all of the coefficients and values for an LP model might be calculated from other data, often referred to as the primary data. It is best to maintain primary data in the spreadsheet and use appropriate formulas to calculate the coefficients and values that are needed for the LP formulation. Then, if the primary data change, appropriate changes will be made automatically in the coefficients for the LP model.)
2. **Reserve separate cells in the spreadsheet to represent each decision variable in the algebraic model.** Although you can use any empty cells in a spreadsheet to represent the decision variables, it is usually best to arrange the cells representing the decision variables in a way that parallels the structure of the data. This is often helpful in setting up formulas for the objective function and constraints. When possible, it is also a good idea to keep the cells representing decision variables in the same area of the spreadsheet. In addition, you should use descriptive labels to clearly identify the meaning of these cells.
3. **Create a formula in a cell in the spreadsheet that corresponds to the objective function in the algebraic model.** The spreadsheet formula corresponding to the objective function is created by referring to the data cells where the objective function coefficients have been entered (or calculated) and to the corresponding cells representing the decision variables.

4. **For each constraint, create a formula in a separate cell in the spreadsheet that corresponds to the left-hand-side (LHS) of the constraint.** The formula corresponding to the LHS of each constraint is created by referring to the data cells where the coefficients for these constraints have been entered (or calculated) and to the appropriate decision variable cells. Many of the constraint formulas have a similar structure. Thus, when possible, you should create constraint formulas that can be copied to implement other constraint formulas. This not only reduces the effort required to implement a model, but also helps avoid hard-to-detect typing errors.

Although each of the previous steps must be performed to implement an LP model in a spreadsheet, they do not have to be performed in the order indicated. It is usually wise to perform step 1 first, followed by step 2. But the order in which steps 3 and 4 are performed often varies from problem to problem.

Also, it is often wise to use shading, background colors, and/or borders to identify the cells representing decision variables, constraints, and the objective function in a model. This allows the user of a spreadsheet to more readily distinguish between cells representing raw data (that can be changed) and other elements of the model. We have more to say about how to design and implement effective spreadsheet models for LP problems. But first, let's see how the previous steps can be used to implement a spreadsheet model using our example problem.

3.4 A SPREADSHEET MODEL FOR THE BLUE RIDGE HOT TUBS PROBLEM

One possible spreadsheet representation for our example problem is given in Figure 3.1 (and in the file named Fig3-1.xls on your data disk). Let's walk through the creation of this model step-by-step so you can see how it relates to the algebraic formulation of the model.

3.4.1 Organizing the Data

One of the first steps in building any spreadsheet model for an LP problem is to organize the data for the model on the spreadsheet. In Figure 3.1, we enter the data for the unit profits for Aqua-Spas and Hydro-Luxes in cells B6 and C6, respectively. Next, the number of pumps, labor hours, and feet of tubing required to produce each type of hot tub are entered in cells B9 through C11. The values in cells B9 and C9 indicate that one pump is required to produce each type of hot tub. The values in cells B10 and C10 show that each Aqua-Spa produced requires 9 hours of labor, and each Hydro-Lux requires 6 hours. Cells B11 and C11 indicate that each Aqua-Spa produced requires 12 feet of tubing, and each Hydro-Lux requires 16 feet. The available number of pumps, labor hours, and feet of tubing are entered in cells E9 through E11. Notice that appropriate labels are also entered to identify all the data elements for the problem.

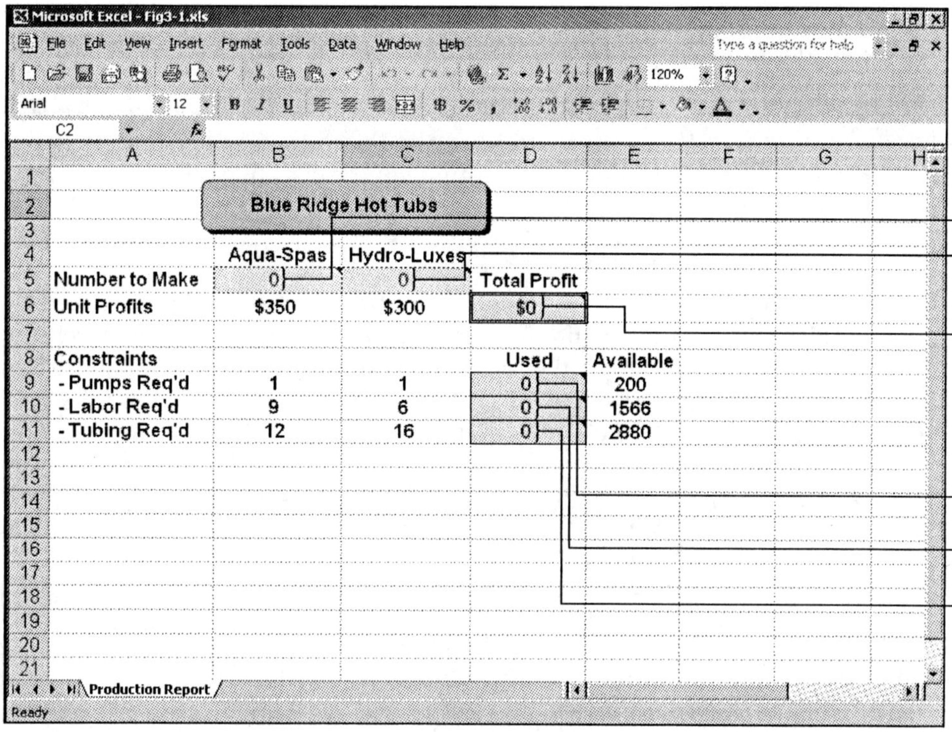

FIGURE 3.1
A spreadsheet model for the Blue Ridge Hot Tub production problem

3.4.2 Representing the Decision Variables

As indicated in Figure 3.1, cells B5 and C5 represent the decision variables X_1 and X_2 in our algebraic model. These cells are shaded and outlined with dashed borders to visually distinguish them from other elements of the model. Values of zero are placed in cells B5 and C5 because we do not know how many Aqua-Spas and Hydro-Luxes should be produced. Shortly, we will use Solver to determine the optimal values for these cells. Figure 3.2 summarizes the relationship between the decision variables in the algebraic model and the corresponding cells in the spreadsheet.

Decision Variables:	X_1	X_2
	↓	↓
Spreadsheet Cells:	B5	C5

FIGURE 3.2
Summary of the relationship between the decision variables and corresponding spreadsheet cells

3.4.3 Representing the Objective Function

The next step in implementing our LP problem is to create a formula in a cell of the spreadsheet to represent the objective function. We can accomplish this in many ways. Because the objective function is $350X_1 + 300X_2$, you might be tempted to enter the formula =350*B5+300*C5 in the spreadsheet. However, if you wanted to change the coefficients in the objective function, you would have to go back and edit this formula to reflect the changes. Because the objective function coefficients are entered in cells B6 and C6, a better way of implementing the objective function is to refer to the values in cells B6 and C6 rather than entering numeric constants in the formula. The formula for the objective function is entered in cell D6 as:

Formula for cell D6: =B6*B5+C6*C5

As shown in Figure 3.1, cell D6 initially returns the value 0 because cells B5 and C5 both contain zeros. Figure 3.3 summarizes the relationship between the algebraic objective function and the formula entered in cell D6. By implementing the objective function in this manner, if the profits earned on the hot tubs ever change, the spreadsheet model can be changed easily and the problem can be resolved to determine the impact of this change on the optimal solution. Note that cell D6 has been shaded and outlined with a double border to distinguish it from other elements of the model.

FIGURE 3.3
Summary of the relationship between the decision variables and corresponding spreadsheet cells

Algebraic Objective:	350 X_1	+	300 X_2
	↓ ↓		↓ ↓
Formula in cell D6:	=B6*B5	+	C6*C5

3.4.4 Representing the Constraints

The next step in building the spreadsheet model involves implementing the constraints of the LP model. Earlier, we said that for each constraint in the algebraic model, you must create a formula in a cell of the spreadsheet that corresponds to the LHS of the constraint. The LHS of each constraint in our model is:

LHS of the pump constraint

$1X_1 + 1X_2 \leq 200$

LHS of the labor constraint

$9X_1 + 6X_2 \leq 1{,}566$

LHS of the tubing constraint

$12X_1 + 16X_2 \leq 2{,}880$

We need to set up three cells in the spreadsheet to represent the LHS formulas of the three constraints. Again, this is done by referring to the data cells containing the coefficients for these constraints and to the cells representing the decision variables. The LHS of the first constraint is entered in cell D9 as:

Formula for cell D9: =B9*B5+C9*C5

Similarly, the LHS of the second and third constraints are entered in cells D10 and D11 as:

Formula for cell D10: =B10*B5+C10*C5

Formula for cell D11: =B11*B5+C11*C5

These formulas calculate the number of pumps, hours of labor, and feet of tubing required to manufacture the number of hot tubs represented in cells B5 and C5. Note that cells D9 through D11 were shaded and outlined with solid borders to distinguish them from the other elements of the model.

Figure 3.4 summarizes the relationship between the LHS formulas of the constraints in the algebraic formulation of our model and their spreadsheet representations.

LHS formula for the pump constraint:	$1\ X_1 + 1\ X_2$
	↓ ↓ ↓ ↓
Formula in cell D9:	=B9*B5 + C9*C5
LHS formula for the labor constraint:	$9\ X_1 + 6\ X_2$
	↓ ↓ ↓ ↓
Formula in cell D10:	=B10*B5 + C10*C5
LHS formula for the tubing constraint:	$12\ X_1 + 16\ X_2$
	↓ ↓ ↓ ↓
Formula in cell D11:	=B11*B5 + C11*C5

FIGURE 3.4
Summary of the relationship between the LHS formulas of the constraints and their spreadsheet representations

We know that Blue Ridge Hot Tubs has 200 pumps, 1,566 labor hours, and 2,880 feet of tubing available during its next production run. In our algebraic formulation of the LP model, these values represent the RHS values for the three constraints. Therefore, we entered the available number of pumps, hours of labor, and feet of tubing in cells E9, E10, and E11, respectively. These terms indicate the upper limits on the values cells D9, D10, and D11 can assume.

3.4.5 Representing the Bounds on the Decision Variables

Now, what about the simple lower bounds on our decision variables represented by $X_1 \geq 0$ and $X_2 \geq 0$? These conditions are quite common in LP problems and are referred to as **nonnegativity conditions** because they indicate that the decision variables can assume only nonnegative values. These conditions might seem like constraints and can, in fact, be implemented like the other constraints. However, Solver allows you to specify simple upper and lower bounds for the decision variables by referring directly to the cells representing the decision variables. Thus, at this point, we have taken no specific action to implement these bounds in our spreadsheet.

3.5 HOW SOLVER VIEWS THE MODEL

After implementing our model in the spreadsheet, we can use Solver to find the optimal solution to the problem. But first, we need to define the following three components of our spreadsheet model for Solver:

1. **Set (or Target) cell.** The cell in the spreadsheet that represents the *objective function* in the model (and whether its value should be maximized or minimized).
2. **Variable (or Changing) cells.** The cells in the spreadsheet that represent the *decision variables* in the model.
3. **Constraint cells.** The cells in the spreadsheet that represent the *LHS formulas* of the constraints in the model (and any upper and lower bounds that apply to these formulas).

These components correspond directly to the cells in the spreadsheet we established when implementing the LP model. For example, in the spreadsheet for our example problem, the set (or target) cell is represented by cell D6, the variable (or changing) cells are represented by cells B5 and C5, and the constraint cells are represented by cells D9, D10, and D11. Figure 3.5 shows these relationships. Figure 3.5 also shows a cell note documenting the purpose of cell D6. Cell notes can be a

FIGURE 3.5
Summary of Solver's view of the model

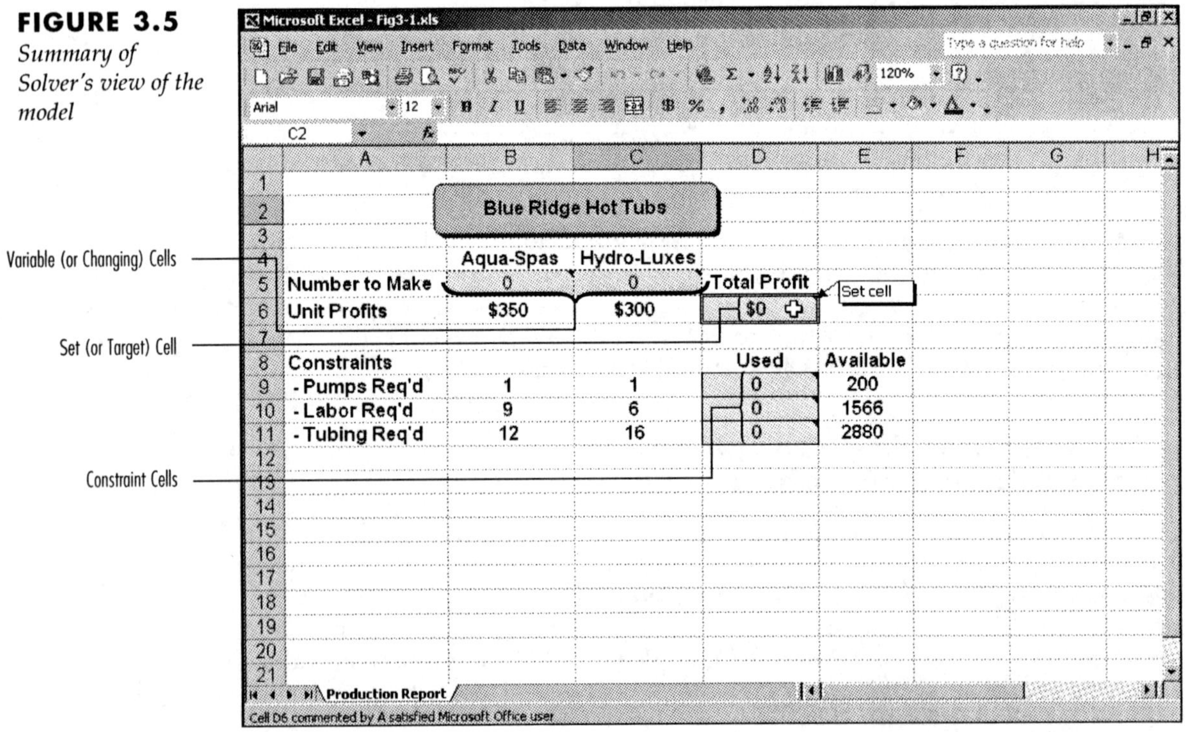

very effective way of describing details about the purpose or meaning of various cells in a model.

By comparing Figure 3.1 with Figure 3.5, you can see the direct connection between the way we formulate LP models algebraically and how Solver views the spreadsheet implementation of the model. The decision variables in the algebraic model correspond to the variable (or changing) cells for Solver. The LHS formulas for the different constraints in the algebraic model correspond to the constraint cells for Solver. Finally, the objective function in the algebraic model corresponds to the set (or target) cell for Solver. So, although the terminology Solver uses to describe spreadsheet LP models is somewhat different from the terminology we use to describe LP models algebraically, the concepts are the same. Figure 3.6 summarizes these differences in terminology.

FIGURE 3.6
Summary of Solver terminology

Terms Used to Describe LP Models Algebraically	Corresponding Terms Used by Solver to Describe Spreadsheet LP Models
Objective function	Set (or target) cell
Decision variables	Variable (or changing) cells
LHS formulas of constraints	Constraint cells

Note that some versions of Solver refer to the cells containing the objective function as the "target" cell, whereas other versions of Solver refer to it simply as the "set" cell. Similarly, some versions of Solver refer to the cells representing the decision variables as "changing" cells, whereas other versions refer to them as "variable" cells. As a result, we may use the terms "target" cell and "set" cell interchangeably in this book to refer to the cell containing the objective function. Similarly, we may use the terms "changing" cells and "variable" cells interchangeably to refer to cells representing decision variables.

A Note About Creating Cell Comments...

It is easy to create cell comments like the one shown for cell D6 in Figure 3.5. To create a comment for a cell:

1. Click the cell to select it.
2. Choose the Comment command on the Insert menu (or press the Shift key and function key F2 simultaneously).
3. Type the comment for the cell, and then select another cell.

The display of cell comments can be turned on or off as follows:

1. Choose the Options command on the Tools menu.
2. Select the appropriate option in the Comments section on the View tab.
3. Click the OK button.

continued

To copy a cell comment from one cell to a series of other cells:

1. Click the cell containing the comment you want to copy.
2. Choose the Copy command on the Edit menu (or press the Ctrl and C keys simultaneously).
3. Select the cells you want to copy the comment to.
4. Select the Paste Special command on the Edit menu (or click the right mouse button and select Paste Special).
5. Select the Comments option button.
6. Click the OK button.

Installing Premium Solver for Education

This book comes with Premium Solver for Education—an upgraded version of the standard Solver that ships with Excel. If you have not already done so, install Premium Solver for Education now by running the program called PremSolv.Exe found on the CD-ROM in the front of this book. To do this, use Windows Explorer to locate the file named PremSolv.Exe and then double-click the file name. (If you are running Excel in a networked environment, consult with your network administrator.) Although most of the examples in this book also work with the standard Solver that comes with Excel, Premium Solver for Education includes several helpful features that are discussed throughout this book.

3.6 USING SOLVER

After implementing an LP model in a spreadsheet, we still need to solve the model. To do this, we must first indicate to Solver which cells in the spreadsheet represent the objective function, the decision variables, and the constraints. To invoke Solver in Excel, choose the Solver command from the Tools menu, as shown in Figure 3.7. This should display one of the Solver Parameters dialog boxes shown in Figure 3.8.

If the Solver Parameters dialog box on your computer looks like the first box in Figure 3.8, click the Premium button. (If the Solver Parameters dialog box on your computer looks like the first box in Figure 3.8 but does not have a Premium button, refer to the previous instruction box titled "Installing Premium Solver for Education.") The second Solver Parameters dialog box, shown in Figure 3.8, displays the user interface for Premium Solver for Education that is used throughout this book.

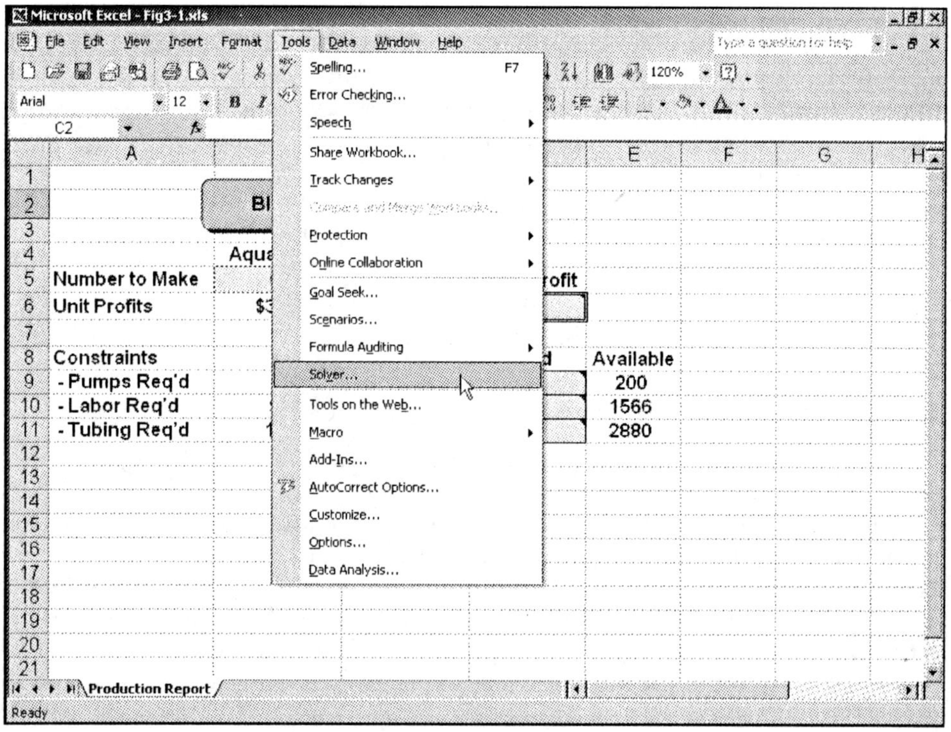

FIGURE 3.7
Command for invoking Solver

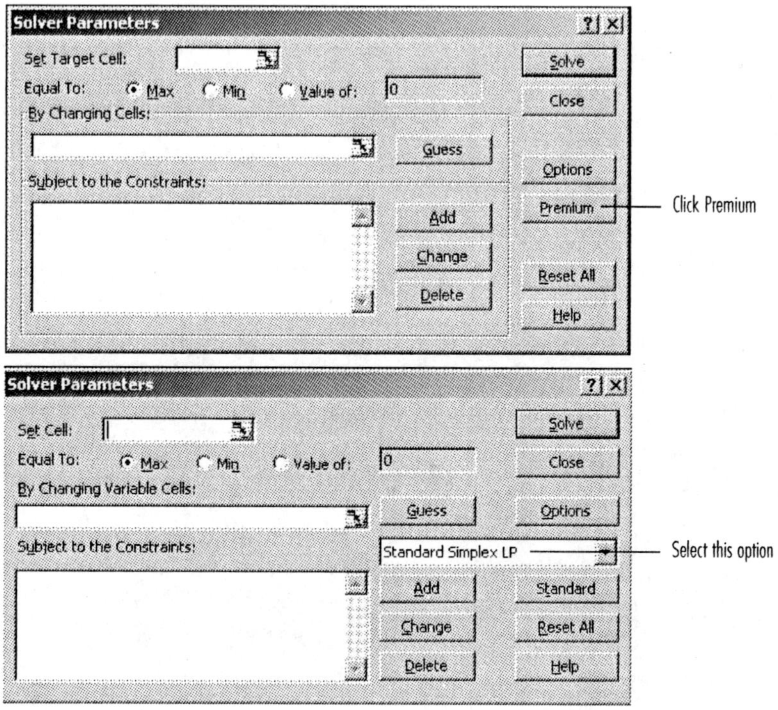

FIGURE 3.8
The Solver Parameters dialog box

Premium Solver for Education provides three different algorithms for solving optimization problems: Standard GRG Nonlinear, Standard Simplex LP, and Standard Evolutionary. If the problem you are trying to solve is an LP problem (that is, an optimization problem with a linear objective function and linear constraints), Solver can use a special algorithm known as the ***simplex method*** to solve the problem. The simplex method provides an efficient way of solving LP problems and, therefore, requires less solution time. Furthermore, using the simplex method allows for expanded sensitivity information about the solution obtained. (chapter 4 discusses this in detail.) In any event, when using Solver to solve an LP problem, it is a good idea to select the Standard Simplex LP option, as indicated in Figure 3.8.

3.6.1 Defining the Set (or Target) Cell

In the Solver Parameters dialog box, specify the location of the cell that represents the objective function by entering it in the Set Cell box, as shown in Figure 3.9.

Notice that cell D6 contains a formula representing the objective function for our problem and that we instructed Solver to try to maximize this value, as specified by the Max button. Select the Min button when you want Solver to find a solution that minimizes the value of the objective. The Value button may be used to find a solution in which the objective function takes on a specific value.

FIGURE 3.9
Specifying the set (or target) cell

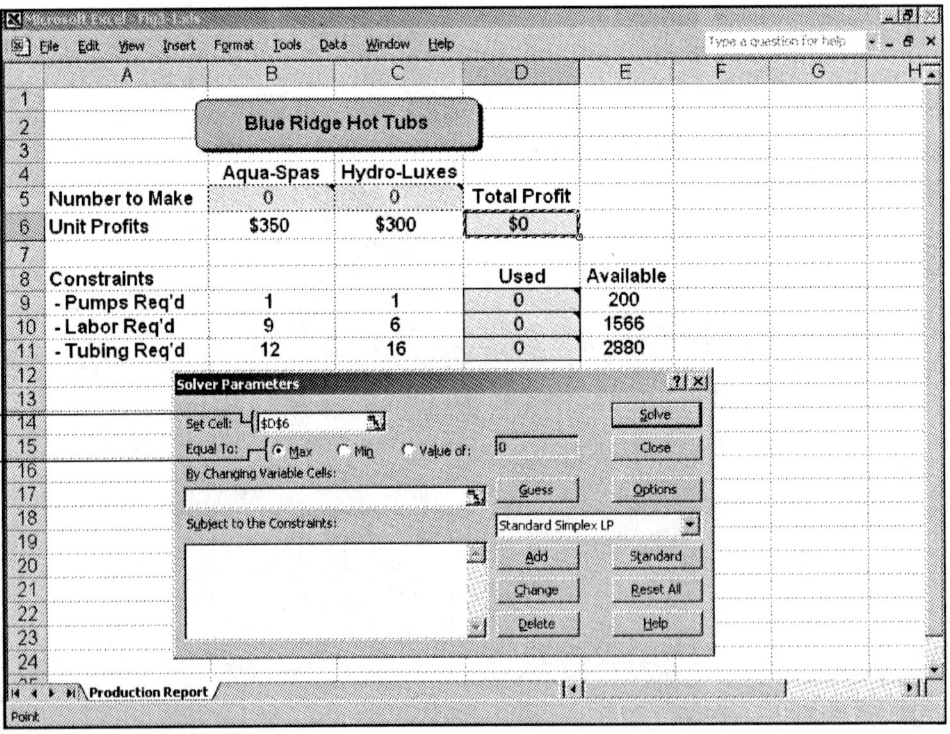

Guess What?

The Guess button in the Solver Parameters dialog box instructs Solver to make an educated guess regarding which cells in the spreadsheet represent decision variables. If you click this button, Solver displays all the cells upon which the value of the set (or target) cell depends. In some cases, this is only the variable cells. In other cases, this is the variable cells plus some additional cells that you will have to edit out of the variable cells box before continuing. In general, it is probably a good idea for you to enter the variable cells manually by clicking on the appropriate cells in your spreadsheet. But if you use the Guess button, remember that you will usually need to remove some of the cells it identifies as variable cells.

3.6.2 Defining the Variable Cells

To solve our LP problem, we also need to indicate which cells represent the decision variables in the model. Again, Solver refers to these cells as variable cells. The variable cells for our example problem are specified as shown in Figure 3.10.

Cells B5 and C5 represent the decision variables for the model. Solver will determine the optimal values for these cells. If the decision variables were not in a contiguous range, we would have to list the individual decision variable cells

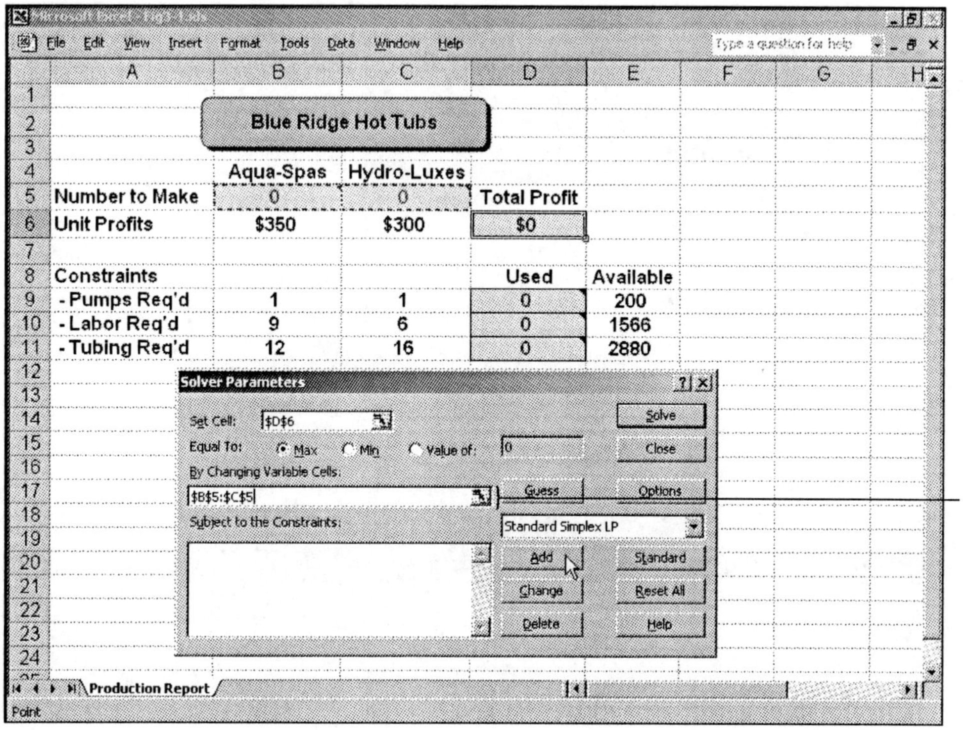

FIGURE 3.10
Specifying the variable (or changing) cells

separated by commas in the By Changing Variable Cells box. Whenever possible, it is best to use contiguous cells to represent the decision variables.

3.6.3 Defining the Constraint Cells

Next, we must define the constraint cells in the spreadsheet and the restrictions that apply to these cells. As mentioned earlier, the constraint cells are the cells in which we implemented the LHS formulas for each constraint in our model. To define the constraint cells, click the Add button shown in Figure 3.10, and then complete the Add Constraint dialog box shown in Figure 3.11. In the Add Constraint dialog box, click the Add button again to define additional constraints. Click the OK button when you have finished defining constraints.

Cells D9 through D11 represent constraint cells whose values must be less than or equal to the values in cells E9 through E11, respectively. If the constraint cells were not in contiguous cells in the spreadsheet, we would have to define the constraint cells repeatedly. As with the variable cells, it is usually best to choose contiguous cells in your spreadsheet to implement the LHS formulas of the constraints in a model.

If you want to define more than one constraint at the same time, as in Figure 3.11, all the constraint cells you select must be the same type (that is, they must all be ≤, ≥, or =). Therefore, it is a good idea to keep constraints of a given type grouped in contiguous cells so you can select them at the same time. For example, in our case, the three constraint cells we selected are all less than or equal to (≤) constraints. However, this consideration should not take precedence over setting up the spreadsheet in the way that communicates its purpose most clearly.

FIGURE 3.11
Specifying the constraint cells

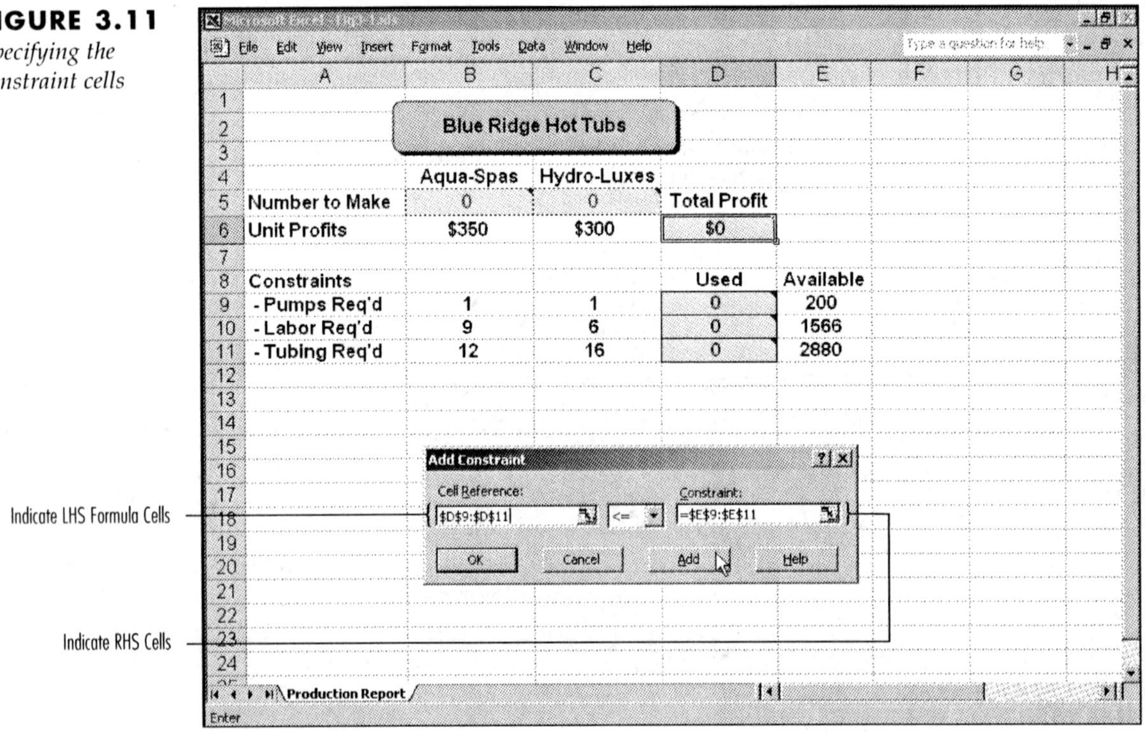

3.6.4 Defining the Nonnegativity Conditions

One final specification we need to make for our model is that the decision variables must be greater than or equal to zero. As mentioned earlier, we can impose these conditions as constraints by placing appropriate restrictions on the values that can be assigned to the cells representing the decision variables (in this case, cells B5 and C5). To do this, we simply add another set of constraints to the model, as shown in Figure 3.12.

Figure 3.12 indicates that cells B5 and C5, which represent the decision variables in our model, must be greater than or equal to zero. Notice that the RHS value of this constraint is a numeric constant that is entered manually. The same type of constraints can also be used if we placed some strictly positive lower bounds on these variables (for example, if we wanted to produce at least 10 Aqua-Spas and at least 10 Hydro-Luxes). However, in that case, it would probably be best to place the minimum required production amounts on the spreadsheet so that these restrictions are clearly displayed. We can then refer to those cells in the spreadsheet when specifying the RHS values for these constraints.

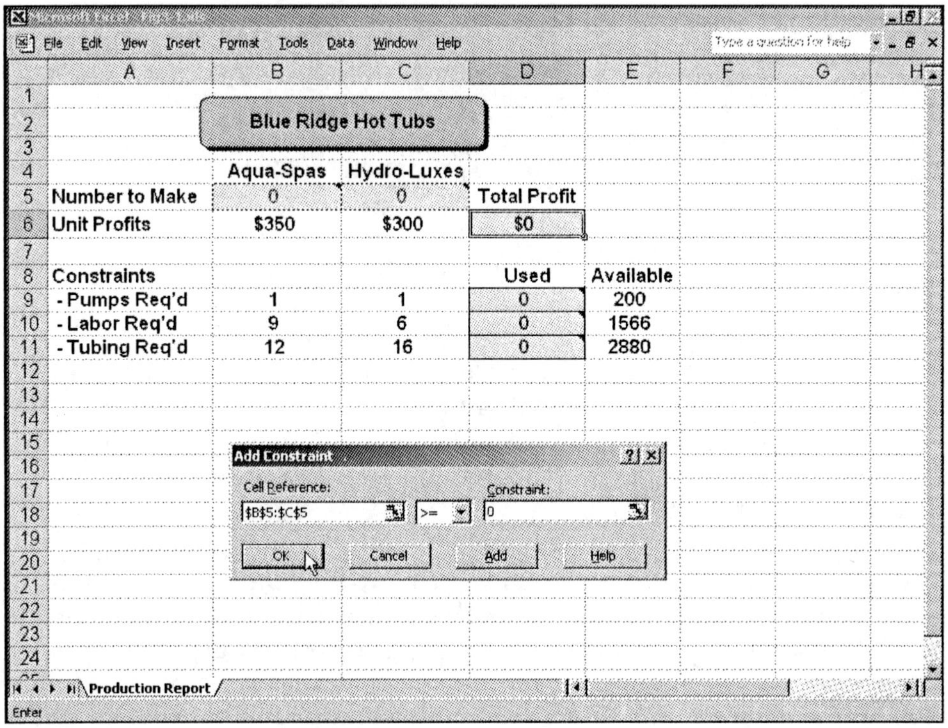

FIGURE 3.12
Adding the nonnegativity conditions for the problem

Important Software Note

There is another way to impose nonnegativity conditions—simply check the Assume Non-Negative check box in the Solver Options dialog box (see Figure 3.14). Checking this box tells Solver to assume that all the variables (or variable cells) in your model that have not been assigned explicit lower bounds should have lower bounds of zero.

3.6.5 Reviewing the Model

After specifying all the constraints for our model, the final Solver Parameters dialog box appears, as shown in Figure 3.13. This dialog box provides a summary of how Solver views our model. It is a good idea to review this information before solving the model to make sure you entered all the parameters accurately and to correct any errors before proceeding.

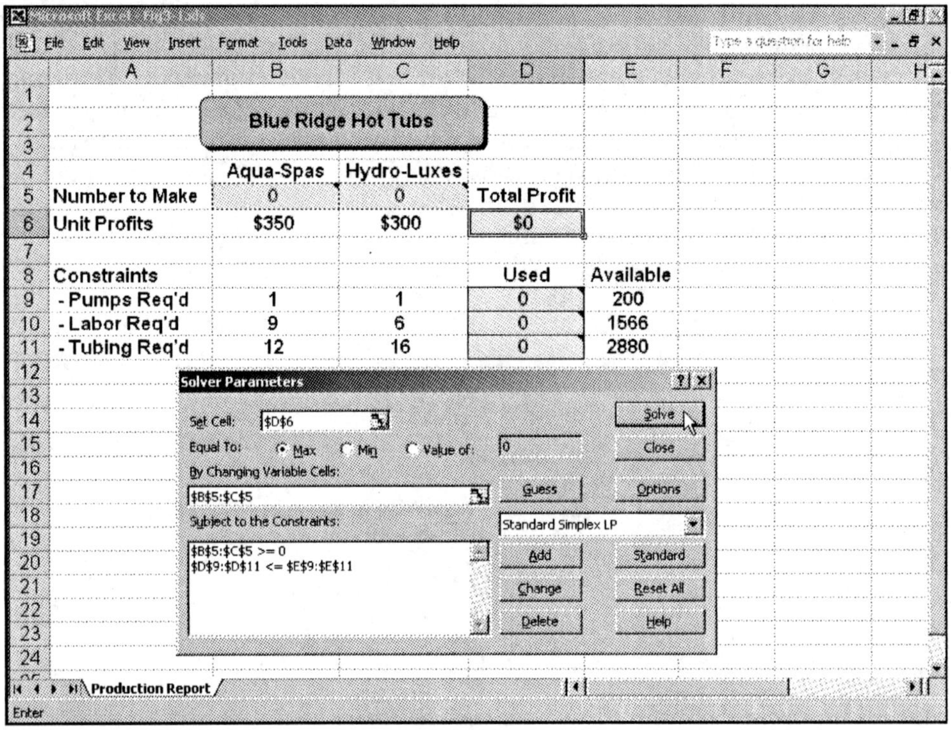

FIGURE 3.13
Summary of how Solver views the model

3.6.6 Options

Solver provides a number of options that affect how it solves a problem. These options are available in the Solver Options dialog box, which you display by clicking the Options button in the Solver Parameters dialog box. Figure 3.14 shows the Solver Options dialog box for the Standard Simplex LP solution algorithm. We will discuss the meanings of several of these options as we proceed. You can also find out more about these options by clicking the Help button in the Solver Options dialog box.

3.6.7 Solving the Model

After entering all the appropriate parameters and choosing any necessary options for our model, the next step is to solve the problem. Click the Solve button in the Solver Parameters dialog box to solve the problem. When Solver finds the optimal solution, it displays the Solver Results dialog box shown in Figure 3.15. If the

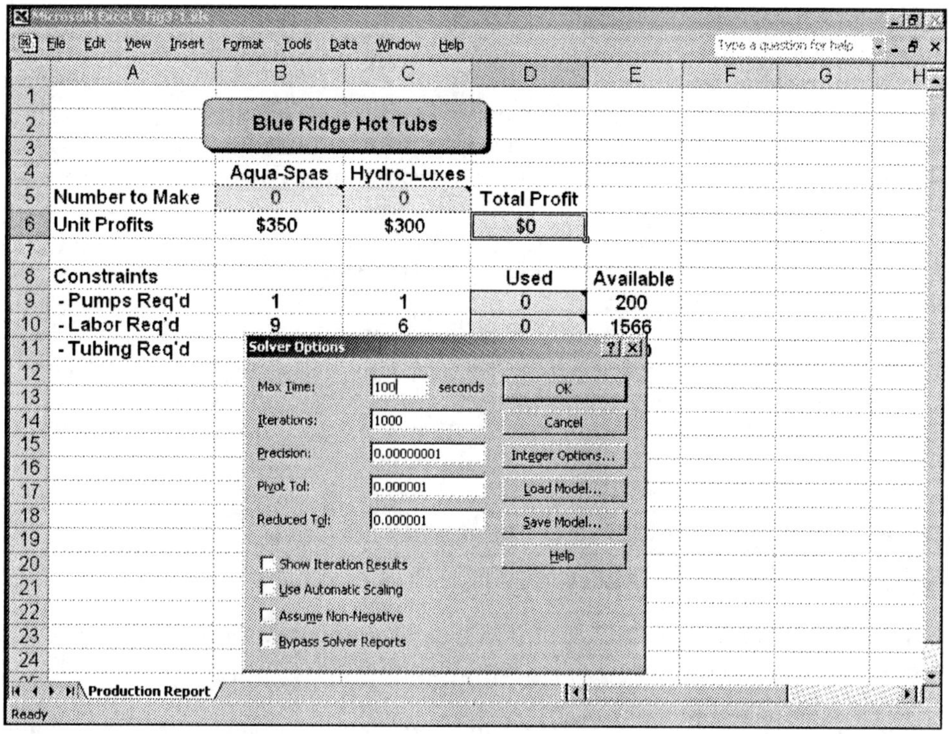

FIGURE 3.14
The Solver Options dialog box

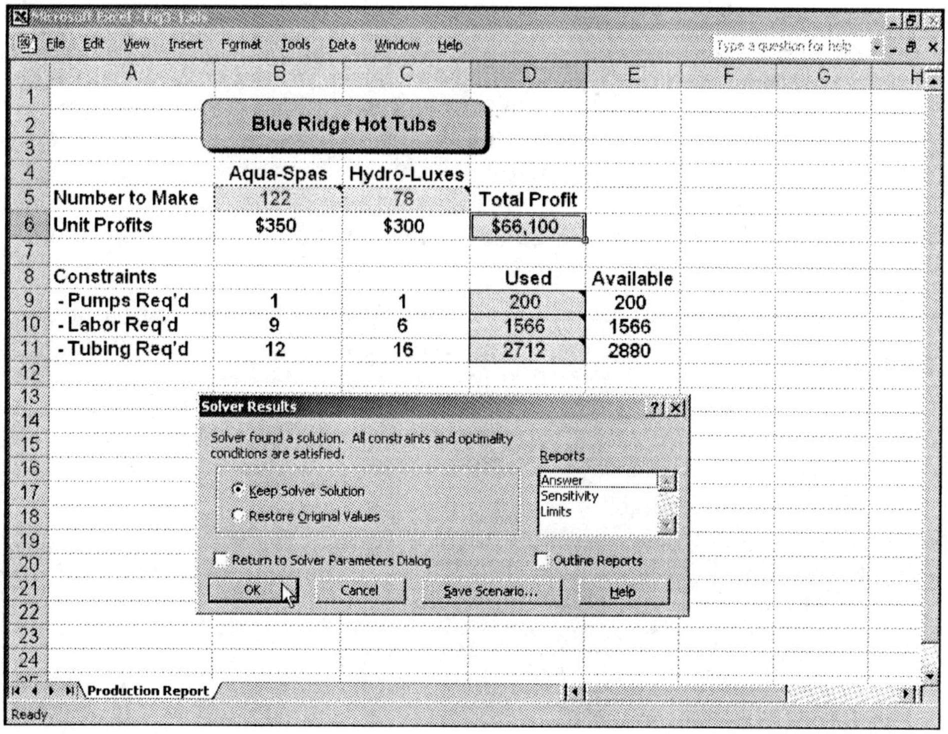

FIGURE 3.15
Optimal solution for the Blue Ridge Hot Tubs problem

values on your screen do not match those in Figure 3.15, click the Restore Original Values option button, click OK, and try again.

This dialog box provides options for keeping the solution found by Solver or restoring the spreadsheet to its original condition. Most often, you'll want to keep Solver's solution unless there is an obvious problem with it. Notice that the Solver Results dialog box also provides options for generating Answer, Sensitivity, and Limits reports. Chapter 4 discusses these options.

As shown in Figure 3.15, Solver determined that the optimal value for cell B5 is 122 and the optimal value for cell C5 is 78. These values correspond to the optimal values for X_1 and X_2 that we determined graphically in chapter 2. The value of the set cell (D6) now indicates that if Blue Ridge Hot Tubs produces and sells 122 Aqua-Spas and 78 Hydro-Luxes, the company will earn a profit of $66,100. Cells D9, D10, and D11 indicate that this solution uses all the 200 available pumps, all the 1,566 available labor hours, and 2,712 of the 2,880 feet of available tubing.

3.7 GOALS AND GUIDELINES FOR SPREADSHEET DESIGN

Now that you have a basic idea of how Solver works and how to set up an LP model in a spreadsheet, we'll walk through several more examples of formulating LP models and solving them with Solver. These problems highlight the wide variety of business problems in which LP can be applied and will also show you some helpful "tricks of the trade" that should help you solve the problems at the end of this chapter. When you work through the end-of-the-chapter problems, you will better appreciate how much thought is required to find a good way to implement a given model.

As we proceed, keep in mind that you can set up these problems more than one way. Creating spreadsheet models that effectively communicate their purpose is very much an art—or at least an acquired skill. Spreadsheets are inherently free-form and impose no particular structure on the way we model problems. As a result, there is no one "right" way to model a problem in a spreadsheet; however, some ways are certainly better (or more logical) than others. To achieve the end result of a logical spreadsheet design, your modeling efforts should be directed toward the following goals:

- **Communication.** A spreadsheet's primary business purpose is that of communicating information to managers. As such, the primary design objective in most spreadsheet modeling tasks is to communicate the relevant aspects of the problem at hand in as clear and intuitively appealing a manner as possible.
- **Reliability.** The output a spreadsheet generates should be correct and consistent. This has an obvious impact on the degree of confidence a manager places in the results of the modeling effort.
- **Auditability.** A manager should be able to retrace the steps followed to generate the different outputs from the model in order to understand the model and verify results. Models that are set up in an intuitively appealing, logical layout tend to be the most auditable.

- **Modifiability.** The data and assumptions upon which we build spreadsheet models can change frequently. A well-designed spreadsheet should be easy to change or enhance in order to meet dynamic user requirements.

In most cases, the spreadsheet design that most clearly communicates its purpose will also be the most reliable, auditable, and modifiable design. As you consider different ways of implementing a spreadsheet model for a particular problem, consider how well the modeling alternatives compare in terms of these goals. Some practical suggestions and guidelines for creating effective spreadsheet models are given in Figure 3.16.

FIGURE 3.16
Guidelines for effective spreadsheet design

Spreadsheet Design Guidelines

- **Organize the data, and then build the model around the data.** After the data is arranged in a visually appealing manner, logical locations for decision variables, constraints, and the objective function tend to naturally suggest themselves. This also tends to enhance the reliability, auditability, and maintainability of the model.
- **Do not embed numeric constants in formulas.** Numeric constants should be placed in individual cells and labeled appropriately. This enhances the reliability and modifiability of the model.
- **Things which are logically related (for example, LHS and RHS of constraints) should be arranged in close physical proximity to one another and in the same columnar or row orientation.** This enhances reliability and auditability of the model.
- **A design that results in formulas that can be copied is probably better than one that does not.** A model with formulas that can copied to complete a series of calculations in a range is less prone to error (more reliable) and tends to be more understandable (auditable). Once a user understands the first formula in a range, he/she understands all the formulas in a range.
- **Column or row totals should be in close proximity to the columns or rows being totaled.** Spreadsheet users often expect numbers at the end of a column or row to represent a total or some other summary measure involving the data in the column or row. Numbers at the ends of columns or rows that do not represent totals can easily be misinterpreted (reducing auditability).
- **The English-reading human eye scans left to right, top to bottom.** This fact should be considered and reflected in the spreadsheet design to enhance the auditability of the model.
- **Use color, shading, borders, and protection to distinguish changeable parameters from other elements of the model.** This enhances the reliability and modifiability of the model.
- **Use text boxes and cell comments to document various elements of the model.** These devices can be used to provide greater detail about a model or particular cells in a model than labels on a spreadsheet may allow.

Spreadsheet-Based LP Solvers Create New Applications for Linear Programming

In 1987, *The Wall Street Journal* reported on an exciting new trend in business—the availability of solvers for personal computers that allowed many businesses to transfer LP models from mainframe computers. Newfoundland Energy Ltd., for example, evaluated its mix of crude oils to purchase with LP on a mainframe for 25 years. Since it began using a personal computer for this application, the company has saved thousands of dollars per year in mainframe access time charges.

The expansion of access to LP also spawned new applications. Therese Fitzpatrick, a nursing administrator at Grant Hospital in Chicago, used spreadsheet optimization to create a staff scheduling model that was projected to save the hospital $80,000 per month in overtime and temporary hiring costs. The task of scheduling 300 nurses so that those with appropriate skills were in the right place at the right time required 20 hours per month. The LP model enabled Therese to do the job in four hours, even with such complicating factors as leaves, vacations, and variations in staffing requirements at different times and days of the week.

Hawley Fuel Corp., a New York wholesaler of coal, found that it could minimize its cost of purchases while still meeting customers' requirements for sulfur and ash content by optimizing a spreadsheet LP model. Charles Howard of Victoria, British Columbia, developed an LP model to increase electricity generation from a dam just by opening and closing the outlet valves at the right time.

Source: Bulkely, William M. "The Right Mix: New Software Makes the Choice Much Easier." *The Wall Street Journal*, March 27, 1987, p. 17.

3.8 MAKE VS. BUY DECISIONS

As mentioned at the beginning of chapter 2, LP is particularly well-suited to problems where scarce or limited resources must be allocated or used in an optimal manner. Numerous examples of these types of problems occur in manufacturing organizations. For example, LP might be used to determine how the various components of a job should be assigned to multipurpose machines in order to minimize the time it takes to complete the job. As another example, a company might receive an order for several items that it cannot fill entirely with its own production capacity. In such a case, the company must determine which items to produce and which items to subcontract (or buy) from an outside supplier. The following is an example of this type of make vs. buy decision.

The Electro-Poly Corporation is the world's leading manufacturer of slip rings. A slip ring is an electrical coupling device that allows current to pass through a spinning or rotating connection—such as a gun turret on a ship, aircraft, or tank. The company recently received a $750,000 order for various quantities of three types of slip rings. Each slip ring requires a certain amount of time to wire and harness. The following table summarizes the requirements for the three models of slip rings.

	Model 1	Model 2	Model 3
Number ordered	3,000	2,000	900
Hours of wiring required per unit	2	1.5	3
Hours of harnessing required per unit	1	2	1

Unfortunately, Electro-Poly does not have enough wiring and harnessing capacity to fill the order by its due date. The company has only 10,000 hours of wiring capacity and 5,000 hours of harnessing capacity available to devote to this order. However, the company can subcontract any portion of this order to one of its competitors. The unit costs of producing each model in-house and buying the finished products from a competitor are summarized below.

	Model 1	Model 2	Model 3
Cost to Make	$50	$83	$130
Cost to Buy	$61	$97	$145

Electro-Poly wants to determine the number of slip rings to make and the number to buy in order to fill the customer order at the least possible cost.

3.8.1 Defining the Decision Variables

To solve the Electro-Poly problem, we need six decision variables to represent the alternatives under consideration. The six variables are:

M_1 = number of model 1 slip rings to make in-house
M_2 = number of model 2 slip rings to make in-house
M_3 = number of model 3 slip rings to make in-house
B_1 = number of model 1 slip rings to buy from competitor
B_2 = number of model 2 slip rings to buy from competitor
B_3 = number of model 3 slip rings to buy from competitor

As mentioned in chapter 2, we do not have to use the symbols $X_1, X_2, \ldots, X_n$ for the decision variables. If other symbols better clarify the model, you are certainly free to use them. In this case, the symbols M_i and B_i help distinguish the **M**ake in-house variables from the **B**uy from competitor variables.

3.8.2 Defining the Objective Function

The objective in this problem is to minimize the total cost of filling the order. Recall that each model 1 slip ring made in-house (each unit of M_1) costs $50; each model 2 slip ring made in-house (each unit of M_2) costs $83; and each model 3 slip ring (each unit of M_3) costs $130. Each model 1 slip ring bought from the competitor (each unit of B_1) costs $61; each model 2 slip ring bought from the competitor (each unit of B_2) costs \$97; and each model 3 slip ring bought from the competitor (each unit of B_3) costs \$145. Thus, the objective is stated mathematically as:

$$\text{MIN:} \quad 50M_1 + 83M_2 + 130M_3 + 61B_1 + 97B_2 + 145B_3$$

3.8.3 Defining the Constraints

Several constraints affect this problem. Two constraints are needed to ensure that the number of slip rings made in-house does not exceed the available capacity for wiring and harnessing. These constraints are stated as:

$$\begin{aligned} 2M_1 + 1.5M_2 + 3M_3 &\leq 10{,}000 \quad \text{\} wiring constraint} \\ 1M_1 + 2M_2 + 1M_3 &\leq 5{,}000 \quad \text{\} harnessing constraint} \end{aligned}$$

Three additional constraints ensure that 3,000 model 1 slip rings, 2,000 model 2 slip rings, and 900 model 3 slip rings are available to fill the order. These constraints are stated as:

$$\begin{aligned} M_1 + B_1 &= 3{,}000 \quad \text{\} demand for model 1} \\ M_2 + B_2 &= 2{,}000 \quad \text{\} demand for model 2} \\ M_3 + B_3 &= 900 \quad \text{\} demand for model 3} \end{aligned}$$

Finally, because none of the variables in the model can assume a value of less than zero, we also need the following nonnegativity condition:

$$M_1, M_2, M_3, B_1, B_2, B_3 \geq 0$$

3.8.4 Implementing the Model

The LP model for Electro-Poly's make vs. buy problem is summarized as:

$$\begin{aligned} \text{MIN:} \quad & 50M_1 + 83M_2 + 130M_3 + 61B_1 + 97B_2 + 145B_3 && \text{\} total cost} \\ \text{Subject to:} \quad & M_1 + B_1 = 3{,}000 && \text{\} demand for model 1} \\ & M_2 + B_2 = 2{,}000 && \text{\} demand for model 2} \\ & M_3 + B_3 = 900 && \text{\} demand for model 3} \\ & 2M_1 + 1.5M_2 + 3M_3 \leq 10{,}000 && \text{\} wiring constraint} \\ & 1M_1 + 2M_2 + 1M_3 \leq 5{,}000 && \text{\} harnessing constraint} \\ & M_1, M_2, M_3, B_1, B_2, B_3 \geq 0 && \text{\} nonnegativity condition} \end{aligned}$$

The data for this model were implemented in the spreadsheet shown in Figure 3.17 (and in the file Fig3-17.xls on your data disk). The coefficients that appear in the objective function are entered in the range B10 through D11. The coefficients for the LHS formulas for the wiring and harnessing constraints are entered in cells B17 through D18, and the corresponding RHS values are entered in cells F17 and F18. Because the LHS formulas for the demand constraints involve simply summing the decision variables, we do not need to list the coefficients for these constraints in the spreadsheet. The RHS values for the demand constraints are entered in cells B14 through D14.

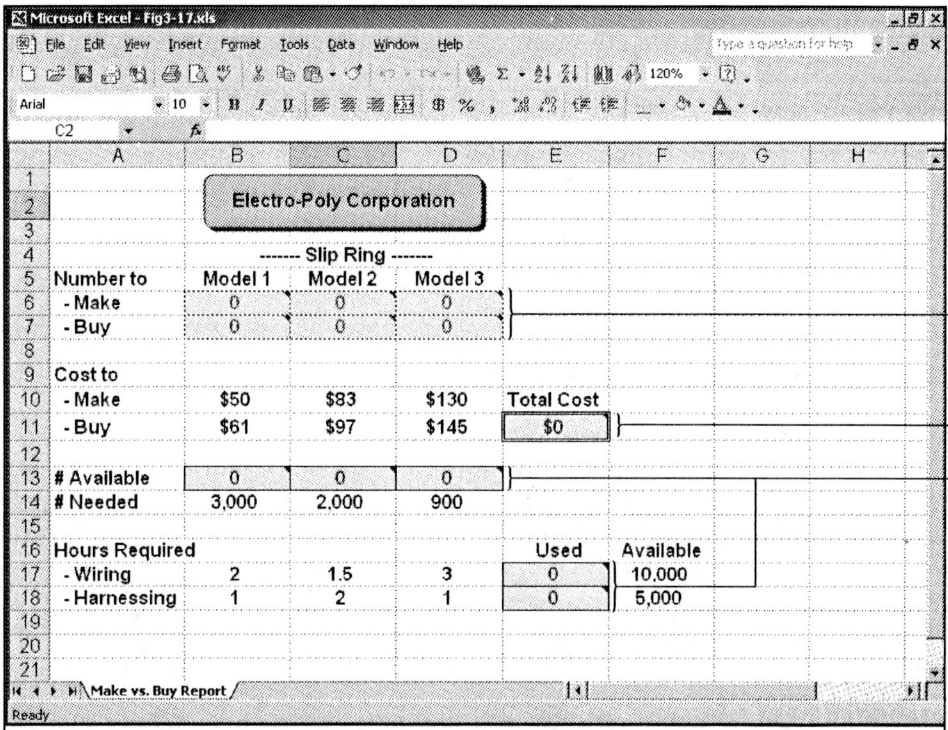

FIGURE 3.17
Spreadsheet model for Electro-Poly's make vs. buy problem

Key Cell Formulas

Cell	Formula	Copied to
B13	=B6+B7	C13:D13
E11	=SUMPRODUCT(B10:D11,B6:D7)	—
E17	=SUMPRODUCT(B17:D17,$B$6:$D$6)	E18

Cells B6 through D7 are reserved to represent the six variables in our algebraic model. So, the objective function could be entered in cell E11 as:

Formula for cell E11: =B10*B6+C10*C6+D10*D6+B11*B7+C11*C7+D11*D7

In this formula, the values in the range B6 through D7 are multiplied by the corresponding values in the range B10 through D11; these individual products are then added together. Therefore, the formula is simply the sum of a collection of products—or a *sum of products.* It turns out that this formula can be implemented in an equivalent (and easier) way as:

Equivalent formula for cell E11: =SUMPRODUCT(B10:D11,B6:D7)

The preceding formula takes the values in the range B10 through D11, multiplies them by the corresponding values in the range B6 through D7, and adds (or sums) these products. The SUMPRODUCT( ) function greatly simplifies the implementation of many formulas required in optimization problems and will be used extensively throughout this book.

Because the LHS of the demand constraint for model 1 slip rings involves adding variables M_1 and B_1, this constraint is implemented in cell B13 by adding the two cells in the spreadsheet that correspond to these variables—cells B6 and B7:

Formula for cell B13: =B6+B7
(Copy to C13 through D13.)

The formula in cell B13 is then copied to cells C13 and D13 to implement the LHS formulas for the constraints for model 2 and model 3 slip rings.

The coefficients for the wiring and harnessing constraints are entered in cells B17 through D18. The LHS formula for the wiring constraint is implemented in cell E17 as:

Formula for cell E17: =SUMPRODUCT(B17:D17,$B$6:$D$6)
(Copy to cell E18.)

This formula is then copied to cell E18 to implement the LHS formula for the harnessing constraint. (In the preceding formula, the dollar signs denote absolute cell references. An **absolute cell reference** will not change if the formula containing the reference is copied to another location.)

3.8.5 Solving the Model

To solve this model, we need to specify the set cell, variable cells, and constraint cells identified in Figure 3.17, just as we did earlier in the Blue Ridge Hot Tubs example. Figure 3.18 shows the Solver parameters required to solve Electro-Poly's make vs. buy problem.

After we click the Solve button in the Solver Parameters dialog box, Solver finds the optimal solution shown in Figure 3.19.

3.8.6 Analyzing the Solution

The optimal solution shown in Figure 3.19 indicates that Electro-Poly should make (in-house) 3,000 model 1 slip rings, 550 model 2 slip rings, and 900 model 3 slip rings (that is, M_1= 3,000, M_2 = 550, M_3 = 900). Additionally, it should buy 1,450 model 2 slip rings from its competitor (that is, B_1 = 0, B_2 = 1,450, B_3 = 0). This solution allows Electro-Poly to fill the customer order at a minimum cost of $453,300. This solution uses 9,525 of the 10,000 hours of available wiring capacity and all 5,000 hours of the harnessing capacity.

FIGURE 3.18
Solver parameters for the make vs. buy problem

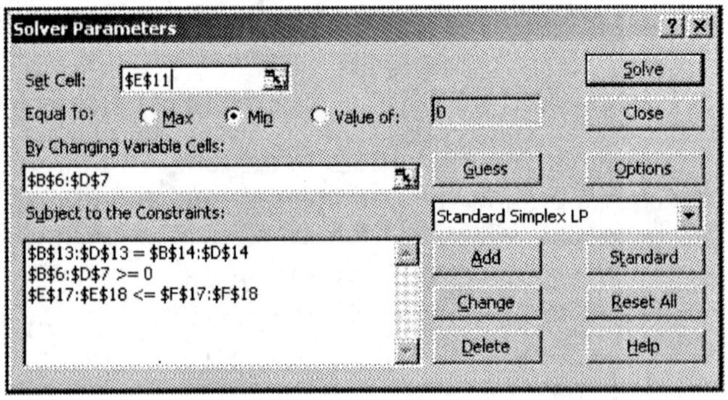

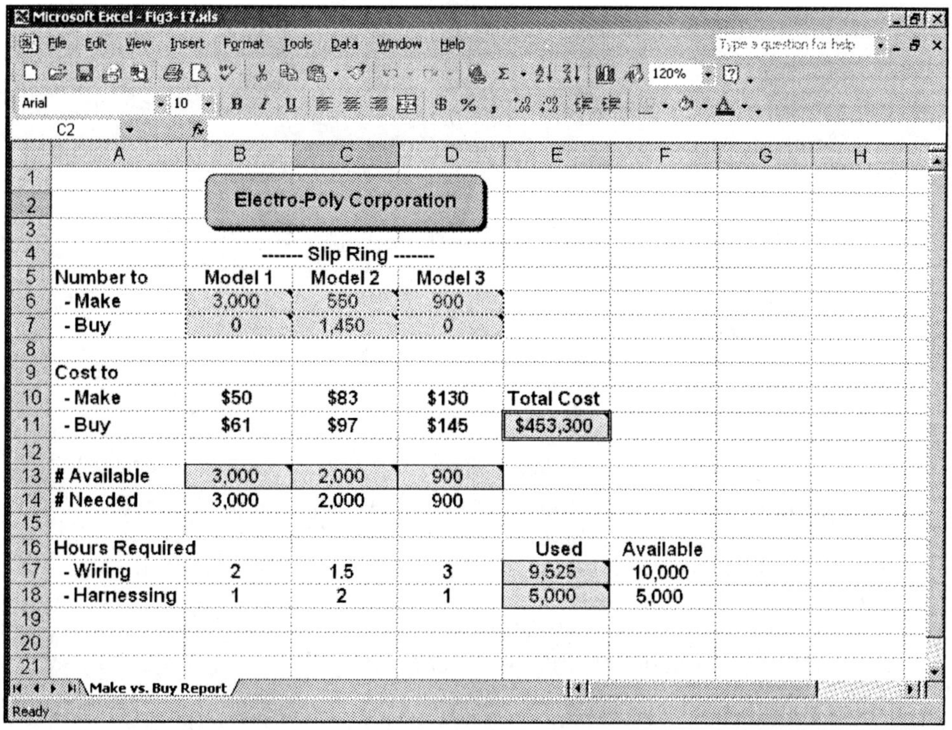

FIGURE 3.19
Optimal solution to Electro-Poly's make vs. buy problem

At first glance, this solution might seem a bit surprising. Electro-Poly has to pay $97 for each model 2 slip ring it purchases from its competitor. This represents a $14 premium over its in-house cost of $83. On the other hand, Electro-Poly has to pay a premium of $11 over its in-house cost to purchase model 1 slip rings from its competitor. It seems as if the optimal solution would be to purchase model 1 slip rings from its competitor rather than model 2 slip rings because the additional cost premium for model 1 slip rings is smaller. However, this argument fails to consider the fact that each model 2 slip ring produced in-house uses twice as much of the company's harnessing capacity as does each model 1 slip ring. Making more model 2 slip rings in-house would deplete the company's harnessing capacity more quickly, and would require buying an excessive number of model 1 slip rings from the competitor. Fortunately, the LP technique automatically considers such trade-offs in determining the optimal solution to the problem.

3.9 AN INVESTMENT PROBLEM

There are numerous problems in the area of finance to which various optimization techniques can be applied. These problems often involve attempting to maximize the return on an investment while meeting certain cash flow requirements and risk constraints. Alternatively, we may want to minimize the risk on an investment while maintaining a certain level of return. We'll consider one such problem here and discuss several other financial engineering problems throughout this text.

Brian Givens is a financial analyst for Retirement Planning Services, Inc. who specializes in designing retirement income portfolios for retirees using corporate bonds. He has just completed a consultation with a client who expects to have $750,000 in liquid assets to invest when she retires next month. Brian and his client agreed to consider upcoming bond issues from the following six companies:

Company	Return	Years to Maturity	Rating
Acme Chemical	8.65%	11	1-Excellent
DynaStar	9.50%	10	3-Good
Eagle Vision	10.00%	6	4-Fair
MicroModeling	8.75%	10	1-Excellent
OptiPro	9.25%	7	3-Good
Sabre Systems	9.00%	13	2-Very Good

The column labeled "Return" in this table represents the expected annual yield on each bond, the column labeled "Years to Maturity" indicates the length of time over which the bonds will be payable, and the column labeled "Rating" indicates an independent underwriter's assessment of the quality or risk associated with each issue.

Brian believes that all of the companies are relatively safe investments. However, to protect his client's income, Brian and his client agreed that no more than 25% of her money should be invested in any one investment and at least half of her money should be invested in long-term bonds that mature in ten or more years. Also, even though DynaStar, Eagle Vision, and OptiPro offer the highest returns, it was agreed that no more than 35% of the money should be invested in these bonds because they also represent the highest risks (*i.e.*, they were rated lower than "very good").

Brian needs to determine how to allocate his client's investments to maximize her income while meeting their agreed upon investment restrictions.

3.9.1 Defining the Decision Variables

In this problem, Brian must decide how much money to invest in each type of bond. Because there are six different investment alternatives, we need the following six decision variables:

X_1 = amount of money to invest in Acme Chemical

X_2 = amount of money to invest in DynaStar

X_3 = amount of money to invest in Eagle Vision

X_4 = amount of money to invest in MicroModeling

X_5 = amount of money to invest in OptiPro

X_6 = amount of money to invest in Sabre Systems

3.9.2 Defining the Objective Function

The objective in this problem is to maximize the investment income for Brian's client. Because each dollar invested in Acme Chemical (X_1) earns 8.65% annually, each dollar invested in DynaStar (X_2) earns 9.50%, and so on, the objective function for the problem is expressed as:

MAX: $.0865X_1 + .095X_2 + .10X_3 + .0875X_4 + .0925X_5 + .09X_6$ } total annual return

3.9.3 Defining the Constraints

Again, there are several constraints that apply to this problem. First, we must ensure that exactly \$750,000 is invested. This is accomplished by the following constraint:

$$X_1 + X_2 + X_3 + X_4 + X_5 + X_6 = 750{,}000$$

Next, we must ensure that no more than 25% of the total be invested in any one investment. Twenty-five percent of \$750,000 is \$187,500. Therefore, Brian can put no more than \$187,500 in any one investment. The following constraints enforce this restriction:

$$X_1 \leq 187{,}500$$
$$X_2 \leq 187{,}500$$
$$X_3 \leq 187{,}500$$
$$X_4 \leq 187{,}500$$
$$X_5 \leq 187{,}500$$
$$X_6 \leq 187{,}500$$

Because the bonds for Eagle Vision (X_3) and OptiPro (X_5) are the only ones that mature in fewer than 10 years, the following constraint ensures that at least half the money (\$375,000) is placed in investments maturing in ten or more years:

$$X_1 + X_2 + X_4 + X_6 \geq 375{,}000$$

Similarly, the following constraint ensures that no more than 35% of the money (\$262,500) is placed in the bonds for DynaStar (X_2), Eagle Vision (X_3), and OptiPro (X_5):

$$X_2 + X_3 + X_5 \leq 262{,}500$$

Finally, because none of the variables in the model can assume a value of less than zero, we also need the following nonnegativity condition:

$$X_1, X_2, X_3, X_4, X_5, X_6 \geq 0$$

3.9.4 Implementing the Model

The LP model for the Retirement Planning Services, Inc. investment problem is summarized as:

MAX: $.0865X_1 + .095X_2 + .10X_3 + .0875X_4 + .0925X_5 + .09X_6$ } total annual return

Subject to:

$X_1 \le 187{,}500$	} 25% restriction per investment
$X_2 \le 187{,}500$	} 25% restriction per investment
$X_3 \le 187{,}500$	} 25% restriction per investment
$X_4 \le 187{,}500$	} 25% restriction per investment
$X_5 \le 187{,}500$	} 25% restriction per investment
$X_6 \le 187{,}500$	} 25% restriction per investment
$X_1 + X_2 + X_3 + X_4 + X_5 + X_6 = 750{,}000$	} total amount invested
$X_1 + X_2 + X_4 + X_6 \ge 375{,}000$	} long-term investment
$X_2 + X_3 + X_5 \le 262{,}500$	} higher-risk investment
$X_1, X_2, X_3, X_4, X_5, X_6 \ge 0$	} nonnegativity conditions

A convenient way of implementing this model is shown in Figure 3.20 (file Fig3-20.xls on your data disk). Each row in this spreadsheet corresponds to one of the investment alternatives. Cells C6 through C11 correspond to the decision variables for the problem (X_1, …, X_6). The maximum value that each of these cells can

FIGURE 3.20
Spreadsheet model for Retirement Planning Services, Inc. bond selection problem

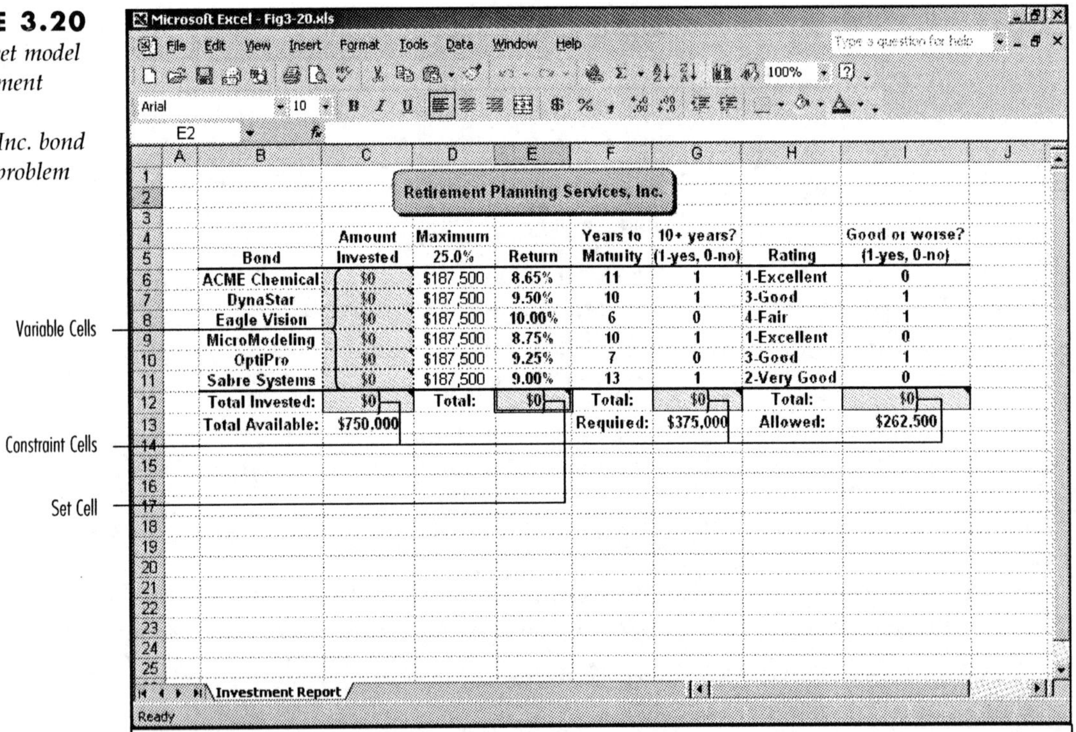

Bond	Amount Invested	Maximum 25.0%	Return	Years to Maturity	10+ years? (1-yes, 0-no)	Rating	Good or worse? (1-yes, 0-no)
ACME Chemical	$0	$187,500	8.65%	11	1	1-Excellent	0
DynaStar	$0	$187,500	9.50%	10	1	3-Good	1
Eagle Vision	$0	$187,500	10.00%	6	0	4-Fair	1
MicroModeling	$0	$187,500	8.75%	10	1	1-Excellent	0
OptiPro	$0	$187,500	9.25%	7	0	3-Good	1
Sabre Systems	$0	$187,500	9.00%	13	1	2-Very Good	0
Total Invested:	$0	Total:	$0	Total:	$0	Total:	$0
Total Available:	$750,000			Required:	$375,000	Allowed:	$262,500

Key Cell Formulas

Cell	Formula	Copied to
C12	=SUM(C6:C11)	—
E12	=SUMPRODUCT(E6:E11,$C$6:$C$11)	G12 and I12

take on is listed in cells D6 through D11. These values correspond to the RHS values for the first six constraints. The sum of cells C6 through C11 is computed in cell C12 as follows and will be restricted to equal the value shown in cell C13:

Formula for cell C12: =SUM(C6:C11)

The annual returns for each investment are listed in cells E6 through E11. The objective function is then implemented conveniently in cell E12 as follows:

Formula for cell E12: =SUMPRODUCT(E6:E11,$C$6:$C$11)

The values in cells G6 through G11 indicate which of these rows correspond to "long-term" investments. Note that the use of ones and zeros in this column makes it convenient to compute the sum of the cells C6, C7, C9, and C11 (representing X_1, X_2, X_4, and X_6) representing the LHS of the "long-term" investment constraint. This is done in cell G12 as follows:

Formula for cell G12: =SUMPRODUCT(G6:G11,$C$6:$C$11)

Similarly, the zeros and ones in cells I6 through I11 indicate the higher-risk investments and allow us to implement the LHS of the "higher-risk investment" constraint as follows:

Formula for cell I12: =SUMPRODUCT(I6:I11,$C$6:$C$11)

Note that the use of zeros and ones in columns G and I to compute the sums of selected decision variables is a very useful modeling technique that makes it easy for the user to change the variables being included in the sums. Also note that the formula for the objective in cell E12 could be copied to cells G12 and I12 to implement LHS formulas for these constraint cells.

3.9.5 Solving the Model

To solve this model, we need to specify the set cell, variable cells, and constraint cells identified in Figure 3.20. Figure 3.21 shows the Solver parameters required to solve this problem. After we click the Solve button in the Solver Parameters dialog box, Solver finds the optimal solution shown in Figure 3.22.

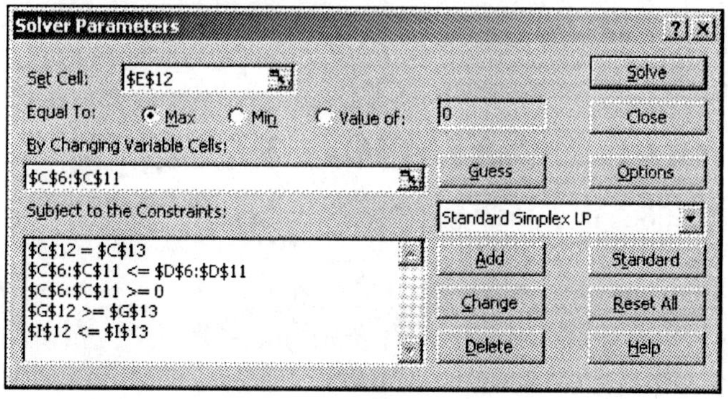

FIGURE 3.21
Solver parameters for the bond selection problem

FIGURE 3.22
Optimal solution to the bond selection problem

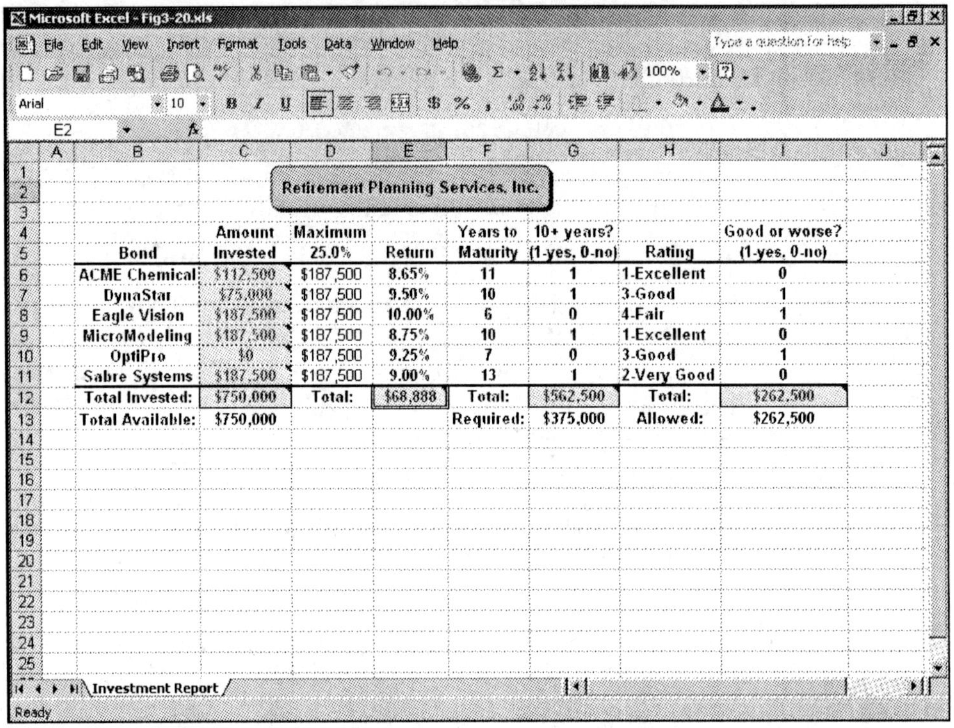

Retirement Planning Services, Inc.

Bond	Amount Invested	Maximum 25.0%	Return	Years to Maturity	10+ years? (1-yes, 0-no)	Rating	Good or worse? (1-yes, 0-no)
ACME Chemical	$112,500	$187,500	8.65%	11	1	1-Excellent	0
DynaStar	$75,000	$187,500	9.50%	10	1	3-Good	1
Eagle Vision	$187,500	$187,500	10.00%	6	0	4-Fair	1
MicroModeling	$187,500	$187,500	8.75%	10	1	1-Excellent	0
OptiPro	$0	$187,500	9.25%	7	0	3-Good	1
Sabre Systems	$187,500	$187,500	9.00%	13	1	2-Very Good	0
Total Invested:	$750,000	Total:	$68,888	Total:	$562,500	Total:	$262,500
Total Available:	$750,000			Required:	$375,000	Allowed:	$262,500

3.9.6 Analyzing the Solution

The solution shown in Figure 3.22 indicates the optimal investment plan places $112,500 in Acme Chemical (X_1), $75,000 in DynaStar ($X_2$), $187,500 in Eagle Vision (X_3), $187,500 in MicroModeling (X_4), $0 in OptiPro ($X_5$), and $187,500 in Sabre Systems (X_6). It is interesting to note that more money is being invested in Acme Chemical than DynaStar and OptiPro even though the return on Acme Chemical is lower than on the returns for DynaStar and OptiPro. This is because DynaStar and OptiPro are both "higher-risk" investments and the 35% limit on "higher-risk" investments is a binding constraint (or is met as a strict equality in the optimal solution). Thus, the optimal solution could be improved if we could put more than 35% of the money into the higher-risk investments.

3.10 A TRANSPORTATION PROBLEM

Many transportation and logistics problems businesses face fall into a category of problems known as network flow problems. We will consider one such example here and study this area in more detail in chapter 5.

Tropicsun is a leading grower and distributor of fresh citrus products with three large citrus groves scattered around central Florida in the cities of Mt. Dora, Eustis, and Clermont. Tropicsun currently has 275,000 bushels of citrus at the grove in Mt. Dora, 400,000 bushels at the grove in Eustis, and 300,000 bushels at the grove in Clermont. Tropicsun has citrus processing plants in

Ocala, Orlando, and Leesburg with processing capacities to handle 200,000, 600,000, and 225,000 bushels, respectively. Tropicsun contracts with a local trucking company to transport its fruit from the groves to the processing plants. The trucking company charges a flat rate for every mile that each bushel of fruit must be transported. Each mile a bushel of fruit travels is known as a bushel-mile. The following table summarizes the distances (in miles) between the groves and processing plants:

	Distances (in miles) Between Groves and Plants		
Grove	**Ocala**	**Orlando**	**Leesburg**
Mt. Dora	21	50	40
Eustis	35	30	22
Clermont	55	20	25

Tropicsun wants to determine how many bushels to ship from each grove to each processing plant in order to minimize the total number of bushel-miles the fruit must be shipped.

3.10.1 Defining the Decision Variables

In this situation, the problem is to determine how many bushels of fruit should be shipped from each grove to each processing plant. The problem is summarized graphically in Figure 3.23.

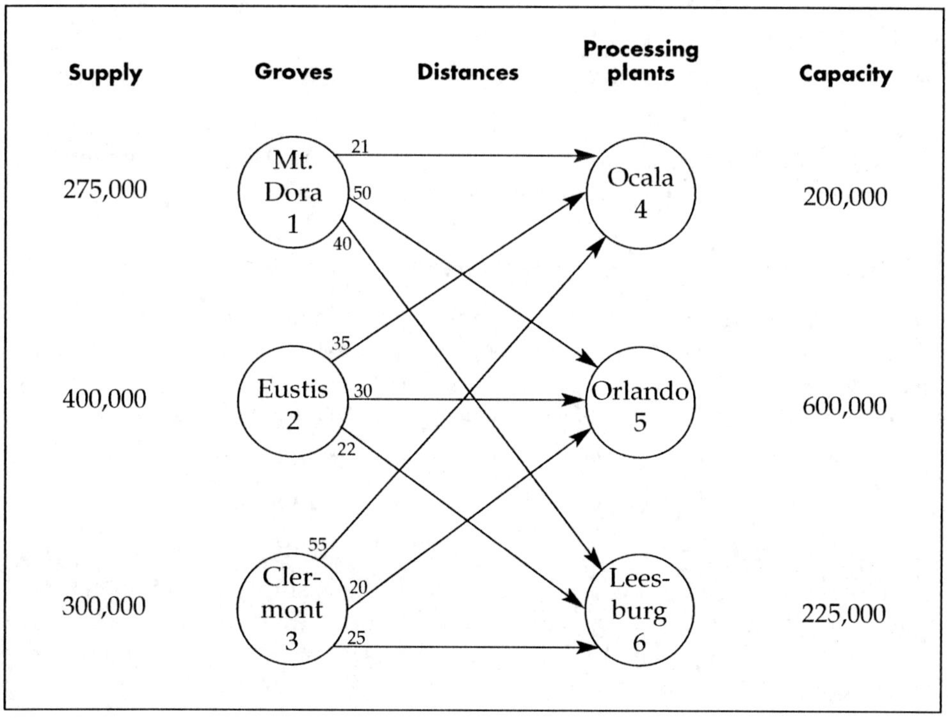

FIGURE 3.23
Diagram for the Tropicsun transportation problem

The circles (or nodes) in Figure 3.23 correspond to the different groves and processing plants in the problem. Note that a number has been assigned to each node. The arrows (or arcs) connecting the various groves and processing plants represent different shipping routes. The decision problem faced by Tropicsun is to determine how many bushels of fruit to ship on each of these routes. Thus, one decision variable is associated with each of the arcs in Figure 3.23. We can define these variables in general as:

X_{ij} = number of bushels to ship from node *i* to node *j*

Specifically, the nine decision variables are:

X_{14} = number of bushels to ship from Mt. Dora (node 1) to Ocala (node 4)
X_{15} = number of bushels to ship from Mt. Dora (node 1) to Orlando (node 5)
X_{16} = number of bushels to ship from Mt. Dora (node 1) to Leesburg (node 6)
X_{24} = number of bushels to ship from Eustis (node 2) to Ocala (node 4)
X_{25} = number of bushels to ship from Eustis (node 2) to Orlando (node 5)
X_{26} = number of bushels to ship from Eustis (node 2) to Leesburg (node 6)
X_{34} = number of bushels to ship from Clermont (node 3) to Ocala (node 4)
X_{35} = number of bushels to ship from Clermont (node 3) to Orlando (node 5)
X_{36} = number of bushels to ship from Clermont (node 3) to Leesburg (node 6)

3.10.2 Defining the Objective Function

The goal in this problem is to determine how many bushels to ship from each grove to each processing plant while minimizing the total distance (or total number of bushel-miles) the fruit must travel. The objective function for this problem is represented by:

$$\text{MIN:} \quad 21X_{14} + 50X_{15} + 40X_{16} + 35X_{24} + 30X_{25} + 22X_{26} + 55X_{34} + 20X_{35} + 25X_{36}$$

The term $21X_{14}$ in this function reflects the fact that each bushel shipped from Mt. Dora (node 1) to Ocala (node 4) must travel 21 miles. The remaining terms in the function express similar relationships for the other shipping routes.

3.10.3 Defining the Constraints

Two physical constraints apply to this problem. First, there is a limit on the amount of fruit that can be shipped to each processing plant. Tropicsun can ship no more than 200,000, 600,000, and 225,000 bushels to Ocala, Orlando, and Leesburg, respectively. These restrictions are reflected by the following constraints:

$$X_{14} + X_{24} + X_{34} \leq 200{,}000 \quad \text{\} capacity restriction for Ocala}$$
$$X_{15} + X_{25} + X_{35} \leq 600{,}000 \quad \text{\} capacity restriction for Orlando}$$
$$X_{16} + X_{26} + X_{36} \leq 225{,}000 \quad \text{\} capacity restriction for Leesburg}$$

The first constraint indicates that the total bushels shipped to Ocala (node 4) from Mt. Dora (node 1), Eustis (node 2), and Clermont (node 3) must be less than or equal to Ocala's capacity of 200,000 bushels. The other two constraints have similar interpretations for Orlando and Leesburg. Notice that the total processing capacity at the plants (1,025,000 bushels) exceeds the total supply of fruit at the groves (975,000 bushels). Therefore, these constraints are less than or equal to constraints because not all the available capacity will be used.

The second set of constraints ensures that the supply of fruit at each grove is shipped to a processing plant. That is, all of the 275,000, 400,000, and 300,000 bushels at Mt. Dora, Eustis, and Clermont, respectively, must be processed somewhere. This is accomplished by the following constraints:

$X_{14} + X_{15} + X_{16} = 275{,}000$ } supply available at Mt. Dora
$X_{24} + X_{25} + X_{26} = 400{,}000$ } supply available at Eustis
$X_{34} + X_{35} + X_{36} = 300{,}000$ } supply available at Clermont

The first constraint indicates that the total amount shipped from Mt. Dora (node 1) to the plants in Ocala (node 4), Orlando (node 5), and Leesburg (node 6) must equal the total amount available at Mt. Dora. This constraint indicates that all the fruit available at Mt. Dora must be shipped somewhere. The other two constraints play similar roles for Eustis and Clermont.

3.10.4 Implementing the Model

The LP model for Tropicsun's fruit transportation problem is summarized as:

MIN: $21X_{14} + 50X_{15} + 40X_{16} + 35X_{24} + 30X_{25} + 22X_{26} + 55X_{34} + 20X_{35} + 25X_{36}$ } total distance fruit is shipped (in bushel-miles)

Subject to:
$X_{14} + X_{24} + X_{34} \leq 200{,}000$ } capacity restriction for Ocala
$X_{15} + X_{25} + X_{35} \leq 600{,}000$ } capacity restriction for Orlando
$X_{16} + X_{26} + X_{36} \leq 225{,}000$ } capacity restriction for Leesburg
$X_{14} + X_{15} + X_{16} = 275{,}000$ } supply available at Mt. Dora
$X_{24} + X_{25} + X_{26} = 400{,}000$ } supply available at Eustis
$X_{34} + X_{35} + X_{36} = 300{,}000$ } supply available at Clermont
$X_{ij} \geq 0$, for all i and j } nonnegativity conditions

The last constraint, as in previous models, indicates that all the decision variables must be nonnegative.

A convenient way to implement this model is shown in Figure 3.24 (and in the file Fig3-24.xls on your data disk). In this spreadsheet, the distances between each grove and plant are summarized in a tabular format in cells C7 through E9. Cells C14 through E16 are reserved for representing the number of bushels of fruit to ship from each grove to each processing plant. Notice that these nine cells correspond directly to the nine decision variables in the algebraic formulation of the model.

The LHS formulas for the three capacity constraints in the model are implemented in cells C17, D17, and E17 in the spreadsheet. To do this, the following formula is entered in cell C17 and copied to cells D17 and E17:

Formula for cell C17: =SUM(C14:C16)
(Copy to D17 and E17.)

FIGURE 3.24
Spreadsheet model for Tropicsun's transportation problem

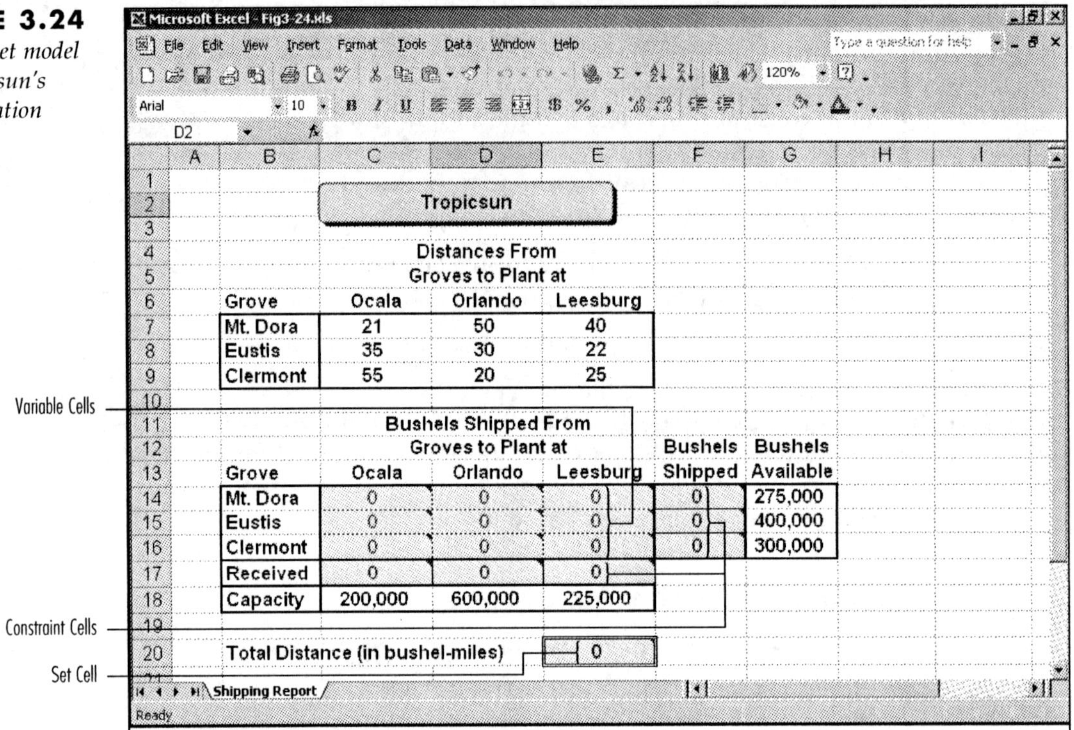

Key Cell Formulas

Cell	**Formula**	**Copied to**
C17	=SUM(C14:C16)	D17:E17
F14	=SUM(C14:E14)	F15:F16
E20	=SUMPRODUCT(C7:E9,C14:E16)	—

These cells represent the total bushels of fruit being shipped to the plants in Ocala, Orlando, and Leesburg, respectively. Cells C18 through E18 contain the RHS values for these constraint cells.

The LHS formulas for the three supply constraints in the model are implemented in cells F14, F15, and F16 as:

Formula for cell F14: =SUM(C14:E14)
(Copy to F15 and F16.)

These cells represent the total bushels of fruit being shipped from the groves at Mt. Dora, Eustis, and Clermont, respectively. Cells G14 through G16 contain the RHS values for these constraint cells.

Finally, the objective function for this model is entered in cell E20 as:

Formula for cell E20: =SUMPRODUCT(C7:E9,C14:E16)

The SUMPRODUCT( ) function multiplies each element in the range C7 through E9 by the corresponding element in the range C14 through E16 and then sums the individual products.

3.10.5 Heuristic Solution for the Model

To appreciate what Solver is accomplishing, let's consider how we might try to solve this problem manually using a heuristic. A **heuristic** is a rule-of-thumb for making decisions that might work well in some instances, but is not guaranteed to produce optimal solutions or decisions. One heuristic we can apply to solve Tropicsun's problem is to always ship as much as possible along the next available path with the shortest distance (or least cost). Using this heuristic, we solve the problem as follows:

1. Because the shortest available path between any grove and processing plant is between Clermont and Orlando (20 miles), we first ship as much as possible through this route. The maximum we can ship through this route is the smaller of the supply at Clermont (300,000 bushels) or the capacity at Orlando (600,000 bushels). So we would ship 300,000 bushels from Clermont to Orlando. This depletes the supply at Clermont.
2. The next shortest available route occurs between Mt. Dora and Ocala (21 miles). The maximum we can ship through this route is the smaller of the supply at Mt. Dora (275,000 bushels) or the capacity at Ocala (200,000 bushels). So we would ship 200,000 bushels from Mt. Dora to Ocala. This depletes the capacity at Ocala.
3. The next shortest available route occurs between Eustis and Leesburg (22 miles). The maximum we can ship through this route is the smaller of the supply at Eustis (400,000 bushels) or the capacity at Leesburg (225,000 bushels). So we would ship 225,000 bushels from Eustis to Leesburg. This depletes the capacity at Leesburg.
4. The next shortest available route occurs between Eustis and Orlando (30 miles). The maximum we can ship through this route is the smaller of the remaining supply at Eustis (175,000 bushels) or the remaining capacity at Orlando (300,000 bushels). So we would ship 175,000 bushels from Eustis to Orlando. This depletes the supply at Eustis.
5. The only remaining route occurs between Mt. Dora and Orlando (because the processing capacities at Ocala and Leesburg have both been depleted). This distance is 50 miles. The maximum we can ship through this route is the smaller of the remaining supply at Mt. Dora (75,000 bushels) and the remaining capacity at Orlando (125,000 bushels). So we would ship the final 75,000 bushels at Mt. Dora to Orlando. This depletes the supply at Mt. Dora.

As shown in Figure 3.25, the solution identified with this heuristic involves shipping the fruit a total of 24,150,000 bushel-miles. All the bushels available at each grove have been shipped to the processing plants and none of the capacities at the processing plants have been exceeded. Therefore, this is a *feasible* solution to the problem. And the logic used to find this solution might lead us to believe it is a reasonably good solution—but is it the *optimal* solution? Is there no other feasible solution to this problem that can make the total distance the fruit has to travel less than 24,150,000 bushel-miles?

FIGURE 3.25
A heuristic solution to the transportation problem

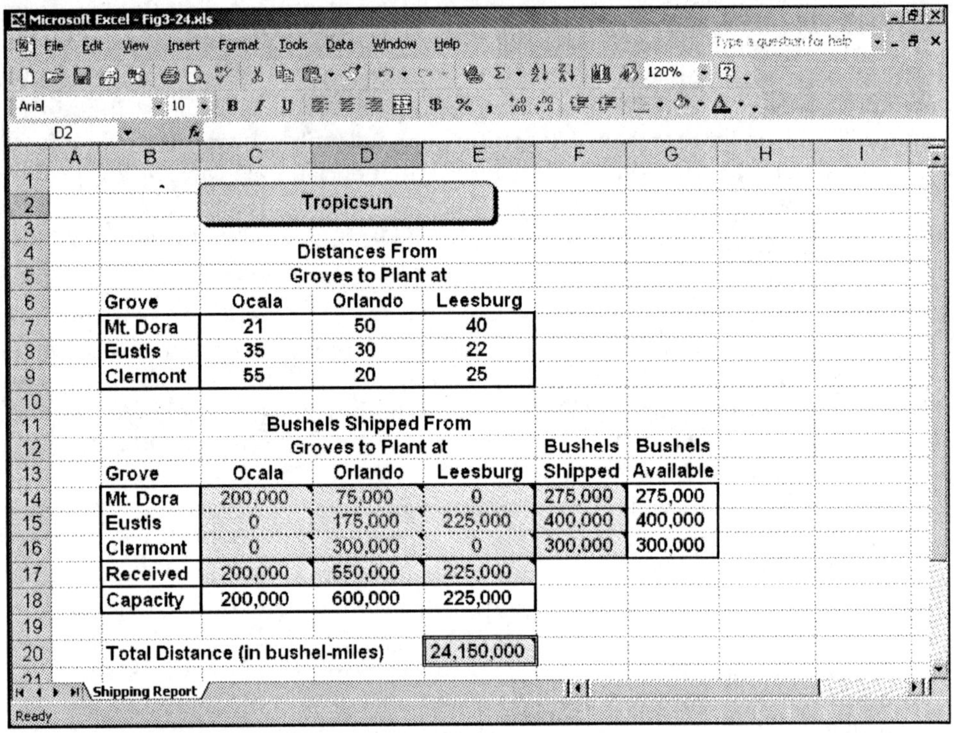

Tropicsun

	Distances From Groves to Plant at		
Grove	Ocala	Orlando	Leesburg
Mt. Dora	21	50	40
Eustis	35	30	22
Clermont	55	20	25

	Bushels Shipped From Groves to Plant at			Bushels	Bushels
Grove	Ocala	Orlando	Leesburg	Shipped	Available
Mt. Dora	200,000	75,000	0	275,000	275,000
Eustis	0	175,000	225,000	400,000	400,000
Clermont	0	300,000	0	300,000	300,000
Received	200,000	550,000	225,000		
Capacity	200,000	600,000	225,000		

Total Distance (in bushel-miles) 24,150,000

3.10.6 Solving the Model

To find the optimal solution to this model, we must indicate to Solver the set cell, variable cells, and constraint cells identified in Figure 3.24. Figure 3.26 shows the Solver parameters required to solve this problem. The optimal solution is shown in Figure 3.27.

3.10.7 Analyzing the Solution

The optimal solution in Figure 3.27 indicates that 200,000 bushels should be shipped from Mt. Dora to Ocala (X_{14} = 200,000) and 75,000 bushels should be shipped from Mt. Dora to Leesburg (X_{16} = 75,000). Of the 400,000 bushels available

FIGURE 3.26
Solver parameters for the transportation problem

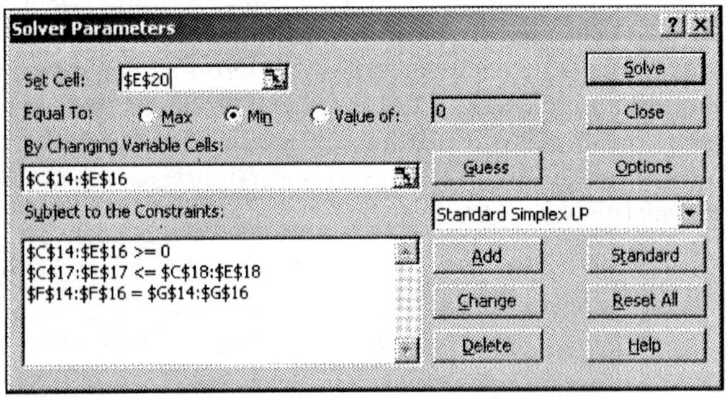

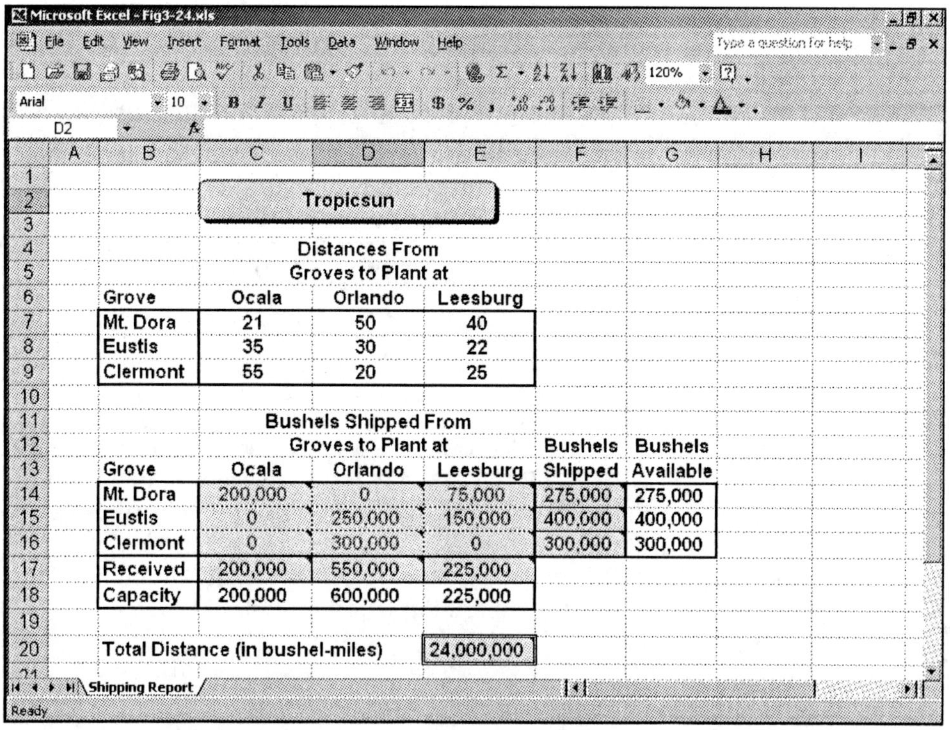

Tropicsun

Grove	Ocala	Orlando	Leesburg
	Distances From Groves to Plant at		
Mt. Dora	21	50	40
Eustis	35	30	22
Clermont	55	20	25

Grove	Ocala	Orlando	Leesburg	Bushels Shipped	Bushels Available
	Bushels Shipped From Groves to Plant at				
Mt. Dora	200,000	0	75,000	275,000	275,000
Eustis	0	250,000	150,000	400,000	400,000
Clermont	0	300,000	0	300,000	300,000
Received	200,000	550,000	225,000		
Capacity	200,000	600,000	225,000		

Total Distance (in bushel-miles) 24,000,000

FIGURE 3.27
Optimal solution to Tropicsun's transportation problem

at the grove in Eustis, 250,000 bushels should be shipped to Orlando for processing (X_{25} = 250,000) and 150,000 bushels should be shipped to Leesburg (X_{26} = 150,000). Finally, all 300,000 bushels available in Clermont should be shipped to Orlando (X_{35} = 300,000). None of the other possible shipping routes will be used.

The solution shown in Figure 3.27 satisfies all the constraints in the model and results in a minimum shipping distance of 24,000,000 bushel-miles, which is better than the heuristic solution identified earlier. Therefore, simple heuristics can sometimes solve LP problems, but as this example illustrates, there is no guarantee that a heuristic solution is the best possible solution.

3.11 A BLENDING PROBLEM

Many business problems involve determining an optimal mix of ingredients. For example, major oil companies must determine the least costly mix of different crude oils and other chemicals to blend together to produce a certain grade of gasoline. Lawn care companies must determine the least costly mix of chemicals and other products to blend together to produce different types of fertilizer. The following is another example of a common blending problem faced in the U.S. agricultural industry, which annually produces goods valued at approximately $200 billion.

Agri-Pro is a company that sells agricultural products to farmers in a number of states. One service it provides to customers is custom feed mixing, whereby a farmer can order a specific amount of livestock feed and specify the amount of corn, grain, and minerals the feed should contain. This is an important service because the proper feed for various farm animals changes regularly depending on the weather, pasture conditions, and so on.

Agri-Pro stocks bulk amounts of four types of feeds that it can mix to meet a given customer's specifications. The following table summarizes the four feeds, their composition of corn, grain, and minerals, and the cost per pound for each type.

	Percent of Nutrient in			
Nutrient	**Feed 1**	**Feed 2**	**Feed 3**	**Feed 4**
Corn	30%	5%	20%	10%
Grain	10%	30%	15%	10%
Minerals	20%	20%	20%	30%
Cost per Pound	$0.25	$0.30	$0.32	$0.15

On average, each U.S. citizen consumes almost 70 pounds of poultry per year. To remain competitive, chicken growers must ensure that they feed the required nutrients to their flocks in the most cost-effective manner. Agri-Pro has just received an order from a local chicken farmer for 8,000 pounds of feed. The farmer wants this feed to contain at least 20% corn, 15% grain, and 15% minerals. What should Agri-Pro do to fill this order at minimum cost?

3.11.1 Defining the Decision Variables

In this problem, Agri-Pro must determine how much of the various feeds to blend together in order to meet the customer's requirements at minimum cost. An algebraic formulation of this problem might use the following four decision variables:

X_1 = pounds of feed 1 to use in the mix
X_2 = pounds of feed 2 to use in the mix
X_3 = pounds of feed 3 to use in the mix
X_4 = pounds of feed 4 to use in the mix

3.11.2 Defining the Objective Function

The objective in this problem is to fill the customer's order at the lowest possible cost. Because each pound of feed 1, 2, 3, and 4 costs $0.25, $0.30, $0.32, and $0.15, respectively, the objective function is represented by:

$$\text{MIN:} \quad .25X_1 + .30X_2 + .32X_3 + .15X_4$$

3.11.3 Defining the Constraints

Four constraints must be met to fulfill the customer's requirements. First, the customer wants a total of 8,000 pounds of feed. This is expressed by the constraint:

$$X_1 + X_2 + X_3 + X_4 = 8{,}000$$

The customer also wants the order to consist of at least 20% corn. Because each pound of feed 1, 2, 3, and 4 consists of 30%, 5%, 20%, and 10% corn, respectively, the total amount of corn in the mix is represented by:

$$.30X_1 + .05X_2 + .20X_3 + .10X_4$$

To ensure that *corn* constitutes at least 20% of the 8,000 pounds of feed, we set up the following constraint:

$$\frac{.30X_1 + .05X_2 + .20X_3 + .10X_4}{8{,}000} \geq .20$$

Similarly, to ensure that *grain* constitutes at least 15% of the 8,000 pounds of feed, we use the constraint:

$$\frac{.10X_1 + .30X_2 + .15X_3 + .10X_4}{8{,}000} \geq .15$$

Finally, to ensure that *minerals* constitute at least 15% of the 8,000 pounds of feed, we use the constraint:

$$\frac{.20X_1 + .20X_2 + .20X_3 + .30X_4}{8{,}000} \geq .15$$

3.11.4 Some Observations About Constraints, Reporting, and Scaling

We need to make some important observations about the constraints for this model. First, these constraints look somewhat different from the usual linear sum of products. However, these constraints are equivalent to a sum of products. For example, the constraint for the required percentage of corn can be expressed as:

$$\frac{.30X_1 + .05X_2 + .20X_3 + .10X_4}{8{,}000} \geq .20$$

or as:

$$\frac{.30X_1}{8{,}000} + \frac{.05X_2}{8{,}000} + \frac{.20X_3}{8{,}000} + \frac{.10X_4}{8{,}000} \geq .20$$

or, if you multiply both sides of the inequality by 8,000, as:

$$.30X_1 + .05X_2 + .20X_3 + .10X_4 \geq 1{,}600$$

All these constraints define exactly the same set of feasible values for $X_1, \ldots, X_4$. Theoretically, we should be able to implement and use *any* of these constraints to solve the problem. However, we need to consider a number of practical issues in determining which form of the constraint to implement.

Notice that the LHS formulas for the first and second versions of the constraint represent the *proportion* of corn in the 8,000 pound order, whereas the LHS in the third version of the constraint represents the *total pounds* of corn in the 8,000 pound order. Because we must implement the LHS formula of one of these constraints in the spreadsheet, we need to decide which number to display in the spreadsheet—the *proportion* (or percentage) of corn in the order, or the *total pounds of corn* in the order. If we know one of these values, we can easily set up a formula to calculate the other value. But, when more than one way to implement a constraint exists (as is usually the case), we need to consider what the value of the LHS portion of the constraint means to the user of the spreadsheet so that the results of the model can be reported as clearly as possible.

Another issue to consider involves *scaling* the model so that it can be solved accurately. For example, suppose we decide to implement the LHS formula for the first or second version of the corn constraint given earlier so that the *proportion* of corn in the 8,000 pound feed order appears in the spreadsheet. The coefficients for the variables in these constraints are *very* small values. In either case, the coefficient for X_2 is 0.05/8,000 or 0.000006250.

As Solver tries to solve an LP problem, it must perform intermediate calculations that make the various coefficients in the model larger or smaller. As numbers become extremely large or small, computers often run into storage or representation problems that force them to use approximations of the actual numbers. This opens the door for problems to occur in the accuracy of the results and, in some cases, can prevent the computer from solving the problem at all. So, if some coefficients in the initial model are extremely large or extremely small, it is a good idea to rescale the problem so that all the coefficients are of similar magnitudes.

3.11.5 Rescaling the Model

To illustrate how a problem is rescaled, consider the following equivalent formulation of the Agri-Pro problem:

X_1 = amount of feed 1 *in thousands of pounds* to use in the mix
X_2 = amount of feed 2 *in thousands of pounds* to use in the mix
X_3 = amount of feed 3 *in thousands of pounds* to use in the mix
X_4 = amount of feed 4 *in thousands of pounds* to use in the mix

The objective function and constraints are represented by:

MIN: $250X_1 + 300X_2 + 320X_3 + 150X_4$ } total cost

Subject to:

$$X_1 + X_2 + X_3 + X_4 = 8 \quad \text{\} pounds of feed required}$$

$$\frac{.30X_1 + .05X_2 + .20X_3 + .10X_4}{8} \geq 0.20 \quad \text{\} min \% of corn required}$$

$$\frac{.10X_1 + .30X_2 + .15X_3 + .10X_4}{8} \geq 0.15 \quad \text{\} min \% of grain required}$$

$$\frac{.20X_1 + .20X_2 + .20X_3 + .30X_4}{8} \geq 0.15 \quad \text{\} min \% of minerals required}$$

$$X_1, X_2, X_3, X_4 \geq 0 \quad \text{\} nonnegativity conditions}$$

Each unit of X_1, X_2, X_3, and X_4 now represents 1,000 pounds of feed 1, 2, 3, and 4, respectively. So the objective now reflects the fact that each unit (or each 1,000 pounds) of X_1, X_2, X_3, and X_4 costs $250, $300, $320, and $150, respectively. The constraints have also been adjusted to reflect the fact that the variables now represent thousands of pounds of the different feeds. Notice that the smallest coefficient in the constraints is now 0.05/8 = 0.00625 and the largest coefficient is 8 (that is, the RHS value for the first constraint). In our original formulation, the smallest coefficient was 0.00000625 and the largest coefficient was 8,000. By rescaling the problem, we dramatically reduced the range between the smallest and largest coefficients in the model.

Automatic Scaling

In solving some earlier problems in this chapter, you might have noticed that the Solver Options dialog box provides an option called Use Automatic Scaling (see Figure 3.14). If you select this option, Solver attempts to rescale the data automatically before solving the problem. Although this option is effective, you should not rely solely on it to solve all scaling problems that occur in your models.

The Assume Linear Model Option

When the Assume Linear Model option is selected, Solver conducts a number of internal tests to verify that the model is truly linear in the objective and constraints. If this option is selected and Solver's tests indicate that the model is not linear, a dialog box appears indicating that the conditions for linearity are not satisfied. The internal tests Solver applies are not always 100% accurate and sometimes indicate that the model is not linear when, in fact, it is. This often occurs when a model is poorly scaled. If you encounter this message and you are certain that your model is linear, re-solving the model might result in Solver identifying the optimal solution. If this does not work, try reformulating your model so that it is more evenly scaled.

3.11.6 Implementing the Model

One way to implement this model in a spreadsheet is shown in Figure 3.28 (and in the file Fig3-28.xls on your data disk). In this spreadsheet, cells B5 through E5 contain the costs of the different types of feeds. The percentage of the different nutrients found in each type of feed is listed in cells B10 through E12.

Cell G6 contains the total amount of feed (in 1,000s of pounds) required for the order, and the minimum percentage of the three types of nutrients required by the customer order are entered in cells G10 through G12. Notice that the values in column G correspond to the RHS values for the various constraints in the model.

In this spreadsheet, cells B6, C6, D6, and E6 are reserved to represent the decision variables X_1, X_2, X_3, and X_4. These cells will ultimately indicate how much of each type of feed should be mixed together to fill the order. The objective function for the problem is implemented in cell F5 using the formula:

Formula for cell F5: =SUMPRODUCT(B5:E5,B6:E6)

The LHS formula for the first constraint involves calculating the sum of the decision variables. This relationship is implemented in cell F6 as:

Formula for cell F6: =SUM(B6:E6)

FIGURE 3.28
Spreadsheet model for Agri-Pro's blending problem

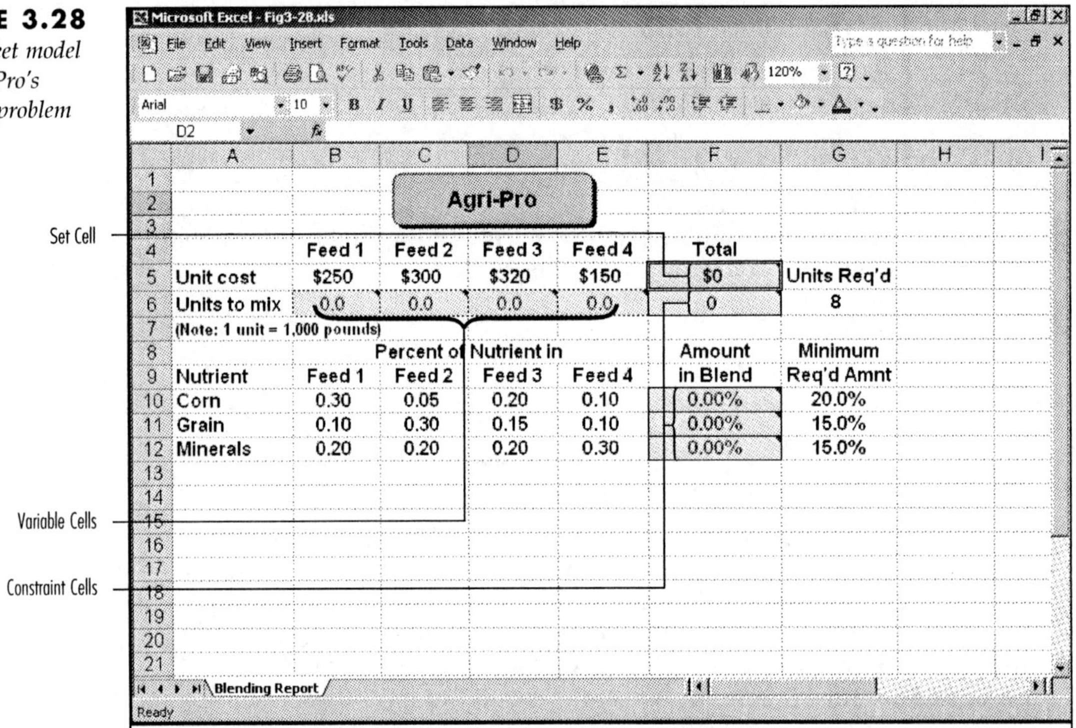

Key Cell Formulas

Cell	Formula	Copied to
F5	=SUMPRODUCT(B5:E5,B6:E6)	—
F6	=SUM(B6:E6)	—
F10	=SUMPRODUCT(B10:E10,$B$6:$E$6)/$G$6	F11:F12

The RHS for this constraint is in cell G6. The LHS formulas for the other three constraints are implemented in cells F10, F11, and F12. Specifically, the LHS formula for the second constraint (representing the proportion of corn in the mix) is implemented in cell F10 as:

Formula for cell F10: =SUMPRODUCT(B10:E10,$B$6:$E$6)/$G$6
(Copy to F11 through F12.)

This formula is then copied to cells F11 and F12 to implement the LHS formulas for the remaining two constraints. Again, cells G10 through G12 contain the RHS values for these constraints.

Notice that this model is implemented in a user-friendly way. Each constraint cell has a logical interpretation that communicates important information. For any given values for the variable cells (B6 through E6) totaling 8,000, the constraint cells (F10 through F12) indicate the *actual* percentage of corn, grain, and minerals in the mix.

3.11.7 Solving the Model

Figure 3.29 shows the Solver parameters required to solve this problem. The optimal solution is shown in Figure 3.30.

3.11.8 Analyzing the Solution

The optimal solution shown in Figure 3.30 indicates that the 8,000 pound feed order is produced at the lowest possible cost by mixing 4,500 pounds of feed 1 ($X_1 = 4.5$) with 2,000 pounds of feed 2 ($X_2 = 2$) and 1,500 pounds of feed 4 ($X_4 = 1.5$). Cell F6 indicates this produces exactly 8,000 pounds of feed. Furthermore, cells F10 through F12 indicate this mix contains 20% corn, 15% grain, and 21.88% minerals. The total cost of producing this mix is $1,950, as indicated by cell F5.

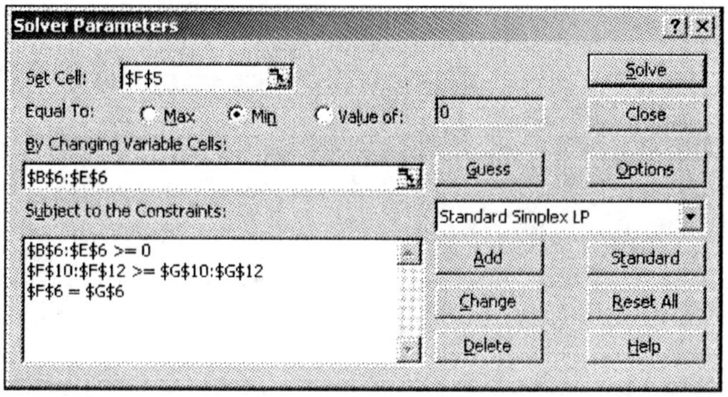

FIGURE 3.29
Solver parameters for the blending problem

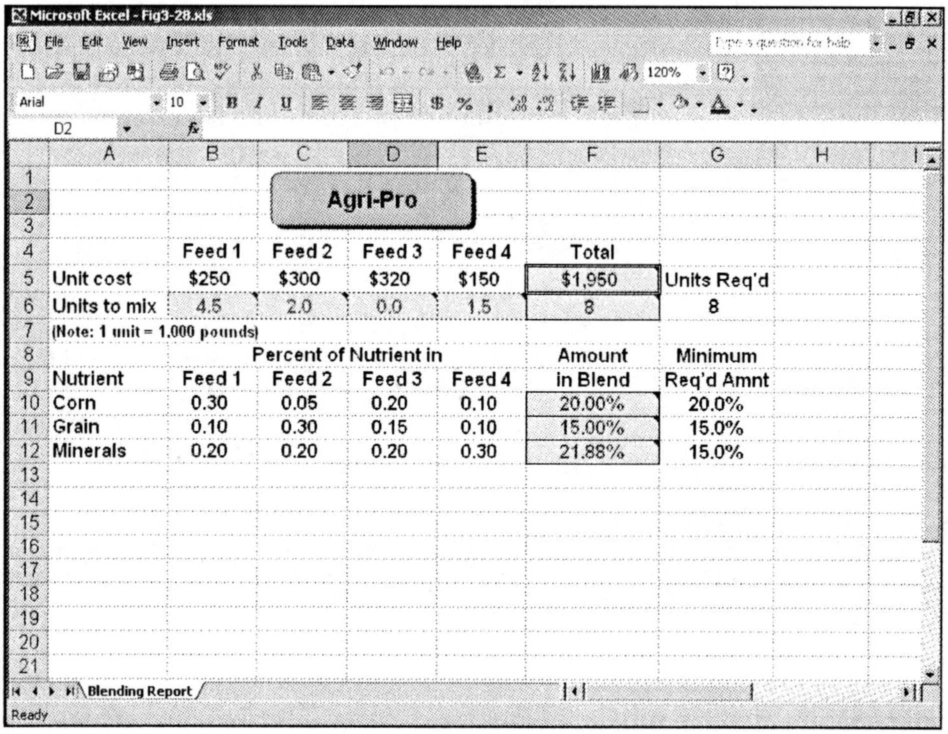

FIGURE 3.30
Optimal solution to Agri-Pro's blending problem

Have You Seen LP at Your Grocery Store?

The next time you are at your local grocery store, make a special trip down the aisle where the pet food is located. On the back of just about any bag of dog or cat food, you should see the following sort of label (taken directly from the author's dog's favorite brand of food):

This product contains:

- At least 21% crude protein
- At least 8% crude fat
- At most 4.5% crude fiber
- At most 12% moisture

In making such statements, the manufacturer guarantees that these nutritional requirements are met by the product. Various ingredients (such as corn, soybeans, meat and bone meal, animal fat, wheat, and rice) are blended to make the product. Most companies are interested in determining the blend of ingredients that satisfies these requirements in the least costly way. Not surprisingly, almost all of the major pet food manufacturing companies use LP extensively in their production process to solve this type of blending problem.

3.12 A PRODUCTION AND INVENTORY PLANNING PROBLEM

One of the most fundamental problems facing manufacturing companies is that of planning their production and inventory levels. This process considers demand forecasts and resource constraints for the next several time periods and determines production and inventory levels for each of these time periods so as to meet the anticipated demand in the most economical way. As the following example illustrates, the multiperiod nature of these problems can be handled very conveniently in a spreadsheet to greatly simplify the production planning process.

> The Upton Corporation manufactures heavy duty air compressors for the home and light industrial markets. Upton is presently trying to plan its production and inventory levels for the next six months. Because of seasonal fluctuations in utility and raw material costs, the per unit cost of producing air compressors varies from month to month—as does the demand for air compressors. Production capacity also varies from month to month due to differences in the number of working days, vacations, and scheduled maintenance and training. The following table summarizes the monthly production costs, demands, and production capacity Upton's management expects to face over the next six months.

	Month					
	1	2	3	4	5	6
Unit Production Cost	\$ 240	\$ 250	\$ 265	\$ 285	\$ 280	\$ 260
Units Demanded	1,000	4,500	6,000	5,500	3,500	4,000
Maximum Production	4,000	3,500	4,000	4,500	4,000	3,500

Given the size of Upton's warehouse, a maximum of 6,000 units can be held in inventory at the end of any month. The owner of the company likes to keep at least 1,500 units in inventory as safety stock to meet unexpected demand contingencies. To maintain a stable workforce, the company wants to produce at no less than one half of its maximum production capacity each month. Upton's controller estimates that the cost of carrying a unit in any given month is approximately equal to 1.5% of the unit production cost in the same month. Upton estimates the number of units carried in inventory each month by averaging the beginning and ending inventory for each month.

There are 2,750 units currently in inventory. Upton wants to identify the production and inventory plan for the next six months that will meet the expected demand each month while minimizing production and inventory costs.

3.12.1 Defining the Decision Variables

The basic decision Upton's management team faces is how many units to manufacture in each of the next six months. We will represent these decision variables as follows:

P_1 = number of units to produce in month 1
P_2 = number of units to produce in month 2
P_3 = number of units to produce in month 3
P_4 = number of units to produce in month 4
P_5 = number of units to produce in month 5
P_6 = number of units to produce in month 6

3.12.2 Defining the Objective Function

The objective in this problem is to minimize the total production and inventory costs. The total production cost is computed easily as:

$$\text{Production Cost} = 240P_1 + 250P_2 + 265P_3 + 285P_4 + 280P_5 + 260P_6$$

The inventory cost is a bit more tricky to compute. The cost of holding a unit in inventory each month is 1.5% of the production cost in the same month. So, the unit inventory cost is \$3.60 in month 1 (*i.e.*, 1.5% × \$240 = \$3.60), \$3.75 in month 2 (*i.e.*, 1.5% × \$250 = \$3.75), and so on. The number of units held each month is to be computed as the average of the beginning and ending inventory for the month. Of course, the beginning inventory in any given month is equal to the ending inventory from the previous month. So if we let B_i represent the beginning inventory for month *i*, the total inventory cost is given by:

$$\text{Inventory Cost} = 3.6(B_1+B_2)/2 + 3.75(B_2+B_3)/2 + 3.98(B_3+B_4)/2 + 4.28(B_4+B_5)/2 + 4.20(B_5+B_6)/2 + 3.9(B_6+B_7)/2$$

Note that the first term in the previous formula computes the inventory cost for month 1 using B_1 as the beginning inventory for month 1 and B_2 as the ending inventory for month 1. Thus, the objective function for this problem is given as:

$$\text{MIN:} \quad \left.\begin{array}{l} 240P_1 + 250P_2 + 265P_3 + 285P_4 + 280P_5 + 260P_6 \\ + 3.6(B_1+B_2)/2 + 3.75(B_2+B_3)/2 + 3.98(B_3+B_4)/2 \\ + 4.28(B_4+B_5)/2 + 4.20(B_5+B_6)/2 + 3.9(B_6+B_7)/2 \end{array}\right\} \text{total cost}$$

3.12.3 Defining the Constraints

There are two sets of constraints that apply to this problem. First, the number of units produced each month cannot exceed the maximum production levels stated in the problem. However, we must also make sure that the number of units produced each month is no less than one half of the maximum production capacity for the month. These conditions can be expressed concisely as follows:

$2{,}000 \le P_1 \le 4{,}000$ } production level for month 1
$1{,}750 \le P_2 \le 3{,}500$ } production level for month 2
$2{,}000 \le P_3 \le 4{,}000$ } production level for month 3
$2{,}250 \le P_4 \le 4{,}500$ } production level for month 4
$2{,}000 \le P_5 \le 4{,}000$ } production level for month 5
$1{,}750 \le P_6 \le 3{,}500$ } production level for month 6

These restrictions simply place the appropriate lower and upper limits on the values each of the decision variables may assume. Similarly, we must ensure that the ending inventory each month falls between the minimum and maximum allowable inventory levels of 1,500 and 6,000, respectively. In general, the ending inventory for any month is computed as:

$$\text{Ending Inventory} = \text{Beginning Inventory} + \text{Units Produced} - \text{Units Sold}$$

Thus, the following restrictions indicate that the ending inventory in each of the next six months (after meeting the demand for the month) must fall between 1,500 and 6,000.

$1{,}500 \le B_1 + P_1 - 1{,}000 \le 6{,}000$ } ending inventory for month 1
$1{,}500 \le B_2 + P_2 - 4{,}500 \le 6{,}000$ } ending inventory for month 2
$1{,}500 \le B_3 + P_3 - 6{,}000 \le 6{,}000$ } ending inventory for month 3
$1{,}500 \le B_4 + P_4 - 5{,}500 \le 6{,}000$ } ending inventory for month 4
$1{,}500 \le B_5 + P_5 - 3{,}500 \le 6{,}000$ } ending inventory for month 5
$1{,}500 \le B_6 + P_6 - 4{,}000 \le 6{,}000$ } ending inventory for month 6

Finally, to ensure that the beginning balance in one month equals the ending balance from the previous month, we have the following additional restrictions:

$$B_2 = B_1 + P_1 - 1{,}000$$
$$B_3 = B_2 + P_2 - 4{,}500$$
$$B_4 = B_3 + P_3 - 6{,}000$$
$$B_5 = B_4 + P_4 - 5{,}500$$
$$B_6 = B_5 + P_5 - 3{,}500$$
$$B_7 = B_6 + P_6 - 4{,}000$$

3.12.4 Implementing the Model

The LP problem for Upton's production and inventory planning problem may be summarized as:

MIN: $240P_1 + 250P_2 + 265P_3 + 285P_4 + 280P_5 + 260P_6 + 3.6(B_1+B_2)/2 + 3.75(B_2+B_3)/2 + 3.98(B_3+B_4)/2 + 4.28(B_4+B_5)/2 + 4.20(B_5 + B_6)/2 + 3.9(B_6+B_7)/2$ } total cost

Subject to:

$2{,}000 \le P_1 \le 4{,}000$ } production level for month 1
$1{,}750 \le P_2 \le 3{,}500$ } production level for month 2
$2{,}000 \le P_3 \le 4{,}000$ } production level for month 3
$2{,}250 \le P_4 \le 4{,}500$ } production level for month 4
$2{,}000 \le P_5 \le 4{,}000$ } production level for month 5
$1{,}750 \le P_6 \le 3{,}500$ } production level for month 6
$1{,}500 \le B_1 + P_1 - 1{,}000 \le 6{,}000$ } ending inventory for month 1
$1{,}500 \le B_2 + P_2 - 4{,}500 \le 6{,}000$ } ending inventory for month 2
$1{,}500 \le B_3 + P_3 - 6{,}000 \le 6{,}000$ } ending inventory for month 3
$1{,}500 \le B_4 + P_4 - 5{,}500 \le 6{,}000$ } ending inventory for month 4
$1{,}500 \le B_5 + P_5 - 3{,}500 \le 6{,}000$ } ending inventory for month 5
$1{,}500 \le B_6 + P_6 - 4{,}000 \le 6{,}000$ } ending inventory for month 6

where:

$$B_2 = B_1 + P_1 - 1{,}000$$
$$B_3 = B_2 + P_2 - 4{,}500$$
$$B_4 = B_3 + P_3 - 6{,}000$$
$$B_5 = B_4 + P_4 - 5{,}500$$
$$B_6 = B_5 + P_5 - 3{,}500$$
$$B_7 = B_6 + P_6 - 4{,}000$$

A convenient way of implementing this model is shown in Figure 3.31 (and file Fig3-31.xls on your data disk). Cells C7 through H7 in this spreadsheet represent the number of air compressors to produce in each month and therefore correspond to the decision variables (P_1 through P_6) in our model. We will place appropriate upper and lower bounds on these cells to enforce the restrictions represented by the first six constraints in our model. The estimated demands for each time period are listed just below the decision variables in cells C8 through H8.

FIGURE 3.31
Spreadsheet model for Upton's production problem

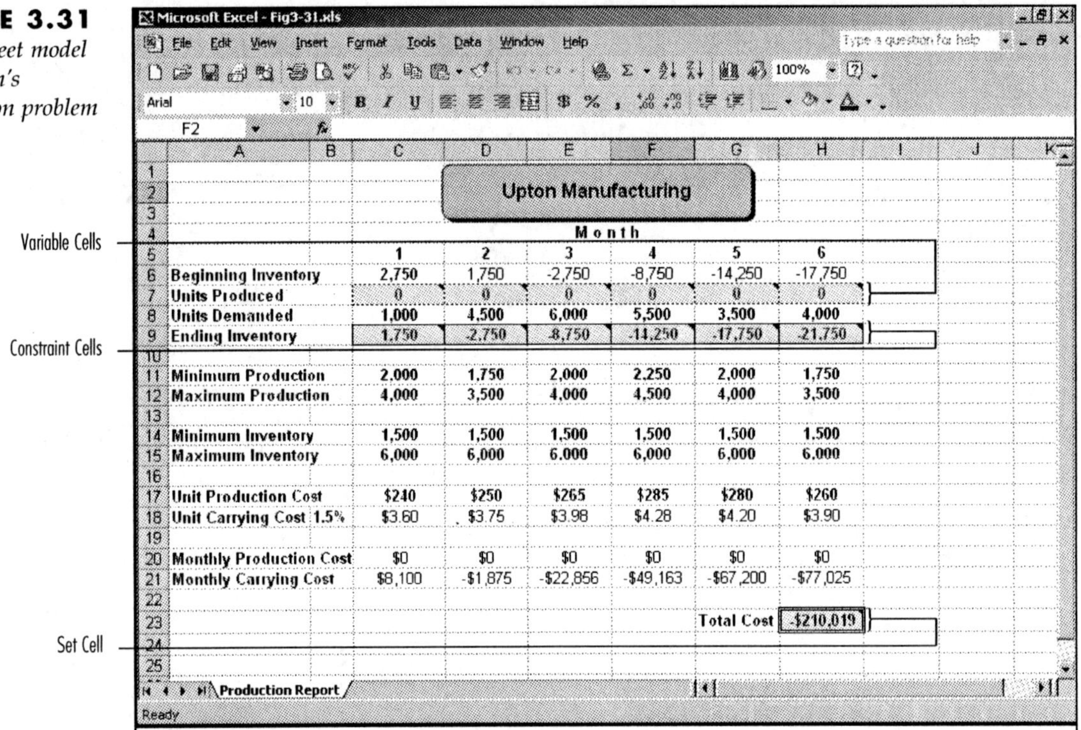

	Month					
	1	2	3	4	5	6
Beginning Inventory	2,750	1,750	-2,750	-8,750	-14,250	-17,750
Units Produced	0	0	0	0	0	0
Units Demanded	1,000	4,500	6,000	5,500	3,500	4,000
Ending Inventory	1,750	-2,750	-8,750	-14,250	-17,750	-21,750
Minimum Production	2,000	1,750	2,000	2,250	2,000	1,750
Maximum Production	4,000	3,500	4,000	4,500	4,000	3,500
Minimum Inventory	1,500	1,500	1,500	1,500	1,500	1,500
Maximum Inventory	6,000	6,000	6,000	6,000	6,000	6,000
Unit Production Cost	$240	$250	$265	$285	$280	$260
Unit Carrying Cost 1.5%	$3.60	$3.75	$3.98	$4.28	$4.20	$3.90
Monthly Production Cost	$0	$0	$0	$0	$0	$0
Monthly Carrying Cost	$8,100	-$1,875	-$22,856	-$49,163	-$67,200	-$77,025
					Total Cost	-$210,019

Key Cell Formulas

Cell	Formula	Copied to
C9	=C6+C7-C8	D9:H9
D6	=C9	E6:H6
C18	=$B$18*C17	D18:H18
C20	=C17*C7	D20:H20
C21	=C18*(C6+C9)/2	D21:H21
H23	=SUM(C20:H21)	—

With the beginning inventory level of 2,750 entered in cell C6, the ending inventory for month 1 is computed in cell C9 as follows:

Formula for cell C9: =C6+C7-C8
(Copy to cells D9 through H9.)

This formula can be copied to cells D9 through H9 to compute the ending inventory levels for each of the remaining months. We will place appropriate lower and upper limits on these cells to enforce the restrictions indicated by the second set of six constraints in our model.

To ensure that the beginning inventory in month 2 equals the ending inventory from month 1, we place the following formula in cell D6:

Formula for cell D6: =C9
(Copy to cells E6 through H6.)

This formula can be copied to cells E6 through H6 to ensure that the beginning inventory levels in each month equal the ending inventory levels from the previous month. It is important to note that because the beginning inventory levels can be calculated directly from the ending inventory levels, there is no need to specify these cells as constraint cells to Solver.

With the monthly unit production costs entered in cell C17 through H17, the monthly unit carrying costs are computed in cells C18 through H18 as follows:

Formula for cell C18: =$B$18*C17
(Copy to cells D18 through H18.)

The total monthly production and inventory costs are then computed in rows 20 and 21 as follows:

Formula for cell C20: =C17*C7
(Copy to cells D20 through H20.)

Formula for cell C21: =C18*(C6+C9)/2
(Copy to cells D21 through H21.)

Finally, the objective function representing the total production and inventory costs for the problem is implemented in cell H23 as follows:

Formula for cell H23: =SUM(C20:H21)

3.12.5 Solving the Model

Figure 3.32 shows the Solver parameters required to solve this problem. The optimal solution is shown in Figure 3.33.

3.12.6 Analyzing the Solution

The optimal solution shown in Figure 3.33 indicates Upton should produce 4,000 units in period 1, 3,500 units in period 2, 4,000 units in period 3, 4,250 units in period 4, 4,000 units in period 5, and 3,500 units in period 6. Although the demand for air compressors in month 1 can be met by the beginning inventory, production in month 1 is required to build inventory for future months in which demand exceeds the available production capacity. Notice that this production schedule calls for the company to operate at full production capacity in all months except month 4. Month 4 is expected to have the highest per unit production cost. Therefore, it is more economical to produce extra units in prior months and hold them in inventory for sale in month 4.

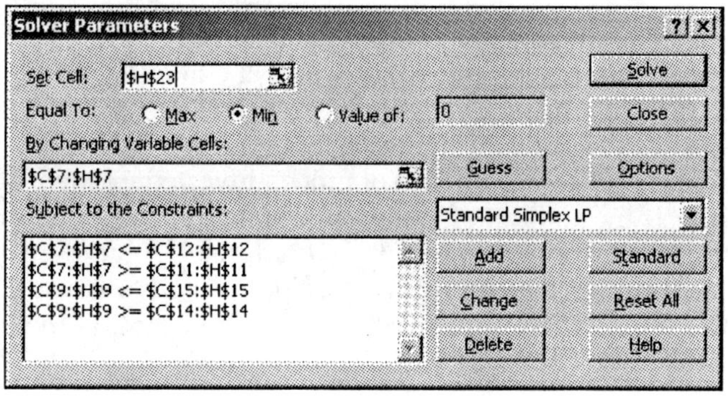

FIGURE 3.32
Solver parameters for the production problem

FIGURE 3.33
Optimal solution to Upton's production problem

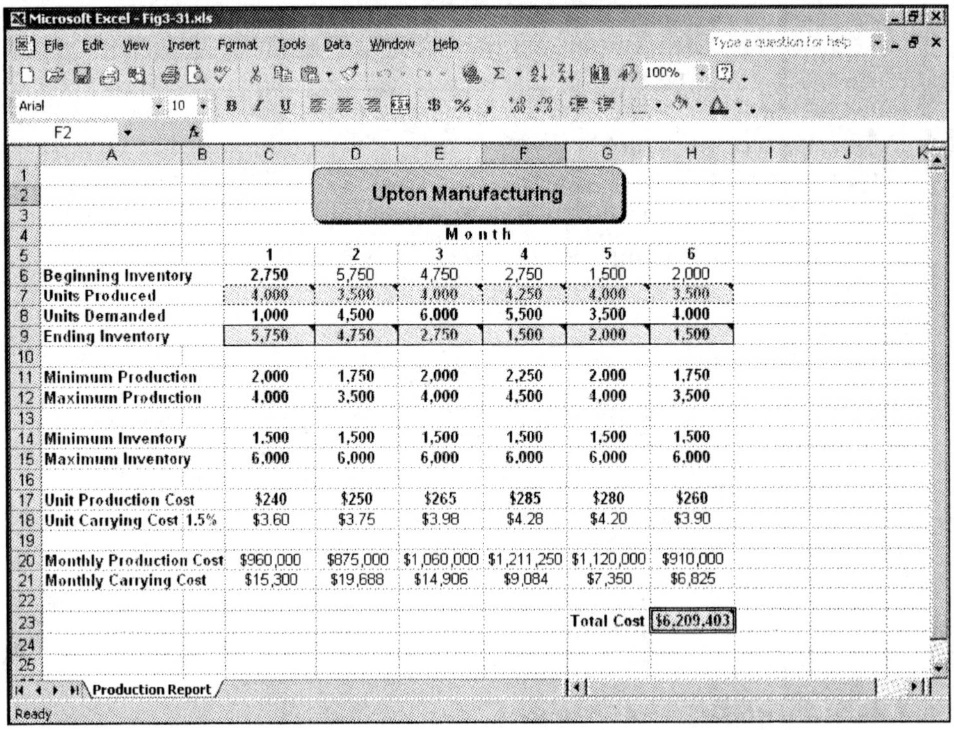

Upton Manufacturing

	Month 1	2	3	4	5	6
Beginning Inventory	2,750	5,750	4,750	2,750	1,500	2,000
Units Produced	4,000	3,500	4,000	4,250	4,000	3,500
Units Demanded	1,000	4,500	6,000	5,500	3,500	4,000
Ending Inventory	5,750	4,750	2,750	1,500	2,000	1,500
Minimum Production	2,000	1,750	2,000	2,250	2,000	1,750
Maximum Production	4,000	3,500	4,000	4,500	4,000	3,500
Minimum Inventory	1,500	1,500	1,500	1,500	1,500	1,500
Maximum Inventory	6,000	6,000	6,000	6,000	6,000	6,000
Unit Production Cost	$240	$250	$265	$285	$280	$260
Unit Carrying Cost 1.5%	$3.60	$3.75	$3.98	$4.28	$4.20	$3.90
Monthly Production Cost	$960,000	$875,000	$1,060,000	$1,211,250	$1,120,000	$910,000
Monthly Carrying Cost	$15,300	$19,688	$14,906	$9,084	$7,350	$6,825
					Total Cost	$6,209,403

It is important to note that although the solution to this problem provides a production plan for the next six months, it does not bind Upton's management team to implement this particular solution throughout the next six months. At an operational level, the management team is most concerned with the decision that must be made now—namely the number of units to schedule for production in month 1. At the end of month 1, Upton's management should update the inventory, demand, and cost estimates, and re-solve the model to identify the production plan for the next six months (presently months 2 through 7). At the end of month 2, this process should be repeated again. Thus, multiperiod planning models such as this should be used repeatedly on a periodic basis as part of a rolling planning process.

3.13 A MULTIPERIOD CASH FLOW PROBLEM

Numerous business problems involve decisions that have a ripple effect on future decisions. In the previous example, we saw how the manufacturing plans for one time period can impact the amount of resources available and the inventory carried in subsequent time periods. Similarly, many financial decisions involve multiple time periods because the amount of money invested or spent at one point in time directly affects the amount of money available in subsequent time periods. In these types of multiperiod problems, it can be difficult to account for the consequences of a current decision on future time periods without an LP model. The formulation of such a model is illustrated next in an example from the world of finance.

Taco-Viva is a small but growing restaurant chain specializing in Mexican fast food. The management of the company has decided to build a new location in Wilmington, North Carolina, and wants to establish a construction fund (or sinking fund) to pay for the new facility. Construction of the restaurant is expected to take six months and cost \$800,000. Taco-Viva's contract with the construction company requires it to make payments of \$250,000 at the end of the second and fourth months, and a final payment of \$300,000 at the end of the sixth month when the restaurant is completed. The company can use four investment opportunities to establish the construction fund; these investments are summarized in the following table:

Investment	Available in Month	Months to Maturity	Yield at Maturity
A	1, 2, 3, 4, 5, 6	1	1.8%
B	1, 3, 5	2	3.5%
C	1, 4	3	5.8%
D	1	6	11.0%

The table indicates that investment A will be available at the beginning of each of the next six months, and funds invested in this manner mature in one month with a yield of 1.8%. Funds can be placed in investment C only at the beginning of months 1 and/or 4, and mature at the end of three months with a yield of 5.8%.

The management of Taco-Viva needs to determine the investment plan that allows them to meet the required schedule of payments while placing the least amount of money in the construction fund.

This is a multiperiod problem because a six-month planning horizon must be considered. That is, Taco-Viva must plan which investment alternatives to use at various times during the next six months.

3.13.1 Defining the Decision Variables

The basic decision faced by the management of Taco-Viva is how much money to invest in each investment vehicle during each time period when the investment opportunities are available. To model this problem, we need different variables to represent each investment/time period combination. This can be done as:

$A_1, A_2, A_3, A_4, A_5, A_6$ = the amount of money (in \$1,000s) placed in investment A at the beginning of months 1, 2, 3, 4, 5, and 6, respectively

B_1, B_3, B_5 = the amount of money (in \$1,000s) placed in investment B at the beginning of months 1, 3, and 5, respectively

C_1, C_4 = the amount of money (in \$1,000s) placed in investment C at the beginning of months 1 and 4, respectively

D_1 = the amount of money (in \$1,000s) placed in investment D at the beginning of month 1

Notice that all variables are expressed in units of thousands of dollars to maintain a reasonable scale for this problem. So, keep in mind that when referring to the amount of money represented by our variables, we mean the amount in thousands of dollars.

3.13.2 Defining the Objective Function

Taco-Viva's management wants to minimize the amount of money it must initially place in the construction fund in order to cover the payments that will be due under the contract. At the beginning of month 1, the company wants to invest some amount of money that, along with its investment earnings, will cover the required payments without an additional infusion of cash from the company. Because A_1, B_1, C_1, and D_1 represent the initial amounts invested by the company in month 1, the objective function for the problem is:

MIN: $A_1 + B_1 + C_1 + D_1$ } total cash invested at the beginning of month 1

3.13.3 Defining the Constraints

To formulate the cash-flow constraints for this problem, it is important to clearly identify: (1) when the different investments can be made, (2) when the different investments will mature, and (3) how much money will be available when each investment matures. Figure 3.34 summarizes this information.

The negative values, represented by –1 in Figure 3.34, indicate when dollars can flow *into* each investment. The positive values indicate how much these same dollars will be worth when the investment matures, or when dollars flow *out* of each investment. The double-headed arrow symbols indicate time periods in which funds remain in a particular investment. For example, the third row of the table in Figure 3.34 indicates that every dollar placed in investment C at the beginning of month 1 will be worth $1.058 when this investment matures three months later—at the *beginning* of month 4. (Note that the beginning of month 4 occurs at virtually the same instant as the *end* of month 3. Thus, there is no prac-

FIGURE 3.34
Cash flow summary table for Taco-Viva's investment opportunities

	Cash Inflow/Outflow at the Beginning of Month						
Investment	**1**	**2**	**3**	**4**	**5**	**6**	**7**
A_1	–1	1.018					
B_1	–1	⟷	1.035				
C_1	–1	⟷	⟷	1.058			
D_1	–1	⟷	⟷	⟷	⟷	⟷	1.11
A_2		–1	1.018				
A_3			–1	1.018			
B_3			–1	⟷	1.035		
A_4				–1	1.018		
C_4				–1	⟷	⟷	1.058
A_5					–1	1.018	
B_5					–1	⟷	1.035
A_6						–1	1.018
Req'd Payments (in $1,000s)	$0	$0	$250	$0	$250	$0	$300

tical difference between the beginning of one time period and the end of the previous time period.)

Assuming that the company invests the amounts represented by A_1, B_1, C_1, and D_1 at the beginning of month 1, how much money will be available to reinvest or make the required payments at the beginning of months 2, 3, 4, 5, 6, and 7? The answer to this question allows us to generate the set of cash-flow constraints needed for this problem.

As indicated by the second column of Figure 3.34, the only funds maturing at the beginning of month 2 are those placed in investment A at the beginning of month 1 (A_1). The value of the funds maturing at the beginning of month 2 is \$$1.018A_1$. Because no payments are required at the beginning of month 2, all the maturing funds must be reinvested. But the only new investment opportunity available at the beginning of month 2 is investment A (A_2). Thus, the amount of money placed in investment A at the beginning of month 2 must be \$$1.018A_1$. This is expressed by the constraint:

$$1.018A_1 = A_2 + 0 \qquad \} \text{ cash flow for month 2}$$

This constraint indicates that the total amount of money maturing at the beginning of month 2 ($1.018A_1$) must equal the amount of money reinvested at the beginning of month 2 (A_2) plus any payment due in month 2 (\$0).

Now, let's consider the cash flows that will occur during month 3. At the beginning of month 3, any funds that were placed in investment B at the beginning of month 1 (B_1) will mature and be worth a total of \$$1.035B_1$. Similarly, any funds placed in investment A at the beginning of month 2 (A_2) will mature and be worth a total of \$$1.018A_2$. Because a payment of \$250,000 is due at the beginning of month 3, we must ensure that the funds maturing at the beginning of month 3 are sufficient to cover this payment, and that any remaining funds are placed in the investment opportunities available at the beginning of month 3 (A_3 and B_3). This requirement can be stated algebraically as:

$$1.035B_1 + 1.018A_2 = A_3 + B_3 + 250 \qquad \} \text{ cash flow for month 3}$$

This constraint indicates that the total amount of money maturing at the beginning of month 3 ($1.035B_1 + 1.018A_2$) must equal the amount of money reinvested at the beginning of month 3 ($A_3 + B_3$) plus the payment due at the beginning of month 3 (\$250,000).

The same logic we applied to generate the cash-flow constraints for months 2 and 3 can also be used to generate cash-flow constraints for the remaining months. Doing so produces a cash-flow constraint for each month that takes on the general form:

$$\begin{pmatrix}\text{Total \$ amount}\\ \text{maturing at the}\\ \text{beginning}\\ \text{of the month}\end{pmatrix} = \begin{pmatrix}\text{Total \$ amount}\\ \text{reinvested at the}\\ \text{beginning}\\ \text{of the month}\end{pmatrix} + \begin{pmatrix}\text{Payment}\\ \text{due at the}\\ \text{beginning}\\ \text{of the month}\end{pmatrix}$$

Using this general definition of the cash-flow relationships, the constraints for the remaining months are represented by:

$1.058C_1 + 1.018A_3 = A_4 + C_4$	} cash flow for month 4
$1.035B_3 + 1.018A_4 = A_5 + B_5 + 250$	} cash flow for month 5
$1.018A_5 = A_6$	} cash flow for month 6
$1.11D_1 + 1.058C_4 + 1.035B_5 + 1.018A_6 = 300$	} cash flow for month 7

To implement these constraints in the spreadsheet, we must express them in a slightly different (but algebraically equivalent) manner. Specifically, to conform to our general definition of an equality constraint ($f(X_1, X_2, \ldots, X_n) = b$) we need to rewrite the cash-flow constraints so that all the *variables* in each constraint appear on the LHS of the equal sign, and a numeric constant appears on the RHS of the equal sign. This can be done as:

$1.018A_1 - 1A_2 = 0$	} cash flow for month 2
$1.035B_1 + 1.018A_2 - 1A_3 - 1B_3 = 250$	} cash flow for month 3
$1.058C_1 + 1.018A_3 - 1A_4 - 1C_4 = 0$	} cash flow for month 4
$1.035B_3 + 1.018A_4 - 1A_5 - 1B_5 = 250$	} cash flow for month 5
$1.018A_5 - 1A_6 = 0$	} cash flow for month 6
$1.11D_1 + 1.058C_4 + 1.035B_5 + 1.018A_6 = 300$	} cash flow for month 7

There are two important points to note about this alternate expression of the constraints. First, each constraint takes on the following general form, which is algebraically equivalent to our previous general definition for the cash-flow constraints:

$$\begin{pmatrix} \text{Total \$ amount} \\ \text{maturing at the} \\ \text{beginning} \\ \text{of the month} \end{pmatrix} - \begin{pmatrix} \text{Total \$ amount} \\ \text{reinvested at the} \\ \text{beginning} \\ \text{of the month} \end{pmatrix} = \begin{pmatrix} \text{Payment} \\ \text{due at the} \\ \text{beginning} \\ \text{of the month} \end{pmatrix}$$

Although the constraints look slightly different in this form, they enforce the same relationships among the variables as expressed by the earlier constraints.

Second, the LHS coefficients in the alternate expression of the constraints correspond directly to the values listed in the cash-flow summary table in Figure 3.34. That is, the coefficients in the constraint for month 2 correspond to the values in the column for month 2 in Figure 3.34; the coefficients for month 3 correspond to the values in the column for month 3, and so on. This relationship is true for all the constraints and will be very helpful in implementing this model in the spreadsheet.

3.13.4 Implementing the Model

The LP model for Taco-Viva's construction fund problem is summarized as:

$$
\begin{array}{llr}
\text{MIN:} & A_1 + B_1 + C_1 + D_1 & \text{\} cash invested at beginning of month 1}
\end{array}
$$

Subject to:

$$
\begin{array}{lll}
1.018A_1 - 1A_2 & = 0 & \text{\} cash flow for month 2} \\
1.035B_1 + 1.018A_2 - 1A_3 - 1B_3 & = 250 & \text{\} cash flow for month 3} \\
1.058C_1 + 1.018A_3 - 1A_4 - 1C_4 & = 0 & \text{\} cash flow for month 4} \\
1.035B_3 + 1.018A_4 - 1A_5 - 1B_5 & = 250 & \text{\} cash flow for month 5} \\
1.018A_5 - 1A_6 & = 0 & \text{\} cash flow for month 6} \\
1.11D_1 + 1.058C_4 + 1.035B_5 + 1.018A_6 & = 300 & \text{\} cash flow for month 7} \\
A_i, B_i, C_i, D_i, \geq 0, \text{ for all } i & & \text{\} nonnegativity conditions}
\end{array}
$$

One approach to implementing this model is shown in Figure 3.35 (and file Fig3-35.xls on your data disk). The first three columns of this spreadsheet summarize the different investment options that are available and the months in which money may flow into and out of these investments. Cells D6 through D17 represent the decision variables in our model and indicate the amount of money (in $1,000s) to be placed in each of the possible investments.

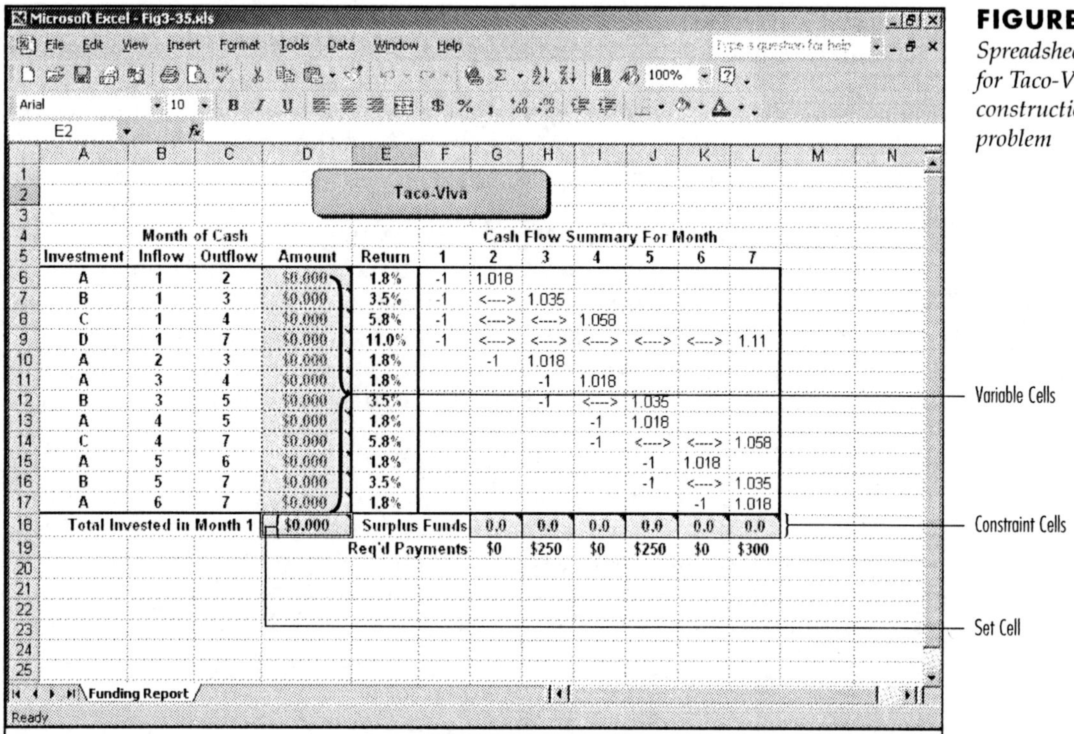

	Month of Cash				Cash Flow Summary For Month						
Investment	Inflow	Outflow	Amount	Return	1	2	3	4	5	6	7
A	1	2	$0.000	1.8%	-1	1.018					
B	1	3	$0.000	3.5%	-1	<---->	1.035				
C	1	4	$0.000	5.8%	-1	<---->	<---->	1.058			
D	1	7	$0.000	11.0%	-1	<---->	<---->	<---->	<---->	<---->	1.11
A	2	3	$0.000	1.8%		-1	1.018				
A	3	4	$0.000	1.8%			-1	1.018			
B	3	5	$0.000	3.5%			-1	<---->	1.035		
A	4	5	$0.000	1.8%				-1	1.018		
C	4	7	$0.000	5.8%				-1	<---->	<---->	1.058
A	5	6	$0.000	1.8%					-1	1.018	
B	5	7	$0.000	3.5%					-1	<---->	1.035
A	6	7	$0.000	1.8%						-1	1.018
Total Invested in Month 1			$0.000	Surplus Funds		0.0	0.0	0.0	0.0	0.0	0.0
				Req'd Payments		$0	$250	$0	$250	$0	$300

FIGURE 3.35
Spreadsheet model for Taco-Viva's construction fund problem

Key Cell Formulas

Cell	Formula	Copied to
D18	=SUMIF(B6:B17,1,D6:D17)	—
F6	=IF($B6=F$5,-1,IF($C6=F$5,1+$E6,IF(AND($B6<F$5,$C6>F$5),"<---->","")))	F6:L17
G18	=SUMPRODUCT(G6:G17,$D$6:$D$17)	H18:L18

The objective function for this problem requires that we compute the total amount of money being invested in month 1. This was done in cell D18 as follows:

Formula for cell D18: =SUMIF(B6:B17,1,D6:D17)

This SUMIF function compares the values in cells B6 through B17 to the value 1 (its second argument). If any of the values in B6 through B17 equal 1, it sums the corresponding values in cells D6 through D17. In this case, the values in cells B6 through B9 all equal 1; therefore, the function returns the sum of the values in cells D6 through D9. Note that although we could have implemented the objective using the formula SUM(D6:D9), the previous SUMIF formula makes for a more modifiable and reliable model. If any of the values in column B are changed to or from 1, the SUMIF function continues to represent the appropriate objective function, whereas the SUM function would not.

Our next job is to implement the cash inflow/outflow table described earlier in Figure 3.34. Recall that each row in Figure 3.34 corresponds to the cash flows associated with a particular investment alternative. This table can be implemented in our spreadsheet using the following formula:

Formula for cell F6: =IF($B6=F$5,-1,IF($C6=F$5,1+$E6,IF(AND($B6<F$5,$C6>F$5),"<---->"," ")))
(Copy to cells F6 through L17.)

This formula first checks to see if the "month of cash inflow" value in column B matches the month indicator value in row 5. If so, the formula returns the value –1. Otherwise, it goes on to check to see if the "month of cash outflow" value in column C matches the month indicator value in row 5. If so, the formula returns a value equal to 1 plus the return for the investment (from column E). If neither of the first two conditions are met, the formula next checks whether the current month indicator in row 5 is larger than the "month of cash inflow" value (column B) and smaller than the "month of cash outflow" value (column C). If so, the formula returns the characters "<---->" to indicate periods in which funds neither flow into or out of a particular investment. Finally, if none of the previous three conditions are met, the formula simply returns an empty (or null) string " ". Although this formula looks a bit intimidating, it is simply a set of three nested IF functions. More importantly, it automatically updates the cash flow summary if any of the values in columns B, C, or E are changed, increasing the reliability and modifiability of the model.

Earlier, we noted that the values listed in columns 2 through 7 of the cash inflow/outflow table correspond directly to the coefficients appearing in the various cash-flow constraints. This property allows us to implement the cash-flow constraints in the spreadsheet conveniently. For example, the LHS formula for the cash-flow constraint for month 2 is implemented in cell G18 through the formula:

Formula in cell G18: =SUMPRODUCT(G6:G17,$D$6:$D$17)
(Copy to H18 through L18.)

This formula multiplies each entry in the range G6 through G17 by the corresponding entry in the range D6 through D17 and then sums these individual products. This formula is copied to cells H18 through L18. (Notice that the SUMPRODUCT( ) formula treats cells containing labels and null strings as if they contained the value zero.) Take a moment now to verify that the formulas in cells

G18 through L18 correspond to the LHS formulas of the cash-flow constraints in our model. Cells G19 through L19 list the RHS values for the cash-flow constraints.

3.13.5 Solving the Model

To find the optimal solution to this model, we must indicate to Solver the set cell, variable cells, and constraint cells identified in Figure 3.35. Figure 3.36 shows the Solver parameters required to solve this model. The optimal solution is shown in Figure 3.37.

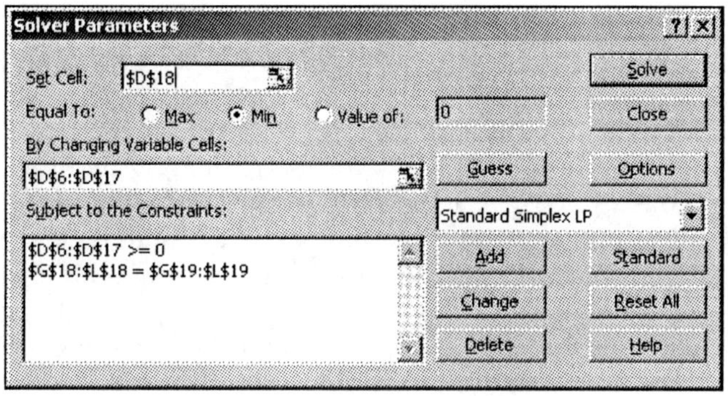

FIGURE 3.36
Solver parameters for the construction fund problem

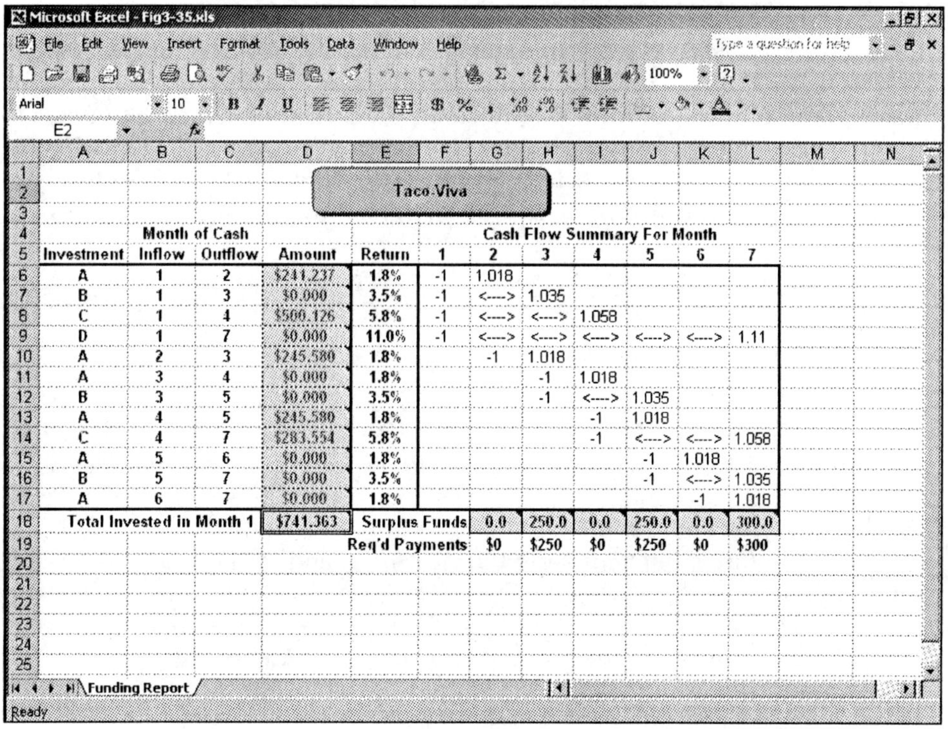

Taco Viva

	Month of Cash				Cash Flow Summary For Month						
Investment	Inflow	Outflow	Amount	Return	1	2	3	4	5	6	7
A	1	2	$241.237	1.8%	-1	1.018					
B	1	3	$0.000	3.5%	-1	<--->	1.035				
C	1	4	$500.126	5.8%	-1	<--->	<--->	1.058			
D	1	7	$0.000	11.0%	-1	<--->	<--->	<--->	<--->	<--->	1.11
A	2	3	$245.580	1.8%		-1	1.018				
A	3	4	$0.000	1.8%			-1	1.018			
B	3	5	$0.000	3.5%			-1	<--->	1.035		
A	4	5	$245.580	1.8%				-1	1.018		
C	4	7	$283.554	5.8%				-1	<--->	<--->	1.058
A	5	6	$0.000	1.8%					-1	1.018	
B	5	7	$0.000	3.5%					-1	<--->	1.035
A	6	7	$0.000	1.8%						-1	1.018
Total Invested in Month 1			$741.363	Surplus Funds		0.0	250.0	0.0	250.0	0.0	300.0
				Req'd Payments		$0	$250	$0	$250	$0	$300

FIGURE 3.37
Optimal solution to Taco-Viva's construction fund problem

3.13.6 Analyzing the Solution

The value of the set cell (D18) in Figure 3.37 indicates that a total of \$741,363 must be invested to meet the payments on Taco-Viva's construction project. Cells D6 and D8 indicate that approximately \$241,237 should be placed in investment A at the beginning of month 1 ($A_1 = 241.237$) and approximately \$500,126 should be placed in investment C ($C_1 = 500.126$).

At the beginning of month 2, the funds placed in investment A at the beginning of month 1 will mature and be worth \$245,580 (241,237 × 1.018 = 245,580). The value in cell D10 indicates these funds should be placed back into investment A at the beginning of month 2 ($A_2 = 245.580$).

At the beginning of month 3, the first \$250,000 payment is due. At that time, the funds placed in investment A at the beginning of month 2 will mature and be worth \$250,000 (1.018 × 245,580 = 250,000)—allowing us to make this payment.

At the beginning of month 4, the funds placed in investment C at the beginning of month 1 will mature and be worth \$529,134. Our solution indicates that \$245,580 of this amount should be placed in investment A ($A_4 = 245.580$) and the rest should be reinvested in investment C ($C_4 = 283.554$).

If you trace through the cash flows for the remaining months, you will discover that our model is doing exactly what it was designed to do. The amount of money scheduled to mature at the beginning of each month is exactly equal to the amount of money scheduled to be reinvested after required payments are made. Thus, out of an infinite number of possible investment schedules, our LP model found the one schedule that requires the least amount of money up front.

3.13.7 Modifying the Taco-Viva Problem to Account for Risk (Optional)

In investment problems like this, it is not uncommon for decision makers to place limits on the amount of risk they are willing to assume. For instance, suppose the chief financial officer (CFO) for Taco-Viva assigned the following risk ratings to each of the possible investments on a scale from 1 to 10 (where 1 represents the least risk and 10 the greatest risk). We will also assume that the CFO wants to determine an investment plan where the weighted average risk level does not exceed 5.

Investment	Risk Rating
A	1
B	3
C	8
D	6

We will need to formulate an additional constraint for each time period to ensure the weighted average risk level never exceeds 5. To see how this can be done, let's start with month 1.

In month 1, funds can be invested in A_1, B_1, C_1, and/or D_1, and each investment is associated with a different degree of risk. To calculate the weighted average risk during month 1, we must multiply the risk factors for each investment by the proportion of money in that investment. This is represented by:

$$\text{Weighted average risk in month 1} = \frac{1A_1 + 3B_1 + 8C_1 + 6D_1}{A_1 + B_1 + C_1 + D_1}$$

We can ensure that the weighted average risk in month 1 does not exceed the value 5 by including the following constraint in our LP model:

$$\frac{1A_1 + 3B_1 + 8C_1 + 6D_1}{A_1 + B_1 + C_1 + D_1} \le 5 \quad \} \text{ risk constraint for month 1}$$

Now, let's consider month 2. According to the column for month 2 in our cash inflow/outflow table, the company can have funds invested in B_1, C_1, D_1, and/or A_2 during this month. Thus, the weighted average risk that occurs in month 2 is defined by:

$$\text{Weighted average risk in month 2} = \frac{3B_1 + 8C_1 + 6D_1 + 1A_2}{B_1 + C_1 + D_1 + A_2}$$

Again, the following constraint ensures that this quantity never exceeds 5:

$$\frac{3B_1 + 8C_1 + 6D_1 + 1A_2}{B_1 + C_1 + D_1 + A_2} \le 5 \quad \} \text{ risk constraint for month 2}$$

The risk constraints for months 3 through 6 are generated in a similar manner, and appear as:

$$\frac{8C_1 + 6D_1 + 1A_3 + 3B_3}{C_1 + D_1 + A_3 + B_3} \le 5 \quad \} \text{ risk constraint for month 3}$$

$$\frac{6D_1 + 3B_3 + 1A_4 + 8C_4}{D_1 + B_3 + A_4 + C_4} \le 5 \quad \} \text{ risk constraint for month 4}$$

$$\frac{6D_1 + 8C_4 + 1A_5 + 3B_5}{D_1 + C_4 + A_5 + B_5} \le 5 \quad \} \text{ risk constraint for month 5}$$

$$\frac{6D_1 + 8C_4 + 3B_5 + 1A_6}{D_1 + C_4 + B_5 + A_6} \le 5 \quad \} \text{ risk constraint for month 6}$$

Although the risk constraints listed here have a very clear meaning, it is easier to implement these constraints in the spreadsheet if we state them in a different (but algebraically equivalent) manner. In particular, it is helpful to eliminate the fractions on the LHS of the inequalities by multiplying each constraint through by its denominator and re-collecting the variables on the LHS of the inequality. The following steps show how to rewrite the risk constraint for month 1:

1. Multiply both sides of the inequality by the denominator:

$$(A_1 + B_1 + C_1 + D_1)\frac{1A_1 + 3B_1 + 8C_1 + 6D_1}{A_1 + B_1 + C_1 + D_1} \le (A_1 + B_1 + C_1 + D_1)5$$

   to obtain:

$$1A_1 + 3B_1 + 8C_1 + 6D_1 \le 5A_1 + 5B_1 + 5C_1 + 5D_1$$

2. Re-collect the variables on the LHS of the inequality sign:

$$(1-5)A_1 + (3-5)B_1 + (8-5)C_1 + (6-5)D_1 \le 0$$

   to obtain:

$$-4A_1 - 2B_1 + 3C_1 + 1D_1 \le 0$$

Thus, the following two constraints are algebraically equivalent:

$$\frac{1A_1 + 3B_1 + 8C_1 + 6D_1}{A_1 + B_1 + C_1 + D_1} \le 5 \qquad \}\text{ risk constraint for month 1}$$

$$-4A_1 - 2B_1 + 3C_1 + 1D_1 \le 0 \qquad \}\text{ risk constraint for month 1}$$

The set of values for A_1, B_1, C_1, and D_1 that satisfies the first of these constraints also satisfies the second constraint (that is, these constraints have exactly the same set of feasible values). So, it does not matter which of these constraints we use to find the optimal solution to the problem.

The remaining risk constraints are simplified in the same way, producing the following constraints:

$$-2B_1 + 3C_1 + 1D_1 - 4A_2 \le 0 \qquad \}\text{ risk constraint for month 2}$$

$$3C_1 + 1D_1 - 4A_3 - 2B_3 \le 0 \qquad \}\text{ risk constraint for month 3}$$

$$1D_1 - 2B_3 - 4A_4 + 3C_4 \le 0 \qquad \}\text{ risk constraint for month 4}$$

$$1D_1 + 3C_4 - 4A_5 - 2B_5 \le 0 \qquad \}\text{ risk constraint for month 5}$$

$$1D_1 + 3C_4 - 2B_5 - 4A_6 \le 0 \qquad \}\text{ risk constraint for month 6}$$

Notice that the coefficient for each variable in these constraints is simply the risk factor for the particular investment minus the maximum allowable weighted average risk value of 5. That is, all A_i variables have coefficients of $1 - 5 = -4$; all B_i variables have coefficients of $3 - 5 = -2$; all C_i variables have coefficients of $8 - 5 = 3$; and all D_i variables have coefficients of $6 - 5 = 1$. This observation will help us implement these constraints efficiently.

3.13.8 Implementing the Risk Constraints

Figure 3.38 (and file Fig3-38.xls on your data disk) shows a split screen that illustrates an easy way to implement the risk constraints for this model. Earlier, we noted that the coefficient for each variable in each risk constraint is simply the risk factor for the particular investment minus the maximum allowable weighted average risk value. Thus, the strategy in Figure 3.38 is to generate these values in the appropriate columns and rows of the spreadsheet so that the SUMPRODUCT( ) function can implement the LHS formulas for the risk constraints.

Recall that the risk constraint for each month involves only the variables representing investments that actually held funds during that month. For any given month, the investments that actually held funds during that month have the value –1 or contain a text entry starting with the "<" symbol (the first character of the "<---->" entries) in the corresponding column of the cash inflow/outflow summary table. For example, during month 2, funds can be invested in B_1, C_1, D_1, and/or A_2. The corresponding cells for month 2 in Figure 3.38 (cells G7, G8, G9, and G10, respectively) each contain either the value –1 or a text entry starting with the "<" symbol. Therefore, to generate the appropriate coefficients for the risk constraints, we can instruct the spreadsheet to scan the cash inflow/outflow summary for cells containing the value –1 or text entries starting with the "<" symbol, and return the correct risk constraint coefficients in the appropriate cells. To do this, we enter the following formula in cell N6:

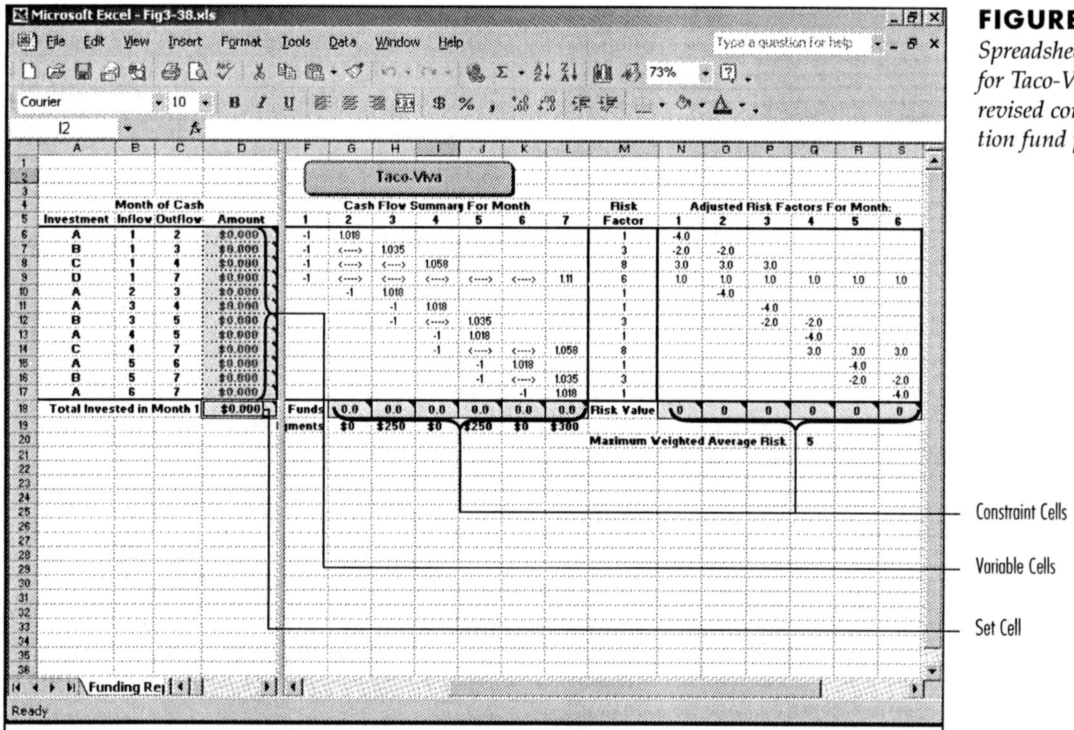

FIGURE 3.38
Spreadsheet model for Taco-Viva's revised construction fund problem

Key Cell Formulas

Cell	Formula	Copied to
D18	=SUMIF(B6:B17,1,D6:D17)	—
F6	=IF($B6=F$5,-1,IF($C6=F$5,1+$E6,IF(AND($B6<F$5,$C6>F$5),"<---->","")))	F6:L17
G18	=SUMPRODUCT(G6:G17,$D$6:$D$17)	H18:L18 and N18:S18
N6	=IF(OR(F6=-1,LEFT(F6)="<"),$M6-$Q$20,"")	N6:S17

Formula in cell N6: =IF(OR(F6=-1,LEFT(F6)="<"),$M6-$Q$20,"")
(Copy to N6 through S17.)

To generate the appropriate value in cell N6, the previous formula checks if cell F6 is equal to –1 or contains a text entry that starts with the "<" symbol. If either of these conditions is true, the function takes the risk factor for the investment from cell M6 and subtracts the maximum allowable risk factor found in cell Q20; otherwise, the function returns a null string (with a value of zero). This formula is copied to the remaining cells in the range N6 through S17, as shown in Figure 3.38.

The values in cells N6 through S17 in Figure 3.38 correspond to the coefficients in the LHS formulas for each of the risk constraints formulated earlier. Thus, the LHS formula for the risk constraint for month 1 is implemented in cell N18 as:

Formula in cell N18: =SUMPRODUCT(N6:N17,$D$6:$D$17)
(Copy to O18 through S18.)

The LHS formulas for the remaining risk constraints are implemented by copying this formula to cells O18 through S18. We will tell Solver that these constraint cells must be less than or equal to zero.

3.13.9 Solving the Model

To find the optimal solution to this model, we must communicate the appropriate information about the new risk constraints to Solver. Figure 3.39 shows the Solver parameters required to solve this model. The optimal solution is shown in Figure 3.40.

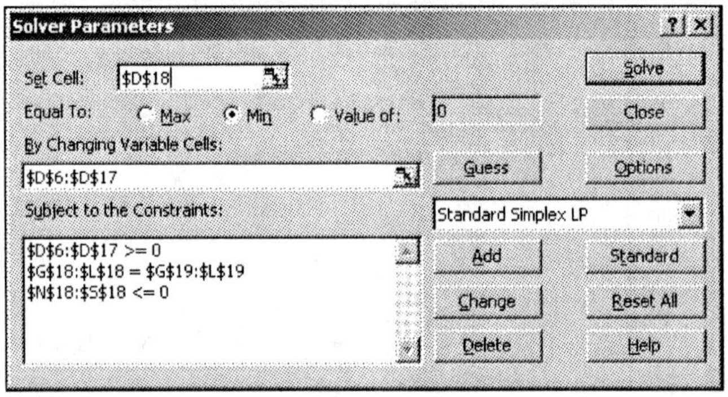

FIGURE 3.39
Solver parameters for the revised construction fund problem

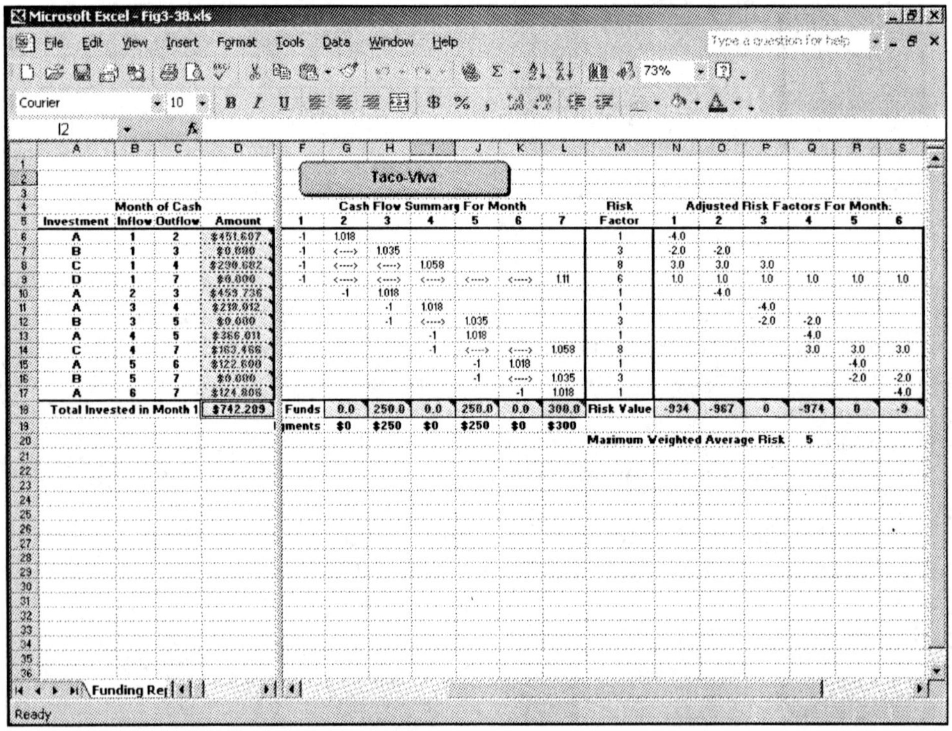

	Month of Cash			Cash Flow Summary For Month							Risk	Adjusted Risk Factors For Month:					
Investment	Inflow	Outflow	Amount	1	2	3	4	5	6	7	Factor	1	2	3	4	5	6
A	1	2	$451.607	-1	1.018						1	-4.0					
B	1	3	$0.000	-1	<---->	1.035					3	-2.0	-2.0				
C	1	4	$290.682	-1	<---->	<---->	1.058				8	3.0	3.0	3.0			
D	1	7	$0.000	-1	<---->	<---->	<---->	<---->	<---->	1.11	6	1.0	1.0	1.0	1.0	1.0	1.0
A	2	3	$453.736		-1	1.018					1		-4.0				
A	3	4	$218.912			-1	1.018				1			-4.0			
B	3	5	$0.000			-1	<---->	1.035			3			-2.0	-2.0		
A	4	5	$366.011				-1	1.018			1				-4.0		
C	4	7	$183.466				-1	<---->	<---->	1.058	8				3.0	3.0	3.0
A	5	6	$122.800					-1	1.018		1					-4.0	
B	5	7	$0.000					-1	<---->	1.035	3					-2.0	-2.0
A	6	7	$124.808						-1	1.018	1						-4.0
Total Invested in Month 1			$742.289	Funds	0.0	250.0	0.0	250.0	0.0	300.0	Risk Value	-934	-967	0	-974	0	-9
				ments	$0	$250	$0	$250	$0	$300							
											Maximum Weighted Average Risk				5		

FIGURE 3.40
Optimal solution to Taco-Viva's revised construction fund problem

3.13.10 Analyzing the Solution

The optimal solution to the revised Taco-Viva problem with risk constraints is quite different than the solution obtained earlier. In particular, the new solution requires that funds be placed in investment A in every time period. This is not too surprising given that investment A has the lowest risk rating. What may be somewhat surprising is that of the remaining investments, B and D are never used. Although these investments have lower risk ratings than investment C, the combination of funds placed in investment A and C allows for the least amount of money to be invested in month 1 while meeting the scheduled payments and keeping the weighted average risk at or below the specified level.

3.14 DATA ENVELOPMENT ANALYSIS

Managers are often interested in determining how efficiently various units within a company operate. Similarly, investment analysts may be interested in comparing the efficiency of several competing companies within an industry. Data Envelopment Analysis (DEA) is an LP-based methodology for performing this type of analysis. DEA determines how efficiently an operating unit (or company) converts inputs to outputs when compared with other units. We will consider how DEA may be applied via the following example.

Mike Lister is a district manager for the Steak & Burger fast-food restaurant chain. The region Mike manages contains 12 company-owned units. Mike is in the process of evaluating the performance of these units during the past year to make recommendations on how much of an annual bonus to pay each unit's manager. He wants to base this decision, in part, on how efficiently each unit has been operated. Mike has collected the data shown in the following table on each of the 12 units. The outputs he has chosen include each unit's net profit (in $100,000s), average customer satisfaction rating, and average monthly cleanliness score. The inputs include total labor hours (in 100,000s) and total operating costs (in $1,000,000s). He wants to apply DEA to this data to determine an efficiency score of each unit.

	Outputs			Inputs	
Unit	**Profit**	**Satisfaction**	**Cleanliness**	**Labor Hours**	**Operating Costs**
1	5.98	7.7	92	4.74	6.75
2	7.18	9.7	99	6.38	7.42
3	4.97	9.3	98	5.04	6.35
4	5.32	7.7	87	3.61	6.34
5	3.39	7.8	94	3.45	4.43
6	4.95	7.9	88	5.25	6.31
7	2.89	8.6	90	2.36	3.23
8	6.40	9.1	100	7.09	8.69
9	6.01	7.3	89	6.49	7.28
10	6.94	8.8	89	7.36	9.07
11	5.86	8.2	93	5.46	6.69
12	8.35	9.6	97	6.58	8.75

3.14.1 Defining the Decision Variables

Using DEA, the efficiency of an arbitrary unit i is defined as follows:

$$\text{Efficiency of unit } i = \frac{\text{Weighted sum of unit } i\text{'s outputs}}{\text{Weighted sum of unit } i\text{'s inputs}} = \frac{\sum_{j=1}^{n_O} O_{ij} w_j}{\sum_{j=1}^{n_I} I_{ij} v_j}$$

Here, O_{ij} represents the value of unit i on *output* j, I_{ij} represents the value of unit i on *input* j, w_j is a nonnegative weight assigned to output j, v_j is a nonnegative weight assigned to input j, n_O is the number of output variables, and n_I is the number of input variables. The problem in DEA is to determine values for the weights w_j and v_j. Thus, w_j and v_j represent the decision variables in a DEA problem.

3.14.2 Defining the Objective

A separate LP problem is solved for each unit in a DEA problem. However, for each unit the objective is the same: to maximize the weighted sum of that unit's outputs. For an arbitrary unit i, the objective is stated as:

$$\text{MAX:} \quad \sum_{j=1}^{n_O} O_{ij} w_j$$

Thus, as each LP problem is solved, the unit under investigation is given the opportunity to select the best possible weights for itself (or the weights that maximize the weighted sum of its output), subject to the following constraints.

3.14.3 Defining the Constraints

It is impossible for any unit to be more than 100% efficient. So as each LP is solved, the unit under investigation cannot select weights for itself that would cause the efficiency for any unit (including itself) to be greater than 100%. Thus, for each individual unit, we require the weighted sum of the unit's outputs to be less than or equal to the weighted sum of its inputs (so the ratio of weighted outputs to weighted inputs does not exceed 100%).

$$\sum_{j=1}^{n_O} O_{kj} w_j \le \sum_{j=1}^{n_I} I_{kj} v_j, \text{ for } k = 1 \text{ to the number of units}$$

or equivalently,

$$\sum_{j=1}^{n_O} O_{kj} w_j - \sum_{j=1}^{n_I} I_{kj} v_j \le 0, \text{ for } k = 1 \text{ to the number of units}$$

To prevent unbounded solutions, we also require the sum of the weighted inputs for the unit under investigation (unit i) to equal one.

$$\sum_{j=1}^{n_I} I_{ij} v_j = 1$$

Because the sum of weighted inputs for the unit under investigation must equal one and its sum of the weighted outputs (being maximized) cannot exceed this value, the maximum efficiency score for the unit under investigation is also one (or 100%). Thus, units that are efficient will have a DEA efficiency score of 100%.

Important Point

When applying DEA, it is assumed that for output variables "more is better" (*e.g.*, profit) and for input variables "less is better" (*e.g.*, costs). Any output or input variables that do not naturally conform to these rules should be transformed before applying DEA. For example, the percentage of defective products produced is not a good choice for an output because fewer defects is actually a good thing. However, the percentage of nondefective products produced would be an acceptable choice for an output because "more is better" in that case.

3.14.4 Implementing the Model

To evaluate the efficiency of unit 1 in our example problem, we would solve the following LP problem:

MAX:	$5.98w_1 + 7.7w_2 + 92w_3$	} weighted output for unit 1
Subject to:	$5.98w_1 + 7.7w_2 + 92w_3 - 4.74v_1 - 6.75v_2 \leq 0$	} efficiency constraint for unit 1
	$7.18w_1 + 9.7w_2 + 99w_3 - 6.38v_1 - 7.42v_2 \leq 0$	} efficiency constraint for unit 2
	and so on to...	
	$8.35w_1 + 9.6w_2 + 97w_3 - 6.58v_1 - 8.75v_2 \leq 0$	} efficiency constraint for unit 12
	$4.74v_1 + 6.75v_2 = 1$	} input constraint for unit 1
	$w_1, w_2, w_3, v_1, v_2 \geq 0$	} nonnegativity conditions

A convenient way to implement this model is shown in Figure 3.41 (and in the file Fig3-41.xls on your data disk).

In Figure 3.41, cells B19 through F19 are reserved to represent the weights for each of the input and output variables. The weighted output for each unit is computed in column G as follows:

Formula for cell G6: =SUMPRODUCT(B6:D6,$B$19:$D$19)
(Copy to G7 through G17.)

FIGURE 3.41
Spreadsheet model for the Steak & Burger DEA problem

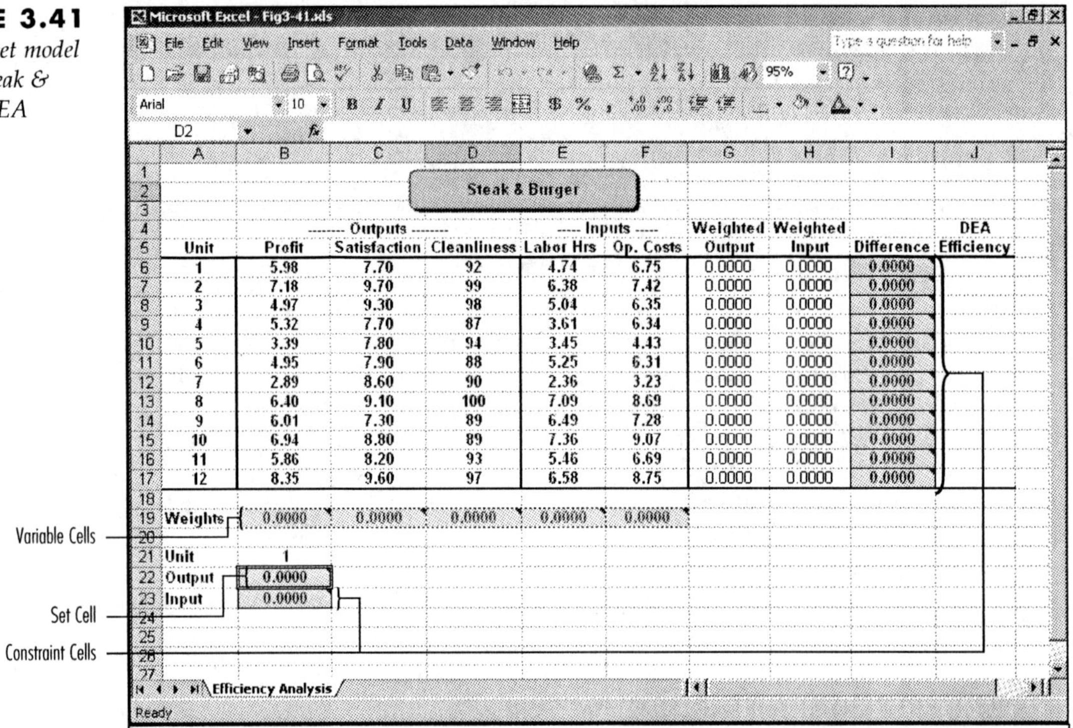

	Outputs			Inputs					
Unit	Profit	Satisfaction	Cleanliness	Labor Hrs	Op. Costs	Weighted Output	Weighted Input	Difference	DEA Efficiency
1	5.98	7.70	92	4.74	6.75	0.0000	0.0000	0.0000	
2	7.18	9.70	99	6.38	7.42	0.0000	0.0000	0.0000	
3	4.97	9.30	98	5.04	6.35	0.0000	0.0000	0.0000	
4	5.32	7.70	87	3.61	6.34	0.0000	0.0000	0.0000	
5	3.39	7.80	94	3.45	4.43	0.0000	0.0000	0.0000	
6	4.95	7.90	88	5.25	6.31	0.0000	0.0000	0.0000	
7	2.89	8.60	90	2.36	3.23	0.0000	0.0000	0.0000	
8	6.40	9.10	100	7.09	8.69	0.0000	0.0000	0.0000	
9	6.01	7.30	89	6.49	7.28	0.0000	0.0000	0.0000	
10	6.94	8.80	89	7.36	9.07	0.0000	0.0000	0.0000	
11	5.86	8.20	93	5.46	6.69	0.0000	0.0000	0.0000	
12	8.35	9.60	97	6.58	8.75	0.0000	0.0000	0.0000	
Weights	0.0000	0.0000	0.0000	0.0000	0.0000				
Unit	1								
Output	0.0000								
Input	0.0000								

Key Cell Formulas

Cell	Formula	Copied to
G6	=SUMPRODUCT (B6:D6,$B$19:$D$19)	G7:G17
H6	=SUMPRODUCT (E6:F6,$E$19:$F$19)	H7:H17
I6	=G6-H6	I7:I17
B22	=INDEX(G6:G17,B21,1)	—
B23	=INDEX(H6:H17,B21,1)	—

Similarly, the weighted input for each unit is computed in column H as:

Formula for cell H6: =SUMPRODUCT(E6:F6,$E$19:$F$19)
(Copy to H7 through H17.)

The differences between the weighted outputs and weighted inputs are computed in column I. We will instruct Solver to constrain these values to be less than or equal to 0.

Formula for cell I6: =G6-H6
(Copy to I7 through I17.)

The weighted output for unit 1 (computed in cell G6) implements the appropriate objective function and could be used as the set cell for Solver in this problem. Similarly, the weighted input for unit 1 is computed in cell H6 and could be constrained to equal 1 (as specified by the input constraint for unit 1 above). However, because we need to solve a separate LP problem for each of the twelve units, it will be more convenient to handle the objective function and input constraint in a slightly different manner. To this end, we reserve cell B21 to indicate the unit number currently under investigation. Cell B22 contains a formula that returns the weighted output for this unit from the list of weighted outputs in column G.

Formula for cell B22: =INDEX(G6:G17,B21,1)

In general, the function INDEX (***range,row number,column number***) returns the value in the specified ***row number*** and ***column number*** of the given ***range.*** Because cell B21 contains the number 1, the previous formula returns the value in the first row and first column of the range G6:G17—or the value in cell G6. Thus, as long as the value of cell B21 represents a valid unit number from 1 to 12, the value in cell B22 will represent the appropriate objective function for the DEA model for that unit. Similarly, the input constraint requiring the weighted inputs for the unit in question to equal 1 can be implemented in cell B23 as follows:

Formula for cell B23: =INDEX(H6:H17,B21,1)

So, for whatever unit number is listed in cell B21, cell B22 represents the appropriate objective function to be maximized and cell B23 represents the weighted input that must be constrained to equal 1. This arrangement greatly simplifies the process of solving the required series of DEA models.

3.14.5 Solving the Model

To solve this model, we specify the set cells, variable cells, and constraints specified in Figure 3.42. Note that exactly the same Solver settings would be used to find the optimal DEA weights for any other unit. The optimal solution for unit 1 is shown in Figure 3.43. Notice that unit 1 achieves an efficiency score of 0.9667 and is therefore slightly inefficient.

To complete the analysis for the remaining units, Mike could change the value in cell B21 manually to 2, 3, ..., 12 and use Solver to reoptimize the worksheet for each unit and record their efficiency scores in column J. However, if there were 120 units rather than 12, this manual approach would become quite cumbersome. Fortunately, it is easy to write a simple macro in Excel to carry out this process for us automatically with the click of a button. To do this, turn on the Control Toolbox command bar and place a command button on your worksheet (as shown in Figure 3.44) as follows:

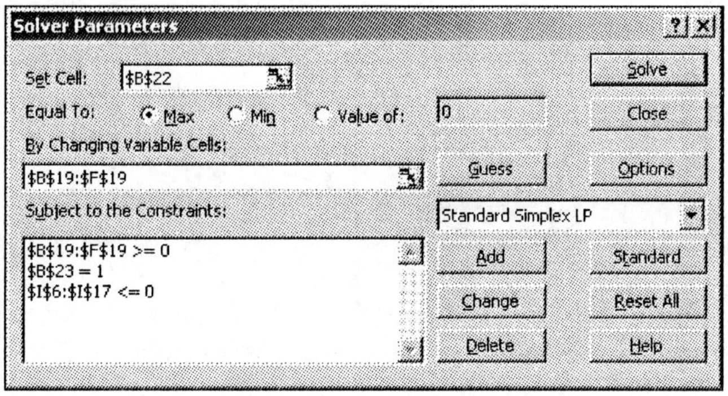

FIGURE 3.42
Solver parameters for the DEA problem

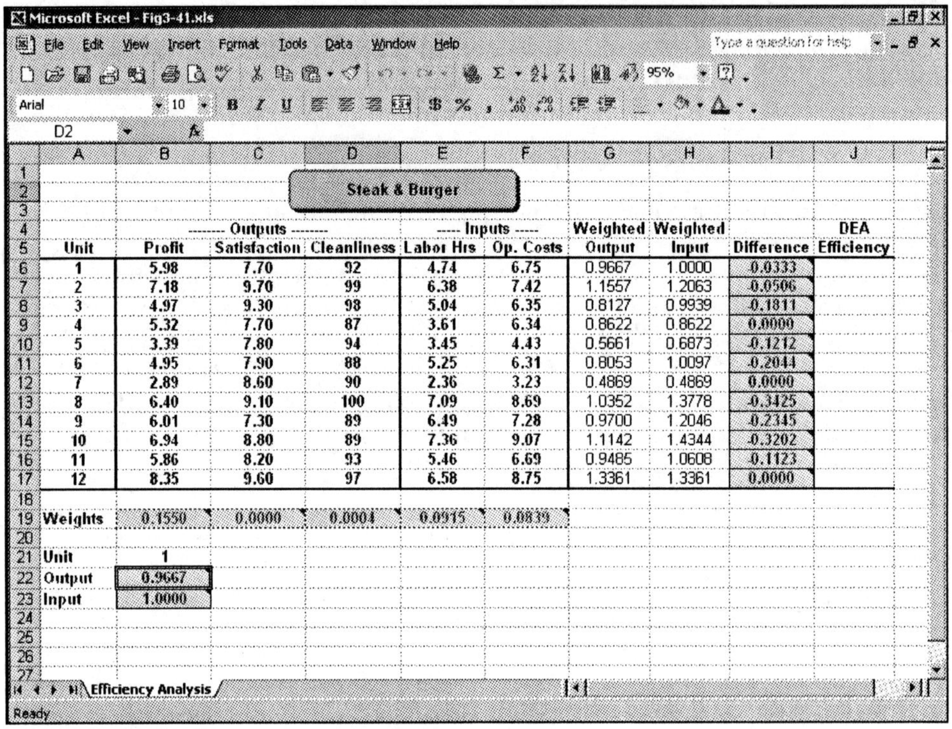

FIGURE 3.43
Optimal DEA solution for unit 1

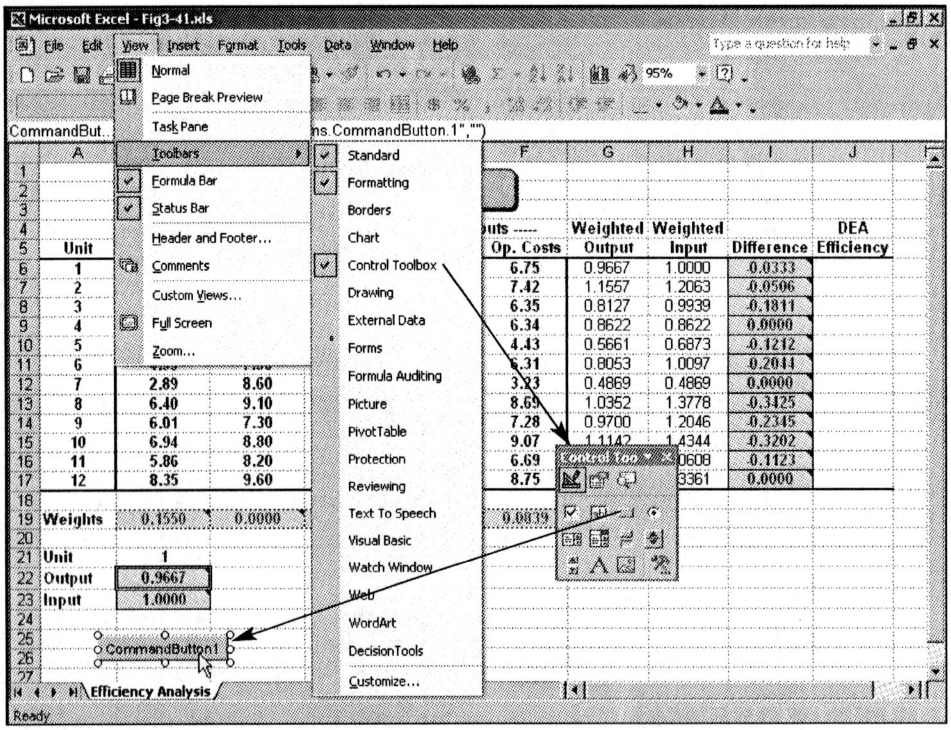

FIGURE 3.44
Using the Control Toolbox to create a command button

1. Click View, Toolbars, Control Toolbox.
2. Click the Command Button icon on the Control Toolbox.
3. Click and drag on your worksheet to draw a command button.

Next, we need to change a few properties of our newly created command button. To do this:

1. Click the command button to make sure it is selected.
2. Click the Properties icon on the Control Toolbox.

These actions cause the Properties window shown in Figure 3.45 to appear. This window lists several properties (or attributes) of the command button that you can change to customize its appearance and behavior. For present purposes, change the command button's property values as follows:

Property	**New Value**
(Name)	DEA
Caption	Run DEA
TakeFocusOnClick	False

Next, double-click the command button. This should launch Excel's Visual Basic Editor and bring up the code window for the command button's click event. Initially, the click event will not have any commands in it. Insert the statements shown in Figure 3.46. These statements will be executed whenever the command button is clicked.

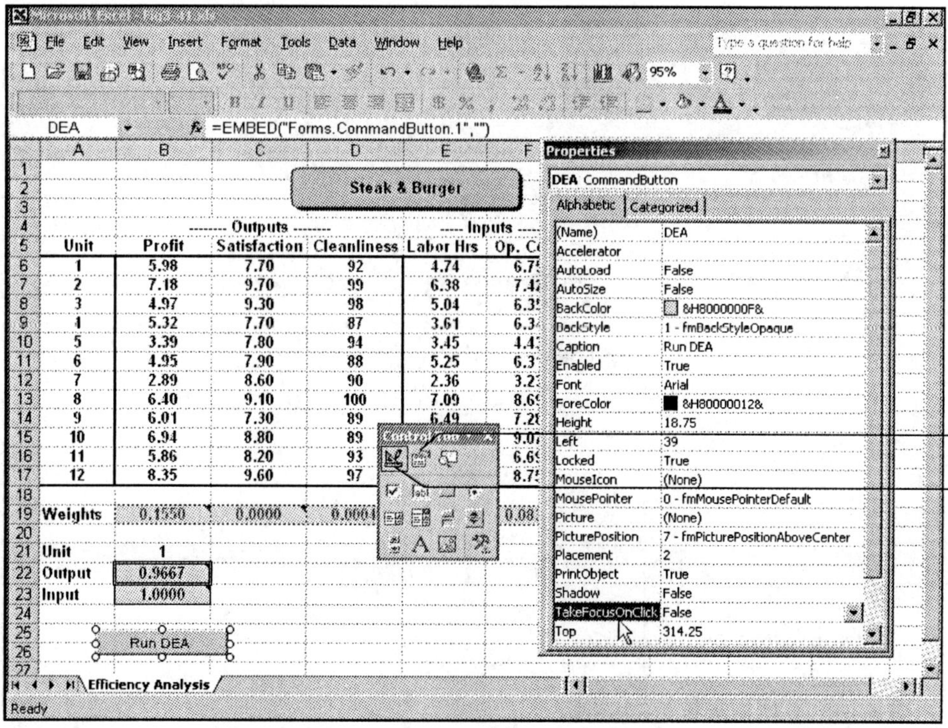

FIGURE 3.45
Adjusting the properties of the command button

Important Software Note

When you place a command button on a worksheet, it is a good idea to set its "TakeFocusOnClick" property to False. This prevents the command button from receiving the focus when it is clicked. "Focus" refers to the object on the screen that is selected or has the computer's attention. An Excel macro cannot perform certain operations if a command button has the focus.

Software Tip

You can easily toggle back and forth between Excel and the Visual Basic Editor by pressing Alt+F11.

If you have any programming experience, you can probably follow the logic behind the programming code listed in Figure 3.46. In a nutshell, the For and Next statements define a loop of code that will be repeated 12 times. During the first execution of the loop, the variable "unit" will equal 1. During the second execution of the loop, the variable "unit" will equal 2, and so on. During each execution of the loop, the following operations take place:

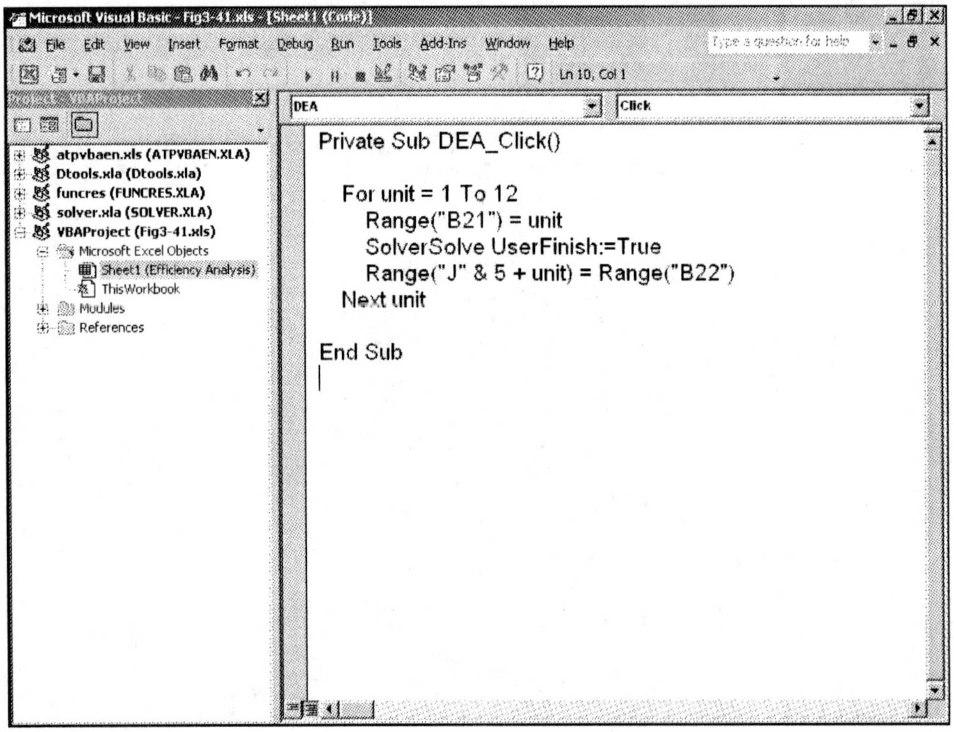

FIGURE 3.46
VBA code for the command button's click event

Macro Statement	**Purpose**
RANGE("B21")=unit	Places the current value of "unit" (the number 1, 2, 3, …, or 12) into cell B21 on the worksheet.
SolverSolve UserFinish:=True	Tells Solver to solve the problem without displaying the usual Solver Results dialog box.
Range("J" & 5 + unit) = Range("B22")	Takes the optimal objective function value in cell B22 and places it in row "5 + unit" (that is, row 6, 7, …, or 17) in column J.

To call Solver from within a macro program, we must first set a reference to the Solver.xla file. You do this from within Excel's Visual Basic editor as follows:

1. Click Tools, References and check the box for solver.xla.
2. Click OK.

We can now test our command button to see if it works. To do this:

1. Close the Visual Basic editor window (or press Alt+F11).
2. Click the Exit Design Mode icon on the Control Toolbox.
3. Click the Run DEA command button.

If everything worked correctly, you should see the results shown in Figure 3.47 (or see the completed file Fig3-47.xls on your data disk).

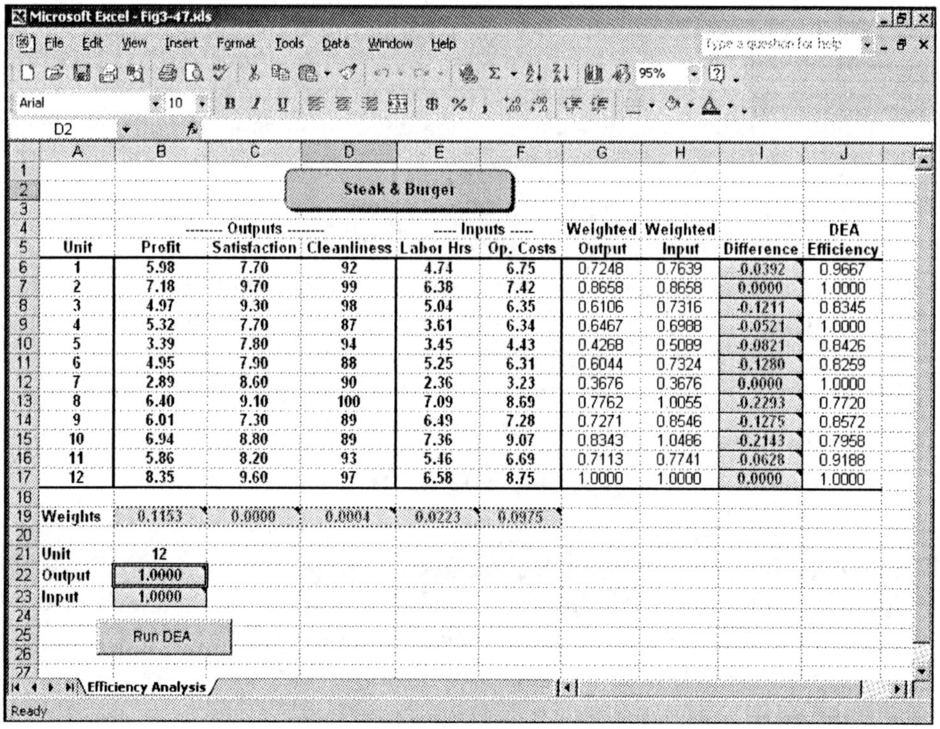

FIGURE 3.47
DEA efficiency scores for all the units

Important Software Note

It is important to remember that command buttons and other controls become operational only after you exit design mode. If you close the Control Toolbox toolbar before clicking the Exit Design Mode icon, you will still be in design mode even after the Control Toolbox is gone and your controls will not operate correctly.

3.14.6 Analyzing the Solution

The solution shown in Figure 3.47 indicates that units 2, 4, 7, and 12 are operating at 100% efficiency (in the DEA sense), while the remaining units are operating less efficiently. Note that an efficiency rating of 100% does not necessarily mean that a unit is operating in the best possible way. It simply means that no linear combination of the other units in the study results in a composite unit that produces at least as much output using the same or less input. On the other hand, for units that are DEA *inefficient,* there exists a linear combination of efficient units that results in a composite unit that produces at least as much output using the same or less input than the inefficient unit. The idea in DEA is that an inefficient unit should be able to operate as efficiently as this hypothetical composite unit formed from a linear combination of the efficient units.

For instance, unit 1 has an efficiency score of 96.67% and is, therefore, somewhat inefficient. Figure 3.48 (in file Fig3-48.xls on your data disk) shows that a weighted average of 26.38% of unit 4, plus 28.15% of unit 7, plus 45.07% of unit 12 produces a hypothetical composite unit with outputs greater than or equal to those of unit 1 and requiring less input than unit 1. The assumption in DEA is that unit 1 should have been able to achieve this same level of performance.

For any inefficient unit, you can determine the linear combination of efficient units that results in a more efficient composite unit as follows:

1. Solve the DEA problem for the unit in question.
2. In the Solver Results dialog box, select the Sensitivity report option.

In the resulting sensitivity report, the absolute value of the Shadow Prices for the "Difference" constraints are the weights that should create a composite unit that is more efficient than the unit in question. The sensitivity report for unit 1 is shown in Figure 3.49.

Want to Know More?

To learn more about writing VBA macros in Excel, see *Excel 2002 Power Programming with VBA* by John Walkenbach published by M&T Books. To learn more about controlling Solver from within macros, see http://www.frontsys.com/macrovba.htm or click the Help button on the Solver Options dialog box.

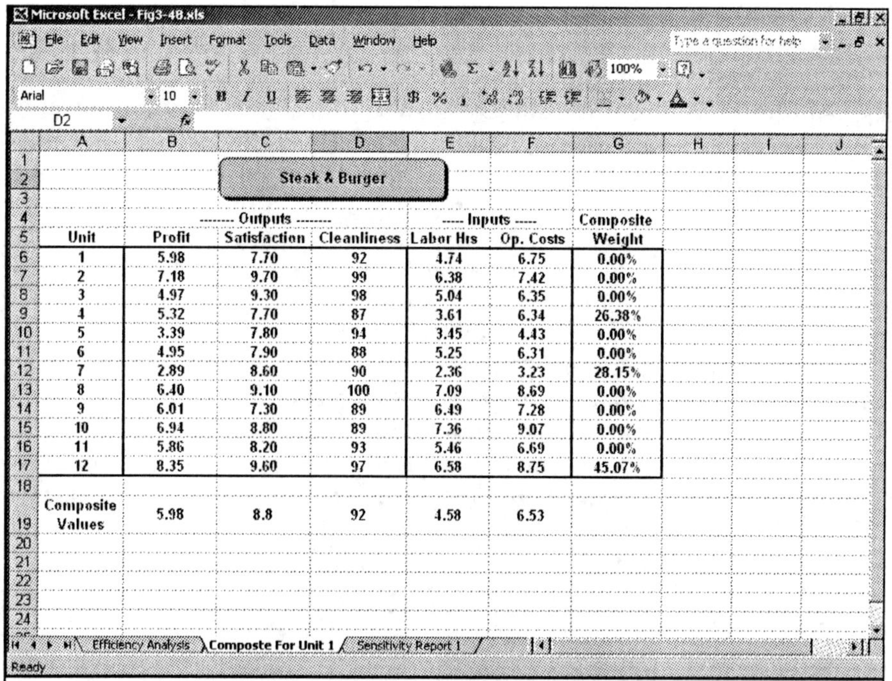

Unit	Profit	Satisfaction	Cleanliness	Labor Hrs	Op. Costs	Composite Weight
1	5.98	7.70	92	4.74	6.75	0.00%
2	7.18	9.70	99	6.38	7.42	0.00%
3	4.97	9.30	98	5.04	6.35	0.00%
4	5.32	7.70	87	3.61	6.34	26.38%
5	3.39	7.80	94	3.45	4.43	0.00%
6	4.95	7.90	88	5.25	6.31	0.00%
7	2.89	8.60	90	2.36	3.23	28.15%
8	6.40	9.10	100	7.09	8.69	0.00%
9	6.01	7.30	89	6.49	7.28	0.00%
10	6.94	8.80	89	7.36	9.07	0.00%
11	5.86	8.20	93	5.46	6.69	0.00%
12	8.35	9.60	97	6.58	8.75	45.07%
Composite Values	5.98	8.8	92	4.58	6.53	

(Outputs: Profit, Satisfaction, Cleanliness; Inputs: Labor Hrs, Op. Costs)

Key Cell Formulas

Cell	Formula	Copied to
B19	=SUMPRODUCT (B6:B17,$G$6:$G$17)	C19:F19

FIGURE 3.48
Example of a composite unit that is more efficient than unit 1

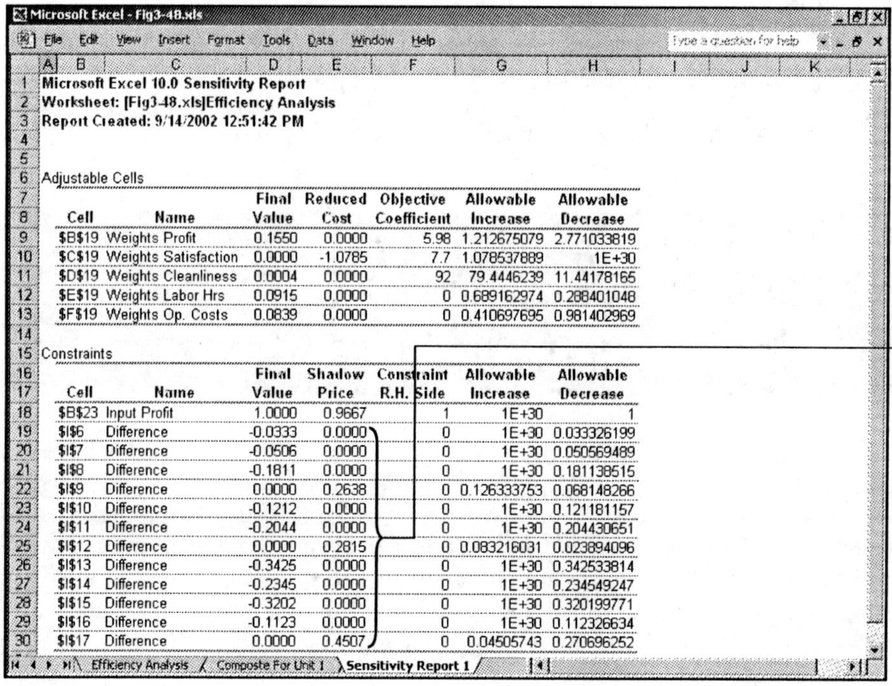

Microsoft Excel 10.0 Sensitivity Report
Worksheet: [Fig3-48.xls]Efficiency Analysis
Report Created: 9/14/2002 12:51:42 PM

Adjustable Cells

Cell	Name	Final Value	Reduced Cost	Objective Coefficient	Allowable Increase	Allowable Decrease
$B$19	Weights Profit	0.1550	0.0000	5.98	1.212675079	2.771033819
$C$19	Weights Satisfaction	0.0000	-1.0785	7.7	1.078537889	1E+30
$D$19	Weights Cleanliness	0.0004	0.0000	92	79.4446239	11.44178165
$E$19	Weights Labor Hrs	0.0915	0.0000	0	0.689162974	0.288401048
$F$19	Weights Op. Costs	0.0839	0.0000	0	0.410697695	0.981402969

Constraints

Cell	Name	Final Value	Shadow Price	Constraint R.H. Side	Allowable Increase	Allowable Decrease
$B$23	Input Profit	1.0000	0.9667	1	1E+30	1
$I$6	Difference	-0.0333	0.0000	0	1E+30	0.033326199
$I$7	Difference	-0.0506	0.0000	0	1E+30	0.050569489
$I$8	Difference	-0.1811	0.0000	0	1E+30	0.181138515
$I$9	Difference	0.0000	0.2638	0	0.126333753	0.068148266
$I$10	Difference	-0.1212	0.0000	0	1E+30	0.121181157
$I$11	Difference	-0.2044	0.0000	0	1E+30	0.204430651
$I$12	Difference	0.0000	0.2815	0	0.083216031	0.023894096
$I$13	Difference	-0.3425	0.0000	0	1E+30	0.342533814
$I$14	Difference	-0.2345	0.0000	0	1E+30	0.234549247
$I$15	Difference	-0.3202	0.0000	0	1E+30	0.320199771
$I$16	Difference	-0.1123	0.0000	0	1E+30	0.112326634
$I$17	Difference	0.0000	0.4507	0	0.04505743	0.270696252

FIGURE 3.49
Sensitivity report for unit 1

3.15 SUMMARY

This chapter described how to formulate an LP problem algebraically, implement it in a spreadsheet, and solve it using Solver. The decision variables in the algebraic formulation of a model correspond to the variable cells in the spreadsheet. The LHS formulas for each constraint in an LP model must be implemented in different cells in the spreadsheet. Also, a cell in the spreadsheet must represent the objective function in the LP model. Thus, there is a direct relationship between the various components of an algebraic formulation of an LP problem and its implementation in a spreadsheet.

There are many ways a given LP problem can be implemented in a spreadsheet. The process of building spreadsheet models is more an art than a science. A good spreadsheet implementation represents the problem in a way that clearly communicates its purpose, is reliable, auditable, and modifiable.

It is possible to use Excel's macro language (known as Visual Basic for Applications or VBA) to automate the process of solving LP models. This is particularly useful in problems in which an analyst might want to solve several related problems in succession.

3.16 REFERENCES

Charnes, C., et al. *Data Envelopment Analysis: Theory, Methodology, and Application.* Boston: Kluwer Academic Publishers, 1994.

Hilal, S., and W. Erickson. "Matching Supplies to Save Lives: Linear Programming the Production of Heart Valves." *Interfaces,* vol. 11, no. 6, 1981.

Lanzenauer, C., et al. "RRSP Flood: LP to the Rescue." *Interfaces,* vol. 17, no. 4, 1987.

McKay, A. "Linear Programming Applications on Microcomputers." *Journal of the Operational Research Society,* vol. 36, July 1985.

Roush, W., et al. "Using Chance-Constrained Programming for Animal Feed Formulation at Agway." *Interfaces,* vol. 24, no. 2, 1994.

Shogan, A. *Management Science.* Englewood Cliffs, NJ: Prentice Hall, 1988.

Subramanian, R., et al., "Coldstart: Fleet Assignment at Delta Airlines," *Interfaces,* vol. 24, no. 1, 1994.

Williams, H. *Model Building in Mathematical Programming.* New York: Wiley, 1990.

THE WORLD OF MANAGEMENT SCIENCE

Optimizing Production, Inventory, and Distribution at Kellogg

The Kellogg Company (http://www.kelloggs.com) is the largest cereal producer in the world and a leading producer of convenience foods. In 1999, Kellogg's worldwide sales totaled nearly $7 billion. Kellogg operates five plants in the United States and Canada and has seven core distribution centers and roughly fifteen co-packers that contract to produce or pack some of Kellogg's products. In the cereal business alone, Kellogg must coordinate the production of 80 products while inventorying and distributing over 600

continued

stock keeping units with roughly 90 production lines and 180 packaging lines. Optimizing this many decision variables is obviously a daunting challenge.

Since 1990, Kellogg has been using a large-scale, multiperiod linear program, called the Kellogg Planning System (KPS), to guide production and distribution decisions. Most large companies like Kellogg employ some sort of enterprise resource planning (ERP). Kellogg's ERP systems is a largely custom, home-grown product, and KPS is custom developed tool to complement the ERP system.

An operational-level version of KPS is used at a weekly level of detail to help determine where products are produced and how finished products and in-process products are shipped between plants and distribution centers. A tactical-level version of KPS is used at a monthly level of detail to help establish plant budgets and make capacity and consolidation decisions. Kellogg attributes annual savings of $40–$45 million to the use of the KPS system.

Source: Brown, G., J. Keegan, B. Vigus, and K. Wood. "The Kellogg Company Optimizes Production, Inventory, and Distribution." *Interfaces*, vol. 35, no. 6, 2001.

QUESTIONS AND PROBLEMS

1. In creating the spreadsheet models for the problems in this chapter, cells in the spreadsheets had to be reserved to represent each of the decision variables in the algebraic models. We reserved these cells in the spreadsheets by entering values of zero in them. Why didn't we place some other value or formula in these cells? Would doing so have made any difference?
2. Four goals should be considered when trying to design an effective spreadsheet model: communication, reliability, auditability, and maintainability. We also noted that a spreadsheet design that results in formulas that can be copied is usually more effective than other designs. Briefly describe how using formulas that can be copied supports the four spreadsheet modeling goals.
3. Refer to question 13 at the end of chapter 2. Implement a spreadsheet model for this problem and solve it using Solver.
4. Refer to question 14 at the end of chapter 2. Implement a spreadsheet model for this problem and solve it using Solver.
5. Refer to question 17 at the end of chapter 2. Implement a spreadsheet model for this problem and solve it using Solver.
6. Refer to question 18 at the end of chapter 2. Implement a spreadsheet model for this problem and solve it using Solver.
7. Refer to question 20 at the end of chapter 2. Implement a spreadsheet model for this problem and solve it using Solver.
8. Refer to question 21 at the end of chapter 2. Implement a spreadsheet model for this problem and solve it using Solver.
9. Refer to question 22 at the end of chapter 2. Implement a spreadsheet model for this problem and solve it using Solver.

10. A furniture manufacturer produces two types of tables (country and contemporary) using three types of machines. The time required to produce the tables on each machine is given in the following table.

Machine	Country	Contemporary	Total Machine Time Available per Week
Router	1.5	2.0	1,000
Sander	3.0	4.5	2,000
Polisher	2.5	1.5	1,500

Country tables sell for $350 and contemporary tables sell for $450. Management has determined that at least 20% of the tables made should be country and at least 30% should be contemporary. How many of each type of table should the company produce if it wants to maximize its revenue?

a. Formulate an LP model for this problem.
b. Create a spreadsheet model for this problem and solve it using Solver.
c. What is the optimal solution?
d. How will your spreadsheet model differ if there are 25 types of tables and 15 machine processes involved in manufacturing them?

11. Aire-Co produces home dehumidifiers at two different plants in Atlanta and Phoenix. The per unit cost of production in Atlanta and Phoenix is $400 and $360, respectively. Each plant can produce a maximum of 300 units per month. Inventory holding costs are assessed at $30 per unit in beginning inventory each month. Aire-Co estimates the demand for its product to be 300, 400, and 500 units, respectively, over the next three months. Aire-Co wants to be able to meet this demand at minimum cost.

a. Formulate an LP model for this problem.
b. Implement your model in a spreadsheet and solve it.
c. What is the optimal solution?
d. How does the solution change if each plant is required to produce at least 50 units per month?
e. How does the solution change if each plant is required to produce at least 100 units per month?

12. A company is trying to determine how to allocate its $145,000 advertising budget for a new product. The company is considering newspaper ads and television commercials as its primary means for advertising. The following table summarizes the costs of advertising in these different media and the number of new customers reached by increasing amounts of advertising.

Media & # of Ads	# of New Customers Reached	Cost per Ad
Newspaper: 1–10	900	$1,000
Newspaper: 11–20	700	$900
Newspaper: 21–30	400	$800
Television: 1–5	10,000	$12,000
Television: 6–10	7,500	$10,000
Television: 11–15	5,000	$8,000

For instance, each of the first ten ads the company places in newspapers will cost $1,000 and is expected to reach 900 new customers. Each of the next 10 newspaper ads will cost $900 and is expected to reach 700 new customers. Note that the number of new customers reached by increasing amounts of advertising decreases as the advertising saturates the market. Assume the company will purchase no more than 30 newspaper ads and no more than 15 television ads.

a. Formulate an LP model for this problem to maximize the number of new customers reached by advertising.
b. Implement your model in a spreadsheet and solve it.
c. What is the optimal solution?
d. Suppose the number of new customers reached by 11–20 newspaper ads is 400 and the number of new customers reached by 21–30 newspaper ads is 700. Make these changes in your spreadsheet and reoptimize the problem. What is the new optimal solution? What (if anything) is wrong with this solution and why?

13. A bank has $650,000 in assets to allocate among investments in bonds, home mortgages, car loans, and personal loans. Bonds are expected to produce a return of 10%, mortgages 8.5%, car loans 9.5%, and personal loans 12.5%. To make sure the portfolio is not too risky, the bank wants to restrict personal loans to no more than the 25% of the total portfolio. The bank also wants to ensure that more money is invested in mortgages than personal loans. They also want to invest more in bonds than personal loans.
    a. Formulate an LP model for this problem with the objective of maximizing the expected return on the portfolio.
    b. Implement your model in a spreadsheet and solve it.
    c. What it the optimal solution?

14. Valu-Com Electronics manufactures five different models of telecommunications interface cards for personal and laptop computers. As summarized in the following table, each of these devices requires differing amounts of printed circuit (PC) board, resistors, memory chips, and assembly.

	Per Unit Requirements				
	HyperLink	**FastLink**	**SpeedLink**	**MicroLink**	**EtherLink**
PC Board (square inches)	20	15	10	8	5
Resistors	28	24	18	12	16
Memory Chips	8	8	4	4	6
Assembly Labor (in hours)	0.75	0.6	0.5	0.65	1

The unit wholesale price and manufacturing cost for each model are as follows.

	Per Unit Revenues and Costs				
	HyperLink	**FastLink**	**SpeedLink**	**MicroLink**	**EtherLink**
Wholesale Price	$189	$149	$129	$169	$139
Manufacturing Cost	$136	$101	$ 96	$137	$101

In their next production period, Valu-Com has 80,000 square inches of PC board, 100,000 resistors, 30,000 memory chips, and 5,000 hours of assembly time available. They can sell all the product they can manufacture, but the marketing department wants to be sure they produce at least 500 units of each product and at least twice as many FastLink cards as HyperLink cards while maximizing profit.

a. Formulate an LP model for this problem.
b. Create a spreadsheet model for this problem and solve it using Solver.
c. What is the optimal solution?
d. Could Valu-Com make more money if they schedule their assembly workers to work overtime?

15. A trust officer at the Blacksburg National Bank needs to determine how to invest $100,000 in the following collection of bonds to maximize the annual return.

Bond	Annual Return	Maturity	Risk	Tax Free
A	9.5%	Long	High	Yes
B	8.0%	Short	Low	Yes
C	9.0%	Long	Low	No
D	9.0%	Long	High	Yes
E	9.0%	Short	High	No

The officer wants to invest at least 50% of the money in short-term issues and no more than 50% in high-risk issues. At least 30% of the funds should go in tax-free investments and at least 40% of the total annual return should be tax free.

a. Formulate an LP model for this problem.
b. Create a spreadsheet model for this problem and solve it using Solver.
c. What is the optimal solution?

16. The Weedwacker Company manufactures two types of lawn trimmers: an electric model and a gas model. The company has contracted to supply a national discount retail chain with a total of 30,000 electric trimmers and 15,000 gas trimmers. However, Weedwacker's production capability is limited in three departments: production, assembly, and packaging. The following table summarizes the hours of processing time available and the processing time required by each department, for both types of trimmers:

	Hours Required per Trimmer		
	Electric	Gas	Hours Available
Production	0.20	0.40	10,000
Assembly	0.30	0.50	15,000
Packaging	0.10	0.10	5,000

The company makes its electric trimmer in-house for $55 and its gas trimmer for $85. Alternatively, it can buy electric and gas trimmers from another source for $67 and $95, respectively. How many gas and electric trimmers should Weedwacker make and how many should it buy from its competitor in order to fulfill its contract in the least costly manner?

a. Formulate an LP model for this problem.
b. Create a spreadsheet model for this problem and solve it using Solver.
c. What is the optimal solution?

17. A manufacturer of prefabricated homes has decided to subcontract four components of the homes. Several companies are interested in receiving this business, but none can handle more than one subcontract. The bids made by the companies for the various subcontracts are summarized in the following table.

Bids by Companies (in $1,000s) for Various Subcontracts

	Company			
Component	**A**	**B**	**C**	**D**
1	185	225	193	207
2	200	190	175	225
3	330	320	315	300
4	375	389	425	445

Assuming all the companies can perform each subcontract equally well, to which company should each subcontract be assigned if the home manufacturer wants to minimize payments to the subcontractors?

a. Formulate an LP model for this problem.
b. Create a spreadsheet model for this problem and solve it using Solver.
c. What is the optimal solution?

18. Tarmac Chemical Corporation produces a special chemical compound—called CHEMIX—that is used extensively in high school chemistry classes. This compound must contain at least 20% sulfur, at least 30% iron oxide, and at least 30% but no more than 45% potassium. Tarmac's marketing department has estimated that it will need at least 600 pounds of this compound to meet the expected demand during the coming school session. Tarmac can buy three compounds to mix together to produce CHEMIX. The makeup of these compounds is shown in the following table.

Compound	Sulfur	Iron Oxide	Potassium
1	20%	60%	20%
2	40%	30%	30%
3	10%	40%	50%

Compounds 1, 2, and 3 cost $5.00, $5.25, and $5.50 per pound, respectively. Tarmac wants to use an LP model to determine the least costly way of producing enough CHEMIX to meet the demand expected for the coming year.

a. Formulate an LP model for this problem.
b. Create a spreadsheet model for this problem and solve it using Solver.
c. What is the optimal solution?

19. Holiday Fruit Company buys oranges and processes them into gift fruit baskets and fresh juice. The company grades the fruit it buys on a scale from 1 (lowest quality) to 5 (highest quality). The following table summarizes Holiday's current inventory of fruit.

Grade	Supply (100s of pounds)
1	90
2	225
3	300
4	100
5	75

Each pound of oranges devoted to fruit baskets results in a marginal profit of \$2.50, whereas each pound devoted to fresh juice results in a marginal profit of \$1.75. Holiday wants the fruit in its baskets to have an average quality grade of at least 3.75 and its fresh juice to have a average quality grade of at least 2.50.

a. Formulate an optimization model for this problem.
b. Implement your model in a spreadsheet and solve it.
c. What it the optimal solution?

20. Riverside Oil Company in eastern Kentucky produces regular and supreme gasoline. Each barrel of regular sells for \$21 and must have an octane rating of at least 90. Each barrel of supreme sells for \$25 and must have an octane rating of at least 97. Each of these types of gasoline are manufactured by mixing different quantities of the following three inputs:

Input	Cost per Barrel	Octane Rating	Barrels Available (in 1000s)
1	\$17.25	100	150
2	\$15.75	87	350
3	\$17.75	110	300

Riverside has orders for 300,000 barrels of regular and 450,000 barrels of supreme. How should the company allocate the available inputs to the production of regular and supreme gasoline if they want to maximize profits?

a. Formulate an LP model for this problem.
b. Create a spreadsheet model for this problem and solve it using Solver.
c. What is the optimal solution?

21. Maintenance at a major theme park in central Florida is an ongoing process that occurs 24 hours a day. Because it is a long drive from most residential areas to the park, employees do not like to work shifts of fewer than eight hours. These 8-hour shifts start every four hours throughout the day. The number of maintenance workers needed at different times throughout the day varies. The following table summarizes the minimum number of employees needed in each 4-hour time period.

Time Period	Minimum Employees Needed
12 A.M. to 4 A.M.	90
4 A.M. to 8 A.M.	215
8 A.M. to 12 P.M.	250
12 P.M. to 4 P.M.	165
4 P.M. to 8 P.M.	300
8 P.M. to 12 A.M.	125

The maintenance supervisor wants to determine the minimum number of employees to schedule that meets the minimum staffing requirements.

a. Formulate an LP model for this problem.
b. Create a spreadsheet model for this problem and solve it using Solver.
c. What is the optimal solution?

22. Radmore Memorial Hospital has a problem in its fluids analysis lab. The lab has available three machines that analyze various fluid samples. Recently, the demand for analyzing blood samples has increased so much that the lab director is having difficulty getting all the samples analyzed quickly enough and

still completing the other fluid work that comes into the lab. The lab works with five types of blood specimens. Any machine can be used to process any of the specimens. However, the amount of time required by each machine varies depending on the type of specimen being analyzed. These times are summarized in the following table.

Required Specimen Processing Time in Minutes

Machine	**Specimen Type** 1	**2**	**3**	**4**	**5**
A	3	4	4	5	3
B	5	3	5	4	5
C	2	5	3	3	4

Each machine can be used a total of 8 hours a day. Blood samples collected on a given day arrive at the lab and are stored overnight and processed the next day. So, at the beginning of each day, the lab director must determine how to allocate the various samples to the machines for analysis. This morning, the lab has 80 type-1 specimens, 75 type-2 specimens, 80 type-3 specimens, 120 type-4 specimens, and 60 type-5 specimens awaiting processing. The lab director wants to know how many of each type of specimen should be analyzed on each machine in order to minimize the total time the machines are devoted to analyzing blood samples.

a. Formulate an LP model for this problem.
b. Create a spreadsheet model for this problem and solve it using Solver.
c. What is the optimal solution?
d. How much processing time will be available on each machine if this solution is implemented?
e. How would the model and solution change if the lab director wanted to balance the use of each machine so that each machine were used approximately the same amount of time?

23. Virginia Tech operates its own power generating plant. The electricity generated by this plant supplies power to the university and to local businesses and residences in the Blacksburg area. The plant burns three types of coal, which produce steam that drives the turbines that generate the electricity. The Environmental Protection Agency (EPA) requires that for each ton of coal burned, the emissions from the coal furnace smoke stacks contain no more than 2,500 parts per million (ppm) of sulfur and no more than 2.8 kilograms (kg) of coal dust. The following table summarizes the amounts of sulfur, coal dust, and steam that result from burning a ton of each type of coal.

Coal	**Sulfur (in ppm)**	**Coal Dust (in kg)**	**Pounds of Steam Produced**
1	1,100	1.7	24,000
2	3,500	3.2	36,000
3	1,300	2.4	28,000

The three types of coal can be mixed and burned in any combination. The resulting emission of sulfur or coal dust and the pounds of steam produced by any mixture are given as the weighted average of the values shown in the table for each type of coal. For example, if the coals are mixed to produce a blend that consists of 35% of coal 1, 40% of coal 2, and 25% of coal 3, the sulfur emission (in ppm) resulting from burning one ton of this blend is:

$$0.35 \times 1{,}100 + 0.40 \times 3{,}500 + 0.25 \times 1{,}300 = 2{,}110$$

The manager of this facility wants to determine the blend of coal that will produce the maximum pounds of steam per ton without violating the EPA requirements.

a. Formulate an LP model for this problem.
b. Create a spreadsheet model for this problem and solve it using Solver.
c. What is the optimal solution?
d. If the furnace can burn up to 30 tons of coal per hour, what is the maximum amount of steam that can be produced per hour?

24. A real estate developer is planning to build an apartment building specifically for graduate students on a parcel of land adjacent to a major university. Four types of apartments can be included in the building: efficiencies, and one-, two-, or three-bedroom units. Each efficiency requires 500 square feet; each one-bedroom apartment requires 700 square feet; each two-bedroom apartment requires 800 square feet; and each three-bedroom unit requires 1,000 square feet. The developer believes that the building should include no more than 15 one-bedroom units, 22 two-bedroom units, and 10 three-bedroom units. Local zoning ordinances do not allow the developer to build more than 40 units in this particular building location, and restrict the building to a maximum of 40,000 square feet. The developer has already agreed to lease 5 one-bedroom units and 8 two-bedroom units to a local rental agency that is a "silent partner" in this endeavor. Market studies indicate that efficiencies can be rented for $350 per month, one-bedrooms for $450 per month, two-bedrooms for $550 per month, and three-bedrooms for $750 per month. How many rental units of each type should the developer include in the building plans in order to maximize the potential rental income from the building?
    a. Formulate an LP model for this problem.
    b. Create a spreadsheet model for this problem and solve it using Solver.
    c. What is the optimal solution?
    d. Which constraint in this model limits the builder's potential rental income from increasing any further?
25. Kentwood Electronics manufactures three components for stereo systems: CD players, tape decks, and stereo tuners. The wholesale price and manufacturing cost of each item are shown in the following table.

Component	Wholesale Price	Manufacturing Cost
CD Player	$150	$75
Tape Deck	$85	$35
Stereo Tuner	$70	$30

Each CD player produced requires 3 hours of assembly; each tape deck requires 2 hours of assembly; and each tuner requires 1 hour of assembly. The marketing department has indicated that it can sell no more than 150,000 CD players, 100,000 tape decks, and 90,000 stereo tuners. However, the demand is expected to be at least 50,000 units of each item, and Kentwood wants to meet this demand. If Kentwood has 400,000 hours of assembly time available, how many CD players, tape decks, and stereo tuners should it produce in order to maximize profits while meeting the minimum demand figures?

a. Formulate an LP model for this problem.
b. Create a spreadsheet model for this problem and solve it using Solver.
c. What is the optimal solution?

26. The Rent-A-Dent car rental company allows its customers to pick up a rental car at one location and return it to any of its locations. Currently, two locations (1 and 2) have 16 and 18 surplus cars, respectively, and four locations (3, 4, 5, and 6) each need 10 cars. The costs of getting the surplus cars from locations 1 and 2 to the other locations are summarized in the following table.

Costs of Transporting Cars Between Locations

	Location 3	Location 4	Location 5	Location 6
Location 1	$54	$17	$23	$30
Location 2	$24	$18	$19	$31

Because 34 surplus cars are available at locations 1 and 2, and 40 cars are needed at locations 3, 4, 5, and 6, some locations will not receive as many cars as they need. However, management wants to make sure that all the surplus cars are sent where they are needed, and that each location needing cars receives at least five.

a. Formulate an LP model for this problem.
b. Create a spreadsheet model for this problem and solve it using Solver.
c. What is the optimal solution?

27. The Sentry Lock Corporation manufactures a popular commercial security lock at plants in Macon, Louisville, Detroit, and Phoenix. The per unit cost of production at each plant is $35.50, $37.50, $39.00, and $36.25, respectively, while the annual production capacity at each plant is 18,000, 15,000, 25,000, and 20,000, respectively. Sentry's locks are sold to retailers through wholesale distributors in seven cities across the United States. The unit cost of shipping from each plant to each distributor is summarized in the following table along with the forecasted demand from each distributor for the coming year.

Unit Shipping Cost to Distributor in

Plants	Tacoma	San Diego	Dallas	Denver	St. Louis	Tampa	Baltimore
Macon	$2.50	$2.75	$1.75	$2.00	$2.10	$1.80	$1.65
Louisville	$1.85	$1.90	$1.50	$1.60	$1.00	$1.90	$1.85
Detroit	$2.30	$2.25	$1.85	$1.25	$1.50	$2.25	$2.00
Phoenix	$1.90	$0.90	$1.60	$1.75	$2.00	$2.50	$2.65
Demand	8,500	14,500	13,500	12,600	18,000	15,000	9,000

Sentry wants to determine the least expensive way of manufacturing and shipping locks from their plants to the distributors. Because the total demand from distributors exceeds the total production capacity for all the plants, Sentry realizes they will not be able to satisfy all the demand for their product, but wants to make sure each distributor will have the opportunity to fill at least 80% of the orders they receive.

a. Create a spreadsheet model for this problem and solve it.
b. What is the optimal solution?

28. A paper recycling company converts newspaper, mixed paper, white office paper, and cardboard into pulp for newsprint, packaging paper, and print stock quality paper. The following table summarizes the yield for each kind of pulp recovered from each ton of recycled material.

	Recycling Yield		
	Newsprint	**Packaging**	**Print Stock**
Newspaper	85%	80%	—
Mixed Paper	90%	80%	70%
White Office Paper	90%	85%	80%
Cardboard	80%	70%	—

For instance, a ton of newspaper can be recycled using a technique that yields 0.85 tons of newsprint pulp. Alternatively, a ton of newspaper can be recycled using a technique that yields 0.80 tons of packaging paper. Similarly, a ton of cardboard can be recycled to yield 0.80 tons of newsprint or 0.70 tons of packaging paper pulp. Note that newspaper and cardboard cannot be converted to print stock pulp using the techniques available to the recycler.

The cost of processing each ton of raw material into the various types of pulp is summarized in the following table along with the amount of each of the four raw materials that can be purchased and their costs.

	Processing Costs per Ton			Purchase Cost	Tons
	Newsprint	**Packaging**	**Print Stock**	**per Ton**	**Available**
Newspaper	$6.50	$11.00	—	$15	600
Mixed Paper	$9.75	$12.25	$9.50	$16	500
White Office Paper	$4.75	$7.75	$8.50	$19	300
Cardboard	$7.50	$8.50	—	$17	400

The recycler wants to determine the least costly way of producing 500 tons of newsprint pulp, 600 tons of packaging paper pulp, and 300 tons of print stock quality pulp.

a. Create a spreadsheet model for this problem and solve it.
b. What is the optimal solution?

29. A winery has the following capacity to produce an exclusive dinner wine at either of its two vineyards at the indicated costs:

Vineyard	Capacity	Cost per Bottle
1	3,500 bottles	$23
2	3,100 bottles	$25

Four Italian restaurants around the country are interested in purchasing this wine. Because the wine is exclusive, they all want to buy as much as they need but will take whatever they can get. The maximum amounts required by the restaurants and the prices they are willing to pay are summarized in the following table.

Restaurant	Maximum Demand	Price
1	1,800 bottles	$69
2	2,300 bottles	$67
3	1,250 bottles	$70
4	1,750 bottles	$66

The costs of shipping a bottle from the vineyards to the restaurants are summarized in the following table.

	Restaurant			
Vineyard	1	2	3	4
1	$7	$8	$13	$9
2	$12	$6	$8	$7

The winery needs to determine the production and shipping plan that allows it to maximize its profits on this wine.

a. Formulate an LP model for this problem.
b. Create a spreadsheet model for this problem and solve it using Solver.
c. What is the optimal solution?

30. Bellows Lumber Yard, Inc. stocks standard length, 25-foot boards, which it cuts to custom lengths to fill individual customer orders. An order has just come in for 5,000 7-foot boards, 1,200 9-foot boards, and 300 11-foot boards. The lumber yard manager has identified six ways to cut the 25-foot boards to fill this order. The six cutting patterns are summarized in the following table.

	Number of Boards Produced		
Cutting Pattern	7 ft	9 ft	11 ft
1	3	0	0
2	2	1	0
3	2	0	1
4	1	2	0
5	0	1	1
6	0	0	2

One possibility (cutting pattern 1) is to cut a 25-foot board into three 7-foot boards, and not to cut any 9- or 11-foot boards. Note that cutting pattern 1 uses a total of 21 feet of board and leaves a 4-foot piece of scrap. Another possibility (cutting pattern 4) is to cut a 25-foot board into one 7-foot board and two 9-foot boards (using all 25 feet of the board). The remaining cutting patterns have similar interpretations. The lumber yard manager wants to fill this order using the fewest number of 25-foot boards as possible. To do this, the manager needs to determine how many 25-foot boards to run through each cutting pattern.

a. Formulate an LP model for this problem.
b. Create a spreadsheet model for this problem and solve it using Solver.
c. What is the optimal solution?
d. Suppose the manager wants to minimize waste. Would the solution change?

31. Howie's Carpet World has just received an order for carpets for a new office building. The order is for 4,000 yards of carpet 4-feet wide, 20,000 yards of carpet 9-feet wide, and 9,000 yards of carpet 12-feet wide. Howie can order two kinds of carpet rolls, which he will then have to cut to fill this order. One type of roll is 14-feet wide, 100-yards long, and costs $1,000 per roll; the other is 18-feet wide, 100-yards long, and costs $1,400 per roll. Howie needs to determine how many of the two types of carpet rolls to order and how they should be cut. He wants to do this in the least costly way possible.
    a. Formulate an LP model for this problem.
    b. Create a spreadsheet model for this problem and solve it using Solver.
    c. What is the optimal solution?
    d. Suppose Howie wants to minimize waste. Would the solution change?
32. The Pitts Barbecue Company makes three kinds of barbecue sauce: Extra Hot, Hot, and Mild. Pitts' vice president of marketing estimates that the company can sell 8,000 cases of its Extra Hot sauce plus 10 extra cases for every dollar it spends promoting this sauce; 10,000 cases of Hot sauce plus 8 extra cases for every dollar spent promoting this sauce; and 12,000 cases of its Mild sauce plus 5 extra cases for every dollar spent promoting this sauce. Although each barbecue sauce sells for $10 per case, the cost of producing the different types of sauce varies. It costs the company $6 to produce a case of Extra Hot sauce, $5.50 to produce a case of Hot sauce, and $5.25 to produce a case of Mild sauce. The president of the company wants to make sure the company manufactures at least the minimum amounts of each sauce that the marketing vice president thinks the company can sell. A budget of $25,000 total has been approved for promoting these items of which at least $5,000 must be spent advertising each item. How many cases of each type of sauce should be made and how do you suggest that the company allocate the promotional budget if it wants to maximize profits?
    a. Formulate an LP model for this problem.
    b. Create a spreadsheet model for this problem and solve it using Solver.
    c. What is the optimal solution?
33. Acme Manufacturing makes a variety of household appliances at a single manufacturing facility. The expected demand for one of these appliances during the next four months is shown in the following table along with the expected production costs and the expected capacity for producing these items.

	Month			
	1	2	3	4
Demand	420	580	310	540
Production Cost	$49.00	$45.00	$46.00	$47.00
Production Capacity	500	520	450	550

Acme estimates it costs $1.50 per month for each unit of this appliance carried in inventory (estimated by averaging the beginning and ending inventory levels each month). Currently, Acme has 120 units in inventory on hand for this product. To maintain a level workforce, the company wants to produce at least 400 units per month. They also want to maintain a safety stock of at least 50 units per month. Acme wants to determine how many of each appliance to manufacture during each of the next four months to meet the expected demand at the lowest possible total cost.

a. Formulate an LP model for this problem.
b. Create a spreadsheet model for this problem and solve it using Solver.
c. What is the optimal solution?
d. How much money could Acme save if they were willing to drop the restriction about producing at least 400 units per month?

34. Paul Bergey is in charge of loading cargo ships for International Cargo Company (ICC) at the port in Newport News, Virginia. Paul is preparing a loading plan for an ICC freighter destined for Ghana. An agricultural commodities dealer wants to transport the following products aboard this ship.

Commodity	Amount Available (tons)	Volume per Ton (cubic feet)	Profit per Ton ($)
1	4,800	40	70
2	2,500	25	50
3	1,200	60	60
4	1,700	55	80

Paul can elect to load any and/or all of the available commodities. However, the ship has three cargo holds with the following capacity restrictions:

Cargo Hold	Weight Capacity (tons)	Volume Capacity (cubic feet)
Forward	3,000	145,000
Center	6,000	180,000
Rear	4,000	155,000

More than one type of commodity can be placed in the same cargo hold. However, because of balance considerations, the weight in the forward cargo hold must be within 10% of the weight in the rear cargo hold and the center cargo hold must be between 40% to 60% of the total weight on board.

a. Formulate an LP model for this problem.
b. Create a spreadsheet model for this problem and solve it using Solver.
c. What is the optimal solution?

35. The Pelletier Corporation has just discovered that it will not have enough warehouse space for the next five months. The additional warehouse space requirements for this period are:

Month	1	2	3	4	5
Additional Space Needed (in 1,000 sq ft)	25	10	20	10	5

To cover its space requirements, the firm plans to lease additional warehouse space on a short-term basis. Over the next five months, a local warehouse has agreed to lease Pelletier any amount of space for any number of months according to the following cost schedule.

Length of Lease (in months)	1	2	3	4	5
Cost per 1000 square feet	$300	$525	$775	$850	$975

This schedule of leasing options is available to Pelletier at the beginning of each of the next five months. For example, the company could elect to lease 5,000 square feet for 4 months beginning in month 1 (at a cost of $850 × 5) and lease 10,000 square feet for 2 months beginning in month 3 (at a cost of $525 × 10).

a. Formulate an LP model for this problem.
b. Create a spreadsheet model for this problem and solve it using Solver.
c. What is the optimal solution?

36. Carter Enterprises is involved in the soybean business in South Carolina, Alabama, and Georgia. The president of the company, Earl Carter, goes to a commodity sale once a month where he buys and sells soybeans in bulk. Carter uses a local warehouse for storing his soybean inventory. This warehouse charges $10 per average ton of soybeans stored per month (based on the average of the beginning and ending inventory each month). The warehouse guarantees Carter the capacity to store up to 400 tons of soybeans at the end of each month. Carter has estimated what he believes the price per ton of soybeans will be during each of the next six months. These prices are summarized in the following table.

Month	Price per Ton
1	$135
2	$110
3	$150
4	$175
5	$130
6	$145

Assume Carter currently has 70 tons of soybeans stored in the warehouse. How many tons of soybeans should Carter buy and sell during each of the next six months to maximize his profit trading soybeans?

a. Formulate an LP model for this problem.
b. Create a spreadsheet model for this problem and solve it using Solver.
c. What is the optimal solution?

37. Jack Potts recently won $1,000,000 in Las Vegas and is trying to determine how to invest his winnings. He has narrowed his decision down to five investments, which are summarized in the following table.

	Summary of Cash Inflows and Outflows (at beginning of years)			
	1	**2**	**3**	**4**
A	−1	0.50	0.80	
B		−1	⟷	1.25
C	−1	⟷	⟷	1.35
D			−1	1.13
E	−1	⟷	1.27	

If Jack invests $1 in investment A at the beginning of year 1, he will receive $0.50 at the beginning of year 2 and another $0.80 at the beginning of year 3. Alternatively, he can invest $1 in investment B at the beginning of year 2 and receive $1.25 at the beginning of year 4. Entries of "<--->" in the table indicate times when no cash inflows or outflows can occur. At the beginning of any year, Jack can place money in a money market account that is expected to yield 8% per year. He wants to keep at least \$50,000 in the money market account at all times and doesn't want to place any more than \$500,000 in any single investment. How would you advise Jack to invest his winnings if he wants to maximize the amount of money he'll have at the beginning of year 4?

a. Formulate an LP model for this problem.
b. Create a spreadsheet model for this problem and solve it using Solver.
c. What is the optimal solution?

38. Fred and Sally Merrit recently inherited a substantial amount of money from a deceased relative. They want to use part of this money to establish an account to pay for their daughter's college education. Their daughter, Lisa, will be starting college 5 years from now. The Merrits estimate that her first year college expenses will amount to \$12,000 and increase \$2,000 per year during each of the remaining three years of her education. The following investments are available to the Merrits:

Investment	Available	Matures	Return at Maturity
A	Every year	1 year	6%
B	1, 3, 5, 7	2 years	14%
C	1, 4	3 years	18%
D	1	7 years	65%

The Merrits want to determine an investment plan that will provide the necessary funds to cover Lisa's anticipated college expenses with the smallest initial investment.

a. Formulate an LP model for this problem.
b. Create a spreadsheet model for this problem and solve it using Solver.
c. What is the optimal solution?

39. Refer to the previous question. Suppose the investments available to the Merrits have the following levels of risk associated with them.

Investment	Risk Factor
A	1
B	3
C	6
D	8

If the Merrits want the weighted average risk level of their investments to not exceed 4, how much money will they need to set aside for Lisa's education and how should they invest it?

a. Formulate an LP model for this problem.
b. Create a spreadsheet model for this problem and solve it using Solver.
c. What is the optimal solution?

40. WinterWearhouse operates a clothing store specializing in ski apparel. Given the seasonal nature of their business, there is often somewhat of an imbalance between when bills must be paid for inventory purchased and when the goods are actually sold and cash is received. Over the next six months, the company expects cash receipts and requirements for bill paying as follows:

	Month					
	1	2	3	4	5	6
Cash Receipts	$100,000	$225,000	$275,000	$350,000	$475,000	625,000
Bills Due	$400,000	$500,000	$600,000	$300,000	$200,000	100,000

The company likes to maintain a cash balance of at least $20,000 and currently has $100,000 cash on hand. The company can borrow money from a local bank for the following term/rate structure: 1-month at 1%, 2-months at 1.75%, 3-months at 2.49%, 4-months at 3.22%, and 5-months at 3.94%. When needed, money is borrowed at the end of a month and repaid, with interest, at the end of the month in which the obligation is due. For instance, if the company borrows $10,000 for 2 months in month 3, they would have to pay back $10,175 at the end of month 5.

a. Create a spreadsheet model for this problem and solve it.
b. What is the optimal solution?
c. Suppose its bank limits WinterWearhouse to borrowing no more than $100,000 at each level in the term/rate structure. How would this restriction change the optimal solution?

41. The chief financial officer for Eagle's Beach Wear and Gift Shop is in the process of planning for the company's cash flows for the next six months. The following table summarizes the expected accounts receivables and planned payments for each of these months (in $100,000s).

	January	February	March	April	May	June
Accounts Receivable Balances Due	1.50	1.00	1.40	2.30	2.00	1.00
Planned Payments (net of discounts)	1.80	1.60	2.20	1.20	0.80	1.20

The company currently has a beginning cash balance of $400,000 and desires to maintain a balance of at least $25,000 in cash at the end of each month. To accomplish this, the company has a number of ways of obtaining short-term funds:

1. **Delay Payments.** In any month, the company's suppliers permit it to delay any or all payments for one month. However, for this consideration, the company forfeits a 2% discount that normally applies when payments are made on time. (Loss of this 2% discount is, in effect, a financing cost.)
2. **Borrow Against Accounts Receivables.** In any month, the company's bank will loan it up to 75% of the accounts receivable balances due that month. These loans must be repaid in the following month and incur an interest charge of 1.5%
3. **Short-Term Loan.** At the beginning of January, the company's bank will also give it a 6-month loan to be repaid in a lump sum at the end of June. Interest on this loan is 1% per month and is payable at the end of each month.

Assume the company earns 0.5% interest each month on cash held at the beginning of the month. Create a spreadsheet model the company can use to determine the least costly cash management plan (*i.e.*, minimal net financing costs) for this 6-month period. What is the optimal solution?

42. The XYZ.com Corporation is implementing a pension plan for its employees. The company intends to start funding the plan with a deposit of $50,000 on January 1, 2004. It plans to invest an additional $12,000 one year later, and continue making additional investments (increasing by $2,000 per year) on January 1 of each year from 2006 through 2018. To fund these payments, the company plans to purchase a number of bonds. Bond 1 costs $970 per unit and will pay a $65 coupon on January 1 of each year from 2005 through 2008 plus a final payment of $1065 on January 1, 2009. Bond 2 costs $980 and will pay a $73 coupon on January 1 of each year from 2005 through 2014 plus a final payment of $1073 on January 1, 2015. Bond 3 costs $1025 and will pay a $85 coupon on January 1 of each year from 2005 through 2017 plus a final payment of $1085 on January 1, 2018. The company's cash holdings earn an interest rate of 4.5%. Assume the company wants to purchase bonds on January 1, 2004 and can buy them in fractional units. How much should the company invest in the various bonds and cash account to fund this plan through January 1, 2018 in the least costly way?
    a. Create a spreadsheet model for this problem and solve it.
    b. What is the optimal solution?
43. A natural gas trading company wants to develop an optimal trading plan for the next 10 days. The following table summarizes the estimated prices (per thousand cubic feet (cf)) at which the company can buy and sell natural gas during this time. The company may buy gas at the "Ask" price and sell gas at the "Bid" price.

Day	Bid	Ask
1	$3.06	$3.22
2	$4.01	$4.10
3	$6.03	$6.13
4	$4.06	$4.19
5	$4.01	$4.05
6	$5.02	$5.12
7	$5.10	$5.28
8	$4.08	$4.23
9	$3.01	$3.15
10	$4.01	$4.18

The company currently has 150,000 cf of gas in storage and has a maximum storage capacity of 500,000 cf. To maintain the required pressure in the gas transmission pipeline system, the company can inject no more than 200,000 cf into the storage facility each day and can extract no more than 180,000 cf per day. Assume extractions occur in the morning and injections occur in the evening. The owner of the storage facility charges a storage fee of 5% of the market (bid) value of the average daily gas inventory. (The average daily inventory is computed as the average of each day's beginning and ending inventory.)

a. Create a spreadsheet model for this problem and solve it.
b. What is the optimal solution?
c. Assuming price forecasts for natural gas change on a daily basis, how would you suggest the company in this problem actually use your model?

44. The Embassy Lodge hotel chain wants to compare its brand efficiency to that of its major competitors using DEA. Embassy collected the following data reported in industry trade publications. Embassy views customers' perceptions of satisfaction and value (scored from 0 to 100 where 100 is best) to be outputs produced as a function of the following inputs: price, convenience, room comfort, climate control, service, and food quality. (All inputs are expressed on scales where less is better.)

Brand	Satisfaction	Value	Price	Convenience	Room Comfort	Climate Control	Service	Food Quality
Embassy Lodge	85	82	70.00	2.3	1.8	2.7	1.5	3.3
Sheritown Inn	96	93	70.00	1.5	1.1	0.2	0.5	0.5
Hynton Hotel	78	87	75.00	2.2	2.4	2.6	2.5	3.2
Vacation Inn	87	88	75.00	1.8	1.6	1.5	1.8	2.3
Merrylot	89	94	80.00	0.5	1.4	0.4	0.9	2.6
FairPrice Inn	93	93	80.00	1.3	0.9	0.2	0.6	2.8
Nights Inn	92	91	85.00	1.4	1.3	0.6	1.4	2.1
Western Hotels	97	92	90.00	0.3	1.7	1.7	1.7	1.8

a. Compute the DEA efficiency for each brand.
b. Which brands are efficient?
c. Is Embassy Lodge efficient? If not, what input and output values should they aspire to in order to become efficient?

45. Fidelity Savings & Loans (FS&L) operates a number of banking facilities throughout the Southeastern United States. The officers of FS&L wants to analyze the efficiency of the various branch offices using DEA. The following data has been selected to represent appropriate input and output measures of each banking facility.

Branch	R.O.A.	New Loans	Satisfaction	Labor Hrs.	Op. Costs
1	5.32	770	92	3.73	6.34
2	3.39	780	94	3.49	4.43
3	4.95	790	93	5.98	6.31
4	6.01	730	82	6.49	7.28
5	6.40	910	98	7.09	8.69
6	2.89	860	90	3.46	3.23
7	6.94	880	89	7.36	9.07
8	7.18	970	99	6.38	7.42
9	5.98	770	94	4.74	6.75
10	4.97	930	91	5.04	6.35

a. Identify the inputs and outputs for FS&L. Are they all measured on the appropriate scale for use with DEA?
b. Compute the DEA efficiency of each branch office.
c. Which offices are DEA efficient?
d. What input and output levels should branch 5 aspire to in order to become efficient?

CASE 3.1: FOREIGN EXCHANGE TRADING AT BALDWIN ENTERPRISES

Baldwin Enterprises is a large manufacturing company with operations and sales divisions located in the United States and several other countries. The CFO of the organization, Wes Hamrick, is concerned about the amount of money Baldwin has been paying in transaction costs in the foreign exchange markets and has asked you to help optimize Baldwin's foreign exchange treasury functions.

With operations in several countries, Baldwin maintains cash assets in several different currencies: U.S. dollars (USD), the European Union's euro (EUR), Great Britian's pound (GBP), Hong Kong dollars (HKD), and Japanese yen (JPY). To meet the different cash flow requirements associated with their operations around the world, Baldwin must often move funds from one location (and currency) to another. For instance, to pay an unexpected maintenance expense at their facility in Japan, Baldwin may need to convert some of their holdings in U.S. dollars to Japanese yen.

The foreign exchange (FX) market is a network of financial institutions and brokers in which individuals, businesses, banks, and governments buy and sell the currencies of different countries. They do so in order to finance international trade, invest or do business abroad, or speculate on currency price changes. The FX market operates 24-hours a day and represents the largest and most liquid marketplace in the global economy. On average, the equivalent of about $1.5 trillion in different currencies is traded daily in the FX market around the world. The liquidity of the market provides businesses with access to international markets for goods and services by providing foreign currency necessary for transactions worldwide (see: http://www.ny.frb.org/fxc).

The FX market operates in much the same way as a stock or commodity market where there is a bid price and ask price for each commodity (or, in this case, currency). A bid price is the price at with the market is willing to buy a particular currency and the ask price is the price at which the market is willing to sell a currency. The ask prices are typically slightly higher than the bid prices for the same currency—representing the transaction cost or the profit earned by the organizations that keep the market liquid.

The following table summarizes the current FX rates for the currencies Baldwin currently holds. The entries in this table represent the conversion rates from the row currencies to the column currencies.

Convert/To	USD	EUR	GBP	HKD	JPY
USD	1	1.01864	0.6409	7.7985	118.55
EUR	0.9724	1	0.6295	7.6552	116.41
GBP	1.5593	1.5881	1	12.154	184.97
HKD	0.12812	0.1304	0.0821	1	15.1005
JPY	0.008435	0.00856	0.0054	0.0658	1

For example, the table indicates that one British pound (GBP) can be exchanged (or sold) for 1.5593 U.S. dollars (USD). Thus, $1.5593 is the bid price, in U.S. dollars, for one British pound. Alternatively, the table indicates one U.S. dollar (USD) can be exchanged (sold) for 0.6409 British pounds (GBP). So, it takes about 1.5603 U.S. dollars (or 1/0.6409) to buy one British pound (or the ask price, in U.S. dollars, for one British pound is roughly $1.5603).

Notice that if you took one British pound, converted it to 1.5593 U.S. dollars, and then converted those 1.5593 dollars back to British pounds, you would wind up with only 0.999355 British pounds (*i.e.*, $1 \times 1.5593 \times 0.6409 = 0.999355$). The money you lose in this exchange is the transaction cost.

Baldwin's current portfolio of cash holdings includes 2 million USD, 5 million EUR, 1 million GBP, 3 million HKD, and 30 million JPY. This portfolio is equivalent to $9,058,710 USD under the current exchange rates (given above). Wes has asked you to design a currency trading plan that would increase Baldwin's euro and yen holdings to 8 million EUR and 54 JPY, respectively, while maintaining the equivalent of at least $250,000 USD in each currency. Baldwin measures transaction costs as the change in the USD equivalent value of the portfolio.

1. Create a spreadsheet model for this problem and solve it.
2. What is the optimal trading plan?
3. What is the optimal transaction cost (in equivalent USD)?
4. Suppose another executive thinks that holding $250,000 USD in each currency is excessive and wants to lower the amount to $50,000 USD in each currency. Does this help to lower the transaction cost? Why or why not?
5. Suppose the exchange rate for converting USD to GBP increased from 0.6409 to 0.6414. What happens to the optimal solution in this case?

CASE 3.2: THE WOLVERINE RETIREMENT FUND

Kelly Jones is a financial analyst for Wolverine Manufacturing, a company that produces engine bearings for the automotive industry. Wolverine is in the process of hammering out a new labor agreement with its unionized workforce. One of the major concerns of the labor union is the funding of Wolverine's retirement plan for their hourly employees. The union believes the company has not been contributing enough money to this fund to cover the benefits it will need to pay to retiring employees. Because of this, the union wants the company to contribute approximately $1.5 million dollars in additional money to this fund over the next 20 years. These extra contributions would begin with an extra payment of $20,000 at the end of one year with annual payments increasing by 12.35% per year for the next 19 years.

The union has asked the company to set up a sinking fund to cover the extra annual payments to the retirement fund. The Wolverines' Chief Financial Officer and the union's chief negotiator have agreed that AAA rated bonds recently issued by three different companies may be used to establish this fund. The following table summarizes the provisions of these bonds.

Company	Maturity	Coupon Payment	Price	Par Value
AC&C	15 years	$80	$847.88	$1,000
IBN	10 years	$90	$938.55	$1,000
MicroHard	20 years	$85	$872.30	$1,000

According to this table, Wolverine may buy bonds issued by AC&C for $847.88 per bond. Each AC&C bond will pay the bondholder $80 per year for the next 15 years, plus an extra payment of $1,000 (the par value) in the fifteenth year. Similar interpretations apply to the information for the IBN and MicroHard bonds. A money market fund yielding 5% may be used to hold any coupon payments that are not needed to meet the company's required retirement fund payment in any given year.

Wolverine's CFO has asked Kelly to determine how much money the company would have to invest and which bonds the company should buy in order to meet the labor union's demands.

1. If you were Kelly, what would you tell the CFO?
2. Suppose the union insists on including one of the following stipulations in the agreement:
   a. No more than half of the total number of bonds purchased may be purchased from a single company.
   b. At least 10% of the total number of bonds must be purchased from each of the companies. Which stipulation should Wolverine agree to?

CASE 3.3: SAVING THE MANATEES

"So how am I going to spend this money," thought Tom Wieboldt as he sat staring at the pictures and posters of manatees around his office. An avid environmentalist, Tom is the president of "Friends of the Manatees"—a nonprofit organization trying to help pass legislation to protect manatees.

Manatees are large, gray-brown aquatic mammals with bodies that taper to a flat, paddle-shaped tail. These gentle and slow-moving creatures grow to an average adult length of 10 feet and weigh an average of 1,000 pounds. Manatees are found in shallow, slow-moving rivers, estuaries, saltwater bays, canals, and coastal areas. In the United States, manatees are concentrated in Florida in the winter, but can be found in summer months as far west as Alabama and as far north as Virginia and the Carolinas. They have no natural enemies, but loss of habitat is the most serious threat facing manatees today. Most human-related manatee deaths occur from collisions with motor boats.

Tom's organization has been supporting a bill before the Florida legislature to restrict the use of motor boats in areas known to be inhabited by manatees. This bill is scheduled to come up for a vote in the legislature. Tom recently received a phone call from a national environmental protection organization indicating that they are going to donate $300,000 to Friends of the Manatees to help increase public awareness about the plight of the manatees and to encourage voters to urge their representatives in the state legislature to vote for this bill. Tom intends to use this money to purchase various types of advertising media to "get the message out" during the four weeks immediately preceding the vote.

Tom is considering several different advertising alternatives: newspapers, TV, radio, billboards, and magazines. A marketing consultant provided Tom with the following data on the costs and effectiveness of the various types of media being considered.

Advertising Medium	Unit Cost	Unit Impact Rating
Half-page, Daily paper	$800	55
Full-page, Daily paper	$1,400	75
Half-page, Sunday paper	$1,200	65
Full-page, Sunday paper	$1,800	80
Daytime TV spot	$2,500	85
Evening TV spot	$3,500	100
Highway Billboards	$750	35
15-second Radio spot	$150	45
30-second Radio spot	$300	55
Half-page, magazine	$500	50
Full-page, magazine	$900	60

According to the marketing consultant, the most effective type of advertising for this type of problem would be short TV ads during the evening prime-time hours. Thus, this type of advertising was given a "unit impact rating" of 100. The other types of advertising were then given assigned unit impact ratings that reflect their expected effectiveness relative to an evening TV ad. For instance, a half-page magazine ad is expected to be have half the effectiveness of an evening TV ad and is therefore given an impact rating of 50.

Tom wants to allocate the $300,000 to these different advertising alternatives in a way that will maximize the impact achieved. However, he realizes it is important to spread his message via several different advertising channels as not everyone listens to the radio and not everyone watches TV in the evenings.

The two most widely read newspapers in the state of Florida are the *Orlando Sentinel* and the *Miami Herald.* During the four weeks prior to the vote, Tom wants to have half-page ads in the daily (Monday–Saturday) versions of each of these papers at least three times per week. He also wants to have one full-page ad in the daily version of each paper the week before the vote and he is willing to run more full-page ads if this would be helpful. He also wants to run full-page ads in the Sunday editions of each paper the Sunday before the vote. Tom never wants to run a full-page and half-page ad in a paper on the same day. So, the maximum number of full and half-page ads that can be run in the daily papers should be 48 (*i.e.,* 4 weeks × 6 days per week × 2 papers = 48). Similarly, the maximum number of full and half-page ads that can be run in the Sunday papers is eight.

Tom wants to have at least one and no more than three daytime TV ads every day during the four-week period. He also wants to have at least one ad on TV every night but no more than two per night.

There are 10 billboard locations throughout the state that are available for use during the four weeks before the vote. Tom definitely wants to have at least one billboard in each of the cities of Orlando, Tampa, and Miami.

Tom believes that the ability to show pictures of the cute, pudgy, lovable manatees in the print media offers a distinct advantage over radio ads. However, the radio ads are relatively inexpensive and may reach some people that the other ads will not reach. Thus, Tom wants to have at least two 15-second and at least two 30-second ads on radio each day. However, he wants to limit the number of radio ads to five 15-second ad and five 30-second ads per day.

There are three different weekly magazines in which Tom can run ads. Tom wants to run full-page ads in each of the magazines at some point during the four-week period. However, he never wants to run full and half-page ads in the same magazine in a given week. Thus, the total number of full and half-page magazine ads selected should not exceed 12 (*i.e.*, 4 weeks × 3 magazines × 1 ad per magazine per week = 12 ads).

Although Tom has some ideas about the minimum and maximum number of ads to run in the various types of media, he's not sure how much money this will take. And if he can afford to meet all the minimums, he's really confused about the best way to spend the remaining funds. So again Tom asks himself, "How am I going to spend this money?"

1. Create a spreadsheet model for this problem and solve it. What is the optimal solution?
2. Of the constraints Tom placed on this problem, which are "binding" or preventing the objective function from being improved further?
3. Suppose Tom was willing to increase the allowable number of evening TV ads. How much would this improve the solution?
4. Suppose Tom was willing to double the allowable number of radio ads aired each day. How much would this improve the solution?

CASE 3.4: REMOVING SNOW IN MONTREAL

Based on: James Campbell and Andre Langevin. "The Snow Disposal Assignment Problem." *Journal of the Operational Research Society*, 1995, pp. 919–929.

Snow removal and disposal are important and expensive activities in Montreal and many northern cities. Although snow can be cleared from streets and sidewalks by plowing and shoveling, in prolonged subfreezing temperatures, the resulting banks of accumulated snow can impede pedestrian and vehicular traffic and must be removed.

To allow timely removal and disposal of snow, a city is divided up into several sectors and snow removal operations are carried out concurrently in each sector. In Montreal, accumulated snow is loaded into trucks and hauled away to disposal sites (*e.g.*, rivers, quarries, sewer chutes, surface holding areas). The different types of disposal sites can accommodate different amounts of snow due to either the physical size of the disposal facility or environmental restrictions on the amount of snow (often contaminated by salt and de-icing chemicals) that can be dumped into rivers. The annual capacities for five different snow disposal sites are given below (in 1,000s of cubic meters).

	Disposal Site				
	1	**2**	**3**	**4**	**5**
Capacity	350	250	500	400	200

The cost of removing and disposing of snow depends mainly on the distance it must be trucked. For planning purposes, the City of Montreal uses the straight-line distance between the center of each sector to each of the various disposal sites as an approximation of the cost involved in transporting snow between these locations. The following table summarizes these distances (in kilometers) for ten sectors in the city.

	Disposal Site				
Sector	**1**	**2**	**3**	**4**	**5**
1	3.4	1.4	4.9	7.4	9.3
2	2.4	2.1	8.3	9.1	8.8
3	1.4	2.9	3.7	9.4	8.6
4	2.6	3.6	4.5	8.2	8.9
5	1.5	3.1	2.1	7.9	8.8
6	4.2	4.9	6.5	7.7	6.1
7	4.8	6.2	9.9	6.2	5.7
8	5.4	6	5.2	7.6	4.9
9	3.1	4.1	6.6	7.5	7.2
10	3.2	6.5	7.1	6	8.3

Using historical snow fall data, the city is able to estimate the annual volume of snow requiring removal in each sector as four times the length of streets in the sectors in meters (*i.e.*, it is assumed each linear meter of street generates 4 cubic meters of snow to remove over an entire year). The following table estimates the snow removal requirements (in 1000s of cubic meters) for each sector in the coming year.

Estimated Annual Snow Removal Requirements

1	2	3	4	5	6	7	8	9	10
153	152	154	138	127	129	111	110	130	135

1. Create a spreadsheet model for this problem and solve it. What is the optimal solution?
2. On average, how many kilometers must snow be trucked for disposal?

Chapter 4

Sensitivity Analysis and the Simplex Method

4.0 INTRODUCTION

In chapters 2 and 3, we studied how to formulate and solve LP models for a variety of decision problems. However, formulating and solving an LP model does not necessarily mean that the original decision problem has been solved. After solving a model, a number of questions often arise about the optimal solution to the LP model. In particular, we might be interested in how sensitive the optimal solution is to changes in various coefficients of the LP model.

Businesses rarely know with certainty what costs will be incurred or the exact amount of resources that will be consumed or available in a given situation or time period. Thus, optimal solutions obtained using models that assume all relevant factors are known with certainty might be viewed with skepticism by management. Sensitivity analysis can help overcome this skepticism and provide a better picture of how the solution to a problem will change if different factors in the model change. Sensitivity analysis also can help answer a number of practical managerial questions that might arise about the solution to an LP problem.

4.1 THE PURPOSE OF SENSITIVITY ANALYSIS

As noted in chapter 2, any problem that can be stated in the following form is an LP problem:

$$
\begin{array}{ll}
\text{MAX (or MIN):} & c_1X_1 + c_2X_2 + \ldots + c_nX_n \\
\text{Subject to:} & a_{11}X_1 + a_{12}X_2 + \ldots + a_{1n}X_n \le b_1 \\
& \vdots \\
& a_{k1}X_1 + a_{k2}X_2 + \ldots + a_{kn}X_n \ge b_k \\
& \vdots \\
& a_{m1}X_1 + a_{m2}X_2 + \ldots + a_{mn}X_n = b_m
\end{array}
$$

All the coefficients in this model (the c_j, a_{ij}, and b_i) represent numeric constants. So, when we formulate and solve an LP problem, we implicitly assume that we can specify the exact values for these coefficients. However, in the real world, these coefficients might change from day to day or minute to minute. For example, the price a company charges for its products can change on a daily, weekly, or monthly basis. Similarly, if a skilled machinist calls in sick, a manufacturer might have less capacity to produce items on a given machine than was originally planned.

Realizing that such uncertainties exist, a manager should consider how sensitive an LP model's solution is to changes or estimation errors that might occur in: (1) the objective function coefficients (the c_j), (2) the constraint coefficients (the a_{ij}), and (3) the RHS values for the constraints (the b_i). A manager also might ask a number of "What if?" questions about these values. For example, what if the cost of a product increases by 7%? What if a reduction in setup time allows for additional capacity on a given machine? What if a worker's suggestion results in a product requiring only two hours of labor rather than three? Sensitivity analysis addresses these issues by assessing the sensitivity of the solution to uncertainty or estimation errors in the model coefficients, as well as the solution's sensitivity to changes in model coefficients that might occur because of human intervention.

4.2 APPROACHES TO SENSITIVITY ANALYSIS

You can perform sensitivity analysis on an LP model in a number of ways. If you want to determine the effect of some change in the model, the most direct approach is to simply change the model and re-solve it. This approach is suitable if the model does not take an excessive amount of time to change or solve. In addition, if you are interested in studying the consequences of *simultaneously* changing several coefficients in the model, this might be the only practical approach to sensitivity analysis.

Solver also provides some sensitivity information after solving an LP problem. As mentioned in chapter 3, one of the benefits of using the simplex method to solve LP problems is its speed—it is considerably faster than the other optimization techniques offered by Solver. However, another advantage of using the simplex method is that it provides more sensitivity analysis information than the other techniques. In particular, the simplex method provides us with information about:

- The range of values the objective function coefficients can assume without changing the optimal solution
- The impact on the optimal objective function value of increases or decreases in the availability of various constrained resources
- The impact on the optimal objective function value of forcing changes in the values of certain decision variables away from their optimal values

- The impact that changes in constraint coefficients will have on the optimal solution to the problem

4.3 AN EXAMPLE PROBLEM

We will again use the Blue Ridge Hot Tubs problem to illustrate the types of sensitivity analysis information available using Solver. The LP formulation of the problem is repeated here, where X_1 represents the number of Aqua-Spas and X_2 represents the number of Hydro-Luxes to be produced:

MAX:	$350X_1 + 300X_2$	} profit
Subject to:	$1X_1 + 1X_2 \leq 200$	} pump constraint
	$9X_1 + 6X_2 \leq 1{,}566$	} labor constraint
	$12X_1 + 16X_2 \leq 2{,}880$	} tubing constraint
	$X_1, X_2 \geq 0$	} nonnegativity conditions

This model is implemented in the spreadsheet shown in Figure 4.1. (See chapter 3 for details on the procedure used to create and solve this spreadsheet model.)

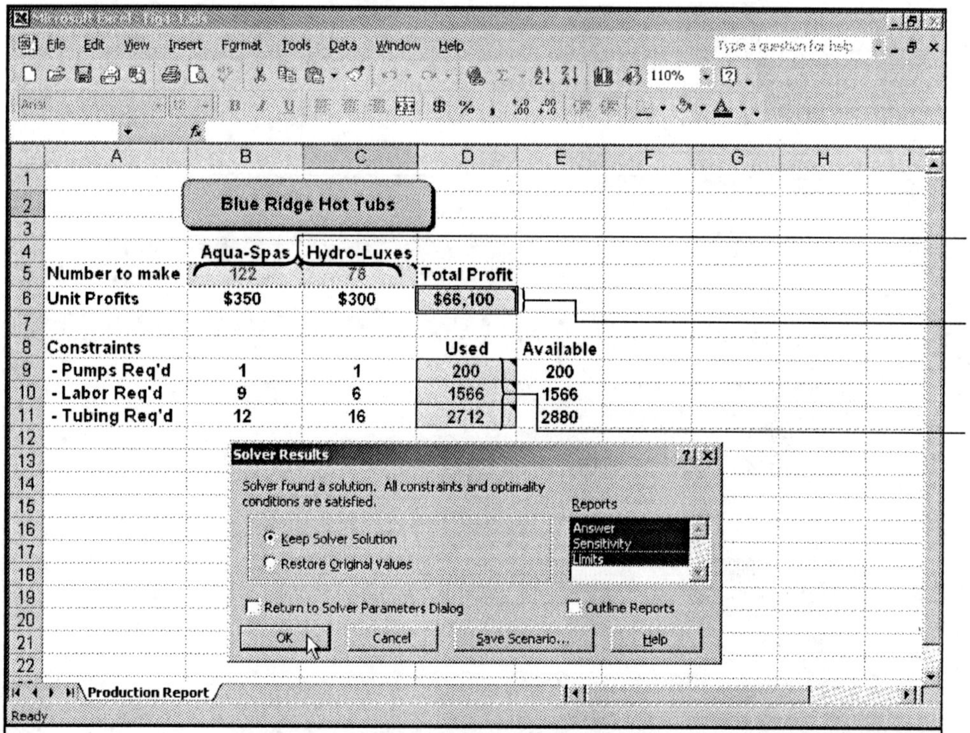

FIGURE 4.1
Spreadsheet model for the Blue Ridge Hot Tubs product mix problem

Key Cell Formulas

Cell	Formula	Copied to
D6	=SUMPRODUCT(B6:C6,$B$5:$C$5)	D9:D11

After solving the LP model, Solver displays the Solver Results dialog box, shown in Figure 4.1. This dialog box provides three report options: Answer, Sensitivity, and Limits. You can select any of these reports after a model has been solved. To select all three reports, highlight the reports, and then click OK. To access each report, click the appropriate tab at the bottom of the screen.

4.4 THE ANSWER REPORT

Figure 4.2 shows the Answer Report for the Blue Ridge Hot Tubs problem. This report summarizes the solution to the problem, and is fairly self-explanatory. The first section of the report summarizes the original and final (optimal) value of the set cell. The next section summarizes the original and final (optimal) values of the adjustable (or changing) cells representing the decision variables.

The final section of this report provides information about the constraints. In particular, the Cell Value column shows the final (optimal) value assumed by each constraint cell. Note that these values correspond to the final value assumed by the LHS formula of each constraint. The Formula column indicates the upper or lower bounds that apply to each constraint cell. The Status column indicates which constraints are binding and which are nonbinding. A constraint is **binding** if it is satisfied as a strict equality in the optimal solution; otherwise, it is **nonbinding**. Notice that the constraints for the number of pumps and amount of labor used are both binding, meaning that *all* the available pumps and labor hours will be used if this solution is implemented. Therefore, these constraints are preventing Blue Ridge Hot Tubs from achieving a higher level of profit.

FIGURE 4.2
Answer Report for the hot tub problem

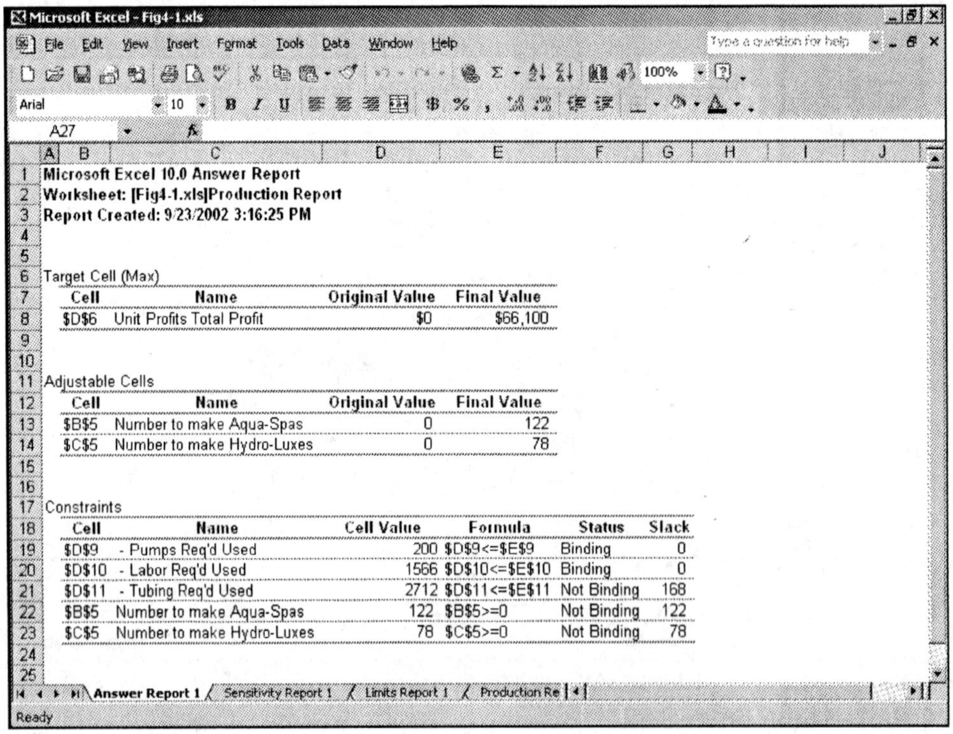
Microsoft Excel 10.0 Answer Report
Worksheet: [Fig4-1.xls]Production Report
Report Created: 9/23/2002 3:16:25 PM

Target Cell (Max)

Cell	Name	Original Value	Final Value
$D$6	Unit Profits Total Profit	$0	$66,100

Adjustable Cells

Cell	Name	Original Value	Final Value
$B$5	Number to make Aqua-Spas	0	122
$C$5	Number to make Hydro-Luxes	0	78

Constraints

Cell	Name	Cell Value	Formula	Status	Slack
$D$9	- Pumps Req'd Used	200	$D$9<=$E$9	Binding	0
$D$10	- Labor Req'd Used	1566	$D$10<=$E$10	Binding	0
$D$11	- Tubing Req'd Used	2712	$D$11<=$E$11	Not Binding	168
$B$5	Number to make Aqua-Spas	122	$B$5>=0	Not Binding	122
$C$5	Number to make Hydro-Luxes	78	$C$5>=0	Not Binding	78

Finally, the values in the Slack column indicate the difference between the LHS and RHS of each constraint. By definition, binding constraints have zero slack and nonbinding constraints have some positive level of slack. The values in the Slack column indicate that if this solution is implemented, all the available pumps and labor hours will be used, but 168 feet of tubing will be left over. The slack values for the nonnegativity conditions indicate the amounts by which the decision variables exceed their respective lowers bounds of zero.

The Answer Report does not provide any information that could not be derived from the solution shown in the spreadsheet model. However, the format of this report gives a convenient summary of the solution that can be incorporated easily into a word-processing document as part of a written report to management.

Report Headings

When creating the reports described in this chapter, Solver will try to use various text entries from the original spreadsheet to generate meaningful headings and labels in the reports. Given the various ways in which a model can be implemented, Solver might not always produce meaningful headings. However, you can change any text entry to make the report more meaningful or descriptive.

4.5 THE SENSITIVITY REPORT

Figure 4.3 shows the Sensitivity Report for the Blue Ridge Hot Tubs problem. This report summarizes information about the variable cells and constraints for our model. This information is useful in evaluating how sensitive the optimal solution is to changes in various coefficients in the model.

4.5.1 Changes in the Objective Function Coefficients

Chapter 2 introduced the level-curve approach to solving a graphical LP problem and showed how to use this approach to solve the Blue Ridge Hot Tubs problem. This graphical solution is repeated in Figure 4.4.

The slope of the original level curve in Figure 4.4 is determined by the coefficients in the objective function of the model (the values 350 and 300). In Figure 4.4 on page 149, we can see that if the slope of the level curve were different, the corner point represented by $X_1 = 0$, $X_2 = 180$ would be the optimal solution. Of course, the only way to change the level curve for the objective function is to change the coefficients in the objective function. So, if the objective function coefficients are at all uncertain, we might be interested in determining how much these values could change before the optimal solution would change.

For example, if the owner of Blue Ridge Hot Tubs does not have complete control over the costs of producing hot tubs (which is likely because he purchases the fiberglass hot tub shells from another company), the profit figures in the objective function of our LP model might not be the exact profits earned on hot tubs

FIGURE 4.3
Sensitivity Report for the hot tub problem

Microsoft Excel - Fig4-1.xls

Microsoft Excel 10.0 Sensitivity Report
Worksheet: [Fig4-1.xls]Production Report
Report Created: 9/23/2002 3:16:25 PM

Adjustable Cells

Cell	Name	Final Value	Reduced Cost	Objective Coefficient	Allowable Increase	Allowable Decrease
$B$5	Number to make Aqua-Spas	122	0.00	350	100	50
$C$5	Number to make Hydro-Luxes	78	0.00	300	50	66.66667

Constraints

Cell	Name	Final Value	Shadow Price	Constraint R.H. Side	Allowable Increase	Allowable Decrease
$D$9	- Pumps Req'd Used	200	200.00	200	7	26
$D$10	- Labor Req'd Used	1566	16.67	1566	234	126
$D$11	- Tubing Req'd Used	2712	0.00	2880	1E+30	168

Answer Report 1 | Sensitivity Report 1 | Limits Report 1 | Production Re

produced in the future. So before the manager decides to produce 122 Aqua-Spas and 78 Hydro-Luxes, he might want to determine how sensitive this solution is to the profit figures in the objective. That is, the manager might want to determine how much the profit figures could change before the optimal solution of $X_1 = 122$, $X_2 = 78$ would change. This information is provided in the Sensitivity Report shown in Figure 4.3.

The original objective function coefficients associated with the variable cells are listed in the Objective Coefficient column in Figure 4.3. The next two columns show the allowable increases and decreases in these values. For example, the objective function value associated with Aqua-Spas (or variable X_1) can increase by as much as $100 or decrease by as much as $50 without changing the optimal

Software Note

When setting up a spreadsheet model for an LP problem for which you intend to generate a sensitivity report, it is a good idea to make sure the cells corresponding to RHS values of constraints contain constants or formulas that do not involve the decision variables. Thus, any RHS formula related directly or indirectly to the decision variables should be moved algebraically to the left-hand side of the constraint before implementing your model. This will help to reduce problems in interpreting Solver's sensitivity report.

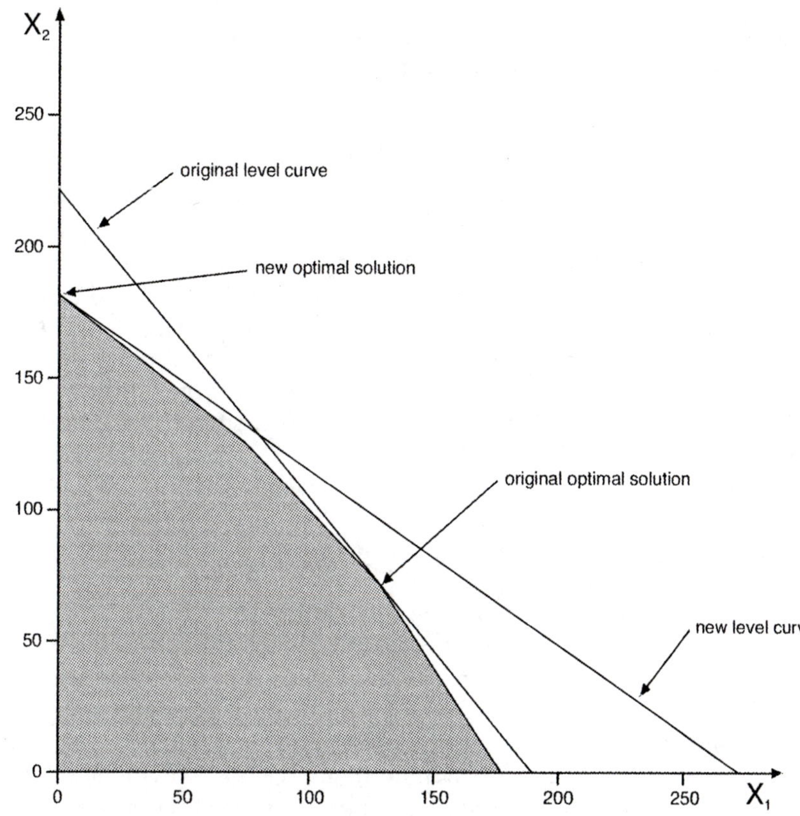

FIGURE 4.4
How changes in the objective function coefficients can change the slope of the level curve and the optimal solution

solution, assuming all other coefficients remain constant. (You can verify this by changing the profit coefficient for Aqua-Spas to any value in the range from $300 to $450 and re-solving the model.) Similarly, the objective function value associated with Hydro-Luxes (or variable X_2) can increase by $50 or decrease by approximately $66.67 without changing the optimal values of the decision variables, assuming all other coefficients remain constant. (Again, you can verify this by re-solving the model with different profit values for Hydro-Luxes.)

4.5.2 A Note About Constancy

The phrase "assuming all other coefficients remain constant" in the previous paragraph underscores the fact that the allowable increases and decreases shown in the Sensitivity Report apply only if *all* the other coefficients in the LP model do not change. The objective coefficient for Aqua-Spas can assume any value from $300 to $450 without changing the optimal solution—*but this is guaranteed to be true only if all the other coefficients in the model remain constant (including the objective function coefficient for X_2).* Similarly, the objective function coefficient for X_2 can assume any value between $233.33 and $350 without changing the optimal solution—*but this is guaranteed to be true only if all the other coefficients in the model remain constant (including the objective function coefficient for X_1).* Later in this chapter, you will see how to determine whether the current solution remains optimal if changes are made in two or more objective coefficients at the same time.

4.5.3 Alternate Optimal Solutions

Sometimes, the allowable increase or allowable decrease for the objective function coefficient for one or more variables will equal zero. In the absence of degeneracy (to be described later), this indicates that alternate optimal solutions exist. You can usually get Solver to produce an alternate optimal solution (when they exist) by: (1) adding a constraint to your model that holds the objective function at the current optimal value, and then (2) attempting to maximize or minimize the value of one of the decision variables that had an objective function coefficient with an allowable increase or decrease of zero. This approach sometimes involves some "trial and error" in step 2, but should cause Solver to produce an alternate optimal solution to your problem.

4.5.4 Changes in the RHS Values

As noted earlier, constraints that have zero slack in the optimal solution to an LP problem are called binding constraints. Binding constraints prevent us from further improving (that is, maximizing or minimizing) the objective function. For example, the Answer Report in Figure 4.2 indicates that the constraints for the number of pumps and hours of labor available are binding, whereas the constraint on the amount of tubing available is nonbinding. This is also evident in Figure 4.3 by comparing the Final Value column with the Constraint R.H. Side column. The values in the Final Value column represent the LHS values of each constraint at the optimal solution. A constraint is binding if its Final Value is equal to its Constraint R.H. Side value.

After solving an LP problem, you might want to determine how much better or worse the solution would be if we had more or less of a given resource. For example, Howie Jones might wonder how much more profit could be earned if additional pumps or labor hours were available. The Shadow Price column in Figure 4.3 provides the answers to such questions.

The **shadow price** for a constraint indicates the amount by which the objective function value changes given a unit *increase* in the RHS value of the constraint, assuming all other coefficients remain constant. If a shadow price is positive, a unit increase in the RHS value of the associated constraint results in an increase in the optimal objective function value. If a shadow price is negative, a unit increase in the RHS value of the associated constraint results in a decrease in the optimal objective function value. To analyze the effects of decreases in the RHS values, you reverse the sign on the shadow price. That is, the negated shadow price for a constraint indicates the amount by which the optimal objective function value changes given a unit *decrease* in the RHS value of the constraint, assuming all other coefficients remain constant. The shadow price values apply provided that the increase or decrease in the RHS value falls within the allowable increase or allowable decrease limits in the Sensitivity Report for each constraint.

For example, Figure 4.3 indicates that the shadow price for the labor constraint is 16.67. Therefore, if the number of available labor hours increased by any amount in the range from 0 to 234 hours, the optimal objective function value changes (increases) by \$16.67 for each additional labor hour. If the number of available labor hours decreased by any amount in the range from 0 to 126 hours, the optimal objective function value changes (decreases) by –\$16.67 for each lost labor hour. A similar interpretation holds for the shadow price for the constraint on the number of pumps. (It is coincidental that the shadow price for the pump constraint (200) is the same as that constraint's RHS and Final Values.)

4.5.5 Shadow Prices for Nonbinding Constraints

Now, let's consider the shadow price for the nonbinding tubing constraint. The tubing constraint has a shadow price of zero with an allowable increase of infinity and an allowable decrease of 168. Therefore, if the RHS value for the tubing constraint increases by *any* amount, the objective function value does not change (or changes by zero). This result is not surprising. Because the optimal solution to this problem leaves 168 feet of tubing unused, *additional* tubing will not produce a better solution. Furthermore, because the optimal solution includes 168 feet of unused tubing, we can reduce the RHS value of this constraint by 168 without affecting the optimal solution.

As this example illustrates, the shadow price of a nonbinding constraint is always zero. There is always some amount by which the RHS value of a nonbinding constraint can be changed without affecting the optimal solution.

4.5.6 A Note About Shadow Prices

One important point needs to be made concerning shadow prices. To illustrate this point, let's suppose that the RHS value of the labor constraint for our example problem increases by 162 hours (from 1,566 to 1,728) due to the addition of new workers. Because this increase is within the allowable increase listed for the labor constraint, you might expect that the optimal objective function value would increase by $\$16.67 \times 162 = \$2{,}700$. That is, the new optimal objective function value would be approximately \$68,800 ($\$66{,}100 + \$16.67 \times 162 = \$68{,}800$). Figure 4.5 shows the re-solved model after increasing the RHS value for the labor constraint by 162 labor hours to 1,728.

In Figure 4.5, the new optimal objective function value is \$68,800, as expected. But this solution involves producing 176 Aqua-Spas and 24 Hydro-Luxes. That is, the optimal solution to the revised problem is *different* from the solution to the original problem shown in Figure 4.1. This is not surprising because changing the RHS of a constraint also changes the feasible region for the problem. The effect of increasing the RHS of the labor constraint is summarized graphically in Figure 4.6 on page 153.

So, although shadow prices indicate how the objective function value changes if a given RHS value changes, they *do not* tell you which values the decision variables need to assume in order to achieve this new objective function value. Determining the new optimal values for the decision variables requires that you make the appropriate changes in the RHS value and re-solve the model.

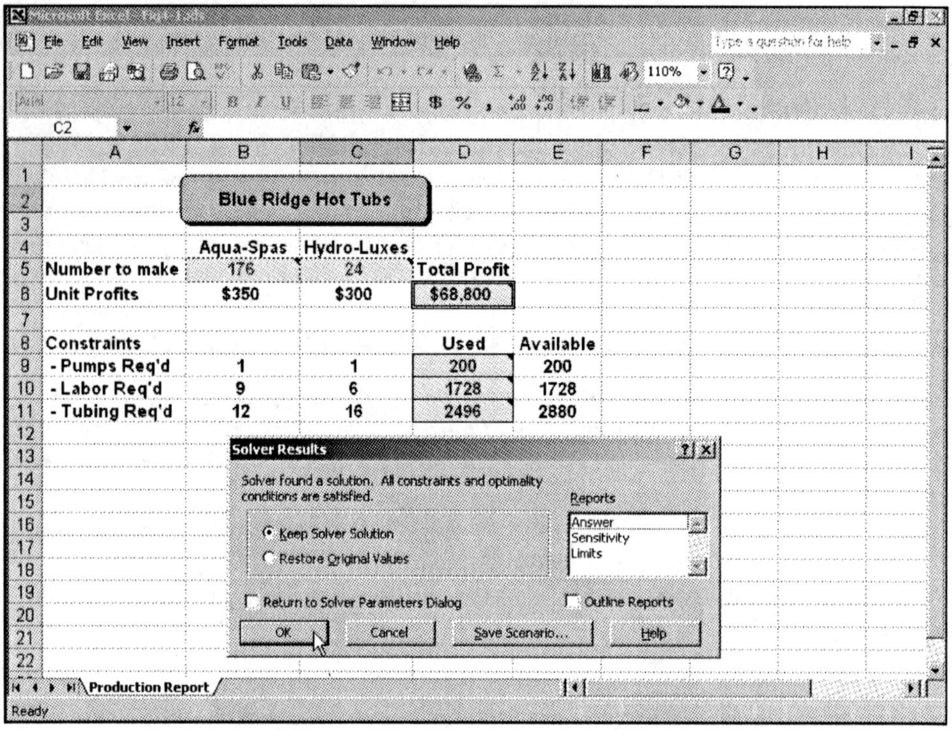

FIGURE 4.5
Solution to the revised hot tub problem with 162 additional labor hours

Another Interpretation of Shadow Prices

Unfortunately, there is no one universally accepted way of reporting shadow prices for constraints. In some software packages, the signs of the shadow prices do not conform to the convention used by Solver. Regardless of which software package you use, there is another way to look at shadow prices that should always lead to a proper interpretation. The absolute value of the shadow price always indicates the amount by which the objective function will be *improved* if the corresponding constraint is *loosened.* A less than or equal to constraint is loosened by *increasing* its RHS value, whereas a greater than or equal to constraint is loosened by *decreasing* its RHS value. (The absolute value of the shadow price can also be interpreted as the amount by which the objective will be made *worse* if the corresponding constraint is *tightened.*)

4.5.7 Shadow Prices and the Value of Additional Resources

In the previous example, an additional 162 hours of labor allowed us to increase profits by $2,700. A question might then arise as to how much we should be willing to pay to acquire these additional 162 hours of labor. The answer to this question is, "It depends. . . ."

If labor is a *variable* cost that was subtracted (along with other variable costs) from the selling price of the hot tubs to determine the marginal profits associated with each type of tub, we should be willing to pay up to $2,700 *above and beyond* what we would ordinarily pay to acquire 162 hours of labor. In this case, notice that both the original and revised profit figures of $66,100 and $68,800, respectively, represent the profit earned *after* the normal labor charge has been paid. Therefore, we could pay a premium of up to $2,700 to acquire the additional 162 hours of labor (or an extra $16.67 per additional labor hour) and still earn at least as much profit as we would have without the additional 162 hours of labor. Thus, if the normal labor rate is $12 per hour, we could pay up to $28.67 per hour to acquire each of the additional 162 hours of labor.

On the other hand, if labor is a sunk cost, which must be paid regardless of how many hot tubs are produced, it would not (or should not) have been subtracted from the selling price of the hot tubs in determining the marginal profit coefficients for each tub produced. In this case, we should be willing to pay a maximum of $16.67 per hour to acquire each of the additional 162 hours of labor.

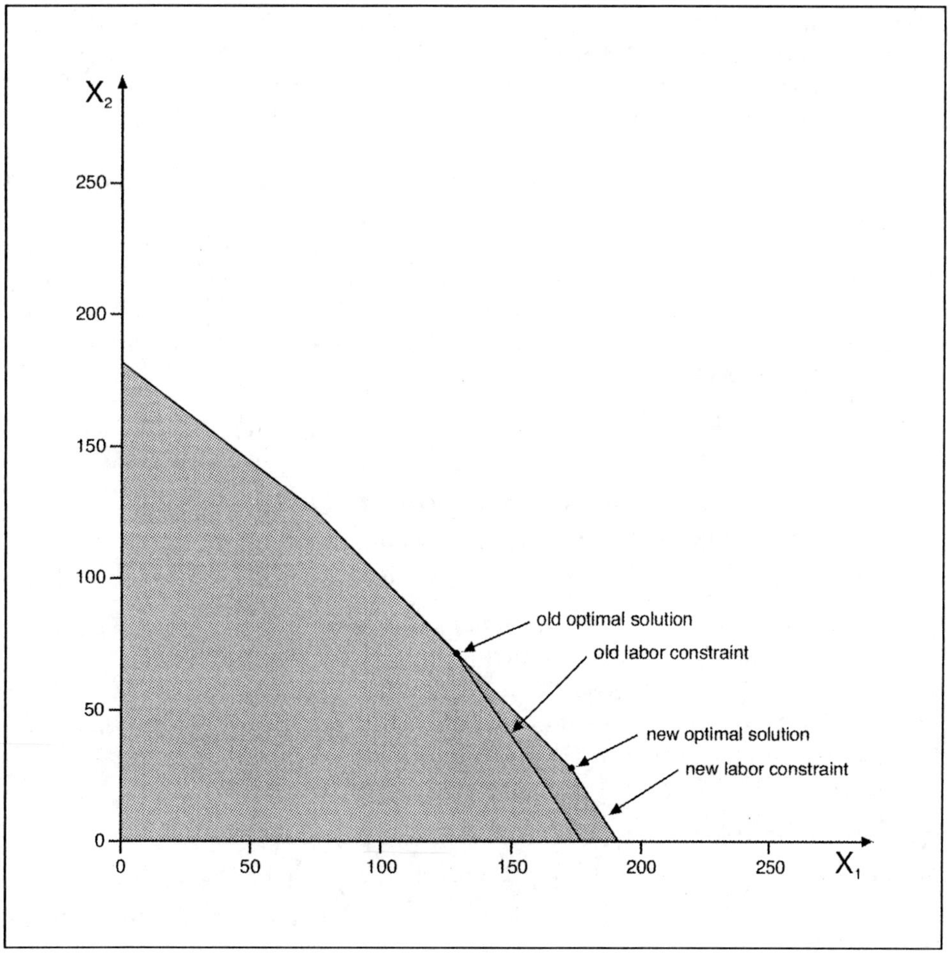

FIGURE 4.6
How changes in the RHS value of a constraint can change the feasible region and optimal solution

4.5.8 Other Uses of Shadow Prices

Because shadow prices represent the marginal values of the resources in an LP problem, they can help us answer a number of other managerial questions that might arise. For example, suppose Blue Ridge Hot Tubs is considering introducing a new model of hot tub called the Typhoon-Lagoon. Suppose that each unit of this new model requires 1 pump, 8 hours of labor, and 13 feet of tubing, and can be sold to generate a marginal profit of $320. Would production of this new model be profitable?

Because Blue Ridge Hot Tubs has limited resources, the production of any Typhoon-Lagoons would consume some of the resources currently devoted to the production of Aqua-Spas and Hydro-Luxes. So, producing Typhoon-Lagoons will reduce the number of pumps, labor hours, and tubing available for producing the other types of hot tubs. The shadow prices in Figure 4.3 indicate that each pump taken away from production of the current products will reduce profits by $200. Similarly, each labor hour taken away from the production of the current products will reduce profits by $16.67. The shadow price for the tubing constraint indicates that the supply of tubing can be reduced without adversely affecting profits.

Because each Typhoon-Lagoon requires 1 pump, 8 hours of labor, and 13 feet of tubing, the diversion of resources required to produce one unit of this new model would cause a reduction in profit of $\$200 \times 1 + \$16.67 \times 8 + \$0 \times 13 = \$333.33$. This reduction would be partially offset by the $320 increase in profit generated by each Typhoon-Lagoon. The net effect of producing each Typhoon-Lagoon would be a $13.33 reduction in profit ($\$320 - \$333.33 = -\$13.33$). Therefore, the production of Typhoon-Lagoons would not be profitable (although the company might choose to produce a small number of Typhoon-Lagoons to enhance its product line for marketing purposes).

Another way to determine whether or not Typhoon-Lagoons should be produced is to add this alternative to our model and solve the resulting LP problem. The LP model for this revised problem is represented as follows, where X_1, X_2, and X_3 represent the number of Aqua-Spas, Hydro-Luxes, and Typhoon-Lagoons to be produced, respectively:

$$\begin{array}{lrl}
\text{MAX:} & 350X_1 + 300X_2 + 320X_3 & \} \text{ profit} \\
\text{Subject to:} & 1X_1 + 1X_2 + 1X_3 \leq 200 & \} \text{ pump constraint} \\
& 9X_1 + 6X_2 + 8X_3 \leq 1{,}566 & \} \text{ labor constraint} \\
& 12X_1 + 16X_2 + 13X_3 \leq 2{,}880 & \} \text{ tubing constraint} \\
& X_1, X_2, X_3 \geq 0 & \} \text{ nonnegativity conditions}
\end{array}$$

This model is implemented and solved in the spreadsheet, as shown in Figure 4.7. Notice that the optimal solution to this problem involves producing 122 Aqua-Spas ($X_1 = 122$), 78 Hydro-Luxes ($X_2 = 78$), and no Typhoon-Lagoons ($X_3 = 0$). So, as expected, the optimal solution does not involve producing Typhoon-Lagoons. Figure 4.8 shows the Sensitivity Report for our revised model.

4.5.9 The Meaning of the Reduced Costs

The Sensitivity Report in Figure 4.8 for our revised model is identical to the sensitivity report for our original model *except* that it includes an additional row in

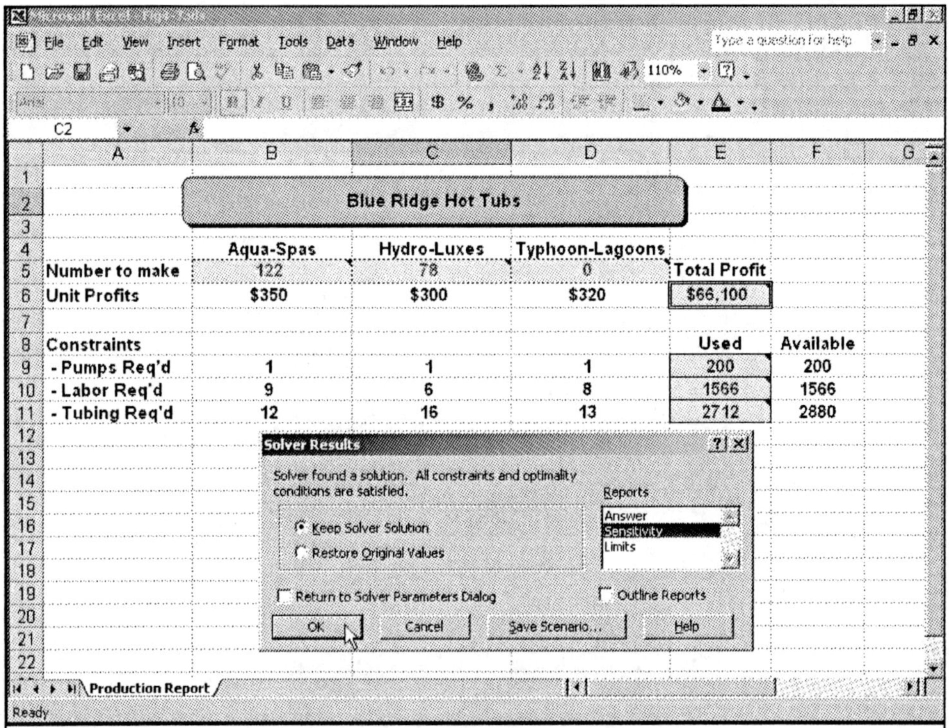

Key Cell Formulas

Cell	Formula	Copied to
E6	=SUMPRODUCT(B6:D6,$B$5:$D$5)	E9:E11

FIGURE 4.7
Spreadsheet model for the revised product mix problem with three hot tub models

the Adjustable cells section. This row reports sensitivity information on the number of Typhoon-Lagoons to produce. Notice that the Reduced Cost column indicates that the reduced cost value for Typhoon-Lagoons is –13.33. This is the same number that we calculated in the previous section when determining whether or not it would be profitable to produce Typhoon-Lagoons.

The reduced cost for each variable is equal to the per-unit amount the product contributes to profits minus the per-unit value of the resources it consumes (where the consumed resources are priced at their shadow prices). For example, the reduced cost of each variable in this problem is calculated as:

Reduced cost of Aqua-Spas	$= 350 - 200 \times 1 - 16.67 \times 9 - 0 \times 12 = 0$
Reduced cost of Hydro-Luxes	$= 300 - 200 \times 1 - 16.67 \times 6 - 0 \times 16 = 0$
Reduced cost of Typhoon-Lagoons	$= 320 - 200 \times 1 - 16.67 \times 8 - 0 \times 13 = -13.33$

The allowable increase in the objective function coefficient for Typhoon-Lagoons equals 13.33. This means that the current solution will remain optimal provided that the marginal profit on Typhoon-Lagoons is less than or equal to $320 + $13.33 = $333.33 (because this would keep its reduced cost less than or equal to zero). However, if the marginal profit for Typhoon-Lagoons is more than $333.33, producing this product would be profitable and the optimal solution to the problem would change.

FIGURE 4.8
Sensitivity Report for the revised product mix problem with three hot tub models

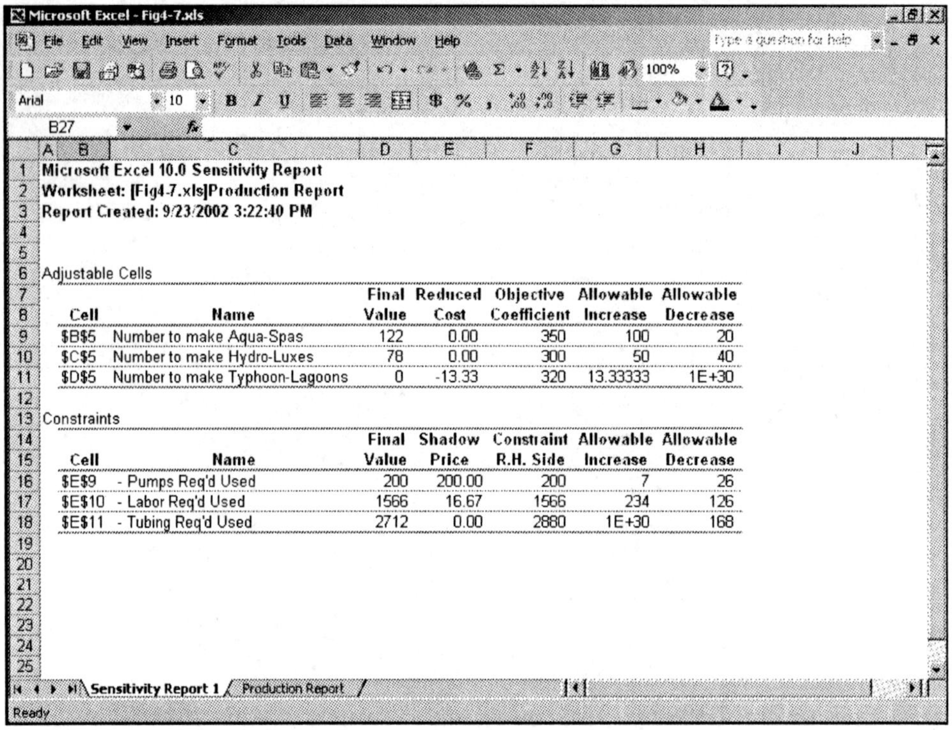

Microsoft Excel 10.0 Sensitivity Report
Worksheet: [Fig4-7.xls]Production Report
Report Created: 9/23/2002 3:22:40 PM

Adjustable Cells

Cell	Name	Final Value	Reduced Cost	Objective Coefficient	Allowable Increase	Allowable Decrease
$B$5	Number to make Aqua-Spas	122	0.00	350	100	20
$C$5	Number to make Hydro-Luxes	78	0.00	300	50	40
$D$5	Number to make Typhoon-Lagoons	0	-13.33	320	13.33333	1E+30

Constraints

Cell	Name	Final Value	Shadow Price	Constraint R.H. Side	Allowable Increase	Allowable Decrease
$E$9	- Pumps Req'd Used	200	200.00	200	7	26
$E$10	- Labor Req'd Used	1566	16.67	1566	234	126
$E$11	- Tubing Req'd Used	2712	0.00	2880	1E+30	168

It is interesting to note that the shadow prices (marginal values) of the resources equate exactly with the marginal profits of the products that, at optimality, assume values between their simple lower and upper bounds. This will always be the case. In the optimal solution to an LP problem, the variables that assume values *between* their simple lower and upper bounds always have reduced cost values of zero. (In our example problem, all the variables have implicit simple upper bounds of positive infinity.) The variables with optimal values equal to their simple lower bounds have reduced cost values that are less than or equal to zero for maximization problems, or greater than or equal to zero for minimization problems. Variables with optimal values equal to their simple upper bounds have reduced cost values that are greater than or equal to zero for maximization problems, or less than or equal to zero for minimization problems. Figure 4.9 summarizes these relationships.

FIGURE 4.9
Summary of optimal reduced cost values

Type of Problem	Optimal Value of Decision Variable	Optimal Value of Reduced Cost
Maximization	at simple lower bound	≤ 0
	between lower and upper bounds	$= 0$
	at simple upper bound	≥ 0
Minimization	at simple lower bound	≥ 0
	between lower and upper bounds	$= 0$
	at simple upper bound	≤ 0

Generally, at optimality, a variable assumes its largest possible value (or is set equal to its simple upper bound) if this variable helps improve the objective function value. In a maximization problem, the variable's reduced cost must be nonnegative to indicate that if the variable's value increased, the objective value would increase (improve). In a minimization problem, the variable's reduced cost must be nonpositive to indicate that if the variable's value increased, the objective value would decrease (improve).

Similar arguments can be made for the optimal reduced costs of variables at their lower bounds. At optimality, a variable assumes its smallest (lower bound) value if it cannot be used to improve the objective value. In a maximization problem, the variable's reduced cost must be nonpositive to indicate that if the variable's value increased, the objective value would decrease (worsen). In a minimization problem, the variable's reduced cost must be nonnegative to indicate that if the variable's value increased, the objective value would increase (worsen).

Key Points

Our discussion of Solver's sensitivity report highlights some key points concerning shadow prices and their relationship to reduced costs. These key points are summarized as:

- The shadow prices of resources equate the marginal value of the resources consumed with the marginal benefit of the goods being produced.
- Resources in excess supply have a shadow price (or marginal value) of zero.
- The reduced cost of a product is the difference between its marginal profit and the marginal value of the resources it consumes.
- Products whose marginal profits are less than the marginal value of the goods required for their production will not be produced in an optimal solution.

4.5.10 Analyzing Changes in Constraint Coefficients

Given what we know about reduced costs and shadow prices, we can now analyze how changes in some constraint coefficients affect the optimal solution to an LP problem. For example, it is unprofitable for Blue Ridge Hot Tubs to manufacture Typhoon-Lagoons assuming that each unit requires 8 hours of labor. However, what would happen if the product could be produced in only 7 hours? The reduced cost value for Typhoon-Lagoons is calculated as:

$$\$320 - \$200 \times 1 - \$16.67 \times 7 - \$0 \times 13 = \$3.31$$

Because this new reduced cost value is positive, producing Typhoon-Lagoons would be profitable in this scenario and the solution shown in Figure 4.7 would no longer be optimal. We could also reach this conclusion by changing the labor requirement for Typhoon-Lagoons in our spreadsheet model and re-solving the problem. In fact, we have to do this to determine the new optimal solution if each Typhoon-Lagoon requires only 7 hours of labor.

As another example, suppose that we wanted to know the maximum amount of labor that is required to assemble a Typhoon-Lagoon while keeping its production economically justifiable. The production of Typhoon-Lagoons would be profitable provided that the reduced cost for the product is greater than or equal to zero. If L_3 represents the amount of labor required to produce a Typhoon-Lagoon, we want to find the maximum value of L_3 that keeps the reduced cost for Typhoon-Lagoons greater than or equal to zero. That is, we want to find the maximum value of L_3 that satisfies the inequality:

$$\$320 - \$200 \times 1 - \$16.67 \times L_3 - \$0 \times 13 \geq 0$$

If we solve this inequality for L_3, we obtain:

$$L_3 \leq \frac{120}{16.67} = 7.20$$

Thus, the production of Typhoon-Lagoons would be economically justified provided that the labor required to produce them does not exceed 7.20 hours per unit. Similar types of questions can be answered using knowledge of the basic relationships between reduced costs, shadow prices, and optimality conditions.

4.5.11 Simultaneous Changes in Objective Function Coefficients

Earlier, we noted that the values in the Allowable Increase and Allowable Decrease columns in the Sensitivity Report for the objective function coefficients indicate the maximum amounts by which each objective coefficient can change without altering the optimal solution—*assuming all other coefficients in the model remain constant.* A technique known as The 100% Rule determines whether the current solution remains optimal when more than one objective function coefficient changes. The following two situations could arise when applying this rule:

Case 1. All variables whose objective function coefficients change have nonzero reduced costs.

Case 2. At least one variable whose objective function coefficient changes has a reduced cost of zero.

In case 1, the current solution remains optimal provided that the objective function coefficient of each changed variable remains within the limits indicated in the Allowable Increase and Allowable Decrease columns of the Sensitivity Report.

Case 2 is a bit more tricky. In case 2, we must perform the following analysis where:

c_j = the original objective function coefficient for variable X_j
Δc_j = the planned change in c_j
I_j = the allowable increase in c_j given in the Sensitivity Report
D_j = the allowable decrease in c_j given in the Sensitivity Report

$$r_j = \begin{cases} \dfrac{\Delta c_j}{I_j}, & \text{if } \Delta c_j \geq 0 \\[2ex] \dfrac{-\Delta c_j}{D_j}, & \text{if } \Delta c_j < 0 \end{cases}$$

Notice that r_j measures the ratio of the planned change in c_j to the maximum allowable change for which the current solution remains optimal. If only one objective function coefficient changed, the current solution remains optimal provided that $r_j \le 1$ (or, if r_j is expressed as a percentage, it must be less than or equal to 100%). Similarly, if more than one objective function coefficient changes, the current solution will remain optimal provided that $\Sigma r_j \le 1$. (Note that if $\Sigma r_j > 1$, the current solution might remain optimal, but this is not guaranteed.)

4.5.12 A Warning About Degeneracy

The solution to an LP problem sometimes exhibits a mathematical anomaly known as ***degeneracy.*** The solution to an LP problem is degenerate if the RHS values of any of the constraints have an allowable increase or allowable decrease of zero. The presence of degeneracy impacts our interpretation of the values on the sensitivity report in a number of important ways:

1. When the solution is degenerate, the methods mentioned earlier for detecting alternate optimal solutions cannot be relied upon.
2. When a solution is degenerate, the reduced costs for the variable cells may not be unique. Additionally, in this case, the objective function coefficients for variable cells must change by at least as much as (and possibly more than) their respective reduced costs before the optimal solution would change.
3. When the solution is degenerate, the allowable increases and decreases for the objective function coefficients still hold and, in fact, the coefficients may have to be changed substantially beyond the allowable increase and decrease limits before the optimal solution changes.
4. When the solution is degenerate, the given shadow prices and their ranges may still be interpreted in the usual way but they may not be unique. That is, a different set of shadow prices and ranges may also apply to the problem (even if the optimal solution is unique).

So before interpreting the results on a sensitivity report, you should always first check to see if the solution is degenerate because this has important ramifications on how the numbers on the report should be interpreted. A complete description of the degeneracy anomaly goes beyond the intended scope of this book. However, degeneracy is sometimes caused by having redundant constraints in an LP model. ***Extreme caution*** (and perhaps consultation with an expert in mathematical programming) is in order if important business decisions are being made based on the sensitivity report for a degenerate LP problem.

4.6 THE LIMITS REPORT

The Limits Report for the original Blue Ridge Hot Tubs problem is shown in Figure 4.10. This report lists the optimal value of the set cell. It then summarizes the optimal values for each variable cell and indicates what values the set cell assumes if each variable cell is set to its upper or lower limits. The values in the Lower Limits column indicate the smallest value each variable cell can assume while the values of all other variable cells remain constant and all the constraints are satisfied. The values in the Upper Limits column indicate the largest value each variable cell can assume while the values of all other variable cells remain constant and all the constraints are satisfied.

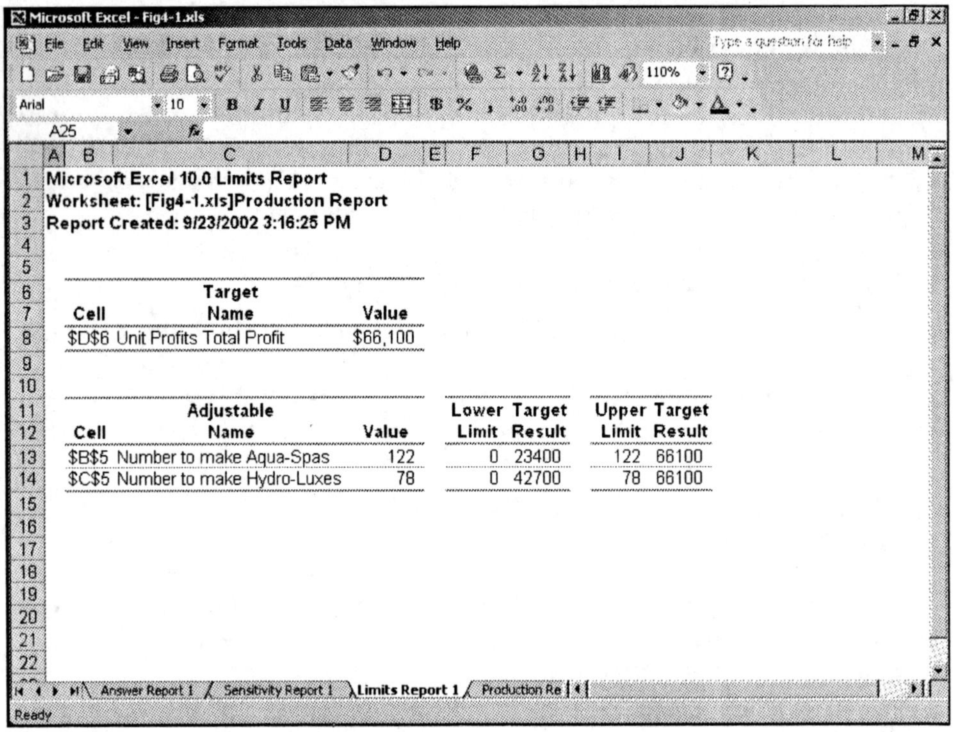

Microsoft Excel 10.0 Limits Report
Worksheet: [Fig4-1.xls]Production Report
Report Created: 9/23/2002 3:16:25 PM

Cell	Target Name	Value
$D$6	Unit Profits Total Profit	$66,100

Cell	Adjustable Name	Value	Lower Limit	Target Result	Upper Limit	Target Result
$B$5	Number to make Aqua-Spas	122	0	23400	122	66100
$C$5	Number to make Hydro-Luxes	78	0	42700	78	66100

FIGURE 4.10
Limits Report for the original Blue Ridge Hot Tubs problem

4.7 THE SENSITIVITY ASSISTANT ADD-IN (OPTIONAL)

This book comes with an Excel add-in called Sensitivity Assistant that provides two additional tools for performing sensitivity analysis on an *ad hoc* basis: Spider Tables and Solver Tables. A Spider Table summarizes the optimal value for one output cell as individual changes are made to various input cells. A Solver Table summarizes the optimal value of multiple output cells as changes are made to a single input cell. As illustrated in the following sections, these tools can be helpful in developing an understanding of how changes in various model parameters affect the optimal solution to a problem.

Installing the Sensitivity Assistant Add-In

To use the Sensitivity Assistant add-in, it must first be installed on your computer. To do this:

1. Copy the file Sensitivity.xla from the CD-ROM accompanying this book to the folder on your hard drive that contains the file Solver.xla. (In most cases, this is either the folder *d:*\Program Files\Microsoft Office\Office\Library\Solver or, for Office XP, *d:*\Program Files\Microsoft Office\Office10\Library\Solver.)

continued

2. In Excel, click Tools, Add-Ins, click the Browse button, locate the Sensitivity.xla file, and click OK.

This instructs your computer to open the Sensitivity Assistant add-in whenever you start Excel. It also causes the "Sensitivity Assistant..." option to be added to the Tools menu in Excel. You can deactivate the Sensitivity Assistant add-in at any time by using the Tools, Add-Ins command again.

4.7.1 Creating Spider Tables and Plots

Recall that the optimal solution to the original Blue Ridge Hot Tubs problem involves producing 122 Aqua-Spas and 78 Hydro-Luxes for a total profit of $66,100. However, this solution assumes there will be exactly 200 pumps, 1,566 labor hours, and 2,880 feet of tubing available. In reality, pumps and tubing are sometimes defective, and workers sometimes call in sick. So, the owner of the company may wonder how sensitive the total profit is to changes in these resources. Although Solver's Sensitivity Report provides some information about this issue, a Spider Table and Plot is sometimes more helpful in communicating this information to management.

Again, a Spider Table summarizes the optimal value for one output cell as individual changes are made to various input cells. In this case, the output cell of interest is cell D6 representing total profit, and the input cells are E9, E10, and E11 representing the availability of pumps, labor, and tubing. Figure 4.11 (and file Fig4-11.xls on your data disk) shows how to set up a Spider Table for this problem.

The upper-left cell in a Spider Table should contain a formula referring to the output cell you want to track. Thus, in Figure 4.11, cell A14 contains a formula that returns the value of cell D6 representing total profit.

Formula for cell A14: =D6

The remaining cells in the first row of a Spider Table should contain formulas referring to the input cells you want to manipulate. Thus, cells B14, C14, and D14 contain formulas referring, respectively, to cells E9, E10, and E11, which represent the resource availability values that we want to manipulate.

Formula for cell B14: =E9

Formula for cell C14: =E10

Formula for cell D14: =E11

The first cell in each remaining row of a Spider Table should contain a percentage value indicating an amount by which to adjust each of the input cells. Thus, in cells A15 through A25, we entered a series of percentages from 90% to 110%. The Spider Table tool will multiply the value of each of the input cells referenced in cells B14 through D14 by each of the percentages listed in cells A15 through A25 and keep a record of the corresponding value of the output cell referenced in cell A14. Specifically, the Spider Table tool will first change the value in

FIGURE 4.11
Set up for creating a Spider Table and Plot

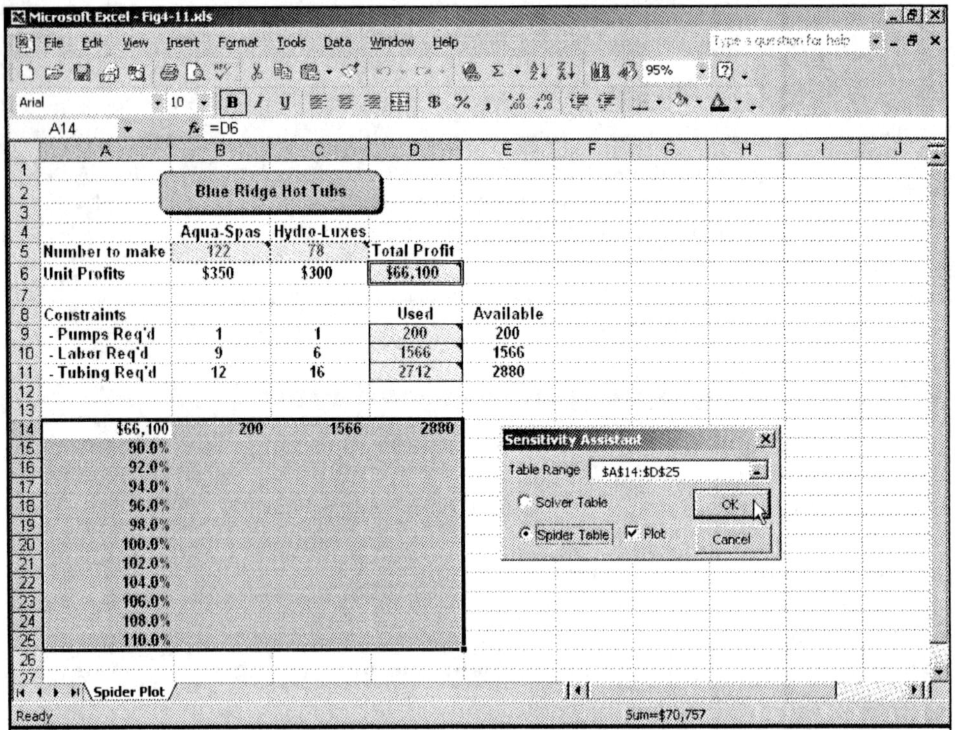

Key Cell Formulas

Cell	Formula	Copied to
A14	=D6	—
B14	=E9	—
C14	=E10	—
D14	=E11	—

cell E9 (representing the number of pumps available) to 180 (or 90% of 200), re-solve the problem, and record the optimal profit in cell B15. It will then change the value in cell E9 to 184 (or 92% of 200), re-solve the problem, and record the optimal profit in cell B16. This process continues until all the input cells have been varied from 90% to 110% and the resulting optimal profit values recorded in the table.

To complete the Spider Table, we would proceed through the following steps. The resulting table and plot is shown in Figure 4.12.

1. Select the range A14:D25.
2. Click Tools, Sensitivity Assistant.
3. Select the Spider Table option.
4. Click OK.

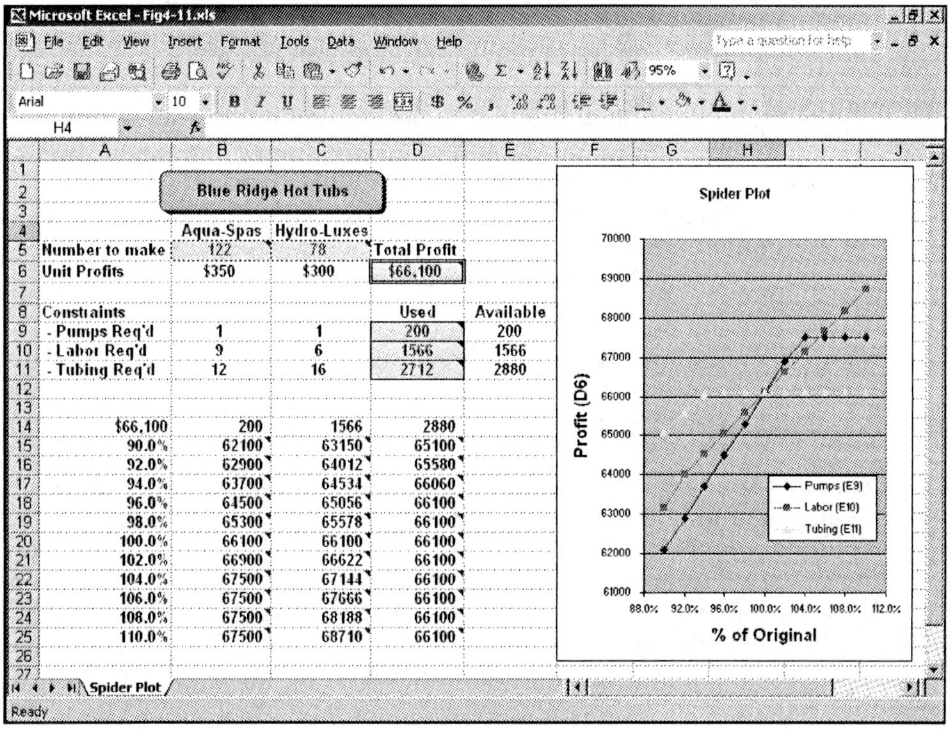

	A	B	C	D	E
1					
2		Blue Ridge Hot Tubs			
3					
4		Aqua-Spas	Hydro-Luxes		
5	Number to make	122	78	Total Profit	
6	Unit Profits	$350	$300	$66,100	
7					
8	Constraints			Used	Available
9	- Pumps Req'd	1	1	200	200
10	- Labor Req'd	9	6	1566	1566
11	- Tubing Req'd	12	16	2712	2880
12					
13					
14	$66,100	200	1566	2880	
15	90.0%	62100	63150	65100	
16	92.0%	62900	64012	65580	
17	94.0%	63700	64534	66060	
18	96.0%	64500	65056	66100	
19	98.0%	65300	65578	66100	
20	100.0%	66100	66100	66100	
21	102.0%	66900	66622	66100	
22	104.0%	67500	67144	66100	
23	106.0%	67500	67666	66100	
24	108.0%	67500	68188	66100	
25	110.0%	67500	68710	66100	

FIGURE 4.12
A Spider Table and Plot showing the relationship between profit and the availability of pumps, labor, and tubing

The rationale for the name of this procedure should be readily apparent from the spider-like plot shown in Figure 4.12. The center point in the graph corresponds to the optimal solution to the original model with 100% of the pumps, labor, and tubing available. Each of the points in the graph show the impact on total profit of varying the original resource levels by the indicated percentage.

It is clear from Figure 4.12 that total profit is relatively insensitive to modest decreases or large increases in the availability of tubing. This is consistent with the sensitivity information regarding tubing shown earlier in Figure 4.8. The optimal solution to the original problem involved using all the pumps and all the labor hours but only 2,712 feet of the 2,880 available feet of tubing. As a result, we could achieve the same level of profit even if the availability of tubing was reduced by 168 feet (or to about 94.2% of its original value). Similarly, because we are not using all of the available tubing, acquiring more tubing would only increase the surplus and not allow for any improvement in profit. Thus, our Spider Table and Plot suggest that the availability of tubing probably should not be a top concern in this problem. On the other hand, the Spider Plot suggests that changes in the availability of pumps and labor have a more pronounced impact on profit and the optimal solution to the problem.

Notes on Setting Up a Spider Table

1. The cell in the upper-left corner of the table range should contain a formula returning the value of the output cell you want to track.
2. The remaining cells in the first row of the table range should contain formulas referring to the input cells you want to manipulate.
3. The first cell in each remaining row of the table range should contain a percentage value indicating an amount by which to multiply each of the input cells.

4.7.2 Creating a Solver Table

The Spider Plot in Figure 4.12 suggests that the total profit earned is most sensitive to changes in the available supply of pumps. We can create a Solver Table to study in greater detail the impact of changes in the available number of pumps. Recall that a Solver Table summarizes the optimal value of multiple output cells as changes are made to a single input cell. In this case, the single input we want to change is cell E9 representing the number of pumps available. We might want to track what happens to several output cells, including the optimal number of Aqua-Spas and Hydro-Luxes (cells B5 and B6), the total profit (cell D6), and the total amount pumps, labor, and tubing used (cells D9, D10, and D11). Figure 4.13 (and file Fig4-13.xls on your data disk) shows how to set up the Solver Table for this problem.

The upper-left cell in a Solver Table should contain a formula referring to the input cell you want to manipulate. Thus, cell A14 contains a formula referring to cell E9, which represents the available number of pumps.

Formula for cell A14: =E9

The remaining cells in the first row of a Solver Table should contain formulas returning the values of the various output cells you want to track. Thus, cells B14 through G14 each contain a formula referring to one of our output cells.

Formula for cell B14: =B5
Formula for cell C14: =C5
Formula for cell D14: =D6
Formula for cell E14: =D9
Formula for cell F14: =D10
Formula for cell G14: =D11

The first cell in each of the remaining rows of the Solver Table should contain a value to be assumed by the input cell. In this case, we entered values from 170 to 220 (in multiples of five) in cells A15 to A25 as representative values for the input cell (E9) representing the available number of pumps. The Solver Table tool will substitute each of the values in cells A15 through A25 into the input cell (E9), re-solve the problem, and then record the resulting values for the output cells referenced in the first row of the table range.

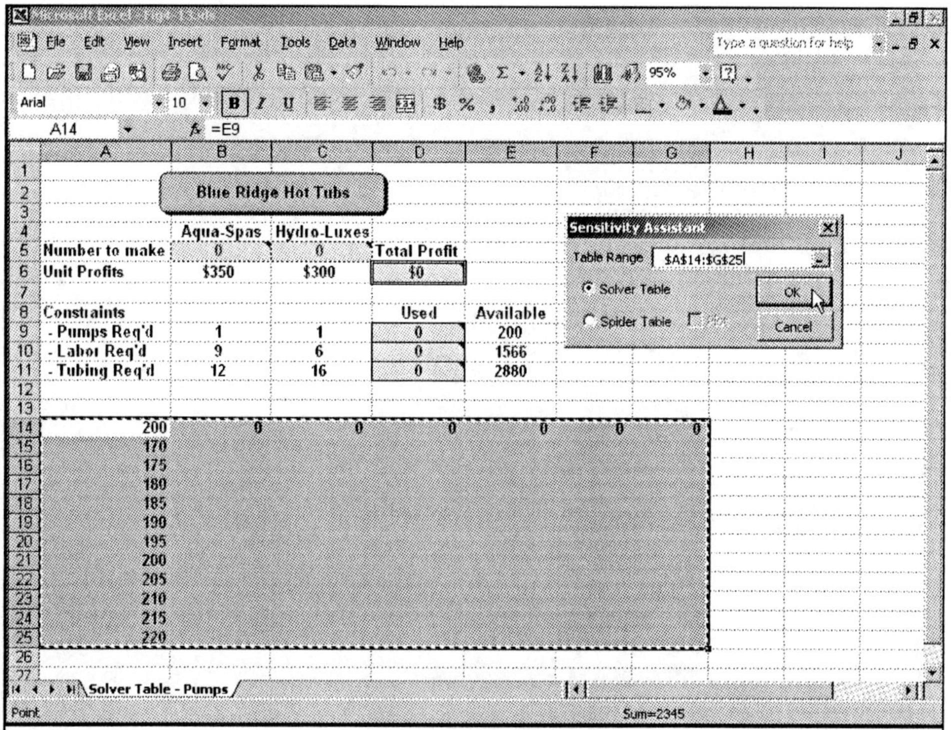

FIGURE 4.13
Set up for creating a Solver Table

Key Cell Formulas

Cell	Formula	Copied to
A14	=E9	—
B14	=B5	—
C14	=C5	—
D14	=D6	—
E14	=D9	—
F14	=D10	—
G14	=D11	—

To complete the Solver Table, we would proceed through the following steps. The resulting table and plot is shown in Figure 4.14.

1. Select the range A14:G25.
2. Click Tools, Sensitivity Assistant.
3. Select the Solver Table option.
4. Click OK.

A number of interesting insights emerge from Figure 4.14. First, comparing columns A and E, as the number of available pumps increases from 170 up to 205, they are always all used. With about 175 pumps, we also begin to use all the available labor. However, when the number of available pumps increases to 210 or more, only 207 pumps can be used because we run out of both tubing and labor at that point. This suggests that the company should not be interested in getting more than 7 additional pumps unless it can also increase the amount of tubing and/or labor available.

FIGURE 4.14
Solver Table showing changes in the optimal solution, profit, and resource usage as the number of pumps changes

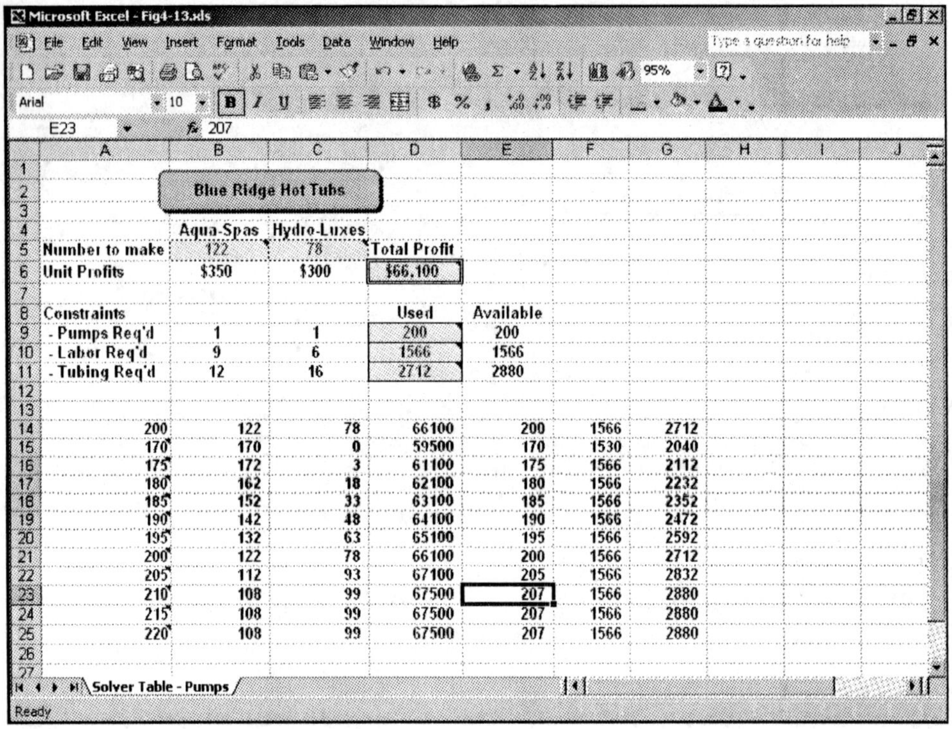

	A	B	C	D	E	F	G
4		Aqua-Spas	Hydro-Luxes				
5	Number to make	122	78	Total Profit			
6	Unit Profits	$350	$300	$66,100			
8	Constraints			Used	Available		
9	- Pumps Req'd	1	1	200	200		
10	- Labor Req'd	9	6	1566	1566		
11	- Tubing Req'd	12	16	2712	2880		
14	200	122	78	66100	200	1566	2712
15	170	170	0	59500	170	1530	2040
16	175	172	3	61100	175	1566	2112
17	180	162	18	62100	180	1566	2232
18	185	152	33	63100	185	1566	2352
19	190	142	48	64100	190	1566	2472
20	195	132	63	65100	195	1566	2592
21	200	122	78	66100	200	1566	2712
22	205	112	93	67100	205	1566	2832
23	210	108	99	67500	207	1566	2880
24	215	108	99	67500	207	1566	2880
25	220	108	99	67500	207	1566	2880

Also note that the addition or subtraction of 5 pumps from the initial supply of 200 causes the optimal objective function value (column D) to change by $1,000. This suggests that if the company has 200 pumps, the marginal value of each pump is about $200 (*i.e.*, $1000/5=$200). Of course, this is equivalent to the ***shadow price*** of pumps shown earlier in Figure 4.8.

Finally, it is interesting to note that when the availability of pumps is between 175 and 205, each increase of 5 pumps causes the optimal number of Aqua-Spas to decrease by 10 and the optimal number of Hydro-Luxes to increase by 15. Thus, one advantage of the Solver Table over the Sensitivity Report is that it tells you not only how much the optimal value of the objective function changes as the number of pumps change, but it can also tell you how the optimal solution changes.

Notes on Setting Up a Solver Table

1. The cell in the upper-left corner of the table range should contain a formula referring to the input cell you want to manipulate.
2. The remaining cells in the first row of the table range should contain formulas returning the values of the output cells you want to track.
3. The first cell in each remaining row of the table range should contain a value to be assumed by the input cell.

4.7.3 Comments

Additional Solver Tables and Spider Tables/Plots could be constructed to analyze every element of the model, including objective function and constraint coefficients. However, these techniques are considered 'computationally expensive' because they require the LP model to be solved repeatedly. For small problems like Blue Ridge Hot Tubs, this is not really a problem. But as problem size and complexity increases, this approach to sensitivity analysis can become impractical.

4.8 THE SIMPLEX METHOD (OPTIONAL)

We have repeatedly mentioned that the simplex method is the preferred method for solving LP problems. This section provides an overview of the simplex method and shows how it relates to some of the items that appear on the Answer Report and the Sensitivity Report.

4.8.1 Creating Equality Constraints Using Slack Variables

Because our original formulation of the LP model for the Blue Ridge Hot Tubs problem has only *two* decision variables (X_1 and X_2), you might be surprised to learn that Solver actually used *five* variables to solve this problem. As you saw in chapter 2 when we plotted the boundary lines for the constraints in an LP problem, it is easier to work with equal to conditions rather than less than or equal to, or greater than or equal to conditions. Similarly, the simplex method requires that *all* constraints in an LP model be expressed as equalities.

To solve an LP problem using the simplex method, Solver temporarily turns all inequality constraints into equality constraints by adding one new variable to each less than or equal to constraint and subtracting one new variable from each greater than or equal to constraint. The new variables used to create equality constraints are called **slack variables.**

For example, consider the less than or equal to constraint:

$$a_{k1}X_1 + a_{k2}X_2 + \dots + a_{kn}X_n \leq b_k$$

Solver can turn this constraint into an equal to constraint by adding the nonnegative slack variable S_k to the LHS of the constraint:

$$a_{k1}X_1 + a_{k2}X_2 + \dots + a_{kn}X_n + S_k = b_k$$

The variable S_k represents the amount by which $a_{k1}X_1 + a_{k2}X_2 + \dots + a_{kn}X_n$ is less than b_k. Now consider the greater than or equal to constraint:

$$a_{k1}X_1 + a_{k2}X_2 + \dots + a_{kn}X_n \geq b_k$$

Solver can turn this constraint into an equal to constraint by subtracting the nonnegative slack variable S_k from the LHS of the constraint:

$$a_{k1}X_1 + a_{k2}X_2 + \dots + a_{kn}X_n - S_k = b_k$$

In this case, the variable S_k represents the amount by which $a_{k1}X_1 + a_{k2}X_2 + \dots + a_{kn}X_n$ exceeds b_k.

To solve the original Blue Ridge Hot Tubs problem using the simplex method, Solver actually solved the following modified problem involving *five* variables:

MAX:	$350X_1 + 300X_2$	} profit
Subject to:	$1X_1 + 1X_2 + S_1 = 200$	} pump constraint
	$9X_1 + 6X_2 + S_2 = 1{,}566$	} labor constraint
	$12X_1 + 16X_2 + S_3 = 2{,}880$	} tubing constraint
	$X_1, X_2, S_1, S_2, S_3 \geq 0$	} nonnegativity conditions

We will refer to X_1 and X_2 as the **structural variables** in the model to distinguish them from the slack variables.

Recall that we did not set up slack variables in the spreadsheet or include them in the formulas in the constraint cells. Solver automatically sets up the slack variables it needs to solve a particular problem. The only time Solver even mentions these variables is when it creates an Answer Report like the one shown in Figure 4.2. The values in the Slack column in the Answer Report correspond to the optimal values of the slack variables.

4.8.2 Basic Feasible Solutions

After all the inequality constraints in an LP problem have been converted into equalities (by adding or subtracting appropriate slack variables), the constraints in the LP model represent a system (or collection) of linear equations. If there are a total of n variables in a system of m equations, one strategy for finding a solution to the system of equations is to select any m variables and try to find values for them that solve the system, assuming all other variables are set equal to their lower bounds (which are usually zero). This strategy requires more variables than constraints in the system of equations—or that $n \geq m$.

The m variables selected to solve the system of equations in an LP model are sometimes called **basic variables,** while the remaining variables are called **nonbasic variables.** If a solution to the system of equations can be obtained using a given set of basic variables (while the nonbasic variables are all set equal to zero), that solution is called a **basic feasible solution.** Every basic feasible solution corresponds to one of the extreme points of the feasible region for the LP problem, and we know that the optimal solution to the LP problem also occurs at an extreme point. So, the challenge in LP is to find the set of basic variables (and their optimal values) that produce the basic feasible solution corresponding to the optimal extreme point of the feasible region.

Because our modified problem involves three constraints and five variables, we could select three basic variables in ten different ways to form possible basic feasible solutions for the problem. Figure 4.15 summarizes the results for these ten options.

The first five solutions in Figure 4.15 are feasible and, therefore, represent basic feasible solutions to this problem. The remaining solutions are infeasible because they violate the nonnegativity conditions. The best feasible alternative shown in Figure 4.15 corresponds to the optimal solution to the problem. In particular, if X_1, X_2, and S_3 are selected as basic variables and S_1 and S_2 are nonbasic and assigned their lower bound values (zero), we try to find values for X_1, X_2, and S_3 that satisfy the following constraints:

	Basic Variables	Nonbasic Variables	Solution	Objective Value
1	S_1, S_2, S_3	X_1, X_2	X_1=0, X_2=0, S_1=200, S_2=1566, S_3=2880	0
2	X_1, S_1, S_3	X_2, S_2	X_1=174, X_2=0, S_1=26, S_2=0, S_3=792	60,900
3	X_1, X_2, S_3	S_1, S_2	X_1=122, X_2=78, S_1=0, S_2=0, S_3=168	66,100
4	X_1, X_2, S_2	S_1, S_3	X_1=80, X_2=120, S_1=0, S_2=126, S_3=0	64,000
5	X_2, S_1, S_2	X_1, S_3	X_1=0, X_2=180, S_1=20, S_2=486, S_3=0	54,000
6*	X_1, X_2, S_1	S_2, S_3	X_1=108, X_2=99, S_1=–7, S_2=0, S_3=0	67,500
7*	X_1, S_1, S_2	X_2, S_3	X_1=240, X_2=0, S_1=–40, S_2=–594, S_3=0	84,000
8*	X_1, S_2, S_3	X_2, S_1	X_1=200, X_2=0, S_1=0, S_2=–234, S_3=480	70,000
9*	X_2, S_2, S_3	X_1, S_1	X_1=0, X_2=200, S_1=0, S_2=366, S_3=–320	60,000
10*	X_2, S_1, S_3	X_1, S_2	X_1=0, X_2=261, S_1=–61, S_2=0, S_3=–1296	78,300

Note: * denotes infeasible solutions

FIGURE 4.15
Possible basic feasible solutions for the original Blue Ridge Hot Tubs problem

$$1X_1 + 1X_2 = 200 \quad \} \text{ pump constraint}$$
$$9X_1 + 6X_2 = 1{,}566 \quad \} \text{ labor constraint}$$
$$12X_1 + 16X_2 + S_3 = 2{,}880 \quad \} \text{ tubing constraint}$$

Notice that S_1 and S_2 in the modified equal to constraints are not included in the above constraint equations because we are assuming that the values of these nonbasic variables are equal to zero (their lower bounds). Using linear algebra, the simplex method determines that the values $X_1 = 122$, $X_2 = 78$, and $S_3 = 168$ satisfy the equations given above. So, a basic feasible solution to this problem is $X_1 = 122$, $X_2 = 78$, $S_1 = 0$, $S_2 = 0$, $S_3 = 168$. As indicated in Figure 4.15, this solution produces an objective function value of $66,100. (Notice that the optimal values for the slack variables S_1, S_2, and S_3 also correspond to the values shown in the Answer Report in Figure 4.2 in the Slack column for constraint cells D9, D10, and D11.) Figure 4.16 shows the relationships between the basic feasible solutions listed in Figure 4.15 and the extreme points of the feasible region for this problem.

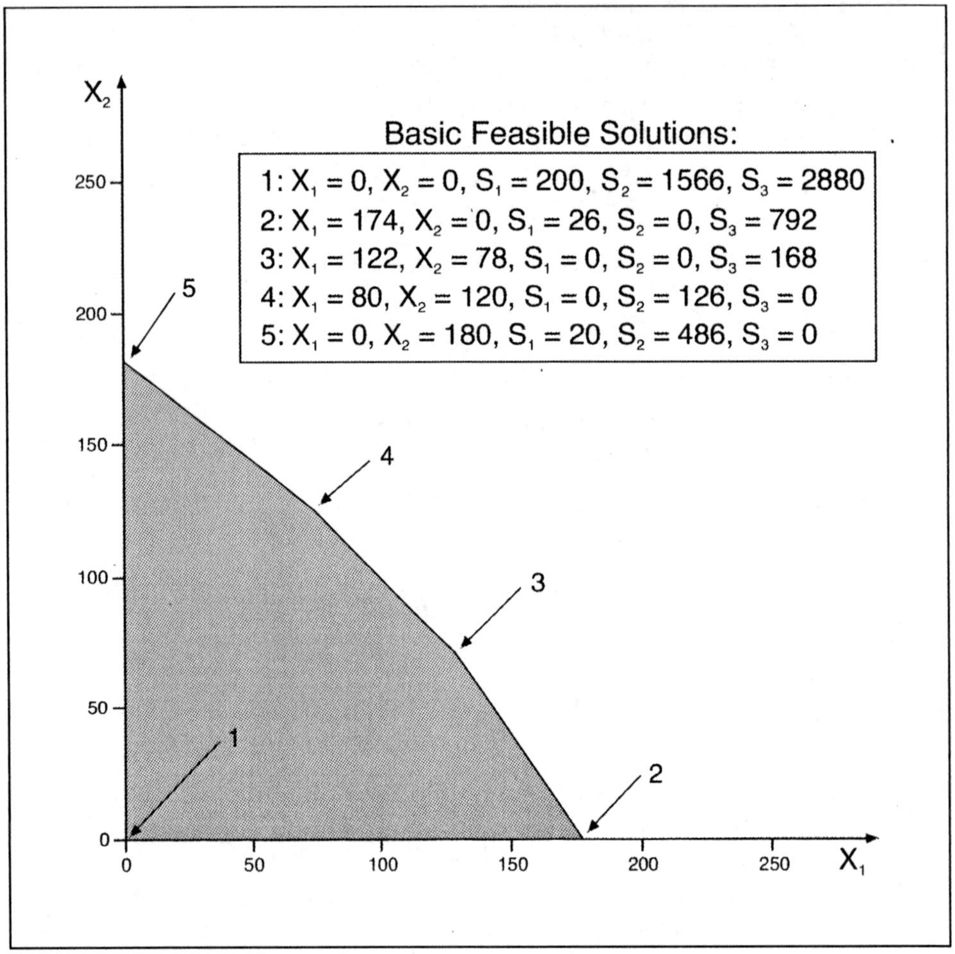

FIGURE 4.16
Illustration of the relationship between basic feasible solutions and extreme points

4.8.3 Finding the Best Solution

The simplex method operates by first identifying any basic feasible solution (or extreme point) for an LP problem, and then moving to an adjacent extreme point, if such a move improves the value of the objective function. When no adjacent extreme point has a better objective function value, the current extreme point is optimal and the simplex method terminates.

The process of moving from one extreme point to an adjacent one is accomplished by switching one of the basic variables with one of the nonbasic variables to create a new basic feasible solution that corresponds to the adjacent extreme point. For example, in Figure 4.16, moving from the first basic feasible solution (point 1) to the second basic feasible solution (point 2) involves making X_1 a basic variable and S_2 a nonbasic variable. Similarly, we can move from point 2 to point 3 by switching basic variables with nonbasic variables. So, starting at point 1 in Figure 4.16, the simplex method could move to point 2, then to the optimal solution at point 3. Alternatively, the simplex method could move from point 1 through points 5 and 4 to reach the optimal solution at point 3. Thus, although there is no guarantee that the simplex method will take the shortest route to the optimal solution of an LP problem, it will find the optimal solution eventually.

To determine whether switching a basic and nonbasic variable will result in a better solution, the simplex method calculates the reduced cost for each nonbasic variable to determine if the objective function could be improved if any of these variables are substituted for one of the basic variables. (Note that unbounded solutions are detected easily in the simplex method by the existence of a nonbasic variable that could improve the objective value by an infinite amount if it were made basic.) This process continues until no further improvement in the objective function value is possible.

4.9 SUMMARY

This chapter described the methods for assessing how sensitive an LP model is to various changes that might occur in the model or its optimal solution. The impact of changes in an LP model can be analyzed easily by re-solving the model. Solver also provides a significant amount of sensitivity information automatically. For LP problems, the maximum amount of sensitivity information is obtained by solving the problem using the simplex method. Before using the information on the Sensitivity Report, you should always first check for the presence of degeneracy because this can have a significant impact on how one should interpret the numbers on this report.

The simplex method considers only the extreme points of the feasible region, and is an efficient way of solving LP problems. In this method, slack variables are first introduced to convert all constraints to equal to constraints. The simplex method systematically moves to better and better corner point solutions until no adjacent extreme point provides an improved objective function value.

4.10 REFERENCES

Bazaraa, M. and J. Jarvis. *Linear Programming and Network Flows*. New York: Wiley, 1990.

Eppen, G., F. Gould and C. Schmidt. *Introductory Management Science*, 4th ed. Englewoods Cliffs, NJ: Prentice-Hall, 1993.

Shogan, A. *Management Science*. Englewood Cliffs, NJ: Prentice Hall, 1988.

Wagner, H. and D. Rubin. "Shadow Prices: Tips and Traps for Managers and Instructors." *Interfaces*, vol. 20, no. 4, 1990.

Winston, W. *Operations Research: Applications and Algorithms*. Belmont, CA: Duxbury Press, 1994.

THE WORLD OF MANAGEMENT SCIENCE

Fuel Management and Allocation Model Helps National Airlines Adapt to Cost and Supply Changes

Fuel is a major component in the cost structure of an airline. Price and availability of fuel can vary from one air terminal to the next, and it is sometimes advantageous for an aircraft to carry more than the necessary minimum for the next leg of its route. Fuel loaded for the purpose of taking advantage of price or availability at a specific location is said to be tankered. A disadvantage of tankering is that fuel consumption increases when an aircraft is carrying more weight.

The use of LP to determine when and where to fuel aircraft saved National Airlines several million dollars during the first two years of implementation. In particular, National Airlines saw its average fuel costs drop 11.75% during a period when the average fuel cost for all domestic trunk airlines increased by 2.87%.

The objective function in the Fuel Management and Allocation Model consists of fuel costs and increases in operating costs from tankering. The constraints in the model address availability, minimum reserves, and aircraft capacities.

A particularly useful feature of the Fuel Management and Allocation Model is a series of reports that assist management in modifying the fuel-loading plan when sudden changes occur in availability or price. Shadow prices, along with the associated range of applicability, provide information about supply changes. Information about changes in price per gallon comes from the allowable increase and decrease for objective function coefficients.

For example, the availability report might indicate that the optimal quantity to purchase at Los Angeles from Shell West is 2,718,013 gallons; but if its supply decreases and fuel must be purchased from the next most attractive vendor, total cost would increase at the rate of $0.0478 per gallon (the shadow price). This fuel would be replaced by a prior purchase of up to 159,293 gallons from Shell East at New Orleans, tankered to Los Angeles.

The price report shows, for example, that vendor substitutions should be made if the current price of Shell West at Los Angeles, $0.3074, increases to $0.32583 or decreases to $0.27036. The report also indicates what that substitution should be.

Source: Darnell, D. Wayne and Carolyn Loflin. "National Airlines Fuel Management and Allocation Model." *Interfaces*, vol. 7, no. 2, February 1977, pp. 1–16.

QUESTIONS AND PROBLEMS

1. Howie Jones used the following information to calculate the profit coefficients for Aqua-Spas and Hydro-Luxes: pumps cost \$225 each, labor costs \$12 per hour, tubing costs \$2 per foot. In addition to pumps, labor, and tubing, the production of Aqua-Spas and Hydro-Luxes consumes, respectively, \$243 and \$246 per unit in other resources that are not in short supply. Using this information, Howie calculated the marginal profits on Aqua-Spas and Hydro-Luxes as:

	Aqua-Spas	**Hydro-Luxes**
Selling Price	\$950	\$875
Pump Cost	–\$225	–\$225
Labor Cost	–\$108	–\$72
Tubing Cost	–\$24	–\$32
Other Variable Costs	–\$243	–\$246
Marginal Profit	\$350	\$300

Howie's accountant reviewed these calculations and thinks Howie made a mistake. For accounting purposes, factory overhead is assigned to products at a rate of \$16 per labor hour. Howie's accountant argues that because Aqua-Spas require nine labor hours, the profit margin on this product should be \$144 less. Similarly, because Hydro-Luxes require six labor hours, the profit margin on this product should be \$96 less. Who is right and why?

2. A variable that assumes an optimal value between its lower and upper bounds has a reduced cost value of zero. Why must this be true? (*Hint:* What if such a variable's reduced cost value is not zero? What does this imply about the value of the objective function?)
3. Implement the following LP problem in a spreadsheet. Use Solver to solve the problem and create a Sensitivity Report. Use this information to answer the following questions:

$$\begin{aligned} \text{MAX:} \quad & 4X_1 + 2X_2 \\ \text{Subject to:} \quad & 2X_1 + 4X_2 \le 20 \\ & 3X_1 + 5X_2 \le 15 \\ & X_1, X_2 \ge 0 \end{aligned}$$

a. What range of values can the objective function coefficient for variable X_1 assume without changing the optimal solution?
b. Is the optimal solution to this problem unique, or are there alternate optimal solutions?
c. How much does the objective function coefficient for variable X_2 have to increase before it enters the optimal solution at a strictly positive level?
d. What is the optimal objective function value if X_2 equals 1?
e. What is the optimal objective function value if the RHS value for the second constraint changes from 15 to 25?
f. Is the current solution still optimal if the coefficient for X_2 in the second constraint changes from 5 to 1? Explain.

4. Implement the following LP model in a spreadsheet. Use Solver to solve the problem and create a Sensitivity Report. Use this information to answer the following questions:

$$
\begin{array}{ll}
\text{MAX:} & 2X_1 + 4X_2 \\
\text{Subject to:} & -X_1 + 2X_2 \leq 8 \\
& X_1 + 2X_2 \leq 12 \\
& X_1 + X_2 \geq 2 \\
& X_1, X_2 \geq 0
\end{array}
$$

a. Which of the constraints are binding at the optimal solution?
b. Is the optimal solution to this problem unique, or is there an alternate optimal solution?
c. What is the optimal solution to this problem if the value of the objective function coefficient for variable X_1 is zero?
d. How much can the objective function coefficient for variable X_2 decrease before changing the optimal solution?
e. Given the objective in this problem, if management could increase the RHS value for any of the constraints for identical costs, which would you choose to increase and why?

5. Implement the following LP model in a spreadsheet. Use Solver to solve the problem and create a Sensitivity Report. Use this information to answer the following questions:

$$
\begin{array}{ll}
\text{MIN:} & 5X_1 + 3X_2 + 4X_3 \\
\text{Subject to:} & X_1 + X_2 + 2X_3 \geq 2 \\
& 5X_1 + 3X_2 + 2X_3 \geq 1 \\
& X_1, X_2, X_3 \geq 0
\end{array}
$$

a. What is the smallest value the objective function coefficient for X_3 can assume without changing the optimal solution?
b. What is the optimal objective function value if the objective function coefficient for X_3 changes to –1? (*Hint:* The answer to this question is not given in the Sensitivity Report. Consider what the new objective function is relative to the constraints.)
c. What is the optimal objective function value if the RHS value of the first constraint increases to 7?
d. What is the optimal objective function value if the RHS value of the first constraint decreases by 1?
e. Will the current solution remain optimal if the objective function coefficients for X_1 and X_3 both decrease by 1?

6. The CitruSun Corporation ships frozen orange juice concentrate from processing plants in Eustis and Clermont to distributors in Miami, Orlando, and Tallahassee. Each plant can produce 20 tons of concentrate each week. The company has just received orders of 10 tons from Miami for the coming week, 15 tons for Orlando, and 10 tons for Tallahassee. The cost per ton for supplying each of the distributors from each of the processing plants is shown in the following table.

	Miami	**Orlando**	**Tallahassee**
Eustis	\$260	\$220	\$290
Clermont	\$230	\$240	\$310

The company wants to determine the least costly plan for filling their orders for the coming week.

a. Formulate an LP model for this problem.
b. Implement the model in a spreadsheet and solve it.
c. What is the optimal solution?
d. Is the optimal solution degenerate?
e. Is the optimal solution unique? If not, identify an alternate optimal solution for the problem.
f. How would the solution change if the plant in Clermont is forced to shut for one day resulting in a loss of four tons of production capacity?
g. What would the optimal objective function value be if the processing capacity in Eustis was reduced by five tons?
h. Interpret the reduced cost for shipping from Eustis to Miami.

7. Use Solver to create Answer and Sensitivity Reports for question 14 at the end of chapter 2 and answer the following questions:
   a. How much excess wiring and testing capacity exists in the optimal solution?
   b. What is the company's total profit if it has 10 additional hours of wiring capacity?
   c. By how much does the profit on alternators need to increase before their production is justified?
   d. Does the optimal solution change if the marginal profit on generators decreases by $50 and the marginal profit on alternators increases by $75?
   e. Suppose the marginal profit on generators decreases by $25. What is the maximum profit that can be earned on alternators without changing the optimal solution?
   f. Suppose the amount of wiring required on alternators is reduced to 1.5 hours. Does this change the optimal solution? Why or why not?
8. Use Solver to create Answer and Sensitivity Reports for question 21 at the end of chapter 2 and answer the following questions:
   a. How much can the price of watermelons drop before it is no longer optimal to plant any watermelons?
   b. How much does the price of cantaloupes have to increase before it is optimal to only grow cantaloupes?
   c. Suppose the price of watermelons drops by $60 per acre and the price of cantaloupes increases by $50 per acre. Is the current solution still optimal?
   d. Suppose the farmer can lease up to 20 acres of land from a neighboring farm to plant additional crops. How many acres should the farmer lease and what is the maximum amount he should pay to lease each acre?
9. Create a Sensitivity Report for Electro-Poly's make vs. buy problem in section 3.8 of chapter 3 and answer the following questions.
   a. Is the solution degenerate?
   b. How much can the cost of making model 1 slip rings increase before it becomes more economical to buy some of them?
   c. Suppose the cost of buying model 2 slip rings decreased by $9 per unit. Would the optimal solution change?
   d. Assume workers in the wiring area normally make $12 per hour and get 50% more when they work overtime. Should Electro-Poly schedule these employees to work overtime to complete this job? If so, how much money would this save?
   e. Assume workers in the harnessing area normally make $12 per hour and get 50% more when they work overtime. Should Electro-Poly schedule these employees to work overtime to complete this job? If so, how much money would this save?

f. Create a Spider Table that shows the effect of varying each of the wiring and harnessing requirements (in cells B17 thru D18) to 90% of their current levels in 1% increments. If Electro-Ploy wanted to invest in training or new technology to reduce one of these values, which one offers the greatest potential for cost savings?

10. Use Solver to create a Sensitivity Report for question 10 at the end of chapter 3 and answer the following questions:
    a. If the company could get 50 more units of routing capacity, should they do it? If so, how much should they be willing to pay for it?
    b. If the company could get 50 more units of sanding capacity, should they do it? If so, how much should they be willing to pay for it?
    c. Suppose the polishing time on country tables could be reduced from 2.5 to 2 units per table. How much should the company be willing to pay to achieve this improvement in efficiency?
    d. Contemporary tables sell for $450. By how much would the selling price have to decrease before we would no longer be willing to produce contemporary tables? Does this make sense? Explain.
11. Use Solver to create a Sensitivity Report for question 14 at the end of chapter 3 and answer the following questions:
    a. Which of the constraints in the problem are binding?
    b. If the company was going to eliminate one of its products, which should it be?
    c. If the company could buy 1,000 additional memory chips at the usual cost, should they do it? If so, how much would profits increase?
    d. Suppose the manufacturing costs used in this analysis were estimated hastily and are known to be somewhat imprecise. Which products would you be most concerned about having more precise cost estimates for before implementing this solution?
    e. Create a Spider Plot showing the sensitivity of the total profit to the selling price of each product (adjusting the original values by 90%, 92%, ..., 110%). According to this graph, total profit is most sensitive to which product?
12. Use Solver to create a Sensitivity Report for question 16 at the end of chapter 3 and answer the following questions:
    a. How much would electric trimmers have to cost in order for the company to consider purchasing these items rather than making them?
    b. If the cost to make gas trimmers increased to $90 per unit, how would the optimal solution change?
    c. How much should the company be willing to pay to acquire additional capacity in the assembly area? Explain.
    d. How much should the company be willing to pay to acquire additional capacity in the production area? Explain.
    e. Prepare a Spider Plot showing the sensitivity of the total cost to changes in costs to make and the costs to buy (adjusting the original values by of 90%, 92%, ..., 110%). Which of these costs is the total cost most sensitive to?
    f. Suppose the hours of production capacity available is uncertain and could vary from 9,500 to 10,500. How does the optimal solution change for every 100-hour change in production capacity within this range?
13. Use Solver to create a Sensitivity Report for question 18 at the end of chapter 3 and answer the following questions.

a. Suppose the cost of the first two compounds increases by $1.00 per pound and the cost of the third compound increases by $0.50 per pound. Does the optimal solution change?
b. How does the solution change if the maximum amount of potassium allowed decreases from 45% to 40%?
c. How much does the cost of the mix increase if the specifications for CHEMIX change to require at least 31% sulfur? (*Hint:* Remember that the shadow price indicates the impact on the objective function if the RHS value of the associated constraint increases by 1.)

14. Use Solver to create a Sensitivity Report for question 19 at the end of chapter 3 and answer the following questions.
    a. What is the maximum level profit that can be achieved for this problem?
    b. Are there alternate optimal solutions to this problem? If so, identify the solution that allows the most grade 5 oranges to be used in fruit baskets while still achieving the maximum profit identified in part a.
    c. If Holiday could acquire 1,000 more pounds of grade 4 oranges at a cost of $2.65 per 100 pounds, should they do it? Why?
    d. Create a Spider Table and Plot showing the change in the total profit obtained by changing the required grade of fruit baskets and juice from 90% to 110% in 1% increments. If the department of agriculture wants to increase the required rating of one of these products, which product should the company lobby for?
15. Use Solver to create a Sensitivity Report for question 20 at the end of chapter 3 and answer the following questions:
    a. Are there alternate optimal solutions to this problem? Explain.
    b. What is the highest possible octane rating for regular gasoline, assuming the company wants to maximize its profits? What is the octane rating for supreme gasoline at this solution?
    c. What is the highest possible octane rating for supreme gasoline, assuming the company wants to maximize its profits? What is the octane rating for regular gasoline at this solution?
    d. Which of the two profit-maximizing solutions identified in parts b and c would you recommend the company implement? Why?
    e. If the company could buy another 150 barrels of input 2 at a cost of $17 per barrel, should they do it? Why?
16. Use Solver to create a Sensitivity Report for question 24 at the end of chapter 3 and answer the following questions:
    a. How many more three-bedroom units can be built in the development if the zoning board does not restrict the developer to 40 units?
    b. By how much does the developer's monthly rental income increase if the zoning board allows the developer to build five more units in the complex?
    c. If the developer built one efficiency unit, what effect does this have on the total rental income?
17. Use Solver to create a Sensitivity Report for question 25 at the end of chapter 3 and answer the following questions:
    a. What total profit level is realized if 100 extra hours of labor are available?
    b. Assume a marginal labor cost of $11 per hour in determining the unit profits of each of the three products. How much should management pay to acquire 100 additional labor hours?
    c. Interpret the reduced cost value for tuners. Why are more tuners not being produced?

18. Use Solver to create a Sensitivity Report for question 26 at the end of chapter 3 and answer the following questions:
    a. Is the optimal solution unique? How can you tell?
    b. Which location is receiving the fewest cars?
    c. Suppose a particular car at location 1 must be sent to location 3 in order to meet a customer's request. How much does this increase costs for the company?
    d. Suppose location 6 must have at least eight cars shipped to it. What impact does this have on the optimal objective function value?
19. Refer to the previous question. Suppose location 1 has 15 cars available rather than 16. Create a Sensitivity Report for this problem and answer the following questions:
    a. Is the optimal solution unique? How can you tell?
    b. According to the Sensitivity Report, by how much should the total cost increase if we force a car to be shipped from location 1 to location 3?
    c. Add a constraint to the model to force one car to be shipped from location 1 to location 3. By how much did the total cost increase?
20. Use Solver to create a Sensitivity Report for question 27 at the end of chapter 3 and answer the following questions:
    a. Is the solution unique?
    b. If Sentry wants to increase their production capacity in order to meet more of the demand for their product, which plant should they use? Explain.
    c. If the cost of shipping from Phoenix to Tacoma increased to $1.98 per unit, would the solution change? Explain.
    d. Could the company make more money if they relaxed the restriction that each distributor must receive at least 80% of the predicted demand? Explain.
    e. How much extra should the company charge the distributor in Tacoma if this distributor insisted on receiving 8,500 units?
21. Use Solver to create a Sensitivity Report for question 28 at the end of chapter 3 and answer the following questions.
    a. Is the solution degenerate?
    b. Is the solution unique?
    c. How much should the recycler be willing to pay to acquire more cardboard?
    d. If the recycler could buy 50 more tons of newspaper at a cost of $18 per ton, should they do it? Why or why not?
    e. What is the recycler's marginal cost of producing each of the three different types of pulp?
    f. By how much would the cost of converting white office paper into newsprint have to drop before it would become economical to use white office paper for this purpose?
    g. By how much would the yield of newsprint pulp per ton of cardboard have to increase before it would become economical to use cardboard for this purpose?
22. Use Solver to create a Sensitivity Report for question 34 at the end of chapter 3 and answer the following questions.
    a. Is the solution degenerate?
    b. Is the solution unique?
    c. How much can the profit per ton on commodity one decrease before the optimal solution would change?

d. Create a Spider Table and Plot showing the change in the total profit obtained by changing the profit per ton on each commodity from 95% to 105% in 1% increments. If the shipping company wanted to increase the price of transporting one of the commodities, which one would have the greatest influence on total profits?

23. Use Solver to create a Sensitivity Report for question 35 at the end of chapter 3 and answer the following questions.
    a. Is the solution degenerate?
    b. Is the solution unique?
    c. Use a Solver Table to determine the maximum price the Pelletier Corporation should be willing to pay for a two-month lease.
    d. Suppose the company is not certain that it will need exactly 20,000 sq. ft. in month 3 and believes that actual amount needed may be as low as 15,000 sq ft or as high as 25,000 sq. ft. Use a Solver Table to determine if this would have any impact on the leasing arrangements the company selects in months 1 and 2.
24. Refer to question 43 in chapter 3 and create a Solver table to answer the following questions.
    a. Suppose the gas producer is in need of an extra 50,000 cf of storage capacity for the next 10 days and wants to buy this capacity from the gas trading firm. What is the least amount of money the gas trading company should demand to provide this capacity?
    b. How much should the gas trading company be willing to pay to increase their available storage capacity to 500,000 cf?
25. Consider the following LP problem:

$$\begin{aligned} \text{MAX:} \quad & 4X_1 + 2X_2 \\ \text{Subject to:} \quad & 2X_1 + 4X_2 \le 20 \\ & 3X_1 + 5X_2 \le 15 \\ & X_1, X_2 \ge 0 \end{aligned}$$

    a. Use slack variables to rewrite this problem so that all its constraints are equal-to constraints.
    b. Identify the different sets of basic variables that might be used to obtain a solution to the problem.
    c. Of the possible sets of basic variables, which lead to feasible solutions and what are the values for all the variables at each of these solutions?
    d. Graph the feasible region for this problem and indicate which basic feasible solution corresponds to each of the extreme points of the feasible region.
    e. What is the value of the objective function at each of the basic feasible solutions?
    f. What is the optimal solution to the problem?
    g. Which constraints are binding at the optimal solution?
26. Consider the following LP problem:

$$\begin{aligned} \text{MAX:} \quad & 2X_1 + 4X_2 \\ \text{Subject to:} \quad & -X_1 + 2X_2 \le 8 \\ & X_1 + 2X_2 \le 12 \\ & X_1 + X_2 \ge 2 \\ & X_1, X_2 \ge 0 \end{aligned}$$

a. Use slack variables to rewrite this problem so that all its constraints are equal-to constraints.
b. Identify the different sets of basic variables that might be used to obtain a solution to the problem.
c. Of the possible sets of basic variables, which lead to feasible solutions and what are the values for all the variables at each of these solutions?
d. Graph the feasible region for this problem and indicate which basic feasible solution corresponds to each of the extreme points of the feasible region.
e. What is the value of the objective function at each of the basic feasible solutions?
f. What is the optimal solution to the problem?
g. Which constraints are binding at the optimal solution?

27. Consider the following LP problem:

MIN:	$5X_1 + 3X_2 + 4X_3$
Subject to:	$X_1 + X_2 + 2X_3 \geq 2$
	$5X_1 + 3X_2 + 2X_3 \geq 1$
	$X_1, X_2, X_3 \geq 0$

a. Use slack variables to rewrite this problem so that all its constraints are equal-to constraints.
b. Identify the different sets of basic variables that might be used to obtain a solution to the problem.
c. Of the possible sets of basic variables, which lead to feasible solutions and what are the values for all the variables at each of these solutions?
d. What is the value of the objective function at each of the basic feasible solutions?
e. What is the optimal solution to the problem?
f. Which constraints are binding at the optimal solution?

28. Consider the following constraint, where S is a slack variable:

$$2X_1 + 4X_2 + S = 16$$

a. What was the original constraint before the slack variable was included?
b. What value of S is associated with each of the following points:
   i) $X_1 = 2, X_2 = 2$
   ii) $X_1 = 8, X_2 = 0$
   iii) $X_1 = 1, X_2 = 3$
   iv) $X_1 = 4, X_2 = 1$

29. Consider the following constraint, where S is a slack variable:

$$3X_1 + 4X_2 - S = 12$$

a. What was the original constraint before the slack variable was included?
b. What value of S is associated with each of the following points:
   i) $X_1 = 5, X_2 = 0$
   ii) $X_1 = 2, X_2 = 2$
   iii) $X_1 = 7, X_2 = 1$
   iv) $X_1 = 4, X_2 = 0$

CASE 4.1: PARKET SISTERS

Contributed by Jack Yurkiewicz. Lubin School of Business, Pace University, New York.

Computers and word processors notwithstanding, the art of writing by hand recently entered a boom era. People are buying fountain pens again, and mechanical pencils are becoming more popular than ever. Joe Script, the president and CEO of Parket Sisters, a small but growing pen and pencil manufacturer, wants to establish a better foothold in the market. The writing market is divided into two main sectors. One, dominated by Mont Blanc, Cross, Parker Brothers, Waterman, Schaffer, and a few others, caters to people who want writing instruments. The product lines from these companies consist of pens and pencils of elaborate design, lifetime warranty, and high price. At the other end of the market are manufacturers like BIC, Pentel, and many companies from the far east, offering good quality items, low price, few trims, and limited diversity. These pens and pencils are meant to be used for a limited time and disposed of when the ink in a ballpoint pen runs out, or when the lead in a mechanical pencil won't retract or extend. In short, these items are not meant for repair.

Joe thinks that there must be a middle ground, and that is where he wants to position his company. Parket Sisters makes high-quality items, with limited trim and diversity, but also offers lifetime warranties. Furthermore, its pens and pencils are ergonomically efficient. Joe knows that some people want the status of the Mont Blanc Meisterstuck pen, for example, but he has never met a person who said that writing with such a pen is enjoyable. The pen is too large and clumsy for smooth writing. Parket Sisters' products, on the other hand, have a reputation for working well, are easy to hold and use, and cause limited "writer's fatigue."

Parket Sisters makes only three items—a ballpoint pen, a mechanical pencil, and a fountain pen. All are available in just one color, black, and are sold mostly in specialty stores and from better catalog companies. The per-unit profit of the items is $3.00 for the ballpoint pen, $3.00 for the mechanical pencil, and $5.00 for the fountain pen. These values take into account labor, the cost of materials, packing, quality control, and so on.

The company is trying to plan its production mix for each week. Joe believes that the company can sell any number of pens and pencils it produces, but production is currently limited by the available resources. Because of a recent strike and certain cash-flow problems, the suppliers of these resources are selling them to Parket Sisters in limited amounts. In particular, Joe can count on getting at most 1,000 ounces of plastic, 1,200 ounces of chrome, and 2,000 ounces of stainless steel each week from his suppliers, and these figures are not likely to change in the near future. Because of Joe's excellent reputation, the suppliers will sell Joe any amount (up to his limit) of the resources he needs when he requires them. That is, the suppliers do not require Joe to buy some fixed quantities of resources in advance of his production of pens and pencils; therefore, these resources can be considered variable costs rather than fixed costs for the pens and pencils.

Each ballpoint pen requires 1.2 ounces of plastic, 0.8 ounces of chrome, and 2 ounces of stainless steel. Each mechanical pencil requires 1.7 ounces of plastic, no chrome, and 3 ounces of stainless steel. Each fountain pen requires 1.2 ounces of plastic, 2.3 ounces of chrome, and 4.5 ounces of stainless steel. Joe believes LP could help him decide what his weekly product mix should consist of.

Getting his notes and notebooks, Joe grapples with the LP formulation. In addition to the constraints of the available resources, he recognizes that the model should include many other constraints (such as labor time availability and materials for packing). However, Joe wants to keep his model simple. He knows that eventually he'll have to take other constraints into account, but as a first-pass model, he'll restrict the constraints to just the three resources: plastic, chrome, and stainless steel.

With only these three constraints, Joe can formulate the problem easily as:

$$
\begin{aligned}
\text{MAX:} \quad & 3.0X_1 + 3.0X_2 + 5.0X_3 \\
\text{Subject to:} \quad & 1.2X_1 + 1.7X_2 + 1.2X_3 \le 1{,}000 \\
& 0.8X_1 + 0X_2 + 2.3X_3 \le 1{,}200 \\
& 2.0X_1 + 3.0X_2 + 4.5X_3 \le 2{,}000 \\
& X_1, X_2, X_3 \ge 0
\end{aligned}
$$

where:

X_1 = the number of ballpoint pens
X_2 = the number of mechanical pencils
X_3 = the number of fountain pens

Joe's knowledge of Excel and the Solver feature is limited so he asks you to enter and solve the problem for him, then answer the following questions. (Assume each question is independent unless otherwise stated.)

1. What should the weekly product mix consist of, and what is the weekly net profit?
2. Is the optimal solution to question 1 degenerate? Explain your response.
3. Is the optimal solution from question 1 unique, or are there alternate answers to this question? Explain your response.
4. What is the marginal value of one more unit of chrome? Of plastic?
5. A local distributor has offered to sell Parket Sisters an additional 500 ounces of stainless steel for $0.60 per ounce more than it ordinarily pays. Should the company buy the steel at this price? Explain your response.
6. If Parket Sisters buys the additional 500 ounces of stainless steel noted in question 5, what is the new optimal product mix and what is the new optimal profit? Explain your response.
7. Suppose that the distributor offers to sell Parket Sisters some additional plastic at a price of only $1.00 over its usual cost of $5.00 per ounce. However, the distributor will sell the plastic only in lot sizes of 500 ounces. Should Parket Sisters buy one such lot? Explain your response.
8. The distributor is willing to sell the plastic in lots of just 100 ounces instead of the usual 500-ounce lots, still at $1.00 over Parket Sisters' cost of $5.00 per ounce. How many lots (if any) should Parket Sisters buy? What is the optimal product mix if the company buys these lots, and what is the optimal profit?
9. Parket Sisters has an opportunity to sell some of its plastic for $6.50 per ounce to another company. The other company (which does not produce pens and pencils and, therefore, is not a competitor) wants to buy 300 ounces of plastic from Parket Sisters. Should Parket Sisters sell the plastic to the other com-

pany? What happens to Parket Sisters' product mix and overall profit if it does sell the plastic? Be as specific as possible.

10. The chrome supplier might have to fulfill an emergency order, and would be able to send only 1,000 ounces of chrome this week instead of the usual 1,200 ounces. If Parket Sisters receives only 1,000 ounces of chrome, what is the optimal product mix and optimal profit? Be as specific as possible.
11. The R&D department at Parket Sisters has been redesigning the mechanical pencil to make it more profitable. The new design requires 1.1 ounces of plastic, 2.0 ounces of chrome, and 2.0 ounces of stainless steel. If the company can sell one of these pencils at a net profit of $3.00, should it approve the new design? Explain your response.
12. If the per-unit profit on ballpoint pens decreases to $2.50, what is the optimal product mix and what is the company's total profit?
13. The marketing department suggested introducing a new felt tip pen that requires 1.8 ounces of plastic, 0.5 ounces of chrome, and 1.3 ounces of stainless steel. What profit must this product generate in order to make it worthwhile to produce?
14. What must the minimum per-unit profit of mechanical pencils be in order to make them worthwhile to produce?
15. Management believes that the company should produce at least 20 mechanical pencils per week to round out its product line. What effect would this have on overall profit? Give a numerical answer.
16. If the profit on a fountain pen is $6.75 instead of $5.00, what is the optimal product mix and optimal profit?

CASE 4.2: KAMM INDUSTRIES

If your home or office is carpeted, there's a good chance that carpet came from Dalton, Georgia—also known as the "Carpet Capital of the World." Manufacturers in the Dalton area produce more than 70 percent of the total output of the $9 billion world-wide carpet industry. Competition in this industry is intense and and forces producers to strive for maximum efficiency and economies of scale. It also forces producers to continually evaluate investments in new technology.

Kamm Industries is one of the leading carpet producers in the Dalton area. Its owner, Geoff Kamm, has asked for you assistance in planning the production schedule for the next quarter (13 weeks). The company has orders for fifteen different types of carpets that the company can either produce on two types of looms: Dobbie looms and Pantera looms. Pantera looms produce standard tufted carpeting. Dobbie looms can also produce standard tufted carpeting but also allow the incorporation of designs (such as flowers or corporate logos) into the carpeting. The following table summarizes the orders for each type of carpet that must be produced in the coming quarter along with their production rates and costs on each type of loom, and the cost of subcontracting each order. Note that the first 4 orders involved special production requirements that can only be achieved on a Dobbie loom or via subcontracting. Assume that any portion of an order may be subcontracted.

	Demand	Dobbie		Pantera		Subcontract
Carpet	Yds	Yd/Hr	Cost/Yd	Yd/Hr	Cost/Yd	Cost/Yd
1	14,000	4.510	$2.66	na	na	$2.77
2	52,000	4.796	2.55	na	na	2.73
3	44,000	4.629	2.64	na	na	2.85
4	20,000	4.256	2.56	na	na	2.73
5	77,500	5.145	1.61	5.428	$1.60	1.76
6	109,500	3.806	1.62	3.935	1.61	1.76
7	120,000	4.168	1.64	4.316	1.61	1.76
8	60,000	5.251	1.48	5.356	1.47	1.59
9	7,500	5.223	1.50	5.277	1.50	1.71
10	69,500	5.216	1.44	5.419	1.42	1.63
11	68,500	3.744	1.64	3.835	1.64	1.80
12	83,000	4.157	1.57	4.291	1.56	1.78
13	10,000	4.422	1.49	4.558	1.48	1.63
14	381,000	5.281	1.31	5.353	1.30	1.44
15	64,000	4.222	1.51	4.288	1.50	1.69

Kamm currently owns and operates 15 Dobbie looms and 80 Pantera looms. To maximize efficiency and keep pace with demand, the company operates 24 hours a day, 7 days a week. Each machine is down for routine maintenance for approximately 2 hours per week. Create a spreadsheet model for this problem that can be used to determine the optimal production plan and answer the following questions.

1. What is the optimal production plan and associated cost?
2. Is the solution degenerate?
3. Is the solution unique?
4. What would happen to the total cost if one of the Dobbie machines broke and could not be used at all during the quarter?
5. What would happen to the total cost if an additional Dobbie machine was purchased and available for the quarter?
6. What would happen to the total cost if one of the Pantera machines broke and could not be used at all during the quarter?
7. What would happen to the total cost if an additional Pantera machine was purchased and available for the quarter?
8. Explain the shadow prices and the values in the "Allowable Increase" column of the Sensitivity Report for the products that are being outsourced.
9. How much money does it cost to produce carpet order 2? How much would the total costs decrease if that order were eliminated? Explain.
10. If the carpets in orders 5 through 15 all sell for the same amount, which type of carpet should Kamm encourage its salesforce to sell more of? Why?
11. If the cost of buying the carpet in order 1 increased to $2.80 per yard, would the optimal solution change? Why?
12. If the cost of buying the carpet in order 15 decreased to $1.65 per yard, would the optimal solution change? Why?

Chapter 5

Network Modeling

5.0 INTRODUCTION

A number of practical decision problems in business fall into a category known as **network flow problems.** These problems share a common characteristic—they can be described or displayed in a graphical form known as a **network.** This chapter focuses on several types of network flow problems: transshipment problems, shortest path problems, maximal flow problems, transportation/assignment problems, and generalized network flow problems. Although specialized solution procedures exist for solving network flow problems, we will consider how to formulate and solve these problems as LP problems. We will also consider a different type of network problem known as the **minimum spanning tree problem.**

5.1 THE TRANSSHIPMENT PROBLEM

Let's begin our study of network flow problems by considering the transshipment problem. As you will see, most of the other types of network flow problems all can be viewed as simple variations of the transshipment problem. So, once you understand how to formulate and solve transshipment problems, the other types of problems will be easy to solve. The following example illustrates the transshipment problem.

The Bavarian Motor Company (BMC) manufactures expensive luxury cars in Hamburg, Germany, and exports cars to sell in the United States. The exported cars are shipped from Hamburg to ports in Newark, New Jersey, and Jacksonville, Florida. From these ports, the cars are transported by rail or truck to distributors located in Boston, Massachusetts; Columbus, Ohio; Atlanta, Georgia; Richmond, Virginia; and Mobile, Alabama. Figure 5.1 shows the possible shipping routes available to the company along with the transportation cost for shipping each car along the indicated path.

Currently, 200 cars are available at the port in Newark and 300 are available in Jacksonville. The numbers of cars needed by the distributors in Boston, Columbus, Atlanta, Richmond, and Mobile are 100, 60, 170, 80, and 70, respectively. BMC wants to determine the least costly way of transporting cars from the ports in Newark and Jacksonville to the cities where they are needed.

5.1.1 Characteristics of Network Flow Problems

Figure 5.1 illustrates a number of characteristics common to all network flow problems. All network flow problems can be represented as a collection of nodes connected by arcs. The circles in Figure 5.1 are called **nodes** in the terminology of network flow problems, and the lines connecting the nodes are called **arcs.** The arcs in a network indicate the valid paths, routes, or connections between the nodes in a network flow problem. When the lines connecting the nodes in a network are arrows that indicate a direction, the arcs in the network are called

FIGURE 5.1
Network representation of the BMC transshipment problem

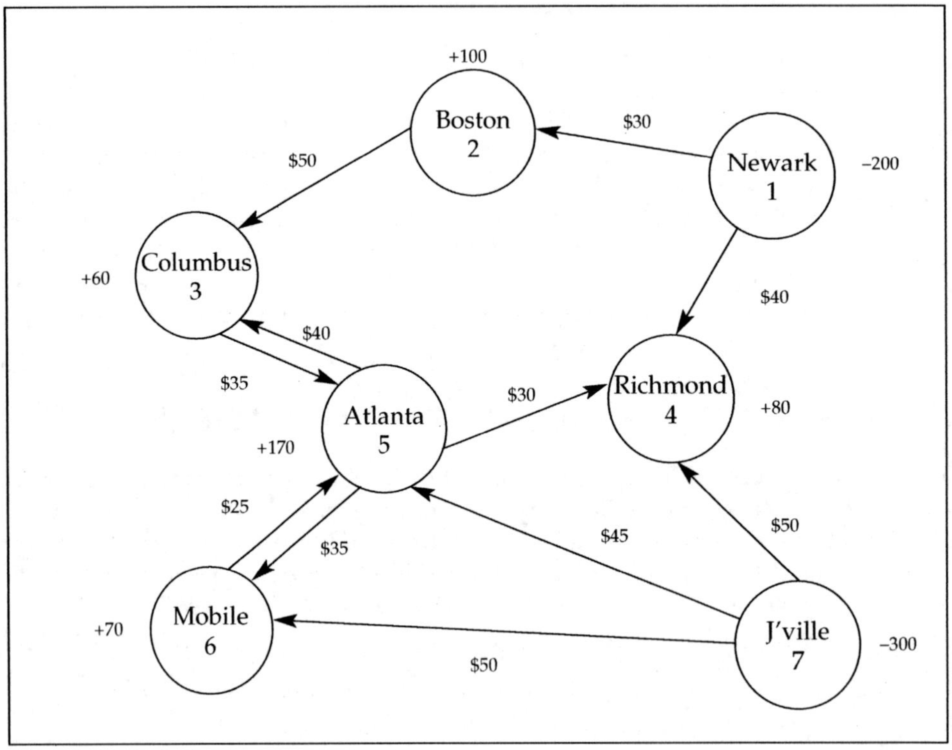

directed arcs. This chapter discusses directed arcs primarily but, for convenience, refers to them as arcs.

The notion of **supply nodes** (or sending nodes) and **demand nodes** (or receiving nodes) is another common element of network flow problems illustrated in Figure 5.1. The nodes representing the port cities of Newark and Jacksonville are both supply nodes because each has a supply of cars to send to other nodes in the network. Richmond represents a demand node because it demands to receive cars from the other nodes. All the other nodes in this network are transshipment nodes. **Transshipment nodes** can both send to and receive from other nodes in the network. For example, the node representing Atlanta in Figure 5.1 is a transshipment node because it can *receive* cars from Jacksonville, Mobile, and Columbus, and it can also send cars to Columbus, Mobile, and Richmond.

The net supply or demand for each node in the network is indicated by a positive or negative number next to each node. **Positive numbers** represent the *demand* at a given node, and **negative numbers** represent the *supply* available at a node. For example, the value +80 next to the node for Richmond indicates that the number of cars needs to increase by 80—or that Richmond has a *demand* for 80 cars. The value –200 next to the node for Newark indicates that the number of cars can be reduced by 200—or that Newark has a *supply* of 200 cars. A transshipment node can have either a net supply or demand, but not both. In this particular problem, all the transshipment nodes have demands. For example, the node representing Mobile in Figure 5.1 has a demand for 70 cars.

5.1.2 The Decision Variables for Network Flow Problems

The goal in a network flow model is to determine how many items should be moved (or flow) across each of the arcs. In our example, BMC needs to determine the least costly method of transporting cars along the various arcs shown in Figure 5.1 to distribute cars where they are needed. Thus, each of the arcs in a network flow model represents a decision variable. Determining the optimal flow for each arc is the equivalent of determining the optimal value for the corresponding decision variable.

It is customary to use numbers to identify each node in a network flow problem. In Figure 5.1, the number 1 identifies the node for Newark, 2 identifies the node for Boston, and so on. You can assign numbers to the nodes in any manner, but it is best to use a series of consecutive integers. The node numbers provide a convenient way to identify the decision variables needed to formulate the LP model for the problem. For each arc in a network flow model, you need to define one decision variable as:

X_{ij} = the number of items shipped (or flowing) *from* node i *to* node j

The network in Figure 5.1 for our example problem contains 11 arcs. Therefore, the LP formulation of this model requires the following 11 decision variables:

X_{12} = the number of cars shipped *from* node 1 (Newark) *to* node 2 (Boston)
X_{14} = the number of cars shipped *from* node 1 (Newark) *to* node 4 (Richmond)
X_{23} = the number of cars shipped *from* node 2 (Boston) *to* node 3 (Columbus)
X_{35} = the number of cars shipped *from* node 3 (Columbus) *to* node 5 (Atlanta)

X_{53} = the number of cars shipped *from* node 5 (Atlanta) *to* node 3 (Columbus)
X_{54} = the number of cars shipped *from* node 5 (Atlanta) *to* node 4 (Richmond)
X_{56} = the number of cars shipped *from* node 5 (Atlanta) *to* node 6 (Mobile)
X_{65} = the number of cars shipped *from* node 6 (Mobile) *to* node 5 (Atlanta)
X_{74} = the number of cars shipped *from* node 7 (Jacksonville) *to* node 4 (Richmond)
X_{75} = the number of cars shipped *from* node 7 (Jacksonville) *to* node 5 (Atlanta)
X_{76} = the number of cars shipped *from* node 7 (Jacksonville) *to* node 6 (Mobile)

5.1.3 The Objective Function for Network Flow Problems

Each unit that flows from node i to node j in a network flow problem usually incurs some cost, c_{ij}. This cost might represent a monetary payment, a distance, or some other type of penalty. The objective in most network flow problems is to minimize the total cost, distance, or penalty that must be incurred to solve the problem. Such problems are known as ***minimum cost network flow problems.***

In our example problem, different monetary costs must be paid for each car shipped across a given arc. For example, it costs \$30 to ship each car from node 1 (Newark) to node 2 (Boston). Because X_{12} represents the number of cars shipped from Newark to Boston, the total cost incurred by cars shipped along this path is determined by $\$30X_{12}$. Similar calculations can be done for the other arcs in the network. Because BMC is interested in minimizing the total shipping costs, the objective function for this problem is expressed as:

$$\begin{aligned}\text{MIN:}\ &+30X_{12}+40X_{14}+50X_{23}+35X_{35}+40X_{53}+30X_{54}\\ &+35X_{56}+25X_{65}+50X_{74}+45X_{75}+50X_{76}\end{aligned}$$

5.1.4 The Constraints for Network Flow Problems

Just as the number of arcs in the network determines the number of variables in the LP formulation of a network flow problem, the number of nodes determines the number of constraints. In particular, there must be one constraint for each node. A simple set of rules, known as the ***Balance-of-Flow Rules,*** applies to constructing the constraints for minimum cost network flow problems. These rules are summarized as follows:

For Minimum Cost Network Flow Problems Where:	Apply This Balance-of-Flow Rule at Each Node:
Total Supply > Total Demand	Inflow – Outflow ≥ Supply or Demand
Total Supply < Total Demand	Inflow – Outflow ≤ Supply or Demand
Total Supply = Total Demand	Inflow – Outflow = Supply or Demand

It should be noted that if the total supply in a network flow problem is less than the total demand, then it will be impossible to satisfy all the demand. The balance-of-flow rule listed for this case assumes that you want to determine the least costly way of distributing the available supply—knowing that it is impossible to satisfy all the demand.

So to apply the correct balance-of-flow rule, we must first compare the total supply in the network to the total demand. In our example problem, there is a total supply of 500 cars and a total demand for 480 cars. Because the total supply exceeds the total demand, we will use the first balance-of-flow rule to formulate our example problem. That is, at each node, we will create a constraint of the form:

$$\text{Inflow} - \text{Outflow} \geq \text{Supply or Demand}$$

For example, consider node 1 (Newark) in Figure 5.1. No arcs flow into this node but two arcs (represented by X_{12} and X_{14}) flow out of the node. According to the balance-of-flow rule, the constraint for this node is:

$$\text{Constraint for node 1:} \qquad -X_{12} - X_{14} \geq -200$$

Notice that the supply at this node is represented by –200 following the convention we established earlier. If we multiply both sides of this equation by –1, we see that it is equivalent to $+X_{12} + X_{14} \leq +200$. (Note that multiplying an inequality by –1 reverses the direction of the inequality.) This constraint indicates that the total number of cars flowing out of Newark must not exceed 200. So, if we include either form of this constraint in the model, we can ensure that no more than 200 cars will be shipped from Newark.

Now consider the constraint for node 2 (Boston) in Figure 5.1. Because Boston has a demand for 100 cars, the balance-of-flow rule requires that the total number of cars coming into Boston from Newark (via X_{12}) minus the total number of cars being shipped out of Boston to Columbus (via X_{23}) must leave at least 100 cars in Boston. This condition is imposed by the constraint:

$$\text{Constraint for node 2:} \qquad +X_{12} - X_{23} \geq +100$$

Note that this constraint makes it possible to leave more than the required number of cars in Boston (*e.g.*, 200 cars could be shipped into Boston and only 50 shipped out, leaving 150 cars in Boston). However, because our objective is to minimize costs, we can be sure that an excess number of cars will never be shipped to any city, because that would result in unnecessary costs being incurred.

Using the balance-of-flow rule, the constraints for each of the remaining nodes in our example problem are represented as:

$$\begin{array}{ll}
\text{Constraint for node 3:} & +X_{23} + X_{53} - X_{35} \geq +60 \\
\text{Constraint for node 4:} & +X_{14} + X_{54} + X_{74} \geq +80 \\
\text{Constraint for node 5:} & +X_{35} + X_{65} + X_{75} - X_{53} - X_{54} - X_{56} \geq +170 \\
\text{Constraint for node 6:} & +X_{56} + X_{76} - X_{65} \geq +70 \\
\text{Constraint for node 7:} & -X_{74} - X_{75} - X_{76} \geq -300
\end{array}$$

Again, each constraint indicates that the flow into a given node minus the flow out of that same node must be greater than or equal to the supply or demand at the node. So, if you draw a graph of a network flow problem like the one in Figure 5.1, it is easy to write out the constraints for the problem by following the balance-of-flow rule. Of course, we also need to specify the following nonnegativity condition for all the decision variables because negative flows should not occur on arcs:

$$X_{ij} \geq 0 \text{ for all } i \text{ and } j$$

5.1.5 Implementing the Model in a Spreadsheet

The formulation for the BMC transshipment problem is summarized as:

MIN: $+30X_{12} + 40X_{14} + 50X_{23} + 35X_{35} + 40X_{53} + 30X_{54} + 35X_{56} + 25X_{65} + 50X_{74} + 45X_{75} + 50X_{76}$ } total shipping cost

Subject to:

$-X_{12} - X_{14} \geq -200$ } flow constraint for node 1

$+X_{12} - X_{23} \geq +100$ } flow constraint for node 2

$+X_{23} + X_{53} - X_{35} \geq +60$ } flow constraint for node 3

$+X_{14} + X_{54} + X_{74} \geq +80$ } flow constraint for node 4

$+X_{35} + X_{65} + X_{75} - X_{53} - X_{54} - X_{56} \geq +170$ } flow constraint for node 5

$+X_{56} + X_{76} - X_{65} \geq +70$ } flow constraint for node 6

$-X_{74} - X_{75} - X_{76} \geq -300$ } flow constraint for node 7

$X_{ij} \geq 0$ for all i and j } nonnegativity conditions

A convenient way of implementing this type of problem is shown in Figure 5.2 (and in the file Fig5-2.xls on your data disk). In this spreadsheet, cells B6 through B16 are used to represent the decision variables for our model (or the number of cars that should flow between each of the cities listed). The unit cost of transporting cars between each city is listed in column G. The objective function for the model is then implemented in cell G18 as follows:

Formula for cell G18: =SUMPRODUCT(B6:B16,G6:G16)

To implement the LHS formulas for the constraints in this model, we need to compute the total inflow minus the total outflow for each node. This is done in cells K6 through K12 as follows:

Formula for cell K6: =SUMIF($E$6:$E$16,I6,$B$6:$B$16)–SUMIF($C$6:$C$16,I6,$B$6:$B$16)
(Copy to cells K7 through K12.)

The first SUMIF function in this formula compares the values in the range E6 through E16 to the value in I6 and, if a match occurs, sums the corresponding value in the range B6 through B16. Of course, this gives us the total number of cars flowing ***into*** Newark (which in this case will always be zero because none of the values in E6 through E16 match the value in I6). The next SUMIF function compares the values in the range C6 through C16 to the value in I6 and, if a match occurs, sums the corresponding values in the range B6 through B16. This gives us the total number of cars flowing ***out of*** Newark (which in this case will always equal the values in cells B6 and B7 because these are the only arcs flowing out of Newark). Copying this formula to cells K7 though K12 allows us to easily calculate the total inflow minus the total outflow for each of the nodes in our problem. The RHS values for these constraint cells are shown in cells L6 though L12.

Figure 5.3 shows the Solver parameters and options required to solve this model. The optimal solution to the problem is shown in Figure 5.4.

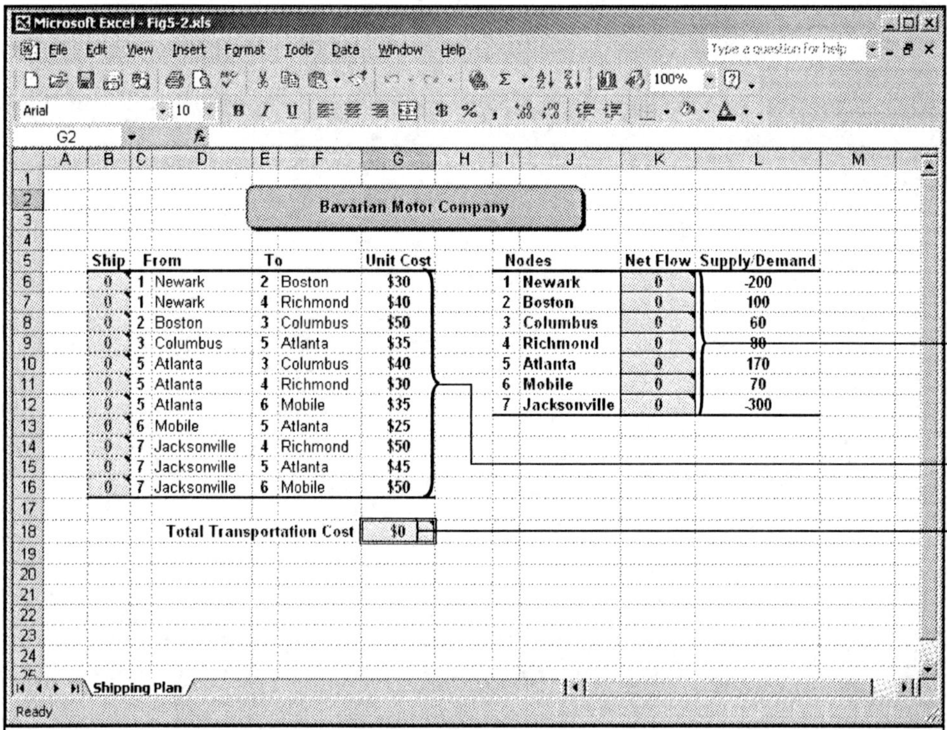

Key Cell Formulas

Cell	Formula	Copied to
D6	=VLOOKUP(C6,$I$6:$J$12,2)	D7:D16 and F6:F16
G18	=SUMPRODUCT(B6:B16,G6:G16)	—
K6	=SUMIF($E$6:$E$16,I6,$B$6:$B$16)-SUMIF($C$6:$C$16,I6,$B$6:$B$16)	K7:K12

FIGURE 5.2
Spreadsheet implementation of the BMC transshipment problem

5.1.6 Analyzing the Solution

Figure 5.4 shows the optimal solution for BMC's transshipment problem. The solution indicates that 120 cars should be shipped from Newark to Boston ($X_{12} = 120$), 80 cars from Newark to Richmond ($X_{14} = 80$), 20 cars from Boston to Columbus

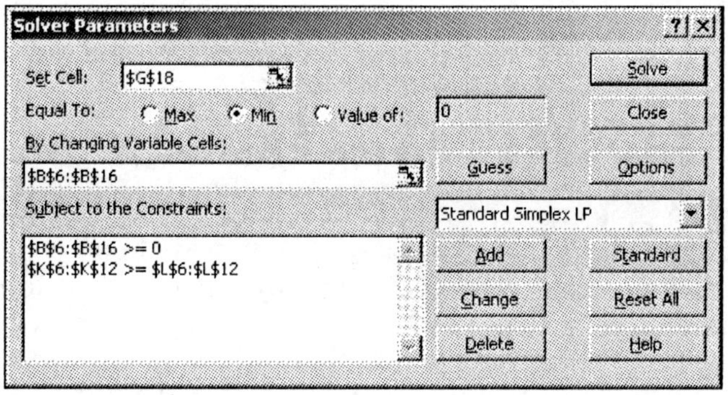

FIGURE 5.3
Solver parameters for the BMC transshipment problem

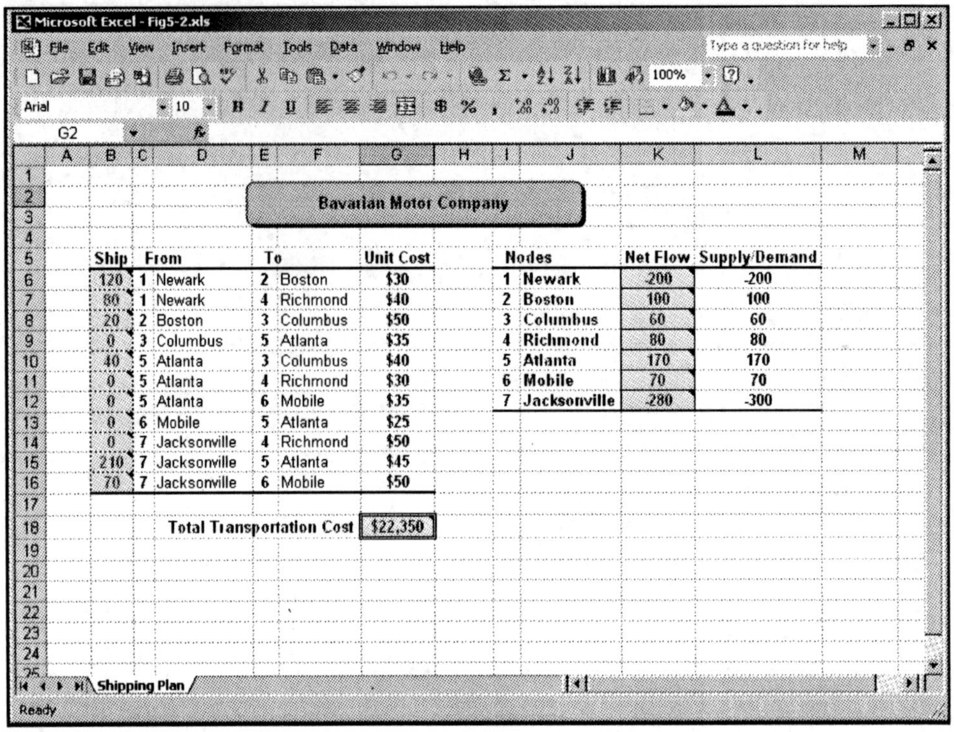

Bavarian Motor Company

Ship	From	To	Unit Cost
120	1 Newark	2 Boston	$30
80	1 Newark	4 Richmond	$40
20	2 Boston	3 Columbus	$50
0	3 Columbus	5 Atlanta	$35
40	5 Atlanta	3 Columbus	$40
0	5 Atlanta	4 Richmond	$30
0	5 Atlanta	6 Mobile	$35
0	6 Mobile	5 Atlanta	$25
0	7 Jacksonville	4 Richmond	$50
210	7 Jacksonville	5 Atlanta	$45
70	7 Jacksonville	6 Mobile	$50
		Total Transportation Cost	$22,350

Nodes	Net Flow	Supply/Demand
1 Newark	-200	-200
2 Boston	100	100
3 Columbus	60	60
4 Richmond	80	80
5 Atlanta	170	170
6 Mobile	70	70
7 Jacksonville	-280	-300

FIGURE 5.4
Optimal solution to the BMC transshipment problem

(X_{23} = 20), 40 cars from Atlanta to Columbus (X_{53} = 40), 210 cars from Jacksonville to Atlanta (X_{75} = 210), and 70 cars from Jacksonville to Mobile (X_{76} = 70). Cell G18 indicates that the total cost associated with this shipping plan is $22,350. The values of the constraint cells in K6 and K12 indicate, respectively, that all 200 cars available at Newark are being shipped and only 280 of the 300 cars available at Jacksonville are being shipped. A comparison of the remaining constraint cells in K7 through K11 with their RHS values in L7 through L11 reveals that the demand at each of these cities is being met by the net flow of cars through each city.

This solution is summarized graphically, as shown in Figure 5.5. The values in the boxes next to each arc indicate the optimal flows for the arcs. The optimal flow for all the other arcs in the problem, which are not shown in Figure 5.5, is 0. Notice that the amount flowing into each node minus the amount flowing out of each node is equal to the supply or demand at the node. For example, 210 cars are being shipped from Jacksonville to Atlanta. Atlanta will keep 170 of the cars (to satisfy the demand at this node) and send the extra 40 to Columbus.

5.2 THE SHORTEST PATH PROBLEM

In many decision problems, we need to determine the shortest (or least costly) route or path through a network from a starting node to an ending node. For example, many cities are developing computerized models of their highways and streets to help emergency vehicles identify the quickest route to a given location. Each street intersection represents a potential node in a network, and the streets connecting the intersections represent arcs. Depending on the day of the week and

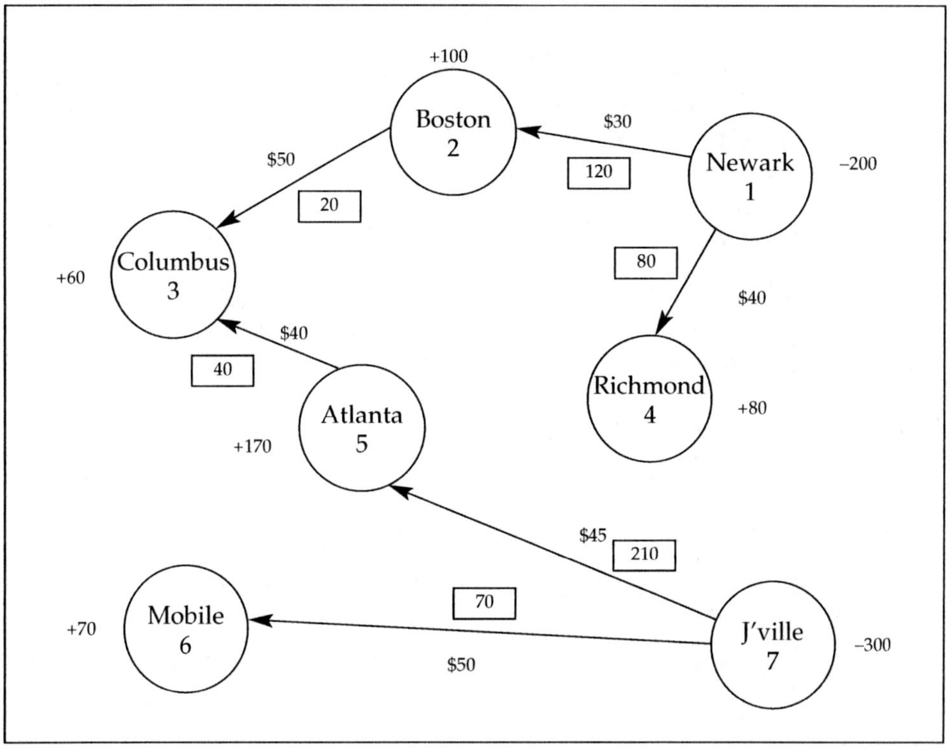

FIGURE 5.5
Network representation of the optimal solution for the BMC transshipment problem

the time of day, the time required to travel various streets can increase or decrease due to changes in traffic patterns. Road construction and maintenance also affect traffic flow patterns. So, the quickest route (or shortest path) for getting from one point in the city to another can change frequently. In emergency situations, lives or property can be lost or saved depending on how quickly emergency vehicles arrive where they are needed. The ability to quickly determine the shortest path to the location of an emergency situation is extremely useful in these situations. The following example illustrates another application of the shortest path problem.

The American Car Association (ACA) provides a variety of travel-related services to its members, including information on vacation destinations, discount hotel reservations, emergency road assistance, and travel route planning. This last service, travel route planning, is one of its most popular services. When members of the ACA are planning to take a driving trip, they call the organization's toll-free 800 number and indicate what cities they will be traveling from and to. The ACA then determines an optimal route for traveling between these cities. The ACA's computer databases of major highways and intestates are kept up-to-date with information on construction delays and detours and estimated travel times along various segments of roadways.

Members of the ACA often have different objectives in planning driving trips. Some are interested in identifying routes that minimize travel times. Others, with more leisure time on their hands, want to identify the most scenic route to their desired destination. The ACA wants to develop an automated system for identifying an optimal travel plan for its members.

To see how the ACA could benefit by solving shortest path problems, consider the simplified network shown in Figure 5.6 for a travel member who wants to drive from Birmingham, Alabama to Virginia Beach, Virginia. The nodes in this graph represent different cities and the arcs indicate the possible travel routes between the cities. For each arc, Figure 5.6 lists both the estimated driving time to travel the road represented by each arc and the number of points that route has received on the ACA's system for rating the scenic quality of the various routes.

Solving this problem as a network flow model requires the various nodes to have some supply or demand. In Figure 5.6, node 1 (Birmingham) has a supply of 1, node 11 (Virginia Beach) has a demand of 1, and all other nodes have a demand (or supply) of 0. If we view this model as a transshipment problem, we want to find either the quickest way or the most scenic way of shipping 1 unit of flow from node 1 to node 11. The route this unit of supply takes corresponds to either the shortest path or the most scenic path through the network, depending on which objective is being pursued.

5.2.1 An LP Model for the Example Problem

Using the balance-of-flow rule, the LP model to minimize the driving time in this problem is represented as:

MIN: $+2.5X_{12} +3X_{13} +1.7X_{23} +2.5X_{24} +1.7X_{35} +2.8X_{36} +2X_{46} +1.5X_{47} +2X_{56} +5X_{59}$
$+3X_{68} +4.7X_{69} +1.5X_{78} +2.3X_{7,10} + 2X_{89} + 1.1X_{8,10} +3.3X_{9,11} +2.7X_{10,11}$

FIGURE 5.6
Network of possible routes for the ACA's shortest path problem

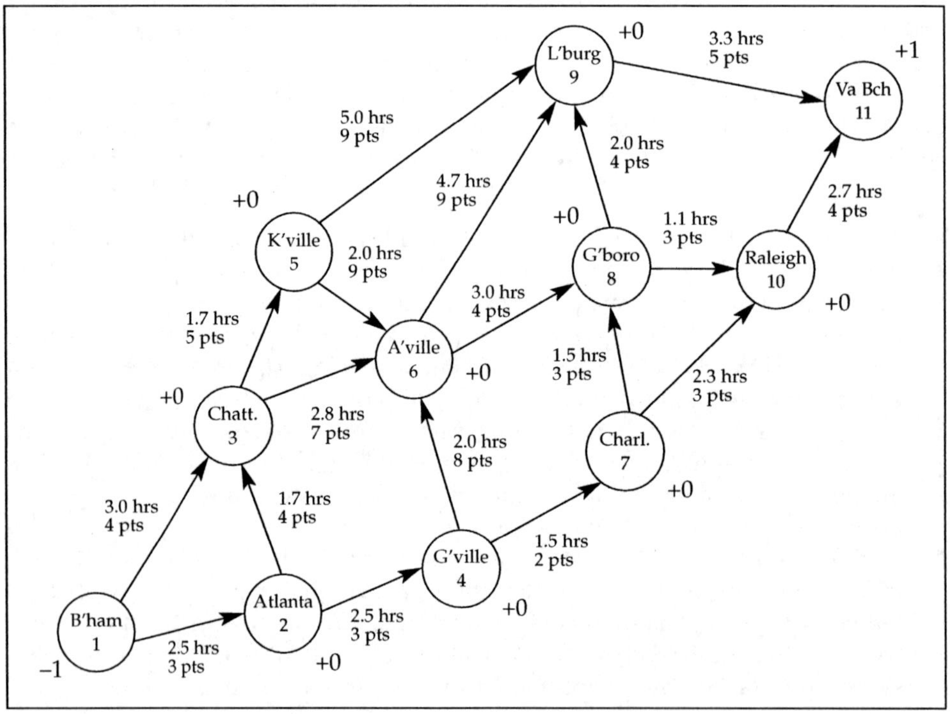

Subject to:

$-X_{12} - X_{13}$	$= -1$	} flow constraint for node 1
$+X_{12} - X_{23} - X_{24}$	$= 0$	} flow constraint for node 2
$+X_{13} + X_{23} - X_{35} - X_{36}$	$= 0$	} flow constraint for node 3
$+X_{24} - X_{46} - X_{47}$	$= 0$	} flow constraint for node 4
$+X_{35} - X_{56} - X_{59}$	$= 0$	} flow constraint for node 5
$+X_{36} + X_{46} + X_{56} - X_{68} - X_{69}$	$= 0$	} flow constraint for node 6
$+X_{47} - X_{78} - X_{7,10}$	$= 0$	} flow constraint for node 7
$+X_{68} + X_{78} - X_{89} - X_{8,10}$	$= 0$	} flow constraint for node 8
$+X_{59} + X_{69} + X_{89} - X_{9,11}$	$= 0$	} flow constraint for node 9
$+X_{7,10} + X_{8,10} - X_{10,11}$	$= 0$	} flow constraint for node 10
$+X_{9,11} + X_{10,11}$	$= +1$	} flow constraint for node 11
$X_{ij} \geq 0$ for all i and j		} nonnegativity conditions

Because the total supply equals the total demand in this problem, the constraint should be stated as equalities. The first constraint in this model ensures that the 1 unit of supply available at node 1 is shipped to node 2 or node 3. The next nine constraints indicate that anything flowing to nodes 2 though node 10 must also flow out of these nodes because each has a demand of 0. For example, if the unit of supply leaves node 1 for node 2 (via X_{12}), the second constraint ensures that it will leave node 2 for node 3 or node 4 (via X_{23} or X_{24}). The last constraint indicates that the unit must ultimately flow to node 11. Thus, the solution to this problem indicates the quickest route for getting from node 1 (Birmingham) to node 11 (Virginia Beach).

5.2.2 The Spreadsheet Model and Solution

The optimal solution to this problem shown in Figure 5.7 (and in the file Fig5-7.xls on your data disk) was obtained using the Solver parameters and options shown in Figure 5.8. Notice that this model includes calculations of both the total expected driving time (cell G26) and total scenic rating points (cell H26) associated with any solution. Either of these cells can be chosen as the objective function according to the client's desires. However, the solution shown in Figure 5.7 minimizes the expected driving time.

The optimal solution shown in Figure 5.7 indicates that the quickest travel plan involves driving from node 1 (Birmingham) to node 2 (Atlanta), then to node 4 (Greenville), then to node 7 (Charlotte), then to node 10 (Raleigh), and finally to node 11 (Virginia Beach). The total expected driving time along this route is 11.5 hours. Also note that this route receives a rating of 15 points on the ACA's scenic rating scale.

Using this spreadsheet, we can also determine the most scenic route by instructing Solver to maximize the value in cell H26. Figure 5.9 shows the optimal solution obtained in this case. This travel plan involves driving from Birmingham to Atlanta, to Chattanooga, to Knoxville, to Asheville, to Lynchburg, and finally, to Virginia Beach. This itinerary receives a rating of 35 points on the ACA's scenic rating scale but takes almost 16 hours of driving time.

FIGURE 5.7
Spreadsheet model and solution showing the route that minimizes estimated driving time for the ACA's shortest path problem

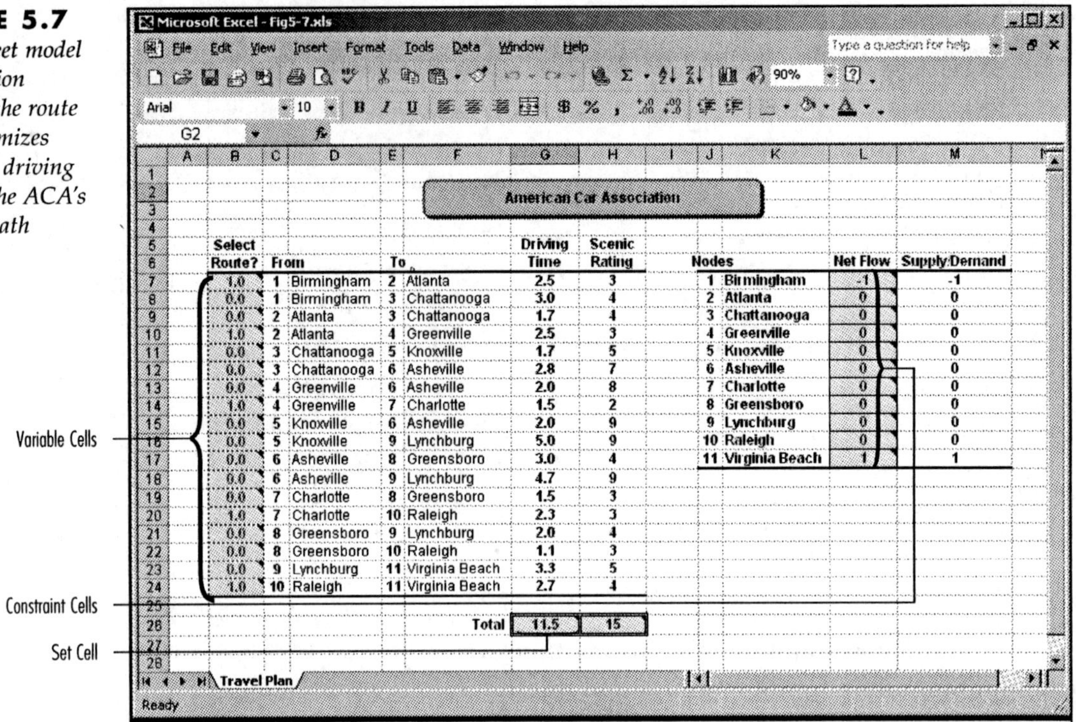

Key Cell Formulas

Cell	Formula	Copied to
D7	=VLOOKUP(C7,$J$7:$K$17,2)	D8:D24 and F7:F24
G26	=SUMPRODUCT(G7:G24,$B$7:$B$24)	H26
L7	=SUMIF($E$7:$E$24,J7,$B$7:$B$24)- SUMIF($C$7:$C$24,J7,$B$7:$B$24)	L8:L17

FIGURE 5.8
Solver parameters for the ACA's shortest path problem

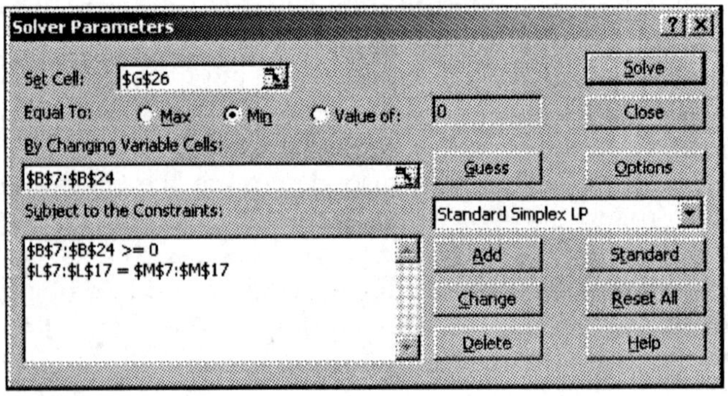

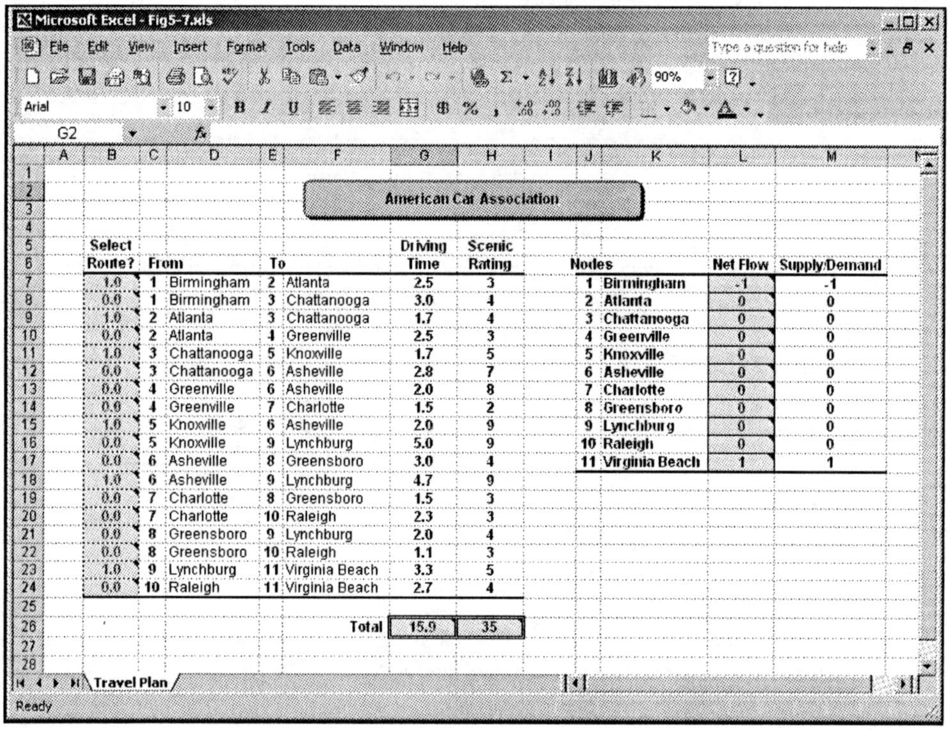

Select Route?	From		To		Driving Time	Scenic Rating
1.0	1	Birmingham	2	Atlanta	2.5	3
0.0	1	Birmingham	3	Chattanooga	3.0	4
1.0	2	Atlanta	3	Chattanooga	1.7	4
0.0	2	Atlanta	4	Greenville	2.5	3
1.0	3	Chattanooga	5	Knoxville	1.7	5
0.0	3	Chattanooga	6	Asheville	2.8	7
0.0	4	Greenville	6	Asheville	2.0	8
0.0	4	Greenville	7	Charlotte	1.5	2
1.0	5	Knoxville	6	Asheville	2.0	9
0.0	5	Knoxville	9	Lynchburg	5.0	9
0.0	6	Asheville	8	Greensboro	3.0	4
1.0	6	Asheville	9	Lynchburg	4.7	9
0.0	7	Charlotte	8	Greensboro	1.5	3
0.0	7	Charlotte	10	Raleigh	2.3	3
0.0	8	Greensboro	9	Lynchburg	2.0	4
0.0	8	Greensboro	10	Raleigh	1.1	3
1.0	9	Lynchburg	11	Virginia Beach	3.3	5
0.0	10	Raleigh	11	Virginia Beach	2.7	4
				Total	15.9	35

Nodes		Net Flow	Supply/Demand
1	Birmingham	-1	-1
2	Atlanta	0	0
3	Chattanooga	0	0
4	Greenville	0	0
5	Knoxville	0	0
6	Asheville	0	0
7	Charlotte	0	0
8	Greensboro	0	0
9	Lynchburg	0	0
10	Raleigh	0	0
11	Virginia Beach	1	1

FIGURE 5.9
Solution showing the most scenic route

5.2.3 Network Flow Models and Integer Solutions

Up to this point, each of the network flow models we have solved generated integer solutions. If you use the simplex method to solve any minimum cost network flow model having integer constraint RHS values, then the optimal solution automatically assumes integer values. This property is helpful because the items flowing through most network flow models represent discrete units (such as cars or people).

Sometimes, it is tempting to place additional constraints (or side constraints) on a network model. For example, in the ACA problem, suppose that the customer wants to get to Virginia Beach in the most scenic way possible within 14 hours of driving time. We can easily add a constraint to the model to keep the total driving time G26 less than or equal to 14 hours. If we then re-solve the model to maximize the scenic rating in cell H26, we obtain the solution shown in Figure 5.10.

Unfortunately, this solution is useless because it produces fractional results. Thus, if we add ***side constraints*** to network flow problems that do not obey the balance-of-flow rule, we can no longer ensure that the solution to the LP formulation of the problems will be integral. If integer solutions are needed for such problems, the integer programming techniques discussed in chapter 6 must be applied.

5.3 THE EQUIPMENT REPLACEMENT PROBLEM

The equipment replacement problem is a common type of business problem that can be modeled as a shortest path problem. This type of problem involves

FIGURE 5.10
Example of a noninteger solution to a network problem with side constraints

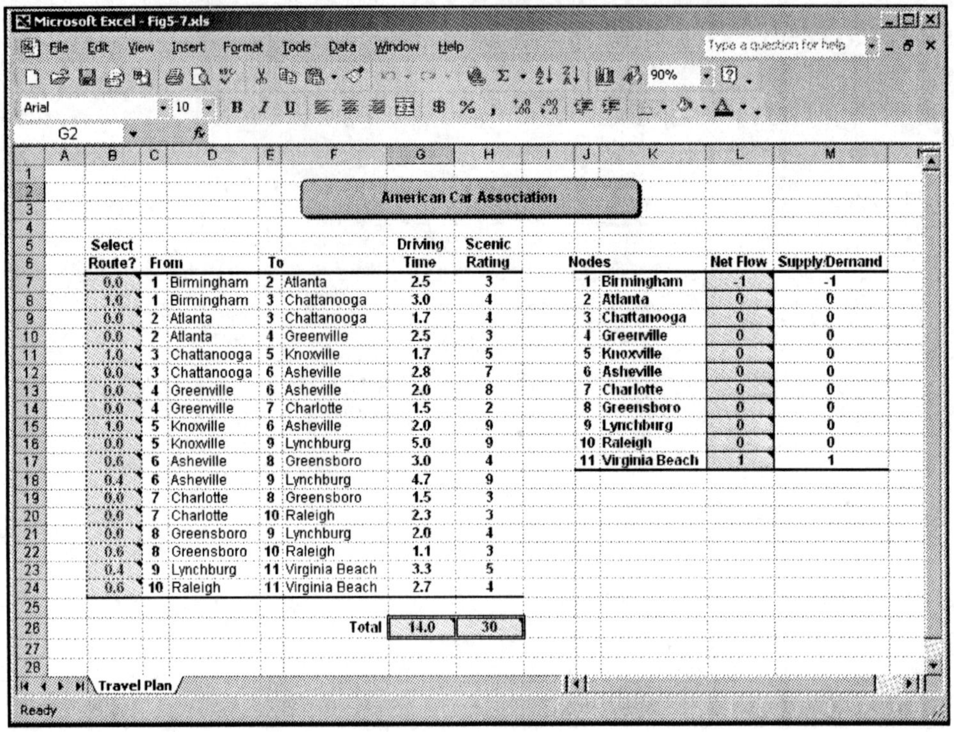

Select Route?	From		To		Driving Time	Scenic Rating
0.0	1	Birmingham	2	Atlanta	2.5	3
1.0	1	Birmingham	3	Chattanooga	3.0	4
0.0	2	Atlanta	3	Chattanooga	1.7	4
0.0	2	Atlanta	4	Greenville	2.5	3
1.0	3	Chattanooga	5	Knoxville	1.7	5
0.0	3	Chattanooga	6	Asheville	2.8	7
0.0	4	Greenville	6	Asheville	2.0	8
0.0	4	Greenville	7	Charlotte	1.5	2
1.0	5	Knoxville	6	Asheville	2.0	9
0.0	5	Knoxville	9	Lynchburg	5.0	9
0.6	6	Asheville	8	Greensboro	3.0	4
0.4	6	Asheville	9	Lynchburg	4.7	9
0.0	7	Charlotte	8	Greensboro	1.5	3
0.0	7	Charlotte	10	Raleigh	2.3	3
0.0	8	Greensboro	9	Lynchburg	2.0	4
0.6	8	Greensboro	10	Raleigh	1.1	3
0.4	9	Lynchburg	11	Virginia Beach	3.3	5
0.6	10	Raleigh	11	Virginia Beach	2.7	4
				Total	14.0	30

Nodes		Net Flow	Supply/Demand
1	Birmingham	-1	-1
2	Atlanta	0	0
3	Chattanooga	0	0
4	Greenville	0	0
5	Knoxville	0	0
6	Asheville	0	0
7	Charlotte	0	0
8	Greensboro	0	0
9	Lynchburg	0	0
10	Raleigh	0	0
11	Virginia Beach	1	1

determining the least costly schedule for replacing equipment over a specified length of time. Consider the following example.

Jose Maderos is the owner of Compu-Train, a small company that provides hands-on software education and training for businesses in and around Boulder, Colorado. Jose leases the computer equipment used in his business and he likes to keep the equipment up-to-date so that it will run the latest, state-of-the-art software in an efficient manner. Because of this, Jose wants to replace his equipment at least every two years.

Jose is currently trying to decide between two different lease contracts his equipment supplier has proposed. Under both contracts Jose would be required to pay $62,000 initially to obtain the equipment he needs. However, the two contracts differ in terms of the amount Jose would have to pay in subsequent years to replace his equipment. Under the first contract, the price to acquire new equipment would increase by 6% per year, but he would be given a trade-in credit of 60% for any equipment that is one year old and 15% for any equipment that is two years old. Under the second contract, the price to acquire new equipment would increase by just 2% per year, but he would only be given a trade-in credit of 30% for any equipment that is one year old and 10% for any equipment that is two years old.

Jose realizes that no matter what he does, he will have to pay $62,000 to obtain the equipment initially. However, he wants to determine which contract would allow him to minimize the remaining leasing costs over the next five years and when he should replace his equipment under the selected contract.

Each of the two contracts Jose is considering can be modeled as a shortest path problem. Figure 5.11 shows how this would be accomplished for the first contract under consideration. Each node corresponds to a point in time during the next five years when Jose can replace his equipment. Each arc in this network represents a choice available to Jose. For example, the arc from node 1 to node 2 indicates that Jose can keep the equipment he initially acquires for one year and then replace it (at the beginning of year 2) for a net cost of \$28,520 ($\$62,000 \times 1.06 - 0.6 \times \$62,000 = \$28,520$). Alternatively, the arc from node 1 to node 3 indicates that Jose can keep his initial equipment for two years and replace it at the beginning of year 3 for a net cost of \$60,363 ($\$62,000 \times 1.06^2 - 0.15 \times \$62,000 = \$60,363$).

The arc from node 2 to node 3 indicates that if Jose replaces his initial equipment at the beginning of year 2, he can keep the new equipment for one year and replace it at the beginning of year 3 at a net cost of \$30,231 (\$62,000 × 1.06^2 – 0.60 × (\$62,000 × 1.06) = \$30,231). The remaining arcs and costs in the network can be interpreted in the same way. Jose's decision problem is to determine the least costly (or shortest) way of getting from node 1 to node 5 in this network.

5.3.1 The Spreadsheet Model and Solution

The LP formulation of Jose's decision problem can be generated from the graph in Figure 5.11 using the balance-of-flow rule in the same manner as the previous network flow problems. The spreadsheet model for this problem was implemented as shown in Figure 5.12 (and in the file Fig5-12.xls on your data disk) and solved using the settings shown in Figure 5.13. To assist Jose in comparing the two different alternatives he faces, notice that an area of the spreadsheet in Figure 5.12 has been reserved to represent assumptions about the annual increase in leasing costs (cell G5), and the trade-in values for one- and two-year old equipment (cells G6 and G7). The rest of the spreadsheet model uses these assumed values to compute the various costs. This enables us to change any of the assumptions and re-solve the model very easily.

The optimal solution to this problem shows that under the provisions of the first contract, Jose should replace his equipment at the beginning of each year at a total cost of \$124,764. This amount is in addition to the \$62,000 he has to pay up front at the beginning of year 1.

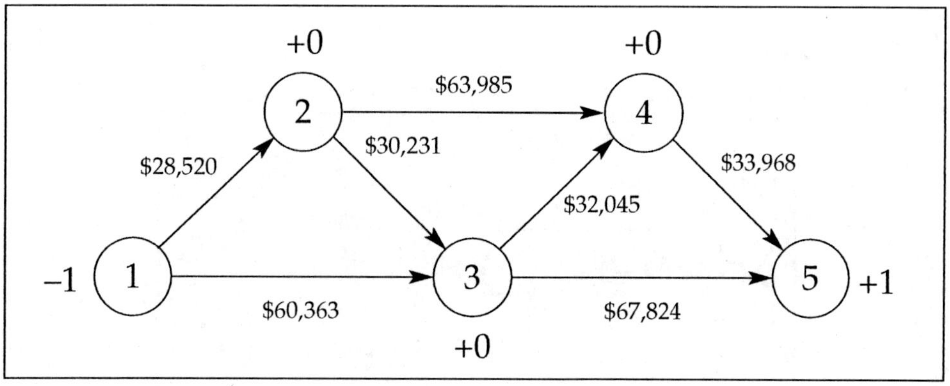

FIGURE 5.11
Network representation of Compu-Train's first contract alternative for its equipment replacement problem

FIGURE 5.12
Spreadsheet model and solution for Compu-Train's first lease contract alternative

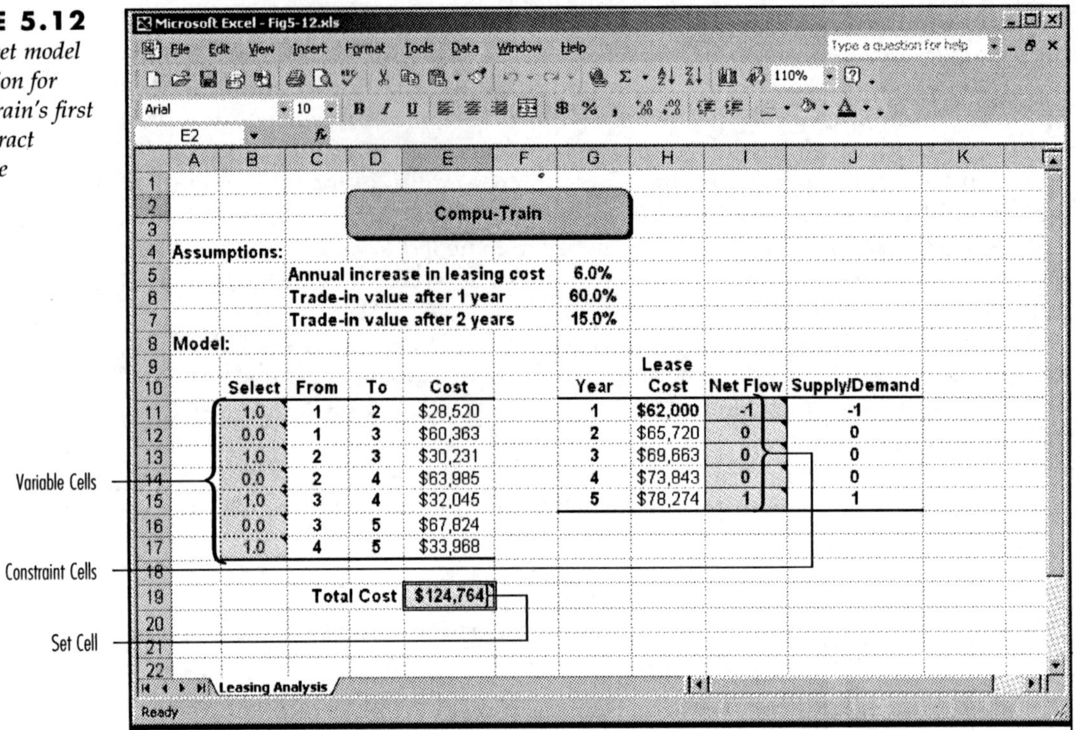

Key Cell Formulas

Cell	Formula	Copied to
E19	=SUMPRODUCT(E11:E17,B11:B17)	—
I11	=SUMIF($D$11:$D$17,G11,$B$11:$B$17) -SUMIF($C$11:$C$17,G11,$B$11:$B$17)	I12:I15
H12	=H11*(1+$G$5)	H13:H15
E11	=VLOOKUP(D11,G$11:J$15,2)-(IF(D11-C11=1,G$6,G$7) *VLOOKUP(C11,G$11:J$15,2))	E12:E17

FIGURE 5.13
Solver parameters for Compu-Train's equipment replacement problem

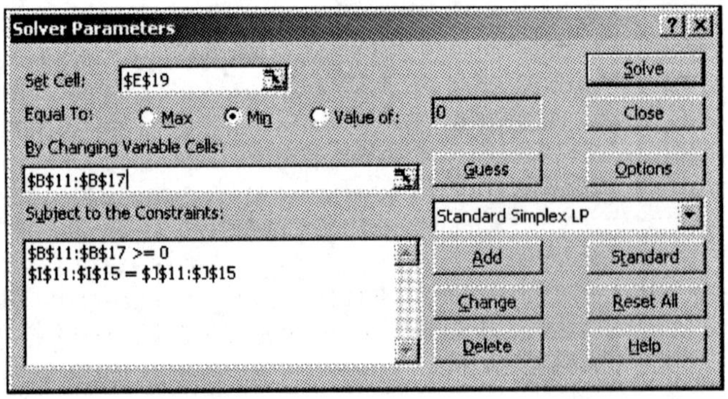

To determine the optimal replacement strategy and costs associated with the second contract, Jose could simply change the assumptions at the top of the spreadsheet and re-solve the model. The results of this are shown in Figure 5.14.

The optimal solution to this problem shows that under the provisions of the second contract, Jose should replace his equipment at the beginning of years 3 and 5 at a total cost of $118,965. Again, this amount is in addition to the $62,000 he has to pay up front at the beginning of year 1. Although the total costs under the second contract are lower than under the first, under the second contract Jose would be working with older equipment during years 2 and 4. Thus, although the solution to these two models makes the financial consequences of the two different alternatives clear, Jose still must decide for himself whether the benefits of the financial cost savings under the second contract outweigh the nonfinancial costs associated with using slightly out-of-date equipment during years 2 and 4. Of course, regardless of which contract Jose decides to go with, he will get to reconsider whether or not to upgrade his equipment at the beginning of each of the next 4 years.

Summary of Shortest Path Problems

You can model any shortest path problem as a transshipment problem by assigning a supply of 1 to the starting node, a demand of 1 to the ending node, and a demand of 0 to all other nodes in the network. Because the examples presented here involved only a small number of paths through each of the networks, it might have been easier to solve these problems simply by enumerating the paths and calculating the total distance of each one. However, in a problem with many nodes and arcs, an automated LP model is preferable to a manual solution approach.

5.4 TRANSPORTATION/ ASSIGNMENT PROBLEMS

Chapter 3 presented an example of another type of network flow problem known as the transportation/assignment problem. The example involved the Tropicsun Company—a grower and distributor of fresh citrus products. The company wanted to determine the least expensive way of transporting freshly picked fruit from three citrus groves to three processing plants. The network representation of the problem is repeated in Figure 5.15.

The network shown in Figure 5.15 differs from the earlier network flow problems in this chapter because it contains no transshipment nodes. Each node in Figure 5.15 is either a sending node or a receiving node. The lack of transshipment nodes is the key feature that distinguishes transportation/assignment problems from other types of network flow problems. As you saw in chapter 3, this property allows you to set up and solve transportation/assignment problems conveniently in a matrix format in the spreadsheet. Although it is possible to solve transportation/assignment problems in the same way in which we solved transshipment problems,

FIGURE 5.14
Solution for Compu-Train's second lease contract alternative

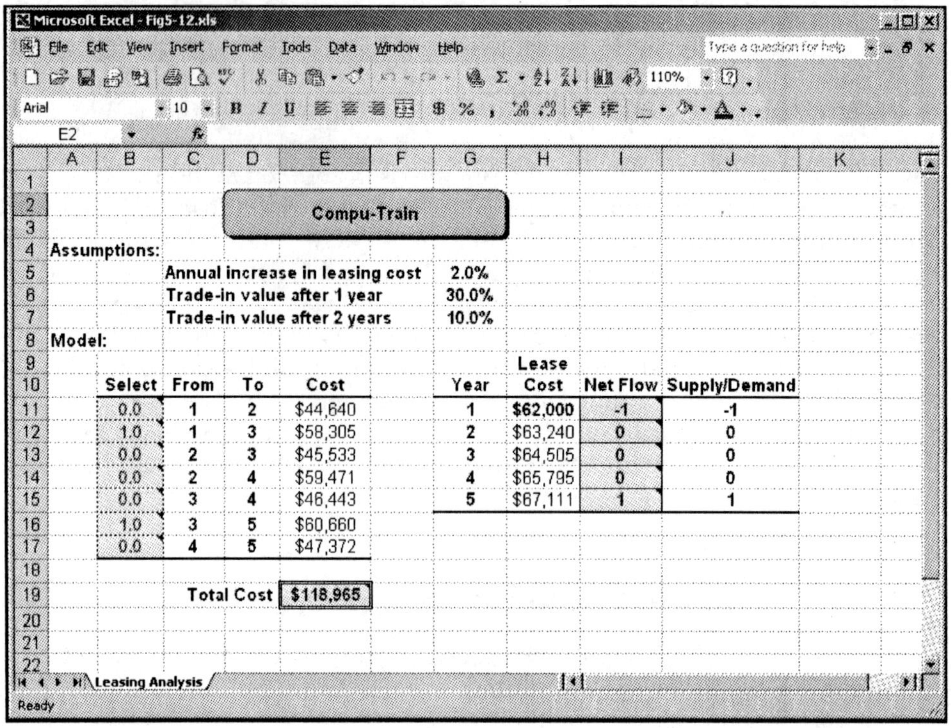

Assumptions:

Annual increase in leasing cost	2.0%
Trade-in value after 1 year	30.0%
Trade-in value after 2 years	10.0%

Model:

Select	From	To	Cost
0.0	1	2	$44,640
1.0	1	3	$58,305
0.0	2	3	$45,533
0.0	2	4	$59,471
0.0	3	4	$46,443
1.0	3	5	$60,660
0.0	4	5	$47,372

Total Cost $118,965

Year	Lease Cost	Net Flow	Supply/Demand
1	$62,000	-1	-1
2	$63,240	0	0
3	$64,505	0	0
4	$65,795	0	0
5	$67,111	1	1

FIGURE 5.15
Network representation of Tropicsun's transportation/assignment problem

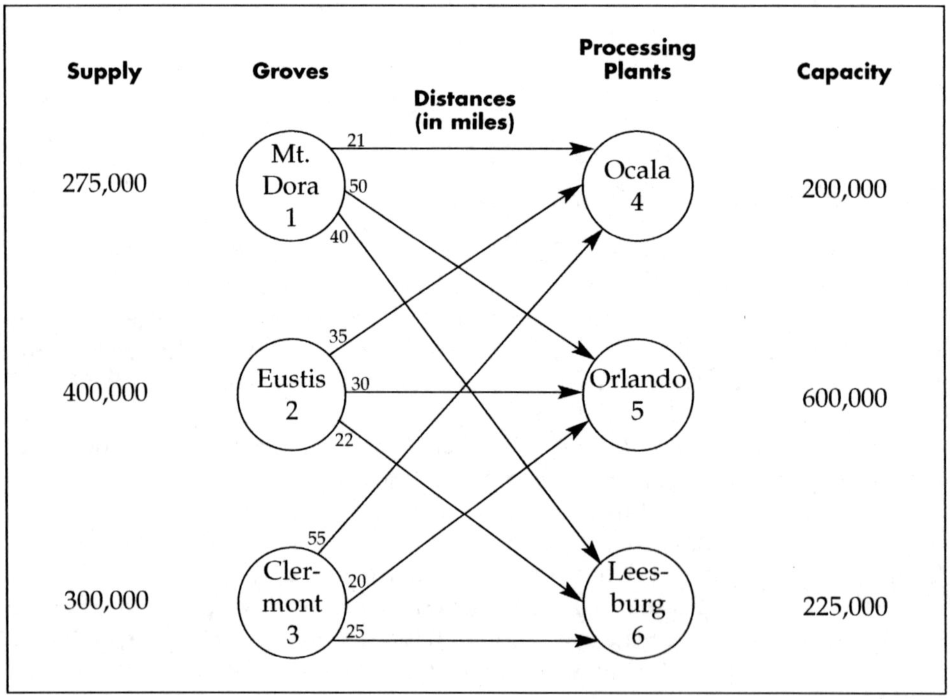

it is much easier to implement and solve these problems using the matrix approach described in chapter 3.

Sometimes, transportation/assignment problems are ***sparse*** or not fully interconnected (meaning not all the supply nodes have arcs connecting them to all the demand nodes). These "missing" arcs can be handled conveniently in the matrix approach to implementation by assigning arbitrarily large costs to the variable cells representing these arcs so that flow on these arcs becomes prohibitively expensive. However, as the number of missing arcs increases, the matrix approach to implementation becomes less and less computationally efficient compared to the procedure described in this chapter.

5.5 GENERALIZED NETWORK FLOW PROBLEMS

In all of the network problems we have considered so far, the amount of flow that exited an arc was always the same as the amount that entered the arc. For example, if we put 40 cars on a train in Jacksonville and sent them to Atlanta, the same 40 cars came off the train in Atlanta. However, there are numerous examples of network flow problems in which a gain or loss occurs on flows across arcs. For instance, if oil or gas is shipped through a leaky pipeline, the amount of oil or gas arriving at the intended destination will be less than the amount originally placed in the pipeline. Similar loss-of-flow examples occur as a result of evaporation of liquids, spoilage of foods and other perishable items, or imperfections in raw materials entering production processes that result in a certain amount of scrap. Many financial cash flow problems can be modeled as network flow problems in which flow gains occur in the form of interest or dividends as money flows through various investments. The following example illustrates the modeling changes required to accommodate these types of problems.

Nancy Grant is the owner of Coal Bank Hollow Recycling, a company that specializes in collecting and recycling paper products. Nancy's company uses two different recycling processes to convert newspaper, mixed paper, white office paper, and cardboard into paper pulp. The amount of paper pulp extracted from the recyclable materials and the cost of extracting the pulp differs depending on which recycling process is used. The following table summarizes the recycling processes:

	Recycling Process 1		Recycling Process 2	
Material	**Cost per Ton**	**Yield**	**Cost per Ton**	**Yield**
Newspaper	$13	90%	$12	85%
Mixed Paper	$11	80%	$13	85%
White Office Paper	$9	95%	$10	90%
Cardboard	$13	75%	$14	85%

For instance, every ton of newspaper subjected to recycling process 1 costs $13 and yields 0.9 tons of paper pulp. The paper pulp produced by the two different recycling processes goes through other operations to be transformed into pulp for newsprint, packaging paper, or print stock quality paper. The yields associated with transforming the recycled pulp into pulp for the final products are summarized in the following table:

	Newsprint Pulp		Packaging Paper Pulp		Print Stock Pulp	
Pulp Source	**Cost per Ton**	**Yield**	**Cost per Ton**	**Yield**	**Cost per Ton**	**Yield**
Recycling Process 1	\$5	95%	\$6	90%	\$8	90%
Recycling Process 2	\$6	90%	\$8	95%	\$7	95%

For instance, a ton of pulp exiting recycling process 2 can be transformed into 0.95 tons of packaging paper at a cost of \$8.

Nancy currently has 70 tons of newspaper, 50 tons of mixed paper, 30 tons of white office paper, and 40 tons of cardboard. She wants to determine the most efficient way of converting these materials into 60 tons of newsprint pulp, 40 tons of packaging paper pulp, and 50 tons of print stock pulp.

Figure 5.16 shows how Nancy's recycling problem can be viewed as a generalized network flow problem. The arcs in this graph indicate the possible flow of recycling material through the production process. On each arc, we have listed both the cost of flow along the arc and the reduction factor that applies to flow along the arc. For instance, the arc from node 1 to node 5 indicates that each ton of newspaper going to recycling process 1 costs \$13 and yields 0.90 tons of paper pulp.

5.5.1 Formulating an LP Model for the Recycling Problem

To formulate the LP model for this problem algebraically, we defined the decision variable X_{ij} to represent the tons of product flowing from node i to node j. The objective is then stated in the usual way as follows:

FIGURE 5.16
Graphical representation of Coal Bank Hollow Recycling's generalized network flow problem

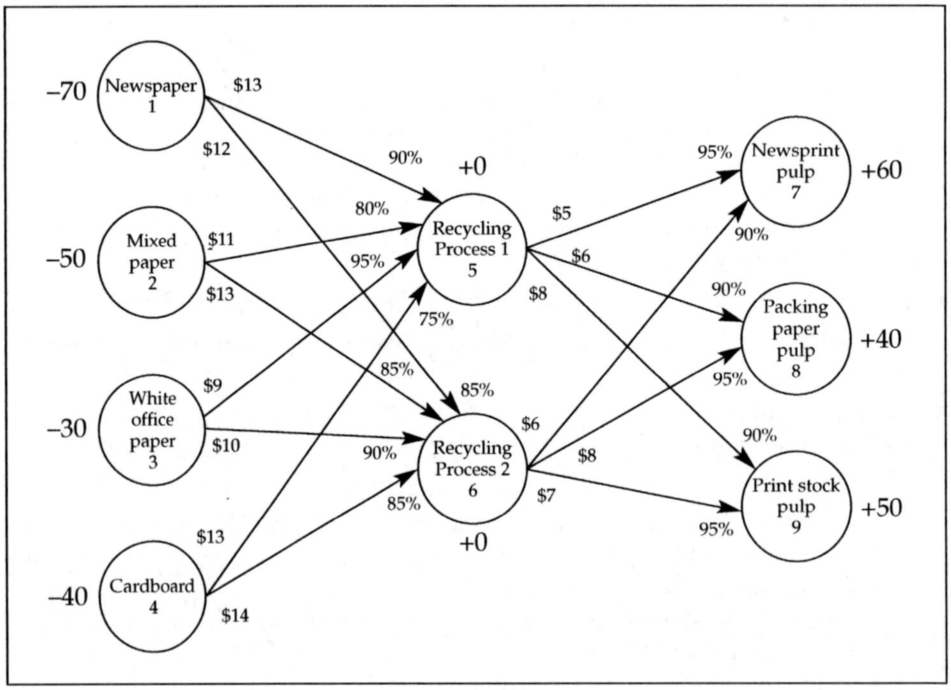

MIN: $13X_{15} + 12X_{16} + 11X_{25} + 13X_{26} + 9X_{35} + 10X_{36} + 13X_{45} + 14X_{46} + 5X_{57} + 6X_{58} + 8X_{59} + 6X_{67} + 8X_{68} + 7X_{69}$

The constraints for this problem may be generated using the balance-of-flow rule for each node. The constraints for the first four nodes (representing the supply of newspaper, mixed paper, white office paper, and cardboard, respectively) are given by:

$-X_{15} - X_{16} \geq -70$ } flow constraint for node 1
$-X_{25} - X_{26} \geq -50$ } flow constraint for node 2
$-X_{35} - X_{36} \geq -30$ } flow constraint for node 3
$-X_{45} - X_{46} \geq -40$ } flow constraint for node 4

These constraints simply indicate that the amount of product flowing out of each of these nodes may not exceed the supply available at each node. (Recall that the constraint given previously for node 1 is equivalent to $+X_{15} + X_{16} \leq +70$.)

Applying the balance-of-flow rule at nodes 5 and 6 (representing the two recycling processes) we obtain:

$+0.9X_{15} + 0.8X_{25} + 0.95X_{35} + 0.75X_{45} - X_{57} - X_{58} - X_{59} \geq 0$ } flow constraint for node 5
$+0.85X_{16} + 0.85X_{26} + 0.9X_{36} + 0.85X_{46} - X_{67} - X_{68} - X_{69} \geq 0$ } flow constraint for node 6

To better understand the logic of these constraints, we will rewrite them in the following algebraically equivalent manner:

$+0.9X_{15} + 0.8X_{25} + 0.95X_{35} + 0.75X_{45} \geq + X_{57} + X_{58} + X_{59}$ } equivalent flow constraint for node 5
$+0.85X_{16} + 0.85X_{26} + 0.9X_{36} + 0.85X_{46} \geq + X_{67} + X_{68} + X_{69}$ } equivalent flow constraint for node 6

Notice that the constraint for node 5 requires that the amount being shipped from node 5 (given by $X_{57} + X_{58} + X_{59}$) cannot exceed the net amount that would be available at node 5 (given by $0.9X_{15} + 0.8X_{25} + 0.95X_{35} + 0.75X_{45}$). Thus, here the yield factors come into play in determining the amount of product that would be available from the recycling processes. A similar interpretation applies to the constraint for node 6.

Finally, applying the balance-of-flow rule to nodes 7, 8, and 9 we obtain the constraints:

$+0.95X_{57} + 0.90X_{67} \geq 60$ } flow constraint for node 7
$+0.9X_{58} + 0.95X_{68} \geq 40$ } flow constraint for node 8
$+0.9X_{59} + 0.95X_{69} \geq 50$ } flow constraint for node 9

The constraint for node 7 ensures that the final amount of product flowing to node 7 ($0.95X_{57} + 0.90X_{67}$) is sufficient to meet the demand for pulp at this node. Again, similar interpretations apply to the constraints for nodes 8 and 9.

5.5.2 Implementing the Model

The model for Coal Bank Hollow Recycling's generalized network flow problem is summarized as:

MIN: $13X_{15} + 12X_{16} + 11X_{25} + 13X_{26} + 9X_{35} + 10X_{36} + 13X_{45} + 14X_{46} + 5X_{57} + 6X_{58} + 8X_{59} + 6X_{67} + 8X_{68} + 7X_{69}$

Subject to:

$-X_{15} - X_{16} \geq -70$ } flow constraint for node 1

$-X_{25} - X_{26} \geq -50$ } flow constraint for node 2

$-X_{35} - X_{36} \geq -30$ } flow constraint for node 3

$-X_{45} - X_{46} \geq -40$ } flow constraint for node 4

$+0.9X_{15} + 0.8X_{25} + 0.95X_{35} + 0.75X_{45} - X_{57} - X_{58} - X_{59} \geq 0$ } flow constraint for node 5

$+0.85X_{16} + 0.85X_{26} + 0.9X_{36} + 0.85X_{46} - X_{67} - X_{68} - X_{69} \geq 0$ } flow constraint for node 6

$+0.95X_{57} + 0.90X_{67} \geq 60$ } flow constraint for node 7

$+0.9X_{58} + 0.95X_{68} \geq 40$ } flow constraint for node 8

$+0.9X_{59} + 0.95X_{69} \geq 50$ } flow constraint for node 9

$X_{ij} \geq 0$ for all i and j } nonnegativity conditions

In all the other network flow models we have seen up to this point, all the coefficients in all the constraints were implicitly always +1 or –1. This is not true in the above model. Thus, we must give special attention to the coefficients in the constraints as we implement this model in the spreadsheet. One approach to implementing this problem is shown in Figure 5.17 (and the file Fig5-17.xls on your data disk).

The spreadsheet in Figure 5.17 is very similar to those of the other network flow problems we have solved. Cells A6 through A19 represent the decision variables (arcs) for our model, and the corresponding unit cost associated with each variable is listed in the range from H6 through H19. The objective function is implemented in cell H21 as:

Formula for cell H21: =SUMPRODUCT(H6:H19,A6:A19)

To implement the LHS formulas for our constraints, we can no longer simply sum the variables flowing into each node and subtract the variables flowing out of the nodes. Instead, we need to first multiply the variables flowing into a node by the appropriate yield factor. With the yield factors entered in column D, the yield-adjusted flow for each arc is computed in column E as follows:

Formula for cell E6: =A6*D6
(Copy to cells E7 through E19.)

Now, to implement the LHS formulas for each node in cells L6 through L14, we will sum the yield-adjusted flows into each node and subtract the raw flow out of each node. This may be done as follows:

Formula for cell L6: =SUMIF($F$6:$F$19,J6,$E$6:$E$19)-
(Copy to cells L7 through L14.) SUMIF($B$6:$B$19,J6,$A$6:$A$19)

Notice that the first SUMIF function in this formula sums the appropriate yield-adjusted flows in column E while the second SUMIF sums the appropriate raw flow values from column A. Thus, although this formula is very similar to the ones used in earlier models, there is a critical difference here that must be carefully noted and understood. The RHS values for these constraint cells are listed in cells M6 through M14.

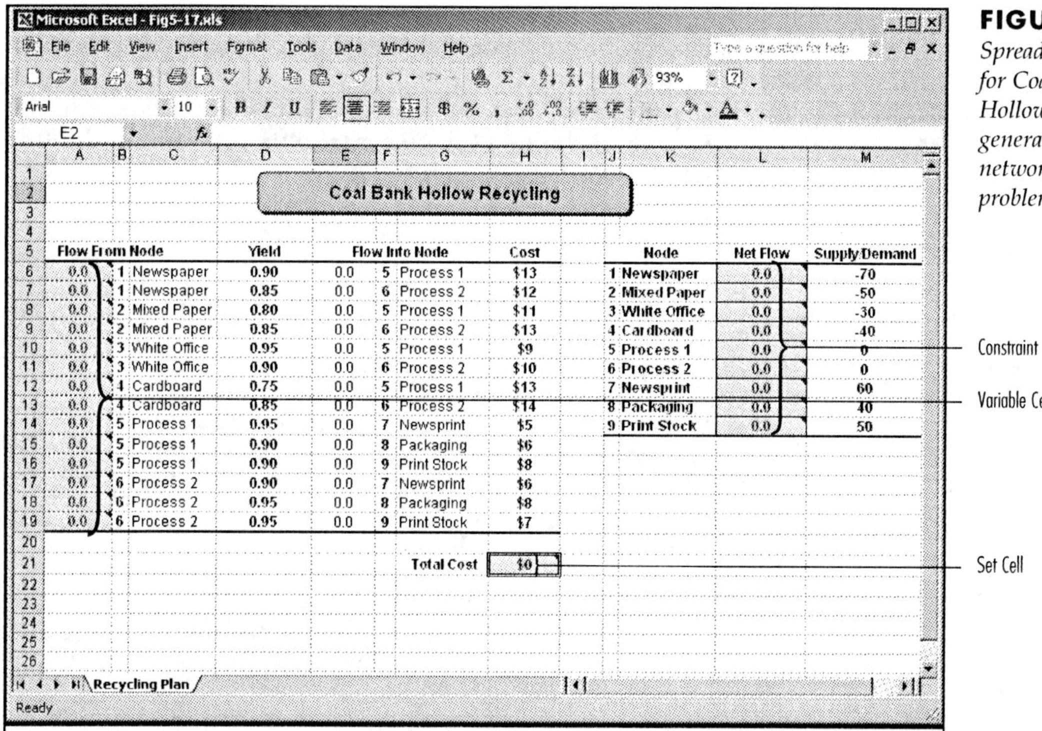

FIGURE 5.17
Spreadsheet model for Coal Bank Hollow Recycling's generalized network flow problem

Key Cell Formulas

Cell	Formula	Copied to
C6	=VLOOKUP(B6,$J$6:$K$14,2)	C7:C19 and G6:G19
E6	=D6*A6	E7:E19
H21	=SUMPRODUCT(H6:H19,A6:A19)	—
L6	=SUMIF($F$6:$F$19,J6,$E$6:$E$19) -SUMIF($B$6:$B$19,J6,$A$6:$A$19)	L7:L14

5.5.3 Analyzing the Solution

The Solver parameters used to solve this problem are shown in Figure 5.18 and the optimal solution is shown in Figure 5.19.

In this solution, 43.4 tons of newspaper, 50 tons of mixed paper, and 30 tons of white office paper are assigned to recycling process 1 (*i.e.*, $X_{15} = 43.4$, $X_{25} = 50$, $X_{35} = 30$). This recycling process then yields a total of 107.6 tons of pulp (*i.e.*, $0.9 \times 43.3 + 0.8 \times 50 + 0.95 \times 30 = 107.6$) of which 63.2 tons are allocated to the production of newsprint pulp ($X_{57} = 63.2$) and 44.4 tons are allocated to the production of pulp for packaging paper ($X_{58} = 44.4$). This allows us to meet the demand for 60 tons of newsprint pulp ($0.95 \times 63.2 = 60$) and 40 tons of packaging paper ($0.90 \times 44.4 = 40$).

The remaining 26.6 tons of newspaper are combined with 35.4 tons of cardboard in recycling process 2 (*i.e.*, $X_{16} = 26.6$, $X_{46} = 35.4$). This results in a yield of 52.6 tons of pulp (*i.e.*, $0.85 \times 26.6 + 0.85 \times 35.4 = 52.6$), which is all devoted to the production of 50 tons of print stock quality pulp ($0.95 \times 52.6 = 50$).

It is important for Nancy to note that this production plan calls for the use of all her supply of newspaper, mixed paper, and white office paper, but leaves about 4.6 tons of cardboard left over. Thus, she should be able to lower her total costs further by acquiring more newspaper, mixed paper, or white office paper. It would be wise for her to see if she could trade her surplus cardboard to another recycler for the material that she is running short on.

FIGURE 5.18
Solver parameters for the recycling problem

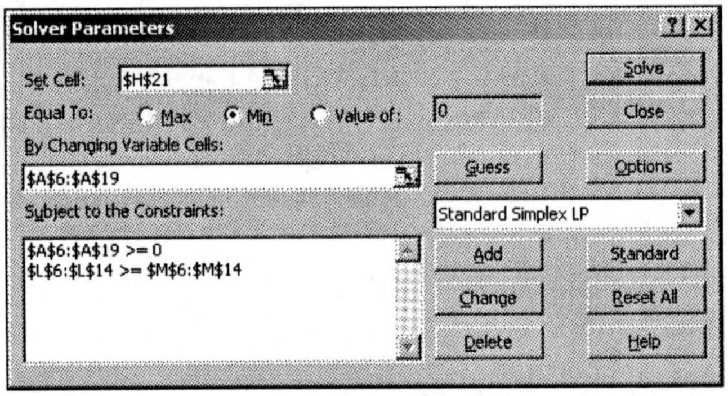

FIGURE 5.19
Optimal solution to Coal Bank Hollow Recycling's generalized network flow problem

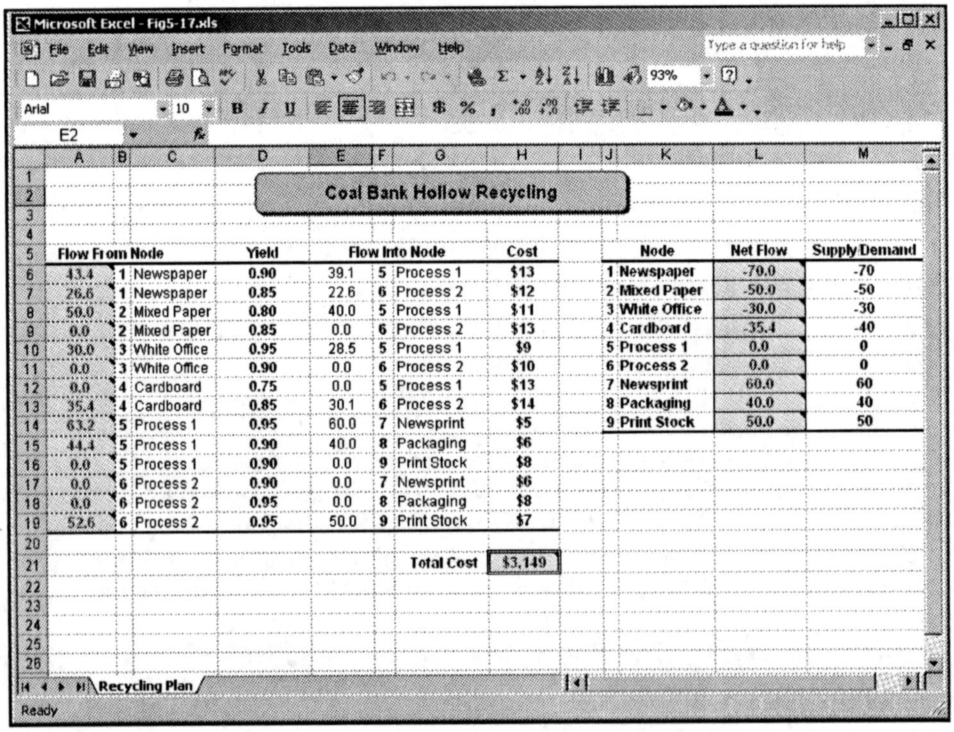

5.5.4 Generalized Network Flow Problems and Feasibility

In generalized network flow problems, the gains and/or losses associated with flows across each arc *effectively* increase and/or decrease the supply available in the network. For example, consider what happens in Figure 5.16 if the supply of newspaper is reduced to 55 tons. Although it *appears* that the total supply in the network (175 tons) still exceeds the total demand (150 tons), if we try to solve the modified problem, Solver will tell us that the problem has no feasible solution. (You may verify this on your own.) So we are not able to satisfy all of the demand due to the loss of material that occurs in the production process.

The point being made here is that with generalized network flow problems, you cannot always tell before solving the problem if the total supply is adequate to meet the total demand. As a result, you cannot always know which balance-of-flow rule to apply. When the issue is unclear, it is safest[1] to first assume that all the demand can be met and (according to the balance-of-flow rule) use constraints of the form: Inflow – Outflow ≥ Supply or Demand. If the resulting problem is infeasible (and there are no errors in the model!), then we know all the demand cannot be satisfied and (according to the balance-of-flow rule) use constraints of the form: Inflow – Outflow ≤ Supply or Demand. In this later case, the solution will identify the least costly way of using the available supply to meet as much of the demand as possible.

Figures 5.20 and 5.21 show, respectively, the Solver parameters and optimal solution for this revised recycling problem with 55 tons of newspaper. Note that this solution uses all of the available supply of each of the recycling materials. Although the solution satisfies all the demand for newsprint pulp and packaging paper pulp, it falls almost 15 tons short of the total demand for print stock pulp.

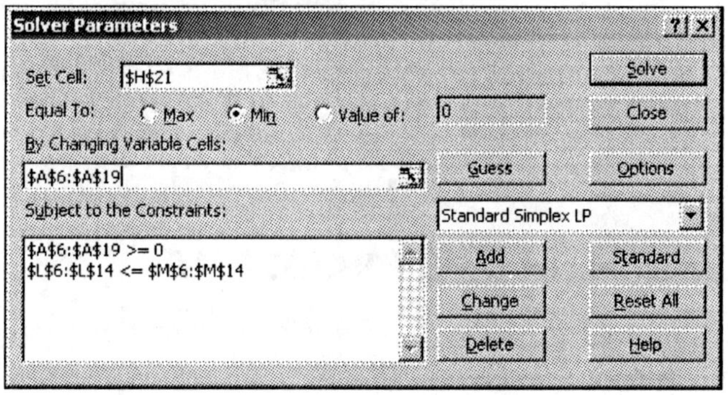

FIGURE 5.20
Solver parameters for modified recycling problem

1 See question 3 at the end of this chapter for more on this issue.

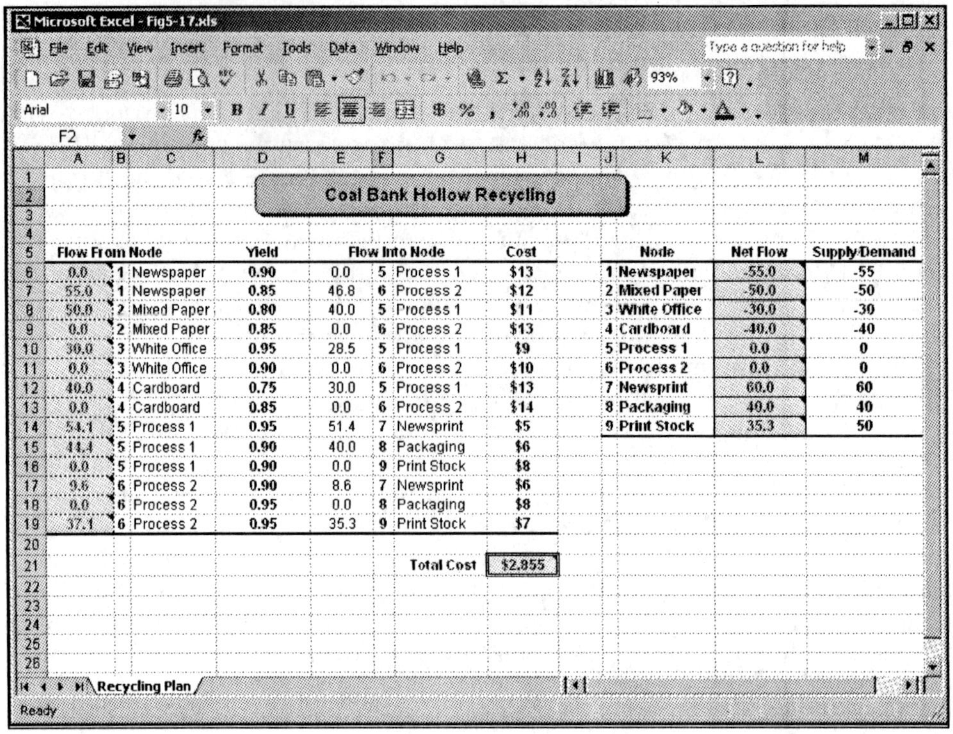

Coal Bank Hollow Recycling

Flow From Node		Yield	Flow Into Node		Cost
0.0	1 Newspaper	0.90	0.0	5 Process 1	$13
55.0	1 Newspaper	0.85	46.8	6 Process 2	$12
50.0	2 Mixed Paper	0.80	40.0	5 Process 1	$11
0.0	2 Mixed Paper	0.85	0.0	6 Process 2	$13
30.0	3 White Office	0.95	28.5	5 Process 1	$9
0.0	3 White Office	0.90	0.0	6 Process 2	$10
40.0	4 Cardboard	0.75	30.0	5 Process 1	$13
0.0	4 Cardboard	0.85	0.0	6 Process 2	$14
54.1	5 Process 1	0.95	51.4	7 Newsprint	$5
44.4	5 Process 1	0.90	40.0	8 Packaging	$6
0.0	5 Process 1	0.90	0.0	9 Print Stock	$8
9.6	6 Process 2	0.90	8.6	7 Newsprint	$6
0.0	6 Process 2	0.95	0.0	8 Packaging	$8
37.1	6 Process 2	0.95	35.3	9 Print Stock	$7
				Total Cost	$2,855

Node	Net Flow	Supply/Demand
1 Newspaper	-55.0	-55
2 Mixed Paper	-50.0	-50
3 White Office	-30.0	-30
4 Cardboard	-40.0	-40
5 Process 1	0.0	0
6 Process 2	0.0	0
7 Newsprint	60.0	60
8 Packaging	40.0	40
9 Print Stock	35.3	50

FIGURE 5.21 *Optimal solution to modified recycling problem*

Important Modeling Point

For generalized network flow problems, the gains and/or losses associated with flows across each arc *effectively* increase and/or decrease the supply available in the network. As a result, it is sometimes difficult to tell in advance whether the total supply is actually adequate to meet the total demand in a generalized network flow problem. When in doubt, it is best to assume the total supply is capable of satisfying the total demand and use Solver to prove (or refute) this assumption.

5.6 MAXIMAL FLOW PROBLEMS

The maximal flow problem (or max flow problem) is a type of network flow problem in which the goal is to determine the maximum amount of flow that can occur in the network. In a maximal flow problem, the amount of flow that can occur over each arc is limited by some capacity restriction. This type of network might be used to model the flow of oil in a pipeline (in which the amount of oil that can flow through a pipe in a unit of time is limited by the diameter of the pipe). Traffic engineers also use this type of network to determine the maximum number of cars that can travel through a collection of streets with different capacities imposed by the number of lanes in the streets and speed limits. The following example illustrates a max flow problem.

5.6.1 An Example of a Maximal Flow Problem

The Northwest Petroleum Company operates an oil field and refinery in Alaska. The crude obtained from the oil field is pumped through the network of pumping substations shown in Figure 5.22 to the company's refinery located 500 miles from the oil field. The amount of oil that can flow through each of the pipelines, represented by the arcs in the network, varies due to differing pipe diameters. The numbers next to the arcs in the network indicate the maximum amount of oil that can flow through the various pipelines (measured in thousands of barrels per hour). The company wants to determine the maximum number of barrels per hour that can flow from the oil field to the refinery.

The max flow problem appears to be very different from the network flow models described earlier because it does not include specific supplies or demands for the nodes. However, you can solve the max flow problem in the same way as a transshipment problem if you add a return arc from the ending node to the starting node, assign a demand of 0 to all the nodes in the network, and attempt to maximize the flow over the return arc. Figure 5.23 shows these modifications to the problem.

To understand the network in Figure 5.23, suppose that k units are shipped from node 6 to node 1 (where k represents some integer). Because node 6 has a supply of 0, it can send k units to node 1 only if these units can be returned through the network to node 6 (to balance the flow at node 6). The capacities on the arcs limit how many units can be returned to node 6. Therefore, the maximum flow through the network corresponds to the largest number of units that can be shipped from node 6 to node 1 and then returned through the network to node 6 (to balance the flow at this node). We can solve an LP model to determine the maximal

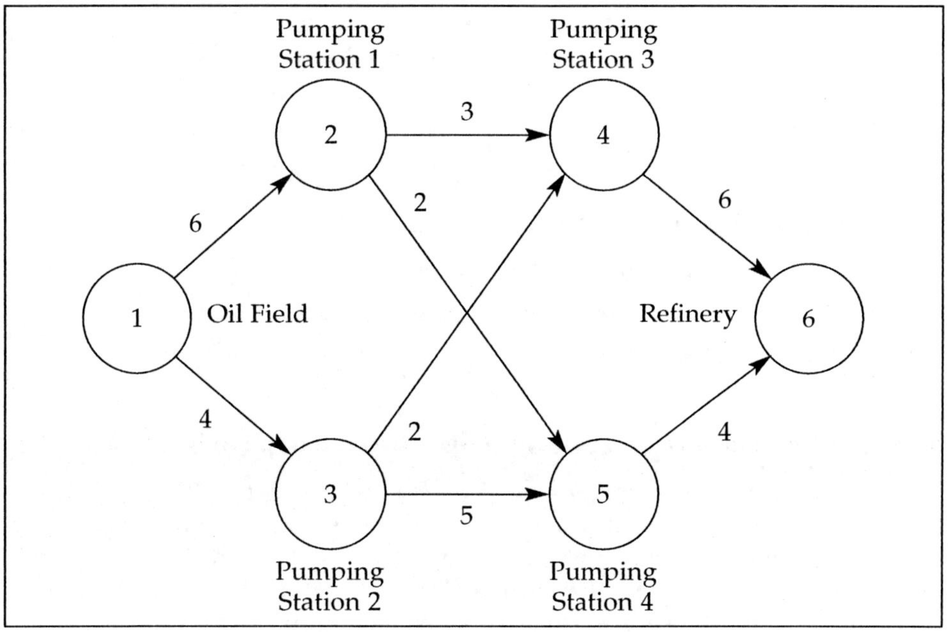

FIGURE 5.22
Network representation of Northwest Petroleum's oil refinery operation

FIGURE 5.23
Network structure of Northwest Petroleum's max flow problem

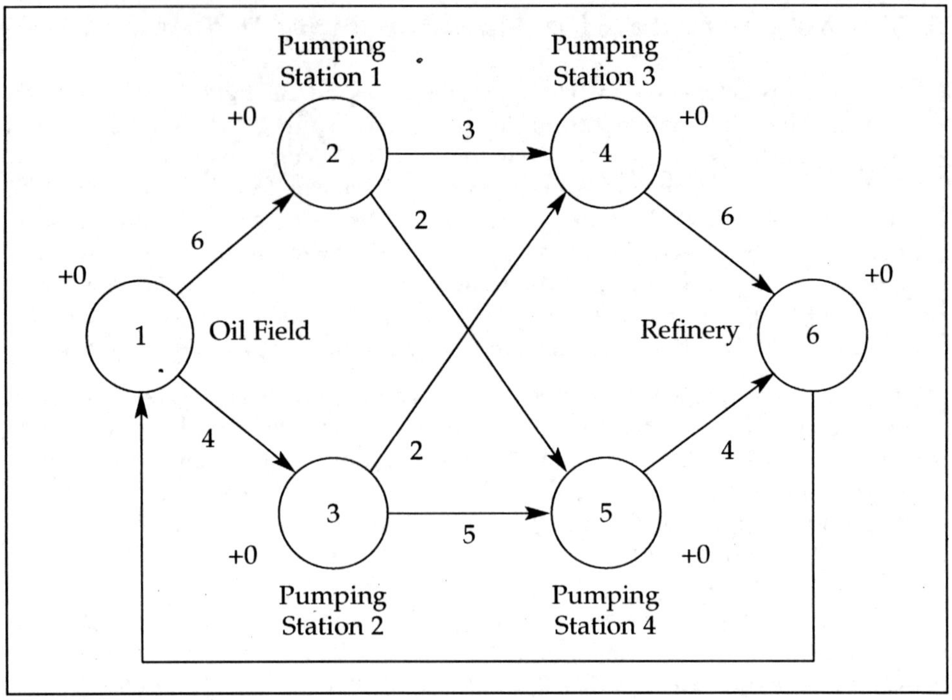

flow by maximizing the flow from node 6 to node 1, given appropriate upper bounds on each arc and the usual balance-of-flow constraints. This model is represented as:

MAX: X_{61}

Subject to:

$$+X_{61} - X_{12} - X_{13} = 0$$
$$+X_{12} - X_{24} - X_{25} = 0$$
$$+X_{13} - X_{34} - X_{35} = 0$$
$$+X_{24} + X_{34} - X_{46} = 0$$
$$+X_{25} + X_{35} - X_{56} = 0$$
$$+X_{46} + X_{56} - X_{61} = 0$$

with the following bounds on the decision variables:

$$0 \le X_{12} \le 6 \qquad 0 \le X_{25} \le 2 \qquad 0 \le X_{46} \le 6$$
$$0 \le X_{13} \le 4 \qquad 0 \le X_{34} \le 2 \qquad 0 \le X_{56} \le 4$$
$$0 \le X_{24} \le 3 \qquad 0 \le X_{35} \le 5 \qquad 0 \le X_{61} \le \infty$$

5.6.2 The Spreadsheet Model and Solution

This model is implemented in the spreadsheet shown in Figure 5.24 (and in the file Fig5-24.xls on your data disk). This spreadsheet model differs from the earlier network models in a few minor, but important, ways. First, column G in Figure 5.24 represents the upper bounds for each arc. Second, the objective function (or set cell) is represented by cell B16, which contains the formula:

Formula in cell B16: =B14

Cell B14 represents the flow from node 6 to node 1 (or X_{61}). This cell corresponds to the variable we want to maximize in the objective function of the LP model. The Solver parameters and options shown in Figure 5.25 are used to obtain the optimal solution shown in Figure 5.24.

Because the arcs leading to node 6 (X_{46} and X_{56}) have a total capacity for 10 units of flow, it might be surprising to learn that only 9 units can flow through the network. However, the optimal solution shown in Figure 5.24 indicates that the maximal flow through the network is just 9 units.

The optimal flows identified in Figure 5.24 for each arc are shown in the boxes next to the capacities for each arc in Figure 5.26. In Figure 5.26, the arc from node 5 to node 6 is at its full capacity of 4 units, whereas the arc from node 4 to node 6 is 1 unit below its full capacity of 6 units. Although the arc from node 4 to node 6 can carry 1 additional unit of flow, it is prevented from doing so because all the arcs flowing to node 4 (X_{24} and X_{34}) are at full capacity.

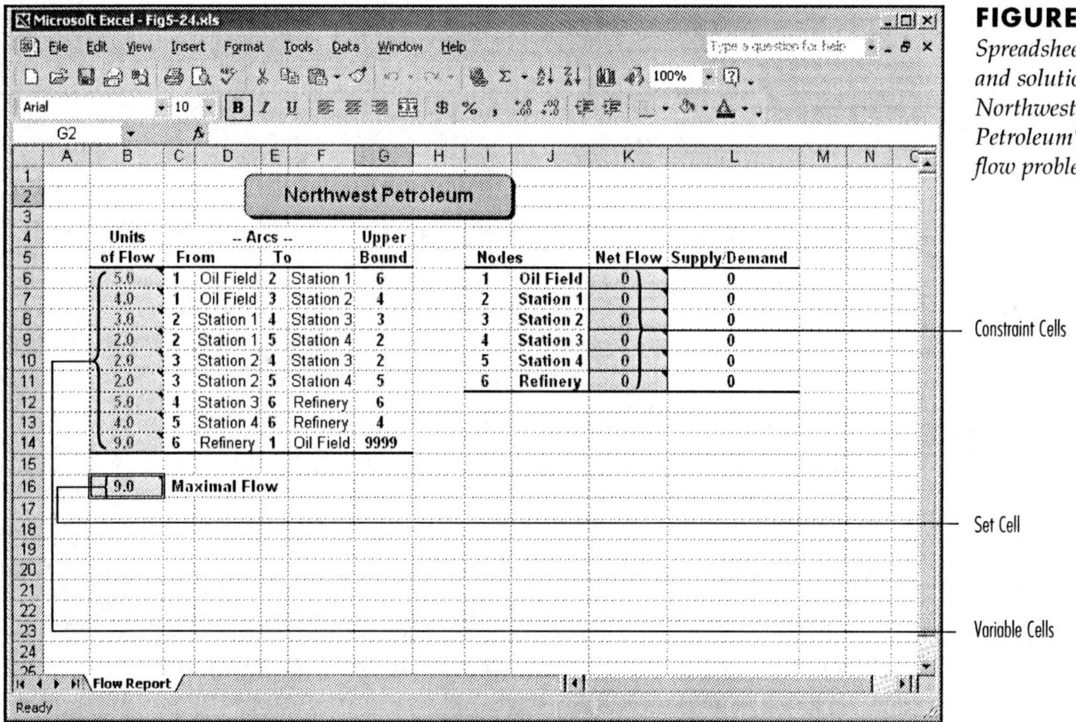

FIGURE 5.24
Spreadsheet model and solution to Northwest Petroleum's max flow problem

Key Cell Formulas

Cell	Formula	Copied to
B16	=B14	—
D6	=VLOOKUP(C6,$I$6:$J$11,2)	D7:D14 and F6:F14
K6	=SUMIF($E$6:$E$14,I6,$B$6:$B$14)-SUMIF($C$6:$C$14,I6,$B$6:$B$14)	K7:K11

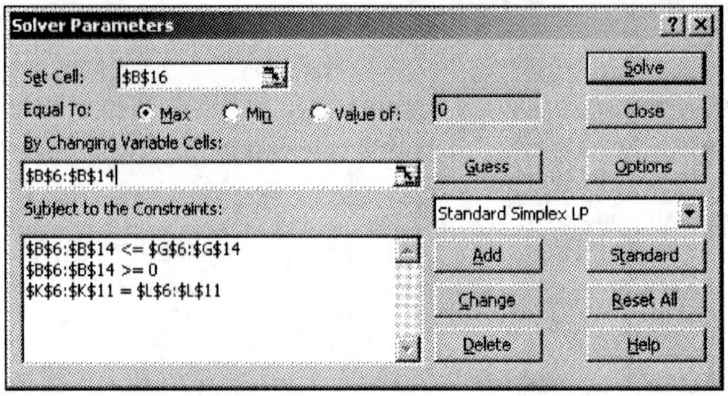

FIGURE 5.25
Solver parameters for Northwest Petroleum's max flow problem

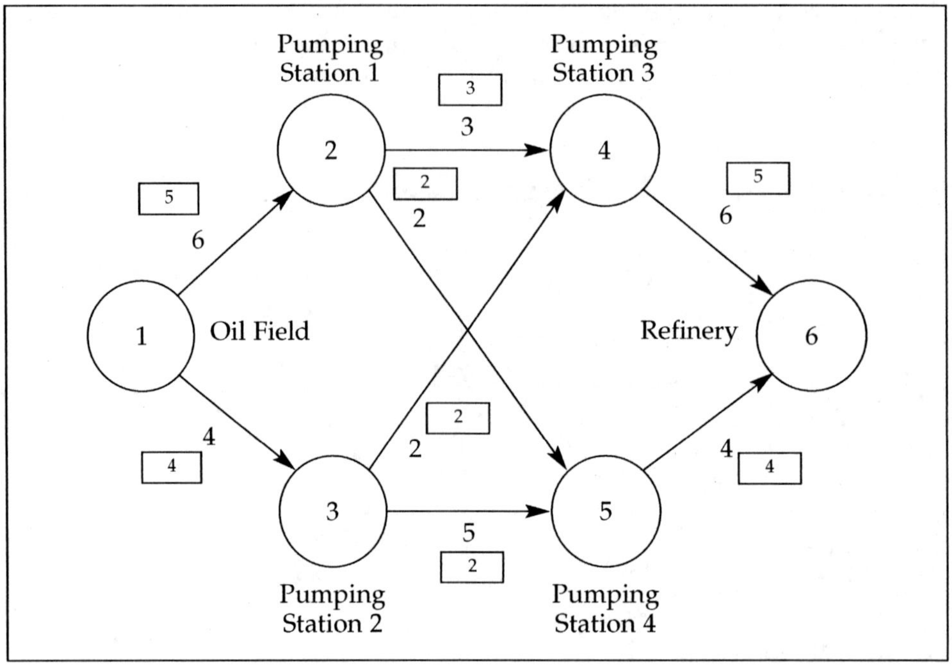

FIGURE 5.26
Network representation of the solution to Northwest Petroleum's max flow problem

A graph like Figure 5.26, which summarizes the optimal flows in a max flow problem, is helpful in identifying where increases in flow capacity would be most effective. For example, from this graph, we can see that even though X_{24} and X_{34} are both at full capacity, increasing their capacity will not necessarily increase the flow through the network. Increasing the capacity of X_{24} would allow for an increased flow through the network because an additional unit could then flow from node 1 to node 2 to node 4 to node 6. However, increasing the capacity of X_{34} would not allow for an increase in the total flow because the arc from node 1 to node 3 is already at full capacity.

5.7 SPECIAL MODELING CONSIDERATIONS

A number of special conditions can arise in network flow problems that require a bit of creativity to model accurately. For example, it is easy to impose minimum or maximum flow restrictions on individual arcs in the networks by placing appropriate lower and upper bounds on the corresponding decision variables. However, in some network flow problems, minimum or maximum flow requirements may apply to the *total* flow emanating from a given node. For example, consider the network flow problem shown in Figure 5.27.

Now suppose that the total flow into node 3 must be at least 50 and the total flow into node 4 must be at least 60. We could easily enforce these conditions with the following constraints:

$$X_{13} + X_{23} \geq 50$$
$$X_{14} + X_{24} \geq 60$$

Unfortunately, these constraints do not conform to the balance-of-flow rule and would require us to impose *side constraints* on the model. An alternative approach to modeling this problem is shown in Figure 5.28.

Two additional nodes and arcs were inserted in Figure 5.28. Note that the arc from node 30 to node 3 has a lower bound (L.B.) of 50. This will ensure that at least 50 units flow into node 3. Node 3 must then distribute this flow to nodes 5 and 6. Similarly, the arc connecting node 40 to node 4 ensures that at least 60 units will flow into node 4. The additional nodes and arcs added to Figure 5.28 are sometimes referred to as ***dummy nodes*** and ***dummy arcs.***

As another example, consider the network in the upper portion of Figure 5.29 in which the flow between two nodes can occur at two different costs. One arc has a cost of \$6 per unit of flow and an upper bound (U.B.) of 35. The other arc has a cost of \$8 per unit of flow with no upper bound on the amount of flow allowed. Note that the minimum cost solution is to send 35 units of flow from node 1 to node 2 across the \$6 arc and 15 units from node 1 to node 2 across the \$8 arc.

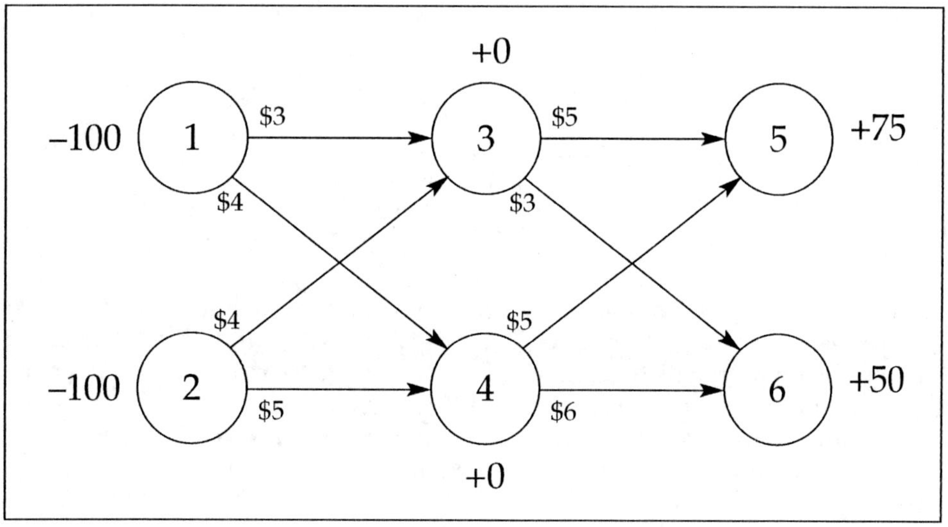

FIGURE 5.27
Example network flow problem

FIGURE 5.28
Revised network flow problem with lower bounds on the total flow into nodes 3 and 4

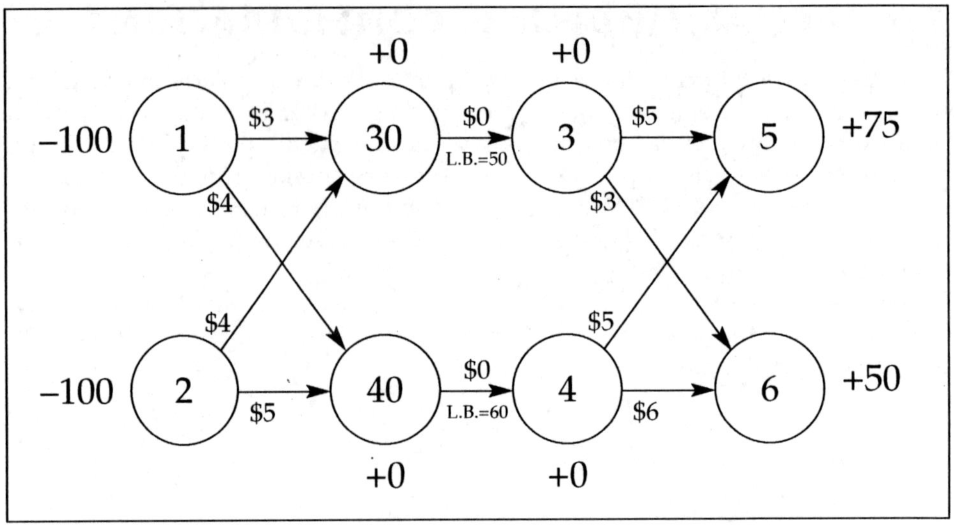

FIGURE 5.29
Alternative networks allowing two different types of flow between two nodes

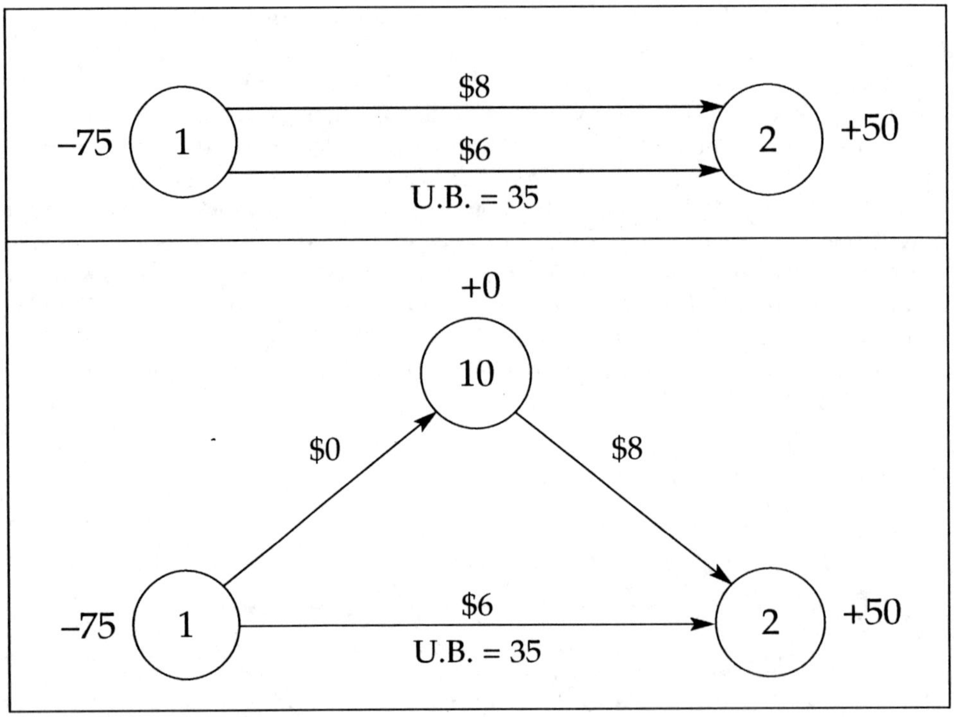

To model this problem mathematically, we would like to have two arcs called X_{12} because both arcs go from node 1 to node 2. However, if both arcs are called X_{12}, there is no way to distinguish one from the other! A solution to this dilemma is shown in the lower portion of Figure 5.29 in which we inserted a dummy node and a dummy arc. Thus, there are now two distinct arcs flowing into node 2: X_{12} and $X_{10,2}$. Flow from node 1 to node 2 across the $8 arc now must first go through node 10.

As a final example, note that upper bounds (or capacity restrictions) on the arcs in a network flow may *effectively* limit the amount of supply that can be sent through the network to meet the demand. As a result, in a network flow problem with flow restrictions (upper bounds) on the arcs, it is sometimes difficult to tell in advance whether the total demand can be met—even if the total supply available exceeds the total demand. This again creates a potential problem in knowing which balance-of-flow rule to use. Consider the example in Figure 5.30.

The upper portion of Figure 5.30 shows a network with a total supply of 200 and total demand of 165. Because the total supply appears to exceed the total demand, we are inclined to apply the balance-of-flow rule that would generate constraints of the form: Inflow – Outflow ≥ Supply or Demand. This balance-of-flow rule requires the total inflow to nodes 3 and 4 to be greater than or equal to their demands of 75 and 80, respectively. However, the upper bounds on the arcs leading into node 3 limit the total flow into this node to 70 units. Similarly, the total flow into node 4 is limited to 70. As a result, there is no feasible solution to the problem. In this case, we cannot resolve the infeasibility by reversing the constraints to be of the form: Inflow – Outflow ≤ Supply or Demand. Although this allows for less than the total amount demanded to be sent to nodes 3 and 4, it now *requires* all the supply to be sent out of nodes 1 and 2. Clearly, some of the 200 units of supply available from nodes 1 and 2 will have nowhere to go if the total flow into nodes 3 and 4 cannot exceed 140 units (as required by the upper bounds on the arcs).

A solution to this predicament is shown in the bottom half of Figure 5.30. Here, we added a dummy demand node (node 0) that is connected directly to nodes 1 and 2 with arcs that impose very large costs on flows to the dummy node. Note that the demand at this dummy node is equal to the total supply in the network.

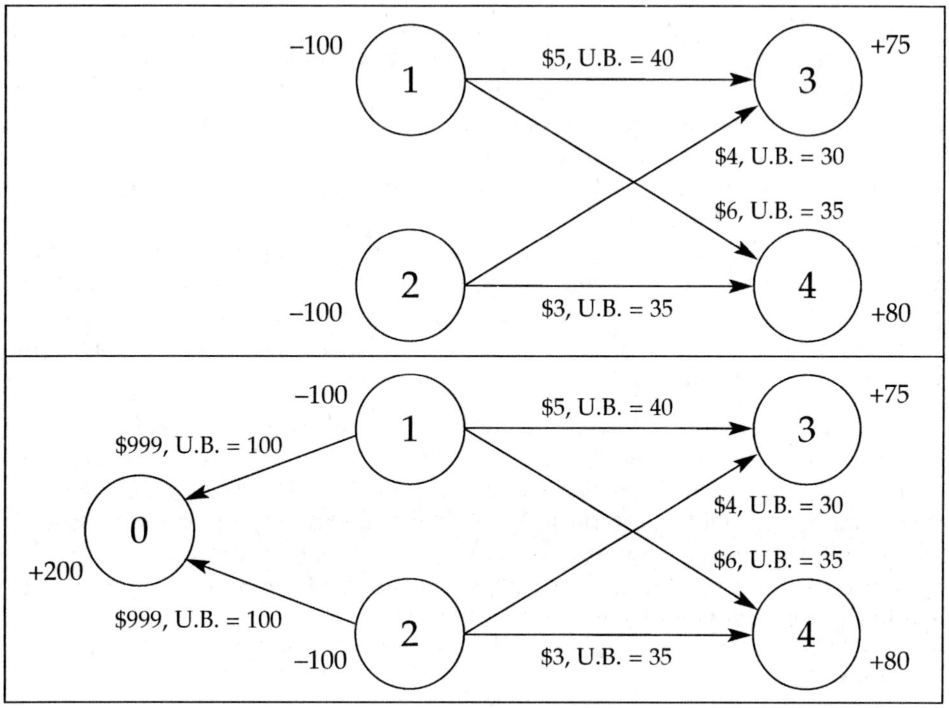

FIGURE 5.30
Example of using a dummy demand node

Now, the total demand exceeds the total supply so the balance-of-flow rule mandates we use constraints of the form: Inflow – Outflow ≤ Supply or Demand. Again, this allows for less than the total amount demanded to be sent to nodes 0, 3, and 4 but *requires* all the supply to be sent out of nodes 1 and 2. Due to the large costs associated with flows from nodes 1 and 2 to the dummy demand node, Solver will ensure that as much of the supply as possible is first sent to nodes 3 and 4. Any remaining supply at nodes 1 and 2 would then be sent to the dummy node. Of course, flows to the dummy node actually represent excess supply or inventory at nodes 1 and 2 that would not actually be shipped anywhere or incur any costs. But using a dummy node in this manner allows us to model and solve the problem accurately.

Dummy nodes and arcs can be helpful in modeling a variety of situations that naturally occur in network problems. The techniques illustrated here are two "tricks of the trade" in network modeling and may prove useful in some of the problems at the end of this chapter.

5.8 MINIMAL SPANNING TREE PROBLEMS

Another type of network problem is known as the minimal spanning tree problem. This type of problem cannot be solved as an LP problem, but is solved easily using a simple manual algorithm.

For a network with n nodes, a **spanning tree** is a set of $n - 1$ arcs that connects all the nodes and contains no loops. A minimum spanning tree problem involves determining the set of arcs that connects all the nodes in a network while minimizing the total length (or cost) of the selected arcs. Consider the following example.

> Jon Fleming is responsible for setting up a local area network (LAN) in the design engineering department of Windstar Aerospace Company. A LAN consists of a number of individual computers connected to a centralized computer or file server. Each computer in the LAN can access information from the file server and communicate with the other computers in the LAN.
>
> Installing a LAN involves connecting all the computers together with communications cables. Individual computers do not have to be connected directly to the file server, but there must be some link between each computer in the network. Figure 5.31 summarizes all the possible connections that Jon can make. Each node in this figure represents one of the computers to be included in the LAN. Each line connecting the nodes represents a possible connection between pairs of computers. The dollar amount on each line represents the cost of making the connection.

The arcs in Figure 5.31 have no specific directional orientation, indicating that information can move in either direction across the arcs. Also note that the communication links represented by the arcs do not exist yet. Jon's challenge is to determine which links to establish. Because the network involves $n = 6$ nodes, a spanning tree for this problem consists of $n - 1 = 5$ arcs that results in a path existing between any pair of nodes. The objective is to find the minimal (least costly) spanning tree for this problem.

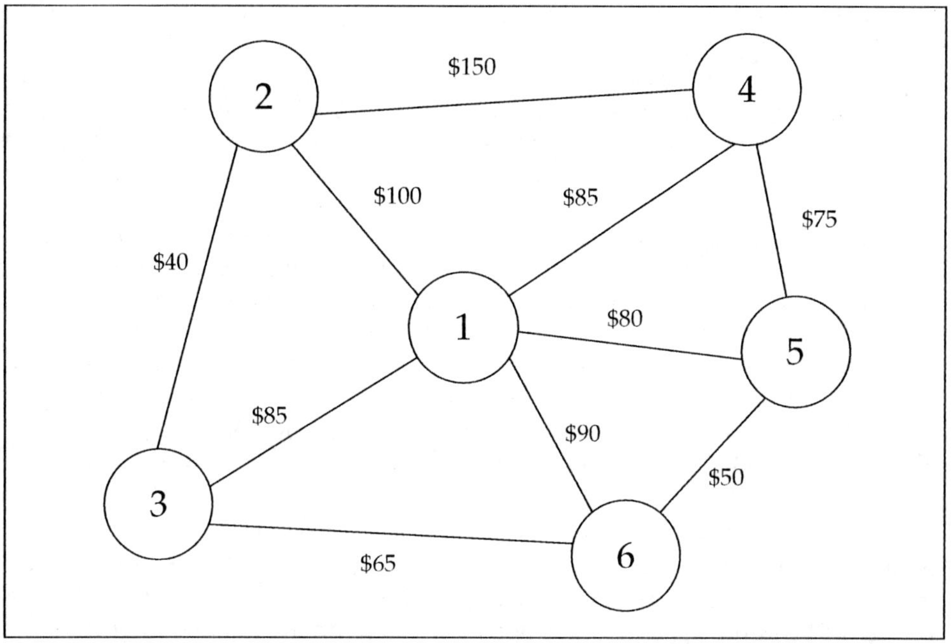

FIGURE 5.31
Network representation of Windstar Aerospace's minimal spanning tree problem

5.8.1 An Algorithm for the Minimal Spanning Tree Problem

You can apply a simple algorithm to solve minimal spanning tree problems. The steps to this algorithm are:

1. Select any node. Call this the current subnetwork.
2. Add to the current subnetwork the cheapest arc that connects any node within the current subnetwork to any node not in the current subnetwork. (Ties for the cheapest arc can be broken arbitrarily.) Call this the current subnetwork.
3. If all the nodes are in the subnetwork, stop; this is the optimal solution. Otherwise, return to step 2.

5.8.2 Solving the Example Problem

You can program this algorithm easily or, for simple problems, execute it manually. The following steps illustrate how to execute the algorithm manually for the example problem shown in Figure 5.31.

Step 1. If we select node 1 in Figure 5.31, then node 1 is the current subnetwork.

Step 2. The cheapest arc connecting the current subnetwork to a node not in the current subnetwork is the $80 arc connecting nodes 1 and 5. This arc and node 5 are added to the current subnetwork.

Step 3. Four nodes (nodes 2, 3, 4, and 6) remain unconnected—therefore, return to step 2.

Step 2. The cheapest arc connecting the current subnetwork to a node not in the current subnetwork is the $50 arc connecting nodes 5 and 6. This arc and node 6 are added to the current subnetwork.

Step 3. Three nodes (nodes 2, 3, and 4) remain unconnected—therefore, return to step 2.

Step 2. The cheapest arc connecting the current subnetwork to a node not in the current subnetwork is the $65 arc connecting nodes 6 and 3. This arc and node 3 are added to the current subnetwork.

Step 3. Two nodes (nodes 2 and 4) remain unconnected—therefore, return to step 2.

Step 2. The cheapest arc connecting the current subnetwork to a node not in the current subnetwork is the $40 arc connecting nodes 3 and 2. This arc and node 2 are added to the current subnetwork.

Step 3. One node (node 4) remains unconnected—therefore, return to step 2.

Step 2. The cheapest arc connecting the current subnetwork to a node not in the current subnetwork is the $75 arc connecting nodes 5 and 4. This arc and node 4 are added to the current subnetwork.

Step 3. All the nodes are now connected. Stop; the current subnetwork is optimal.

Figure 5.32 shows the optimal (minimal) spanning tree generated by this algorithm. The algorithm described here produces the optimal (minimal) spanning tree regardless of which node is selected initially in step 1. You can verify this by solving the example problem again starting with a different node in step 1.

5.9 SUMMARY

This chapter presented several business problems modeled as network flow problems, including transshipment problems, shortest path problems, maximal flow problems, transportation/assignment problems, and generalized network flow

FIGURE 5.32
Optimal solution to Windstar Aerospace's minimal spanning tree problem

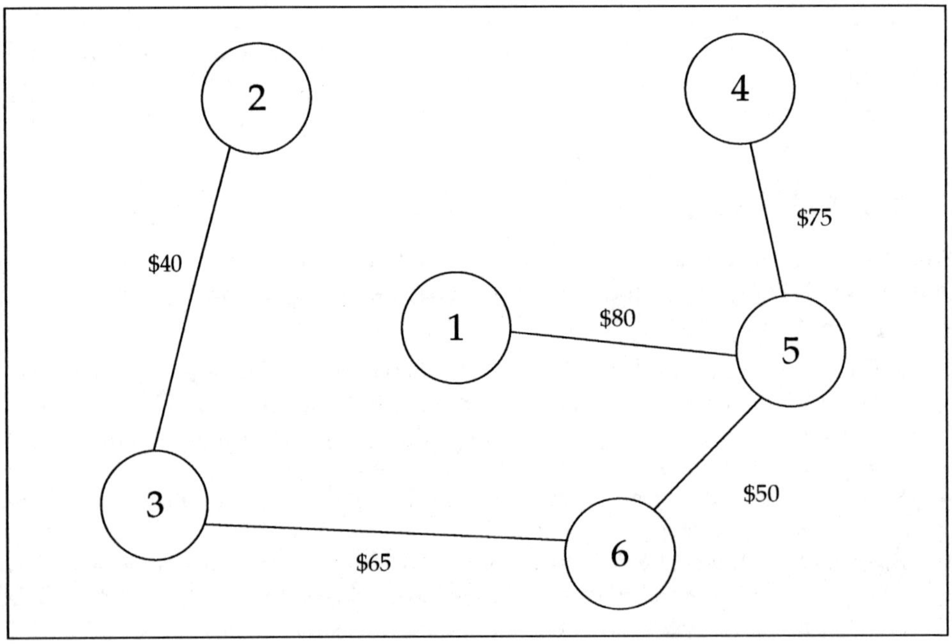

models. It also introduced the minimal spanning tree problem and presented a simple algorithm for solving this type of problem manually.

Although special algorithms exist for solving network flow problems, you can also formulate and solve them as LP problems. The constraints in an LP formulation of a network flow problem have a special structure that enables you to implement and solve these models easily in a spreadsheet. Although there might be more efficient ways of solving network flow problems, the methods discussed in this chapter are often the most practical. For extremely complex network flow problems, you might need to use a specialized algorithm. Unfortunately, you are unlikely to find this type of software at your local software store. However, various network optimization packages can be found in the technical/scientific directories on the Internet.

5.10 REFERENCES

Glassey, R. and V. Gupta. "A Linear Programming Analysis of Paper Recycling," *Studies in Mathematical Programming.* New York: North-Holland, 1978.

Glover, F. and D. Klingman. "Network Applications in Industry and Government." *AIIE Transactions,* vol. 9, no. 4, 1977.

Glover, F., D. Klingman, and N. Phillips. *Network Models and Their Applications in Practice.* New York: Wiley, 1992.

Hansen, P. and R. Wendell. "A Note on Airline Commuting." *Interfaces,* vol. 11, no. 12, 1982.

Phillips, D. and A. Diaz. *Fundamentals of Network Analysis.* Englewood Cliffs, NJ: Prentice Hall, 1981.

Vemuganti, R., et al. "Network Models for Fleet Management." *Decision Sciences,* vol. 20, Winter 1989.

THE WORLD OF MANAGEMENT SCIENCE

Yellow Freight System Boosts Profits and Quality with Network Optimization

One of the largest motor carriers in the United States, Yellow Freight System, Inc. of Overland Park, Kansas, uses network modeling and optimization to assist management in load planning, routing empty trucks, routing trailers, dropping or adding direct service routes, and strategic planning of terminal size and location. The system, called SYSNET, operates on a network of Sun workstations optimizing over a million network flow variables. The company also uses a tactical planning room equipped with graphical display tools that allow planning meetings to be conducted interactively with the system.

The company competes in the less-than-truckload (LTL) segment of the trucking market. That is, they contract for shipments of any size, regardless of whether the shipment fills the trailer. To operate efficiently, Yellow Freight must consolidate and transfer shipments at 23 break-bulk terminals located throughout the United States. At these terminals, shipments might

continued

be reloaded into different trailers depending on the final destination. Each break-bulk terminal serves several end-of-line terminals, in a hub-and-spoke network. Normally, shipments are sent by truck to the break-bulk dedicated to the origination point. Local managers occasionally try to save costs by loading direct, which means bypassing a break-bulk and sending a truckload of consolidated shipments directly to the final destination. Before SYSNET, these decisions were made in the field without accurate information on how they would affect costs and reliability in the entire system.

Since its implementation in 1989, SYSNET has scored high with upper management. Often, the first response to a new proposal is, "Has it been run through SYSNET?" The benefits attributed to the new system include:

- an increase of 11.6% in freight loaded directly, saving $4.7 million annually
- better routing of trailers, saving $1 million annually
- savings of $1.42 million annually by increasing the average number of pounds loaded per trailer
- reduction in claims for damaged merchandise
- a 27% reduction in the number of late deliveries
- tactical planning projects with SYSNET in 1990 that identified $10 million in annual savings

Equally important has been the effect on the management philosophy and culture at Yellow Freight. Management now has greater control over network operations; tradition, intuition, and "gut feel" have been replaced with formal analytical tools; and Yellow Freight is better able to act as a partner with customers in total quality management and just-in-time inventory systems.

Source: Braklow, John W., William W. Graham, Stephen M. Hassler, Ken E. Peck, and Warren B. Powell. "Interactive Optimization Improves Service and Performance for Yellow Freight System." *Interfaces*, 22:1, January–February 1992, pp. 147–172.

QUESTIONS AND PROBLEMS

1. This chapter followed the convention of using negative numbers to represent the supply at a node and positive numbers to represent the demand at a node. Another convention is just the opposite—using positive numbers to represent supply and negative numbers to represent demand. How would the balance-of-flow rule presented in this chapter need to be changed to accommodate this alternate convention?
2. To use the balance-of-flow rule presented in this chapter, constraints for supply nodes must have negative RHS values. Some LP software packages cannot solve problems in which the constraints have negative RHS values. How should the balance-of-flow rules be modified to produce LP models that can be solved with such software packages?
3. Consider the revised Coal Bank Hollow recycling problem discussed in section 5.5.4 of this chapter. We said that it is safest to assume the supply in a generalized network flow problem is capable of meeting the demand (until Solver proves otherwise).

a. Solve the problem in Figure 5.17 (and file Fig5-17.xls on your data disk) assuming 80 tons of newspaper is available and that the supply is NOT adequate to meet the demand. How much of each of the raw recycling materials is used? How much demand for each product is met? What is the cost of this solution?
b. Solve the problem again assuming that the supply is adequate to meet the demand. How much of each of the raw recycling materials is used? How much demand for each product is met? What is the cost of this solution?
c. Which one is better? Why?
d. Suppose there are 55 tons of newspaper available. Figure 5.19 shows the least cost solution for distributing the supply in this case. In that solution, the demand for newsprint pulp and packaging pulp is met but the we are almost 15 tons short on packaging paper pulp. How much can this shortage be reduced and how much extra would it cost to do so?

4. Consider the generalized transportation problem shown in Figure 5.33. How can this problem be transformed into an equivalent transportation problem? Draw the network for the equivalent problem.
5. Draw the network representation of the following network flow problem.

MIN: $+7X_{12} + 6X_{14} + 3X_{23} + 4x_{24} + 5X_{32} + 9X_{43} + 8X_{52} + 5X_{54}$

Subject to:

$-X_{12} - X_{14} = -5$

$+X_{12} + X_{52} + X_{32} - X_{23} - X_{24} = +4$

$-X_{32} + X_{23} + X_{43} = +8$

$+X_{14} + X_{24} + X_{54} - X_{43} = +0$

$-X_{52} - X_{54} = -7$

$X_{ij} \geq 0$ for all i and j

6. Draw the network representation of the following network flow problem (on page 224). What kind of network flow problem is this?

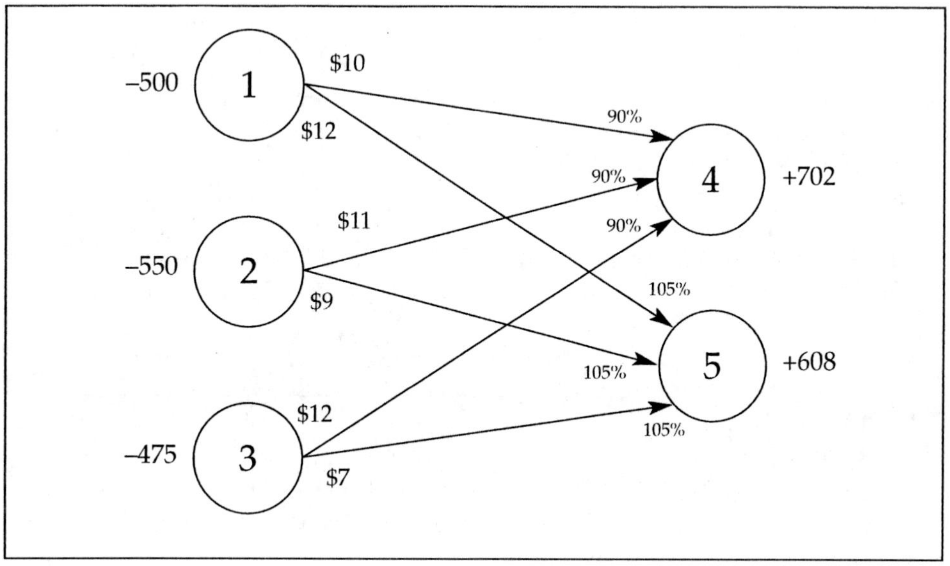

FIGURE 5.33
Graph of a generalized network flow problem

MIN: $+2X_{13} + 6X_{14} + 5X_{15} + 4X_{23} + 3X_{24} + 7X_{25}$

Subject to: $-X_{13} - X_{14} - X_{15} = -8$

$-X_{23} - X_{24} - X_{25} = -7$

$+X_{13} + X_{23} = +5$

$+X_{14} + X_{24} = +5$

$+X_{15} + X_{25} = +5$

$X_{ij} \geq 0$ for all i and j

7. Refer to the equipment replacement problem discussed in section 5.3 of this chapter. In addition to the lease costs described for the problem, suppose that it costs Compu-Train $2,000 extra in labor costs whenever they replace their existing computers with new ones. What effect does this have on the formulation and solution of the problem? Which of the two leasing contracts is optimal in this case?
8. SunNet is a residential Internet Service Provider (ISP) in the central Florida area. Presently, the company operates one centralized facility that all of its clients call into for Internet access. To improve service, the company is planning to open three satellite offices in the cities of Pine Hills, Eustis, and Sanford. The company has identified five different regions to be serviced by these three offices. The following table summarizes the number of customers in each region, the service capacity at each office, and the average monthly per customer cost of providing service to each region from each office. Table entries of "n.a." indicate infeasible region to service center combinations. SunNet wants to determine how many customers from each region to assign to each service center in order to minimize cost.

Region	Pine Hills	Eustis	Sanford	Customers
1	$6.50	$7.50	n.a	30,000
2	$7.00	$8.00	n.a	40,000
3	$8.25	$7.25	$6.75	25,000
4	n.a.	$7.75	$7.00	35,000
5	n.a.	$7.50	$6.75	33,000
Capacity	60,000	70,000	40,000	

   a. Draw a network flow model to represent this problem.
   b. Implement your model in Excel and solve it.
   c. What is the optimal solution?
9. Acme Manufacturing makes a variety of household appliances at a single manufacturing facility. The expected demand for one of these appliances during the next four months is shown in the following table along with the expected production costs and the expected capacity for producing these items.

	Month			
	1	2	3	4
Demand	420	580	310	540
Production Cost	$49.00	$45.00	$46.00	$47.00
Production Capacity	500	520	450	550

Acme estimates it costs $1.50 per month for each unit of this appliance carried in inventory at the end of each month. Currently, Acme has 120 units in inventory on hand for this product. To maintain a level workforce, the company wants to produce at least 400 units per month. They also want to maintain a safety stock of at least 50 units per month. Acme wants to determine how many of each appliance to manufacture during each of the next four months to meet the expected demand at the lowest possible total cost.

a. Draw a network flow model for this problem.
b. Create a spreadsheet model for this problem and solve it using Solver.
c. What is the optimal solution?
d. How much money could Acme save if they were willing to drop the restriction about producing at least 400 units per month?

10. Jacobs Manufacturing produces a popular custom accessory for pick-up trucks at plants in Huntington, West Virginia, and Bakersfield, California, and ships them to distributors in Dallas, Texas; Chicago, Illinois; Denver, Colorado; and Atlanta, Georgia. The plants in Huntington and Bakersfield have, respectively, the capacity to produce 3,000 and 4,000 units per month. For the month of October, costs of shipping a carton of 10 units from each plant to each distributor are summarized in the following table.

	Shipping Cost per Container			
	Dallas	**Chicago**	**Denver**	**Atlanta**
Huntington	$19	$15	$14	$12
Bakersfield	$16	$18	$11	$13

Jacobs has been notified that these shipping rates will each increase by $1.50 on November 1. Each distributor has ordered 1,500 units of Jacobs' product for October and 2,000 units for November. In any month, Jacobs can send each distributor up to 500 units more than they have ordered if Jacobs provides a $2 per unit discount on the excess (which the distributor must hold in inventory from one month to the next). In October, the per unit cost of production in Huntington and Bakersfield are $12 and $16, respectively. In November, Jacobs expects the cost of production at both plants to be $14 per unit. The company wants to develop a production and distribution plan for the months of October and November that would allow them to meet the expected demand from each distributor at the minimum cost.

a. Draw a network flow model for this problem.
b. Implement your model in a spreadsheet and solve it.
c. What is the optimal solution?

11. A construction company wants to determine the optimal replacement policy for the earth mover it owns. The company has a policy of not keeping an earth mover for more than five years, and has estimated the annual operating costs and trade-in values for earth movers during each of the five years they might be kept as:

	Age in Years				
	0–1	**1–2**	**2–3**	**3–4**	**4–5**
Operating Cost	$ 8,000	$9,100	$10,700	$9,200	$11,000
Trade-in Value	$14,000	$9,000	$ 6,000	$3,500	$ 2,000

Assume that new earth movers currently cost $25,000 and are increasing in cost by 4.5% per year. The company wants to determine when it should plan on replacing its current, 2-year-old earth mover. Use a 5-year planning horizon.

a. Draw the network representation of this problem.
b. Write out the LP formulation of this problem.
c. Solve the problem using Solver. Interpret your solution.

12. The Ortega Food Company needs to ship 100 cases of hot tamales from its warehouse in San Diego to a distributor in New York City at minimum cost. The costs associated with shipping 100 cases between various cities are:

	To					
From	Los Angeles	Denver	St. Louis	Memphis	Chicago	New York
San Diego	5	13	—	45	—	105
Los Angeles	—	27	19	50	—	95
Denver	—	—	14	30	32	—
St. Louis	—	14	—	35	24	—
Memphis	—	—	35	—	18	25
Chicago	—	—	24	18	—	17

a. Draw the network representation of this problem.
b. Write out the LP formulation of this problem.
c. Solve the problem using Solver. Interpret your solution.

13. A cotton grower in south Georgia produces cotton on farms in Statesboro and Brooklet, ships it to cotton gins in Claxton and Millen where it is processed, and then sends it to distribution centers in Savannah, Perry, and Valdosta where it is sold to customers for $60 per ton. Any surplus cotton is sold to a government warehouse in Hinesville for $25 per ton. The cost of growing and harvesting a ton of cotton at the farms in Statesboro and Brooklet is $20 and $22, respectively. There are presently 700 and 500 tons of cotton available in Statesboro and Brooklet, respectively. The cost of transporting the cotton from the farms to the gins and the government warehouse is shown in the following table.

	Claxton	Millen	Hinesville
Statesboro	$4.00	$3.00	$4.50
Brooklet	$3.50	$3.00	$3.50

The gin in Claxton has the capacity to process 700 tons of cotton at a cost of $10 per ton. The gin in Millen can process 600 tons at a cost of $11 per ton. Each gin must use at least one half of its available capacity. The cost of shipping a ton of cotton from each gin to each distribution center is summarized in the following table.

	Savannah	Perry	Valdosta
Claxton	$10	$16	$15
Millen	$12	$18	$17

Assume the demand for cotton in Savannah, Perry, and Valdosta is 400, 300, and 450 tons, respectively.

a. Draw a network flow model to represent this problem.
b. Implement your model in Excel and solve it.
c. What is the optimal solution?

14. A furniture manufacturer has warehouses in cities represented by nodes 1, 2, and 3 in Figure 5.34. The values on the arcs indicate the per unit shipping costs required to transport living room suites between the various cities. The supply of living room suites at each warehouse is indicated by the negative number next to nodes 1, 2, and 3. The demand for living room suites is indicated by the positive number next to the remaining nodes.
    a. Identify the supply, demand, and transshipment nodes in this problem.
    b. Use Solver to determine the least costly shipping plan for this problem.
15. The graph in Figure 5.35 represents various flows that can occur through a sewage treatment plant with the numbers on the arcs representing the maximum flow (in tons of sewage per hour) that can be accommodated. Formulate an LP model to determine the maximum tons of sewage per hour that can be processed by this plant.
16. A company has three warehouses that supply four stores with a given product. Each warehouse has 30 units of the product. Stores 1, 2, 3, and 4 require 20, 25, 30, and 35 units of the product, respectively. The per unit shipping costs from each warehouse to each store are:

	Store			
Warehouse	**1**	**2**	**3**	**4**
1	5	4	6	5
2	3	6	4	4
3	4	3	3	2

a. Draw the network representation of this problem. What kind of problem is this?

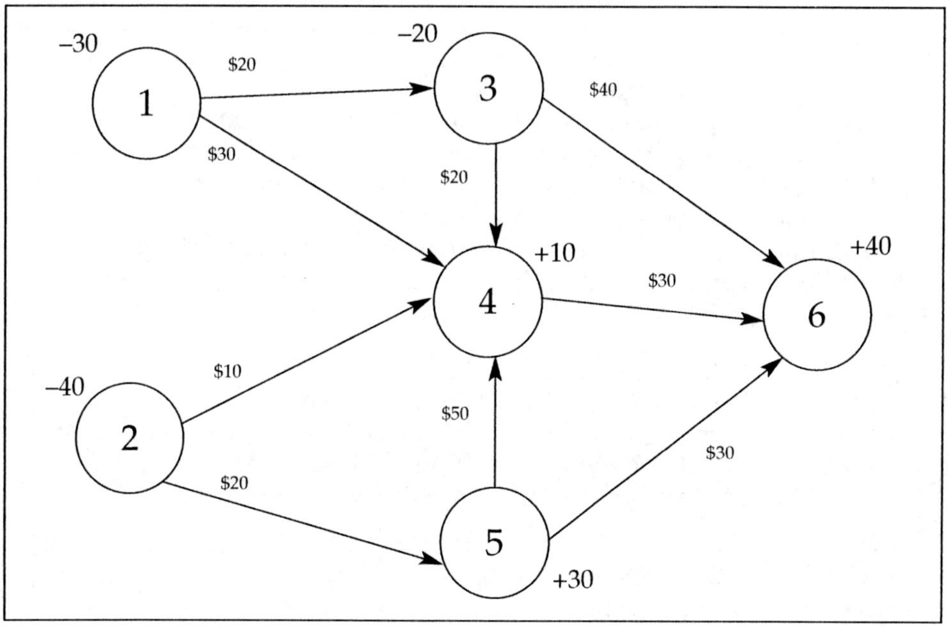

FIGURE 5.34
Network flow model for the furniture manufacturing problem

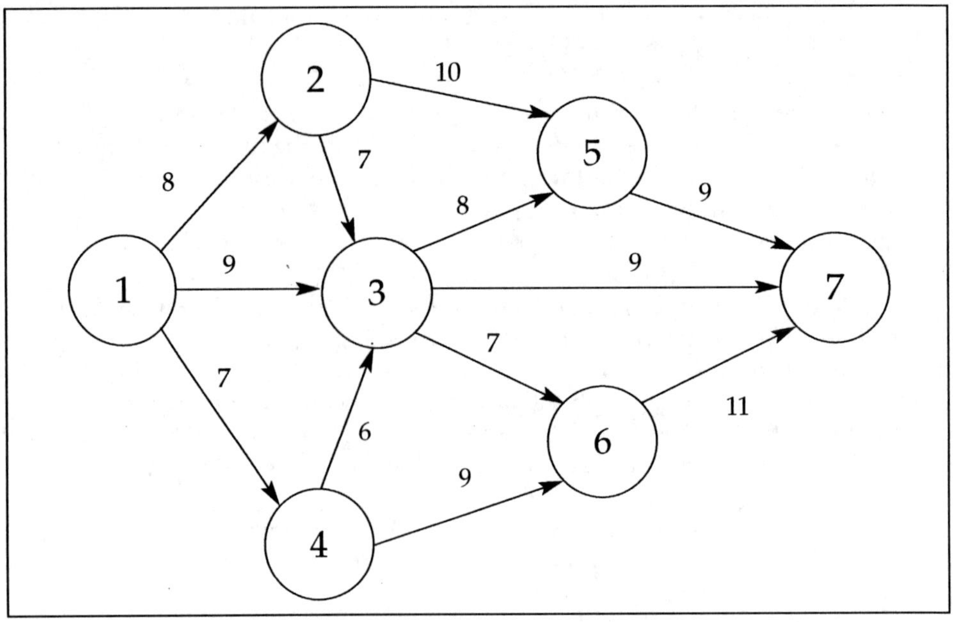

FIGURE 5.35
Network flow model for the sewage treatment plant

b. Formulate an LP model to determine the least expensive shipping plan to fill the demands at the stores.
c. Solve the problem using Solver.
d. Suppose that shipments are not allowed between warehouse 1 and store 2 or between warehouse 2 and store 3. What is the easiest way to modify the spreadsheet so that you can solve this modified problem? What is the optimal solution to the modified problem?

17. A used-car broker needs to transport his inventory of cars from locations 1 and 2 in Figure 5.36 to used-car auctions being held at locations 4 and 5. The costs of transporting cars along each of the routes are indicated on the arcs. The trucks used to carry the cars can hold a maximum of 10 cars. Therefore, the maximum number of cars that can flow over any arc is 10.
   a. Formulate an LP model to determine the least costly method of distributing the cars from locations 1 and 2 so that 20 cars will be available for sale at location 4, and 10 cars will be available for sale at location 5.
   b. Use Solver to find the optimal solution to this problem.
18. An information systems consultant who lives in Dallas must spend the majority of the month of March onsite with a client in San Diego. Her travel schedule for the month is as follows:

Leave Dallas	Leave San Diego
Monday, March 2	Friday, March 6
Monday, March 9	Thursday, March 12
Tuesday, March 17	Friday, March 20
Monday, March 23	Wednesday, March 25

The usual round-trip ticket price between Dallas and San Diego is $750. However, the airline offers a 25% discount if the dates on a round-trip ticket cover less than 7 nights and include a weekend. A 35% discount is offered for

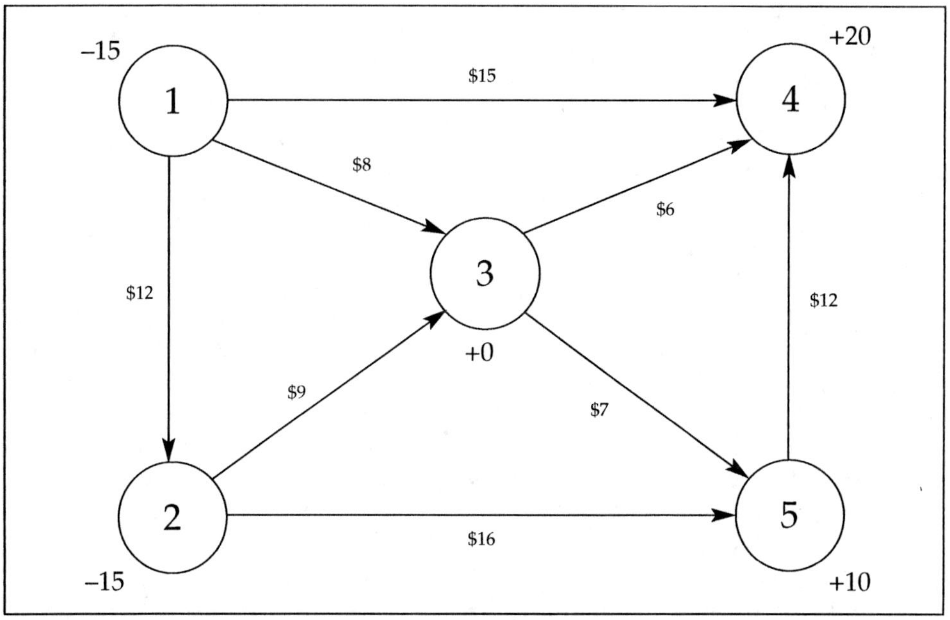

FIGURE 5.36
Network flow model for the used-car problem

round-trip tickets covering 10 or more nights, and a 45% discount is available for round-trip tickets covering 20 or more nights. The consultant can purchase four round-trip tickets in any manner that allows her to leave Dallas and San Diego on the days indicated.

a. Draw a network flow model for this problem.
b. Implement the problem in a spreadsheet and solve it.
c. What is the optimal solution? How much does this save for four full-cost round-trip tickets?

19. The Conch Oil Company needs to transport 30 million barrels of crude oil from a port in Doha, Qatar in the Persian Gulf to three refineries throughout Europe. The refineries are in Rotterdam, Netherlands; Toulon, France; and Palermo, Italy, and require 6 million, 15 million, and 9 million barrels, respectively. The oil can be transported to the refineries in three different ways. First, oil may be shipped from Qatar to Rotterdam, Toulon, and Palermo on supertankers traveling around Africa at costs of $1.20, $1.40, and $1.35 per barrel, respectively. Conch is contractually obligated to send at least 25% of its oil via these supertankers. Alternatively, oil can be shipped from Doha to Suez, Egypt at a cost of $0.35 per barrel, then through the Suez Canal to Port Said at a cost of $0.20 per barrel, then from Port Said to Rotterdam, Toulon, and Palermo at per barrel costs of $0.27, $0.23, and $0.19, respectively. Finally, up to 15 million barrels of the oil shipped from Doha to Suez can then be sent via pipeline Damietta, Egypt at $0.16 per barrel. From Damietta, it can shipped to Rotterdam, Toulon, and Palermo at costs of $0.25, $0.20, and $0.15, respectively.
    a. Draw a network flow model for this problem.
    b. Implement your model in a spreadsheet and solve it.
    c. What is the optimal solution?
20. Omega Airlines has several nonstop flights between Atlanta and Los Angeles every day. The schedules of these flights are shown in the following table.

Flight	Departs Atlanta	Arrives in L.A.	Flight	Departs L.A.	Arrives in Atlanta
1	6 A.M.	8 A.M.	1	5 A.M.	9 A.M.
2	8 A.M.	10 A.M.	2	6 A.M.	10 A.M.
3	10 A.M.	Noon	3	9 A.M.	1 P.M.
4	Noon	2 P.M.	4	Noon	4 P.M.
5	4 P.M.	6 P.M.	5	2 P.M.	6 P.M.
6	6 P.M.	8 P.M.	6	5 P.M.	9 P.M.
7	7 P.M.	9 P.M.	7	7 P.M.	11 P.M.

Omega wants to determine the optimal way of assigning flight crews to these different flights. The company wants to ensure that the crews always return to the city from which they left each day. FAA regulations require at least one hour of rest for flight crews between flights. However, flight crews become irritated if they are forced to wait for extremely long periods of time between flights, so Omega wants to find an assignment of flight schedules that minimizes these waiting periods.

a. Draw a network flow model for this problem.
b. Implement the problem in a spreadsheet and solve it.
c. What is the optimal solution? What is the longest period of time a flight crew has to wait between flights according to your solution?
d. Are there alternate optimal solutions to this problem? If so, do any alternate optimal solutions result in a smaller maximum waiting period between flights?

21. Joe Jones wants to establish a construction fund (or sinking fund) to pay for a new bowling alley he is having built. Construction of the bowling alley is expected to take six months and cost $300,000. Joe's contract with the construction company requires him to make payments of $50,000 at the end of the second and fourth months, and a final payment of $200,000 at the end of the sixth month when the bowling alley is completed. Joe has identified four investments that he can use to establish the construction fund; these investments are summarized in the following table:

Investment	Available in Month	Months to Maturity	Yield at Maturity
A	1, 2, 3, 4, 5, 6	1	1.2%
B	1, 3, 5	2	3.5%
C	1, 4	3	5.8%
D	1	6	11.0%

The table indicates that investment A will be available at the beginning of each of the next six months, and funds invested in this manner mature in one month with a yield of 1.2%. Similarly, funds can be placed in investment C only at the beginning of months 1 and/or 4, and mature at the end of three months with a yield of 5.8%. Joe wants to minimize the amount of money he must invest in month 1 to meet the required payments for this project.

a. Draw a network flow model for this problem.
b. Create a spreadsheet model for this problem and solve it.
c. What is the optimal solution?

22. Telephone calls for the YakLine, a discount long distance carrier, are routed through a variety of switching devices that interconnect various network hubs

in different cities. The maximum number of calls that can be handled by each segment of their network is shown in the following table:

Network Segments	Calls (in 1,000s)
Washington, DC to Chicago	800
Washington, DC to Kansas City	650
Washington, DC to Dallas	700
Chicago to Dallas	725
Chicago to Denver	700
Kansas City to Denver	750
Kansas City to Dallas	625
Denver to San Francisco	900
Dallas to San Francisco	725

YakLine wants to determine the maximum number of calls that can go from their east coast operations hub in Washington, DC to their west coast operations hub in San Francisco.

a. Draw a network flow model for this problem.
b. Create a spreadsheet model for this problem and solve it.
c. What is the optimal solution?

23. Union Express has 60 tons of cargo that needs to be shipped from Boston to Dallas. The shipping capacity on each of the routes Union Express planes fly each night is shown in the following table:

Nightly Flight Segments	Capacity (in tons)
Boston to Baltimore	30
Boston to Pittsburgh	25
Boston to Cincinnati	35
Baltimore to Atlanta	10
Baltimore to Cincinnati	5
Pittsburgh to Atlanta	15
Pittsburgh to Chicago	20
Cincinnati to Chicago	15
Cincinnati to Memphis	5
Atlanta to Memphis	25
Atlanta to Dallas	10
Chicago to Memphis	20
Chicago to Dallas	15
Memphis to Dallas	30
Memphis to Chicago	15

Will Union Express be able to move all 60 tons from Boston to Dallas in one night?

a. Draw a network flow model for this problem.
b. Create a spreadsheet model for the problem and solve it.
c. What is the maximum flow for this network?

24. E-mail messages sent over the Internet are broken up into electronic packets that may take a variety of different paths to reach their destination where the original message is reassembled. Suppose the nodes in the graph shown in Figure 5.37 represents a series of computer hubs on the Internet and the arcs represent connections between them. Suppose the values on the arcs represent the number packets per minute (in 1,000,000s) that can be transmitted over each arc.

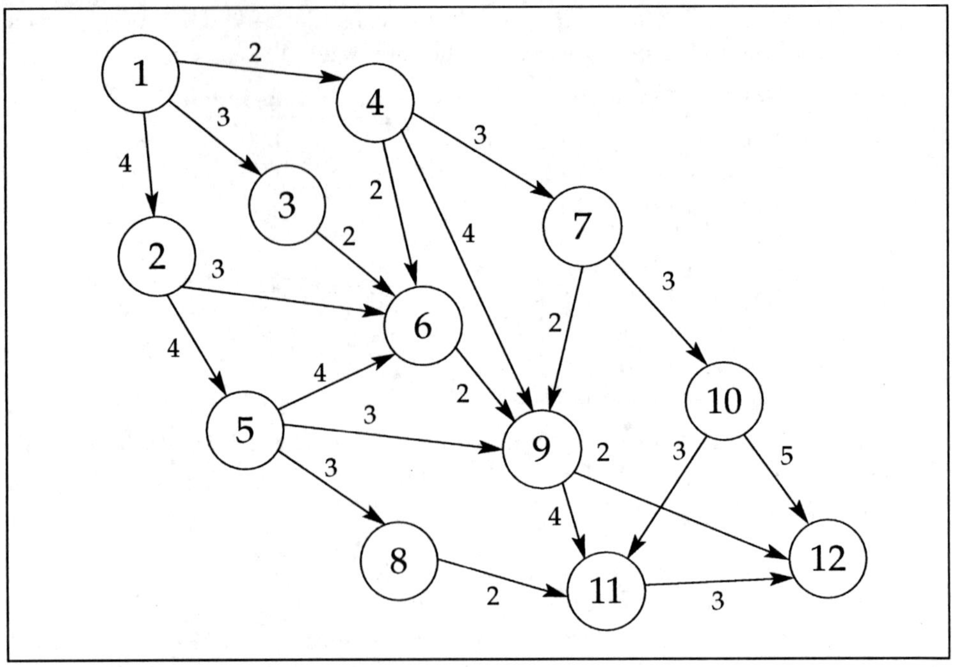

FIGURE 5.37
Network hubs and interconnections for the e-mail problem

a. Implement a network flow model to determine the maximum number of packets that can flow from node 1 to node 12 in one minute.
b. What is the maximum flow?

25. The Britts & Straggon company manufactures small engines at three different plants. From the plants, the engines are transported to two different warehouse facilities before being distributed to three wholesale distributors. The per unit manufacturing cost at each plant is shown in the following table in addition to the minimum required and maximum available daily production capacities.

Plant	Manufacturing Cost	Minimum Required Production	Maximum Production Capacity
1	$13	150	400
2	$15	150	300
3	$12	150	600

The unit cost of transporting engines from each plant to each warehouse is shown in the following table.

Plant	Warehouse 1	Warehouse 2
1	$4	$5
2	$6	$4
3	$3	$5

The unit cost of shipping engines from each warehouse to each distributor is shown in the following table along with the daily demand for each distributor.

Warehouse	Distributor 1	Distributor 2	Distributor 3
1	$6	$4	$3
2	$3	$5	$2
Demand	300	600	100

Each warehouse can process up to 500 engines per day.

a. Draw a network flow model to represent this problem.
b. Implement your model in Excel and solve it.
c. What is the optimal solution?

26. A new airport being built will have three terminals and two baggage pickup areas. An automated baggage delivery system has been designed to transport the baggage from each terminal to the two baggage pickup areas. This system is depicted graphically in Figure 5.38, where nodes 1, 2, and 3 represent the terminals, and nodes 7 and 8 represent the baggage pickup areas. The maximum number of bags per minute that can be handled by each part of the system is indicated by the value on each arc in the network.
    a. Formulate an LP model to determine the maximum number of bags per minute that can be delivered by this system.
    b. Use Solver to find the optimal solution to this problem.
27. Bull Dog Express runs a small airline that offers commuter flights between several cities in Georgia. The airline flies into and out of small airports only. These airports have limits on the number of flights Bull Dog Express can make each day. The airline can make five round-trip flights daily between Savannah and Macon, four round-trip flights daily between Macon and Albany, two round-trip flights daily between Macon and Atlanta, two round-trip flights daily between Macon and Athens, two round-trip flights daily between Athens and Atlanta, and two round-trip flights daily from Albany to Atlanta. The airline

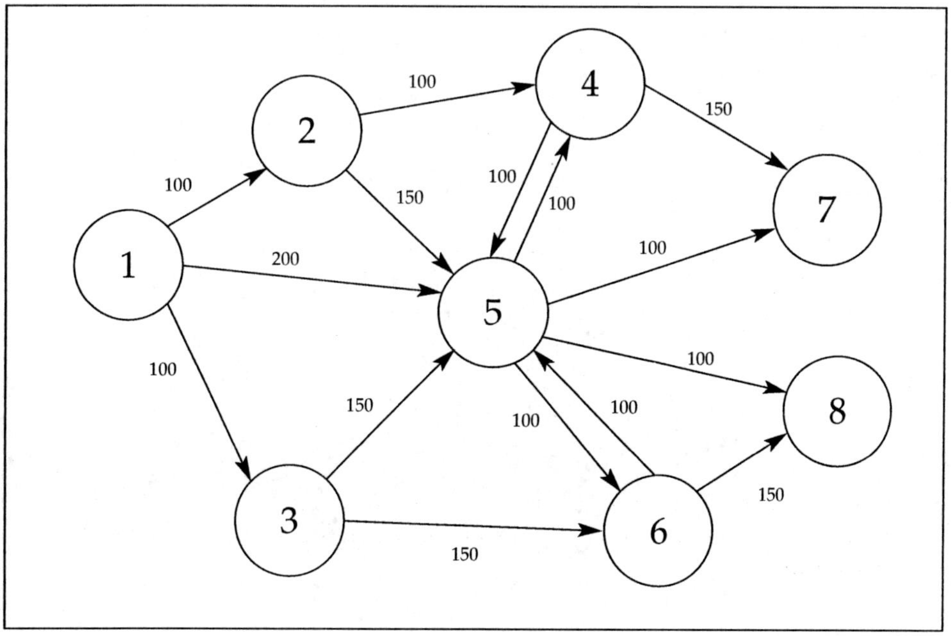

FIGURE 5.38
Network flow model for the airport terminal problem

wants to determine the maximum number of times connecting flights from Savannah to Atlanta can be offered in a single day.

a. Draw the network representation of this problem.
b. Formulate an LP model for this problem. What kind of problem is this?
c. Use Solver to determine the optimal solution to this problem.

28. The U.S. Department of Transportation (DOT) is planning to build a new interstate to run from Detroit, Michigan, to Charleston, South Carolina. A number of different routes have been proposed and are summarized in Figure 5.39, where node 1 represents Detroit and node 12 represents Charleston. The numbers on the arcs indicate the estimated construction costs of the various links (in millions of dollars). It is estimated that all of the routes will require approximately the same total driving time to make the trip from Detroit to Charleston. Thus, the DOT is interested in identifying the least costly alternative.
    a. Formulate an LP model to determine the least costly construction plan.
    b. Use Solver to determine the optimal solution to this problem.
29. A building contractor is designing the ductwork for the heating and air conditioning system in a new, single-story medical building. Figure 5.40 summarizes the possible connections between the primary air handling unit (node 1) and the various air outlets to be placed in the building (nodes 2 through 9). The arcs in the network represent possible ductwork connections, and the values on the arcs represent the feet of ductwork required.

    Starting at node 1, use the minimal spanning tree algorithm to determine how much ductwork should be installed to provide air access to each vent while requiring the least amount of ductwork.

FIGURE 5.39
Possible routes for the interstate construction problem

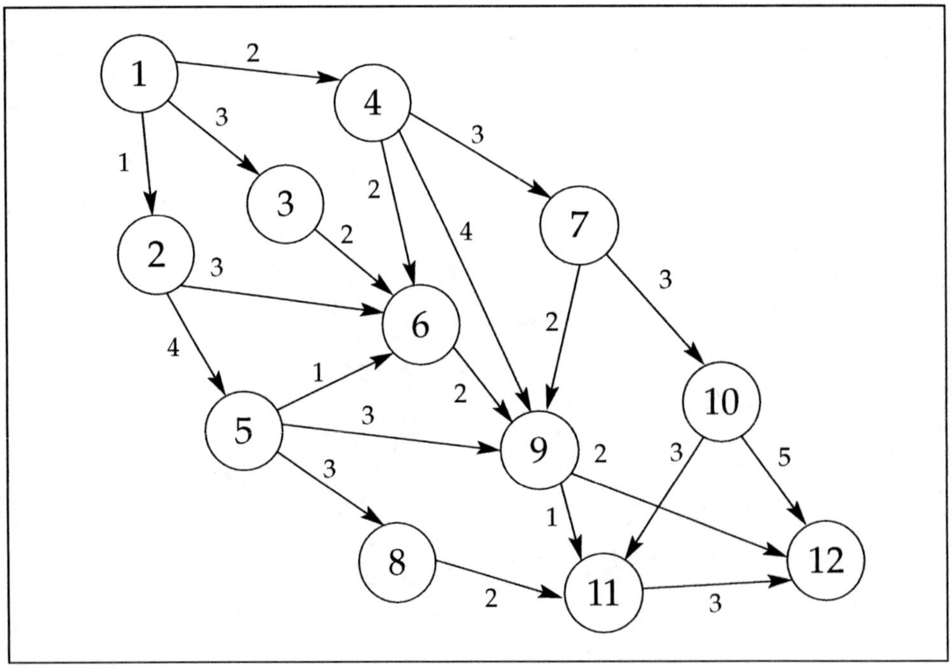

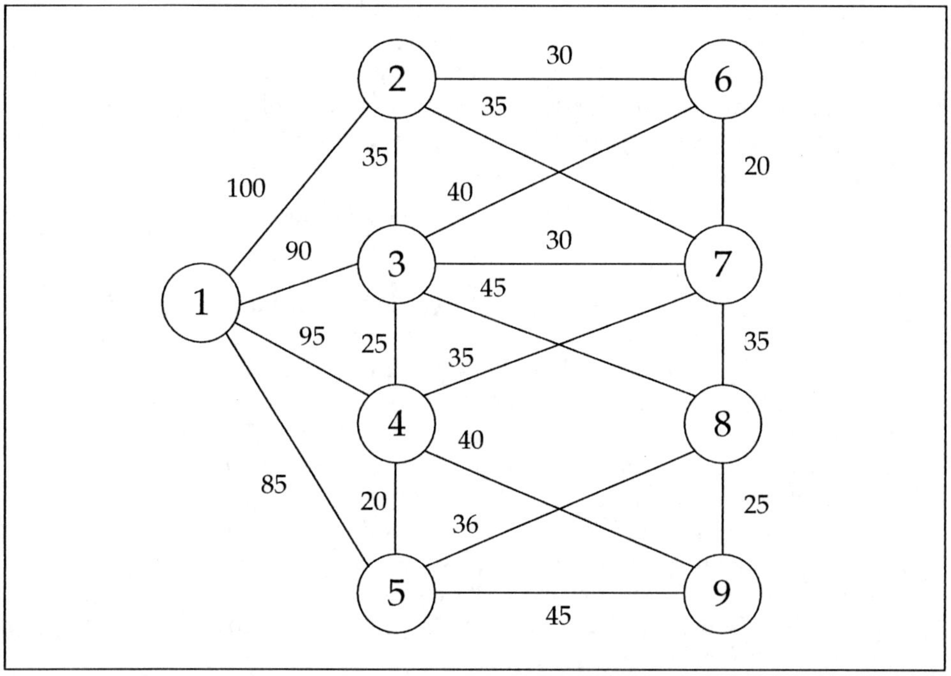

FIGURE 5.40
Network representation of the ductwork problem

30. As rush coordinator for the Alpha Beta Chi (ABC) sorority, Kim Grant asked each pledge to identify five existing members of ABC whom she would most like to have as a big sister. Kim then asks the pledges to rank order these potential big sisters from 5 down to 1, where 5 represents the person they most want as a big sister, 4 represents their next choice, and so on. These rankings are summarized in the following table:

	Big Sisters														
Pledges	**1**	**2**	**3**	**4**	**5**	**6**	**7**	**8**	**9**	**10**	**11**	**12**	**13**	**14**	**15**
1			5		3			1			2				4
2		5		2		1		4		3					
3	2		3			4		5				1			
4		5	4				1		2						3
5		3			5					2			4	1	

After much consideration, Kim decides that this problem is similar to some of the problems she encountered in a management science class she took during her sophomore year. She knows that every pledge must be assigned a big sister, and each potential big sister can be assigned no more than one pledge. Ideally, Kim wants to assign each pledge to the big sister to whom she gave a ranking of 5. The sum of the rankings for such an assignment is 25 because each of the 5 pledges would be assigned to the big sister they ranked as number 5. But in the previous table, that would involve assigning pledges 2 and 4 to the same big sister, which is not allowable. Kim figures that the next best strategy is to determine the assignment that maximizes the sum of the rankings.

a. Create a spreadsheet model for Kim's problem and solve it.
b. Which pledges should be assigned to which big sisters?
c. Can you think of another objective that Kim might use to solve her problem?

31. The manager of catering services for the Roanoker Hotel has a problem. The banquet hall at the hotel is booked each evening during the coming week for groups who have reserved the following numbers of tables:

Day	Monday	Tuesday	Wednesday	Thursday	Friday
Tables Reserved	400	300	250	400	350

The hotel has 500 tablecloths that can be used for these banquets. However, the tablecloths used at each banquet will have to be cleaned before they can be used again. A local cleaning service will pick up the soiled tablecloths each evening after the banquet and offers overnight cleaning for \$2 per tablecloth, or 2-day service for \$1 per tablecloth (*i.e.*, a tablecloth picked up Monday night can be ready Tuesday for \$2 or ready for use Wednesday for \$1). There are no tablecloth losses and all tablecloths must be cleaned. Due to the cleaner's capacity restrictions, the overnight service can be performed only on up to 250 tablecloths, and overnight service is not available on tablecloths picked up Friday night. All cloths used on Friday must be ready for use again by Monday. The hotel wants to determine the least costly plan for having their tablecloths cleaned.

a. Draw a network flow model for this problem. (*Hint:* Express the supplies and demands as minimum required and maximum allowable flows over selected arcs.)
b. Create a spreadsheet model for this problem and solve it. What is the optimal solution?

CASE 5.1: OLD DOMINION ENERGY

The United States is the biggest consumer of natural gas, and the second largest natural gas producer in the world. According to the U.S. Energy Information Administration (EIA), in 2001 the U.S. consumed 22.7 trillion cubic feet of natural gas. Stemming from phased deregulation, the transportation and delivery of natural gas from wellheads has grown since the '80s and there are now more than 278,000 miles of gas pipeline nationwide (see: http://www.platts.com/features/usgasguide/pipelines.shtml). With more electric power companies turning to natural gas as a cleaner-burning fuel, natural gas is expected to grow even more quickly over the next 20 years.

To ensure an adequate supply of natural gas, gas storage facilities have been built in numerous places along the pipeline. Energy companies can buy gas when prices are low and store it in these facilities for use or sale at a later date. Because energy consumption is influenced greatly by the weather (which is not entirely predictable), imbalances often arise in the supply and demand for gas in different parts of the country. Gas traders constantly monitor these market conditions and look for opportunities to sell gas from storage facilities when the price offered at a certain location is high enough. This decision is complicated by the fact that is costs different amounts of money to transport gas through different segments of the nationwide pipeline and the capacity available in different parts of the pipeline is constantly changing. Thus, when a trader sees an opportunity to sell at a favorable price, he or she must quickly see how much capacity is available in the network and create deals with individual pipeline operators for the necessary capacity to move gas from storage to the buyer.

Bruce McDaniel is a gas trader for Old Dominion Energy (ODE), Inc. The network in Figure 5.41 represents a portion of the gas pipeline where ODE does business. The values next to each arc in this network are of the form (x,y) where x is the cost per thousand cubic feet (cf) of transporting gas along the arc, and y is the available transmission capacity of the arc in thousands of cubic feet. Note that the arcs in this network are bidirectional (*i.e.*, gas can flow in either direction at the prices and capacities listed).

Bruce currently has 100,000 cf of gas in storage at Katy. Industrial customers in Joliet are offering $4.35 per thousand cf for up to 35,000 cf of gas. Buyers in Leidy are offering $4.63 per thousand cf for up to 60,000 cf of gas. Create a spreadsheet model to help Bruce answer the following questions.

a. Given the available capacity in the network, how much gas can be shipped from Katy to Leidy? From Katy to Joliet?
b. How much gas should Bruce offer to sell to Joliet and Leidy if he wants to maximize profits?
c. Is Bruce able to meet all the demand from both customers? If not, why not?
d. If Bruce wanted to try to pay more to obtain additional capacity on some of the pipelines, which ones should he investigate and why?

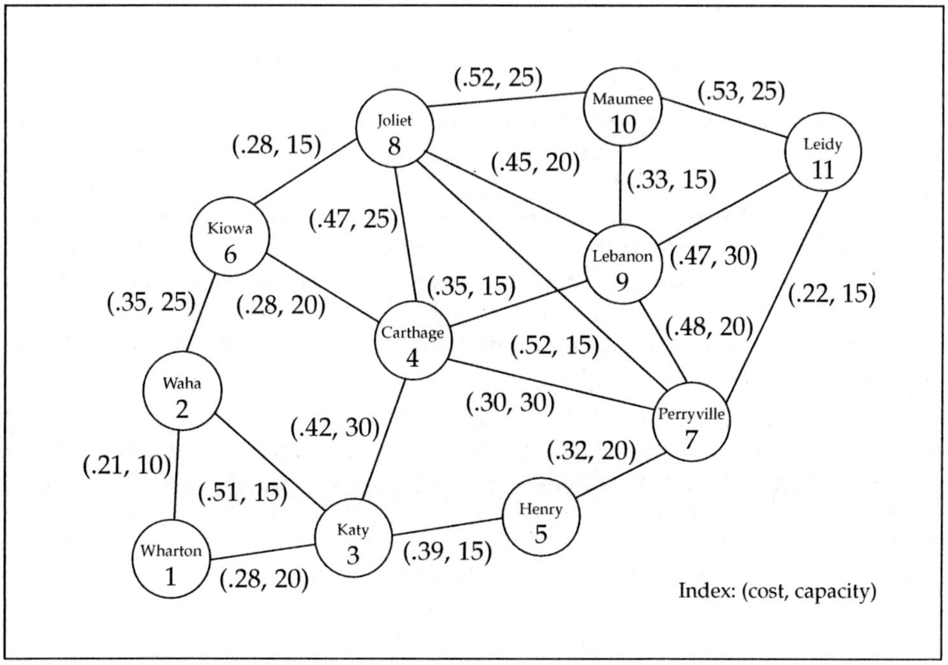

FIGURE 5.41
Gas pipeline network for Old Dominion Energy

CASE 5.2: US EXPRESS

US Express is an overnight package delivery company based in Atlanta, Georgia. Jet fuel is one of the largest operating costs incurred by the company and they want your assistance in managing this cost. The price of jet fuel varies considerably at different airports around the country. As a result, it seems that it might be wise to 'fill up' on jet fuel at airports where it is least expensive. However, the amount of fuel an airliner burns depends, in part, on the weight of the plane—and excess fuel makes an airplane heavier and, therefore, less fuel-efficient. Similarly, more fuel is burned on flights from the east coast to the west coast (going against the jet stream) than from the west coast to the east coast (going with the jet stream).

The following table summarizes the flight schedule (or rotation) flown nightly by one of the company's planes. For each flight segment, the table summarizes the minimum required and maximum allowable amount of fuel on board at takeoff and the cost of fuel at each point of departure. The final column provides a linear function relating fuel consumption to the amount of fuel on board at takeoff.

Segment	Depart	Arrive	Minimum fuel level at takeoff (in 1000s)	Maximum fuel level at takeoff (in 1000s)	Cost per gallon	Fuel used in flight with G gallons (in 1000s) on board at takeoff
1	Atlanta	San Francisco	21	31	$0.92	$3.20 + 0.45 \times G$
2	San Francisco	Los Angeles	7	20	$0.85	$2.25 + 0.65 \times G$
3	Los Angeles	Chicago	18	31	$0.87	$1.80 + 0.35 \times G$
4	Chicago	Atlanta	16	31	$1.02	$2.20 + 0.60 \times G$

For instance, if the plane leaves Atlanta for San Francisco with 25,000 gallons on board, it should arrive in San Francisco with approximately $25 - (3.2 + 0.45 \times 25) = 10.55$ thousand gallons of fuel.

The company has many other planes that fly different schedules each night, so the potential cost savings from efficient fuel purchasing is quite significant. But before turning you loose on all of their flight schedules, the company wants you to create a spreadsheet model to determine the most economical fuel purchasing plan for the previous schedule. (*Hint:* Keep in mind that the most fuel you would purchase at any departure point is the maximum allowable fuel level for takeoff at that point. Also, assume that whatever fuel is on board when the plane returns to Atlanta at the end of the rotation will still be on board when the plane leaves Atlanta the next evening.)

a. Draw the network diagram for this problem.
b. Implement the model for this problem in your spreadsheet and solve it.
c. How much fuel should US Express purchase at each departure point and what is the cost of this purchasing plan?

CASE 5.3: THE MAJOR ELECTRIC CORPORATION

Henry Lee is the Vice President of Purchasing for the consumer electronics division of the Major Electric Corporation (MEC). The company recently introduced a new type of video camcorder that has taken the market by storm. Although Henry is pleased with the strong demand for this product in the market place, it has been a challenge to keep up with MEC's distributors' orders of this camcorder. His current challenge is how to meet requests from MEC's major distributors in Pittsburgh, Denver, Baltimore, and Houston who have placed orders of 10,000, 20,000, 30,000, and 25,000 units, respectively, for delivery in two months (there is a one-month manufacturing and one-month shipping lead time for this product).

MEC has contracts with companies in Hong Kong, Korea, and Singapore who manufacture camcorders for the company under the MEC label. These contracts require MEC to order a specified minimum number of units each month at a guaranteed per unit cost. The contracts also specify the maximum number of units that may be ordered at this price. The following table summarizes these contracts:

	Monthly Purchasing Contract Provisions		
Supplier	**Unit Cost**	**Minimum Required**	**Maximum Allowed**
Hong Kong	$375	20,000	30,000
Korea	$390	25,000	40,000
Singapore	$365	15,000	30,000

MEC also has a standing contract with a shipping company to transport product from each of these suppliers to ports in San Francisco and San Diego. The cost of shipping from each supplier to each port is given in the following table along with the minimum required and maximum allowable number of shipping cartons each month:

	Monthly Shipping Contract Provisions					
	San Francisco Requirements			San Diego Shipping Requirements		
Supplier	**Cost per Container**	**Minimum Containers**	**Maximum Containers**	**Cost per Container**	**Minimum Containers**	**Maximum Containers**
Hong Kong	$2,000	5	20	$2,300	5	20
Korea	$1,800	10	30	$2,100	10	30
Singapore	$2,400	5	25	$2,200	5	15

Under the terms of this contract, MEC guarantees it will send at least 20 but no more than 65 shipping containers to San Francisco each month, and at least 30 but no more than 70 shipping containers to San Diego each month.

Each shipping container can hold 1,000 video cameras and will ultimately be trucked from the seaports on to the distributors. Again, MEC has a standing contract with a trucking company to provide trucking services each month. The cost of trucking a shipping container from each port to each distributor is summarized in the following table.

Unit Shipping Cost per Container

	Pittsburgh	Denver	Baltimore	Houston
San Francisco	$1,100	$ 850	$1,200	$1,000
San Diego	$1,200	$1,000	$1,100	$ 900

As with the other contracts, to obtain the prices given above, MEC is required to use a certain minimum amount of trucking capacity on each route each month and may not exceed certain maximum shipping amounts without incurring cost penalties. These minimum and maximum shipping restrictions are summarized in the following table.

Minimum Required and Maximum Allowable Number of Shipping Containers per Month

	Pittsburgh		Denver		Baltimore		Houston	
	Min	Max	Min	Max	Min	Max	Min	Max
San Francisco	3	7	6	12	10	18	5	15
San Diego	4	6	5	14	5	20	10	20

Henry is left with the task of sorting through all this information to determine the least purchasing and distribution plan to fill the distributor's requests. But because he and his wife have tickets to the symphony for this evening, he has asked you to take a look at this problem and give him your recommendations at 9:00 tomorrow morning.

a. Create a network flow model for this problem. (*Hint:* Consider inserting intermediate nodes in your network to assist in meeting the minimum monthly purchase restrictions for each supplier and the minimum monthly shipping requirements for each port.)
b. Implement a spreadsheet model for this problem and solve it.
c. What is the optimal solution?

CASE 5.4: TURNER AIRLINES

Fred Turner is a successful entrepreneur in Atlanta, Georgia who has just hit upon his next moneymaking idea. Recently, Fred was planning to fly to Washington, DC early one morning for a business meeting. Fred's own personal Leer jet happened to have a mechanical problem that morning, which forced Fred to try to book a flight on a commercial carrier. Much to his dismay, Fred learned that all the flights to DC were overbooked but he was told might be able to get a seat if he waited at the gate as a standby passenger. When Fred arrived at the gate, he was surprised to find several people waiting, hoping to get on a flight as a standby passenger.

When Fred saw this situation, he immediately saw a business opportunity. He knew that the route from Atlanta to Washington, DC was a popular one as these airports are two of the busiest in the world. And the frustration he saw on the faces of those waiting in line with him convinced him that there was money to be made here. Fred knew that it would be difficult to compete head to head against the established, full-service, international airlines. But he figured he could begin a flight service to fill the niche to business travelers wanting to travel between Atlanta and DC.

Fred called some of his business associates and put some people to work on this idea. A month later, their marketing research revealed that there were several times during every business day when travelers want to hop a plane going between Atlanta and DC. They also discovered that many business travelers would prefer to fly to Dulles Airport in Washington, whereas most airlines fly to Washington's Reagan Airport. The following table summarizes the flight schedules where there is considerable unmet demand and the estimate revenues and variable costs that would be incurred in operating these flights.

Depart	Time	Arrive	Time	Est. Revenue	Variable Cost
Atlanta	8 A.M.	Dulles	10 A.M.	$1,600	$ 850
Atlanta	10 A.M.	Dulles	12 noon	$1,400	$ 900
Atlanta	1 P.M.	Dulles	3 P.M.	$1,450	$ 920
Atlanta	4 P.M.	Dulles	6 P.M.	$1,900	$ 950
Dulles	9 A.M.	Atlanta	11 A.M.	$1,400	$ 850
Dulles	11 A.M.	Atlanta	1 P.M.	$1,650	$1,080
Dulles	1 P.M.	Atlanta	3 P.M.	$1,700	$ 900
Dulles	5 P.M.	Atlanta	7 P.M.	$1,900	$1,025

In addition to the costs given, the airport in Atlanta charges a $600 servicing charge for planes left there overnight, whereas Dulles Airport charges $700. Of course, there are also the costs of buying or leasing aircraft, hiring pilots, etc. Before pursuing this any further, Fred wants to know if the proposed flight schedule is profitable and how many planes it would take to implement it. And he has turned to you for help.

a. Draw the graph of the network flow problem Fred should solve to determine the minimum number of planes required to implement the proposed flight schedule in the most efficient manner.
b. Implement a model for this network in a spreadsheet and solve it.
c. Describe the optimal solution to the problem.
d. Suppose there was adequate demand to run two flights from Atlanta to Washington leaving Atlanta at 4 P.M. and arriving at Dulles at 6 P.M. Would this be more profitable than the current schedule? Should Fred be willing to sacrifice any of the current flights to add this second flight out of Atlanta at 4 P.M.?

CASE 5.5 MANEUVERS IN THE SENATE

Contributed by Jack Yurkiewicz. Lubin School of Business, Pace University.

Sherill Wiley, the only reporter from Channel Four covering United States congressional proceedings, knows that the public's perception of partisan politics in the Senate is not entirely correct. Although Republicans and Democrats are often at loggerheads over many national issues—such as the crime bill, health care reform, and others—members of the two parties frequently vote together on bills that are considered beneficial to both. Sherill was surprised at the level of cooperation between the parties when passing legislation that benefits a particular region. For example, if a Democratic senator from the west was sponsoring a bill that would provide funding to divert water from a river so that part of his sun-drenched state would eventually receive it, quite a few Republican senators would vote for such a bill. The Republican senators know that when they need votes for a project that would be advantageous for their states, the Democratic senators would return the favor and vote for that bill.

Richard Kennely, the leading Republican in the Senate and a strong conservative from a Midwest state, has little if any direct interaction with Robin Doll. Doll, a senator from a New England state, is the Senate's most liberal Democrat. The two senators have never served on a committee together or participated in a joint task force. Yet the two often rely on each other and their respective parties when voting on many fiscal issues.

Senator Doll recently added an amendment to a finance bill that would provide funding for research on the effects of using a mouse when working on a computer. Several universities from Doll's state submitted grant proposals to do this research, citing the widespread use of the mouse and the growing number of people who complain of wrist and arm fatigue as a result. If the bill and the attached amendment pass, the universities in Doll's state would be the main beneficiaries of the funding. Sherill knows that Senator Kennely, who was recently on national television railing against what he referred to as "excessive spending for trivial research," would be the main opponent to the bill. Senator Doll cannot directly influence Senator Kennely's position or vote. But she can contact other senators with whom she has influence, pleading her case and hoping that they, in turn, will influence others who might eventually influence Senator Kennely to vote in favor of the bill.

After many years as a reporter in Washington, Sherill has developed a sense of the amount of influence one senator has on another, based on party affiliation, school ties, past favors, mutual interests, and so on. She even developed a numerical system, on a scale from 0 to 10 that quantifies the amount of influence one senator has on another. A 10 means that a particular senator is almost guaranteed to secure the vote of another senator and a 0 means that there is no interaction at all between two senators. Sherill created a table that shows the senators' names and the amount of influence each has on the other.

Sherill saw Senators Abbott, Bartle, Crumb, Dodge, and Fernandez leave Senator Doll's office one morning last week. Looking at her influence table, she notes that Doll's influence on Abbott rates a 7, on Bartle a 6, a 9 for Crumb, only a 3 for Dodge, and a 4 for Fernandez. Later that week, Senator Abbott called in Senators Bartle and Dodge for a strategy meeting. Abbott's influence on Bartle is a 7 and on Dodge a 5.

Bartle next met with Senators Dodge, Evans, and Fernandez. Bartle's influence rating on these senators is a 4 on Dodge and on Evans, and a 5 on Fernandez. The senators continued to hold meetings with each other and with Senators Gene and Harris. Sherill summarized the influence rating of all the senators in the following table:

From–To	Abbott	Bartle	Crumb	Dodge	Evans	Fernandez	Gene	Harris	Kennely
Doll	7	6	9	3	4				
Abbott		7		5					
Bartle				4	4	5			
Crumb		5			3				
Dodge					6		5		6
Evans				6		8			7
Fernandez					8			2	5
Gene									8
Harris									2

Sherill believes that if all the senators (other than Doll) bear at least 20 total units of influence on Senator Kennely, he would not be able to resist and he would have to vote for Senator Doll's bill. With Kennely's support, the bill would definitely pass because the rest of the Republicans and Democrats will follow their leaders.

Considering the amount of networking that takes place between the senators, Sherill thinks she can build and solve a network model to predict if the bill will pass or not.

Formulate a network model for Sherill and solve it. Will the bill pass? (*Hint:* Make a node for each senator.)

Chapter 6

Integer Linear Programming

6.0 INTRODUCTION

When some or all of the decision variables in an LP problem are restricted to assuming only integer values, the resulting problem is referred to as an **integer linear programming** (ILP) problem. Many practical business problems need integer solutions. For example, when scheduling workers, a company needs to determine the optimal number of employees to assign to each shift. If we formulate this problem as an LP problem, its optimal solution could involve allocating fractional numbers of workers (for example, 7.33 workers) to different shifts; but this is not an integer feasible solution. Similarly, if an airline is trying to decide how many 767s, 757s, and A-300s to purchase for its fleet, it must obtain an integer solution because the airline cannot buy fractions of planes.

This chapter discusses how to solve optimization problems in which certain decision variables must assume only integer values. This chapter also shows how the use of integer variables allows us to build more accurate models for a number of business problems.

6.1 INTEGRALITY CONDITIONS

To illustrate some of the issues involved in an ILP problem, let's consider again the decision problem faced by Howie Jones, the owner of Blue Ridge Hot Tubs, described in chapters 2, 3, and 4. This company sells two models of hot tubs, the Aqua-Spa and the Hydro-Lux, which it produces by purchasing prefabricated fiberglass hot tub shells and installing a common water pump and an appropriate amount of tubing. Each Aqua-Spa produced requires 1 pump, 9 hours of labor, and 12 feet of tubing, and contributes $350 to profits. Each Hydro-Lux produced requires 1 pump, 6 hours of labor, and 16 feet of tubing, and contributes $300 to profits. Assuming the company has 200 pumps, 1,566 labor hours, and 2,880 feet of tubing available, we created the following LP formulation for this problem where X_1 and X_2 represent the number of Aqua-Spas and Hydro-Luxes to produce:

MAX:	$350X_1 + 300X_2$	} profit
Subject to:	$1X_1 + 1X_2 \leq 200$	} pump constraint
	$9X_1 + 6X_2 \leq 1{,}566$	} labor constraint
	$12X_1 + 16X_2 \leq 2{,}880$	} tubing constraint
	$X_1, X_2 \geq 0$	} nonnegativity conditions

Blue Ridge Hot Tubs is undoubtedly interested in obtaining the best possible *integer solution* to this problem because hot tubs can be sold only as discrete units. Thus, we can be sure the company wants to find the *optimal integer solution* to this problem. So, in addition to the constraints stated previously, we add the following integrality condition to the formulation of the problem:

$$X_1 \text{ and } X_2 \text{ must be integers}$$

An **integrality condition** indicates that some (or all) of the variables in the formulation must assume only **integer values.** We refer to such variables as the integer variables in a problem. In contrast, variables that are not required to assume strictly integer values are referred to as **continuous variables.** Although it is easy to state integrality conditions for a problem, such conditions often make a problem more difficult (and sometimes impossible) to solve.

6.2 RELAXATION

One approach to finding the optimal integer solution to a problem is to relax, or ignore, the integrality conditions and solve the problem as if it were a standard LP problem where all the variables are assumed to be continuous. This model is sometimes referred to as the **LP relaxation** of the original ILP problem. Consider the following ILP problem:

MAX:	$2X_1 + 3X_2$
Subject to:	$X_1 + 3X_2 \leq 8.25$
	$2.5X_1 + X_2 \leq 8.75$
	$X_1, X_2 \geq 0$
	X_1, X_2 must be integers

The LP relaxation for this problem is represented by:

MAX:	$2X_1 + 3X_2$
Subject to:	$X_1 + 3X_2 \leq 8.25$
	$2.5X_1 + X_2 \leq 8.75$
	$X_1, X_2 \geq 0$

The only difference between the ILP and its LP relaxation is that all integrality conditions imposed by the ILP are dropped in the relaxation. However, as illustrated in Figure 6.1, this change has a significant impact on the feasible regions for the two problems.

As shown in Figure 6.1, the feasible region for the ILP consists of only 11 discrete points. On the other hand, the feasible region for its LP relaxation consists of an infinite number of points represented by the shaded area. This figure illustrates an important point about the relationship between the feasible region of an ILP and its LP relaxation. The feasible region of the LP relaxation of an ILP problem *always* encompasses *all* the feasible integer solutions to the original ILP problem. Although the relaxed feasible region might include additional noninteger solutions, it will *not* include any integer solutions that are not feasible solutions to the original ILP.

6.3 SOLVING THE RELAXED PROBLEM

The LP relaxation of an ILP problem is often easy to solve using the simplex method. As explained in chapter 2, an optimal solution to an LP problem occurs at one of the corner points of its feasible region (assuming that the problem has a bounded optimal solution). Thus, if we are extremely lucky, the optimal solution to the LP relaxation of an ILP problem might occur at an integer corner point of the relaxed feasible region. In this case, we find the optimal integer solution to the ILP problem simply by solving its LP relaxation. This is exactly what happened in

FIGURE 6.1
Integer feasible region vs. LP feasible region

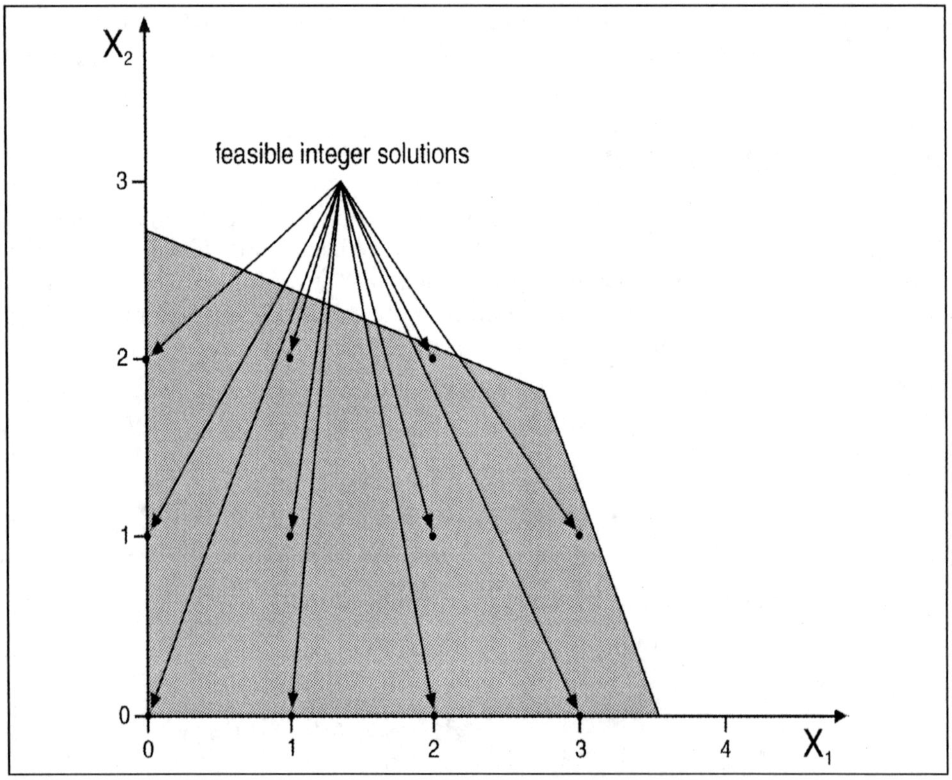

chapters 2 and 3 when we originally solved the relaxed LP model for the hot tub problem. Figure 6.2 (and the file Fig6-2.xls on your data disk) shows the solution to this problem.

The optimal solution to the relaxed LP formulation of the hot tub problem assigns integer values to the decision variables ($X_1 = 122$ and $X_2 = 78$). So in this case, the relaxed LP problem happens to have an integer-valued optimal solution. However, as you might expect, this will not always be the case.

Suppose, for example, that Blue Ridge Hot Tubs has only 1,520 hours of labor and 2,650 feet of tubing available during their next production cycle. The company might be interested in solving the following ILP problem:

MAX:	$350X_1 + 300X_2$	} profit
Subject to:	$1X_1 + 1X_2 \leq 200$	} pump constraint
	$9X_1 + 6X_2 \leq 1{,}520$	} labor constraint
	$12X_1 + 16X_2 \leq 2{,}650$	} tubing constraint
	$X_1, X_2 \geq 0$	} nonnegativity conditions
	X_1, X_2 must be integers	} integrality conditions

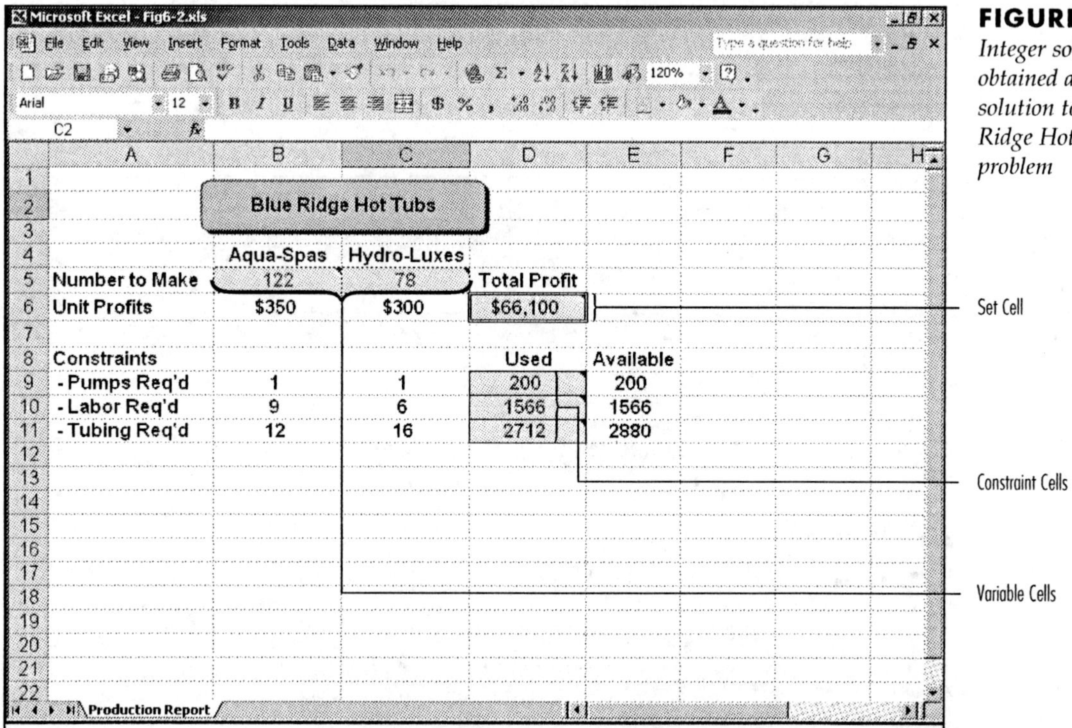

FIGURE 6.2
Integer solution obtained as optimal solution to the Blue Ridge Hot Tubs LP problem

Key Cell Formulas

Cell	Formula	Copied to
D6	=B6*$B$5+C6*$C$5	D9:D11

If we relax the integrality conditions and solve the resulting LP problem, we obtain the solution shown in Figure 6.3. This solution indicates that producing 116.9444 Aqua-Spas and 77.9167 Hydro-Luxes will generate a maximum profit of $64,306. But this solution violates the integrality conditions stated in the original problem. As a general rule, the optimal solution to the LP relaxation of an ILP problem is not guaranteed to produce an integer solution. In such cases, other techniques must be applied to find the optimal integer solution for the problem being solved. (There are some exceptions to this rule. In particular, the network flow problems discussed in chapter 5 often can be viewed as ILP problems. For reasons that go beyond the scope of this text, the LP relaxation of network flow problems will always have integer solutions if the supplies and/or demands at each node are integers and the problem is solved using the simplex method.)

6.4 BOUNDS

Before discussing how to solve ILP problems, an important point must be made about the relationship between the optimal solution to an ILP problem and the optimal solution to its LP relaxation: *The objective function value for the optimal solution to the ILP problem can never be better than the objective function value for the optimal solution to its LP relaxation.*

For example, the solution shown in Figure 6.3 indicates that if the company could produce (and sell) fractional numbers of hot tubs, it could make a maximum profit of $64,306 by producing 116.9444 Aqua-Spas and 77.9167 Hydro-Luxes. No other feasible solution (integer or otherwise) could result in a better value of the

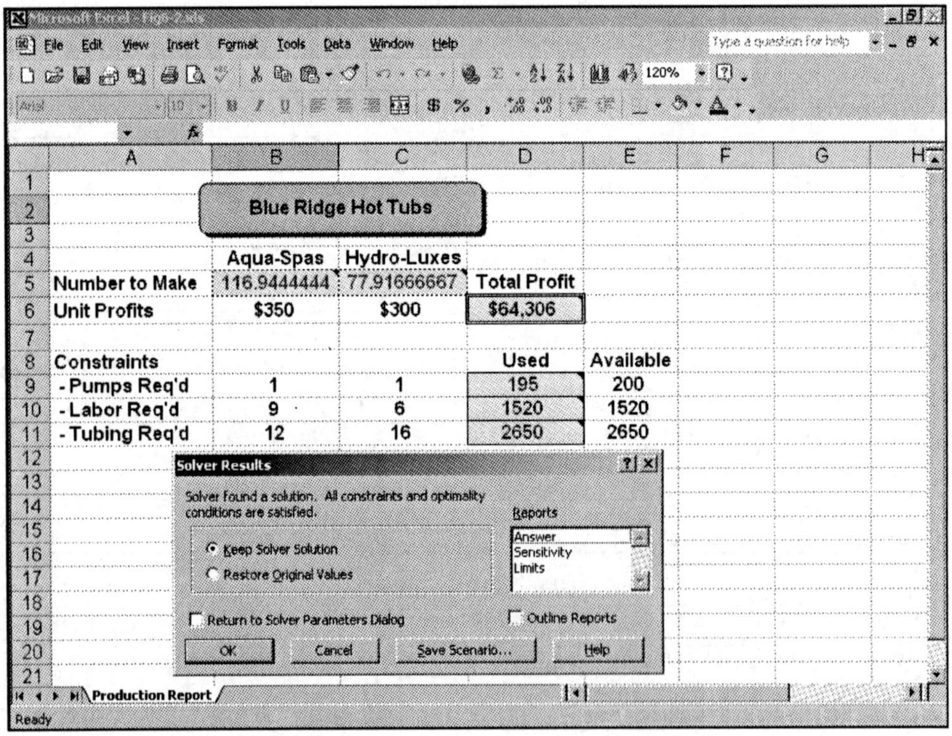

FIGURE 6.3
Noninteger solution obtained as optimal solution to the revised Blue Ridge Hot Tubs LP problem

objective function. If a better feasible solution existed, the optimization procedure would have identified this better solution as optimal because our aim was to maximize the value of the objective function.

Although solving the LP relaxation of the revised hot tub problem might not provide the optimal integer solution to our original ILP problem, it does indicate that the objective function value of the optimal integer solution cannot possibly be greater than $64,306. This information can be important in helping us evaluate the quality of integer solutions we might discover during our search for the optimal solution.

Key Concept

For *maximization* problems, the objective function value at the optimal solution to the LP relaxation represents an *upper bound* on the optimal objective function value of the original ILP problem. For *minimization* problems, the objective function value at the optimal solution to the LP relaxation represents a *lower bound* on the optimal objective function value of the original ILP problem.

6.5 ROUNDING

As mentioned earlier, the solution to the LP relaxation of an ILP problem might satisfy the ILP problem's integrality conditions and, therefore, represent the optimal integer solution to the problem. But what should we do if this is not the case (as usually happens)? One technique that frequently is applied involves rounding the relaxed LP solution.

When the solution to the LP relaxation of an ILP problem does not result in an integer solution, it is tempting to think that simply rounding this solution will generate the optimal integer solution. Unfortunately, this is not the case. For example, if the values for the decision variables shown in Figure 6.3 are manually rounded up to their closest integer values, as shown in Figure 6.4, the resulting solution is infeasible. The company cannot manufacture 117 Aqua-Spas and 78 Hydro-Luxes because this would involve using more labor and tubing than are available.

Because rounding up does not always work, perhaps we should round down, or truncate, the values for the decision variables identified in the LP relaxation. As shown in Figure 6.5, this results in a feasible solution where 116 Aqua-Spas and 77 Hydro-Luxes are manufactured for a total profit of $63,700. However, this approach presents two possible problems. First, rounding down could also result in an infeasible solution, as shown in Figure 6.6 on page 251.

Another problem with rounding down is that even if it results in a feasible integer solution to the problem, there is no guarantee that it is the *optimal* integer solution. For example, the integer solution obtained by rounding down shown in Figure 6.5 produced a total profit of $63,700. However, as shown in Figure 6.7 on page 252, a better integer solution exists for this problem. If the company produces 118 Aqua-Spas and 76 Hydro-Luxes, it can achieve a total profit of $64,100 (which is

FIGURE 6.4
Infeasible integer solution obtained by rounding up

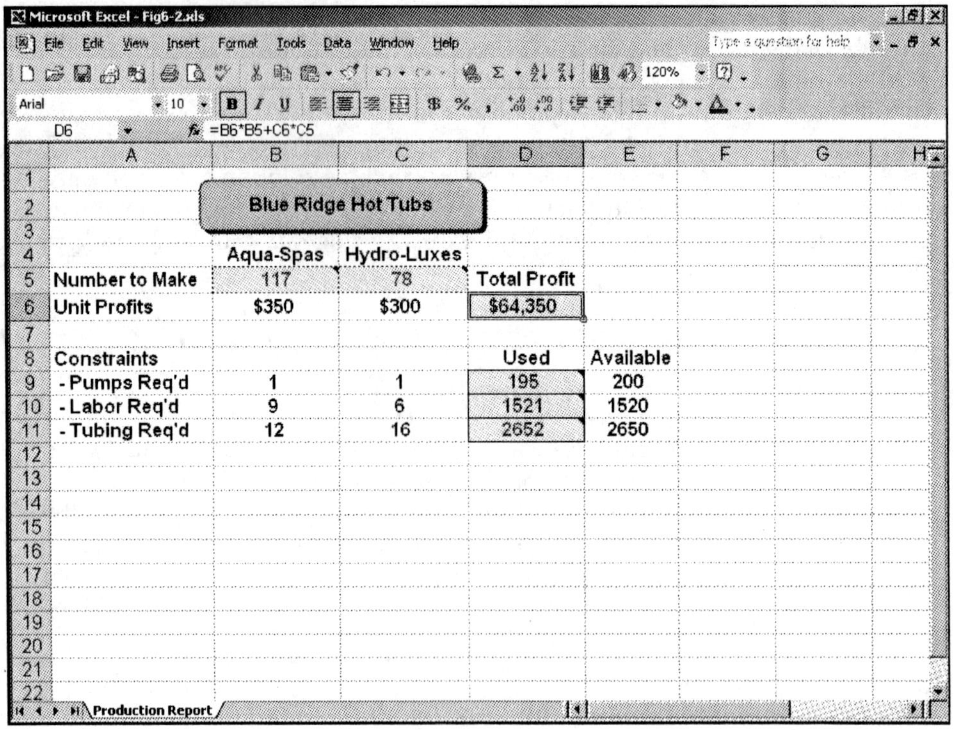

	A	B	C	D	E
2		Blue Ridge Hot Tubs			
4		Aqua-Spas	Hydro-Luxes		
5	Number to Make	117	78	Total Profit	
6	Unit Profits	$350	$300	$64,350	
8	Constraints			Used	Available
9	- Pumps Req'd	1	1	195	200
10	- Labor Req'd	9	6	1521	1520
11	- Tubing Req'd	12	16	2652	2650

FIGURE 6.5
Feasible integer solution obtained by rounding down

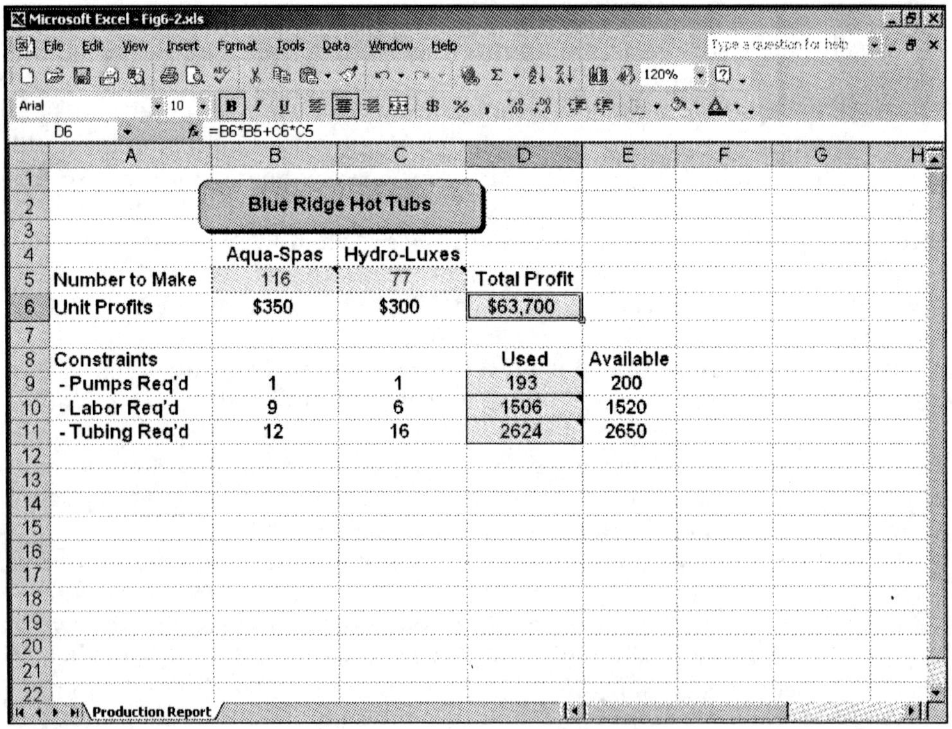

	A	B	C	D	E
2		Blue Ridge Hot Tubs			
4		Aqua-Spas	Hydro-Luxes		
5	Number to Make	116	77	Total Profit	
6	Unit Profits	$350	$300	$63,700	
8	Constraints			Used	Available
9	- Pumps Req'd	1	1	193	200
10	- Labor Req'd	9	6	1506	1520
11	- Tubing Req'd	12	16	2624	2650

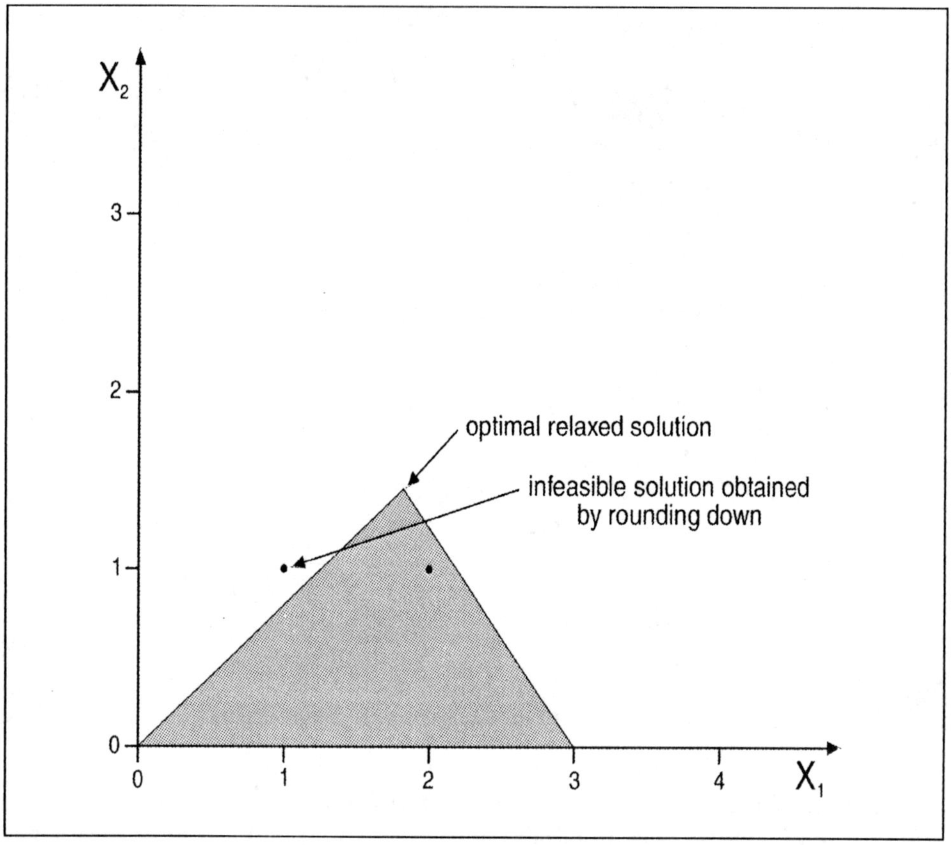

FIGURE 6.6
How rounding down can result in an infeasible integer solution

the optimal integer solution to this problem). Simply rounding the solution to the LP relaxation of an ILP problem is not guaranteed to provide the optimal integer solution. Although the integer solution obtained in this problem by rounding is very close to the optimal integer solution, rounding does not always work this well.

As we have seen, the solution to the LP relaxation of an ILP is not guaranteed to produce an integer solution, and rounding the solution to the LP relaxation is not guaranteed to produce the optimal integer solution. Therefore, we need another way to find the optimal integer solution to an ILP problem. Various procedures have been developed for this purpose. The most effective and widely used of these procedures is the branch-and-bound **(B&B) algorithm.** The B&B algorithm theoretically allows us to solve any ILP problem by solving a series of LP problems called candidate problems. For those who are interested, a discussion of how the B&B algorithm works is given at the end of this chapter.

6.6 STOPPING RULES

Finding the optimal solution for simple ILP problems can sometimes require the evaluation of hundreds of candidate problems. More complex problems can require the evaluation of thousands of candidate problems, which can be a very time-consuming task even for the fastest computers. For this reason, many ILP

FIGURE 6.7
Optimal integer solution to the revised Blue Ridge Hot Tubs problem

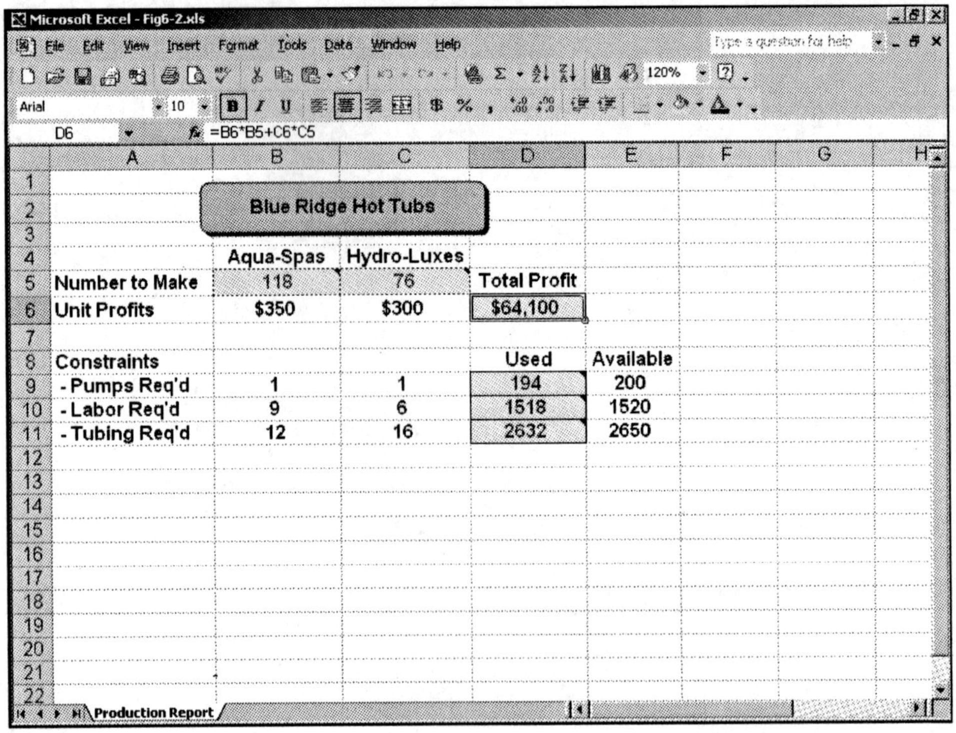

packages allow you to specify a suboptimality tolerance of X% (where X is some numeric value), which tells the B&B algorithm to stop when it finds an integer solution that is no more than X% worse than the optimal integer solution. This is another area where obtaining upper or lower bounds on the optimal integer solution can be helpful.

As noted earlier, if we relax all the integrality conditions in an ILP with a maximization objective and solve the resulting LP problem, the objective function value at the optimal solution to the relaxed problem provides an upper bound on the optimal integer solution. For example, when we relaxed the integrality conditions for the revised Blue Ridge Hot Tubs problem and solved it as an LP, we obtained the solution shown in Figure 6.3, which has an objective function value of $64,306. Thus, we know that the optimal integer solution to this problem cannot have an objective function value greater than $64,306. Now, suppose the owner of Blue Ridge Hot Tubs is willing to settle for any integer solution to their problem that is no more than 5% below the optimal integer solution. It is easy to determine that 95% of $64,306 is $61,090 (0.95 × $64,306 = $61,090). Therefore, any integer solution with an objective function value of at least $61,090 can be no worse than 5% below the optimal integer solution.

Specifying suboptimality tolerances can be helpful if you are willing to settle for a good but suboptimal solution to a difficult ILP problem. However, most B&B packages employ some sort of default suboptimality tolerance and, therefore, might produce a suboptimal solution to the ILP problem without indicating that a better solution might exist. (We will look at an example where this occurs shortly.) It is important to be aware of suboptimality tolerances because they can determine whether or not the true optimal solution to an ILP problem is found.

6.7 SOLVING ILP PROBLEMS USING SOLVER

Now that you have some understanding of the effort required to solve ILP problems, you can appreciate how using Solver simplifies this process. This section shows how to use Solver with the revised Blue Ridge Hot Tubs problem.

Figure 6.8 shows the Solver parameters required to solve the revised Blue Ridge Hot Tubs problem as a standard LP problem. However, none of these parameters indicate that the cells representing the decision variables (cells B5 and C5) must assume integer values. To communicate this to Solver, we need to add constraints to the problem by clicking the Add button.

Clicking this button displays the Add Constraint dialog box shown in Figure 6.9. In this dialog box, cells B5 through C5 are specified as the cell references for the additional constraints. Because we want these cells to assume only integer values, we need to select the **int** option from the drop-down menu, as shown in Figure 6.9.

After clicking the OK button, we return to the Solver Parameters dialog box shown in Figure 6.10. This dialog box now indicates that cells B5 and C5 are constrained to assume only integer values. We can now click the Solve button to determine the optimal solution to the problem, shown in Figure 6.11 on page 255.

The Solver Results dialog box in Figure 6.11 indicates that Solver found a solution within tolerance that satisfies all constraints. Thus, we might suspect that the optimal integer solution to this problem involves producing 116 Aqua-Spas and 78 Hydro-Luxes for a total profit of $64,000. However, if you refer back to Figure 6.7, you will recall that an even better integer solution to this problem can be obtained by producing 118 Aqua-Spas and 76 Hydro-Luxes for a total profit

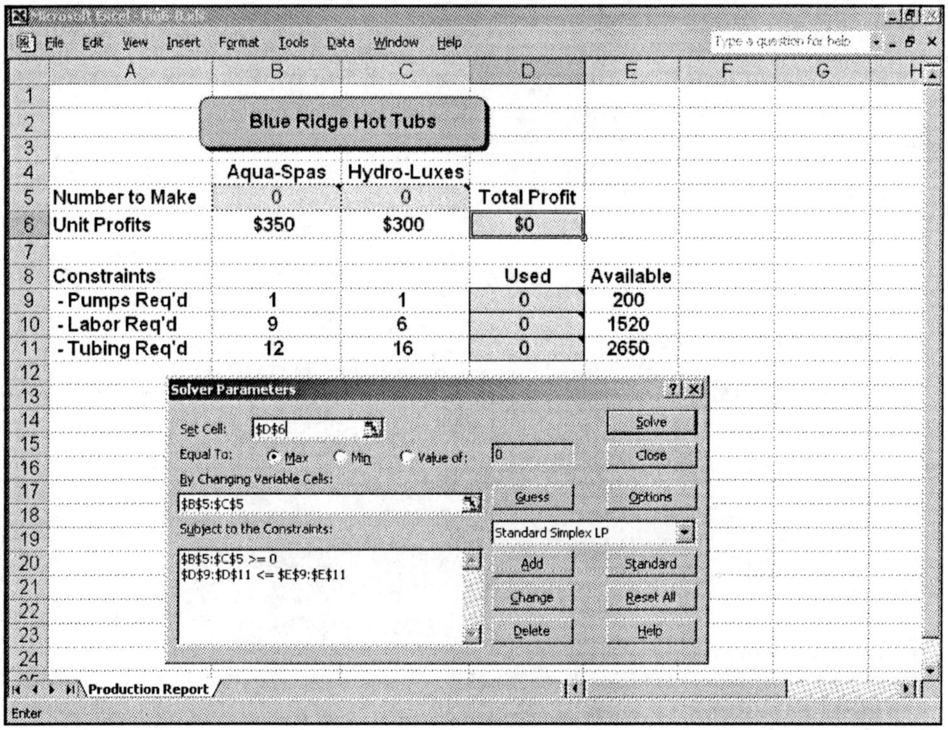

FIGURE 6.8
Solver parameters for the relaxed Blue Ridge Hot Tubs problem

FIGURE 6.9
Selecting integer constraints

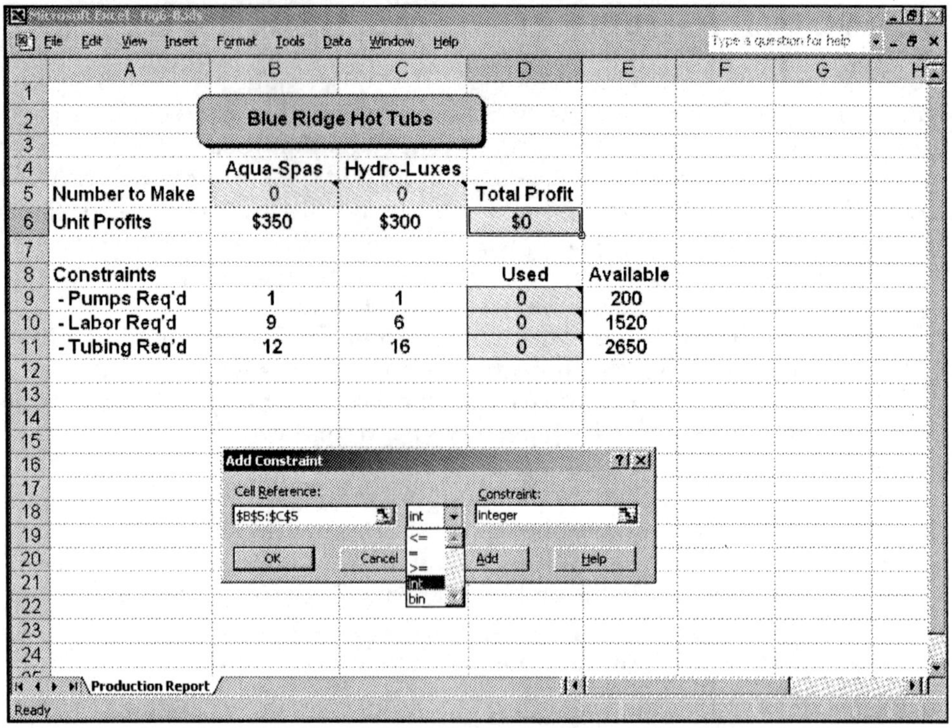

FIGURE 6.10
Solver parameters for the revised Blue Ridge Hot Tubs problem with integer constraints

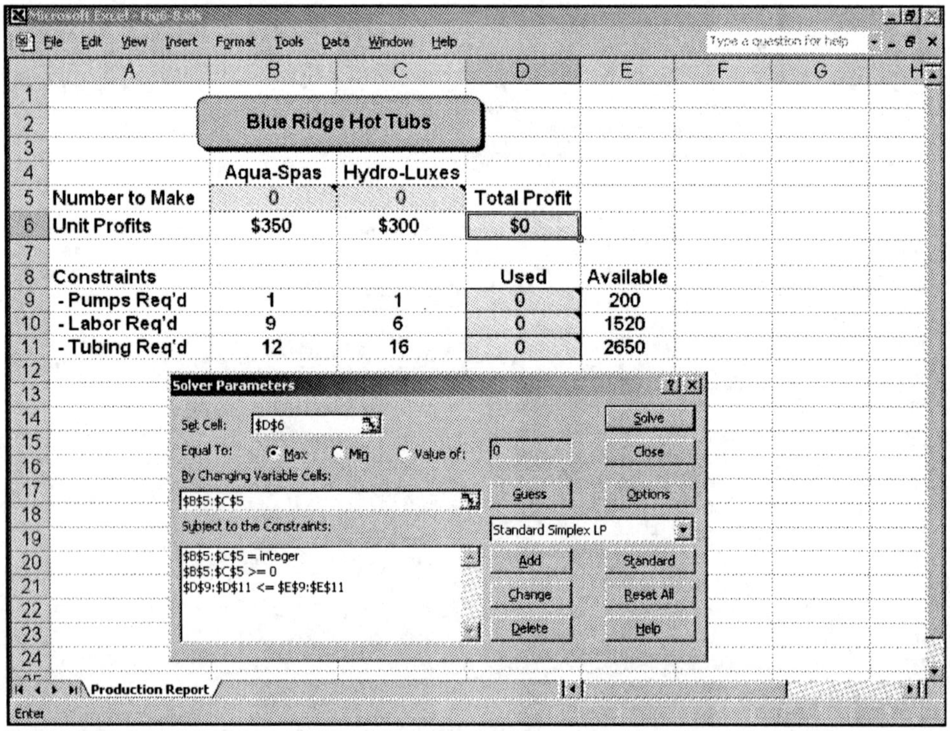

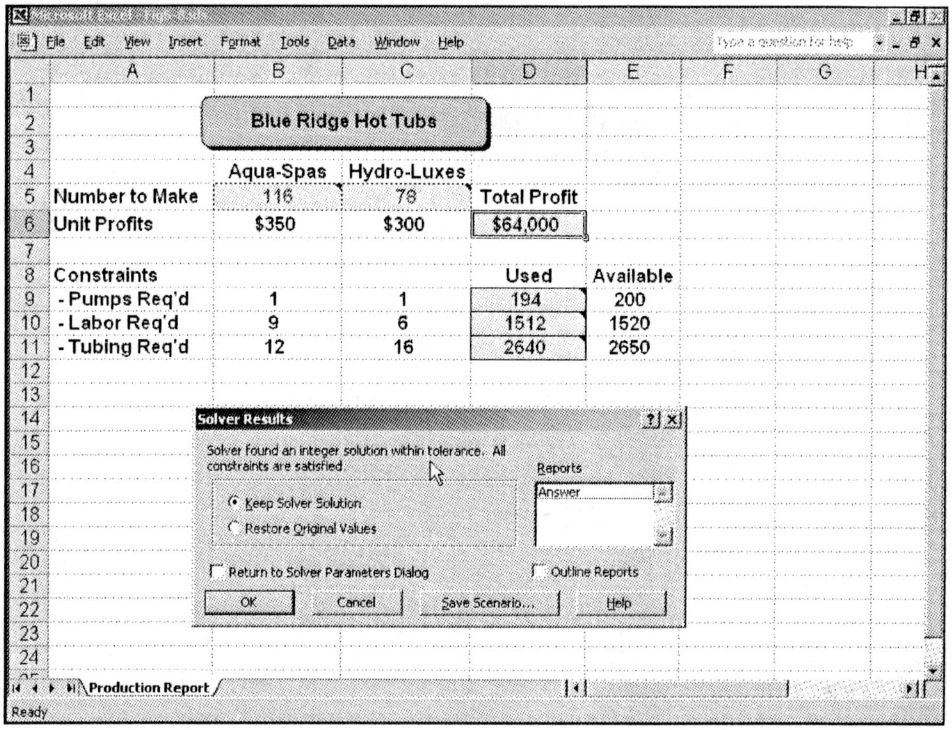

FIGURE 6.11
Solution to the revised Blue Ridge Hot Tubs problem with integer constraints

of $64,100. So why did Solver select an integer solution with a total profit of $64,000 when a better integer solution exists? The answer lies in Solver's suboptimality tolerance factor.

By default, Solver uses a suboptimality tolerance factor of 5%. So, when Solver found the integer solution with the objective function value of $64,000 shown in Figure 6.11, it determined that this solution was within 5% of the optimal integer solution and, therefore, it abandoned its search. (Note the message in Figure 6.11, "Solver found an integer solution within tolerance.") To ensure that Solver finds the best possible solution to an ILP problem, we must change its suboptimality tolerance factor by clicking the Options button in the Solver Parameters dialog box and then click the Integer Options button in the Solver Options dialog box. Figure 6.12 shows the resulting Integer Options dialog box.

As shown in Figure 6.12, you can set a number of options to control Solver's operations. The Tolerance option represents Solver's suboptimality tolerance value. To make sure Solver finds the best possible solution to an ILP problem, we must change this setting from its default value of 0.05 to 0. If we do this and resolve the current problem, we obtain the solution shown in Figure 6.13. This solution is the best possible integer solution to the problem.

6.8 OTHER ILP PROBLEMS

Many decision problems encountered in business can be modeled as ILPs. As we have seen from the Blue Ridge Hot Tubs example, some problems that are initially

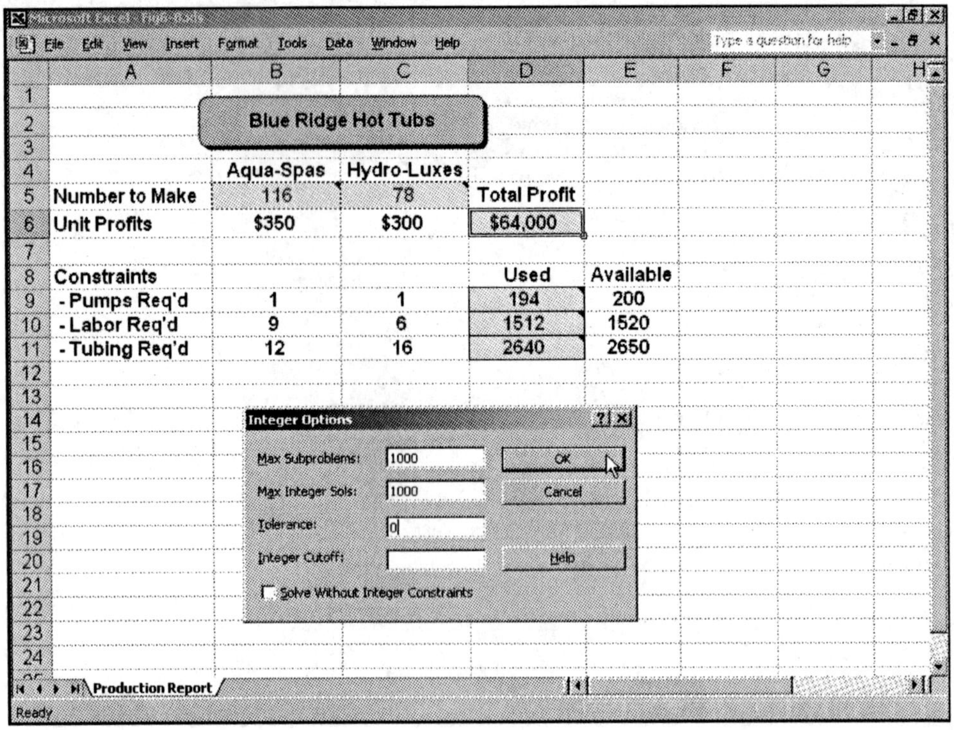

FIGURE 6.12
Changing the suboptimality tolerance factor

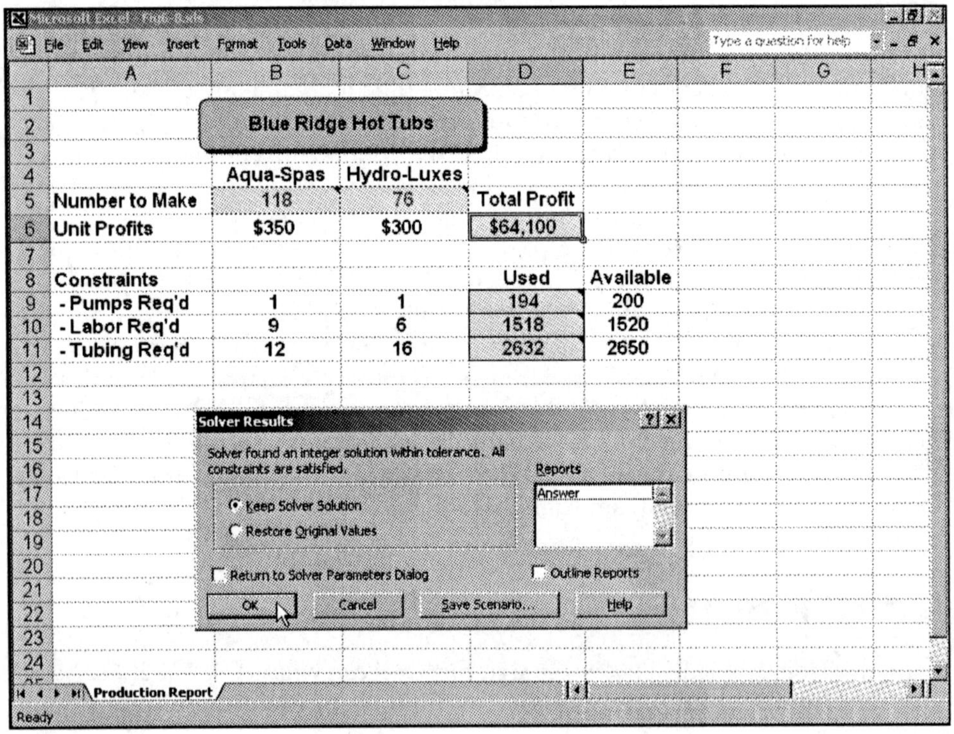

FIGURE 6.13
Optimal integer solution to the revised Blue Ridge Hot Tubs problem

formulated as LP problems might turn into ILP formulations if they require integer solutions. However, the importance of ILP extends beyond simply allowing us to obtain integer solutions to LP problems.

The ability to constrain certain variables to assume only integer values enables us to model a number of important conditions more accurately. For example, up to this point, we have not considered the impact of quantity discounts, setup or lump-sum costs, or batch size restrictions on a given decision problem. Without ILP techniques, we could not model these decision issues. We now consider several examples that illustrate the expanded modeling capabilities available through the use of integer variables.

6.9 AN EMPLOYEE SCHEDULING PROBLEM

Anyone responsible for creating work schedules for a number of employees can appreciate the difficulties in this task. It can be very difficult to develop a feasible schedule, much less an optimal schedule. Trying to ensure that a sufficient number of workers is available when needed is a complicated task when you must consider multiple shifts, rest breaks, and lunch or dinner breaks. However, some sophisticated LP models have been devised to solve these problems. Although a discussion of these models is beyond the scope of this text, we will consider a simple example of an employee scheduling problem to give you an idea of how LP models are applied in this area.

Air-Express is an express shipping service that guarantees overnight delivery of packages anywhere in the continental United States. The company has various operations centers, called hubs, at airports in major cities across the country. Packages are received at hubs from other locations and then shipped to intermediate hubs or to their final destinations.

The manager of the Air-Express hub in Baltimore, Maryland, is concerned about labor costs at the hub and is interested in determining the most effective way to schedule workers. The hub operates seven days a week, and the number of packages it handles each day varies from one day to the next. Using historical data on the average number of packages received each day, the manager estimates the number of workers needed to handle the packages as:

Day of Week	Workers Required
Sunday	18
Monday	27
Tuesday	22
Wednesday	26
Thursday	25
Friday	21
Saturday	19

The package handlers working for Air-Express are unionized and are guaranteed a five-day work week with two consecutive days off. The base wage for the handlers is \$655 per week. Because most workers prefer to have Saturday or Sunday off, the union has negotiated bonuses of \$25 per day for its members who work on these days. The possible shifts and salaries for package handlers are:

Shift	Days Off	Wage
1	Sunday and Monday	$680
2	Monday and Tuesday	$705
3	Tuesday and Wednesday	$705
4	Wednesday and Thursday	$705
5	Thursday and Friday	$705
6	Friday and Saturday	$680
7	Saturday and Sunday	$655

The manager wants to keep the total wage expense for the hub as low as possible. With this in mind, how many package handlers should be assigned to each shift if the manager wants to have a sufficient number of workers available each day?

6.9.1 Defining the Decision Variables

In this problem, the manager must decide how many workers to assign to each shift. Because there are seven possible shifts, we need the following seven decision variables:

X_1 = the number of workers assigned to shift 1
X_2 = the number of workers assigned to shift 2
X_3 = the number of workers assigned to shift 3
X_4 = the number of workers assigned to shift 4
X_5 = the number of workers assigned to shift 5
X_6 = the number of workers assigned to shift 6
X_7 = the number of workers assigned to shift 7

6.9.2 Defining the Objective Function

The objective in this problem is to minimize the total wages paid. Each worker on shift 1 and 6 is paid $680 per week, and each worker on shift 7 is paid $655. All other workers are paid $705 per week. Thus, the objective of minimizing the total wage expense is expressed as:

$$\text{MIN: } 680X_1 + 705X_2 + 705X_3 + 705X_4 + 705X_5 + 680X_6 + 655X_7 \} \text{ total wage expense}$$

6.9.3 Defining the Constraints

The constraints for this problem must ensure that at least 18 workers are scheduled for Sunday, at least 27 are scheduled for Monday, and so on. We need one constraint for each day of the week.

To make sure that at least 18 workers are available on Sunday, we must determine which decision variables represent shifts that are scheduled to work on Sunday. Because shifts 1 and 7 are the only shifts that have Sunday scheduled as a day off, the remaining shifts, 2 through 6, all are scheduled to work on Sunday. The following constraint ensures that at least 18 workers are available on Sunday:

$0X_1 + 1X_2 + 1X_3 + 1X_4 + 1X_5 + 1X_6 + 0X_7 \geq 18$ } workers required on Sunday

Because workers on shifts 1 and 2 have Monday off, the constraint for Monday should ensure that the sum of the variables representing the number of workers on the remaining shifts, 3 through 7, is at least 27. This constraint is expressed as:

$0X_1 + 0X_2 + 1X_3 + 1X_4 + 1X_5 + 1X_6 + 1X_7 \geq 27$ } workers required on Monday

Constraints for the remaining days of the week are generated easily by applying the same logic used in generating the previous two constraints. The resulting constraints are stated as:

$1X_1 + 0X_2 + 0X_3 + 1X_4 + 1X_5 + 1X_6 + 1X_7 \geq 22$ } workers required on Tuesday
$1X_1 + 1X_2 + 0X_3 + 0X_4 + 1X_5 + 1X_6 + 1X_7 \geq 26$ } workers required on Wednesday
$1X_1 + 1X_2 + 1X_3 + 0X_4 + 0X_5 + 1X_6 + 1X_7 \geq 25$ } workers required on Thursday
$1X_1 + 1X_2 + 1X_3 + 1X_4 + 0X_5 + 0X_6 + 1X_7 \geq 21$ } workers required on Friday
$1X_1 + 1X_2 + 1X_3 + 1X_4 + 1X_5 + 0X_6 + 0X_7 \geq 19$ } workers required on Saturday

Finally, all our decision variables must assume nonnegative integer values. These conditions are stated as:

$$X_1, X_2, X_3, X_4, X_5, X_6, X_7 \geq 0$$
All X_i must be integers

6.9.4 A Note About the Constraints

At this point, you might wonder why the constraints for each day are greater than or equal to rather than equal to constraints. For example, if Air-Express needs only 19 people on Saturday, why do we have a constraint that allows *more* than 19 people to be scheduled? The answer to this question relates to feasibility. Suppose we restate the problem so that all the constraints are equal to constraints. There are two possible outcomes for this problem: (1) it might have a feasible optimal solution, or (2) it might not have a feasible solution.

In the first case, if the formulation using equal to constraints has a feasible optimal solution, this same solution also must be a feasible solution to our formulation using greater than or equal to constraints. Because both formulations have the same objective function, the solution to our original formulation could not be worse (in terms of the optimal objective function value) than a formulation using equal to constraints.

In the second case, if the formulation using equal to constraints has no feasible solution, there is no schedule where the *exact* number of employees required can be scheduled each day. To find a feasible solution in this case, we would need to make the constraints less restrictive by allowing for more than the required number of employees to be scheduled (that is, using greater than or equal to constraints).

Therefore, using greater than or equal to constraints does not preclude a solution where the exact number of workers needed is scheduled for each shift, if such a schedule is feasible and optimal. If such a schedule is not feasible or not optimal, the formulation using greater than or equal to constraints also guarantees that a feasible optimal solution to the problem will be obtained.

6.9.5 Implementing the Model

The LP model for the Air-Express scheduling problem is summarized as:

MIN: $680X_1 + 705X_2 + 705X_3 + 705X_4 + 705X_5 + 680X_6 + 655X_7$ } total wage expense

Subject to:

$0X_1 + 1X_2 + 1X_3 + 1X_4 + 1X_5 + 1X_6 + 0X_7 \geq 18$ } workers required on Sunday
$0X_1 + 0X_2 + 1X_3 + 1X_4 + 1X_5 + 1X_6 + 1X_7 \geq 27$ } workers required on Monday
$1X_1 + 0X_2 + 0X_3 + 1X_4 + 1X_5 + 1X_6 + 1X_7 \geq 22$ } workers required on Tuesday
$1X_1 + 1X_2 + 0X_3 + 0X_4 + 1X_5 + 1X_6 + 1X_7 \geq 26$ } workers required on Wednesday
$1X_1 + 1X_2 + 1X_3 + 0X_4 + 0X_5 + 1X_6 + 1X_7 \geq 25$ } workers required on Thursday
$1X_1 + 1X_2 + 1X_3 + 1X_4 + 0X_5 + 0X_6 + 1X_7 \geq 21$ } workers required on Friday
$1X_1 + 1X_2 + 1X_3 + 1X_4 + 1X_5 + 0X_6 + 0X_7 \geq 19$ } workers required on Saturday
$X_1, X_2, X_3, X_4, X_5, X_6, X_7 \geq 0$
All X_i must be integers

A convenient way of implementing this model is shown in Figure 6.14 (and in the file Fig6-14.xls on your data disk). Each row in the table shown in this spreadsheet corresponds to one of the seven shifts in the problem. For each day of the week, entries have been made to indicate which shifts are scheduled to be on or off. For example, shift 1 is scheduled off Sunday and Monday, and works on the remaining days of the week. Notice that the values for each day of the week in Figure 6.14 correspond directly to the coefficients in the constraint in our LP model for the same day of the week. The required number of workers for each day is listed in cells B13 through H13 and corresponds to the RHS values of each constraint. The wages to be paid to each worker on the various shifts are listed in cells J5 through J11 and correspond to the objective function coefficients in our model.

Cells I5 through I11 indicate the number of workers assigned to each shift, and correspond to the decision variables X_1 through X_7 in our algebraic formulation of the LP model. The LHS formula for each constraint is implemented easily using the SUMPRODUCT( ) function. For example, the formula in cell B12 implements the LHS of the constraint for the number of workers needed on Sunday as:

Formula for cell B12: =SUMPRODUCT(B5:B11,$I$5:$I$11)
(Copy to C12 through H12 and J12.)

This formula is then copied to cells C12 through H12 to implement the LHS formulas of the remaining constraints. With the coefficients for the objective function entered in cells J5 through J11, the previous formula is also copied to cell J12 to implement the objective function for this model.

6.9.6 Solving the Model

Figure 6.15 shows the Solver parameters required to solve this problem. The optimal solution is shown in Figure 6.16 on page 262.

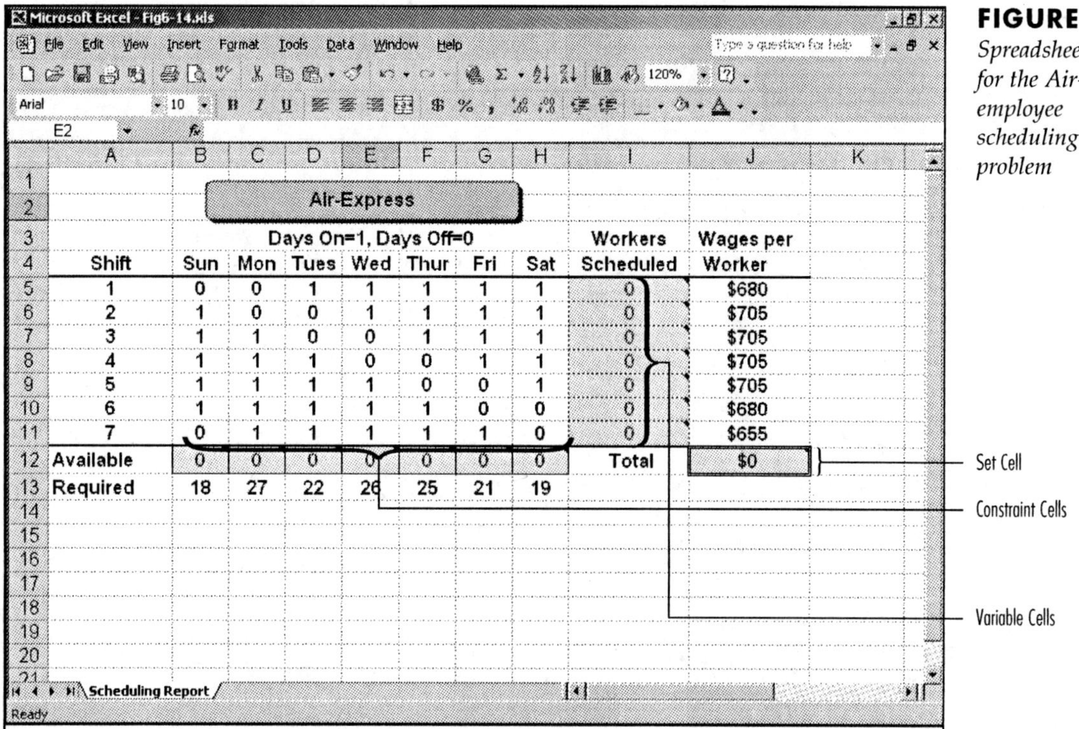

Key Cell Formulas

Cell	Formula	Copied to
B12	=SUMPRODUCT(B5:B11,$I$5:$I$11)	C12:H12 and J12

FIGURE 6.14
Spreadsheet model for the Air-Express employee scheduling problem

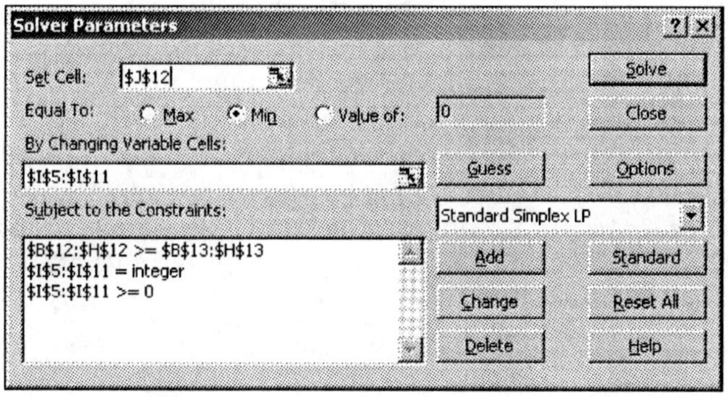

FIGURE 6.15
Solver parameters for the Air-Express scheduling problem

6.9.7 Analyzing the Solution

The optimal solution to this problem is shown in Figure 6.16. This solution ensures that the available number of employees is at least as great as the required number of employees for each day. The minimum total wage expense associated with this solution is $22,540.

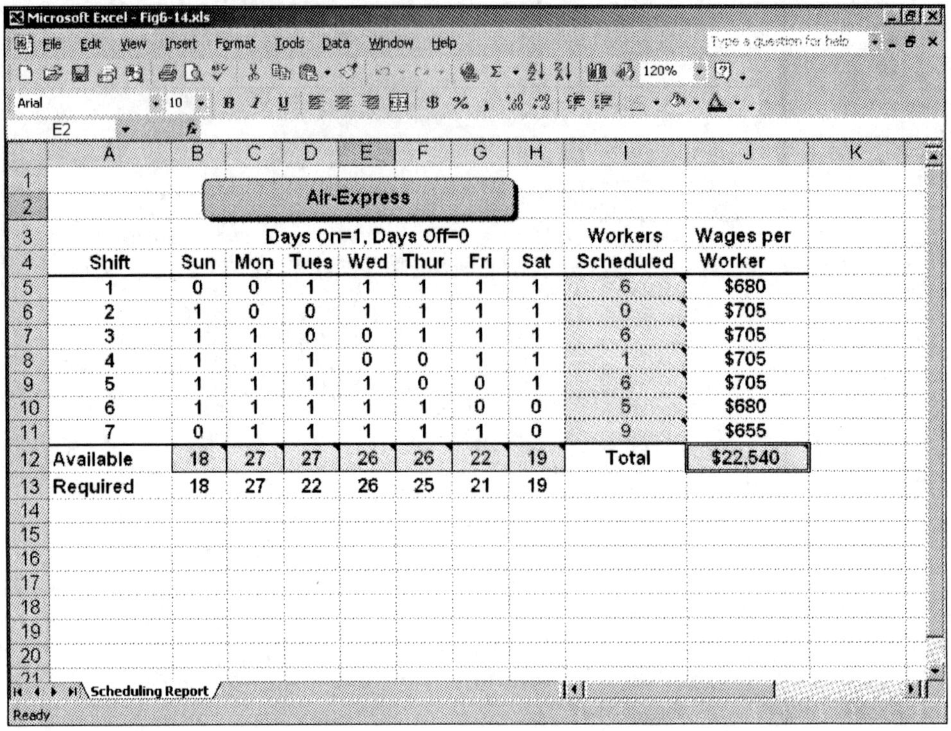

Shift	Sun	Mon	Tues	Wed	Thur	Fri	Sat	Workers Scheduled	Wages per Worker
1	0	0	1	1	1	1	1	6	$680
2	1	0	0	1	1	1	1	0	$705
3	1	1	0	0	1	1	1	6	$705
4	1	1	1	0	0	1	1	1	$705
5	1	1	1	1	0	0	1	6	$705
6	1	1	1	1	1	0	0	5	$680
7	0	1	1	1	1	1	0	9	$655
Available	18	27	27	26	26	22	19	Total	$22,540
Required	18	27	22	26	25	21	19		

FIGURE 6.16
Optimal solution to the Air-Express employee scheduling problem

6.10 BINARY VARIABLES

As mentioned earlier, some LP problems naturally evolve into ILP problems when we realize that we need to obtain integer solutions. For example, in the Air-Express problem discussed in the previous section, we needed to determine the number of workers to assign to each of seven shifts. Because workers are discrete units, we needed to impose integrality conditions on the decision variables in this model representing the number of workers scheduled for each shift. To do so, we changed the continuous variables in the model into **general integer variables,** or variables that could assume any integer value (provided that the constraints of the problem are not violated). In many other situations, we might want to use **binary integer variables** (or binary variables), which can assume *only two* integer values: 0 and 1. Binary variables can be useful in a number of practical modeling situations, as illustrated in the following examples.

6.11 A CAPITAL BUDGETING PROBLEM

In a capital budgeting problem, a decision maker is presented with several potential projects or investment alternatives and must determine which projects or investments to choose. The projects or investments typically require different amounts of various resources (for example, money, equipment, personnel) and generate different cash flows to the company. The cash flows for each project or investment are converted to a net present value (NPV). The problem is to determine which set of projects or investments to select in order to achieve the maximum possible NPV. Consider the following example:

In his position as vice president of research and development (R&D) for CRT Technologies, Mark Schwartz is responsible for evaluating and choosing which R&D projects to support. The company received 18 R&D proposals from its scientists and engineers, and identified six projects as being consistent with the company's mission. However, the company does not have the funds available to undertake all six projects. Mark must determine which of the projects to select. The funding requirements for each project are summarized in the following table along with the NPV the company expects each project to generate.

		Capital (in $1,000s) Required in				
Project	**Expected NPV (in $1,000s)**	**Year 1**	**Year 2**	**Year 3**	**Year 4**	**Year 5**
1	$141	$ 75	$25	$20	$15	$10
2	$187	$ 90	$35	$ 0	$ 0	$30
3	$121	$ 60	$15	$15	$15	$15
4	$ 83	$ 30	$20	$10	$ 5	$ 5
5	$265	$100	$25	$20	$20	$20
6	$127	$ 50	$20	$10	$30	$40

The company currently has $250,000 available to invest in new projects. It has budgeted $75,000 for continued support for these projects in year 2 and $50,000 per year for years 3, 4, and 5. Surplus funds in any year are reappropriated for other uses within the company and may not be carried over to future years.

6.11.1 Defining the Decision Variables

Mark must decide which of the six projects to select. Thus, we need six variables to represent the alternatives under consideration. We will let $X_1, X_2, ..., X_6$ represent the six decision variables for this problem and assume they operate as:

$$X_i = \begin{cases} 1, \text{ if project } i \text{ is selected} \\ 0, \text{ otherwise} \end{cases} \quad i = 1, 2, \ldots, 6$$

Each decision variable in this problem is a binary variable that assumes the value 1 if the associated project is selected, or the value 0 if the associated project is not selected. In essence, each variable acts like an "on/off switch" to indicate whether or not a given project has been selected.

6.11.2 Defining the Objective Function

The objective in this problem is to maximize the total NPV of the selected projects. This is stated mathematically as:

$$\text{MAX:} \quad 141X_1 + 187X_2 + 121X_3 + 83X_4 + 265X_5 + 127X_6$$

Notice that this objective function simply sums the NPV figures for the selected projects.

6.11.3 Defining the Constraints

We need one capital constraint for each year to ensure that the selected projects do not require more capital than is available. This set of constraints is represented by:

$$75X_1 + 90X_2 + 60X_3 + 30X_4 + 100X_5 + 50X_6 \leq 250 \quad \} \text{ year 1 capital constraint}$$
$$25X_1 + 35X_2 + 15X_3 + 20X_4 + 25X_5 + 20X_6 \leq 75 \quad \} \text{ year 2 capital constraint}$$
$$20X_1 + 0X_2 + 15X_3 + 10X_4 + 20X_5 + 10X_6 \leq 50 \quad \} \text{ year 3 capital constraint}$$
$$15X_1 + 0X_2 + 15X_3 + 5X_4 + 20X_5 + 30X_6 \leq 50 \quad \} \text{ year 4 capital constraint}$$
$$10X_1 + 30X_2 + 15X_3 + 5X_4 + 20X_5 + 40X_6 \leq 50 \quad \} \text{ year 5 capital constraint}$$

6.11.4 Setting Up the Binary Variables

In our formulation of this problem, we assume that each decision variable is a binary variable. We must include this assumption in the formal statement of our model by adding the constraints:

All X_i must be binary.

Important Software Note

Starting with Excel 8.0 in Office 97, Solver provides a feature that allows you to indicate that certain variable cells represent binary variables. When you are adding constraints, the drop-down list box (see Figure 6.9) used to indicate the type of constraint ("<=", ">=", "=", "int") includes another option labeled "bin" for binary. If you are using Excel 8.0 (or Premium Solver for Education), you can simply select the "bin" option for variable cells that represent binary variables. However, if you are using an older version of Excel, you will need to add all three sets of constraints (">=0", "<=1", and integer) to any variable cells that you want Solver to treat as binary variables.

6.11.5 Implementing the Model

The ILP model for the CRT Technologies project selection problem is summarized as:

$$\begin{aligned}
\text{MAX:} \quad & 141X_1 + 187X_2 + 121X_3 + 83X_4 + 265X_5 + 127X_6 \\
\text{Subject to:} \quad & 75X_1 + 90X_2 + 60X_3 + 30X_4 + 100X_5 + 50X_6 \leq 250 \\
& 25X_1 + 35X_2 + 15X_3 + 20X_4 + 25X_5 + 20X_6 \leq 75 \\
& 20X_1 + 0X_2 + 15X_3 + 10X_4 + 20X_5 + 10X_6 \leq 50 \\
& 15X_1 + 0X_2 + 15X_3 + 5X_4 + 20X_5 + 30X_6 \leq 50 \\
& 10X_1 + 30X_2 + 15X_3 + 5X_4 + 20X_5 + 40X_6 \leq 50 \\
& \text{All } X_i \text{ must be binary.}
\end{aligned}$$

This model is implemented in the spreadsheet shown in Figure 6.17 (and in the file Fig6-17.xls on your data disk). In this spreadsheet, the data for each project are listed in a separate row.

Cells B6 through B11 contain values of 0 to indicate that they are reserved for representing the six variables in our algebraic model. The LHS formula for the capital constraint is entered in cell D12 then copied to cells E12 through H12, as:

Formula for cell D12: =SUMPRODUCT(D6:D11,$B$6:$B$11)
(Copy to E12 through H12.)

The RHS values for the constraints are listed in cells D13 through H13. Finally, the objective function of the model is implemented in cell D15 as:

Formula for cell D15: =SUMPRODUCT(C6:C11,$B$6:$B$11)

6.11.6 Solving the Model

To solve this model, we must tell Solver where we have implemented our objective function, decision variables, and constraints. The Solver Parameters dialog box shown in Figure 6.18 indicates that the objective function is implemented in

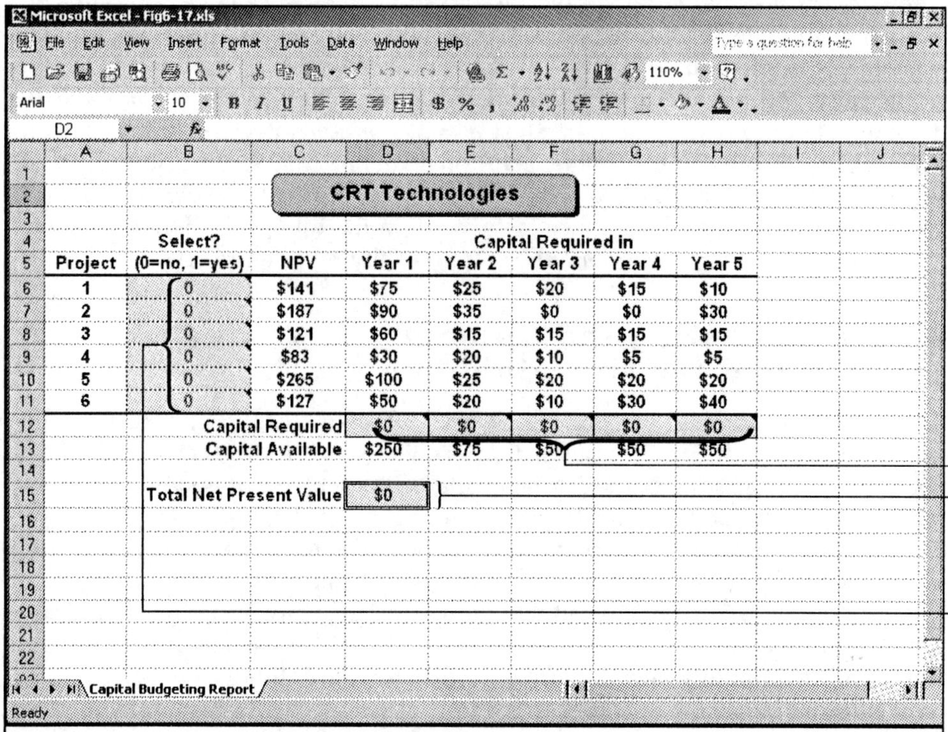

FIGURE 6.17
Spreadsheet model for the CRT Technologies project selection problem

Key Cell Formulas

Cell	Formula	Copied to
D12	=SUMPRODUCT(D6:D11,$B$6:$B$11)	E12:H12
D15	=SUMPRODUCT(C6:C11,$B$6:$B$11)	—

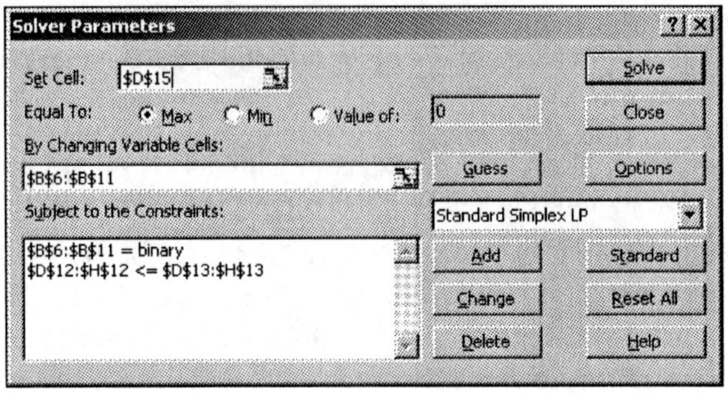

FIGURE 6.18
Solver parameters for the CRT Technologies project selection problem

cell D15 and that the decision variables are represented by cells B6 through B11. Also, notice that only two sets of constraints are specified for this problem.

The first set of constraints ensures that cells B6 through B11 will operate as binary variables. Notice that we implemented these constraints by referring to the cells in the spreadsheet that represent our decision variables—we do not have to set up separate cells in the spreadsheet to implement these constraints. The last set of constraints shown in the dialog box indicates that the values in cells D12 through H12 must be less than or equal to the values in cells D13 through H13 when the problem is solved. These conditions correspond to the capital constraints in the problem.

Because this model contains six decision variables and each variable can assume only one of two values, at most $2^6 = 64$ possible integer solutions exist for this problem. Some of these integer solutions will not fall in the feasible region, so we might suspect that this problem will not be too difficult to solve optimally. If we set the suboptimality tolerance factor to 0 (in the Integer Options dialog box) and solve the problem, we obtain the solution shown in Figure 6.19.

6.11.7 Comparing the Optimal Solution to a Heuristic Solution

The optimal solution shown in Figure 6.19 indicates that if CRT Technologies selects projects 1, 4, and 5, it can achieve a total NPV of $489,000. Although this solution does not use all of the capital available in each year, it is still the best possible integer solution to the problem.

Another approach to solving this problem is to create a ranked list of the projects in decreasing order by NPV and then select projects from this list, in order, until the capital is depleted. As shown in Figure 6.20, if we apply this heuristic to the current problem, we would select projects 5 and 2, but we could not select any more projects due to a lack of capital in year 5. This solution would generate a total NPV of $452,000. Again, we can see the potential benefit of optimization techniques over heuristic solution techniques.

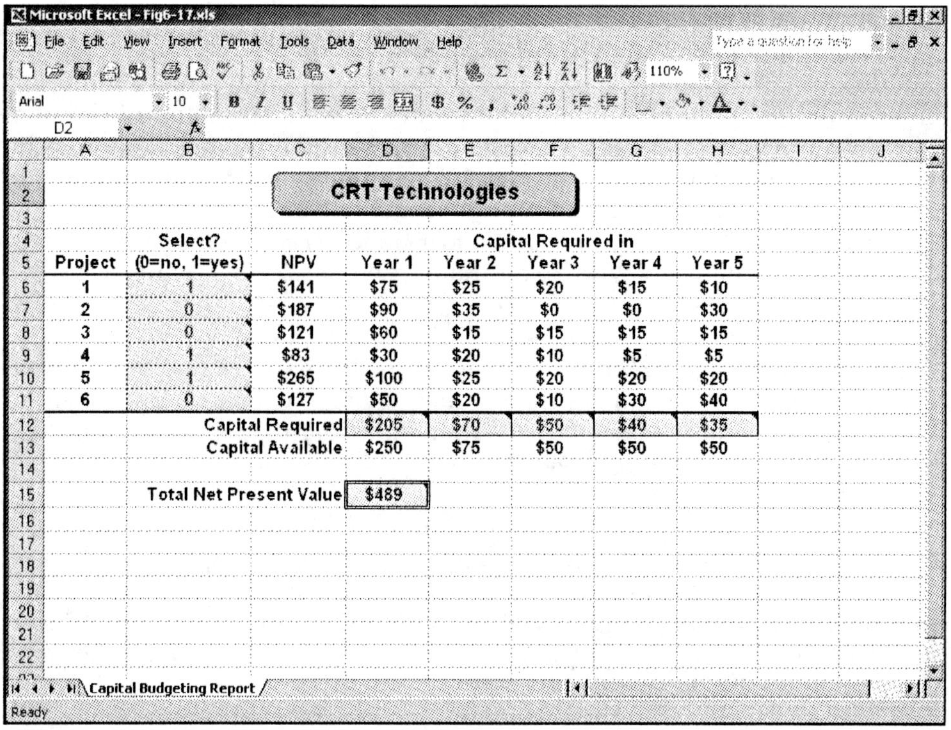

CRT Technologies

Project	Select? (0=no, 1=yes)	NPV	Capital Required in Year 1	Year 2	Year 3	Year 4	Year 5
1	1	$141	$75	$25	$20	$15	$10
2	0	$187	$90	$35	$0	$0	$30
3	0	$121	$60	$15	$15	$15	$15
4	1	$83	$30	$20	$10	$5	$5
5	1	$265	$100	$25	$20	$20	$20
6	0	$127	$50	$20	$10	$30	$40
	Capital Required		$205	$70	$50	$40	$35
	Capital Available		$250	$75	$50	$50	$50
	Total Net Present Value		$489				

FIGURE 6.19 *Optimal integer solution to the CRT Technologies project selection problem*

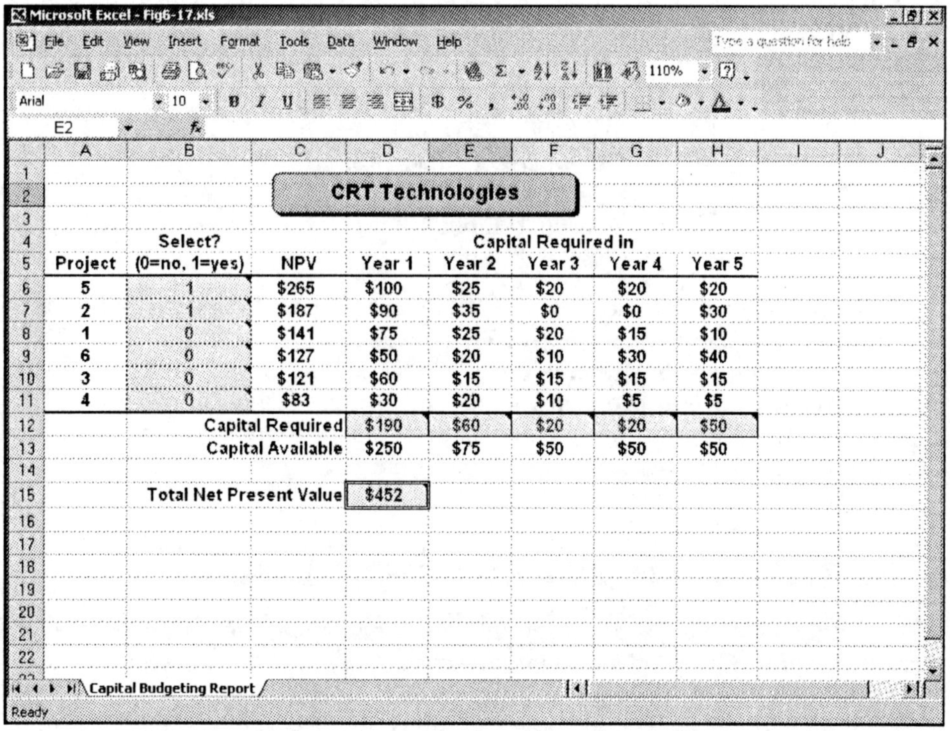

CRT Technologies

Project	Select? (0=no, 1=yes)	NPV	Capital Required in Year 1	Year 2	Year 3	Year 4	Year 5
5	1	$265	$100	$25	$20	$20	$20
2	1	$187	$90	$35	$0	$0	$30
1	0	$141	$75	$25	$20	$15	$10
6	0	$127	$50	$20	$10	$30	$40
3	0	$121	$60	$15	$15	$15	$15
4	0	$83	$30	$20	$10	$5	$5
	Capital Required		$190	$60	$20	$20	$50
	Capital Available		$250	$75	$50	$50	$50
	Total Net Present Value		$452				

FIGURE 6.20 *A suboptimal heuristic solution to the CRT Technologies project selection problem*

6.12 BINARY VARIABLES AND LOGICAL CONDITIONS

Binary variables can be used to model a number of logical conditions that might apply in a variety of problems. For example, in the CRT Technologies problem, several of the projects under consideration (for example, projects 1, 3, and 6) might represent alternative approaches for producing a certain part for a product. The company might want to limit the solution to include *no more than one* of these three alternatives. The following type of constraint accomplishes this restriction:

$$X_1 + X_3 + X_6 \leq 1$$

Because X_1, X_3, and X_6 represent binary variables, no more than one of them can assume the value 1 and still satisfy the previous constraint. If we want to ensure that the solution includes *exactly one* of these alternatives, we could include the following constraint in our model:

$$X_1 + X_3 + X_6 = 1$$

As an example of another type of logical condition, suppose that project 4 involves a cellular communications technology that will not be available to the company unless it undertakes project 5. In other words, the company cannot select project 4 unless it also selects project 5. This type of relationship can be imposed on the solution with the constraint:

$$X_4 - X_5 \leq 0$$

The four possible combinations of values for X_4 and X_5 and their relationships to the previous constraint are summarized as:

Value of			
X_4	**X_5**	**Meaning**	**Feasible?**
0	0	Do not select either project	Yes
1	1	Select both projects	Yes
0	1	Select 5, but not 4	Yes
1	0	Select 4, but not 5	No

As indicated in this table, the previous constraint prohibits any solution in which project 4 is selected and project 5 is not selected.

As these examples illustrate, you can model certain logical conditions using binary variables. Several problems at the end of this chapter allow you to use binary variables (and your own creativity) to formulate models for decision problems that involve these types of logical conditions.

6.13 THE FIXED-CHARGE PROBLEM

In most of the LP problems discussed in earlier chapters, we formulated objective functions to maximize profits or minimize costs. In each of these cases, we associated a per-unit cost or per-unit profit with each decision variable to create the objective function. However, in some situations, the decision to produce a product results in a lump-sum cost, or fixed-charge, in addition to a per-unit cost or profit. These types of problems are known as **fixed-charge** or fixed-cost problems. The following are some examples of fixed-costs:

- the cost to lease, rent, or purchase a piece of equipment or a vehicle that will be required if a particular action is taken
- the setup cost required to prepare a machine or production line to produce a different type of product
- the cost to construct a new production line or facility that will be required if a particular decision is made
- the cost of hiring additional personnel that will be required if a particular decision is made

In each of these examples, the fixed costs are *new* costs that will be incurred if a particular action or decision is made. In this respect, fixed costs are different from **sunk costs,** which are costs that will be incurred regardless of what decision is made. Sunk costs are irrelevant for decision-making purposes because, by definition, decisions do not influence these costs. On the other hand, fixed costs are important factors in decision making because the decision determines whether or not these costs will be incurred. The following example illustrates the formulation and solution of a fixed-charge problem.

Remington Manufacturing is planning its next production cycle. The company can produce three products, each of which must undergo machining, grinding, and assembly operations. The following table summarizes the hours of machining, grinding, and assembly required by each unit of each product, and the total hours of capacity available for each operation.

	Hours Required By			
Operation	**Product 1**	**Product 2**	**Product 3**	**Total Hours Available**
Machining	2	3	6	600
Grinding	6	3	4	300
Assembly	5	6	2	400

The cost accounting department has estimated that each unit of product 1 manufactured and sold will contribute $48 to profit, and each unit of products 2 and 3 contributes $55 and $50, respectively. However, manufacturing a unit of product 1 requires a setup operation on the production line that costs $1,000. Similar setups are required for products 2 and 3 at costs of $800 and $900, respectively. The marketing department believes it can sell all the products produced. Therefore, the management of Remington wants to determine the most profitable mix of products to produce.

6.13.1 Defining the Decision Variables

Although only three products are under consideration in this problem, we need six variables to formulate the problem accurately. We can define these variables as:

$$X_i = \text{the amount of product } i \text{ to be produced, } i = 1, 2, 3$$

$$Y_i = \begin{cases} 1, \text{ if } X_i > 0 \\ 0, \text{ if } X_i = 0 \end{cases}, i = 1, 2, 3$$

We need three variables, X_1, X_2, and X_3, to correspond to the amount of products 1, 2, and 3 produced. Each of the X_i variables has a corresponding binary variable, Y_i, that will equal 1 if X_i assumes any positive value, or will equal 0 if X_i is 0. For now, do not be concerned about how this relationship between the X_i and Y_i is enforced. We will explore that soon.

6.13.2 Defining the Objective Function

Given our definition of the decision variables, the objective function for our model is stated as:

$$\text{MAX:} \quad 48X_1 + 55X_2 + 50X_3 - 1000Y_1 - 800Y_2 - 900Y_3$$

The first three terms in this function calculate the marginal profit generated by the number of products 1, 2, and 3 sold. The last three terms in this function subtract the fixed costs for the products produced. For example, if X_1 assumes a positive value, we know from our definition of the Y_i variables that Y_1 should equal 1. And if $Y_1 = 1$, the value of the objective function will be reduced by \$1,000 to reflect payment of the setup cost. On the other hand, if $X_1 = 0$, we know that $Y_1 = 0$. Therefore, if no units of X_1 are produced, the setup cost for product 1 will not be incurred in the objective. Similar relationships exist between X_2 and Y_2 and between X_3 and Y_3.

6.13.3 Defining the Constraints

Several sets of constraints apply to this problem. Capacity constraints are needed to ensure that the number of machining, grinding, and assembly hours used does not exceed the number of hours available for each of these resources. These constraints are stated as:

$$2X_1 + 3X_2 + 6X_3 \leq 600 \quad \text{\} machining constraint}$$
$$6X_1 + 3X_2 + 4X_3 \leq 300 \quad \text{\} grinding constraint}$$
$$5X_1 + 6X_2 + 2X_3 \leq 400 \quad \text{\} assembly constraint}$$

We also need to include nonnegativity conditions on the X_i variables as:

$$X_i \geq 0,\ i = 1, 2, 3$$

The following constraint on the Y_i variables is needed to ensure that they operate as binary variables:

$$\text{All } Y_i \text{ must be binary}$$

As mentioned earlier, we must ensure that the required relationship between the X_i and Y_i variables is enforced. In particular, the value of the Y_i variables can be determined from the X_i variables. Therefore, we need constraints to establish this *link* between the value of the Y_i variables and the X_i variables. These linking constraints are represented by:

$$X_1 \leq M_1Y_1$$
$$X_2 \leq M_2Y_2$$
$$X_3 \leq M_3Y_3$$

In each of these constraints, the M_i is a numeric constant that represents an upper bound on the optimal value of the X_i. Let's assume that all the M_i are arbitrarily large numbers; for example, $M_i = 10{,}000$. Then, each constraint sets up a link between the value of the X_i and the Y_i. For example, if any X_i variables in the previous constraints assume a value greater than 0, the corresponding Y_i variable must assume the value 1 or the constraint will be violated. On the other hand, if any of the X_i variables are equal to 0, the corresponding Y_i variables could equal 0 or 1 and still satisfy the constraint. However, if we consider the objective function to this problem, we know that when given a choice, Solver will always set the Y_i equal to 0 (rather than 1) because this results in a better objective function value. Therefore, we can conclude that if any X_i variables are equal to 0, Solver will set the corresponding Y_i variable equal to 0 because this is feasible and results in a better objective function value.

6.13.4 Determining Values for "Big M"

The M_i values used in the linking constraints are sometimes referred to as Big M values because they can be assigned arbitrarily large values. However, for reasons that go beyond the scope of this text, these types of problems are much easier to solve if the M_i values are kept as small as possible. As indicated earlier, the M_i values impose upper bounds on the values of the X_i. So, if a problem indicates that a company could manufacture and sell no more than 60 units of X_1, for example, we could let $M_1 = 60$. However, even if upper bounds for the X_i are not explicitly indicated, it is sometimes easy to derive implicit upper bounds for these variables.

Let's consider the variable X_1 in the Remington problem. What is the maximum number of units of X_1 that can be produced in this problem? Referring back to our capacity constraints, if the company produces 0 units of X_2 and X_3, it would run out of machining capacity after producing $600/2 = 300$ units of X_1. Similarly, it would run out of grinding capacity after producing $300/6 = 50$ units of X_1, and it would run out of assembly capacity after producing $400/5 = 80$ units of X_1. Therefore, the maximum number of units of X_1 the company can produce is 50. Using similar logic, we can determine that the maximum units of X_2 the company can produce is $\text{MIN}(600/3, 300/3, 400/6) = 66.67$, and the maximum units of X_3 is $\text{MIN}(600/6, 300/4, 400/2) = 75$. Thus, for this problem reasonable upper bounds for X_1, X_2, and X_3 are represented by $M_1 = 50$, $M_2 = 67$, and $M_3 = 75$, respectively. (Note that the method illustrated here for obtaining reasonable values for the M_i does not apply if any of the coefficients in the machining, grinding, or assembly constraints are negative. Why is this?) When possible, you should determine reasonable values for the M_i in this type of problem. However, if this is not possible, you can assign arbitrarily large values to the M_i.

6.13.5 Implementing the Model

Using the values for the M_i calculated earlier, our ILP formulation of Remington's production planning model is summarized as:

MAX:	$48X_1 + 55X_2 + 50X_3 - 1000Y_1 - 800Y_2 - 900Y_3$	
Subject to:	$2X_1 + 3X_2 + 6X_3 \leq 600$	} machining constraint
	$6X_1 + 3X_2 + 4X_3 \leq 300$	} grinding constraint

$$
\begin{array}{ll}
5X_1 + 6X_2 + 2X_3 \le 400 & \} \text{ assembly constraint} \\
X_1 - 50Y_1 \le 0 & \\
X_2 - 67Y_2 \le 0 & \Big\} \text{ linking constraints} \\
X_3 - 75Y_3 \le 0 & \\
\text{All } Y_i \text{ must be binary} & \} \text{ binary constraints} \\
X_i \ge 0,\ i = 1, 2, 3 & \} \text{ nonnegativity conditions}
\end{array}
$$

This model expresses the linking constraints in a slightly different (but algebraically equivalent) manner in order to follow our convention of having all the variables on the LHS of the inequality and a constant on the RHS. This model is implemented in the spreadsheet shown in Figure 6.21 (and in the file Fig6-21.xls on your data disk).

In the spreadsheet in Figure 6.21, cells B5, C5, and D5 represent the variables X_1, X_2, and X_3, and cells B15, C15, and D15 represent Y_1, Y_2, and Y_3. The coefficients for the objective function are in cells B7 through D8. The objective function is implemented in cell F8 with the formula:

FIGURE 6.21
Spreadsheet model for Remington's fixed-charge problem

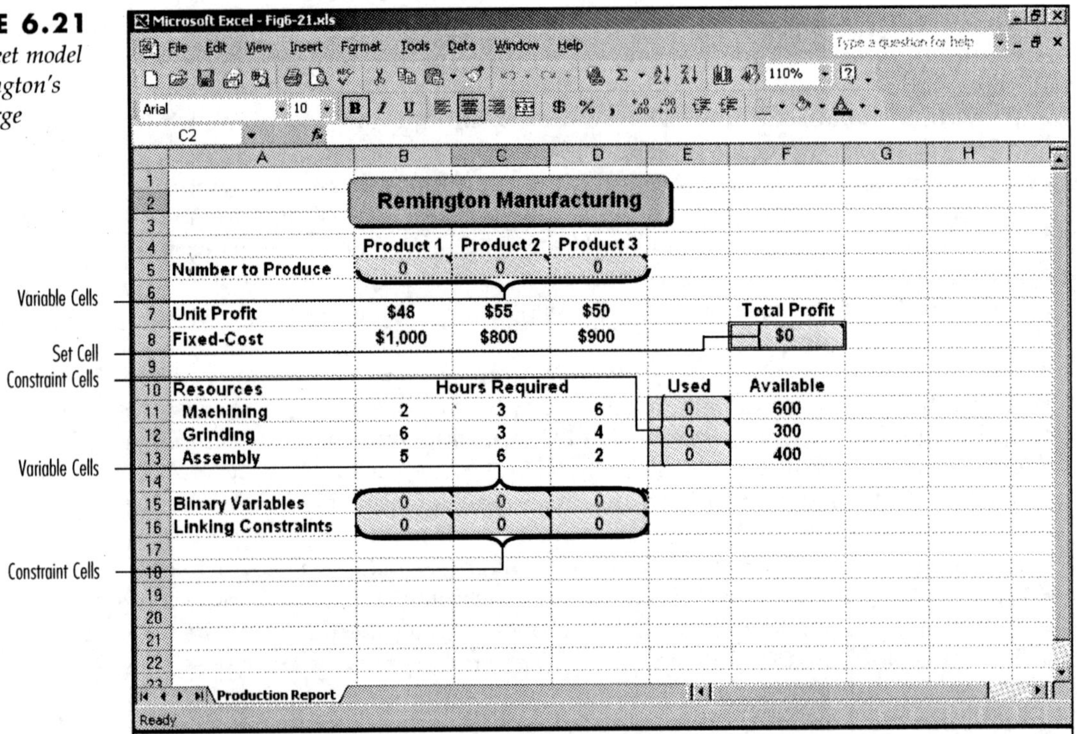

Key Cell Formulas

Cell	Formula	Copied to
B16	=B5-MIN($F$11/B11,$F$12/B12,$F$13/B13)*B15	C16:D16
E11	=SUMPRODUCT(B11:D11,$B$5:$D$5)	E12:E13
F8	=SUMPRODUCT(B7:D7,B5:D5) -SUMPRODUCT(B8:D8,B15:D15)	—

Formula for cell F8: =SUMPRODUCT(B7:D7,B5:D5)–SUMPRODUCT(B8:D8,B15:D15)

Cells B11 through D13 contain the coefficients for the machining, grinding, and assembly constraints. The LHS formulas for these constraints are implemented in cells E11 through E13, and cells F11 through F13 contain the RHS values for these constraints. Finally, the LHS formulas for the linking constraints are entered in cells B16 through D16 as:

Formula for cell B16: =B5-MIN($F$11/B11,$F$12/B12,$F$13/B13)*B15
(Copy to cells C16 through D16.)

Instead of entering the values for M_i in these constraints, we implemented formulas that would automatically calculate correct M_i values if the user of this spreadsheet changed any of the coefficients or RHS values in the capacity constraints.

Potential Pitfall

It is important to note that we are treating cells B15, C15, and D15, which represent the binary variables Y_1, Y_2, and Y_3, just like any other cells representing decision variables. We simply entered values of 0 into these cells to indicate that they represent decision variables. Ultimately, Solver will determine what values should be placed in these cells so that all the constraints are satisfied and the objective function is maximized. Some people try to make Solver's job "easier" by placing IF( ) functions in these cells to determine whether the values should be 0 or 1 depending on the values of cells B5, C5, and D5, which correspond to the variables X_1, X_2, and X_3. Although this approach seems to make sense, it can produce unwanted results. Using IF( ) functions in this way introduces *nonlinearities* in the spreadsheet model that can prevent Solver from finding the optimal solution to the problem. In chapter 8, Nonlinear Programming, we will see that nonlinear programming problems are very difficult to solve optimally. Thus, it is best to create a model so that it can be solved using linear optimization methods.

6.13.6 Solving the Model

The Solver Parameters dialog box shown in Figure 6.22 indicates the settings required to solve this problem. Notice that the ranges B5 through D5 and B15 through D15, which correspond to the X_i and Y_i variables, are both listed as ranges of cells that can be changed. Also, notice the necessary binary constraint is imposed on cells B15 through D15.

Because so few integer variables exist in this problem, we should be able to obtain an optimal integer solution easily. If we set the suboptimality tolerance to 0 in the Integer Options dialog box and instruct Solver to assume a linear model, we obtain the optimal solution to this problem, as shown in Figure 6.23.

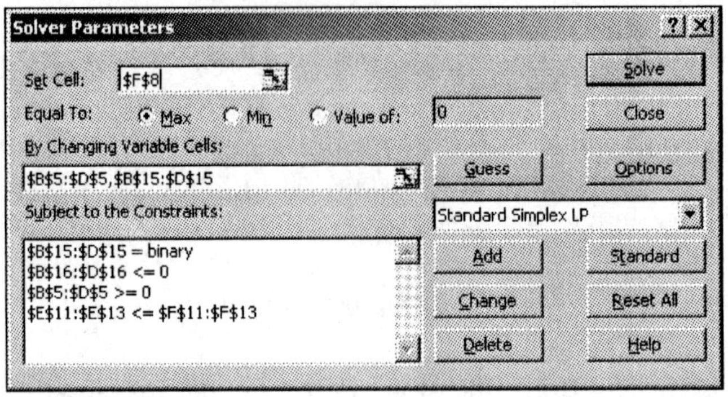

FIGURE 6.22 *Solver parameters for Remington's fixed-charge problem*

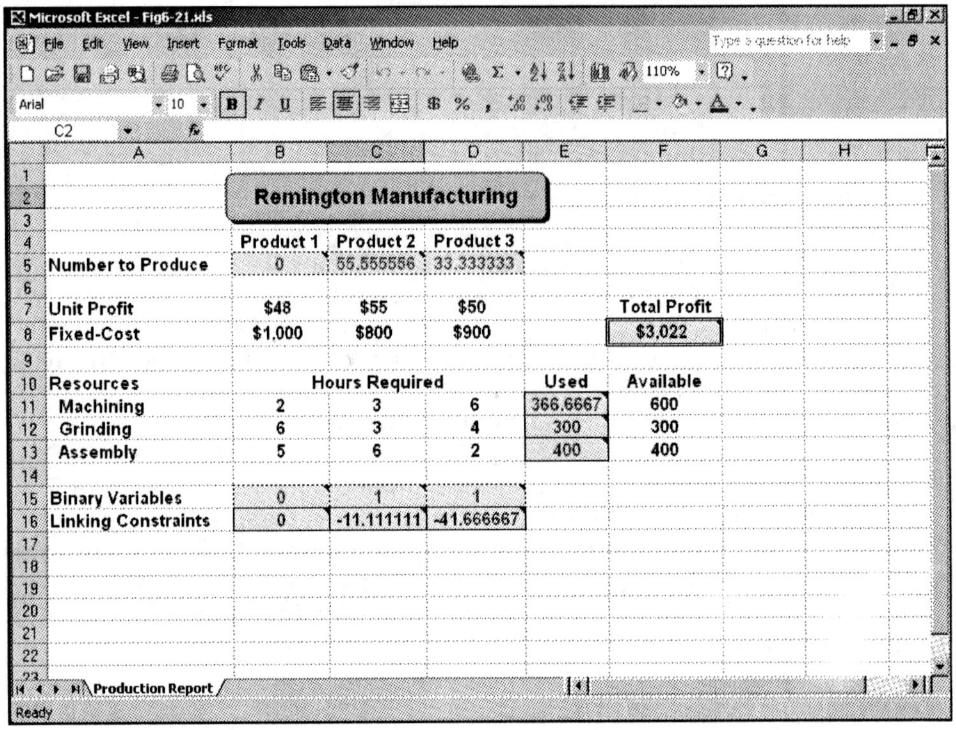

FIGURE 6.23 *Optimal mixed-integer solution to Remington's fixed-charge problem*

6.13.7 Analyzing the Solution

The solution shown in Figure 6.23 indicates that the company should produce 0 units of product 1, 55.55 units of product 2, and 33.33 units of product 3 ($X_1 = 0$, $X_2 = 55.55$, and $X_3 = 33.33$). Solver assigned values of 0, 1, and 1 to cells B15, C15, and D15 ($Y_1 = 0$, $Y_2 = 1$, and $Y_3 = 1$). Thus, Solver maintained the proper relationship between X_i and Y_i because the linking constraints were specified for this problem.

The values in B16, C16, and D16 indicate the amounts by which the values for X_1, X_2, and X_3 (in cells B5, C5, and D5) fall below the upper bounds imposed by their respective linking constraints. Thus, the optimal value of X_2 is approximately

11.11 units below its upper bound of 66.67 and the optimal value of X_3 is approximately 41.67 units below its upper bound of 75. Because the optimal value of Y_1 is zero, the linking constraint for X_1 and Y_1 imposes an upper bound of zero on X_1. Thus, the value in cell B16 indicates that the optimal value of X_1 is zero units below its upper bound of zero.

Because our formulation of this model did not specify that the X_i must be integers, we should not be surprised by the fractional values obtained for these variables in this solution. If we round the values of X_2 and X_3 down to 55 and 33, we obtain an integer feasible solution with an objective function value of $2,975. If we want to find the optimal all-integer solution, we can add the appropriate integrality condition for the X_i to the constraint set and then re-solve the problem. This optimal all-integer solution is shown in Figure 6.24.

Note that more computational effort is required to obtain the all-integer solution shown in Figure 6.24 versus the effort required to obtain the mixed-integer solution shown in Figure 6.23. This additional work resulted in only a $5 improvement in the objective function over the all-integer solution we obtained from rounding down the solution in Figure 6.23. This highlights two important points. First, problems involving binary integer variables are often easier to solve than problems involving general integer variables. Second, good near-optimal solutions often can be obtained by rounding, so this approach is not necessarily ineffective—and could be the only practical solution available for large ILPs that are difficult to solve.

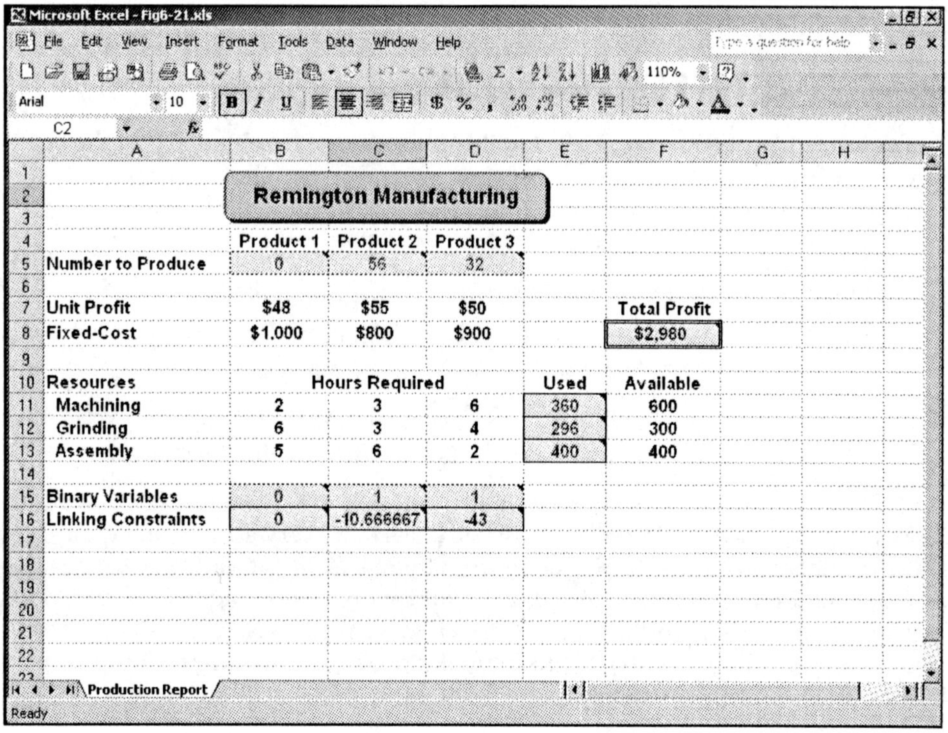

FIGURE 6.24
Optimal all-integer solution to Remington's fixed-charge problem

6.14 MINIMUM ORDER/PURCHASE SIZE

Many investment, production, and distribution problems have minimum purchase amounts or minimum production lot size requirements that must be met. For example, a particular investment opportunity might require a minimum investment of $25,000. Or, a supplier of a given part used in a production process might require a minimum order of 10 units. Similarly, many manufacturing companies have a policy of not producing any units of a given item unless a certain minimum lot size will be produced.

To see how these types of minimum order/purchase requirements can be modeled, suppose that in the previous problem, Remington Manufacturing did not want to produce any units of product 3 (X_3) unless it produced at least 40 units of this product. This type of restriction is modeled as:

$$X_3 \leq M_3Y_3$$
$$X_3 \geq 40Y_3$$

The first constraint is the same type of linking constraint described earlier, in which M_3 represents an upper bound on X_3 (or an arbitrarily large number) and Y_3 represents a binary variable. If X_3 assumes any positive value, Y_3 must equal 1 (if $X_3 > 0$, then $Y_3 = 1$). However, according to the second constraint, if Y_3 equals 1, then X_3 must be greater than or equal to 40 (if $Y_3 = 1$, then $X_3 \geq 40$). On the other hand, if X_3 equals 0, Y_3 must also equal 0 in order to satisfy both constraints. Together, these two constraints ensure that if X_3 assumes any positive value, that value must be at least 40. This example illustrates how binary variables can be used to model a practical condition that is likely to occur in a variety of decision problems.

6.15 QUANTITY DISCOUNTS

In all of the LP problems considered to this point, we have assumed that the profit or cost coefficients in the objective function were constant. For example, consider our revised Blue Ridge Hot Tubs problem, which is represented by:

MAX:	$350X_1 + 300X_2$	} profit
Subject to:	$1X_1 + 1X_2 \leq 200$	} pump constraint
	$9X_1 + 6X_2 \leq 1{,}520$	} labor constraint
	$12X_1 + 16X_2 \leq 2{,}650$	} tubing constraint
	$X_1, X_2 \geq 0$	} nonnegativity conditions
	X_1, X_2 must be integers	} integrality conditions

This model assumes that *every* additional Aqua-Spa (X_1) manufactured and sold results in a $350 increase in profit. It also assumes that every additional Hydro-Lux (X_2) manufactured and sold results in a $300 increase in profit. However, as the production of these products increases, quantity discounts might be obtained on component parts that would cause the profit margin on these items to increase.

For example, suppose that if the company produces more than 75 Aqua-Spas, it will be able to obtain quantity discounts and other economies of scale that would increase the profit margin to \$375 per unit for each unit produced in excess of 75. Similarly, suppose that if the company produces more than 50 Hydro-Luxes, it will be able to increase its profit margin to \$325 for each unit produced in excess of 50. That is, each of the first 75 units of X_1 and the first 50 units of X_2 would produce profits of \$350 and \$300 per unit, respectively, and each additional unit of X_1 and X_2 would produce profits of \$375 and \$325 per unit, respectively. How do we model this type of problem?

6.15.1 Formulating the Model

To accommodate the different profit rates that can be generated by producing Aqua-Spas and Hydro-Luxes, we need to define new variables for the problem, where

X_{11} = the number of Aqua-Spas produced at \$350 profit per unit

X_{12} = the number of Aqua-Spas produced at \$375 profit per unit

X_{21} = the number of Hydro-Luxes produced at \$300 profit per unit

X_{22} = the number of Hydro-Luxes produced at \$325 profit per unit

Using these variables, we can begin to reformulate our problem as:

$$\begin{array}{llr}
\text{MAX:} & 350X_{11} + 375X_{12} + 300X_{21} + 325X_{22} & \\
\text{Subject to:} & 1X_{11} + 1X_{12} + 1X_{21} + 1X_{22} \leq 200 & \}\text{ pump constraint} \\
 & 9X_{11} + 9X_{12} + 6X_{21} + 6X_{22} \leq 1{,}520 & \}\text{ labor constraint} \\
 & 12X_{11} + 12X_{12} + 16X_{21} + 16X_{22} \leq 2{,}650 & \}\text{ tubing constraint} \\
 & \text{All } X_{ij} \geq 0 & \}\text{ simple lower bounds} \\
 & \text{All } X_{ij} \text{ must be integers} & \}\text{ integrality conditions}
\end{array}$$

This formulation is not complete. Notice that the variable X_{12} would always be preferred over X_{11} because X_{12} requires exactly the same resources as X_{11} and generates a larger per-unit profit. The same relationship holds between X_{22} and X_{21}. Thus, the optimal solution to the problem is $X_{11} = 0$, $X_{12} = 118$, $X_{21} = 0$, and $X_{22} = 76$. However, this solution is not allowable because we cannot produce any units of X_{12} until we have produced 75 units of X_{11}; and we cannot produce any units of X_{22} until we have produced 50 units of X_{21}. Therefore, we must identify some additional constraints to ensure that these conditions are met.

6.15.2 The Missing Constraints

To ensure that the model does not allow any units of X_{12} to be produced unless we have produced 75 units of X_{11}, consider the constraints:

$$X_{12} \leq M_{12}Y_1$$
$$X_{11} \geq 75Y_1$$

In the first constraint, M_{12} represents some arbitrarily large numeric constant and Y_1 represents a binary variable. The first constraint requires that $Y_1 = 1$ if any units of X_{12} are produced (if $X_{12} > 0$, then $Y_1 = 1$). However, if $Y_1 = 1$, then the second constraint would require X_{11} to be at least 75. According to the second constraint, the only way that fewer than 75 units of X_{11} can be produced is if $Y_1 = 0$, which, by the first constraint, implies $X_{12} = 0$. These two constraints do not allow any units of X_{12} to be produced unless at least 75 units of X_{11} have been produced. The following constraints ensure that the model does not allow any units of X_{22} to be produced unless we have produced 50 units of X_{21}:

$$X_{22} \leq M_{22}Y_2$$
$$X_{21} \geq 50Y_2$$

If we include these new constraints in our previous formulation (along with the constraints necessary to make Y_1 and Y_2 operate as binary variables), we would have an accurate formulation of the decision problem. The optimal solution to this problem is $X_{11} = 75$, $X_{12} = 43$, $X_{21} = 50$, $X_{22} = 26$.

6.16 A CONTRACT AWARD PROBLEM

Other conditions often arise in decision problems that can be modeled effectively using binary variables. The following example, which involves awarding contracts, illustrates some of these conditions.

B&G Construction is a commercial building company located in Tampa, Florida. The company has recently signed contracts to construct four buildings in different locations throughout southern Florida. Each building project requires large amounts of cement to be delivered to the building sites. At B&G's request, three cement companies have submitted bids for supplying the cement for these jobs. The following table summarizes the prices the three companies charge per delivered ton of cement and the maximum amount of cement that each company can provide.

	Cost per Delivered Ton of Cement				
	Project 1	**Project 2**	**Project 3**	**Project 4**	**Max. Supply**
Company 1	\$120	\$115	\$130	\$125	525
Company 2	\$100	\$150	\$110	\$105	450
Company 3	\$140	\$ 95	\$145	\$165	550
Total Tons Needed	450	275	300	350	

For example, company 1 can supply a maximum of 525 tons of cement, and each ton delivered to projects 1, 2, 3, and 4 will cost \$120, \$115, \$130, and \$125, respectively. The costs vary primarily because of the different distances between the cement plants and the construction sites. The numbers in the last row of the table indicate the total amount of cement (in tons) required for each project.

In addition to the maximum supplies listed, each cement company placed special conditions on its bid. Specifically, company 1 indicated that it will not supply orders of less than 150 tons for any of the construction projects. Company 2 indicated that it can supply more than 200 tons to no more than one of the projects. Company 3 indicated that it will accept only orders that total 200 tons, 400 tons, or 550 tons.

B&G can contract with more than one supplier to meet the cement requirements for a given project. The problem is to determine what amounts to purchase from each supplier to meet the demands for each project at the least total cost.

This problem seems like a transportation problem in which we want to determine how much cement should be shipped from each cement company to each construction project in order to meet the demands of the projects at a minimum cost. However, the special conditions imposed by each supplier require side constraints, which are not usually found in a standard transportation problem. First, we'll discuss the formulation of the objective function and the transportation constraints. Then, we'll consider how to implement the side constraints required by the special conditions in the problem.

6.16.1 Formulating the Model: The Objective Function and Transportation Constraints

To begin formulating this problem, we need to define our decision variables as:

X_{ij} = tons of cement purchased from company i for construction project j

The objective function to minimize total cost is represented by:

$$\begin{aligned}\text{MIN:}\quad & 120X_{11} + 115X_{12} + 130X_{13} + 125X_{14}\\ & +100X_{21} + 150X_{22} + 110X_{23} + 105X_{24}\\ & +140X_{31} + 95X_{32} + 145X_{33} + 165X_{34}\end{aligned}$$

To ensure that the maximum supply of cement from each company is not exceeded, we need the following constraints:

$$X_{11} + X_{12} + X_{13} + X_{14} \leq 525 \quad \text{\} supply from company 1}$$
$$X_{21} + X_{22} + X_{23} + X_{24} \leq 450 \quad \text{\} supply from company 2}$$
$$X_{31} + X_{32} + X_{33} + X_{34} \leq 550 \quad \text{\} supply from company 3}$$

To ensure that the requirement for cement at each construction project is met, we need the following constraints:

$$X_{11} + X_{21} + X_{31} = 450 \quad \text{\} demand for cement at project 1}$$
$$X_{12} + X_{22} + X_{32} = 275 \quad \text{\} demand for cement at project 2}$$
$$X_{13} + X_{23} + X_{33} = 300 \quad \text{\} demand for cement at project 3}$$
$$X_{14} + X_{24} + X_{34} = 350 \quad \text{\} demand for cement at project 4}$$

6.16.2 Implementing the Transportation Constraints

The objective function and the constraints of this problem are implemented in the spreadsheet model shown in Figure 6.25 (and in the file Fig6-25.xls on your data disk).

In this spreadsheet, the costs per delivered ton of cement are shown in cells B6 through E8. Cells B12 through E14 represent the decision variables in the model. The objective function is entered in cell G17 as:

Formula for cell G17: =SUMPRODUCT(B6:E8,B12:E14)

The LHS formulas of the supply constraints are entered in cells F12 through F14 as:

Formula for cell F12: =SUM(B12:E12)
(Copy to F13 through F14.)

FIGURE 6.25
Spreadsheet model for the transportation portion of B&G's contract award problem

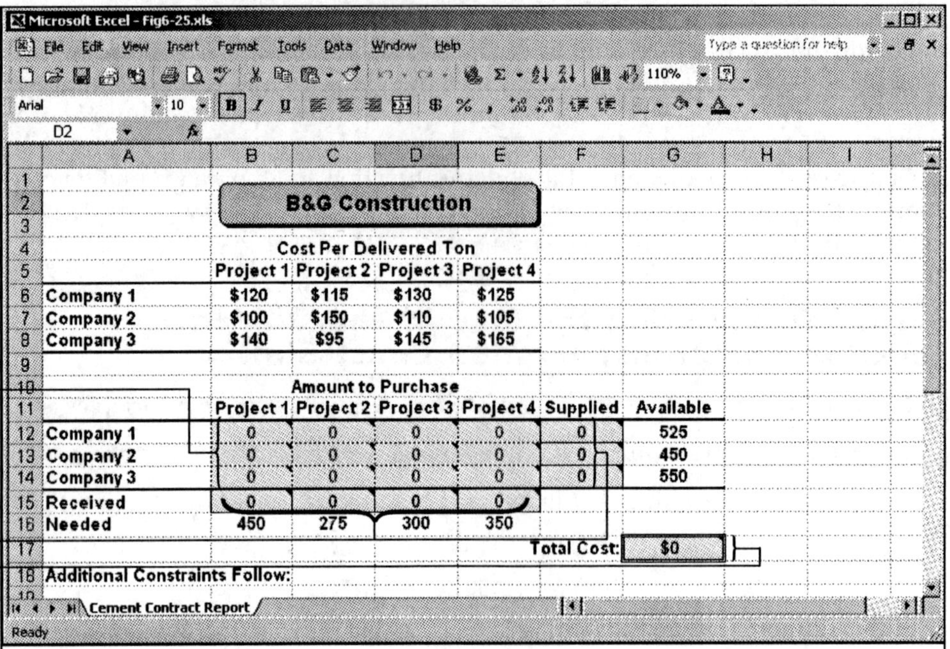

Key Cell Formulas

Cell	Formula	Copied to
B15	=SUM(B12:B14)	C15:E15
F12	=SUM(B12:E12)	F13:F14
G17	=SUMPRODUCT(B6:E8,B12:E14)	—

Cells G12 through G14 contain the RHS values for these constraints. The LHS formulas for the demand constraints are entered in cells B15 through E15 as:

Formula for cell B15: =SUM(B12:B14)
(Copy to C15 through E15.)

Cells B16 through E16 contain the RHS values for these constraints.

6.16.3 Formulating the Model: The Side Constraints

Company 1 indicated that it will not accept orders for less than 150 tons for any of the construction projects. This minimum-size order restriction is modeled by the following eight constraints, where the Y_{ij} represent binary variables:

$X_{11} \leq 525Y_{11}$ (implement as $X_{11} - 525Y_{11} \leq 0$)
$X_{12} \leq 525Y_{12}$ (implement as $X_{12} - 525Y_{12} \leq 0$)
$X_{13} \leq 525Y_{13}$ (implement as $X_{13} - 525Y_{13} \leq 0$)
$X_{14} \leq 525Y_{14}$ (implement as $X_{14} - 525Y_{14} \leq 0$)
$X_{11} \geq 150Y_{11}$ (implement as $X_{11} - 150Y_{11} \geq 0$)
$X_{12} \geq 150Y_{12}$ (implement as $X_{12} - 150Y_{12} \geq 0$)

$$X_{13} \geq 150Y_{13} \qquad \text{(implement as } X_{13} - 150Y_{13} \geq 0\text{)}$$
$$X_{14} \geq 150Y_{14} \qquad \text{(implement as } X_{14} - 150Y_{14} \geq 0\text{)}$$

Each constraint has an algebraically equivalent constraint, which will ultimately be used in implementing the constraint in the spreadsheet. The first four constraints represent linking constraints that ensure if X_{11}, X_{12}, X_{13}, or X_{14} is greater than 0, then its associated binary variable (Y_{11}, Y_{12}, Y_{13}, or Y_{14}) must equal 1. (These constraints also indicate that 525 is the maximum value that can be assumed by X_{11}, X_{12}, X_{13}, and X_{14}.) The next four constraints ensure that if X_{11}, X_{12}, X_{13}, or X_{14} is greater than 0, it must be at least 150. We include these constraints in the formulation of this model to ensure that any order given to company 1 is for at least 150 tons of cement.

Company 2 indicated that it can supply more than 200 tons to no more than one of the projects. This type of restriction is represented by the following set of constraints where, again, the Y_{ij} represent binary variables:

$$X_{21} \leq 200 + 250Y_{21} \qquad \text{(implement as } X_{21} - 200 - 250Y_{21} \leq 0\text{)}$$
$$X_{22} \leq 200 + 250Y_{22} \qquad \text{(implement as } X_{22} - 200 - 250Y_{22} \leq 0\text{)}$$
$$X_{23} \leq 200 + 250Y_{23} \qquad \text{(implement as } X_{23} - 200 - 250Y_{23} \leq 0\text{)}$$
$$X_{24} \leq 200 + 250Y_{24} \qquad \text{(implement as } X_{24} - 200 - 250Y_{24} \leq 0\text{)}$$
$$Y_{21} + Y_{22} + Y_{23} + Y_{24} \leq 1 \qquad \text{(implement as is)}$$

The first constraint indicates that the amount supplied from company 2 for project 1 must be less than 200 if $Y_{21} = 0$, or less than 450 (the maximum supply from company 2) if $Y_{21} = 1$. The next three constraints have similar interpretations for the amount supplied from company 2 to projects 2, 3, and 4, respectively. The last constraint indicates that at most, one of Y_{21}, Y_{22}, Y_{23}, and Y_{24} can equal 1. Therefore, only one of the projects can receive more than 200 tons of cement from company 2.

The final set of constraints for this problem addresses company 3's stipulation that it will accept only orders totaling 200, 400, or 550 tons. This type of condition is modeled using binary Y_{ij} variables as:

$$X_{31} + X_{32} + X_{33} + X_{34} = 200Y_{31} + 400Y_{32} + 550Y_{33}$$
$$\text{(implement as } X_{31} + X_{32} + X_{33} + X_{34} - 200Y_{31} - 400Y_{32} - 550Y_{33} = 0\text{)}$$
$$Y_{31} + Y_{32} + Y_{33} \leq 1 \text{ (implement as is)}$$

These constraints allow for the total amount ordered from company 3 to assume four distinct values. If $Y_{31} = Y_{32} = Y_{33} = 0$, then no cement will be ordered from company 3. If $Y_{31} = 1$, then 200 tons must be ordered. If $Y_{32} = 1$, then 400 tons must be ordered. Finally, if $Y_{33} = 1$, then 550 tons must be ordered from company 3. These two constraints enforce the special condition imposed by company 3.

6.16.4 Implementing the Side Constraints

Although the side constraints in this problem allow us to impose important restrictions on the feasible solutions that can be considered, these constraints serve more of a "mechanical" purpose—to make the model work—but are not of primary interest to management. Thus, it is often convenient to implement side constraints in an out-of-the-way area of the spreadsheet so that they do not detract from the primary purpose of the spreadsheet, in this case, to determine how much cement to order from each potential supplier. Figure 6.26 shows how the side constraints for the current problem can be implemented in a spreadsheet.

To implement the side constraints for company 1, we enter the batch-size restriction of 150 in cell B20 and reserve cells B21 through E21 to represent the binary variables Y_{11}, Y_{12}, Y_{13}, and Y_{14}. The LHS formulas for the linking constraints for company 1 are implemented in cells B22 through E22 as:

Formula for cell B22: =B12-$G$12*B21
(Copy to C22 through E22.)

Cell F22 contains a reminder for us to tell Solver that these cells must be less than or equal to 0. The LHS formulas for the batch-size constraints for company 1 are implemented in cells B23 through E23 as:

Formula for cell B23: =B12-$B$20*B21
(Copy to C23 through E23.)

Cell F23 contains a reminder for us to tell Solver that these cells must be greater than or equal to 0.

FIGURE 6.26
Spreadsheet model for the side constraints in B&G's contract award problem

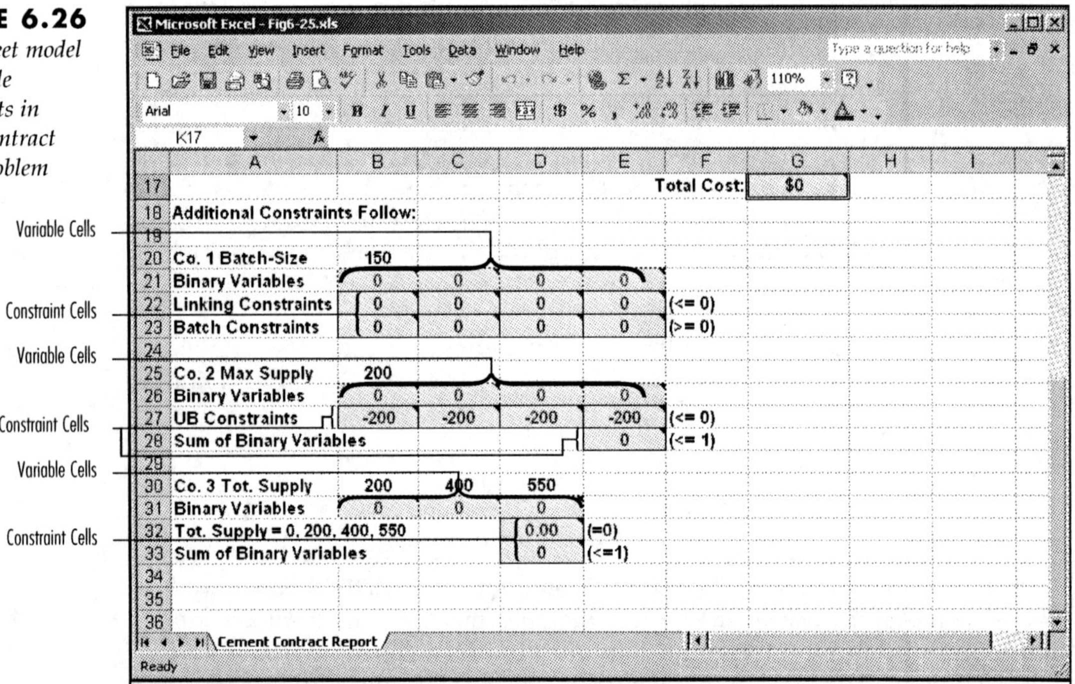

Key Cell Formulas

Cell	Formula	Copied to
B22	=B12-$G$12*B21	C22:E22
B23	=B12-$B$20*B21	C23:E23
B27	=B13-$B$25-($G$13-$B$25)*B26	C27:E27
E28	=SUM(B26:E26)	—
D32	=SUM(B14:E14)-SUMPRODUCT(B30:D30,B31:D31)	—
D33	=SUM(B31:D31)	—

To implement the side constraints for company 2, we enter the maximum supply value of 200 in cell B25 and reserve cells B26 through E26 to represent the binary variables Y_{21}, Y_{22}, Y_{23}, and Y_{24}. The LHS formulas for the maximum supply constraints are implemented in cells B27 through E27 as:

Formula for cell B27: =B13-$B$25-($G$13-$B$25)*B26
(Copy to C27 through E27.)

Cell F27 reminds us to tell Solver that these cells must be less than or equal to 0. As discussed earlier, to ensure that no more than one order from company 2 exceeds 200 tons, the sum of the binary variables for company 2 cannot exceed 1. The LHS formula for this constraint is entered in cell E28 as:

Formula for cell E28: =SUM(B26:E26)

Cell F28 reminds us to tell Solver that this cell must be less than or equal to 1.

To implement the side constraints for company 3, the three possible total order amounts are entered in cells B30 through D30. Cells B31 through D31 are reserved to represent the binary variables Y_{31}, Y_{32}, and Y_{33}. The LHS formula for company 3's total supply side constraint is entered in cell D32 as:

Formula for cell D32: =SUM(B14:E14)-SUMPRODUCT(B30:D30,B31:D31)

Cell E32 reminds us to tell Solver that cell D32 must equal 0. Finally, to ensure that no more than one of the binary variables for company 3 is set equal to 1, we enter the sum of these variables in cell D33 as:

Formula for cell D33: =SUM(B31:D31)

Cell E33 reminds us to tell Solver that this cell must be less than or equal to 1.

6.16.5 Solving the Model

Due to the large number of variables and constraints in this problem, we summarized the Solver parameters required for this problem in Figure 6.27. Note that all of the cells representing binary variables must be identified as variable cells and must be constrained to assume only integer values between 0 and 1.

6.16.6 Analyzing the Solution

An optimal solution to this problem is shown in Figure 6.28 on page 285 (there are alternate optimal solutions to this problem). In this solution, the amounts of cement required by each construction project are met exactly. Also, each condition imposed by the side constraints for each company is met. Specifically, the orders awarded to company 1 are for at least 150 tons; only one of the orders awarded to company 2 exceeds 200 tons; and the sum of the orders awarded to company 3 is exactly equal to 400 tons.

FIGURE 6.27
Solver parameters and options for B&G's contract award problem

Solver parameters

Set Target Cell: G17
Equal to: Min
By Changing Cells: B12:E14,B21:E21,B26:E26,B31:D31
Subject to the Constraints:

- B12:E14 ≥ 0
- B21:E21 = binary
- B26:E26 = binary
- B31:E31 = binary
- F12:F14 ≤ G12:G14
- B15:E15 = B16:E16
- B22:E22 ≤ 0
- B23:E23 ≥ 0
- B27:E27 ≤ 0
- E28 ≤ 1
- D32 = 0
- D33 ≤ 1

Solver options

Standard Simplex LP	Integer Tolerance = 0%
Use Automatic Scaling	Iterations = 100

6.17 THE BRANCH-AND-BOUND ALGORITHM (OPTIONAL)

As mentioned earlier, a special procedure, known as the branch-and-bound (B&B) algorithm is required to solve ILPs. Although we can easily indicate the presence of integer variables in a model, it usually requires quite a bit of effort on Solver's part to actually solve an ILP problem using the B&B algorithm. To better appreciate and understand what is involved in the B&B algorithm, let's consider how it works.

The B&B algorithm starts by relaxing all the integrality conditions in an ILP and solving the resulting LP problem. As noted earlier, if we are lucky, the optimal solution to the relaxed LP problem might happen to satisfy the original integrality conditions. If this occurs, then we are done—the optimal solution to the LP relaxation is also the optimal solution to the ILP. However, it is more likely that the optimal solution to the LP will violate one or more of the original integrality conditions. For example, consider the problem whose integer and relaxed feasible regions were shown in Figure 6.1 and are repeated in Figure 6.29 on page 286:

$$\begin{aligned} \text{MAX:} \quad & 2X_1 + 3X_2 \\ \text{Subject to:} \quad & X_1 + 3X_2 \le 8.25 \\ & 2.5X_1 + X_2 \le 8.75 \end{aligned}$$

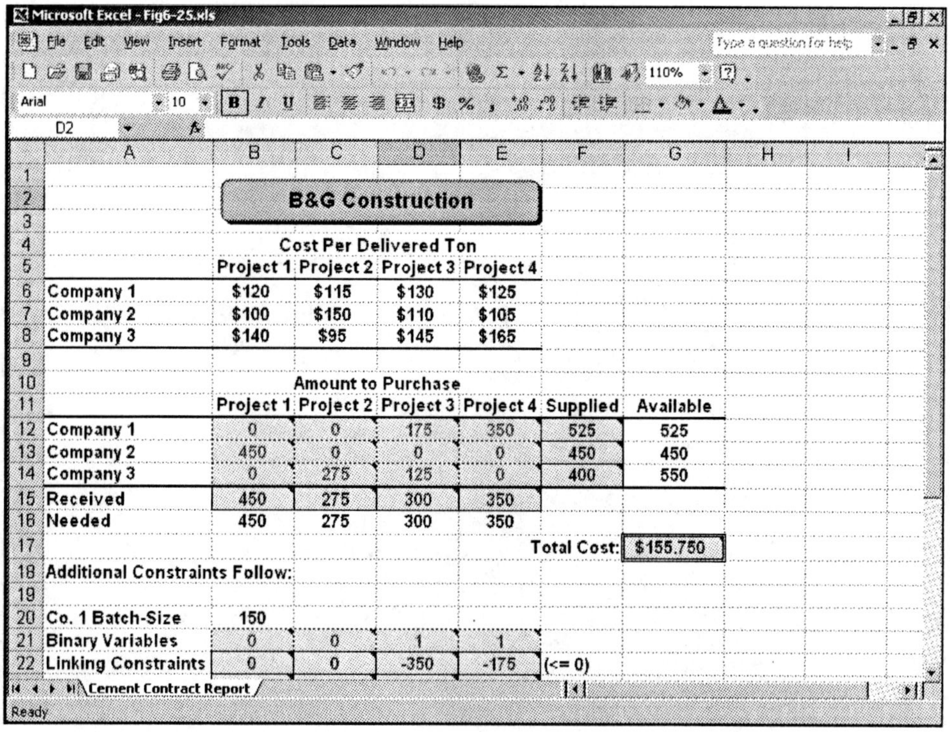

	B&G Construction					
	Cost Per Delivered Ton					
	Project 1	Project 2	Project 3	Project 4		
Company 1	$120	$115	$130	$125		
Company 2	$100	$150	$110	$105		
Company 3	$140	$95	$145	$165		
	Amount to Purchase					
	Project 1	Project 2	Project 3	Project 4	Supplied	Available
Company 1	0	0	175	350	525	525
Company 2	450	0	0	0	450	450
Company 3	0	275	125	0	400	550
Received	450	275	300	350		
Needed	450	275	300	350		
					Total Cost:	$155,750
Additional Constraints Follow:						
Co. 1 Batch-Size	150					
Binary Variables	0	0	1	1		
Linking Constraints	0	0	-350	-175	(<= 0)	

FIGURE 6.28
Optimal solution to B&G's contract award problem

$$X_1, X_2 \geq 0$$
$$X_1, X_2 \text{ must be integers}$$

If we relax the integrality conditions in this problem and solve the resulting LP problem, we obtain the solution $X_1 = 2.769$, $X_2 = 1.826$ shown in Figure 6.29. This solution clearly violates the integrality conditions stated in the original problem. Part of the difficulty here is that none of the corner points of the relaxed feasible region are integer feasible (other than the origin). We know that the optimal solution to an LP problem will occur at a corner point of its feasible region but, in this case, none of those corner points (except the origin) correspond to integer solutions. Thus, we need to modify the problem so that the integer feasible solutions to the problem occur at corner points of the relaxed feasible region. This is accomplished by branching.

6.17.1 Branching

Any integer variable in an ILP that assumes a fractional value in the optimal solution to the relaxed problem can be designated as a **branching variable.** For example, the variables X_1 and X_2 in the previous problem should assume only integer values but were assigned the values $X_1 = 2.769$ and $X_2 = 1.826$ in the optimal solution to the LP relaxation of the problem. Either of these variables could be selected as branching variables.

Let's arbitrarily choose X_1 as our branching variable. Because the current value of X_1 is not integer feasible, we want to eliminate this solution from further consideration. Many other solutions in this same vicinity of the relaxed feasible

FIGURE 6.29
Solution to LP relaxation at noninteger corner point

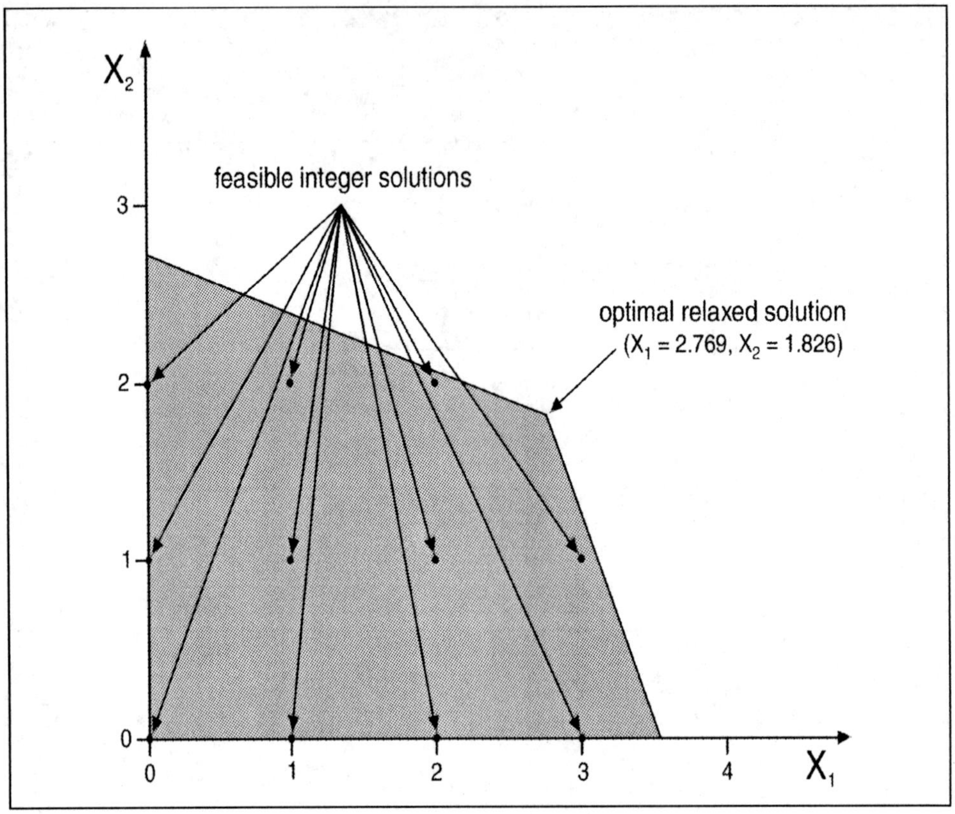

region can be eliminated as well. That is, X_1 must assume a value less than or equal to 2 ($X_1 \le 2$) or greater than or equal to 3 ($X_1 \ge 3$) in the optimal integer solution to the ILP. Therefore, all other possible solutions where X_1 assumes values between 2 and 3 (such as the current solution where $X_1 = 2.769$) can be eliminated from consideration. By branching on X_1, our original ILP problem can be subdivided into the following two candidate problems:

Problem I: MAX: $2X_1 + 3X_2$

Subject to:

$$X_1 + 3X_2 \le 8.25$$
$$2.5X_1 + X_2 \le 8.75$$
$$X_1 \le 2$$
$$X_1, X_2 \ge 0$$
X_1, X_2 must be integers

Problem II: MAX: $2X_1 + 3X_2$

Subject to:

$$X_1 + 3X_2 \le 8.25$$
$$2.5X_1 + X_2 \le 8.75$$
$$X_1 \ge 3$$
$$X_1, X_2 \ge 0$$
X_1, X_2 must be integers

The integer and relaxed feasible regions for each candidate problem are shown in Figure 6.30. Notice that a portion of the relaxed feasible region shown in Figure 6.29 has been eliminated in Figure 6.30, but none of the feasible integer solutions shown in Figure 6.29 have been eliminated. This is a general property of the branching operation in the B&B algorithm. Also notice that several feasible integer solutions now occur on the boundary lines of the feasible regions shown in Figure 6.30. More importantly, one of these feasible integer solutions occurs at an extreme point of the relaxed feasible region for problem I (at the point $X_1 = 2$, $X_2 = 0$). If we relax the integrality conditions in problem I and solve the resulting LP, we could obtain an integer solution because one of the corner points of the relaxed feasible region corresponds to such a point. (However, this integer feasible extreme point still might not be the optimal solution to the relaxed LP problem.)

6.17.2 Bounding

The next step in the B&B algorithm is to select one of the existing candidate problems for further analysis. Let's arbitrarily select problem I. If we relax the integrality conditions in problem I and solve the resulting LP, we obtain the solution $X_1 = 2$, $X_2 = 2.083$ and an objective function value of 10.25. This value represents an upper bound on the best possible integer solution that can be obtained from problem I. That is, because the relaxed solution to problem I is not integer feasible, we have not yet found the best possible integer solution for this problem. However, we do know that the objective function value of the best possible integer solution

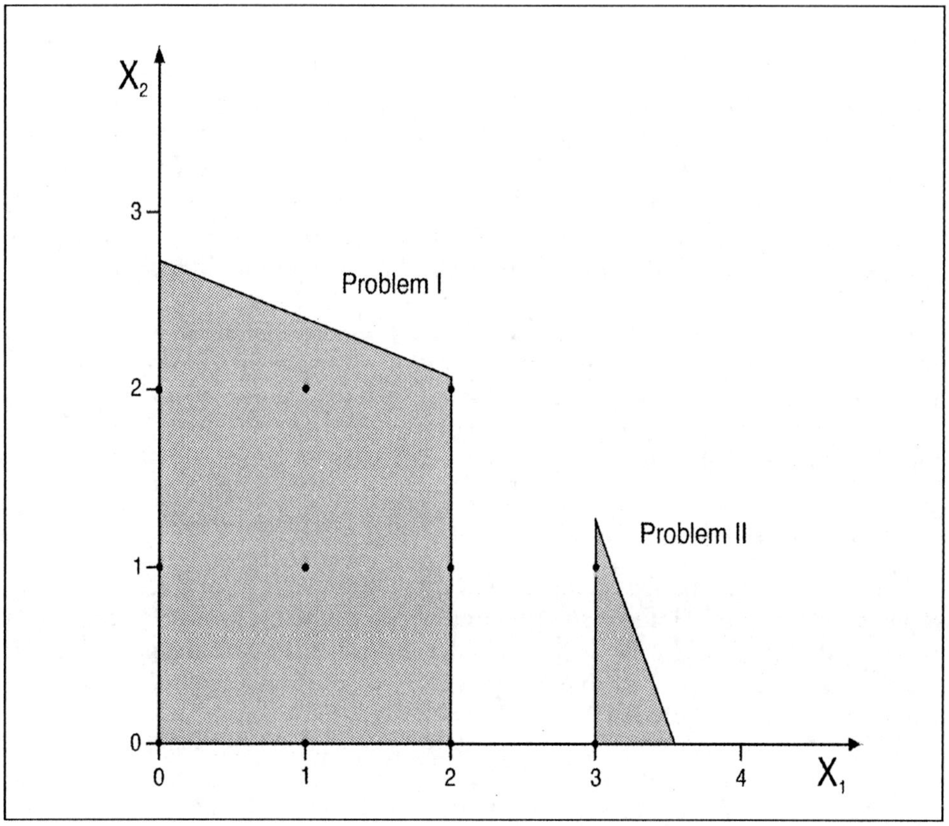

FIGURE 6.30
Feasible solutions to the candidate problems after the first branch

that can be obtained from problem I can be no greater than 10.25. As we shall see, this information can be useful in reducing the amount of work required to locate the optimal integer solution to an ILP problem.

6.17.3 Branching Again

Because the relaxed solution to problem I is not entirely integer feasible, the B&B algorithm proceeds by selecting X_2 as a branching variable and creating two additional candidate problems from problem I. These problems are represented as:

Problem III: MAX: $2X_1 + 3X_2$

Subject to:

$X_1 + 3X_2 \leq 8.25$

$2.5X_1 + X_2 \leq 8.75$

$X_1 \leq 2$

$X_2 \leq 2$

$X_1, X_2 \geq 0$

X_1, X_2 must be integers

Problem IV: MAX: $2X_1 + 3X_2$

Subject to:

$X_1 + 3X_2 \leq 8.25$

$2.5X_1 + X_2 \leq 8.75$

$X_1 \leq 2$

$X_2 \geq 3$

$X_1, X_2 \geq 0$

X_1, X_2 must be integers

Problem III is created by adding the constraint $X_2 \leq 2$ to problem I. Problem IV is created by adding the constraint $X_2 \geq 3$ to problem I. Thus, our previous solution to problem I (where $X_2 = 2.083$) will be eliminated from consideration as a possible solution to the LP relaxations of problems III and IV.

Problem IV is infeasible because there are no feasible solutions where $X_2 \geq 3$. The integer and relaxed feasible regions for problems II and III are summarized in Figure 6.31.

All of the corner points to the relaxed feasible region of problem III correspond to integer feasible solutions. Thus, if we relax the integrality conditions in problem III and solve the resulting LP problem, we must obtain an integer feasible solution. The solution to problem III is represented by $X_1 = 2$, $X_2 = 2$ and has an objective function value of 10.

6.17.4 Bounding Again

Although we have obtained an integer feasible solution to our problem, we won't know if it is the *optimal* integer solution until we evaluate the remaining candidate problem (that is, problem II). If we relax the integrality conditions in problem II and solve the resulting LP problem, we obtain the solution $X_1 = 3$, $X_2 = 1.25$ with an objective function value of 9.75.

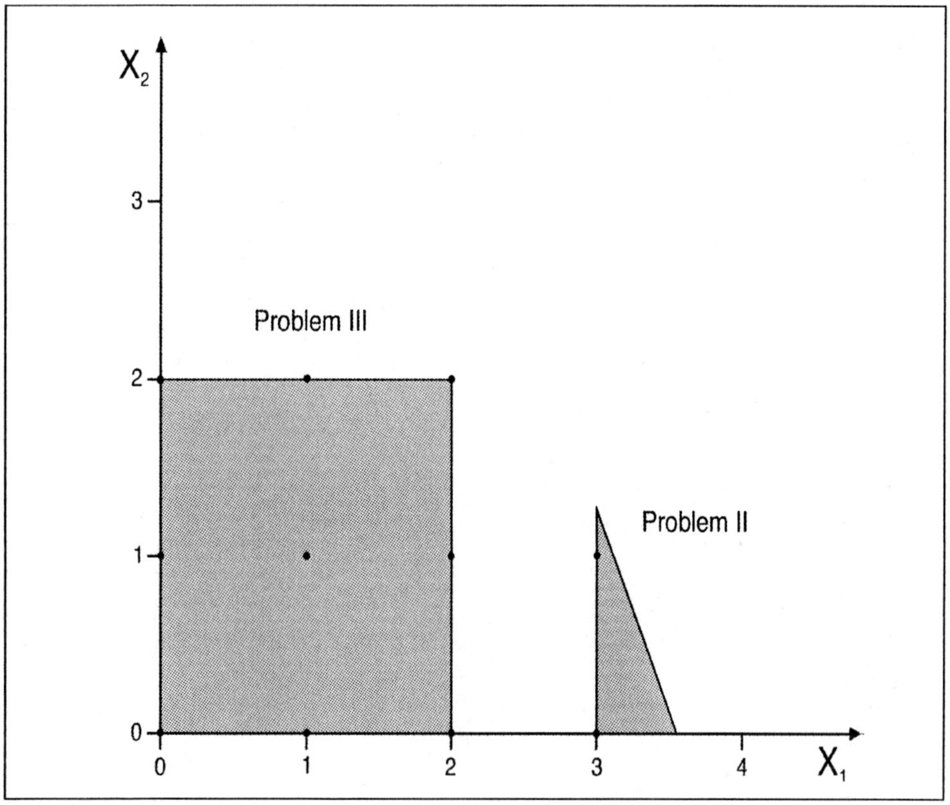

FIGURE 6.31
Feasible solutions to the candidate problems after the second branch

Because the solution to problem II is not integer feasible, we might be inclined to branch on X_2 in a further attempt to determine the best possible integer solution for problem II. However, this is not necessary. Earlier we noted that for *maximization* ILP problems, the objective function value at the optimal solution to the LP relaxation of the problem represents an *upper bound* on the optimal objective function value of the original ILP problem. This means that even though we do not yet know the optimal integer solution to problem II, we do know that its objective function value cannot be greater than 9.75. And because 9.75 is worse than the objective function value for the integer solution obtained from problem III, we cannot find a better integer solution by continuing to branch problem II. Therefore, problem II can be eliminated from further consideration. Because we have no more candidate problems to consider, we can conclude that the optimal integer solution to our problem is $X_1 = 2, X_2 = 2$ with an optimal objective function value of 10.

6.17.5 Summary of B&B Example

The steps involved in the solution to our example problem can be represented graphically in the form of a *branch-and-bound tree,* as shown in Figure 6.32. Although Figure 6.29 indicates that 11 integer solutions exist for this problem, we do not have to locate all of them in order to prove that the integer solution we found is the optimal solution. The bounding operation of the B&B algorithm eliminated

FIGURE 6.32
Branch-and-bound tree for the example problem

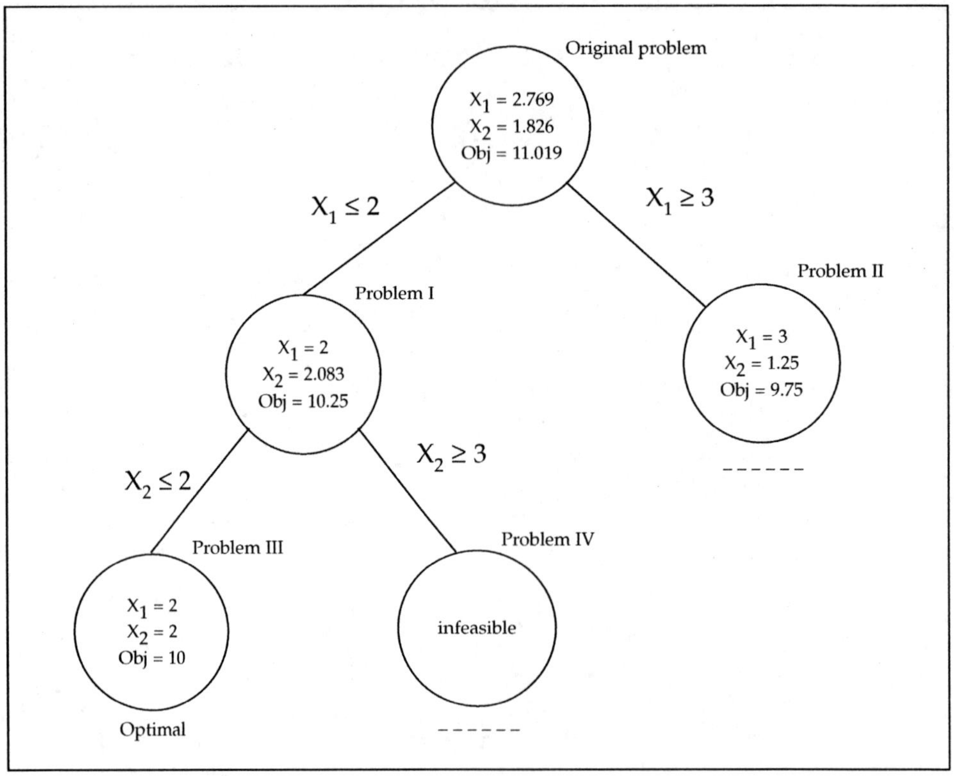

the need to explicitly enumerate all the integer feasible solutions and select the best of those as the optimal solution.

If the relaxed solution to problem II was greater than 10 (say 12.5), then the B&B algorithm would have continued branching from this problem in an attempt to find a better integer solution (an integer solution with an objective function value greater than 10). Similarly, if problem IV had a feasible noninteger solution, we would have needed to perform further branching from that problem if its relaxed objective value was better than that of the best known integer feasible solution. Thus, the first integer solution obtained using B&B will not always be the optimal integer solution. A more detailed description of the operations of the B&B algorithm is given in Figure 6.33.

6.18 SUMMARY

This chapter discussed the issues involved in formulating and solving ILP problems. In some cases, acceptable integer solutions to ILP problems can be obtained by rounding the solution to the LP relaxation of the problem. However, this procedure can lead to suboptimal solutions, which might still be viable if you can show that the solution obtained by rounding is within an acceptable distance from the optimal integer solution. This approach might be the only practical way to obtain integer solutions for some ILP problems.

FIGURE 6.33
Detailed description of the B&B algorithm for solving ILP problems

The Branch-and-Bound Algorithm

1. Relax all the integrality conditions in ILP and solve the resulting LP problem. If the optimal solution to the relaxed LP problem happens to satisfy the original integrality conditions, stop—this is the optimal integer solution. Otherwise, proceed to step 2.
2. If the problem being solved is a maximization problem, let Z_{best} = –infinity. If it is a minimization problem, let Z_{best} = +infinity. (In general, Z_{best} represents the objective function value of the best known integer solution as the algorithm proceeds.)
3. Let X_j represent one of the variables that violated the integrality conditions in the solution to the problem that was solved most recently, and let b_j represent its noninteger value. Let $INT(b_j)$ represent the largest integer that is less than b_j. Create two new candidate problems: one by appending the constraint $X_j \le INT(b_j)$ to the most recently solved LP problem, and the other by appending the constraint $X_j \ge INT(b_j)+1$ to the most recently solved LP problem. Place both of these new LP problems in a list of candidate problems to be solved.
4. If the list of candidate problems is empty, proceed to step 9. Otherwise, remove a candidate problem from the list, relax any integrality conditions in the problem, and solve it.
5. If there is no solution to the current candidate problem (that is, it is infeasible), proceed to step 4. Otherwise, let Z_{cp} denote the optimal objective function value for the current candidate problem.
6. If Z_{cp} is not better than Z_{best} (for a maximization problem $Z_{cp} \le = Z_{best}$ or for a minimization problem $Z_{cp} \ge = Z_{best}$), proceed to step 4.
7. If the solution to the current candidate problem *does not* satisfy the original integrality conditions, proceed to step 3.
8. If the solution to the current candidate problem *does* satisfy the original integrality conditions, a better integer solution has been found. Thus, let $Z_{best} = Z_{cp}$ and save the solution obtained for this candidate problem. Then go back to step 4.
9. Stop. The optimal solution has been found and has an objective function value given by the current value of Z_{best}.

The B&B algorithm is a powerful technique for solving ILP problems. A great deal of skill and creativity are involved in formulating ILPs so that they can be solved efficiently using the B&B technique. Binary variables can be useful in overcoming a number of the simplifying assumptions often made in the formulation of LP models. Here again, quite a bit of creativity might be required on the part of the model builder to identify the constraints to implement various logical conditions in a given problem.

6.19 REFERENCES

Bean, J., et al. "Selecting Tenants in a Shopping Mall." *Interfaces,* vol. 18, no. 2, 1988.

Calloway, R., M. Cummins, and J. Freeland. "Solving Spreadsheet-Based Integer Programming Models: An Example from the Telecommunications Industry." *Decision Sciences,* vol. 21, 1990.

Nauss, R. and R. Markland. "Theory and Application of an Optimizing Procedure for the Lock Box Location Analysis." *Management Science,* vol. 27, no. 8, 1981.

Nemhauser, G. and L. Wolsey. *Integer and Combinatorial Optimization.* New York: Wiley, 1988.

Peiser, R. and S. Andrus. "Phasing of Income-Producing Real Estate." *Interfaces,* vol. 13, no. 1, 1983.

Schindler, S. and T. Semmel. "Station Staffing at Pan American World Airways." *Interfaces,* vol. 23, no. 3, 1993.

Stowe, J. "An Integer Programming Solution for the Optimal Credit Investigation/Credit Granting Sequence." *Financial Management,* vol. 14, Summer 1985.

THE WORLD OF MANAGEMENT SCIENCE

Who Eats the Float?—Maryland National Improves Check Clearing Operations and Cuts Costs

Maryland National Bank (MNB) of Baltimore typically processes about 500,000 checks worth over $250,000,000 each day. Those checks not drawn on MNB or a local bank must be cleared via the Federal Reserve System, a private clearing bank, or a "direct send" by courier service to the bank on which they were drawn.

Because funds are not available until the check clears, banks try to maximize the availability of current funds by reducing the float—the time interval required for a check to clear. Banks publish an availability schedule listing the number of days before funds from a deposited check are available to the customer. If clearing time is longer than the schedule, the bank must "eat the float." If the check is cleared through the Federal Reserve and clearing takes longer than the Federal Reserve availability schedule, then the Federal Reserve "eats the float." If clearing time is actually less than the local bank's availability schedule, the customer "eats the float." The cost of float is related to the daily cost of capital.

MNB uses a system based on binary integer LP to decide the timing and method to be used for each bundle of checks of a certain type (called a cash letter). Total clearing costs (the objective function) include float costs, clearing charges from the Federal Reserve or private clearing banks, and transportation costs for direct sends. Constraints ensure that exactly one method is chosen for each check type and that a method can be used only at a time that method is available. Use of this system saves the bank $100,000 annually.

Source: Markland, Robert E., and Robert M. Nauss. "Improving Transit Check Clearing Operations at Maryland National Bank." *Interfaces,* vol. 13, no. 1, February 1983, pp. 1–9.

QUESTIONS AND PROBLEMS

1. As shown in Figure 6.1, the feasible region for an ILP consists of a relatively small, *finite* number of points, whereas the feasible region of its LP relaxation consists of an *infinite* number of points. Why, then, are ILPs so much harder to solve than LPs?
2. Identify reasonable values for M_{12} and M_{22} in the example on quantity discounts presented in section 6.15.2 of this chapter.
3. The following questions refer to the CRT Technologies project selection example presented in this chapter. Formulate a constraint to implement the conditions described in each of the following statements.
   a. Out of projects 1, 2, 4, and 6, CRT's management wants to select exactly two projects.
   b. Project 2 can be selected only if project 3 is selected and vice versa.
   c. Project 5 cannot be undertaken unless both projects 3 and 4 are also undertaken.
   d. If projects 2 and 4 are undertaken, then project 5 must also be undertaken.
4. In the CRT Technologies project selection example in this chapter, the problem indicates that surplus funds in any year are reappropriated and cannot be carried over to the next year. Suppose this is no longer the case and surplus funds may be carried over to future years.
   a. Modify the spreadsheet model given for this problem to reflect this change in assumptions.
   b. What is the optimal solution to the revised problem?
5. The following questions refer to the Blue Ridge Hot Tubs example discussed in this chapter.
   a. Suppose Howie Jones has to purchase a single piece of equipment for \$1,000 in order to produce any Aqua-Spas or Hydro-Luxes. How will this affect the formulation of the model of his decision problem?
   b. Suppose Howie must buy one piece of equipment that costs \$900 in order to produce any Aqua-Spas and a different piece of equipment that costs \$800 in order to produce any Hydro-Luxes. How will this affect the formulation of the model for his problem?
6. Garden City Beach is a popular summer vacation destination for thousands of people. Each summer, the city hires temporary lifeguards to ensure the safety of the vacationing public. Garden City's lifeguards are assigned to work five consecutive days each week and then have two days off. However, the city's insurance company requires them to have at least the following number of lifeguards on duty each day of the week:

Day	Lifeguards
Sunday	18
Monday	17
Tuesday	16
Wednesday	16
Thursday	16
Friday	14
Saturday	19

The city manager wants to determine the minimum number of lifeguards that will have to be hired.

a. Formulate an ILP for this problem.
b. Implement your model in a spreadsheet and solve it.
c. What is the optimal solution?
d. Several lifeguards have expressed a preference to be off on Saturdays and Sundays. What is the maximum number of lifeguards that can be off on the weekend without increasing the total number of lifeguards required?

7. Snookers Restaurant is open from 8:00 A.M. to 10:00 P.M. daily. Besides the hours they are open for business, workers are needed an hour before opening and an hour after closing for setup and clean up activities. The restaurant operates with both full-time and part-time workers on the following shifts:

Shift	Daily Pay Rate
7:00 A.M.–11:00 A.M.	$32
7:00 A.M.–3:00 P.M.	$80
11:00 A.M.–3:00 P.M.	$32
11:00 A.M.–7:00 P.M.	$80
3:00 P.M.–7:00 P.M.	$32
3:00 P.M.–11:00 P.M.	$80
7:00 P.M.–11:00 P.M.	$32

The following numbers of workers are needed during each of the indicated time blocks.

Hours	Workers Needed
7:00 A.M.–11:00 A.M.	11
11:00 A.M.–1:00 P.M.	24
1:00 P.M.–3:00 P.M.	16
3:00 P.M.–5:00 P.M.	10
5:00 P.M.–7:00 P.M.	22
7:00 P.M.–9:00 P.M.	17
9:00 P.M.–11:00 P.M.	6

At least one full time worker must be available during the hour before opening and after closing. Additionally, at least 30% of the employees should be full-time (8-hour) workers during the restaurant's busy periods from 11:00 A.M.–1:00 P.M. and 5:00 P.M.–7:00 P.M.

a. Formulate an ILP for this problem with the objective of minimizing total daily labor costs.
b. Implement your model in a spreadsheet and solve it.
c. What is the optimal solution?

8. A power company is considering how to increase its generating capacity to meet expected demand in its growing service area. Currently, the company has 750 megawatts (MW) of generating capacity but projects it will need the following minimum generating capacities in each of the next five years:

	Year				
	1	2	3	4	5
Minimum Capacity in Megawatts (MW)	350	250	500	400	200

The company can increase its generating capacity by purchasing four different types of generators: 10 MW, 25 MW, 50 MW, and/or 100 MW. The cost of acquiring and installing each of the four types of generators in each of the next five years is summarized in the following table:

	Cost of Generator (in $1,000s) in Year				
Generator Size	**1**	**2**	**3**	**4**	**5**
10 MW	$300	$250	$200	$170	$145
25 MW	$460	$375	$350	$280	$235
50 MW	$670	$558	$465	$380	$320
100 MW	$950	$790	$670	$550	$460

a. Formulate a mathematical programming model to determine the least costly way of expanding the company's generating assests to the minimum required levels.
b. Implement your model in a spreadsheet and solve it.
c. What is the optimal solution?

9. Health Care Systems of Florida (HCSF) is planning to build a number of new emergency-care clinics in central Florida. HCSF management has divided a map of the area into seven regions. They want to locate the emergency centers so that all seven regions will be conveniently served by at least one facility. Five possible sites are available for constructing the new facilities. The regions that can be served conveniently by each site are indicated by an X in the following table:

	Possible Building Sites				
Region	**Sanford**	**Altamonte**	**Apopka**	**Casselberry**	**Maitland**
1	X		X		
2	X	X		X	X
3		X		X	
4			X		X
5	X	X			
6			X		X
7				X	X
Cost ($1,000s)	$450	$650	$550	$500	$525

a. Formulate an ILP problem to determine which sites should be selected in order to provide convenient service to all locations in the least costly manner.
b. Implement your model in a spreadsheet and solve it.
c. What is the optimal solution?

10. Kentwood Electronics manufactures three components for stereo systems: CD players, tape decks, and stereo tuners. The wholesale price and manufacturing cost of each item are:

Component	Wholesale Price	Manufacturing Cost
CD Player	$150	$75
Tape Deck	$ 85	$35
Stereo Tuner	$ 70	$30

Each CD player produced requires three hours of assembly; each tape deck requires two hours of assembly; and each tuner requires one hour of assembly. However, the company manufactures these products only in batches of 150—partial batches are not allowed. The marketing department believes it can sell no more than 150,000 CD players, 100,000 tape decks, and 90,000 stereo tuners. It expects a demand for at least 50,000 units of each item and wants to be able to meet this demand. If Kentwood has 400,000 hours of assembly time available, how many batches of CD players, tape decks, and stereo tuners should it produce in order to maximize profits while meeting the minimum demand figures supplied by marketing?

a. Formulate an ILP model for this problem. (*Hint:* Let your decision variables represent the number of batches of each item to produce.)
b. Create a spreadsheet model for this problem and solve it.
c. What is the optimal solution?

11. Radford Castings can produce brake shoes on six different machines. The following table summarizes the manufacturing costs associated with producing the brake shoes on each machine along with the available capacity on each machine. If the company has received an order for 1,800 brake shoes, how should it schedule these machines?

Machine	Fixed Cost	Variable Cost	Capacity
1	$1,000	$21	500
2	$ 950	$23	600
3	$ 875	$25	750
4	$ 850	$24	400
5	$ 800	$20	600
6	$ 700	$26	800

a. Formulate an ILP model for this problem.
b. Create a spreadsheet model for this problem and solve it.
c. What is the optimal solution?

12. The teenage daughter of a recently deceased movie star inherited a number of items from her famous father's estate. Rather than convert these assets to cash immediately, her financial advisor has recommended that she let some of these assets appreciate in value before disposing of them. An appraiser has given the following estimates of the assets' worth (in $1,000s) for each of the next five years.

	Year 1	Year 2	Year 3	Year 4	Year 5
Car	$ 35	$ 37	$ 39	$ 42	$ 45
Piano	$ 16	$ 17	$ 18	$ 19	$ 20
Necklace	$125	$130	$136	$139	$144
Desk	$ 25	$ 27	$ 29	$ 30	$ 33
Golf Clubs	$ 40	$ 43	$ 46	$ 50	$ 52
Humidor	$ 5	$ 7	$ 8	$ 10	$ 11

Knowing this teenager's propensity to spend money, her financial advisor wants to develop a plan to dispose of these assets that will maximize the amount of money received and ensure that at least $30,000 of new funds become available each year to pay her college tuition.

a. Formulate an ILP model for this problem.
b. Create a spreadsheet model for this problem and solve it.
c. What is the optimal solution?

13. A developer of video game software has seven proposals for new games. Unfortunately, the company cannot develop all the proposals because its budget for new projects is limited to $950,000 and it has only 20 programmers to assign to new projects. The financial requirements, returns, and the number of programmers required by each project are summarized in the following table. Projects 2 and 6 require specialized programming knowledge that only one of the programmers has. Both of these projects cannot be selected because the programmer with the necessary skills can be assigned to only one of the projects. (Note: All dollar amounts represent thousands.)

Project	Programmers Required	Capital Required	Estimated NPV
1	7	$250	$650
2	6	$175	$550
3	9	$300	$600
4	5	$150	$450
5	6	$145	$375
6	4	$160	$525
7	8	$325	$750

a. Formulate an ILP model for this problem.
b. Create a spreadsheet model for this problem and solve it.
c. What is the optimal solution?

14. Tropicsun is a leading grower and distributor of fresh citrus products with three large citrus groves scattered around central Florida in the cities of Mt. Dora, Eustis, and Clermont. Tropicsun currently has 275,000 bushels of citrus at the grove in Mt. Dora, 400,000 bushels at the grove in Eustis, and 300,000 at the grove in Clermont. Tropicsun has citrus processing plants in Ocala, Orlando, and Leesburg with processing capacities to handle 200,000, 600,000, and 225,000 bushels, respectively. Tropicsun contracts with a local trucking company to transport its fruit from the groves to the processing plants. The trucking company charges a flat rate of $8 per mile regardless of how many bushels of fruit are transported. The following table summarizes the distances (in miles) between each grove and processing plant:

Distances (in Miles) Between Groves and Plants

	Processing Plant		
Grove	Ocala	Orlando	Leesburg
Mt. Dora	21	50	40
Eustis	35	30	22
Clermont	55	20	25

Tropicsun wants to determine how many bushels to ship from each grove to each processing plant in order to minimize the total transportation cost.
a. Formulate an ILP model for this problem.
b. Create a spreadsheet model for this problem and solve it.
c. What is the optimal solution?

15. A manufacturer is considering alternatives for building new plants in order to be located closer to three of its primary customers with whom it intends to develop long-term, sole-supplier relationships. The net cost of manufacturing and transporting each unit of the product to its customers will vary depending on where the plant is built and the production capacity of the plant. These costs are summarized in the following table:

	Net Cost per Unit to Supply Customer		
Plant	**X**	**Y**	**Z**
1	35	30	45
2	45	40	50
3	70	65	50
4	20	45	25
5	65	45	45

The annual demand for products from customers X, Y, and Z is expected to be 40,000, 25,000, and 35,000 units, respectively. The annual production capacity and construction costs for each plant are:

Plant	Production Capacity	Construction Cost (in $1,000s)
1	40,000	$1,325
2	30,000	$1,100
3	50,000	$1,500
4	20,000	$1,200
5	40,000	$1,400

The company wants to determine which plant to build in order to satisfy customer demand at a minimum total cost.

a. Formulate an ILP model for this problem.
b. Create a spreadsheet model for this problem and solve it.
c. What is the optimal solution?

16. Refer to the previous question. Suppose plants 1 and 2 represent different building alternatives for the same site (that is, only one of these plants can be built). Similarly, suppose plants 4 and 5 represent different building alternatives for another site.

a. What additional constraints are required to model these new conditions?
b. Revise the spreadsheet to reflect these additional constraints and solve the resulting problem.
c. What is the optimal solution?

17. A company manufactures three products: A, B, and C. The company currently has an order for three units of product A, 7 units of product B, and 4 units of product C. There is no inventory for any of these products. All three products require special processing that can be done on one of two machines. The cost of producing each product on each machine is summarized in the following table:

	Cost of Producing a Unit of Product		
Machine	**A**	**B**	**C**
1	$13	$ 9	$10
2	$11	$12	$ 8

The time required to produce each product on each machine is summarized in the following table:

Time (Hours) Needed to Produce a Unit of Product

Machine	A	B	C
1	0.4	1.1	0.9
2	0.5	1.2	1.3

Assume machine 1 can be used for eight hours and machine 2 can be used for six hours. Each machine must undergo a special setup operation to prepare it to produce each product. After completing this setup for a product, any number of that product type can be produced. The setup costs for producing each product on each machine are summarized in the following table.

Setup Costs for Producing a Unit of Product

Machine	A	B	C
1	$55	$93	$60
2	$65	$58	$75

a. Formulate an ILP model to determine how many units of each product to produce on each machine in order to meet demand at a minimum cost.
b. Implement your model in a spreadsheet and solve it.
c. What is the optimal solution?

18. Clampett Oil purchases crude oil products from suppliers in Texas (TX), Oklahoma (OK), Pennsylvania (PA), and Alabama (AL), from which it refines four end products: gasoline, kerosene, heating oil, and asphalt. Because of differences in the quality and chemical characteristics of the oil from the different suppliers, the amount of each end product that can be refined from a barrel of crude oil varies depending on the source of the crude. Additionally, the amount of crude available from each source varies, as does the cost of a barrel of crude from each supplier. These values are summarized in the following table. For example, the first line of this table indicates that a barrel of crude oil from Texas can be refined into 2 barrels of gasoline, 2.8 barrels of kerosene, 1.7 barrels of heating oil, or 2.4 barrels of asphalt. Each supplier requires a minimum purchase of at least 500 barrels.

Raw Material Characteristics

Crude Oils	Barrels Available	Possible Production per Barrel				Cost Per Barrel	Trucking Cost
		Gas	Kero.	Heat	Asphalt		
TX	1,500	2.00	2.80	1.70	2.40	$22	$1,500
OK	2,000	1.80	2.30	1.75	1.90	$21	$1,700
PA	1,500	2.30	2.20	1.60	2.60	$22	$1,500
AL	1,800	2.10	2.60	1.90	2.40	$23	$1,400

The company owns a tanker truck that picks up whatever crude oil it purchases. This truck can hold 2,000 barrels of crude oil. The cost of sending the truck to pick up oil from the various locations is shown in the column labeled "Trucking Cost." The company's plans for its next production cycle specify 750 barrels of gasoline, 800 barrels of kerosene, 1,000 barrels of heating oil, and 300 barrels of asphalt to be produced.

a. Formulate an ILP model that can be solved to determine the purchasing plan that will allow the company to implement its production plan at the least cost.
b. Implement this model in a spreadsheet and solve it.
c. What is the optimal solution?

19. The Clampett Oil Company has a tanker truck that it uses to deliver fuel to customers. The tanker has five different storage compartments with capacities to hold 2,500, 2,000, 1,500, 1,800, and 2,300 gallons, respectively. The company has an order to deliver 2,700 gallons of diesel fuel; 3,500 gallons of regular unleaded gasoline; and 4,200 gallons of premium unleaded gasoline. If each storage compartment can hold only one type of fuel, how should Clampett Oil load the tanker? If it is impossible to load the truck with the full order, the company wants to minimize the total number of gallons by which the order is short. (*Hint:* Consider using slack variables to represent shortage amounts.)
    a. Formulate an ILP model for this problem.
    b. Implement this model in a spreadsheet and solve it.
    c. What is the optimal solution?

20. Dan Boyd is a financial planner trying to determine how to invest $100,000 for one of his clients. The cash flows for the investments under consideration are summarized in the following table:

Summary of Cash In-Flows and Out-Flows (at Beginning of Year)

	A	B	C	D	E
2001	–1.00	0.00	–1.00	0.00	–1.00
2002	+0.45	–1.00	0.00	0.00	0.00
2003	+1.05	0.00	0.00	–1.00	1.25
2004	0.00	+1.30	+1.65	+1.30	0.00

For example, if Dan invests $1 in investment A at the beginning of 2001, he will receive $0.45 at the beginning of 2002 and another $1.05 at the beginning of 2003. Alternatively, he can invest $1 in investment B at the beginning of 2002 and receive $1.30 at the beginning of 2004. Entries of "0.00" in the previous table indicate times when no cash in-flows or out-flows can occur. At the beginning of a year, Dan can place any or all of the available money in a money market account that is expected to yield 5% per year. The minimum required investment for each of the possible investments is $50,000. How should Dan plan his investments if he wants to maximize the amount of money available to his client in 2004?
    a. Formulate an ILP model for this problem.
    b. Create a spreadsheet model for this problem and solve it using Solver.
    c. What is the optimal solution?

21. The Mega-Bucks Corporation is planning its production schedule for the next four weeks and is forecasting the following demand for compound X—a key raw material used in its production process:

Compound X

Week	Required
1	400 lbs.
2	150 lbs.
3	200 lbs.
4	350 lbs.

The company currently has no compound X on hand. The supplier of this product delivers only in batch sizes that are multiples of 100 pounds (0, 100, 200, 300, and so on). The price of this material is $125 per 100 pounds. Deliveries can be arranged weekly, but there is a delivery charge of $50. Mega-Bucks estimates that it costs $15 for each 100 pounds of compound X held in inventory from one week to the next. Assuming Mega-Bucks does not want more than 50 pounds of compound X in inventory at the end of week 4, how much should it order each week so that the demand for this product will be met in the least costly manner?

a. Formulate an ILP model for this problem.
b. Create a spreadsheet model for this problem and solve it using Solver.
c. What is the optimal solution?

22. An automobile manufacturer is considering mechanical design changes in one of its top-selling cars to reduce the weight of the car by at least 400 pounds to improve its fuel efficiency. Design engineers have identified ten changes that could be made in the car to make it lighter (for example, using composite body pieces rather than metal). The weight saved by each design change and the estimated costs of implementing each change are summarized in the following table:

Design Change	Weight Saved	Cost
1	50 lbs.	$150,000
2	75 lbs.	350,000
3	25 lbs.	50,000
4	150 lbs.	450,000
5	60 lbs.	90,000
6	95 lbs.	35,000
7	200 lbs.	650,000
8	40 lbs.	75,000
9	80 lbs.	110,000
10	30 lbs.	30,000

Changes 4 and 7 represent alternative ways of modifying the engine block and, therefore, only one of these options could be selected. The company wants to determine which changes to make in order to reduce the total weight of the car by at least 400 pounds in the least costly manner.

a. Formulate an ILP model for this problem.
b. Create a spreadsheet model for this problem and solve it.
c. What is the optimal solution?

23. Darten Restaurants owns and operates several different restaurant chains including Red Snapper and the Olive Grove. The company is considering opening a number of new units in Ohio. There are ten different sites available

for the company to build new restaurants and the company can build either type of restaurant at a given site. The following table summarizes the estimated net present value (NPV) of the cash flows resulting from locating each type of restaurant at each of the sites and also indicates which sites are within 15 miles of each other. (Note: Dollars are in millions.)

Site	Red Snapper NPV	Olive Grove NPV	Other Sites within 15 Miles
1	$11.8	$16.2	2, 3, 4
2	13.3	13.8	1, 3, 5
3	19.0	14.6	1, 2, 4, 5
4	17.8	12.4	1, 3
5	10.0	13.7	2, 3, 9
6	16.1	19.0	7
7	13.3	10.8	6, 8
8	18.8	15.2	7
9	17.2	15.9	5, 10
10	14.4	16.8	9

a. Suppose the company does not want to build two units from the same chain within 15 miles of each other (for example, it does not want to build two Red Snappers within 15 miles of each other nor is it willing to build two Olive Groves within 15 miles of each other). Create a spreadsheet model to determine which (if any) restaurant it should build at each site in order to maximize total NPV.
b. What is the optimal solution?
c. Now additionally suppose the company does not want to build a Red Snapper unless it also builds an Olive Grove at another site within 15 miles. Modify your spreadsheet model to determine which (if any) restaurant it should build at each site in order to maximize total NPV.
d. What is the optimal solution?

24. Paul Bergey is in charge of loading cargo ships for International Cargo Company (ICC) at the port in Newport News, Virginia. Paul is preparing a loading plan for an ICC freighter destined for Ghana. An agricultural commodities dealer wants to transport the following products aboard this ship.

Commodity	Amount Available (tons)	Volume per Ton (cubic feet)	Profit per Ton ($)
1	4,800	40	70
2	2,500	25	50
3	1,200	60	60
4	1,700	55	80

Paul can elect to load any and/or all of the available commodities. However, the ship has three cargo holds with the following capacity restrictions:

Cargo Hold	Weight Capacity (tons)	Volume Capacity (cubic feet)
Forward	3,000	145,000
Center	6,000	180,000
Rear	4,000	155,000

Only one type of commodity can be placed into any cargo hold. However, because of balance considerations, the weight in the forward cargo hold must be within 10% of the weight in the rear cargo hold and the center cargo hold must be between 40% to 60% of the total weight on board.

a. Formulate an ILP model for this problem.
b. Create a spreadsheet model for this problem and solve it using Solver.
c. What is the optimal solution?

25. KPS Communications is planning to bring wireless Internet access to the town of Ames, Iowa. Using a geographic information system, KPS has divided Ames into the following 5 by 5 grid. The values in each block of the grid indicate the expected annual revenue (in $1,000s) KPS will receive if wireless Internet service is provided to the geographic area represented by each block.

Expected Annual Revenue by Area (in $1,000s)

$34	$43	$62	$42	$34
$64	$43	$71	$48	$65
$57	$57	$51	$61	$30
$32	$38	$70	$56	$40
$68	$73	$30	$56	$44

KPS can build wireless towers in any block in the grid at a cost of $150,000 per tower. Each tower can provide wireless service to the block it is in and to all adjacent blocks. (Blocks are considered to be adjacent if they share a side. Blocks touching only at cornerpoint are not considered adjacent.) KPS wants to determine how many towers to build and where to build them in order to maximize profits in the first year of operations. (Note: If a block can receive wireless service from two different towers, the revenue for that block should only be counted once.)

a. Create a spreadsheet model for this problem and solve it.
b. What is the optimal solution and how much money will KPS make in the first year?
c. Suppose KPS is required to provide wireless service to all of the blocks. What is the optimal solution and how much money will KPS make in the first year?

26. The emergency services coordinator for Clarke County is interested in locating the county's two ambulances to maximize the number of residents that can be reached within four minutes in emergency situations. The county is divided into five regions, and the average times required to travel from one region to the next are summarized in the following table:

	To Region				
From Region	**1**	**2**	**3**	**4**	**5**
1	0	4	6	3	2
2	4	0	2	3	6
3	6	2	0	5	3
4	3	3	5	0	7
5	2	6	3	7	0

The population in regions 1, 2, 3, 4, and 5 are estimated as 45,000, 65,000, 28,000, 52,000, and 43,000, respectively. In which two regions should the ambulances be placed?

a. Formulate an ILP model for this problem.
b. Implement your model in a spreadsheet and solve it.
c. What is the optimal solution?

27. Ken Stark is an operations analyst for an insurance company in Muncie, Indiana. Over the next 6 weeks, the company needs to send 2,028,415 pieces of marketing literature to customers in the 16 states shown in the following table.

State	Mailing Pieces
AZ	82,380
CA	212,954
CT	63,796
GA	136,562
IL	296,479
MA	99,070
ME	38,848
MN	86,207
MT	33,309
NC	170,997
NJ	104,974
NV	29,608
OH	260,858
OR	63,605
TX	214,076
VA	134,692
TOTAL	**2,028,415**

To coordinate with other marketing efforts, all the mailings for a given state must go out the same week (*i.e.*, if Ken decides to schedule mailings for Georgia in week 2, then all of the 136,562 pieces of mail for Georgia must be sent that week). Ken wants to balance the workload in each week as much as possible and, in particular, wants to minimize the maximum amount of mail to be processed in any given week during the 6-week period.

a. Create a spreadsheet model to determine which states should be processed each week in order to achieve Ken's objective.
b. What is the optimal solution?

28. The CoolAire Company manufactures air conditioners that are sold to five different retail customers across the United States. The company is evaluating its manufacturing and logistics strategy to ensure that it is operating in the most efficient manner possible. The company can produce air conditioners at six plants across the country and stock these units in any of four different warehouses. The cost of manufacturing and shipping a unit between each plant and warehouse is summarized in the following table along with the monthly capacity and fixed cost of operating each plant.

	Warehouse 1	Warehouse 2	Warehouse 3	Warehouse 4	Fixed Cost	Capacity
Plant 1	$700	$1,000	$900	$1,200	$55,000	300
Plant 2	$800	$ 500	$600	$ 700	$40,000	200
Plant 3	$850	$ 600	$700	$ 500	$45,000	300
Plant 4	$600	$ 800	$500	$ 600	$50,000	250
Plant 5	$500	$ 600	$450	$ 700	$42,000	350
Plant 6	$700	$ 600	$750	$ 500	$40,000	400

Similarly, the per-unit cost of shipping units from each warehouse to each customer is shown in the following table, along with the monthly fixed cost of operating each warehouse.

	Customer 1	Customer 2	Customer 3	Customer 4	Customer 5	Fixed Cost
Warehouse 1	$40	$80	$60	$90	$50	$40,000
Warehouse 2	$60	$50	$75	$40	$35	$50,000
Warehouse 3	$55	$40	$65	$60	$80	$35,000
Warehouse 4	$80	$30	$80	$50	$60	$60,000

The monthly demand from each customer is summarized in the following table.

	Customer 1	Customer 2	Customer 3	Customer 4	Customer 5
Demand	200	300	200	150	250

CoolAire wants to determine which plants and warehouses it should operate to meet demand in the most cost-effective manner.

a. Create a spreadsheet model for this problem and solve it.
b. Which plants and warehouses should CoolAire operate?
c. What is the optimal shipping plan?

29. CaroliNet is an Internet service provider for residential consumers in the state of North Carolina. The company is planning to expand and offer Internet service in South Carolina as well. The company wants to establish a set of hubs throughout the state in such a way to ensure that all residents of the state can access at least one of their hubs via a local phone call. Local phone service is available between all adjacent counties throughout the state. Figure 6.34 (and the file Fig6-34.xls on your data disk) show an Excel spreadsheet with a matrix indicating county adjacencies throughout the state. That is, values of 1 in the matrix indicate counties that are adjacent to one another, whereas values of 0 indicate counties that are not adjacent to one another. (Note that a county is also considered to be adjacent to itself.)
    a. Assume CaroliNet wants to minimize the number of hubs they must install. In what counties should the hubs be installed?
    b. Suppose CaroliNet is willing to install hubs in exactly ten different counties. In what counties should the hubs be installed if the company wants to maximize their service coverage?
30. Solve the following problem manually using the B&B algorithm. You can use the computer to solve the individual problems generated. Create a branch-and-bound tree to display the steps you complete.

FIGURE 6.34
County adjacency matrix for the CaroliNet ISP location problem

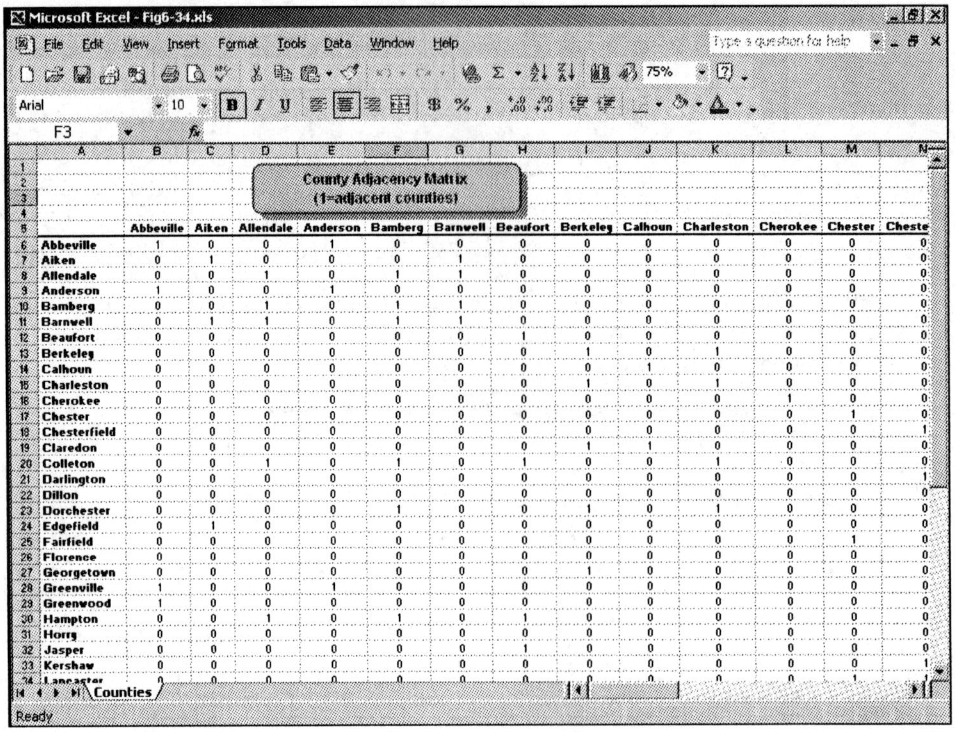

County Adjacency Matrix
(1=adjacent counties)

	Abbeville	Aiken	Allendale	Anderson	Bamberg	Barnwell	Beaufort	Berkeley	Calhoun	Charleston	Cherokee	Chester	Cheste
Abbeville	1	0	0	1	0	0	0	0	0	0	0	0	0
Aiken	0	1	0	0	0	1	0	0	0	0	0	0	0
Allendale	0	0	1	0	1	1	0	0	0	0	0	0	0
Anderson	1	0	0	1	0	0	0	0	0	0	0	0	0
Bamberg	0	0	1	0	1	1	0	0	0	0	0	0	0
Barnwell	0	1	1	0	1	1	0	0	0	0	0	0	0
Beaufort	0	0	0	0	0	0	1	0	0	0	0	0	0
Berkeley	0	0	0	0	0	0	0	1	0	1	0	0	0
Calhoun	0	0	0	0	0	0	0	0	1	0	0	0	0
Charleston	0	0	0	0	0	0	0	1	0	1	0	0	0
Cherokee	0	0	0	0	0	0	0	0	0	0	1	0	0
Chester	0	0	0	0	0	0	0	0	0	0	0	1	0
Chesterfield	0	0	0	0	0	0	0	0	0	0	0	0	1
Claredon	0	0	0	0	0	0	0	1	1	0	0	0	0
Colleton	0	0	1	0	1	0	1	0	0	1	0	0	0
Darlington	0	0	0	0	0	0	0	0	0	0	0	0	1
Dillon	0	0	0	0	0	0	0	0	0	0	0	0	0
Dorchester	0	0	0	0	1	0	0	1	0	1	0	0	0
Edgefield	0	1	0	0	0	0	0	0	0	0	0	0	0
Fairfield	0	0	0	0	0	0	0	0	0	0	0	1	0
Florence	0	0	0	0	0	0	0	0	0	0	0	0	0
Georgetown	0	0	0	0	0	0	0	1	0	0	0	0	0
Greenville	1	0	0	1	0	0	0	0	0	0	0	0	0
Greenwood	1	0	0	0	0	0	0	0	0	0	0	0	0
Hampton	0	0	1	0	1	0	1	0	0	0	0	0	0
Horry	0	0	0	0	0	0	0	0	0	0	0	0	0
Jasper	0	0	0	0	0	0	1	0	0	0	0	0	0
Kershaw	0	0	0	0	0	0	0	0	0	0	0	0	1
Lancaster	0	0	0	0	0	0	0	0	0	0	0	1	1

$$
\begin{aligned}
\text{MAX:} \quad & 6X_1 + 8X_2 \\
\text{Subject to:} \quad & 6X_1 + 3X_2 \leq 18 \\
& 2X_1 + 3X_2 \leq 9 \\
& X_1, X_2 \geq 0 \\
& X_1, X_2 \text{ must be integers}
\end{aligned}
$$

31. During the execution of the B&B algorithm, many candidate problems are likely to be generated and awaiting further analysis. In the B&B example in this chapter, we chose the next candidate problem to analyze in a rather arbitrary way. What other, more structured ways might we use to select the next candidate problem? What are the pros and cons of these techniques?

CASE 6.1: POWER DISPATCHING AT OLD DOMINION

The demand for electricity varies greatly during the day. Because large amounts of electricity cannot be stored economically, electric power companies cannot manufacture electricity and hold it in inventory until it is needed. Instead, power companies must balance the production of power with the demand for power in real time. One of the greatest uncertainties in forecasting the demand for electricity is the weather. Most power companies employ meteorologists who constantly monitor weather patterns and update computer models that predict the demand for power over a rolling, seven-day planning horizon. This forecasted seven-day window of demand is referred to as the company's load-profile and is typically updated every hour basis.

Every power company has a base-load demand that is relatively constant. To satisfy this base-load demand, a power company utilizes its most economical, low-cost power generating assets and keeps them running continuously. To meet additional demands for power above the base-load, a power company must dispatch (or turn on) other generators. These other generators are sometimes called "peakers" because they help the power company meet the highest demands or peak-loads. It costs different amounts of money to bring different types of peakers on-line. And because different peakers use different types of fuel (*e.g.*, coal, gas, bio-mass), their operating costs per megawatt (MW) generated also differ. Thus, dispatchers for a power company continually have to decide which generator to bring on-line or turn off to meet their load profile in the least costly manner.

The Old Dominion Power (ODP) Company provides electrical power throughout Virginia and the Carolinas. Suppose ODP's peak-load profile (that is the estimated load above base-load) in MWs is currently estimated as follows:

	Day						
	1	2	3	4	5	6	7
Load (in MWs)	4,300	3,700	3,900	4,000	4,700	4,800	3,600

ODP currently has three peaking generators off-line that are available to help meet this load. The generators have the following operating characteristics:

Generator Location	Startup Cost	Cost per Day	Maximum MW Capacity per Day
New River	$800	$200 + $5 per MW	2,100
Galax	$1,000	$300 + $4 per MW	1,900
James River	$700	$250 + $7 per MW	3,000

To get an off-line generator up and running, a startup cost must be paid. Once a generator is running, it can continue to run indefinitely without having to pay this startup cost again. However, if the generator is turned off at any point, the setup cost must be paid again to get it back up and running. Each day that a generator runs, there is both a fixed and variable cost that must be paid. For example, any day that the New River generator is on-line, it incurs a fixed cost of $200 plus $5 per MW generated. So, even if this generator is not producing any MWs, it still costs $200 per day to keep it running (so as to avoid a restart). When they are running, each generator can supply up to the maximum daily MWs listed in the final column of the table.

1. Formulate a mathematical programming model for ODP's power dispatching problem.
2. Implement your model in a spreadsheet and solve it.
3. What is the optimal solution?
4. Suppose ODP can sometimes buy power from a competitor. How much should ODP be willing to pay to acquire 300 MW of power on day 1? Explain your answer.
5. What concerns, if any, would you have about implementing this plan?

CASE 6.2: THE MASTERDEBT LOCKBOX PROBLEM

MasterDebt is a national credit card company with thousands of card holders located across the United States. Every day throughout the month, MasterDebt sends out statements to different customers summarizing their charges for the previous month. Customers then have 30 days to remit a payment for their bills. MasterDebt includes a preaddressed envelope with each statement for customers to use in making their payments.

One of the critical problems facing MasterDebt involves determining which address to put on the preaddressed envelopes sent to various parts of the country. The amount of time that elapses between when a customer writes his check and when MasterDebt receives the cash for the check is referred to as ***float.*** Checks can spend several days floating in the mail and in processing before being cashed. This float time represents lost revenue to MasterDebt because if they could receive and cash these checks immediately, they could earn additional interest on these funds.

To reduce the interest being lost from floating checks, MasterDebt wants to implement a lockbox system to speed the processing of checks. Under such a system, MasterDebt might have all their customers on the West Coast send their payments to a bank in Sacramento which, for a fee, processes the checks and deposits the proceeds in a MasterDebt account. Similarly, MasterDebt might arrange for a similar service with a bank on the East Coast for their customers there. Such lockbox systems are a common method companies use to improve their cash flows.

MasterDebt has identified six different cities as possible lockbox sites. The annual fixed cost of operating a lockbox in each of the possible locations is shown in the following table.

Annual Lockbox Operating Costs (in $1,000s)

Sacramento	Denver	Chicago	Dallas	New York	Atlanta
$25	$30	$35	$35	$30	$35

An analysis was done to determine the average number of days a check floats when sent from seven different regions of the country to each of these six cities. The results of this analysis are summarized in the following table. This table indicates, for instance, that a check sent from the central region of the country to New York spends an average of three days in the mail and in processing before MasterDebt actually receives the cash for the check.

Average Days of Float Between Regions and Possible Lockbox Locations

	Sacramento	Denver	Chicago	Dallas	New York	Atlanta
Central	4	2	2	2	3	3
Mid-Atlantic	6	4	3	4	2	2
Midwest	3	2	3	2	5	4
Northeast	6	4	2	5	2	3
Northwest	2	3	5	4	6	7
Southeast	7	4	3	2	4	2
Southwest	2	3	6	2	7	6

Further analysis was done to determine the average amount of payments being sent from each region of the country. These results are shown next.

Average Daily Payments (in $1,000s) by Region

	Payments
Central	$45
Mid-Atlantic	$65
Midwest	$50
Northeast	$90
Northwest	$70
Southeast	$80
Southwest	$60

Thus, if payments from the Central Region are sent to New York, on any given day, there is an average of $135,000 in undeposited checks from the Central Region. Because MasterDebt can earn 15% on cash deposits, it would be losing $20,250 per year in potential interest on these checks alone.

a. Which of the six potential lockbox locations should MasterDebt use and to which lockbox location should each region be assigned?
b. How would your solution change if a maximum of four regions could be assigned to any lockbox location?

CASE 6.3: REMOVING MORE SNOW IN MONTREAL

Based on: Campbell, J. and Langevin, A. "The Snow Disposal Assignment Problem." *Journal of the Operational Research Society*, 1995, pp. 919–929.

Snow removal and disposal are important and expensive activities in Montreal and many northern cities. Although snow can be cleared from streets and sidewalks by plowing and shoveling, in prolonged sub-freezing temperatures, the resulting banks of accumulated snow can impede pedestrian and vehicular traffic and must be removed.

To allow timely removal and disposal of snow, a city is divided up into several sectors and snow removal operations are carried out concurrently in each sector. In Montreal, accumulated snow is loaded onto trucks and hauled away to disposal sites (*e.g.*, rivers, quarries, sewer chutes, surface holding areas). For contractual reasons, each sector may be assigned to only a ***single*** disposal site. (However, each disposal site may receive snow from multiple sectors.) The different types of disposal sites can accommodate different amounts of snow due to either the physical size of the disposal facility or environmental restrictions on the amount of snow (often contaminated by salt and de-icing chemicals) that can be dumped into rivers. The annual capacities for five different snow disposal sites are shown in the following table (in 1,000s of cubic meters).

	Disposal Site				
	1	**2**	**3**	**4**	**5**
Capacity	350	250	500	400	200

The cost of removing and disposing of snow depends mainly on the distance it must be trucked. For planning purposes, the city of Montreal uses the straight-line distance between the center of each sector to each of the various disposal sites as an approximation of the cost involved in transporting snow between these locations. The following table summarizes these distances (in kilometers) for ten sectors in the city.

	Disposal Site				
Sector	**1**	**2**	**3**	**4**	**5**
1	3.4	1.4	4.9	7.4	9.3
2	2.4	2.1	8.3	9.1	8.8
3	1.4	2.9	3.7	9.4	8.6
4	2.6	3.6	4.5	8.2	8.9
5	1.5	3.1	2.1	7.9	8.8
6	4.2	4.9	6.5	7.7	6.1
7	4.8	6.2	9.9	6.2	5.7
8	5.4	6.0	5.2	7.6	4.9
9	3.1	4.1	6.6	7.5	7.2
10	3.2	6.5	7.1	6.0	8.3

Using historical snowfall data, the city is able to estimate the annual volume of snow requiring removal in each sector as four times the length of streets in the sectors in meters (*i.e.*, it is assumed each linear meter of street generates four cubic meters of snow to remove over an entire year). The following table estimates the snow removal requirements (in 1,000s of cubic meters) for each sector in the coming year.

Estimated Annual Snow Removal Requirements

1	2	3	4	5	6	7	8	9	10
153	152	154	138	127	129	111	110	130	135

1. Create a spreadsheet that Montreal could use to determine the most efficient snow removal plan for the coming year. Assume it costs $0.10 to transport one cubic meter of snow one kilometer.
2. What is the optimal solution?
3. How much will it cost Montreal to implement your snow disposal plan?
4. Ignoring the capacity restrictions at the disposal sites, how many different assignments of sectors to disposal sites are possible?
5. Suppose Montreal can increase the capacity of a single disposal site by 100,000 cubic meters. Which disposal site's capacity (if any) should be increased and how much should the city be willing to pay to obtain this extra disposal capacity?

CASE 6.4: PLANNING A TOUR OF NEW YORK CITY

Contributed by Jack Yurkiewicz. Lubin School of Business, Pace University.

John Peters kept humming the score from *On the Town*, his favorite Broadway show and movie musical, over and over. *On the Town* is a whimsical lark written by Leonard Bernstein in the 1940s that tells the story of three sailors on a 24-hour shore leave in New York City. The sailors wanted to see as many sights as possible in the short time they had. John remembers seeing the movie version of the musical for the first time and being awed by the sights of the city, particularly the Statue of Liberty, Rockefeller Center, and the many museums. Since seeing the movie, John's great wish has been to visit New York City.

Now, John has an opportunity to fulfill his wish. John works as an accountant for a firm in Idaho and is being sent by his company on a business trip to Europe. He must stop in New York City to get his connecting flight, and with some juggling of the airline schedules, John managed to arrange a two-day stopover in New York City. In those two days, John wants to see as much of the city as he can.

What should John see? He has about 20 hours total in which to visit some of the many attractions that the city has to offer. These 20 hours take into account the travel time between sights, time for food and rest, times when the attractions are closed, and so on. There are literally hundreds of places to visit, so John knows that he has to narrow down his choices. He decides to consult the *Michelin Guide,* which is known for its reliable and accurate assessments of the various sights in both foreign and domestic cities. The attractions are rated by stars. A three-star attraction is very highly recommended, a two-star attraction is recommended, a one-star rating indicates the attraction is interesting, and a no-star rating indicates that the attraction is worth seeing only if time allows. Because of the limited time John has, he feels that he should visit only three- and two-star attractions; anything less would not be worth his time on this trip.

The *Michelin Guide* indicates that New York City has almost two dozen three-star attractions and almost three dozen two-star attractions. Because almost all these attractions are on Manhattan Island (New York City), John will ignore sights in the other four boroughs. Based on his interests, John further decides to omit some three-star and two-star attractions, including the Bronx Zoo, Rockefeller Center, and The Cloisters. After reading more about each attraction, he came up with a list of 11 possible attractions he wants to visit. John knows that he cannot do justice to these 11 attractions in just 20 hours. The *Michelin Guide* gives recommendations for the number of hours that a visitor should spend at each attraction. John knows that these are rough time estimates. For example, he could easily spend the entire 20 hours at the Metropolitan Museum of Art, one of the world's great art galleries, instead of just the five hours recommended by the *Michelin Guide.* However, spending one hour there would not be enough either, and if he had to do that, perhaps he would just skip that sight entirely.

John decides that he will not spend more than three hours at any one attraction, no matter how much there is to see or do there. To keep matters simple, he decides to measure the time spent at an attraction in intervals of hours; that is, all visitation times are rounded to the nearest hour. Thus, he could spend 1, 2, or 3 hours at a sight, or even 0 hours (which means he will not visit that sight at all). John is more interested in some attractions than others, and visiting these for longer times will be more enjoyable for him than visiting less desirable sights. Thus, a three-hour visit to the Frick Collection, described by Michelin as "one of the most beautiful private museums in the world," housing everything from Old Masters to Louis XVI furniture, will give him less enjoyment than a three-hour visit to the Metropolitan Museum of Art. This is not only because the Metropolitan offers more to see, but the Frick Collection requires less time to see everything than the Metropolitan. So a one-hour visit to the Frick Collection will give him more enjoyment than a one-hour visit to the Metropolitan. John must consider the number of sights to see at an attraction, how much time he has to spend there, and how desirable it is for him to visit the attraction.

John put all these factors in the following table. The table shows the attraction, its assigned number of Michelin stars, how much time the *Michelin Guide* recommends a visitor spend there, and how much enjoyment John will get from spending 1, 2, or 3 hours at the attraction. He measures enjoyment on an arbitrary scale of 0 to 100.

			Actual Visit Time			
			0 hrs	1 hr	2 hrs	3 hrs
Attraction	**Stars**	***Michelin Guide's* Recommended Visit Time**	**Enjoyment Rating**			
Statue of Liberty	***	4.0	0	10	50	80
World Trade Center Memorial	***	2.5	0	50	90	95
Greenwich Village	**	2.0	0	30	40	60
Empire State Building	***	2.0	0	25	75	90
United Nations	***	3.0	0	40	50	75
Museum of Modern Art	***	2.5	0	35	50	75
Frick Collection	***	2.5	0	40	50	60
Whitney Museum	**	1.5	0	20	45	65
Metropolitan Museum of Art	***	5.0	0	40	60	100
Guggenheim Museum	**	1.5	0	20	30	65
Museum of Natural History	***	4.0	0	20	50	90

a. How much time should John spend visiting each attraction?

Chapter 12

Introduction to Simulation Using Crystal Ball

12.0 INTRODUCTION

Chapter 1 discussed how the calculations in a spreadsheet can be viewed as a mathematical model that defines a functional relationship between various input variables (or independent variables) and one or more bottom-line performance measures (or dependent variables). The following equation expresses this relationship:

$$Y = f(X_1, X_2, ..., X_k)$$

In many spreadsheets, the values of various input cells are determined by the person using the spreadsheet. These input cells correspond to the independent variables $X_1, X_2, ..., X_k$ in the previous equation. Various formulas (represented by $f(\ )$ above) are entered in other cells of the spreadsheet to transform the values of the input cells into some bottom-line output (denoted by Y above). Simulation is a technique that is helpful in analyzing models in which the value to be assumed by one or more independent variables is uncertain.

This chapter discusses how to perform simulation using a popular commercial spreadsheet add-in called Crystal Ball, created and distributed by Decisioneering, Inc. A limited-life (140-day) version of Crystal Ball and related products comes on the CD-ROM accompanying this book. Decisioneering offers students one and two year extensions of this software at very affordable prices. You can find additional information about Crystal Ball and these extension options at http://www.decisioneering.com.

12.1 RANDOM VARIABLES AND RISK

In order to compute a value for the bottom-line performance measure of a spreadsheet model, each input cell must be assigned a specific value so that all the related calculations can be performed. However, some uncertainty often exists regarding the value that should be assumed by one or more independent variables (or input cells) in the spreadsheet. This is particularly true in spreadsheet models that represent future conditions. A **random variable** is any variable whose value cannot be predicted or set with certainty. Thus, many input variables in a spreadsheet model represent random variables whose actual values cannot be predicted with certainty.

For example, projections of the cost of raw materials, future interest rates, future numbers of employees, and expected product demand are random variables because their true values are unknown and will be determined in the future. If we cannot say with certainty what value one or more input variables in a model will assume, we also cannot say with certainty what value the dependent variable will assume. This uncertainty associated with the value of the dependent variable introduces an element of risk to the decision-making problem. Specifically, if the dependent variable represents some bottom-line performance measure that managers use to make decisions, and its value is uncertain, any decisions made on the basis of this value are based on uncertain (or incomplete) information. When such a decision is made, some chance exists that the decision will not produce the intended results. This chance, or uncertainty, represents an element of **risk** in the decision-making problem.

The term "risk" also implies the *potential* for loss. The fact that a decision's outcome is uncertain does not mean that the decision is particularly risky. For example, whenever we put money into a soft drink machine, there is a chance that the machine will take our money and not deliver the product. However, most of us would not consider this risk to be particularly great. From past experience, we know that the chance of not receiving the product is small. But even if the machine takes our money and does not deliver the product, most of us would not consider this to be a tremendous loss. Thus, the amount of risk involved in a given decision-making situation is a function of the uncertainty in the outcome of the decision and the magnitude of the potential loss. A proper assessment of the risk present in a decision-making situation should address both of these issues, as the examples in this chapter will demonstrate.

12.2 WHY ANALYZE RISK?

Many spreadsheets built by business people contain *estimated* values for the uncertain input variables in their models. If a manager cannot say with certainty what value a particular cell in a spreadsheet will assume, this cell most likely represents a random variable. Ordinarily, the manager will attempt to make an informed guess about the values such cells will assume. The manager hopes that inserting the expected, or most likely, values for all the uncertain cells in a spreadsheet will provide the most likely value for the cell containing the bottom-line performance measure (Y). The problem with this type of analysis is that it tells the decision maker nothing about the variability of the performance measure.

For example, in analyzing a particular investment opportunity, we might determine that the expected return on a $1,000 investment is $10,000 within two years. But how much variability exists in the possible outcomes? If all the potential outcomes are scattered closely around $10,000 (say from $9,000 to $11,000), then the investment opportunity might still be attractive. If, on the other hand, the potential outcomes are scattered widely around $10,000 (say from –$30,000 up to +$50,000), then the investment opportunity might be unattractive. Although these two scenarios might have the same expected or average value, the risks involved are quite different. Thus, even if we can determine the expected outcome of a decision using a spreadsheet, it is just as important, if not more so, to consider the risk involved in the decision.

12.3 METHODS OF RISK ANALYSIS

Several techniques are available to help managers analyze risk. Three of the most common are best-case/worst-case analysis, what-if analysis, and simulation. Of these methods, simulation is the most powerful and, therefore, is the technique that we will focus on in this chapter. Although the other techniques might not be completely effective in risk analysis, they are probably used more often than simulation by most managers in business today. This is largely due to the fact that most managers are unaware of the spreadsheet's ability to perform simulation and of the benefits provided by this technique. So before discussing simulation, let's first briefly look at the other methods of risk analysis to understand their strengths and weaknesses.

12.3.1 Best-Case/Worst-Case Analysis

If we don't know what value a particular cell in a spreadsheet will assume, we could enter a number that we think is the most likely value for the uncertain cell. If we enter such numbers for all the uncertain cells in the spreadsheet, we can easily calculate the most likely value of the bottom-line performance measure. This is also called the **base-case** scenario. However, this scenario gives us no information about how far away the actual outcome might be from this expected, or most likely, value.

One simple solution to this problem is to calculate the value of the bottom-line performance measure using the **best-case,** or most optimistic, and **worst-case,** or most pessimistic, values for the uncertain input cells. These additional scenarios show the range of possible values that might be assumed by the bottom-line performance measure. As indicated in the earlier example about the $1,000 investment, knowing the range of possible outcomes is very helpful in assessing the risk involved in different alternatives. However, simply knowing the best-case and worst-case outcomes tells us nothing about the distribution of possible values within this range, nor does it tell us the probability of either scenario occurring.

Figure 12.1 displays several probability distributions that might be associated with the value of a bottom-line performance measure within a given range. Each of these distributions describes variables that have identical ranges and similar average values. But each distribution is very different in terms of the risk it represents to the decision maker. The appeal of best-case/worst-case analysis is that it is easy to do. Its weakness is that it tells us nothing about the shape of the distribution associated with the bottom-line performance measure. As we will see later, knowing the shape of the distribution of the bottom-line performance measure can be critically important in helping us answer a number of managerial questions.

12.3.2 What-If Analysis

Prior to the introduction of electronic spreadsheets in the early 1980s, the use of best-case/worst-case analysis was often the only feasible way for a manager to analyze the risk associated with a decision. This process was extremely time-consuming, error prone, and tedious, using only a piece of paper, pencil, and calculator to recalculate the performance measure of a model using different values for the uncertain inputs. The arrival of personal computers and electronic spreadsheets made it much easier for a manager to play out a large number of scenarios in addition to the best and worst cases—which is the essence of what-if analysis.

In **what-if analysis,** a manager changes the values of the uncertain input variables to see what happens to the bottom-line performance measure. By making a series of such changes, a manager can gain some insight into how sensitive the performance measure is to changes to the input variables. Although many managers perform this type of manual what-if analysis, it has three major flaws.

First, if the values selected for the independent variables are based only on the manager's judgement, the resulting sample values of the performance measure are likely to be biased. That is, if several uncertain variables can each assume some range of values, it would be difficult to ensure that the manager tests a fair, or representative, sample of all possible combinations of these values. To select values for the uncertain variables that correctly reflect their random variations, the values must be randomly selected from a distribution, or pool, of values that reflects the appropriate range of possible values, as well as the appropriate relative frequencies of these variables.

FIGURE 12.1
Possible distributions of performance measure values within a given range

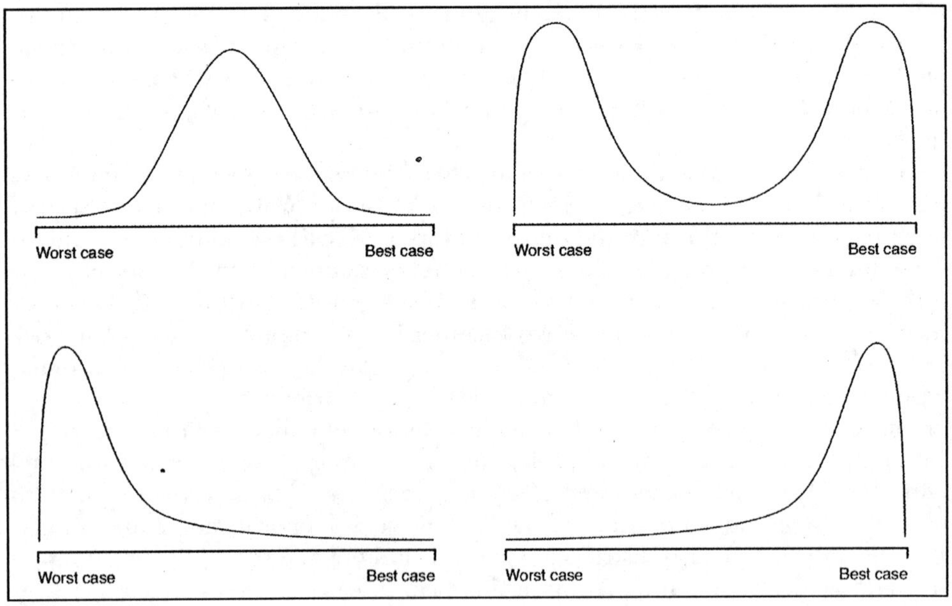

Second, hundreds or thousands of what-if scenarios might be required to create a valid representation of the underlying variability in the bottom-line performance measure. No one would want to perform these scenarios manually nor would anyone be able to make sense of the resulting stream of numbers that would flash on the screen.

The third problem with what-if analysis is that the insight the manager might gain from playing out various scenarios is of little value when recommending a decision to top management. What-if analysis simply does not supply the manager with the tangible evidence (facts and figures) needed to justify why a given decision was made or recommended. Additionally, what-if analysis does not address the problem identified in our earlier discussion of best-case/worst-case analysis—it does not allow us to estimate the distribution of the performance measure in a formal enough manner. Thus, what-if analysis is a step in the right direction, but it is not quite a large enough step to allow managers to analyze risk effectively in the decisions they face.

12.3.3 Simulation

Simulation is a technique that measures and describes various characteristics of the bottom-line performance measure of a model when one or more values for the independent variables are uncertain. If any independent variables in a model are random variables, the dependent variable (Y) also represents a random variable. The objective in simulation is to describe the distribution and characteristics of the possible values of the bottom-line performance measure Y, given the possible values and behavior of the independent variables $X_1, X_2, ..., X_k$.

The idea behind simulation is similar to the notion of playing out many what-if scenarios. The difference is that the process of assigning values to the cells in the spreadsheet that represent random variables is automated so that: (1) the values are assigned in a non-biased way, and (2) the spreadsheet user is relieved of the burden of determining these values. With simulation, we repeatedly and randomly generate sample values for each uncertain input variable ($X_1, X_2, ..., X_k$) in our model and then compute the resulting value of our bottom-line performance measure (Y). We can then use the sample values of Y to estimate the true distribution and other characteristics of the performance measure Y. For example, we can use the sample observations to construct a frequency distribution of the performance measure, to estimate the range of values over which the performance measure might vary, to estimate its mean and variance, and to estimate the probability that the actual value of the performance measure will be greater than (or less than) a particular value. All these measures provide greater insight into the risk associated with a given decision than a single value calculated based on the expected values for the uncertain independent variables.

12.4 A CORPORATE HEALTH INSURANCE EXAMPLE

The following example demonstrates the mechanics of preparing a spreadsheet model for risk analysis using simulation. The example presents a fairly simple model to illustrate the process and give a sense of the amount of effort involved.

However, the process for performing simulation is basically the same regardless of the size of the model.

> Lisa Pon has just been hired as an analyst in the corporate planning department of Hungry Dawg Restaurants. Her first assignment is to determine how much money the company needs to accrue in the coming year to pay for its employees' health insurance claims. Hungry Dawg is a large, growing chain of restaurants that specializes in traditional southern foods. The company has become large enough that it no longer buys insurance from a private insurance company. The company is now self-insured, meaning that it pays health insurance claims with its own money (although it contracts with an outside company to handle the administrative details of processing claims and writing checks).
>
> The money the company uses to pay claims comes from two sources: employee contributions (or premiums deducted from employees' paychecks), and company funds (the company must pay whatever costs are not covered by employee contributions). Each employee covered by the health plan contributes $125 per month. However, the number of employees covered by the plan changes from month to month as employees are hired and fired, quit, or simply add or drop health insurance coverage. A total of 18,533 employees were covered by the plan last month. The average monthly health claim per covered employee was $250 last month.

An example of how most analysts would model this problem is shown in Figure 12.2 (and in the file Fig12-2.xls on your data disk). The spreadsheet begins with a listing of the initial conditions and assumptions for the problem. For example, cell D5 indicates that 18,533 employees are currently covered by the health plan, and cell D6 indicates that the average monthly claim per covered employee is $250. The average monthly contribution per employee is $125, as shown in cell D7. The values in cells D5 and D6 are unlikely to stay the same for the entire year. Thus, we need to make some assumptions about the rate at which these values are likely to increase during the year. For example, we might assume that the number of covered employees will increase by about 2% per month, and that the average claim per employee will increase at a rate of 1% per month. These assumptions are reflected in cells F5 and F6. The average contribution per employee is assumed to be constant over the coming year.

On Uncertainty and Decision-Making…

"Uncertainty is the most difficult thing about decision-making. In the face of uncertainty, some people react with paralysis, or they do exhaustive research to avoid making a decision. The best decision-making happens when the mental environment is focused. In a physical environment, you focus on something physical. In tennis, that might be the spinning seams of the ball. In a mental environment, you focus on the facts at hand. That fined-tuned focus doesn't leave room for fears and doubts to enter. Doubts knock at the door of our consciousness, but you don't have to have them in for tea and crumpets."—Timothy Gallwey, author of *The Inner Game of Tennis* and *The Inner Game of Work.*

Hungry Dawg Restaurants

Initial Conditions		Assumptions		
Number of Covered Employees	18,533	Increasing	2%	per month
Average Claim per Employee	$250	Increasing	1%	per month
Amount Contributed per Employee	$125	Constant		

Month	Number of Employees	Employee Contributions	Avg Claim per Emp.	Total Claims	Company Cost
1	18,904	$2,362,958	$252.50	$4,773,174	$2,410,217
2	19,282	$2,410,217	$255.03	$4,917,324	$2,507,107
3	19,667	$2,458,421	$257.58	$5,065,827	$2,607,406
4	20,061	$2,507,589	$260.15	$5,218,815	$2,711,226
5	20,462	$2,557,741	$262.75	$5,376,423	$2,818,682
6	20,871	$2,608,896	$265.38	$5,538,791	$2,929,895
7	21,289	$2,661,074	$268.03	$5,706,063	$3,044,989
8	21,714	$2,714,295	$270.71	$5,878,386	$3,164,091
9	22,149	$2,768,581	$273.42	$6,055,913	$3,287,332
10	22,592	$2,823,953	$276.16	$6,238,802	$3,414,849
11	23,043	$2,880,432	$278.92	$6,427,214	$3,546,782
12	23,504	$2,938,041	$281.71	$6,621,315	$3,683,275
				Total Company Cost	$36,125,850

FIGURE 12.2 *Original corporate health insurance model with expected values for uncertain variables*

Using the assumed rate of increase in the number of covered employees (cell F5), we can create formulas for cells B11 through B22 that cause the number of covered employees to increase by the assumed amount each month. (The details of these formulas are covered later.) The expected monthly employee contributions shown in column C are calculated as $125 times the number of employees in each month. We can use the assumed rate of increase in average monthly claims (cell F6) to create formulas for cells D11 through D22 that cause the average claim per employee to increase at the assumed rate. The total claims for each month (shown in column E) are calculated as the average claim figures in column D times the number of employees for each month in column B. Because the company must pay for any claims that are not covered by the employee contributions, the company cost figures in column G are calculated as the total claims minus the employee contributions (column E minus column C). Finally, cell G23 sums the company cost figures listed in column G, and shows that the company can expect to contribute $36,125,850 of its revenues toward paying the health insurance claims of its employees in the coming year.

12.4.1 A Critique of the Base Case Model

Now, let's consider the model we just described. The example model assumes that the number of covered employees will increase by *exactly* 2% each month and that the average claim per covered employee will increase by *exactly* 1% each month. Although these values might be reasonable approximations of what might happen, they are unlikely to reflect exactly what will happen. In fact, the number of employees covered by the health plan each month is likely to vary randomly around the average increase per month—that is, the number might decrease in some months and increase by more than 2% in others. Similarly, the average claim per covered employee might be lower than expected in certain months and higher than expected in others.

Both of these figures are likely to exhibit some uncertainty or random behavior, even if they do move in the general upward direction assumed throughout the year. So, we cannot say with certainty that the total cost figure of $36,125,850 is exactly what the company will have to contribute toward health claims in the coming year. It is simply a prediction of what might happen. The actual outcome could be smaller or larger than this estimate. Using the original model, we have no idea how much larger or smaller the actual result could be—nor do we have any idea of how the actual values are distributed around this estimate. We do not know if there is a 10%, 50%, or 90% chance of the actual total costs exceeding this estimate. To determine the variability or risk inherent in the bottom-line performance measure of total company costs, we will apply the technique of simulation to our model.

12.5 SPREADSHEET SIMULATION USING CRYSTAL BALL

To perform simulation in a spreadsheet, we must first place a **random number generator** (RNG) formula in each cell that represents a random, or uncertain, independent variable. Each RNG provides a sample observation from an appropriate distribution that represents the range and frequency of possible values for the variable. Once the RNGs are in place, new sample values are provided automatically each time the spreadsheet is recalculated. We can recalculate the spreadsheet n times, where n is the desired number of replications or scenarios, and the value of the bottom-line performance measure will be stored after each replication. We can analyze these stored observations to gain insights into the behavior and characteristics of the performance measure.

The process of simulation involves a lot of work but, fortunately, the spreadsheet can do most of the work for us fairly easily. In particular, the spreadsheet add-in package Crystal Ball is designed specifically to make spreadsheet simulation a simple process. The Crystal Ball software provides the following capabilities, which are not otherwise available while working in Excel: additional functions that are helpful in generating the random numbers needed in simulation; additional commands that are helpful in setting up and running the simulation; and graphical and statistical summaries of the simulation data. As we shall see, these capabilities make simulation a relatively easy technique to apply in spreadsheets.

12.5.1 Starting Crystal Ball

If you are running Crystal Ball from a local area network (LAN) or in a computer lab, your instructor or LAN coordinator should give you directions on how to access this software. If you have installed Crystal Ball on your own computer, you can load Crystal Ball from within Excel as follows:

1. Click Tools.
2. Click Add-Ins.
3. Check the Crystal Ball option.
4. Click OK.

This loads the memory resident portion of Crystal Ball and causes the Cell, Run, and CBTools menus to appear on the main menu bar. Crystal Ball also provides the custom toolbar shown in Figure 12.3. We will refer to the various icons on this toolbar throughout this chapter. You can display this toolbar in Excel as follows:

1. Click View.
2. Click Toolbars.
3. Check the Crystal Ball option.
4. Click OK.

12.6 RANDOM NUMBER GENERATORS

As mentioned earlier, the first step in spreadsheet simulation is to place an RNG formula in each cell that contains an uncertain value. Each of these formulas will generate (or return) a number that represents a randomly selected value from a distribution, or pool, of values. The distributions that these samples are taken from should be representative of the underlying pool of values expected to occur in each uncertain cell.

Crystal Ball provides several functions that can be used to create the RNGs required for simulating a model. Figure 12.4 describes some of the most useful RNGs.

The functions listed in Figure 12.4 allow us to generate a variety of random numbers easily. For example, if we think that the behavior of an uncertain cell could be modeled as a normally distributed random variable with a mean of 125 and standard deviation of 10, then according to Figure 12.4 we could enter the formula =CB.Normal(125,10) in this cell. (The arguments in this function could also be formulas and could refer to other cells in the spreadsheet.) Whenever the spreadsheet is recalculated, Crystal Ball would then return a randomly selected value from a normal distribution with a mean of 125 and standard deviation of 10 for this cell.

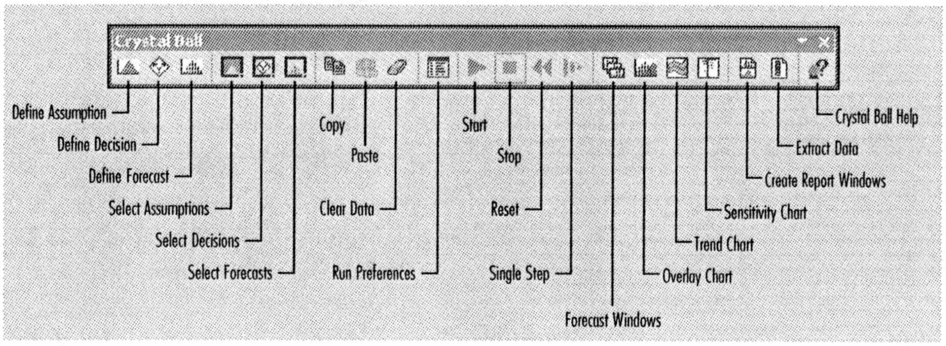

FIGURE 12.3
The Crystal Ball toolbar in Excel

FIGURE 12.4
Commonly used RNGs supplied with @RISK

Distribution	RNG	Description
Binomial	CB.Binomial(*p*,*n*)	Returns the number of "successes" in a sample of size *n* where each trial has a probability *p* of "success."
Custom	CB.Custom(*range*)	Returns a random number from a custom probability distribution defined by a 2 or 3 column range in a worksheet. The first two columns in the range must represent, respectively, lower and upper limits for the values generated. (If the upper limit column is the same as the lower limit, the upper limit may be omitted.) The last column in the range indicates the probability for values within lower and upper limits.
Poisson	CB.Poisson(λ)	Returns a random number of events occurring per some unit of measure (for example, arrivals per hour, defects per yard, and so on). The parameter λ represents the average number of events occurring per unit of measure.
Continuous Uniform	CB.Uniform(*min*,*max*)	Returns a value in the range from a minimum (*min*) to a maximum (*max*). Each value in this range is equally likely to occur.
Exponential	CB.Exponential(λ)	Returns a value from an exponential distribution with mean λ. Often used to model the time between events or the lifetime of a device with a constant probability of failure.
Normal	CB.Normal(μ,σ,*min*,*max*)	Returns a value from a normal distribution with mean μ and standard deviation σ. If *min* and *max* are specified, the distribution is truncated to this range.
Triangular	CB.Triangular(*min*,*most likely*,*max*)	Returns a value from a triangular distribution covering the range specified by a minimum (*min*) and a maximum (*max*). The shape of the distribution is then determined by the size of the *most likely* value relative to *min* and *max*.

Similarly, a cell in our spreadsheet might have a 30% chance of assuming the value 10, a 50% chance of assuming the value 20, and a 20% chance of assuming the value 30. To model the behavior of this random variable using the CB.Custom RNG, we might first set up a worksheet like the one shown in Figure 12.5.

We could use the formula =CB.Custom(A2:B4) to model this random behavior. If we recalculated the spreadsheet many times, this formula would return the value 10 approximately 30% of the time, the value 20 approximately 50% of the time, and the value 30 approximately 20% of the time.

The arguments, or parameters, required by the RNG functions allow us to generate random numbers from distributions with a wide variety of shapes. Figures 12.6 and 12.7 illustrate some example distributions. Additional information about these and other RNGs provided by Crystal Ball is available in the appendices of the Crystal Ball manual and in the on-line Help facility in Crystal Ball.

	A	B
1	Value	Probability
2	10	0.3
3	20	0.5
4	30	0.2

FIGURE 12.5
Sample worksheet to illustrate the CB.Custom function

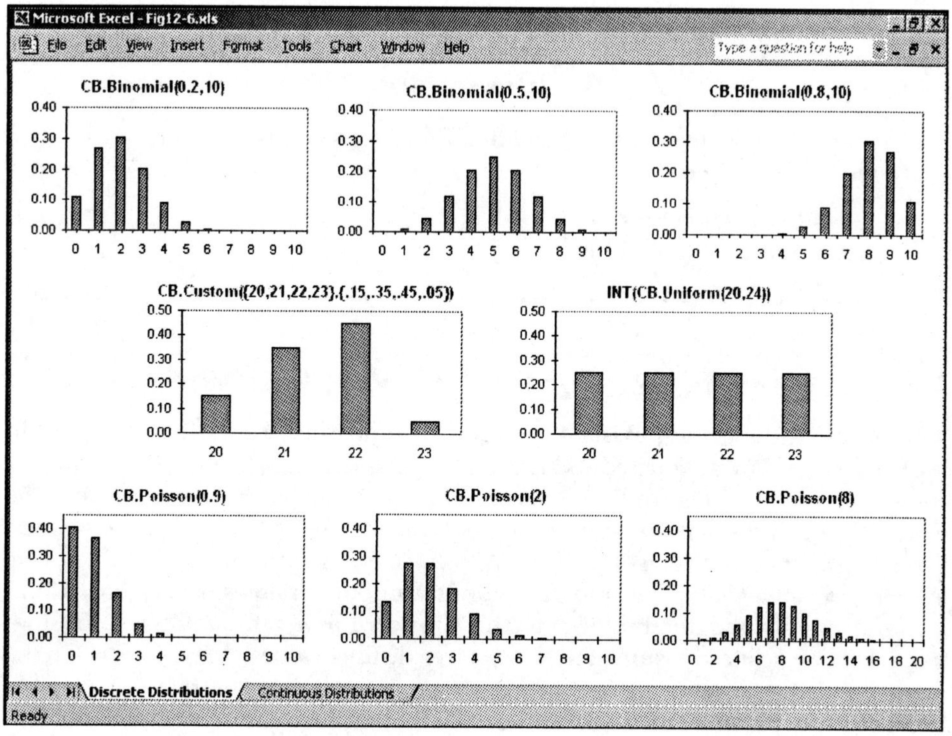

FIGURE 12.6
Examples of distributions associated with selected discrete RNGs

FIGURE 12.7
Examples of distributions associated with selected continuous RNGs

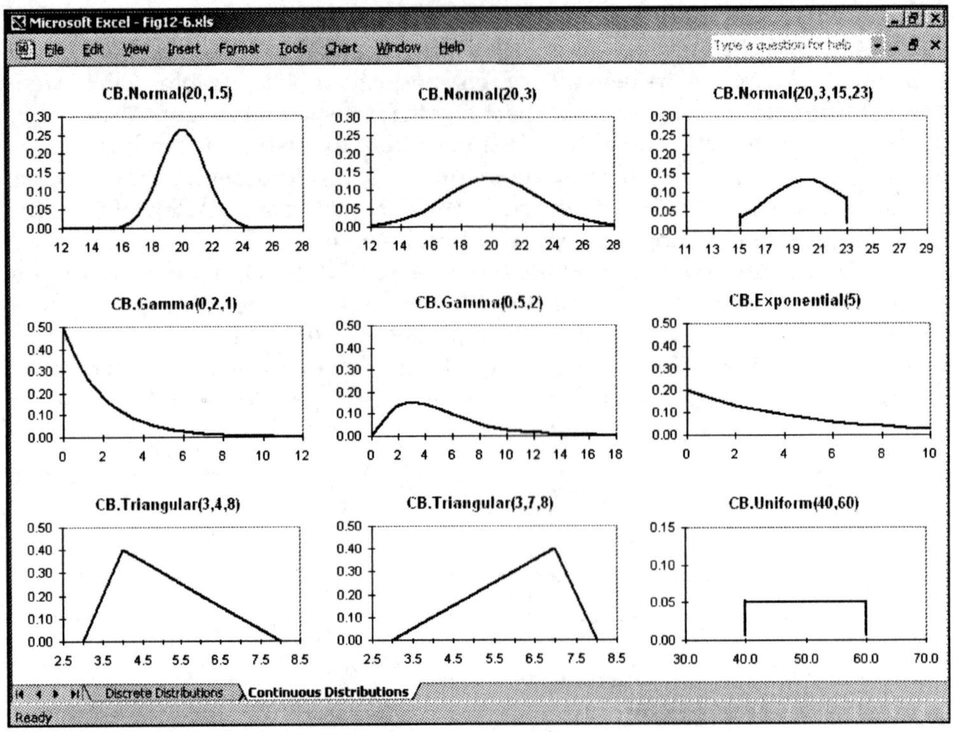

Software Note

A listing of all the available Crystal Ball RNG functions is available in Excel. To view this listing:

1. Click Insert, Function.
2. Select the Crystal Ball function category.

12.6.1 Discrete vs. Continuous Random Variables

An important distinction exists between the graphs in Figures 12.6 and 12.7. In particular, the RNGs depicted in Figure 12.6 generate *discrete* outcomes, whereas those represented in Figure 12.7 generate *continuous* outcomes. That is, some of the RNGs listed in Figure 12.4 can return only a distinct set of individual values, whereas the other RNGs can return any value from an infinite set of values. The distinction between discrete and continuous random variables is very important.

For example, the number of defective tires on a new car is a discrete random variable because it can assume only one of five distinct values: 0, 1, 2, 3, or 4. On the other hand, the amount of fuel in a new car is a continuous random variable because it can assume any value between 0 and the maximum capacity of the fuel tank. Thus, when selecting an RNG for an uncertain variable in a model, it is important to consider whether the variable can assume discrete or continuous values.

12.7 PREPARING THE MODEL FOR SIMULATION

To apply simulation to the model for Hungry Dawg Restaurants described earlier, we must first select appropriate RNGs for the uncertain variables in the model. If available, historical data on the uncertain variables could be analyzed to determine appropriate RNGs for these variables. (Crystal Ball's Batch Fit tool can be used for this purpose.) If past data are not available, or if we have some reason to expect the future behavior of a variable to be significantly different from the past, then we must use judgement in selecting appropriate RNGs to model the random behavior of the uncertain variables.

For our example problem, let's assume that by analyzing historical data, we determined that the change in the number of covered employees from one month to the next is expected to vary uniformly between a 3% decrease and a 7% increase. (Note that this should cause the *average* change in the number of employees to be a 2% increase, because 0.02 is the midpoint between –0.03 and +0.07.) Further, assume that we can model the average monthly claim per covered employee as a normally distributed random variable with the mean (μ) increasing by 1% per month and a standard deviation (σ) of approximately $3. (Note that this will cause the *average* increase in claims per covered employee from one month to the next to be approximately 1%.) These assumptions are reflected in cells F5 through H6 at the top of Figure 12.8 (and in the file Fig12-8.xls on your data disk).

To implement the formula to generate a random number of employees covered by the health plan, we will use the CB.Uniform( ) function described in Figure 12.4. Because the change in the number of employees from one month to the next can vary between a 3% decrease and a 7% increase, the number of employees in the current month is equal to the number of employees in the previous month multiplied by the sum of 1 plus the percentage change. Applying this logic, we obtain the following equation for the number of employees in a given month:

Number of employees in current month = Number of employees in previous month × CB.Uniform(0.97,1.07)

If the CB.Uniform( ) function returns the value 0.97, this formula causes the number of employees in the current month to equal 97% of the number in the previous month (a 3% decrease). Alternatively, if the CB.Uniform( ) function returns the value 1.07, this formula causes the number of employees in the current month to equal 107% of the number in the previous month (a 7% increase). All the values between these two extremes (between 0.97 and 1.07) are also possible and equally likely to occur. The following formulas were used to create formulas that randomly generate the number of employees in each month in Figure 12.8:

Formula for cell B11: =D5*CB.Uniform(1-F5,1+H5)

Formula for cell B12: =B11*CB.Uniform(1-$F$5,1+$H$5)
(Copy to B13 through B22.)

Note that the terms "1–$F$5" and "1+$H$5" in the above formulas generate the values 0.97 and 1.07, respectively.

FIGURE 12.8
Modified corporate health insurance model with RNGs replacing expected values for uncertain variables

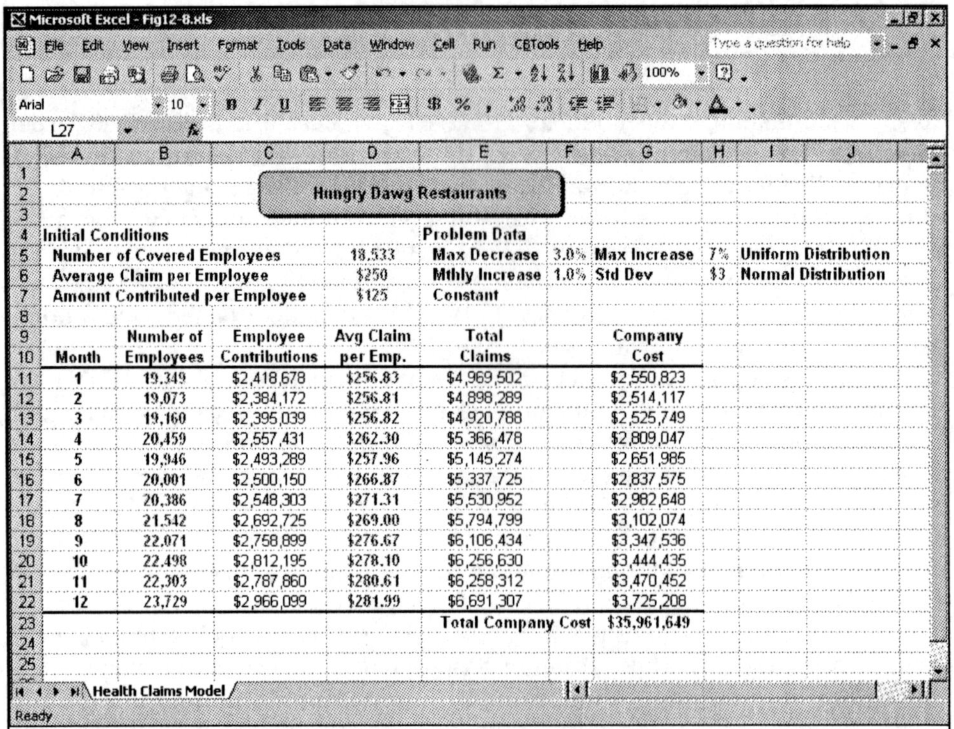

			Hungry Dawg Restaurants					
Initial Conditions				Problem Data				
Number of Covered Employees			18,533	Max Decrease	3.0%	Max Increase	7%	Uniform Distribution
Average Claim per Employee			$250	Mthly Increase	1.0%	Std Dev	$3	Normal Distribution
Amount Contributed per Employee			$125	Constant				

Month	Number of Employees	Employee Contributions	Avg Claim per Emp.	Total Claims	Company Cost
1	19,349	$2,418,678	$256.83	$4,969,502	$2,550,823
2	19,073	$2,384,172	$256.81	$4,898,289	$2,514,117
3	19,160	$2,395,039	$256.82	$4,920,788	$2,525,749
4	20,459	$2,557,431	$262.30	$5,366,478	$2,809,047
5	19,946	$2,493,289	$257.96	$5,145,274	$2,651,985
6	20,001	$2,500,150	$266.87	$5,337,725	$2,837,575
7	20,386	$2,548,303	$271.31	$5,530,952	$2,982,648
8	21,542	$2,692,725	$269.00	$5,794,799	$3,102,074
9	22,071	$2,758,899	$276.67	$6,106,434	$3,347,536
10	22,498	$2,812,195	$278.10	$6,256,630	$3,444,435
11	22,303	$2,787,860	$280.61	$6,258,312	$3,470,452
12	23,729	$2,966,099	$281.99	$6,691,307	$3,725,208
				Total Company Cost	$35,961,649

Key Cell Formulas

Cell	Formula	Copied to
B11	=D5*CB.Uniform(1-F5,1+H5)	—
B12	=B11*CB.Uniform(1-$F$5,1+$H$5)	B13:B22
C11	=$D$7*B11	C12:C22
D11	=CB.Normal($D$6*(1+$F$6)^A11,$H$6)	D12:D22
E11	=D11*B11	E12:E22
G11	=E11-C11	G12:G22
G23	=SUM(G11:G22)	—

To implement the formula to generate the average claims per covered employee in each month, we will use the CB.Normal( ) function described in Figure 12.4. This formula requires that we supply the value of the mean (μ) and standard deviation (σ) of the distribution from which we want to sample. The assumed $3 standard deviation (σ) for the average monthly claim, shown in cell H6 in Figure 12.8, is constant from month to month. Thus, the only remaining problem is to figure out the proper mean value (μ) for each month.

In this case, the mean for any given month should be 1% larger than the mean in the previous month. For example, the mean for month 1 is:

$$\text{Mean in month 1} = (\text{original mean}) \times 1.01$$

and the mean for month 2 is:

$$\text{Mean in month 2} = (\text{mean in month 1}) \times 1.01$$

If we substitute the previous definition of the mean in month 1 into the previous equation, we obtain:

$$\text{Mean in month 2} = (\text{original mean}) \times (1.01)^2$$

Similarly, the mean in month 3 is:

$$\text{Mean in month 3} = (\text{mean in month 2}) \times 1.01 = (\text{original mean}) \times (1.01)^3$$

So in general, the mean (μ) for month n is:

$$\text{Mean in month } n = (\text{original mean}) \times (1.01)^n$$

Thus, to generate the average claim per covered employee in each month, we use the following formula:

Formula for cell D11: =CB.Normal($D$6*(1+$F$6)^A11,$H$6)
(Copy to D12 through D22.)

The term "$D$6*(1+$F$6)^A11" in this formula implements the general definition of the mean (μ) in month n.

After entering the appropriate RNGs, each time we press the recalculate key (the function key [F9]), the RNGs automatically select new values for all the cells in the spreadsheet that represent uncertain (or random) variables. Similarly, with each recalculation, a new value for the bottom-line performance measure (total company cost) appears in cell G23. Thus, by pressing the recalculate key several times, we can observe representative values of the company's total cost for health claims. This also helps to verify that we implemented the RNGs correctly and that they are generating appropriate values for each uncertain cell.

Why Don't Your Numbers Change?

By default, Crystal Ball displays the mean (or average) value of the distribution for cells containing RNG functions. To make Crystal Ball display new values for your RNG cells whenever you manually recalculate the spreadsheet, click Cell, Cell Preferences, and deselect the check box labeled "Set to Distribution Mean."

12.7.1 Alternate RNG Entry

Crystal Ball also offers an alternate way of entering RNGs in spreadsheet models. If you select a worksheet cell that contains a value and then click the Define Assumption icon on the Crystal Ball toolbar shown in Figure 12.3 (or click Cells, Define Assumption), the Distribution Gallery in Figure 12.9 appears.

After selecting one of the distributions shown in Figure 12.9, another dialog box appears prompting you to enter various parameters for the distribution you selected. Although this feature can be helpful in visualizing distributions, RNGs entered in this manner are stored internally in Crystal Ball rather than as functions in the individual cells. This makes it more difficult to build and verify models. As a result, this author prefers to use the functions shown in Figure 12.4 to create the RNGs required in spreadsheet simulation. However, you should be aware that

FIGURE 12.9
The Crystal Ball Distribution Gallery

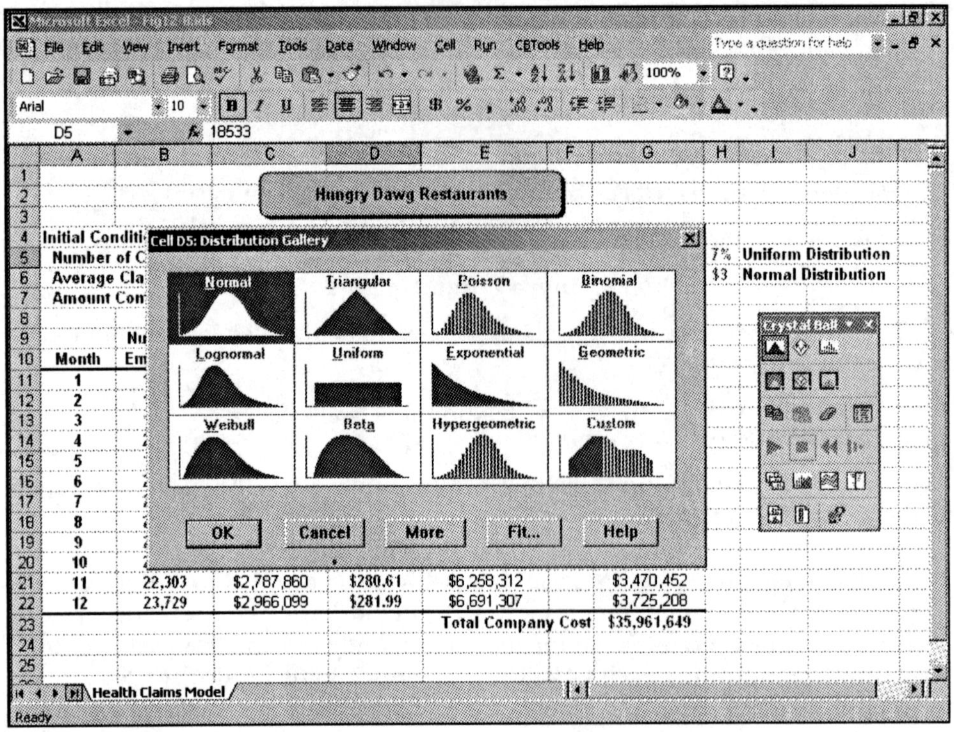

certain capabilities of Crystal Ball (*e.g.*, the Sensitivity Chart and Correlation Matrix tool) require assumption cells to be defined using the Distribution Gallery.

12.8 RUNNING THE SIMULATION

The next step in performing the simulation involves recalculating the spreadsheet several hundred or several thousand times and recording the resulting values generated for the output cell, or bottom-line performance measure. Fortunately, Crystal Ball can do this for us if we indicate how many times we want it to recalculate (or replicate) the model and which cell(s) in the spreadsheet we want to track.

12.8.1 Selecting the Output Cells to Track

We can use the Define Forecast button on the Crystal Ball toolbar (see Figure 12.3) to indicate the output cell (or cells) that we want Crystal Ball to track during the simulation. In the current example, cell G23 represents the output cell we want Crystal Ball to track. To indicate this:

1. Click cell G23.
2. Click the Define Forecast icon on the Crystal Ball toolbar (or click Cells, Define Forecast). (This causes the dialog box in Figure 12.10 to appear. If you see a button labeled More, click it.)
3. Make the indicated selections.
4. Click OK.

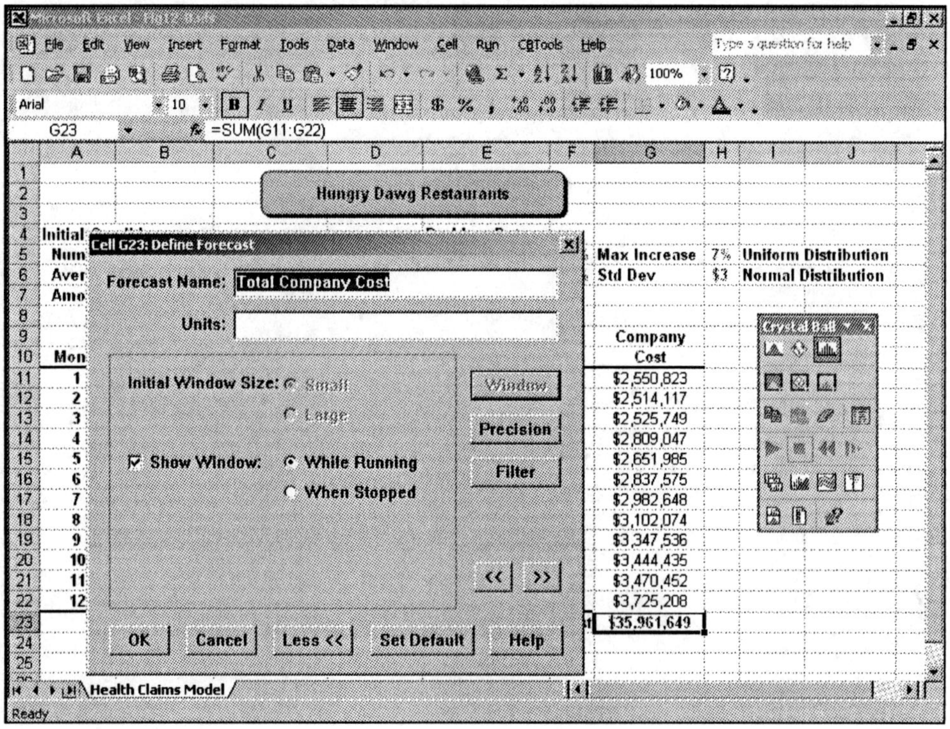

FIGURE 12.10
Defining a forecast cell

In some simulations, we might want to analyze several performance measures. In such a case, we can follow the preceding procedure repeatedly to select additional output cells to track.

> **Software Note...**
>
> When you define assumption, decision, or forecast cells, Crystal Ball automatically changes the background color of the cells to distinguish these cells from others on the spreadsheet. You can change the default colors Crystal Ball uses (or suppress this behavior entirely) by clicking Cell followed by Cell Preferences.

12.8.2 Selecting the Number of Iterations

Figure 12.11 shows the Trials card in the Run Preferences dialog box for Crystal Ball. The "Maximum Number of Trials" option in this dialog box allows us to specify the number of iterations (or replications) to include in our simulation. Thus, to indicate that we want to perform 500 replications of our model:

1. Click the Run Preferences icon on the Crystal Ball toolbar (or click Run, Run Preferences).
2. Type 500 in the box labeled "Maximum Number of Trials."
3. Click OK.

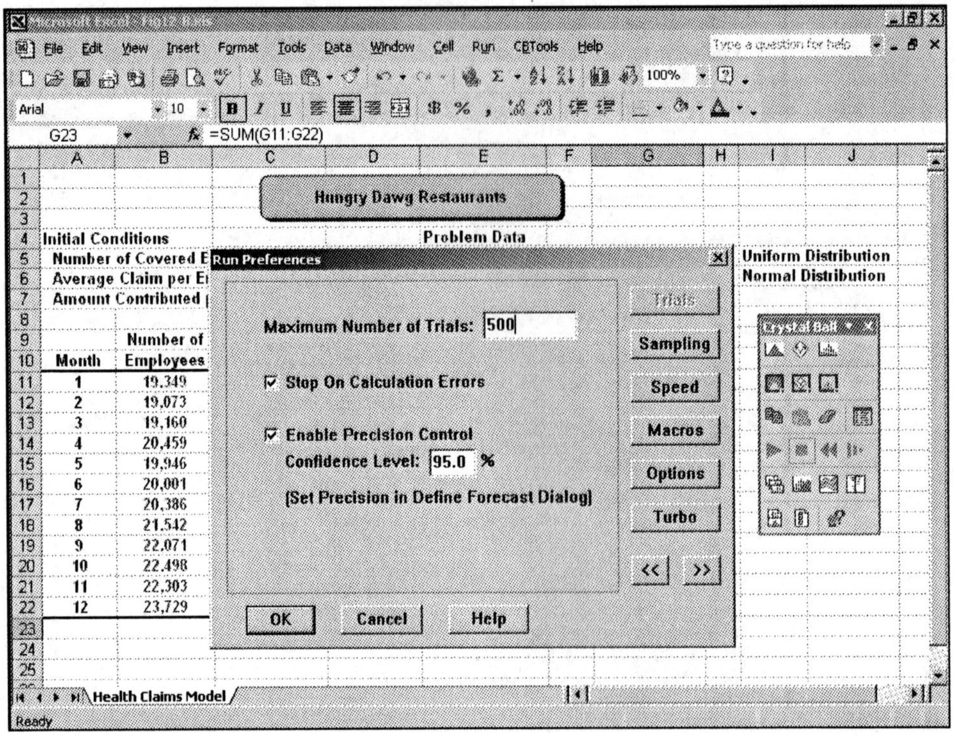

FIGURE 12.11
Trials options in the Run Preferences dialog box

12.8.3 Determining the Sample Size

You might wonder why we selected 500 replications. Why not 250, or 1000? Unfortunately, there is no easy answer to this question. Remember that the goal in simulation is to estimate various characteristics about the bottom-line performance measure(s) under consideration. For example, we might want to estimate the mean value of the performance measure and the shape of its probability distribution. However, a different value of the bottom-line performance measure occurs each time we manually recalculate the model in Figure 12.8. Thus, there is an infinite number of possibilities—or an **infinite population**—of total company cost values associated with this model.

We cannot analyze all of these infinite possibilities. But by taking a large enough sample from this infinite population, we can make reasonably accurate estimates about the characteristics of the underlying infinite population of values. The larger the sample we take (that is, the more replications we do), the more accurate our final results will be. But, performing many replications takes time, so we must make a trade-off in terms of estimation accuracy versus convenience. Thus, there is no simple answer to the question of how many replications to perform, but, as a bare minimum you should always perform at least 100 replications, and more as time permits or accuracy demands.

12.8.4 Running the Simulation

Having identified the output cells to track and the number of replications to perform, we now need to instruct Crystal Ball to perform the simulation by clicking the Start icon on the Crystal Ball toolbar in Figure 12.3 (or by clicking Run, Run). Crystal Ball then begins to perform the specified number of replications. Depending on the number of iterations selected, the size of the model, and the speed of your computer, it could take anywhere from several seconds to several minutes for these computations to be carried out.

For our example problem, Crystal Ball performs 500 recalculations of the model, keeping track of the value in cell G23 for each replication. By default, Crystal Ball updates the computer screen after each replication, which can be very time-consuming. If you select the "When Stopped" option shown in Figure 12.10, Crystal Ball will not update the screen after each replication and will perform the replications more quickly.

12.9 DATA ANALYSIS

As mentioned earlier, the objective of performing simulation is to estimate various characteristics of the performance measure resulting from uncertainty in some or all of the input variables. After performing the replications, Crystal Ball summarizes the output data, as shown in Figure 12.12. The summary statistics are shown by clicking View, Statistics.

12.9.1 The Best Case and the Worst Case

As shown in Figure 12.12, the average (or mean) value for cell G23 is approximately $36.2 million. (If you are working through this example on a computer, the

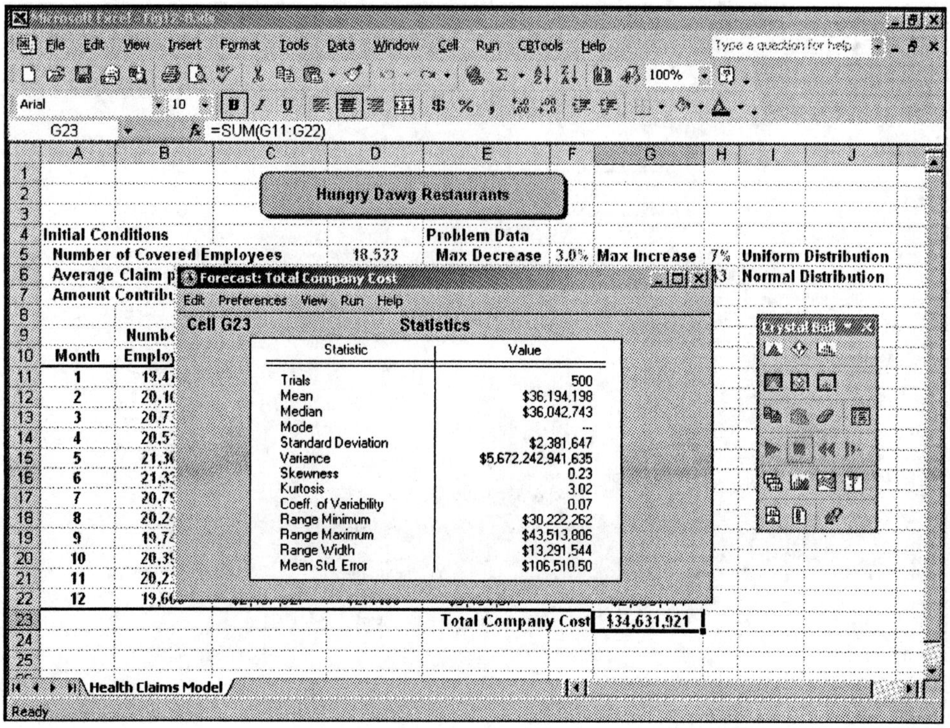

FIGURE 12.12
Summary statistics for simulation results

graphs and statistics you generate may be somewhat different from the results shown here because you may be working with a different sample of 500 observations.) However, decision makers usually want to know the best-case and worst-case scenarios to get an idea of the range of possible outcomes they might face. This information is available from the simulation results, as shown by the Range Minimum and Range Maximum values listed in Figure 12.12.

Although the average total cost value observed in the 500 replications is $36.2 million, in one case the total cost is approximately $30.2 million (representing the best case) and in another case the total cost is approximately $43.5 million (representing the worst case). These figures should give the decision maker a good idea about the range of possible cost values that might occur. Note that these values might be difficult to determine manually in a complex model with many uncertain independent variables.

12.9.2 Viewing the Distribution of the Output Cells

The best- and worst-case scenarios are the most extreme outcomes, and might not be likely to occur. To determine the likelihood of these outcomes requires that we know something about the shape of the distribution of our bottom-line performance measure. To view a graph of the distribution of the results of the 500 replications generated for the output cell in our model, click View, Frequency Chart.

A histogram of the simulation data for cell G23 appears. This graph, shown in Figure 12.13, provides a visual summary of the approximate shape of the probability distribution associated with the output cell tracked by Crystal Ball during the simulation.

FIGURE 12.13
Frequency distribution of possible total costs

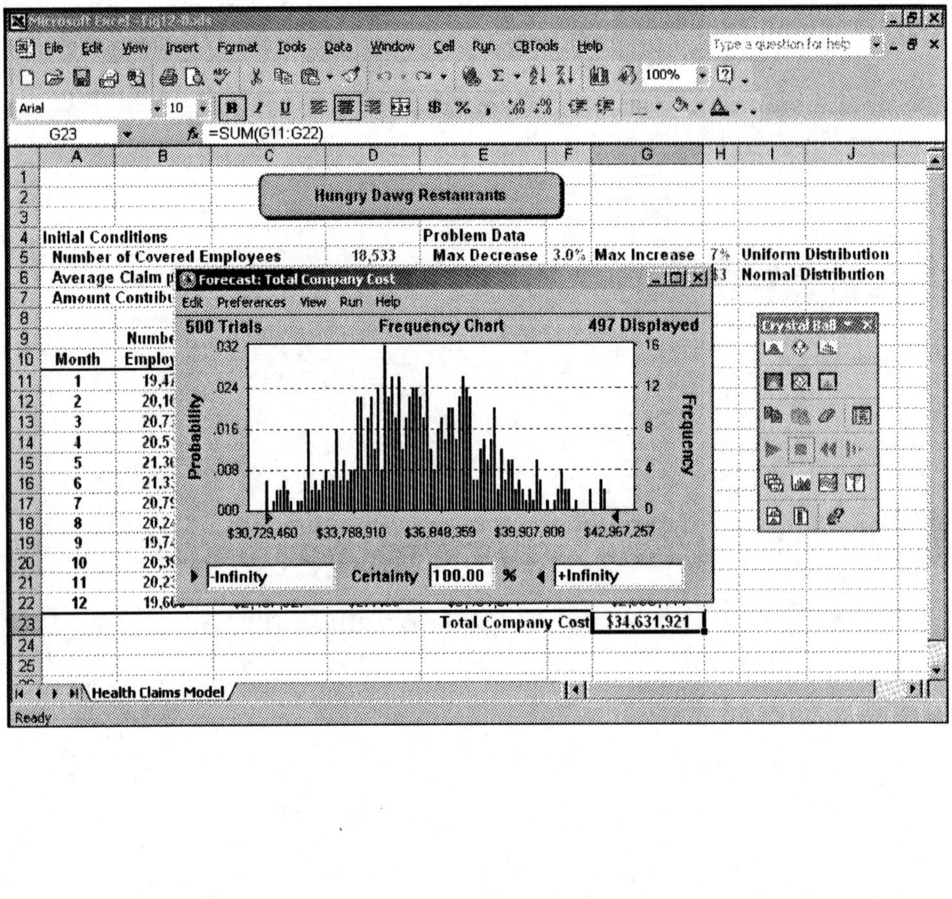

As shown in Figure 12.13, the shape of the distribution associated with the total cost variable is somewhat bell-shaped, with a maximum value around $43 million and a minimum value around $30 million. Thus, we now have a clear idea of the shape of the distribution associated with our bottom-line performance measure—one of the goals in simulation.

If we tracked more than one output cell during the simulation, we could display histograms of the values occurring in these other cells by clicking Run, Forecast Windows.

12.9.3 Viewing the Cumulative Distribution of the Output Cells

At times, we might want to view a graph of the cumulative probability distribution associated with one of the output cells tracked during a simulation. For example, suppose that the chief financial officer (CFO) for Hungry Dawg would rather accrue an excess of money to pay health claims than not accrue enough money. The CFO might want to know what amount the company should accrue so that there is only a 10% chance of coming up short of funds at the end of the year. So, how much money would you recommend be accrued?

Figure 12.14 shows a graph of the cumulative probability distribution of the values that occurred in cell G23 during the simulation. This graph could help us answer the preceding question. To change the graph shown in Figure 12.13 to the cumulative distribution graph shown in Figure 12.14:

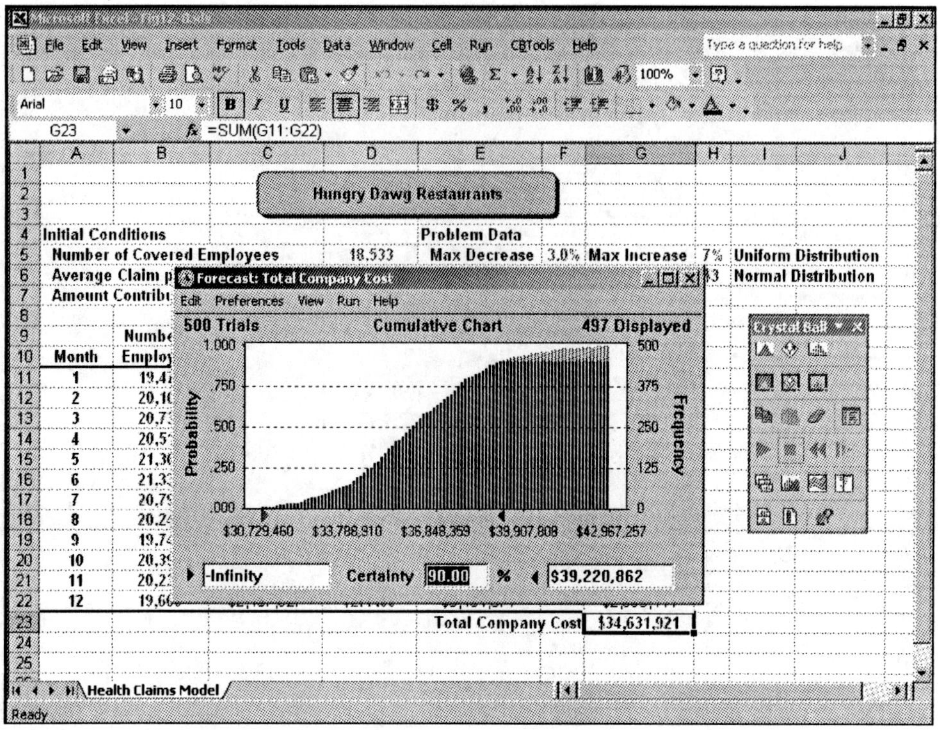

FIGURE 12.14
Cumulative distribution of possible total costs

1. Click View.
2. Click Cumulative Chart.
3. Click and drag the right-hand arrow on the X-axis until the certainty level is 90%.

This graph displays the probability of the selected output cell taking on a value smaller than each value on the X-axis. For example, this graph indicates that approximately a 25% chance exists of the output cell (Total Company Cost) assuming a value smaller than approximately $34.5 million. Similarly, this graph indicates that roughly a 75% chance exists of total costs being less than approximately $38 million (or a 20% chance of total costs exceeding approximately $38 million). Thus, from this graph, we would estimate that roughly a 10% chance exists of the company's costs exceeding approximately $39.2 million.

12.9.4 Obtaining Other Cumulative Probabilities

We can also answer the CFO's question from information in the Percentiles window shown in Figure 12.15 (click View, Percentiles). This window reveals a number of percentile values for the output cell G23. For example, the 10th percentile of the values generated for the output cell is $33,205,394—or 10% of the 500 values generated for cell G23 are less than or equal to this value. Similarly, the 90th percentile of the distribution of values is $39,220,862. Thus, based on these results, if the company accrues $39.2 million, we would expect that only a 10% chance exists of the actual company costs exceeding this amount.

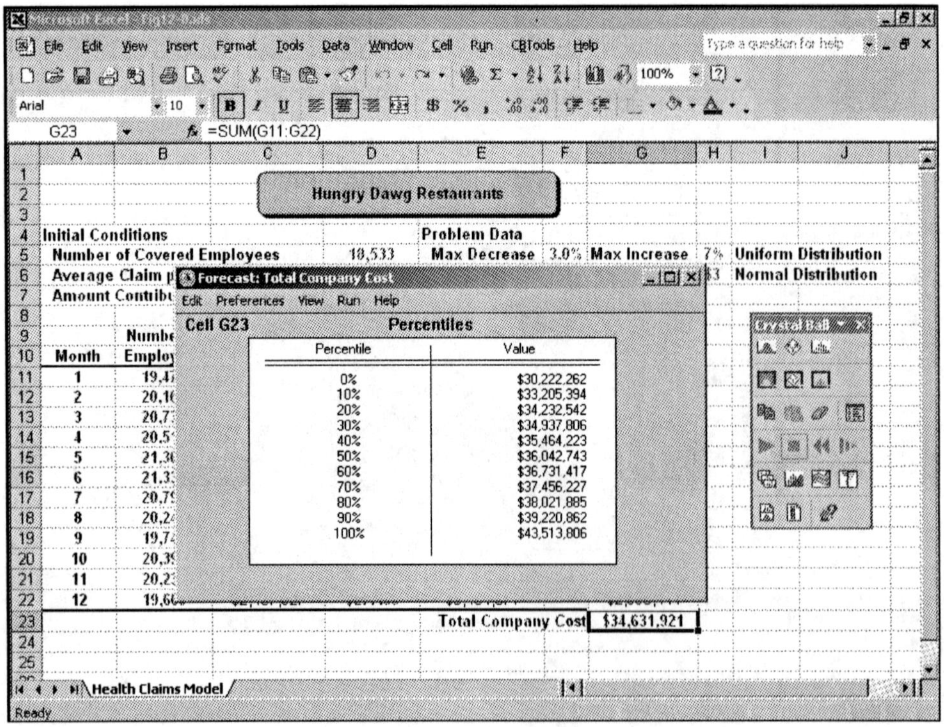

FIGURE 12.15
Percentiles of the distribution of possible total costs

The ability to perform this type of analysis highlights the power and value of simulation and Crystal Ball. For example, how could we have answered the CFO's question about how much money to accrue using best-case/worst-case analysis or what-if analysis? The fact is, we could not answer the question with any degree of accuracy without using simulation.

12.10 INCORPORATING GRAPHS AND STATISTICS INTO A SPREADSHEET

At times, you will want to save some of the graphs or statistics created by Crystal Ball. You can do so by selecting the Create Report option from the Run menu. This option displays the dialog box shown in Figure 12.16. This dialog box provides options for saving different results to Excel. Crystal Ball automatically saves all the selected graphs and statistics in a worksheet in a new workbook.

Similarly, you might want to save the actual replication data generated during the simulation to a separate file for further analysis. You can do so by selecting the Extract Data option from the Run menu. This option displays the dialog box shown in Figure 12.17. Here again, Crystal Ball automatically saves all the selected data items in a worksheet in a new workbook.

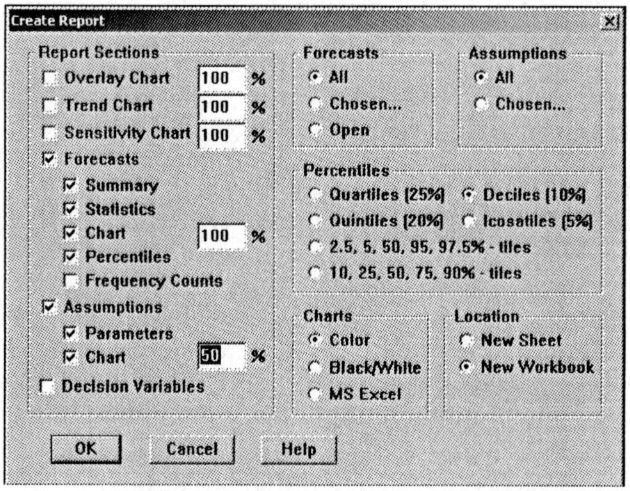

FIGURE 12.16
Saving charts and statistics from the simulation

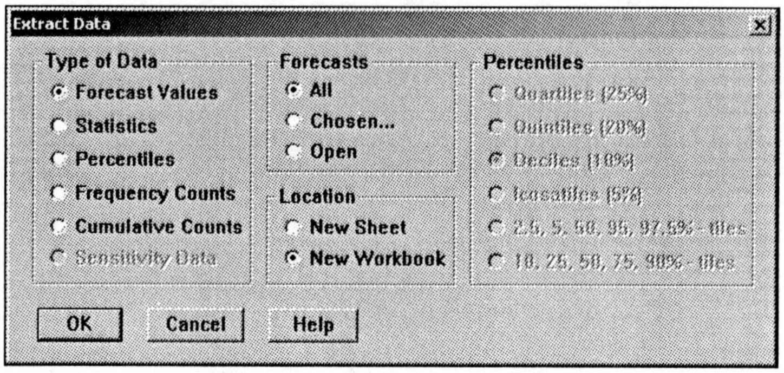

FIGURE 12.17
Saving data from the simulation

12.11 THE UNCERTAINTY OF SAMPLING

To this point, we have used simulation to generate 500 observations on our bottom-line performance measure and then calculated various statistics to describe the characteristics and behavior of the performance measure. For example, Figure 12.12 indicates that the mean company cost value in our sample is $36,194,198, and Figure 12.14 shows that a 90% chance exists of this performance measure assuming a value less than $39,220,862. But what if we repeat this process and generate another 500 observations? Would the sample mean for the new 500 observations also be exactly $36,194,198? Or would exactly 90% of the observations in the new sample be less than $39,220,862?

The answer to both these questions is "probably not." The sample of 500 observations used in our analysis was taken from a population of values that is theoretically infinite in size. That is, if we had enough time and our computer had enough memory, we could generate an infinite number of values for our bottom-line performance measure. Theoretically, we could then analyze this infinite population of values to determine its true mean value, its true standard deviation, and the true probability of the performance measure being less than $39,220,862. Unfortunately, we do not have the time or computer resources to determine these true characteristics (or parameters) of the population. The best we can do is take a sample from this population and, based on our sample, make estimates about the true characteristics of the underlying population. Our estimates will differ depending on the sample we choose and the size of the sample.

So, the mean of the sample we take is probably not equal to the true mean we would observe if we could analyze the entire population of values for our performance measure. The sample mean we calculate is just an estimate of the true population mean. In our example problem, we estimated that a 90% chance exists for our output variable to assume a value less than $39,220,862. However, this most likely is not equal to the true probability we would calculate if we could analyze the entire population. Thus, there is some element of uncertainty surrounding the statistical estimates resulting from simulation because we are using a sample to make inferences about the population. Fortunately, there are ways of measuring and describing the amount of uncertainty present in some of the estimates we make about the population under study. This is typically done by constructing confidence intervals for the population parameters being estimated.

12.11.1 Constructing a Confidence Interval for the True Population Mean

Constructing a confidence interval for the true population mean is a simple process. If $\bar{y}$ and s represent, respectively, the mean and standard deviation of a sample of size n from any population, then assuming n is sufficiently large ($n \geq 30$), the Central Limit Theorem tells us that the lower and upper limits of a 95% confidence interval for the true mean of the population are represented by:

$$\text{95\% Lower Confidence Limit} = \bar{y} - 1.96 \times \frac{s}{\sqrt{n}}$$

$$\text{95\% Upper Confidence Limit} = \bar{y} + 1.96 \times \frac{s}{\sqrt{n}}$$

Although we can be fairly certain that the sample mean we calculate from our sample data is not equal to the true population mean, we can be 95% confident that the true mean of the population falls somewhere between the lower and upper limits given previously. If we want a 90% or 99% confidence interval, we must change the value 1.96 in the previous equation to 1.645 or 2.575, respectively. The values 1.645, 1.96, and 2.575 represent the 95, 97.5, and 99.5 percentiles of the standard normal distribution. Any percentile of the standard normal distribution can be obtained easily using Excel's NORMSINV( ) function.

For our example, the lower and upper limits of a 95% confidence interval for the true mean of the population of total company cost values can be calculated easily, as shown in cells B9 and B10 in Figure 12.18. (The sample mean and standard deviation shown in Figure 12.18 were obtained from Figure 12.12.) The formulas for these cells are:

Formula for cell B9: =B4-NORMSINV(1-B7/2)*B5/SQRT(B6)

Formula for cell B10: =B4+NORMSINV(1-B7/2)*B5/SQRT(B6)

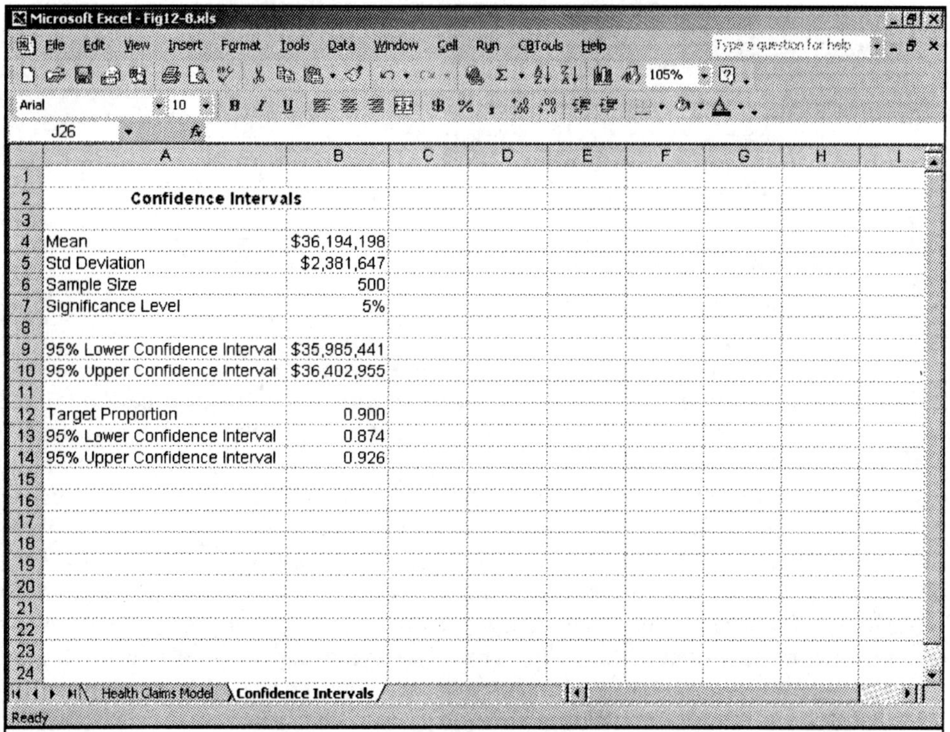

	A	B
2	**Confidence Intervals**	
4	Mean	$36,194,198
5	Std Deviation	$2,381,647
6	Sample Size	500
7	Significance Level	5%
9	95% Lower Confidence Interval	$35,985,441
10	95% Upper Confidence Interval	$36,402,955
12	Target Proportion	0.900
13	95% Lower Confidence Interval	0.874
14	95% Upper Confidence Interval	0.926

Key Cell Formulas

Cell	Formula	Copied to
B9	=B4-NORMSINV(1-B7/2)*B5/SQRT(B6)	—
B10	=B4+NORMSINV(1-B7/2)*B5/SQRT(B6)	—
B13	=B12-NORMSINV(1-B7/2)*SQRT(B12*(1-B12)/B6)	—
B14	=B12+NORMSINV(1-B7/2)*SQRT(B12*(1-B12)/B6)	—

FIGURE 12.18
Confidence intervals for the population mean and population proportion

Thus, we can be 95% confident that the true mean of the population of total company cost values falls somewhere in the interval from \$35,985,441 to \$36,402,955.

12.11.2 Constructing a Confidence Interval for a Population Proportion

In our example, we estimated that 90% of the population of total company cost values fall below \$39,220,862 based on our sample of 500 observations. However, if we could evaluate the entire population of total cost values, we might find that only 80% of these values fall below \$39,220,862. Or, we might find that 99% of the entire population falls below this mark. It would be helpful to determine how accurate the 90% value is. So, at times, we might want to construct a confidence interval for the true proportion of a population that falls below (or above) some value, for example Y_p.

To see how this is done, let $\overline{p}$ denote the proportion of observations in a sample of size n that falls below some value Y_p. Assuming that n is sufficiently large ($n \geq 30$), the Central Limit Theorem tells us that the lower and upper limits of a 95% confidence interval for the true proportion of the population falling below Y_p are represented by:

$$95\%\ \text{Lower Confidence Limit} = \overline{p} - 1.96 \times \sqrt{\frac{\overline{p}(1-\overline{p})}{n}}$$

$$95\%\ \text{Upper Confidence Limit} = \overline{p} + 1.96 \times \sqrt{\frac{\overline{p}(1-\overline{p})}{n}}$$

Although we can be fairly certain that the proportion of observations falling below Y_p in our sample is not equal to the true proportion of the population falling below Y_p, we can be 95% confident that the true proportion of the population falling below Y_p is contained within the lower and upper limits given previously. Again, if we want a 90% or 99% confidence interval, we must change the value 1.96 in the previous equations to 1.645 or 2.575, respectively.

Using these formulas, we can calculate the lower and upper limits of a 95% confidence interval for the true proportion of the population falling below \$39,220,862. From our simulation results, we know that 90% of the observations in our sample are less than \$39,220,862. Thus, our estimated value of $\overline{p}$ is 0.90. This value was entered into cell B12 in Figure 12.18. The upper and lower limits of a 95% confidence interval for the true proportion of the population falling below \$39,220,862 are calculated in cells B13 and B14 of Figure 12.18 using the following formulas:

Formula for cell B13:	=B12-NORMSINV(1-B7/2)*SQRT(B12*(1-B12)/B6)
Formula for cell B14:	=B12+NORMSINV(1-B7/2)*SQRT(B12*(1-B12)/B6)

We can be 95% confident that the true proportion of the population of total cost values falling below \$39,220,862 is between 0.874 and 0.926. Because this interval is fairly tight around the value 0.90, we can be reasonably certain that the \$39,220,862 figure quoted to the CFO has approximately a 10% chance of being exceeded.

12.11.3 Sample Sizes and Confidence Interval Widths

The formulas for the confidence intervals in the previous section depend directly on the number of replications (n) in the simulation. As the number of replications (n) increases, the width of the confidence interval decreases (or becomes more precise). Thus, for a given level of confidence (for example, 95%), the only way to make the upper and lower limits of the interval closer together (or tighter) is to make n larger—that is, use a larger sample size. A larger sample should provide more information about the population and, therefore, allow us to be more accurate in estimating the true parameters of the population.

12.12 THE BENEFITS OF SIMULATION

What have we accomplished through simulation? Are we really better off than if we had just used the results of the original model proposed in Figure 12.2? The estimated value for the expected total cost to the company in Figure 12.2 is comparable to that obtained through simulation (although this might not always be the case). But remember that the goal of modeling is to give us greater insight into a problem to help us make more informed decisions.

The results of our simulation analysis do give us greater insight into the example problem. In particular, we now have some idea of the best- and worst-case total cost outcomes for the company. We have a better idea of the distribution and variability of the possible outcomes, and a more precise idea about where the mean of the distribution is located. We also now have a way of determining how likely it is for the actual outcome to fall above or below some value. Thus, in addition to our greater insight and understanding of the problem, we also have solid empirical evidence (the facts and figures) to support our recommendations.

12.13 ADDITIONAL USES OF SIMULATION

Earlier, we indicated that simulation is a technique that *describes* the behavior or characteristics of a bottom-line performance measure. The next several examples show how describing the behavior of a performance measure gives a manager a useful tool in determining the optimal value for one or more controllable parameters in a decision problem. These examples reinforce the mechanics of using simulation and also demonstrate some additional capabilities of Crystal Ball.

Applying Simulation in Personal Financial Planning

A recent article in the *Wall Street Journal* highlighted the importance of simulation in evaluating the risk in personal financial investments. "Many people are taking a lot more risk than they realize. They are walking around with a false sense of security," said Christopher Cordaro, an investment adviser at Bugen Stuart Korn & Cordaro of Chatman, N.J. Using one on-line retirement calculator, after entering information about your finances and assumptions about investment gains, the screen shows a green or red light indicating whether you have saved enough to retire. What is doesn't tell you is whether there is a 95% chance or just a 60% chance that your plan will succeed. "How certain are you about the green light—is it just about to turn yellow and you're just sneaking by?" Mr. Cordaro asked.

Although any planning is better than nothing, traditional planning models spit out answers that create "the illusion that the number is a certainty, when it isn't," said Ross Levin, a Minneapolis investment adviser who uses simulation. Mutual-fund firm T. Rowe Price applied simulation to its recently launched Retirement Income Manager, a personalized consultation service that helps retirees understand how much income they can afford without outliving their assets or depleting funds they want to leave to heirs. A number of independent financial planning companies are now also using simulation software (see the Advisor Tools section of http://www.financeware.com).

In the face of widely divergent possibilities, the number crunching involved in simulation can bring some peace of mind. Steven Haas of Randolph, N.J., was not sure whether he had saved enough to accept an early retirement package from AT&T at age 53. After his financial advisor used simulation to determine he had a 95% probability that his money would last until he reached age 110, Mr. Haas took the package and retired. Mr. Haas reported that by using simulation, "I found that even under significantly negative scenarios we could live comfortably. It relieved a lot of anxiety."

Adapted from "Monte Carlo Financial Simulator May Be a Good Bet for Planning," *Wall Street Journal*, Section C1, April 27, 2000 by Karen Hube.

12.14 A RESERVATION MANAGEMENT EXAMPLE

Businesses that allow customers to make reservations for services (such as airlines, hotels, and car rental companies) know that some percentage of the reservations made will not be used for one reason or another, leaving these companies with a difficult decision problem. If they accept reservations for only the number of customers that can actually be served, then a portion of the company's assets will be underutilized when some customers with reservations fail to arrive. On the other hand, if they overbook (or accept more reservations than can be handled), then at times, more customers will arrive than can actually be served. This typically results in additional financial costs to the company and often generates ill-will among those customers who cannot be served. The following example illustrates how simulation might be used to help a company determine the optimal number of reservations to accept.

Marty Ford is an operations analyst for Piedmont Commuter Airlines (PCA). Recently, Marty was asked to make a recommendation on how many reservations PCA should book on Flight 343—a flight from a small regional airport in New England to a major hub at Boston's Logan airport. The plane used on Flight 343 is a small twin-engine turbo-prop with 19 passenger seats available. PCA sells nonrefundable tickets for Flight 343 for $150 per seat.

Industry statistics show that for every ticket sold for a commuter flight, a 0.10 probability exists that the ticket holder will not be on the flight. Thus, if PCA sells 19 tickets for this flight, there is a fairly good chance that one or more seats on the plane will be empty. Of course, empty seats represent lost potential revenue to the company. On the other hand, if PCA overbooks this flight and more than 19 passengers show up, some of them will have to be bumped to a later flight.

To compensate for the inconvenience of being bumped, PCA gives these passengers vouchers for a free meal, a free flight at a later date, and sometimes also pays for them to stay overnight in a hotel near the airport. PCA pays an average of $325 (including the cost of lost goodwill) for each passenger that gets bumped. Marty wants to determine if PCA can increase profits by overbooking this flight and, if so, how many reservations should be accepted to produce the maximum average profit. To assist in the analysis, Marty analyzed market research data for this flight that reveals the following probability distribution of demand for this flight:

Seats Demanded	**14**	**15**	**16**	**17**	**18**	**19**	**20**	**21**	**22**	**23**	**24**	**25**
Probability	0.03	0.05	0.07	0.09	0.11	0.15	0.18	0.14	0.08	0.05	0.03	0.02

12.14.1 Implementing the Model

A spreadsheet model for this problem is shown in Figure 12.19 (and in the file Fig12-19.xls on your data disk). The spreadsheet begins by listing the relevant data from the problem, including the number of seats available on the plane, the price PCA charges for each seat, the probability of a no-show (a ticketed passenger not arriving in time for the flight), the cost of bumping passengers, and the number of reservations that will be accepted.

The distribution of demand for seats on the flight is summarized in columns E and F. Using this data, the number of seats demanded for a particular flight is randomly generated in cell C10 as follows:

Formula for cell C10: = CB.Custom(E5:F16)

The number of tickets actually sold for a flight cannot exceed the number of reservations the company is willing to accept. Thus, the number of tickets sold is calculated in cell C11 as follows:

Formula for cell C11: =MIN(C10,C8)

FIGURE 12.19
Spreadsheet model for the overbooking problem

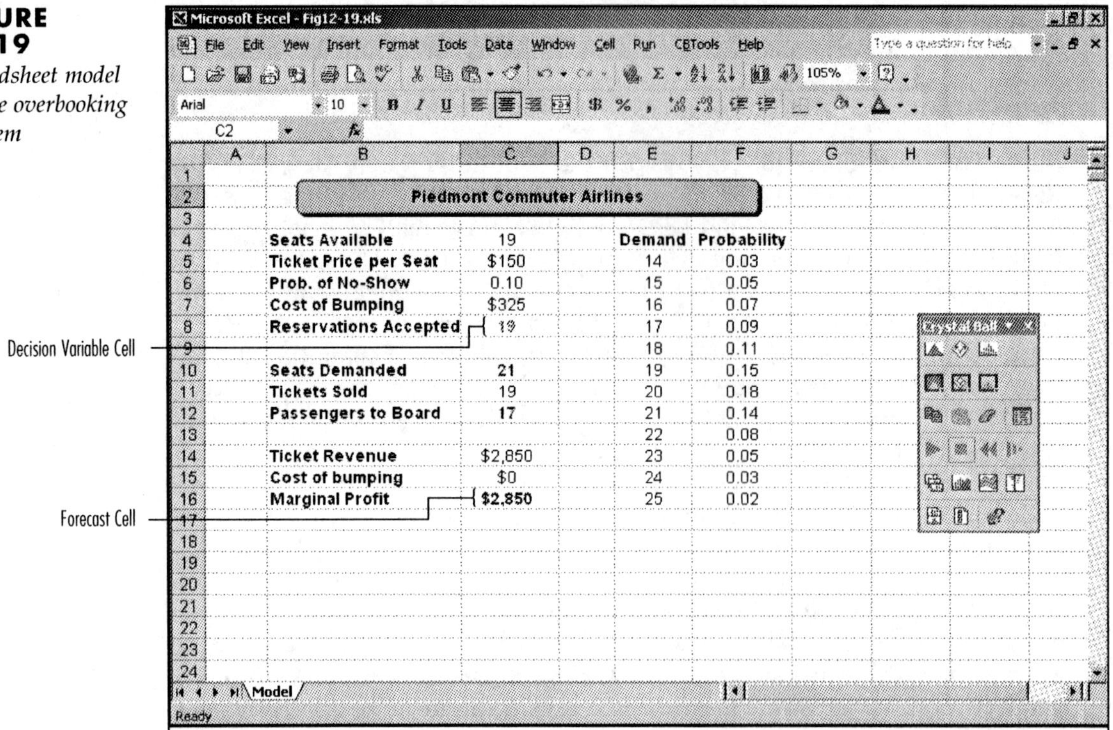

Key Cell Formulas

Cell	Formula	Copied to
C10	=CB.Custom(E5: F16)	—
C11	=MIN(C10,C8)	—
C12	=CB.Binomial(1-C6,C11)	—
C14	=C11*C5	—
C15	=MAX(C12-C4,0)*C7	—
C16	=C14-C15	—

Because each ticketed passenger has a 0.10 probability of being a no-show, a 0.9 probability exists that each ticketed passenger will arrive in time to board the flight. Thus, the CB.Binomial( ) function (described in Figure 12.4) is used in cell C12 to model the number of ticketed passengers that actually arrive for a flight:

Formula for cell C12: =CB.Binomial(1-C6,C11)

Cell C14 represents the ticket revenue PCA earns based on the number of tickets it sells for each flight. The formula for this cell is:

Formula for cell C14: =C11*C5

Cell C15 computes the costs PCA incurs when passengers must be bumped (*i.e.*, when the number of passengers wanting to board exceeds the number of available seats).

Formula for cell C15: = MAX(C12-C4,0)*C7

Finally, cell C16 computes the marginal profit PCA earns on each flight.

Formula for cell C16: =C14-C15

12.14.2 Using the Decision Table Tool

Marty wants to determine the number of reservations to accept that, on average, will result in the highest marginal profit. To do so, he needs to simulate what would happen to the marginal profit cell (C16) if 19, 20, 21, …, 25 reservations were accepted. Fortunately, Crystal Ball includes a tool called Decision Table that simplifies this type of analysis. To use Decision Table, first indicate the marginal profit cell (C16) to be a forecast cell in the usual way:

1. Select C16.
2. Click the Define Forecast icon on the Crystal Ball toolbar (or click Cell, Define Forecast on the main menu).

Next, define cell C8 (number of reservations accepted) to be a decision variable that may assume integer values from 19 to 25. To do this:

1. Select cell C8.
2. Click Cell, Define Decision.
3. Fill in the values shown in Figure 12.20.
4. Click OK.

When comparing different values for one or more decision variables, it is best if each possible solution is evaluated using exactly the same series of random

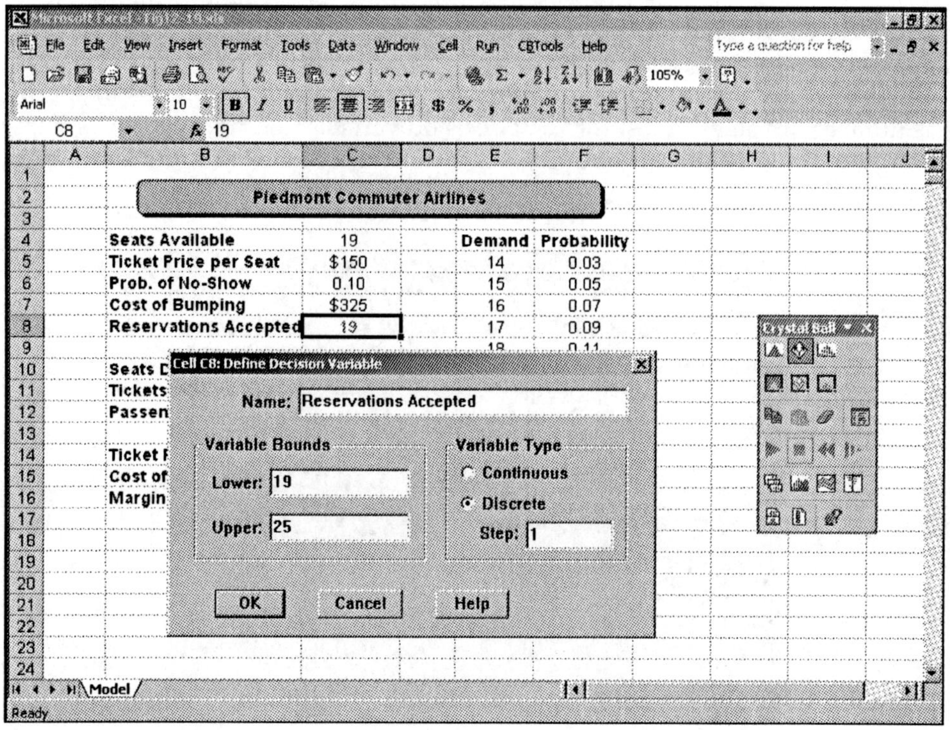

FIGURE 12.20
Defining reservations accepted as a decision variable

numbers. In this way, any difference in the performance of two possible solutions can be attributed to the decision variables' values and not the result of a more favorable set of random numbers for one of the solutions. You can ensure that Crystal Ball uses the same set of random numbers for each simulation by selecting the "Use Same Sequence of Random Numbers" option and supplying an "Initial Seed Value" under the Sampling option on Crystal Ball's Run Preferences dialog box shown in Figure 12.21.

The Sampling Method options shown in Figure 12.21 also have an impact on the accuracy of the results of a simulation run. Using the Monte Carlo option, Crystal Ball is free to select any value for a particular RNG during each replication of the model. For example, Crystal Ball might repeatedly generate several very extreme (and rare!) values from the upper tail of a normal distribution. The Latin Hypercube option guards against this by ensuring that a fair representation of values is generated from the entire distribution for each RNG. As you might imagine, the Latin Hypercube sampling option requires a bit more work during each replication of the model, but it tends to generate more accurate simulation results in a fewer number of trials.

After setting a random number seed as shown in Figure 12.21, we are ready to use the Decision Table tool. To invoke the Decision Table tool:

1. Click the CBTools menu option.
2. Click Decision Table.

The dialog box shown in Figure 12.22 appears prompting us to select the forecast (or target) cell we want to track. Here, we select the "Marginal Profit" option and click the Next button.

In the next dialog box, shown in Figure 12.23, we select the decision variable we want to evaluate. In this case, there is only one variable (Reservations Accepted). However, the Decision Table tool allows you to select up to two decision variables to analyze simultaneously.

The next dialog box, shown in Figure 12.24 on page 628, allows us to specify the number of values to test for each decision variable and the number of iterations (trials) to use for each resulting simulation run. In our case, there are seven

FIGURE 12.21
Crystal Ball's Run Preferences dialog box

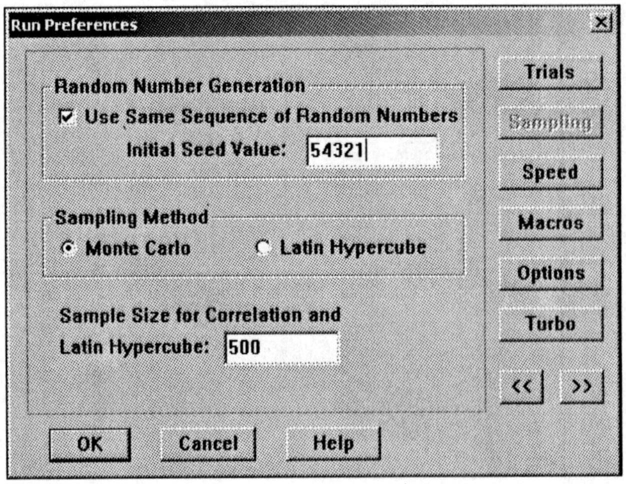

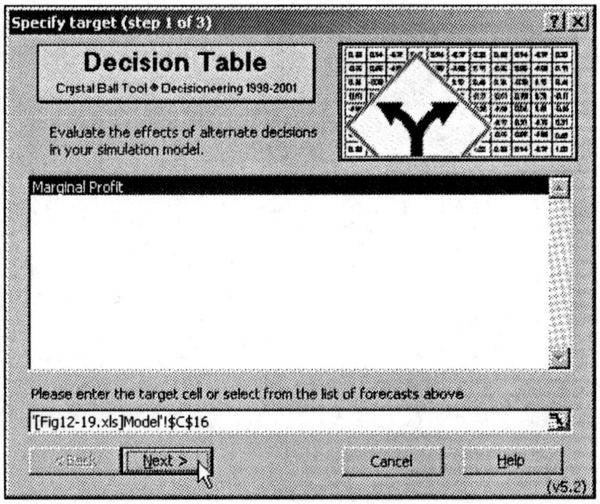

FIGURE 12.22
Specifying the target cell for the Decision Table tool

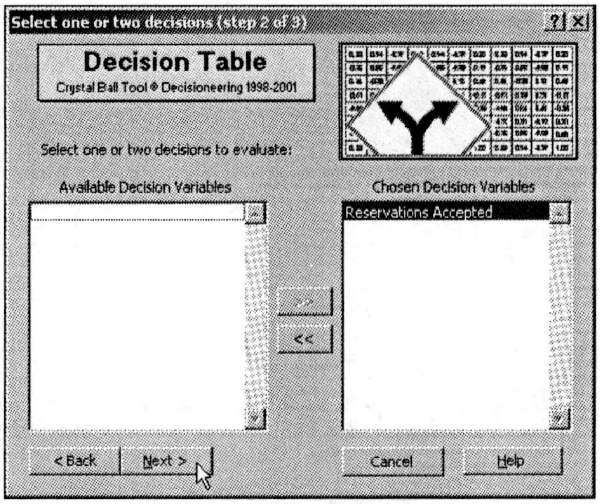

FIGURE 12.23
Choosing the decision variable with the Decision Table tool

possible discrete values for Reservations Accepted (*i.e.*, 19, 20, 21, …, 25) and we want to test them all. However, for continuous decision variables that can assume any value within some interval, it is impossible to test all the possible values and we must tell the Decision Table tool the number of possible values to try.

When you click the Start button in Figure 12.24, the Decision Table tool runs a separate simulation for each of the seven possible values we indicated for the decision variable. When it is finished, the Decision Table tool creates a new workbook like the one shown in Figure 12.25 summarizing the average value of the forecast cell (Marginal Profit) for each of the seven simulations. These values indicate that the average marginal profit reaches a maximum value of $2,774 when PCA accepts 21 reservations. We can easily create a bar chart from this data to graphically represent the differences in the average profits under each scenario.

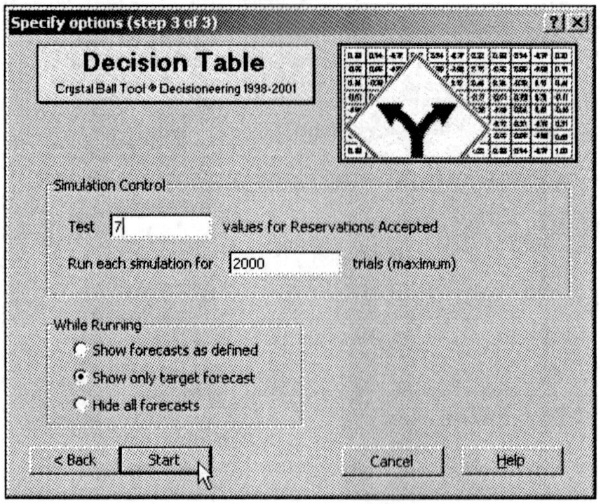

FIGURE 12.24
Setting options with the Decision Table tool

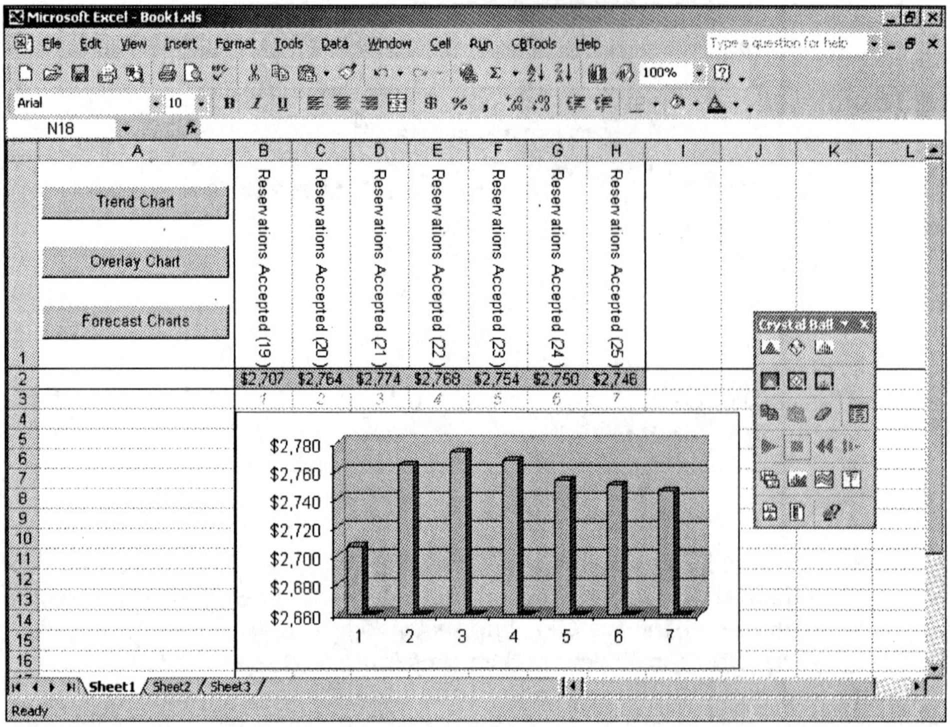

FIGURE 12.25
Results of the Decision Table tool

You can also select one or more of the average profit values on row 2 in Figure 12.25 and display a Trend Chart, Overlay Chart, or Forecast Chart for the selected values. Figure 12.26 shows an Overlay Chart comparing the distributions of values generated in simulation 3 (where up to 21 reservations were accepted) and simulation 7 (where up to 25 reservations were accepted). This type of chart is often helpful in comparing the riskiness of different decision alternatives.

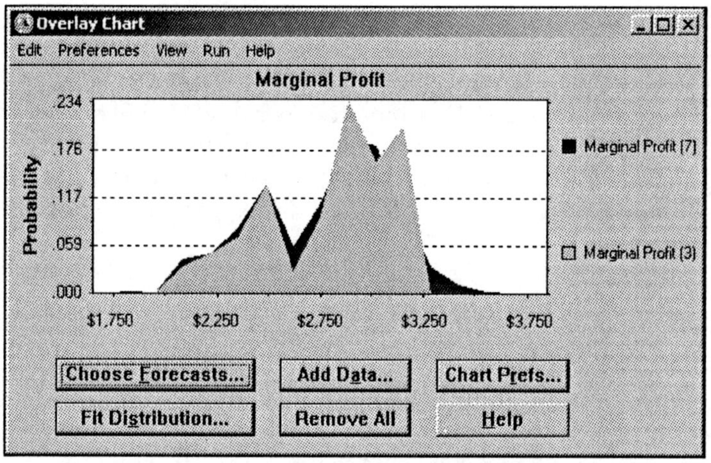

FIGURE 12.26
Overlay chart comparing outcome distributions for 21 and 25 reservations accepted

12.15 AN INVENTORY CONTROL EXAMPLE

According to the *Wall Street Journal,* U.S. businesses recently had a combined inventory worth $884.77 billion dollars. Because so much money is tied up in inventories, businesses face many important decisions regarding the management of these assets. Frequently asked questions regarding inventory include:

- What's the best level of inventory for a business to maintain?
- When should goods be reordered (or manufactured)?
- How much safety stock should be held in inventory?

The study of inventory control principles is split into two distinct areas—one assumes that demand is known (or deterministic), and the other assumes that demand is random (or stochastic). If demand is known, various formulas can be derived that provide answers to the previous questions (an example of one such formula is given in the discussion of the EOQ model in chapter 8.) However, when demand for a product is uncertain or random, answers to the previous questions cannot be expressed in terms of a simple formula. In these situations, the technique of simulation proves to be a useful tool, as illustrated in the following example.

Laura Tanner is the owner of Millennium Computer Corporation (MCC), a retail computer store in Austin, Texas. Competition in retail computer sales is fierce—both in terms of price and service. Laura is concerned about the number of stockouts occurring on a popular type of computer monitor. Stockouts are very costly to the business because when customers cannot buy this item at MCC, they simply buy it from a competing store and MCC loses the sale (there are no backorders). Laura measures the effects of stockouts on her business in terms of service level, or the percentage of total demand that can be satisfied from inventory.

Laura has been following the policy of ordering 50 monitors whenever her daily ending inventory position (defined as ending inventory on hand plus outstanding orders) falls below her reorder point of 28 units. Laura places the order at the beginning of the next day. Orders are delivered at the beginning of the day and, therefore, can be used to satisfy demand on that day. For example, if the ending inventory position on day 2 is less than 28, Laura places the order at the beginning of day 3. If the actual time between order and delivery, or lead time, turns out to be four days, then the order arrives at the start of day 7. The current level of on-hand inventory is 50 units and no orders are pending.

MCC sells an average of six monitors per day. However, the actual number sold on any given day can vary. By reviewing her sales records for the past several months, Laura determined that the actual daily demand for this monitor is a random variable that can be described by the following probability distribution:

Units Demanded	**0**	**1**	**2**	**3**	**4**	**5**	**6**	**7**	**8**	**9**	**10**
Probability	0.01	0.02	0.04	0.06	0.09	0.14	0.18	0.22	0.16	0.06	0.02

The manufacturer of this computer monitor is located in California. Although it takes an average of four days for MCC to receive an order from this company, Laura has determined that the lead time of a shipment of monitors is also a random variable that can be described by the following probability distribution:

Lead Time (days)	**3**	**4**	**5**
Probability	0.2	0.6	0.2

One way to guard against stockouts and improve the service level is to increase the reorder point for the item so that more inventory is on hand to meet the demand occurring during the lead time. However, there are holding costs associated with keeping more inventory on hand. Laura wants to evaluate her current ordering policy for this item and determine if it might be possible to improve the service level without increasing the average amount of inventory on hand.

12.15.1 Creating the RNGs

To solve this problem, we need to build a model to represent the inventory of computer monitors during an average month of 30 days. This model must account for the random daily demands that can occur and the random lead times encountered when orders are placed. First, we will consider how to create RNGs to model the daily demands and order lead times. The data for these variables are entered in the spreadsheet as shown in Figure 12.27 (and in the file Fig12-27.xls on your data disk).

The order lead time and daily demand variables are both examples of *general, discrete* random variables because the possible outcomes they assume consist solely of integers, and the probabilities associated with each outcome are not equal (or not uniform). Thus, using the CB.Custom( ) function described in Figure 12.5, the RNGs for each variable are:

RNG for order lead time: =CB.Custom(Data!$C$7:$D$9)

RNG for daily demand: =CB.Custom(Data!$F$7:$G$17)

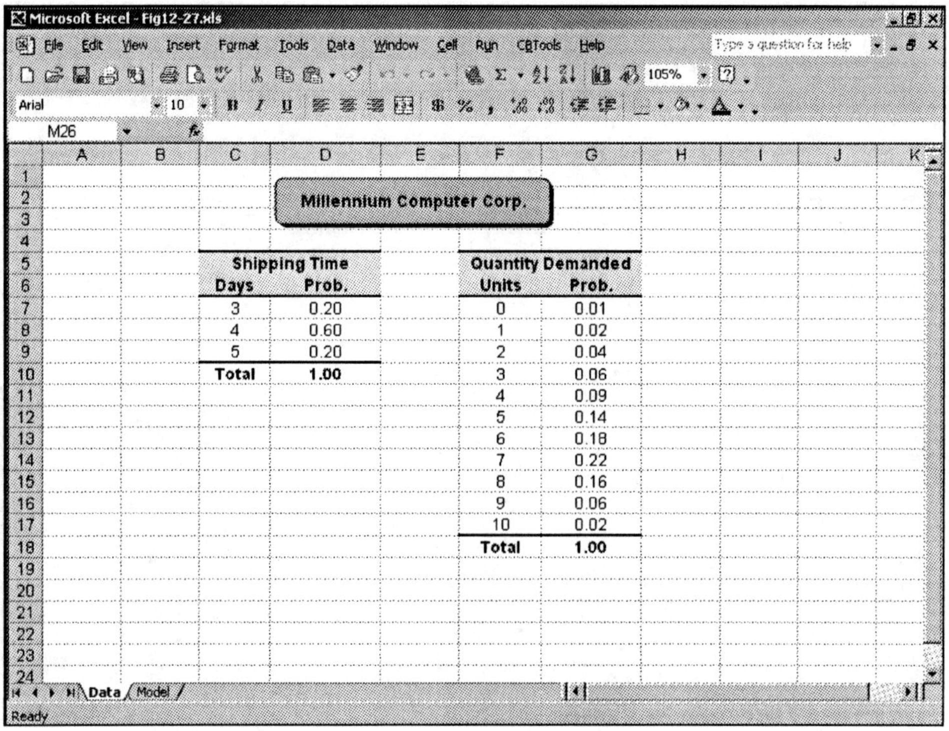

FIGURE 12.27
RNG data for MCC's inventory problem

12.15.2 Implementing the Model

Now that we have a way of generating the random numbers needed in this problem, we can consider how the model should be built. Figure 12.28 shows the model representing 30 days of inventory activity. Notice that cells M5 and M6 have been reserved to represent, respectively, the reorder point and order quantity for the model.

The inventory on hand at the beginning of each day is calculated in column B in Figure 12.28. The beginning inventory for each day is simply the ending inventory from the previous day. The formulas in column B are:

Formula for cell B6: =50

Formula for cell B7: =F6
(Copy to B8 through B35.)

Column C represents the number of units scheduled to be received each day. We will discuss the formulas in column C after we discuss columns H, I, and J, which relate to ordering and order lead times.

In column D, we use the technique described earlier to generate random daily demands, as:

Formula for cell D6: =CB.Custom(Data!$F$7:$G$17)
(Copy to D7 through D35.)

Because it is possible for demand to exceed the available supply, column E indicates how much of the daily demand can be met. If the beginning inventory (in column B) plus the ordered units received (in column C) is greater than or

FIGURE 12.28
Spreadsheet model for MCC's inventory problem

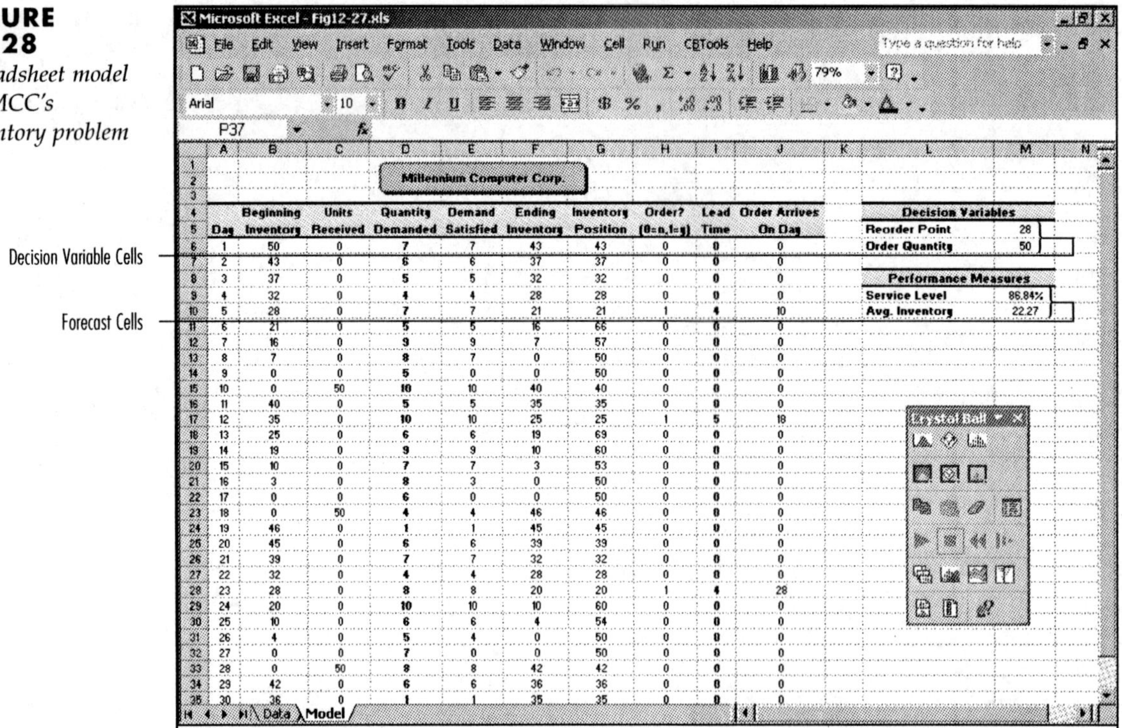

Day	Beginning Inventory	Units Received	Quantity Demanded	Demand Satisfied	Ending Inventory	Inventory Position	Order? (0=n,1=y)	Lead Time	Order Arrives On Day
1	50	0	7	7	43	43	0	0	0
2	43	0	6	6	37	37	0	0	0
3	37	0	5	5	32	32	0	0	0
4	32	0	4	4	28	28	0	0	0
5	28	0	7	7	21	21	1	4	10
6	21	0	5	5	16	66	0	0	0
7	16	0	9	9	7	57	0	0	0
8	7	0	8	7	0	50	0	0	0
9	0	0	5	0	0	50	0	0	0
10	0	50	10	10	40	40	0	0	0
11	40	0	5	5	35	35	0	0	0
12	35	0	10	10	25	25	1	5	18
13	25	0	6	6	19	69	0	0	0
14	19	0	9	9	10	60	0	0	0
15	10	0	7	7	3	53	0	0	0
16	3	0	8	3	0	50	0	0	0
17	0	0	6	0	0	50	0	0	0
18	0	50	4	4	46	46	0	0	0
19	46	0	1	1	45	45	0	0	0
20	45	0	6	6	39	39	0	0	0
21	39	0	7	7	32	32	0	0	0
22	32	0	4	4	28	28	0	0	0
23	28	0	8	8	20	20	1	4	28
24	20	0	10	10	10	60	0	0	0
25	10	0	6	6	4	54	0	0	0
26	4	0	5	4	0	50	0	0	0
27	0	0	7	0	0	50	0	0	0
28	0	50	8	8	42	42	0	0	0
29	42	0	6	6	36	36	0	0	0
30	36	0	1	1	35	35	0	0	0

Key Cell Formulas

Cell	Formula	Copied to
B6	=50	—
B7	=F6	B8:B35
C7	=COUNTIF($J$6:J6,A7)*$M$6	C8:C35
D6	=CB.Custom(Data!$F$7:$G$17)	D7:D35
E6	=MIN(D6,B6+C6)	E7:E35
F6	=B6+C6-E6	F7:F35
G6	=F6	—
G7	=G6-E7+IF(H6=1,$M$6,0)	G8:G35
H6	=IF(G6<$M$5,1,0)	H7:H35
I6	=IF(H6=0,0,CB.Custom(Data!$C$7:$D$9))	I7:I35
J6	=IF(I6=0,0,A6+1+I6)	J7:J35
M9	=SUM(E6:E35)/SUM(D6:D35)	—
M10	=AVERAGE(B6:B35)	—

equal to the actual demand, then all the demand can be satisfied; otherwise, MCC can sell only as many units as are available. This condition is modeled as:

Formula for cell E6: =MIN(D6,B6+C6)
(Copy to E7 through E35.)

The values in column F represent the on-hand inventory at the end of each day, and are calculated as:

Formula for cell F6: =B6+C6-E6
(Copy to F7 through F35.)

To determine whether to place an order, we first must calculate the inventory position, which was defined earlier as the ending inventory plus any outstanding orders. This is implemented in column G as:

Formula for cell G6: =F6

Formula for cell G7: =G6-E7+IF(H6=1,$M$6,0)
(Copy to G8 through G35.)

Column H indicates if an order should be placed based on inventory position and the reorder point, as:

Formula for cell H6: =IF(G6<$M$5,1,0)
(Copy to H7 through H35.)

If an order is placed, then we must generate the random lead time required to receive the order. This is done in column I as:

Formula for cell I6: =IF(H6=0,0,CB.Custom(Data!$C$7:$D$9))
(Copy to I7 through I35.)

This formula returns the value 0 if no order was placed (if H6=0); otherwise, it returns a random lead time value (if H6=1).

If an order is placed, column J indicates the day on which the order will be received based on its random lead time in column I. This is done as:

Formula for cell J6: =IF(I6=0,0,A6+1+I6)
(Copy to J7 through J35.)

The values in column C are coordinated with those in column J. The nonzero values in column J indicate the days on which orders will be received. For example, cell J10 indicates that an order will be received on day 10. The actual receipt of this order is reflected by the value of 50 in cell C15, which represents the receipt of an order at the beginning of day 10. The formula in cell C15 that achieves this is:

Formula for cell C15: =COUNTIF($J$6:J14,A15)*$M$6

This formula counts how many times the value in cell A15 (representing day 10) appears as a scheduled receipt day between days 1 through 9 in column J. This represents the number of orders scheduled to be received on day 10. We then multiply this by the order quantity (50), given in cell M6 to determine the total units to be received on day 10. Thus, the values in column C are generated as:

Formula for cell C6: =0

Formula for cell C7: =COUNTIF($J$6:J6,A7)*$M$6
(Copy to C8 through C35.)

The service level for the model is calculated in cell M9 using the values in columns D and E as:

Formula for cell M9: =SUM(E6:E35)/SUM(D6:D35)

Again, the service level represents the proportion of total demand that can be satisfied from inventory. The value in cell M9 indicates that in the scenario shown, 86.84% of the total demand is satisfied.

The average inventory level is calculated in cell M10 by averaging the values in column B. This is accomplished as follows:

Formula for cell M10: =AVERAGE(B6:B35)

12.15.3 Replicating the Model

The model in Figure 12.28 indicates one possible scenario that could occur if Laura uses a reorder point of 28 units for the computer monitor. Figure 12.29 shows the results of using Crystal Ball to replicate this model 500 times, tracking the values in cells M9 (service level) and M10 (average inventory) as forecast cells.

Figure 12.29 indicates that MCC's current reorder point (28 units) and order quantity (50 units) results in an average service level of approximately 96.07% (with a minimum value of 85.05% and a maximum value of 100%) and an average inventory level of almost 26 monitors (with a minimum value of 20 and a maximum value of 33).

12.15.4 Optimizing the Model

Suppose Laura wants to determine a reorder point and order quantity that provides an average service level of 98% while keeping the average inventory level as low as possible. One way to do this is to run additional simulations at various reorder point and inventory level combinations trying to find the combination of settings that produce the desired behavior. However, as you might imagine, this could be very time-consuming.

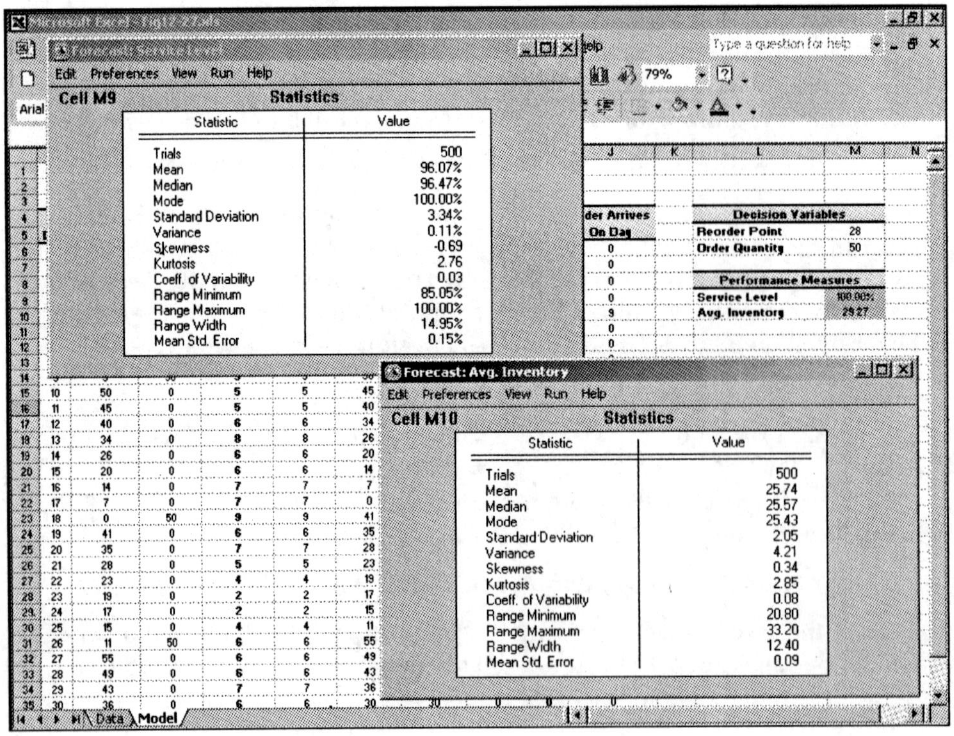

FIGURE 12.29
Results of 500 replications of the MCC model

Fortunately, Crystal Ball Professional includes a product called OptQuest that is designed to solve this type of problem. In order to use OptQuest, we must first use Crystal Ball to define cells M5 (reorder point) and M6 (order quantity) to be decision variable cells. We will assume Laura wants to consider discrete reorder points in the range from 20 and 50 and discrete order quantity values in the range from 20 to 70. To do this:

1. Select cells M5 and M6.
2. Click the Define Decision icon on the Crystal Ball toolbar (or click Cell, Define Decision).
3. Enter lower and upper bounds for each cell and a discrete step size of 1.
4. Click OK.

Note that cells M9 (service level) and M10 (average inventory level) should already be selected as forecast cells from our earlier simulation run.

Again, when comparing different values for one or more decision variables, it is best if each possible solution is evaluated using exactly the same series of random numbers. We can ensure that Crystal Ball uses the same set of random numbers for each simulation by selecting the "Use Same Sequence of Random Numbers" option and supplying an "Initial Seed Value" under the Sampling option on Crystal Ball's Run Preferences dialog box (shown earlier in Figure 12.21).

To optimize a simulation model, OptQuest requires at least one Assumption cell to be defined on the worksheet. Because we built the model in Figure 12.28 using Crystal Ball's built-in RNG functions, it does not contain any Assumption cells. However, we can circumvent this limitation by defining any unused cell in the worksheet to be an Assumption cell. This was done in Figure 12.28 as follows:

1. Select cell E2 and enter the value 9 (or any other numeric value).
2. Click Cell, Define Assumption.
3. Click OK twice.

Important Software Note

OptQuest requires at least one Assumption cell to be defined in the workbook being optimized. If you use Crystal Ball's built-in RNG functions to implement your model (as is the preference of this author), your workbook may not contain any Assumption cells. To circumvent this limitation of OptQuest, simply define one Assumption cell in any unused cell in your workbook. This cell will have no influence on the results of the model, but its presence is required for OptQuest to optimize the Decision cells in your model.

After the decision variable cells, forecast cells, random number seed, and an Assumption cell are specified using Crystal Ball, you may start an OptQuest session for the model as follows:

1. Click CBTools, OptQuest.
2. In OptQuest, click File, New.

The resulting OptQuest screen is shown in Figure 12.30. This screen shows the decision variables for the current problem along with the bounds and restrictions we have placed on these variables. Click the OK button on this screen to accept these selections.

The next step is to tell OptQuest about the objectives we want it to pursue. This is done using the Forecast Selection window shown in Figure 12.31.

In the window shown in Figure 12.31, we indicated we want OptQuest to minimize the value of the "Avg. Inventory" cell. We also placed a lower bound of 0.98 on the "Service Level" cell and indicated this is a requirement that must be enforced. (Note that you can make changes to the various cells in the Forecast Selection window by clicking on the appropriate cell.) Click the OK button on this screen to accept these selections.

FIGURE 12.30
OptQuest's Decision Variable Selection screen

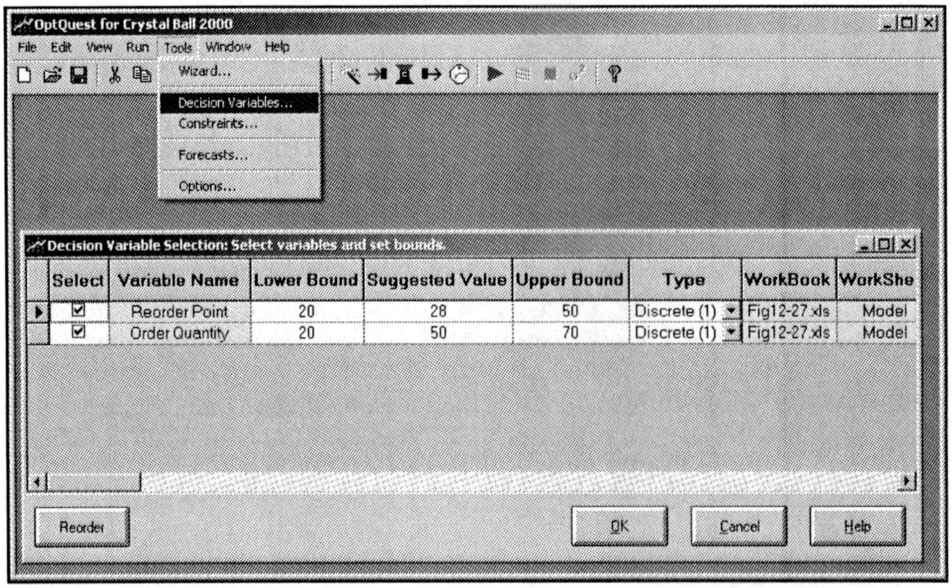

FIGURE 12.31
OptQuest's Forecast Selection screen

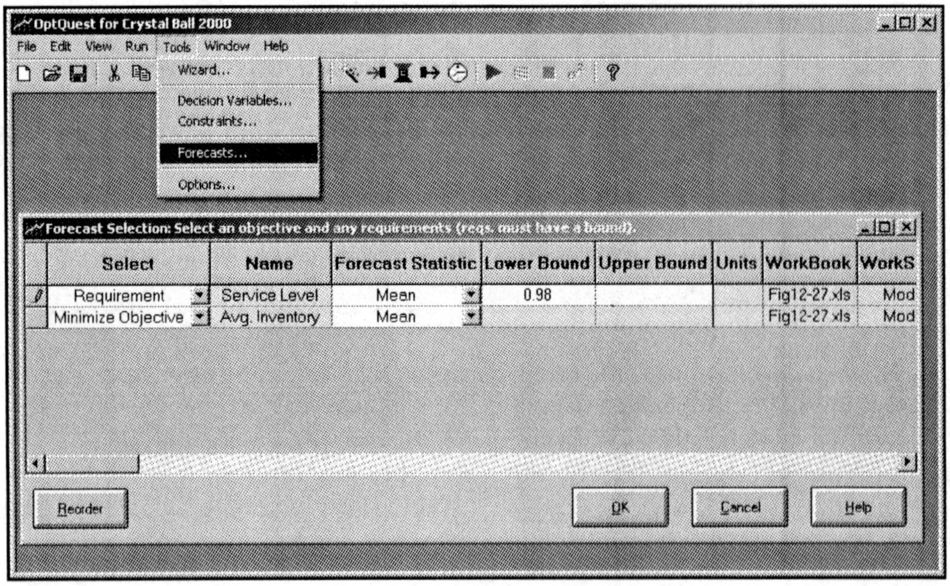

Next, we use the Options window shown in Figure 12.32 to indicate the amount of time we want OptQuest to search for solutions to the problem. It is important to remember that a separate simulation must be run for each combination of the decision variables that OptQuest chooses. OptQuest uses a number of heuristics to search intelligently for the best combination of decision variables. However, this is still inherently a very computationally intensive and time-consuming process and complicated models may take hours (or days) of solution time. Note that we are giving OptQuest ten minutes to search for a solution to the MCC problem.

With all the appropriate options set, click the Start icon (or click Run, Start). OptQuest then runs multiple simulations using different combinations of values for the decision variables. The Performance Graph and Status and Solutions windows shown in Figure 12.33 provide a summary of OptQuest's efforts on the problem. Ultimately, OptQuest found that a reorder point of 34 and order quantity of 20 resulted in an average service level of 98.4% while requiring an average inventory of approximately 18 units per month. Thus, MCC can simultaneously increase its service level and reduce its average inventory level by using the new ordering policy identified by OptQuest.

12.15.5 Comment on Using OptQuest

When using OptQuest to solve a problem, it is often a good idea to reduce the number of trials Crystal Ball performs during each simulation. This allows OptQuest to explore more possible combinations of decision variable values (solutions) in the allotted amount of time. Then after OptQuest identifies a solution for the problem, you can implement that solution in your model (click Edit, Copy to Excel in OptQuest) and rerun Crystal Ball with a higher number of trials to get a better idea of how well the suggested solution actually performs.

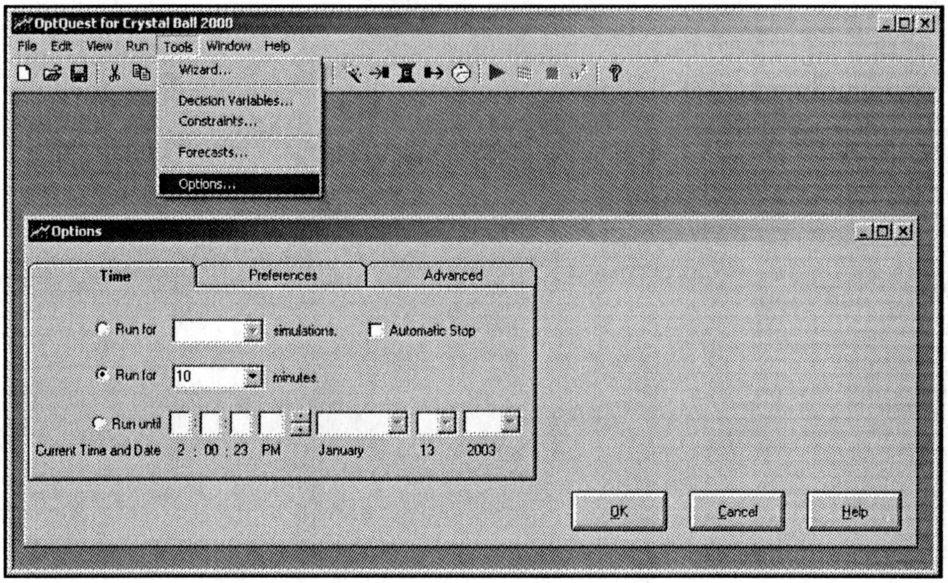

FIGURE 12.32
OptQuest's Options screen

FIGURE 12.33
OptQuest results

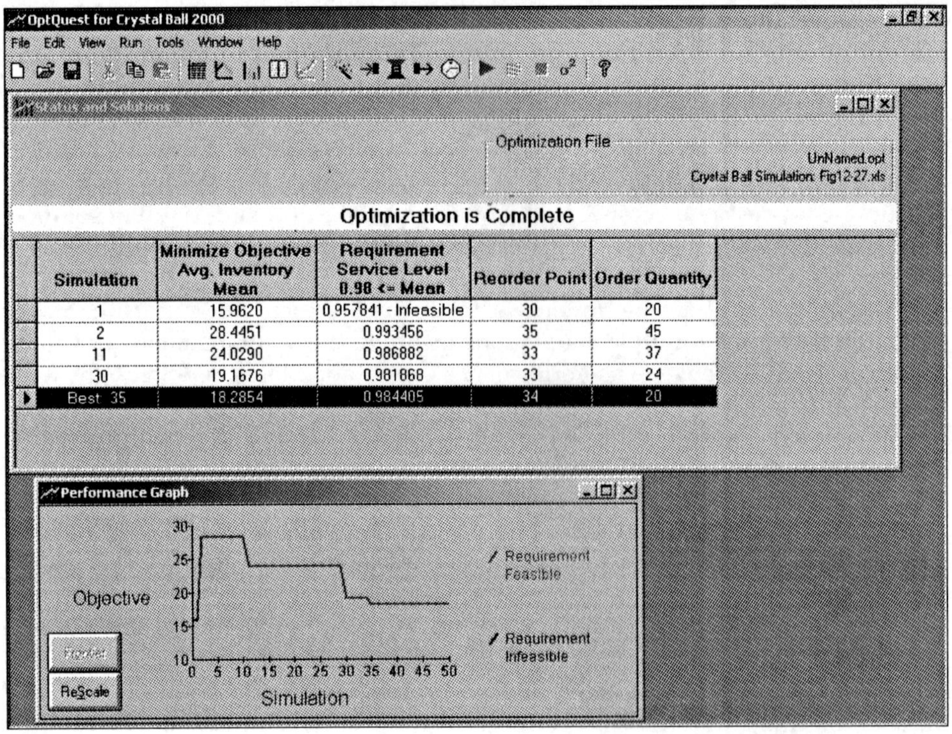

12.16 A PROJECT SELECTION EXAMPLE

In chapter 6, we saw how Solver can be used in project selection problems in which the payoff for each project is assumed to be known with certainty. In many cases, a great deal of uncertainty exists with respect to the ultimate payoff that will be received if a particular project is undertaken. In these situations, Crystal Ball and OptQuest offer an alternate means for deciding which project(s) to undertake. Consider the following example.

TRC Technologies has $2 million to invest in new R&D projects. The following table summarizes the initial cost, probability of success, and revenue potential for each of the projects.

			Revenue Potential ($000s)		
Project	**Initial Cost ($000s)**	**Probability of Success**	**Min.**	**Most Likely**	**Max.**
1	$250.0	90%	$ 600	$ 750	$ 900
2	$650.0	70%	$1,250	$1,500	$1,600
3	$250.0	60%	$ 500	$ 600	$ 750
4	$500.0	40%	$1,600	$1,800	$1,900
5	$700.0	80%	$1,150	$1,200	$1,400
6	$ 30.0	60%	$ 150	$ 180	$ 250
7	$350.0	70%	$ 750	$ 900	$1,000
8	$ 70.0	90%	$ 220	$ 250	$ 320

TRC's management wants to determine the set of projects that will maximize the firm's expected profit.

12.16.1 A Spreadsheet Model

A spreadsheet model for this problem is shown in Figure 12.34 (and the file Fig12-34.xls on your data disk). Cells C6 through C13 in this spreadsheet indicate which projects will be selected. Using Crystal Ball, we can define these cells to be decision variables that must take on discrete values between zero and one—or operate as binary variables. The values shown in cells C6 though C13 were assigned arbitrarily. We will use OptQuest to determine the optimal values for these variables.

In cell D14, we compute the total initial investment require by the selected projects as follows:

Formula for cell D14: =SUMPRODUCT(D6:D13,C6:C13)

In cell D16, we calculate the amount of unused or surplus investment funds. Using Crystal Ball, we will define this to be a forecast cell. Using OptQuest, we can

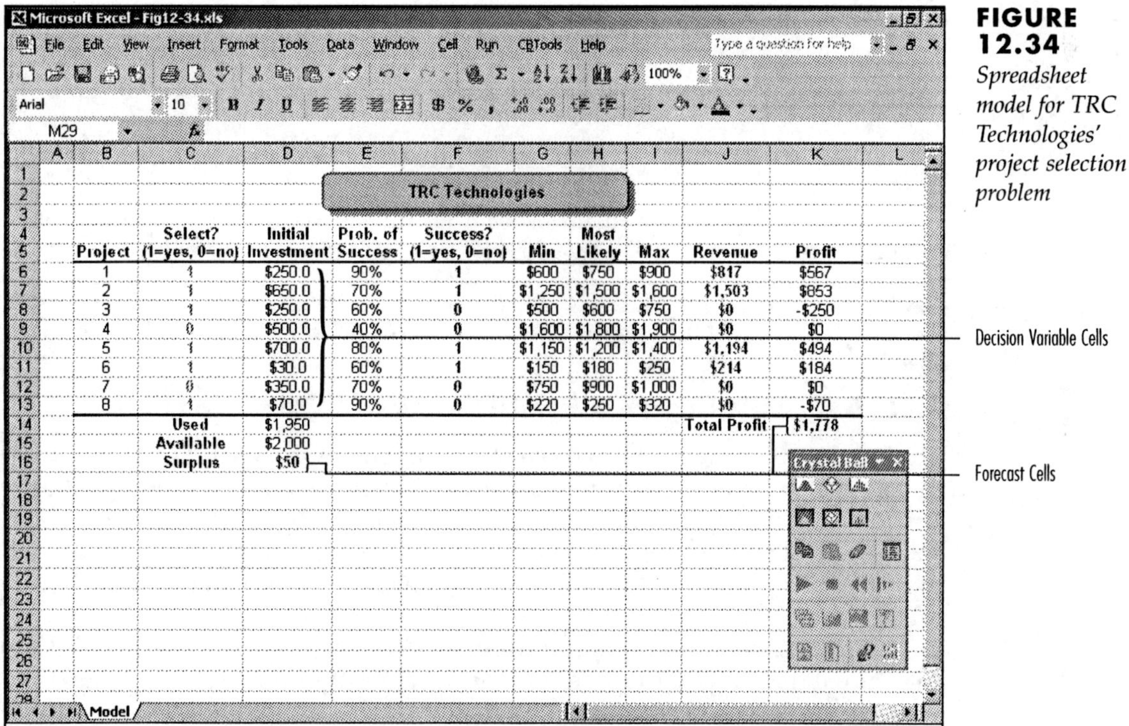

Project	Select? (1=yes, 0=no)	Initial Investment	Prob. of Success	Success? (1=yes, 0=no)	Min	Most Likely	Max	Revenue	Profit
1	1	$250.0	90%	1	$600	$750	$900	$817	$567
2	1	$650.0	70%	1	$1,250	$1,500	$1,600	$1,503	$853
3	1	$250.0	60%	0	$500	$600	$750	$0	-$250
4	0	$500.0	40%	0	$1,600	$1,800	$1,900	$0	$0
5	1	$700.0	80%	1	$1,150	$1,200	$1,400	$1,194	$494
6	1	$30.0	60%	1	$150	$180	$250	$214	$184
7	0	$350.0	70%	0	$750	$900	$1,000	$0	$0
8	1	$70.0	90%	0	$220	$250	$320	$0	-$70
	Used	$1,950						Total Profit	$1,778
	Available	$2,000							
	Surplus	$50							

FIGURE 12.34 *Spreadsheet model for TRC Technologies' project selection problem*

Key Cell Formulas

Cell	Formula	Copied to
D14	=SUMPRODUCT(D6:D13,C6:C13)	—
D16	=D15-D14	—
F6	=IF(C6=1,CB.Binomial(E6,1),0)	F7:F13
J6	=IF(F6=1,CB.Triangular(G6,H6,I6),0)	J7:J13
K6	=J6-C6*D6	K7:K13
K14	=SUM(K6:K13)	—

place a lower bound requirement of zero on the value of this cell to ensure that the projects selected do not require more than $2 million in initial investment funds.

Formula for cell D16: =D15-D14

A project has the potential to be successful only if it is selected. The success or failure of each project may be modeled using a binomial random variable using a single trial and the probability of success given in column E. Thus, we model the potential success of selected projects in column F as follows:

Formula for cell F6: =IF(C6=1,CB.Binomial(E6,1),0)
(Copy to cells F7 through F13.)

If a project is selected and successful, there is uncertainty about the revenue that it will generate. Because we have estimates of the minimum, most likely, and maximum possible revenue for each project, we will model the revenues for selected, successful projects using a triangular distribution. This is accomplished in column J as follows:

Formula for cell J6: =IF(F6=1,CB.Triangular(G6,H6,I6),0)
(Copy to cells J7 through J13.)

The profit associated with each project is computed in column K as follows:

Formula for cell K6: =J6-C6*D6
(Copy to cells K7 through K13.)

Cell K14 computes the total profit for each replication of the model. We will define this as a forecast cell using Crystal Ball and attempt to maximize its value using OptQuest.

Formula for cell K14: =SUM(K6:K13)

12.16.2 Solving the Problem with OptQuest

The OptQuest settings used to solve this problem are shown in Figure 12.35 and the optimal solution is shown in Figure 12.36. (Additionally, remember that at least one Assumption cell must be defined in the workbook to use OptQuest.) This solution involves selecting projects 1, 2, 4, 6, 7, and 8, requiring an initial investment of $1.85 million and resulting in an expected profit of approximately $1.5 million.

To investigate this solution in a bit more detail, we can copy it back into Crystal Ball (click Edit, Copy to Excel in OptQuest), run 2,000 replications, and view the statistics and frequency distribution associated with the solution. These results are shown in Figures 12.37 and 12.38 on page 642, respectively.

Although the expected (mean) profit associated with this solution is approximately $1.5 million, the range of the possible outcomes is fairly wide (approximately $5.4 million). The worst-case outcome observed with this solution resulted in approximately a $1.67 million loss, whereas the best-case outcome resulted in approximately a $3.76 million profit. Because each of the projects are a one-time occurrence that can either succeed or fail, the decision makers in this problem do not have the luxury of repeatedly selecting this set of projects over and over and realizing the average profit level of $1.5 million over time. Also, from Figure 12.38, we see that there is about a 9% chance of losing money if this solution is

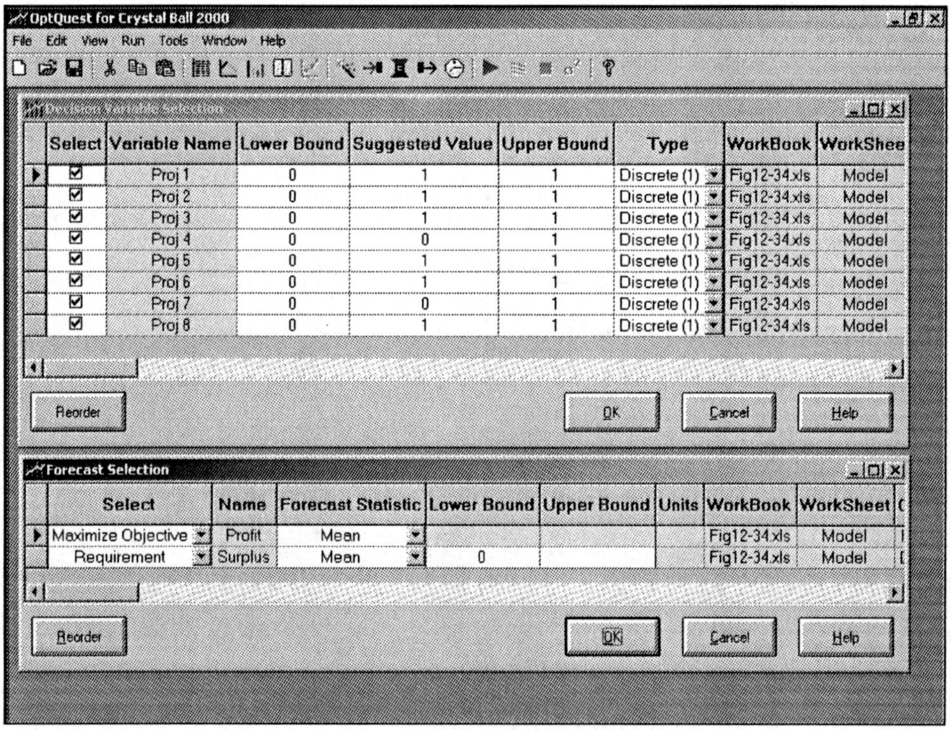

FIGURE 12.35
OptQuest settings for the project selection problem

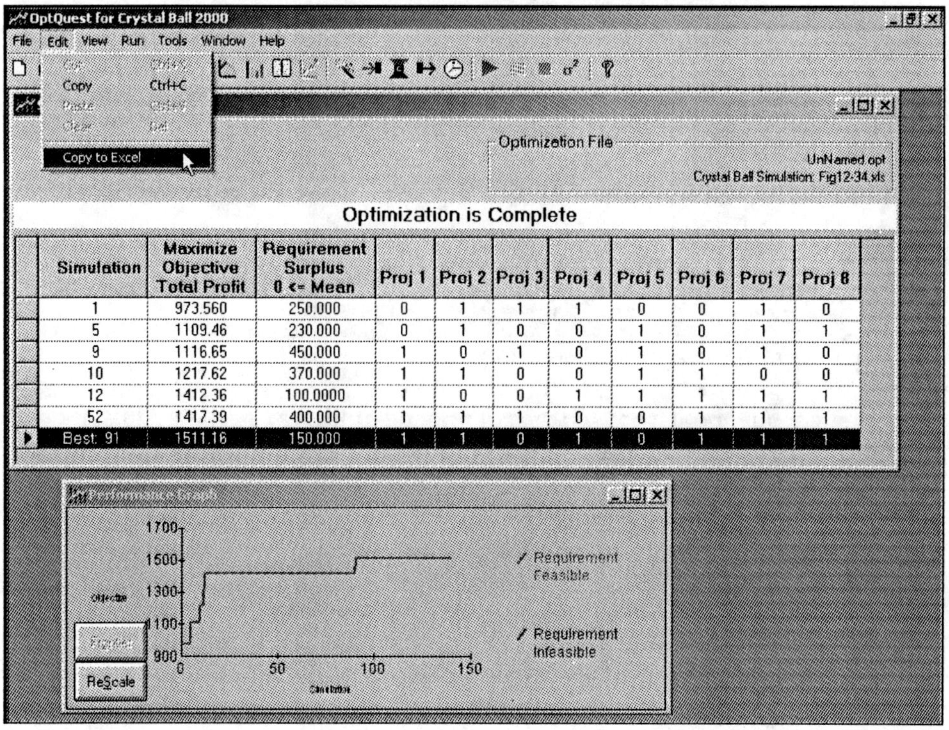

FIGURE 12.36
Optimal solution to the project selection problem

FIGURE 12.37
Statistics for the project selection problem

Forecast: Total Profit
Edit Preferences View Run Help
Cell K14 — Statistics

Statistic	Value
Trials	2,000
Mean	$1,511
Median	$1,560
Mode	---
Standard Deviation	$1,186
Variance	$1,406,930
Skewness	-0.01
Kurtosis	2.36
Coeff. of Variability	0.78
Range Minimum	($1,677)
Range Maximum	$3,762
Range Width	$5,438
Mean Std. Error	$26.52

FIGURE 12.38
Frequency distributions for the project selection problem

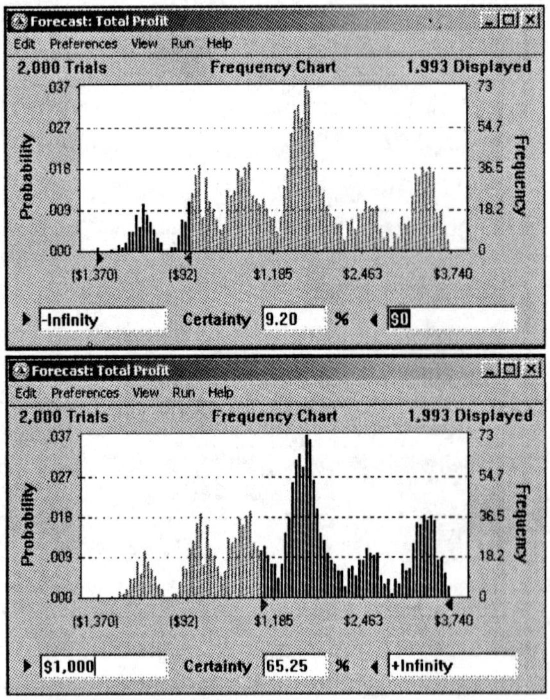

implemented, but about a 65% chance of making at least $1 million. Thus, there is a significant risk associated with this solution that is not apparent if one simply looks at its expected profit level of $1.5 million.

12.16.3 Considering Other Solutions

The decision makers in this problem might be interested in considering other alternatives. Because each of the projects has the potential to fail and lose money, the only way to completely avoid the possibility of a loss is not to invest in any of the projects. Unfortunately, this also completely avoids the possibility of earning profit! In most situations, greater levels of risk are required to achieve higher levels of return.

After considering the earlier solution and their attitudes toward risk and return, suppose the decision makers at TRC decide that they are comfortable with a 9% chance of losing money. But while assuming this risk, they want to ensure that they maximize the chance of earning a profit of at least $1 million. In order to solve this problem with OptQuest, we first need to define an additional forecast cell in our spreadsheet that indicates when losses occur. This was done as shown in Figure 12.39 by placing the following formula in cell K15:

Formula for cell K15: =IF(K14<0,1,0)

The OptQuest Forecast Selections settings required to solve this problem are shown in Figure 12.40. Notice that we now require that the mean value of the losses cell (K15) cannot exceed 9% for any feasible solution. Also, we are now attempting to maximize the number of times that the profit value falls above $1 million.

OptQuests's solution to this problem is shown in Figure 12.41. This solution indicates TRC should accept projects 1, 2, 5, 6, and 7, consuming $1.98 million in initial capital. To investigate this solution in more detail, we copy this solution back into our spreadsheet (in OptQuest click Edit, Copy to Excel), run 2,000 replications, and generate the solution statistics and frequency distribution shown in Figures 12.42 and 12.43 on page 645, respectively.

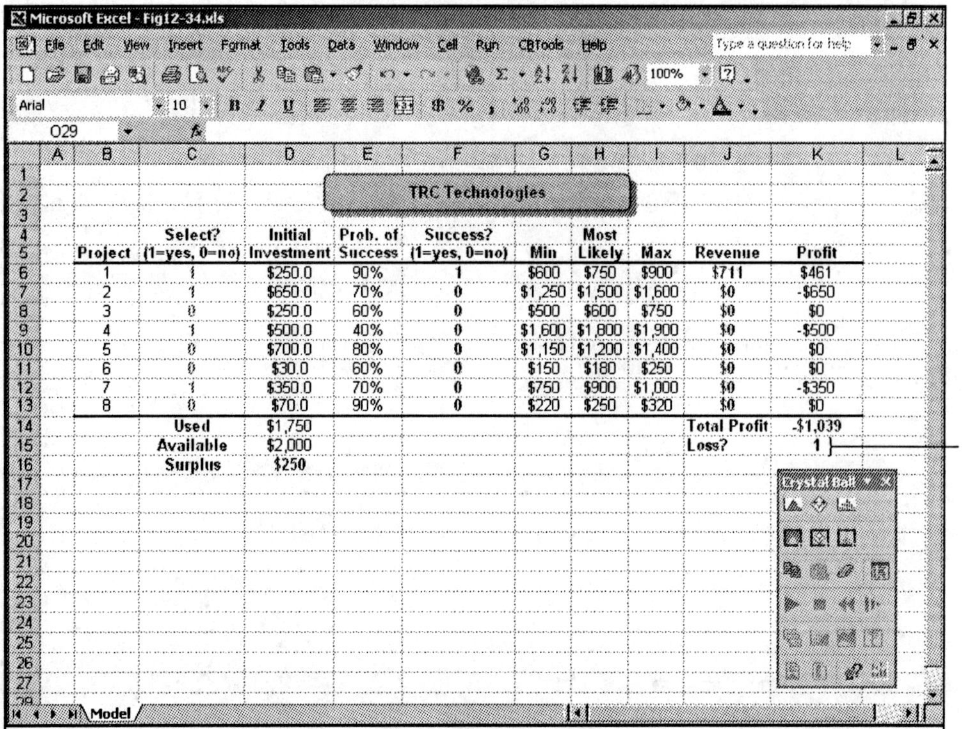

Project	Select? (1=yes, 0=no)	Initial Investment	Prob. of Success	Success? (1=yes, 0=no)	Min	Most Likely	Max	Revenue	Profit
1	1	$250.0	90%	1	$600	$750	$900	$711	$461
2	1	$650.0	70%	0	$1,250	$1,500	$1,600	$0	-$650
3	0	$250.0	60%	0	$500	$600	$750	$0	$0
4	1	$500.0	40%	0	$1,600	$1,800	$1,900	$0	-$500
5	0	$700.0	80%	0	$1,150	$1,200	$1,400	$0	$0
6	0	$30.0	60%	0	$150	$180	$250	$0	$0
7	1	$350.0	70%	0	$750	$900	$1,000	$0	-$350
8	0	$70.0	90%	0	$220	$250	$320	$0	$0
	Used	$1,750						Total Profit	-$1,039
	Available	$2,000						Loss?	1
	Surplus	$250							

Additional Forecast Cell

FIGURE 12.39
Spreadsheet for the revised project selection model

Key Cell Formulas

Cell	Formula	Copied to
K15	=IF(K14<0,1,0)	—

FIGURE 12.40
OptQuest settings for the revised project selection problem

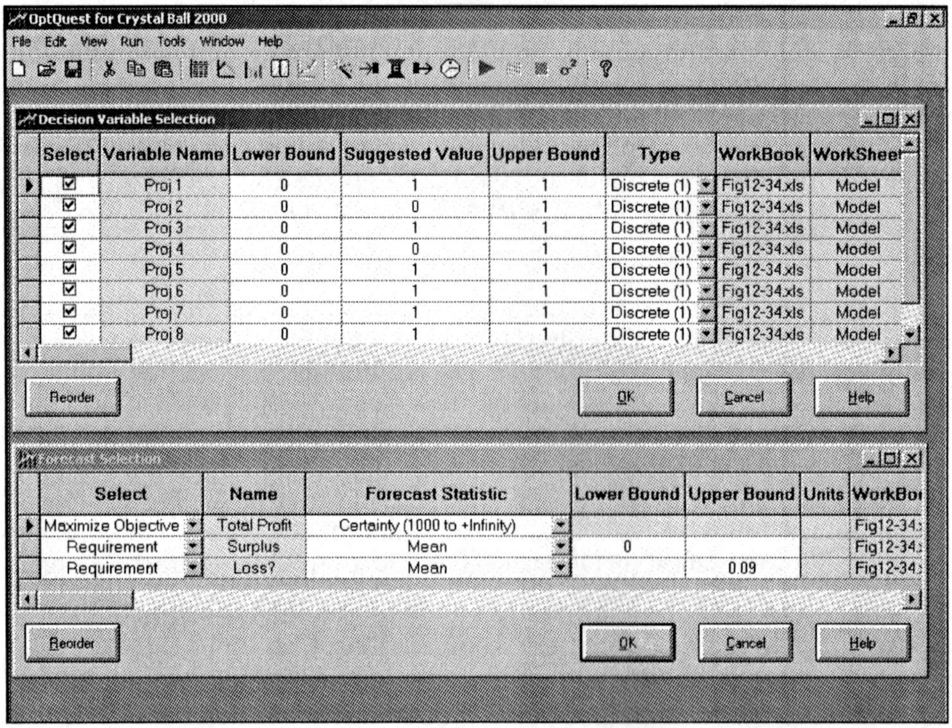

FIGURE 12.41
OptQuest solution for the revised project selection problem

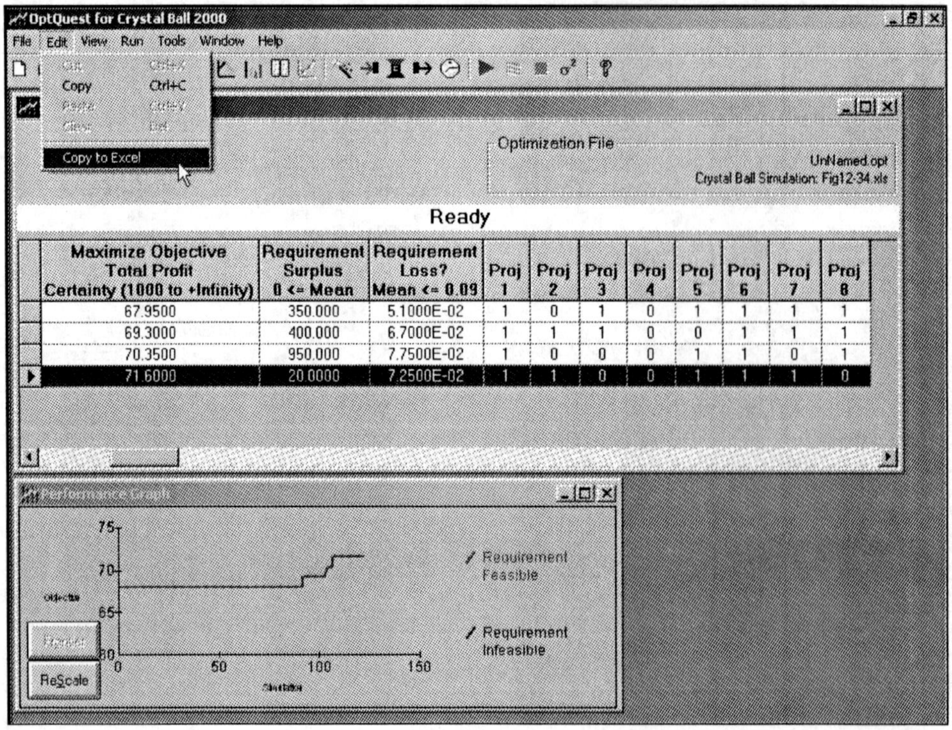

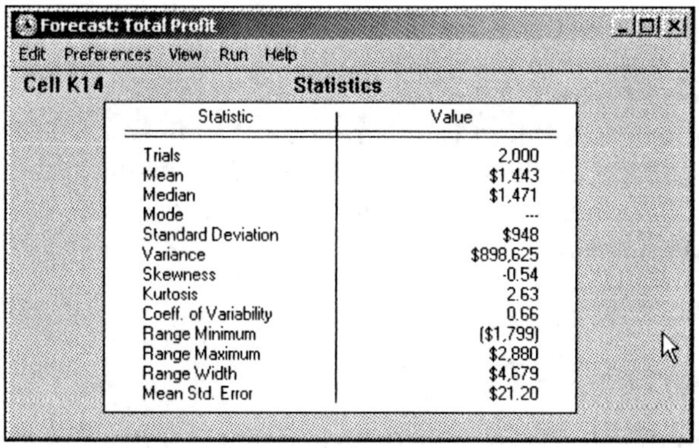

FIGURE 12.42
Statistics for the revised project selection problem

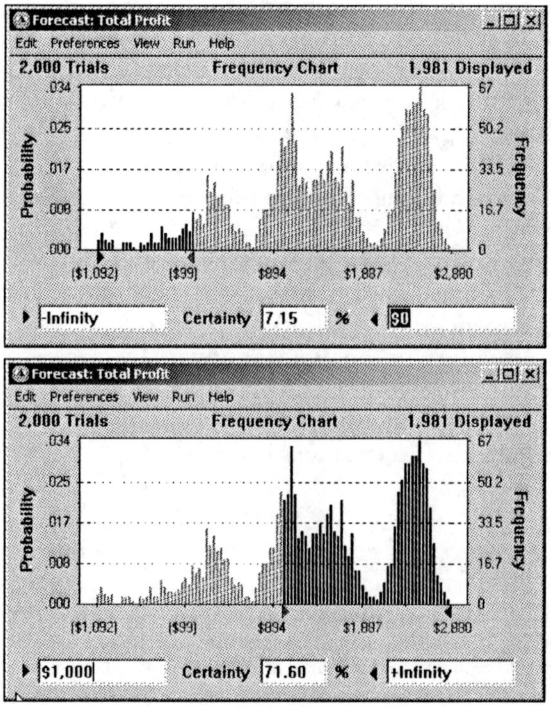

FIGURE 12.43
Frequency distribution for the revised project selection problem

The statistics for this solution are shown in Figure 12.42. Notice that the expected (mean) profit for this solution is about $1.44 million, representing a decrease of approximately $68,000 from the earlier solution. The range of possible outcomes has also decreased to about $4.7 million, with a worst-case outcome of a $1.8 million loss, and a best-case outcome of approximately a $2.9 million profit. As shown in Figure 12.43, this solution *reduces* the chances of realizing a loss to approximately 7% and *increases* the chances of making at least $1 million to almost 72%. Thus, although the best possible outcome realized under this solution ($2.9 million) is not as large as that of the earlier solution ($3.8 million), it reduces the downside risk in the problem and makes it more likely for the company to earn at least $1 million—but it also requires a slightly larger initial investment. It is also interesting to note that the probability of *all* the selected projects being successful under this solution is 0.2116 (*i.e.*, 0.2116=.9×.7×.8×.6×.7), whereas the probability of all selected projects being successful under the first solution is only 0.0953 (*i.e.*, 0.0953=.9×.7×.4×.6×.7×.9).

So, what is the best solution to this problem? It depends on the risk attitudes and preferences of the decision makers at TRC. However, the simulation techniques we have described clearly provide valuable insights into the risks associated with various solutions.

12.17 SUMMARY

This chapter introduced the concept of risk analysis and simulation. Many of the input cells in a spreadsheet represent random variables whose values cannot be determined with certainty. Any uncertainty in the input cells flows through the spreadsheet model to create a related uncertainty in the value of the output cell(s). Decisions made on the basis of these uncertain values involve some degree of risk.

Various methods of risk analysis are available, including best-case/worst-case analysis, what-if analysis, and simulation. Of these three methods, simulation is the only technique that provides hard evidence (facts and figures) that can be used objectively in making decisions. This chapter introduced the use of the Crystal Ball add-in to perform spreadsheet simulation. To simulate a model, RNGs are used to select representative values for each uncertain independent variable in the model. This process is repeated over and over to generate a sample of representative values for the dependent variable(s) in the model. The variability and distribution of the sample values for the dependent variable(s) can then be analyzed to gain insight into the possible outcomes that might occur. We also illustrated the use of OptQuest in determining the optimal value of controllable parameters or decision variables in simulation models.

12.18 REFERENCES

Banks, J. and J. Carson. *Discrete-Event Simulation.* Englewood Cliffs, NJ: Prentice Hall, 1984.

Crystal Ball 2000 User Manual. Decisioneering, Inc., Denver, CO, 2001.

Evans, J. and D. Olson. *Introduction to Simulation and Risk Analysis.* Upper Saddle River, NJ: Prentice Hall, 1998.

Hamzawi, S. "Management and Planning of Airport Gate Capacity: A Microcomputer-Based Gate Assignment Simulation Model." *Transportation Planning and Technology,* vol. 11, 1986.

Kaplan, A. and S. Frazza. "Empirical Inventory Simulation: A Case Study." *Decision Sciences,* vol. 14, January 1983.

Khoshnevis, B. *Discrete Systems Simulation.* New York: McGraw-Hill, 1994.

Law, A. and W. Kelton. *Simulation Modeling and Analysis.* New York: McGraw-Hill, 1990.

Marcus, A. "The Magellan Fund and Market Efficiency." *Journal of Portfolio Management,* Fall 1990.

OptQuest for Crystal Ball 2000 User Manual. Decisioneering Inc., Denver, CO, 2001.

Russell, R. and R. Hickle. "Simulation of a CD Portfolio." *Interfaces,* vol. 16, no. 3, 1986.

Vollman, T., W. Berry and C. Whybark. *Manufacturing Planning and Control Systems.* Homewood, IL: Irwin, 1987.

Watson, H. *Computer Simulation in Business.* New York: Wiley, 1981.

THE WORLD OF MANAGEMENT SCIENCE

The U.S. Postal Service Moves to the Fast Lane

Mail flows into the U.S. Postal Service at the rate of 500 million pieces per day, and it comes in many forms. There are standard-sized letters with 9-digit ZIP codes (with or without imprinted bar codes), 5-digit ZIP codes, typed addresses that can be read by optical character readers, handwritten addresses that are barely decipherable, Christmas cards in red envelopes addressed in red ink, and so on. The enormous task of sorting all these pieces at the sending post office and at the destination has caused postal management to consider and adopt many new forms of technology. These include operator-assisted mechanized sorters, optical character readers (last-line and multiple-line), and bar code sorters. Implementation of new technology brings with it associated policy decisions, such as rate discounts for bar coding by the customer, finer sorting at the origin, and so on.

A simulation model called META (model for evaluating technology alternatives) assists management in evaluating new technologies, configurations, and operating plans. Using distributions based on experience or projections of the effects of new policies, META simulates a random stream of mail of different types; routes the mail through the system configuration being tested; and prints reports detailing total pieces handled, capacity utilization, work hours required, space requirements, and cost.

META has been used on several projects associated with the Postal Service corporate automation plan. These include facilities planning, benefits of alternative sorting plans, justification of efforts to enhance address readability, planning studies for reducing the time carriers spend sorting vs. delivering, and identification of mail types that offer the greatest potential for cost savings.

According to the Associate Postmaster General, "... META became the vehicle to help steer our organization on an entirely new course at a speed we had never before experienced."

Source: Cebry, Michael E., Anura H. deSilva and Fred J. DiLisio. "Management Science in Automating Postal Operations: Facility and Equipment Planning in the United States Postal Service." *Interfaces,* vol. 22, no. 1, January–February 1992, pp. 110–130.

QUESTIONS AND PROBLEMS

1. Under what condition(s) is it appropriate to use simulation to analyze a model? That is, what characteristics should a model possess in order for simulation to be used?
2. The graph of the probability distribution of a normally distributed random variable with a mean of 20 and standard deviation of 3 is shown in Figure 12.7.
   a. Use the CB.Normal( ) function to generate 100 sample values from this distribution.

b. Produce a histogram of the 100 sample values you generated. Does your histogram look like the graph for this distribution in Figure 12.7?
c. Repeat this experiment, with 1,000 sample values.
d. Produce a histogram for the 1,000 sample values you generated. Does the histogram now more closely resemble the graph in Figure 12.7 for this distribution?
e. Why does your second histogram look more "normal" than the first one?

3. Refer to the Hungry Dawg Restaurant example presented in this chapter. Health claim costs actually tend to be seasonal, with higher levels of claims occurring during the summer months (when kids are out of school and more likely to injure themselves) and during December (when people schedule elective procedures before the next year's deductible must be paid). The following table summarizes the seasonal adjustment factors that apply to RNGs for average claims in the Hungry Dawg problem. For instance, the average claim for month 6 should be multiplied by 115% and claims for month 1 should be multiplied by 80%.

Month	**1**	**2**	**3**	**4**	**5**	**6**	**7**	**8**	**9**	**10**	**11**	**12**
Seasonal Factor	0.80	0.85	0.87	0.92	0.93	1.15	1.20	1.18	1.03	0.95	0.98	1.14

Suppose the company maintains an account from which it pays health insurance claims. Assume there is $2.5 million in the account at the beginning of month 1. Each month, employee contributions are deposited into this account and claims are paid from the account.

a. Modify the spreadsheet shown in Figure 12.8 to include the cash flows in this account. If the company deposits $3 million in this account every month, what is the probability that the account will have insufficient funds to pay claims at some point during the year? Use 1000 replications. (*Hint:* You can use the COUNTIF( ) function to count the number of months in a year in which the ending balance in the account is below 0.)
b. If the company wants to deposit an equal amount of money in this account each month, what should this amount be if they want there to only be a 5% chance of having insufficient funds?

4. One of the examples in this chapter dealt with determining the optimal reorder point for a computer monitor sold by Millennium Computer Corp. Suppose that it costs MCC $0.30 per day in holding costs for each monitor in beginning inventory, and it costs $20 to place an order. Each monitor sold generates a profit of $45, and each lost sale results in an opportunity cost of $65 (including the lost profit of $45 and $20 in lost goodwill). Modify the spreadsheet shown in Figure 12.26 to determine the reorder point and order quantity that maximize the average monthly profit associated with this monitor.

5. A debate recently erupted about the optimal strategy for playing a game on the TV show called "Let's Make a Deal." In one of the games on this show, the contestant would be given the choice of prizes behind three closed doors. A valuable prize was behind one door and worthless prizes were behind the other two doors. After the contestant selected a door, the host would open one of the two remaining doors to reveal one of the worthless prizes. Then, before opening the selected door, the host would give the contestant the opportunity to switch his or her selection to the other door that had not been opened. The question is, should the contestant switch?

a. Suppose a contestant is allowed to play this game 500 times, always picks door number 1, and never switches when given the option. If the valuable prize is equally likely to be behind each door at the beginning of each play, how many times would the contestant win the valuable prize? Use simulation to answer this question.

b. Now suppose the contestant is allowed to play this game another 500 times. This time the player always selects door number 1 initially and switches when given the option. Using simulation, how many times would the contestant win the valuable prize?

c. If you were a contestant on this show, what would you do if given the option of switching doors?

6. WVTU is a television station that has 20 thirty-second advertising slots during their regularly scheduled programming each evening. The station is now selling advertising for the first few days in November. They could sell all the slots immediately for $4,500 each, but because November 7 will be an election day, the station manager knows she may be able to sell slots at the last minute to political candidates in tight races for a price of $8,000 each. The demand for these last minute slots is estimated as follows:

	Demand											
	8	**9**	**10**	**11**	**12**	**13**	**14**	**15**	**16**	**17**	**18**	**19**
Probability	0.03	0.05	0.10	0.15	0.20	0.15	0.10	0.05	0.05	0.05	0.05	0.02

Slots not sold in advance and not sold to political candidates at the last minute can be sold to local advertisers at a price of $2,000.

a. If the station manager sells all the advertising slots in advance, how much revenue will the station receive?

b. How many advertising slots should be sold in advance if the station manager wants to maximize expected revenue?

c. If the station manager sells in advance the number of slots identified in the previous question, what is the probability that the total revenue received will exceed the amount identified in part a where all slots are sold in advance?

7. The owner of a ski apparel store in Winter Park, CO must make a decision in July regarding the number of ski jackets to order for the following ski season. Each ski jacket costs $54 each and can be sold during the ski season for $145. Any unsold jackets at the end of the season are sold for $45. The demand for jackets is expected to follow a Poisson distribution with a mean of 80. The store owner can order jackets in lot sizes of 10 units.

a. How many jackets should the store owner order if she wants to maximize her expected profit?

b. What are the best-case and worst-case outcomes the owner may face on this product if she implements your suggestion?

c. How likely is it that the store owner will make at least $7,000 if she implements your suggestion?

d. How likely is it that the store owner will make between $6,000 to $7,000 if she implements your suggestion?

8. The owner of a golf shop in Myrtle Beach, SC must decide how many sets of beginner golf clubs to order for the coming tourist season. Demand for golf clubs is random but follows a Poisson distribution with the means indicated

in the following table for each month. The expected selling price of the clubs is also shown for each month.

	May	June	July	August	September	October
Average Demand	60	90	70	50	30	40
Selling Price	$145	$140	$130	$110	$80	$60

In May, each set of clubs can be ordered at a cost of $75. This price is expected to drop 5% a month during the remainder of season. Each month, the owner of the shop also gives away a free set of clubs to anyone who makes a hole-in-one from a short practice tee next to the shop. The number of people making a hole-in-one on this tee each month follows a Poisson distribution with a mean of 3. Any sets of clubs left over at the end of October are sold for $45 per set.

a. How many sets of clubs should the shop owner order if he wants to maximize the expected profit on this product?
b. What are the best-case and worst-case outcomes the owner may face on this product if he implements your suggestion?
c. How likely is it that the store owner will make at least $17,000 if he implements your suggestion?
d. How likely is it that the store owner will make between $12,000 to $14,000 if he implements your suggestion?
e. What percentage of the total demand for this product (excluding the free giveaways) will the owner be able to meet if he implements your suggestion?

9. Large Lots is planning a seven-day promotion on a discontinued model of 31" color television sets. At a price of $575 per set, the daily demand for this type of TV has been estimated as follows:

	Units Demanded per Day					
	0	1	2	3	4	5
Probability	0.15	0.20	0.30	0.20	0.10	0.05

Large Lots can order up to 50 of these TVs from a surplus dealer at a cost of $325. This dealer has offered to buy back any unsold sets at the end of the promotion for $250 each.

a. How many TVs should Large Lots order if it wants to maximize the expected profit on this promotion?
b. What is the expected level of profit?
c. Suppose the surplus dealer will only buy back a maximum of four sets at the end of the promotion. Would this change your answer? If so, how?

10. The monthly demand for the latest computer at Newland Computers follows a normal distribution with a mean of 350 and standard deviation of 75. Newland purchases these computers for $1,200 and sells them for $2,300. It costs the company $100 to place an order and $12 for every computer held in inventory at the end of each month. Currently, the company places an order for 1000 computers whenever the inventory at the end of a month falls below 100 units. Assume the beginning inventory is 400 units, unmet demand in any month is lost to competitors, and orders placed at the end of one month arrive at the beginning of the next month.

a. Create a spreadsheet model to simulate the profit the company will earn on this product over the next two years. Use 1000 replications. What is the average level of profit the company will earn?
b. Suppose the company wants to determine the optimum reorder point and order quantity. Which combination of reorder point and order quantity will provide the highest average profit over the next two years?

11. The manager of Moore's Catalog Showroom is trying to predict how much revenue will be generated by each major department in the store during 2003. The manager has estimated the minimum and maximum growth rates possible for revenues in each department. The manager believes that any of the possible growth rates between the minimum and maximum values are equally likely to occur. These estimates are summarized in the following table:

		Growth Rates	
Department	**2002 Revenues**	**Minimum**	**Maximum**
Electronics	$6,342,213	2%	10%
Garden Supplies	$1,203,231	–4%	5%
Jewelry	$4,367,342	–2%	6%
Sporting Goods	$3,543,532	–1%	8%
Toys	$4,342,132	4%	15%

Create a spreadsheet to simulate the total revenues that could occur in the coming year. Run 500 replications of the model and do the following:
a. Construct a 95% confidence interval for the average level of revenues the manager could expect for 2003.
b. According to your model, what are the chances that total revenues in 2003 will be more than 5% larger than those in 2002?

12. The Harriet Hotel in downtown Boston has 100 rooms that rent for $150 per night. It costs the hotel $30 per room in variable costs (cleaning, bathroom items, etc.) each night a room is occupied. For each reservation accepted, there is a 5% chance that the guest will not arrive. If the hotel overbooks, it costs $200 to compensate guests whose reservations cannot be honored.
a. How many reservations should the hotel accept if it wants to maximize the average daily profit? Use 1000 replications for each reservation level you consider.

13. Lynn Price recently completed her MBA and accepted a job with an electronics manufacturing company. Although she likes her job, she is also looking forward to retiring one day. To ensure that her retirement is comfortable, Lynn intends to invest $3,000 of her salary into a tax-sheltered retirement fund at the end of each year. Lynn is not certain what rate of return this investment will earn each year, but she expects each year's rate of return could be modeled appropriately as a normally distributed random variable with a mean of 12.5% and standard deviation of 2%.
a. If Lynn is 30 years old, how much money should she expect to have in her retirement fund at age 60? (Use 1000 replications.)
b. Construct a 95% confidence interval for the average amount Lynn will have at age 60.
c. What is the probability that Lynn will have more than $1 million in her retirement fund when she reaches age 60?

d. How much should Lynn invest each year if she wants there to be a 90% chance of having at least $1 million in her retirement fund at age 60?
e. Suppose that Lynn contributes $3,000 annually to her retirement fund for eight years and then terminates these annual contributions. How much of her salary would she have contributed to this retirement plan and how much money could she expect to have accumulated at age 60?
f. Now suppose that Lynn contributes nothing to her retirement fund for eight years and then begins contributing $3,000 annually until age 60. How much of her salary would she have contributed to this retirement plan and how much money could she expect to have accumulated at age 60?
g. What should Lynn (and you) learn from the answers to questions e and f?

14. Employees of Georgia-Atlantic are permitted to contribute a portion of their earnings (in increments of $500) to a flexible spending account from which they can pay medical expenses not covered by the company's health insurance program. Contributions to an employees' "flex" account are not subject to income taxes. However, the employee forfeits any amount contributed to the "flex" account that is not spent during the year. Suppose Greg Davis makes $60,000 per year from Georgia-Atlantic and pays a marginal tax rate of 33%. Greg and his wife estimate that in the coming year their normal medical expenses not covered by the health insurance program could be as small as $500, as large as $5,000, and most likely about $1,300. However, Greg also believes there is a 5% chance that an abnormal medical event could occur which might add $10,000 to the normal expenses paid from their flex account. If their uncovered medical claims exceed their contribution to their "flex" account, they will have to cover these expenses with the after-tax money Greg brings home.
a. Use simulation to determine the amount of money Greg should contribute to his flexible spending account in the coming year if he wants to maximize his disposable income (after taxes and all medical expenses are paid). Use 1000 replications for each level of "flex" account contribution you consider.

15. Acme Equipment Company is considering the development of a new machine that would be marketed to tire manufacturers. Research and development costs for the project are expected to be about $4 million but could vary between $3 and $6 million. The market life for the product is estimated to be 3 to 8 years with all intervening possibilities being equally likely. The company thinks it will sell 250 units per year, but acknowledges that this figure could be as low as 50 or as high as 350. The company will sell the machine for about $23,000. Finally, the cost of manufacturing the machine is expected to be $14,000 but could be as low as $12,000 or as high as $18,000. The company's cost of capital is 15%.
a. Use appropriate RNGs to create a spreadsheet to calculate the possible net present values (NPVs) that could result from taking on this project.
b. Replicate the model 1000 times. What is the expected NPV for this project?
c. What is the probability of this project generating a positive NPV for the company?

16. Representatives from the American Heart Association are planning to go door-to-door throughout a community, soliciting contributions. From past experience, they know that when someone answers the door, 80% of the time it is a female and 20% of the time it is a male. They also know that 70% of the females

who answer the door make a donation, whereas only 40% of the males who answer the door make donations. The amount of money that females contribute follows a normal distribution with a mean of \$20 and standard deviation of \$3. The amount of money males contribute follows a normal distribution with a mean of \$10 and standard deviation of \$2.

a. Create a spreadsheet model that simulates what might happen whenever a representative of the American Heart Association knocks on a door and someone answers.
b. Replicate your model 1000 times. What is the average contribution the Heart Association can expect to receive when someone answers the door?
c. Suppose that the Heart Association plans to visit 300 homes on a given Saturday. If no one is home at 25% of the residences, what is the total amount that the Heart Association can expect to receive in donations?

17. After spending ten years as an assistant manager for a large restaurant chain, Ray Clark has decided to become his own boss. The owner of a local submarine sandwich store wants to sell the store to Ray for \$65,000 to be paid in installments of \$13,000 in each of the next five years. According to the current owner, the store brings in revenue of about \$110,000 per year and incurs operating costs of about 63% of sales. Thus, once the store is paid for, Ray should make about \$35,000–\$40,000 per year before taxes. Until the store is paid for, he will make substantially less—but he will be his own boss. Realizing that some uncertainty is involved in this decision, Ray wants to simulate what level of net income he can expect to earn during the next five years as he operates and pays for the store. In particular, he wants to see what could happen if sales are allowed to vary uniformly between \$90,000 and \$120,000, and if operating costs are allowed to vary uniformly between 60% and 65% of sales. Assume that Ray's payments for the store are not deductible for tax purposes and that he is in the 28% tax bracket.
    a. Create a spreadsheet model to simulate the annual net income Ray would receive during each of the next five years if he decides to buy the store.
    b. Given the money he has in savings, Ray thinks he can get by for the next five years if he can make at least \$12,000 from the store each year. Replicate the model 500 times and track: 1) the minimum amount of money Ray makes over the five-year period represented by each replication, and 2) the total amount Ray makes during the five-year period represented by each replication.
    c. What is the probability that Ray will make at least \$12,000 in each of the next five years?
    d. What is the probability that Ray will make at least \$60,000 total over the next five years?
18. Road Racer Sports, Inc. is a mail-order business dedicated to the running enthusiast. The company sends out full-color catalogs several times a year to several hundred thousand people on its mailing list. Production and mailing costs are fairly expensive for direct mail advertising, averaging about \$3.25 per catalog. As a result, management does not want to continue sending catalogs to persons who do not buy enough to cover the costs of the catalogs they receive. Currently, the company removes a customer from their mailing list if they receive six consecutive catalogs without placing an order. The following table summarizes the probability of a customer placing an order.

Last Order	Prob. of Order
1 catalog ago	0.40
2 catalogs ago	0.34
3 catalogs ago	0.25
4 catalogs ago	0.17
5 catalogs ago	0.09
6 catalogs ago	0.03

According to the first row in this table, if a customer receives a catalog and places an order, there is a 40% chance he will place another order when he receives his next catalog. The second row indicates there is a 34% chance a customer will receive a catalog, place an order, and then not order again until they receive two more catalogs. The remaining rows in this table have similar interpretations.

a. How much profit must the company earn on an average order in order to cover the cost of printing and distributing the catalogs?

b. Approximately what percentage of the names on the mailing list will be purged before each catalog mailing?

19. Sammy Slick works for a company that allows him to contribute up to 10% of his earnings into a tax-deferred savings plan. The company matches a portion of the contributions its employees make based on the organization's financial performance. Although the minimum match is 25% of the employee's contributions and the maximum match is 100%, in most years the company match is about 50%. Sammy is currently 30 years old and makes $35,000. He wants to retire at age 60. He expects his salary to increase in any given year to be at least 2% per year, at most 6%, and most likely 3%. The funds contributed by Sammy and his employer are invested in mutual funds. Sammy expects the annual return on his investments to vary according to a normal distribution with a mean of 12.5% and standard deviation of 2%.

    a. If Sammy contributes 10% of his income to this plan, how much money could he expect to have at age 60?

    b. Suppose Sammy makes 10% contributions to this plan for eight years, from age 30 to 37, and then stops contributing. How much of his own money would he have invested and how much money could he expect to have at age 60?

    c. Now suppose Sammy contributes nothing to the plan his first eight years and then contributes 10% for twenty-three years from age 38 to age 60. How much of his own money would he have invested and how much money could he expect to have at age 60?

    d. What do you learn from Sammy's example?

20. Bob Davidson owns a newsstand outside the Waterstone office building complex in Atlanta, near Hartsfield International Airport. He buys his papers wholesale at $0.50 per paper and sells them for $0.75. Bob wonders what is the optimal number of papers to order each day. Based on history, he has found that demand (even though it is discrete) can be modeled by a normal distribution with a mean of 50 and standard deviation of 5. When he has more papers than customers, he can recycle all the extra papers the next day and receive $0.05 per paper. On the other hand, if he has more customers than

papers, he loses some goodwill in addition to the lost profit on the potential sale of $0.25. Bob estimates the incremental lost goodwill costs five days' worth of business (that is, dissatisfied customers will go to a competitor the next week, but come back to him the week after that).

a. Create a spreadsheet model to determine the optimal number of papers to order each day. Use 500 replications and round the demand values generated by the normal RNG to the closest integer value.
b. Construct a 95% confidence interval for the expected payoff from the optimal decision.

21. Vinton Auto Insurance is trying to decide how much money to keep in liquid assets to cover insurance claims. In the past, the company held some of the premiums it received in interest-bearing checking accounts and put the rest into investments that are not quite as liquid, but tend to generate a higher investment return. The company wants to study cash flows to determine how much money it should keep in liquid assets to pay claims. After reviewing historical data, the company determined that the average repair bill per claim is normally distributed with a mean of $1,700 and standard deviation of $400. It also determined that the number of repair claims filed each week is a random variable that follows the probability distribution shown in the following table:

Number of Repair Claims	Probability
1	0.05
2	0.06
3	0.10
4	0.17
5	0.28
6	0.14
7	0.08
8	0.07
9	0.05

In addition to repair claims, the company also receives claims for cars that have been "totaled" and cannot be repaired. A 20% chance of receiving this type of claim exists in any week. These claims for "totaled" cars typically cost anywhere from $2,000 to $35,000, with $13,000 being the most common cost.

a. Create a spreadsheet model of the total claims cost incurred by the company in any week.
b. Replicate the model 1000 times and create a histogram of the distribution of total cost values that were generated.
c. What is the average cost the company should expect to pay each week?
d. Suppose that the company decides to keep $20,000 cash on hand to pay claims. What is the probability that this amount would not be adequate to cover claims in any week?
e. Create a 95% confidence interval for the true probability of claims exceeding $20,000 in a given week.

22. The owner of a local car dealership has just received a call from a regional distributor stating that a $5,000 bonus will be awarded if the owner's dealership sells at least 10 new cars next Saturday. On an average Saturday, this dealership has 75 potential customers look at new cars, but there is no way to determine exactly how many customers will come this particular Saturday. The owner is fairly certain that the number would not be less than 40, but also thinks it would be unrealistic to expect more than 120 (which is the largest number of customers to ever show up in one day). The owner determined that, on average, about one out of ten customers who look at cars at the dealership actually purchase a car—or, a 0.10 probability (or 10% chance) exists that any given customer will buy a new car.
    a. Create a spreadsheet model for this problem and generate 1000 random outcomes for the number of cars the dealership might sell next Saturday.
    b. What is the probability that the dealership will earn the $5,000 bonus?
    c. If you were this dealer, what is the maximum amount of money you would be willing to spend on sales incentives to try to earn this bonus?
23. Dr. Sarah Benson is an ophthalmologist who, in addition to prescribing glasses and contact lenses, performs optical laser surgery to correct nearsightedness. This surgery is fairly easy and inexpensive to perform. Thus, it represents a potential gold mine for her practice. To inform the public about this procedure, Dr. Benson advertises in the local paper and holds information sessions in her office one night a week at which she shows a videotape about the procedure and answers any questions potential patients might have. The room where these meetings are held can seat ten people, and reservations are required. The number of people attending each session varies from week to week. Dr. Benson cancels the meeting if two or fewer people have made reservations. Using data from the previous year, Dr. Benson determined that the distribution of reservations is as follows:

Number of Reservations	**0**	**1**	**2**	**3**	**4**	**5**	**6**	**7**	**8**	**9**	**10**
Probability	0.02	0.05	0.08	0.16	0.26	0.18	0.11	0.07	0.05	0.01	0.01

    Using data from the past year, Dr. Benson determined that each person who attends an information session has a 0.25 probability of electing to have the surgery. Of those who do not, most cite the cost of the procedure—$2,000—as their major concern.
    a. On average, how much revenue does Dr. Benson's practice in laser surgery generate each week? (Use 1000 replications.)
    b. On average, how much revenue would the laser surgery generate each week if Dr. Benson did not cancel sessions with two or fewer reservations?
    c. Dr. Benson believes that 40% of the people attending the information sessions would have the surgery if she reduced the price to $1,500. Under this scenario, how much revenue could Dr. Benson expect to realize per week from laser surgery?
24. Calls to the 24-hour customer support line for Richman Financial Services occur randomly following a Poisson distribution with the following average rates during different hours of the day:

Time Period	Avg Calls Per Hour	Time Period	Avg Calls Per Hour
Midnight–1 A.M.	2	Noon–1 P.M.	35
1 A.M.–2 A.M.	2	1 P.M.–2 P.M.	20
2 A.M.–3 A.M.	2	2 P.M.–3 P.M.	20
3 A.M.–4 A.M.	4	3 P.M.–4 P.M.	20
4 A.M.–5 A.M.	4	4 P.M.–5 P.M.	18
5 A.M.–6 A.M.	8	5 P.M.–6 P.M.	18
6 A.M.–7 A.M.	12	6 P.M.–7 P.M.	15
7 A.M.–8 A.M.	18	7 P.M.–8 P.M.	10
8 A.M.–9 A.M.	25	8 P.M.–9 P.M.	6
9 A.M.–10 A.M.	30	9 P.M.–10 P.M.	5
10 A.M.–11 A.M.	25	10 P.M.–11 P.M.	4
11 A.M.–Noon	20	11 P.M.–Midnight	2

The Richman's customer service representatives spend approximately seven minutes on each call and are assigned to work eight-hour shifts that begin at the top of each hour. Richman wants to ensure that, on average, they can provide a 98% service level.

a. Determine the customer service schedule that allows Richman to achieve their service level objective using the fewest number of employees.
b. According to your solution, how many customer service representatives should Richman employ and how should they be scheduled?

25. A European call option gives a person the right to buy a particular stock at a given price (the strike price) on a specific date in the future (the expiration date). This type of call option is typically sold at the net present value of the expected value of the option on its expiration date. Suppose you own a call option with a strike price of \$54. If the stock is worth \$59 on the expiration date, you would exercise your option and buy the stock, making a \$5 profit. On the other hand, if the stock is worth \$47 on the expiration date, you would not exercise your option and make \$0 profit. Researchers have suggested the following model for simulating the movement of stock prices:

$$P_{k+1} = P_k\,(1 + \mu t + z\sigma\sqrt{t}\,)$$

where:

P_k = price of the stock at time period k
$\mu = v + 0.5\sigma^2$
v = the stock's expected annual growth rate
σ = the standard deviation on the stock's annual growth rate
t = time period interval (expressed in years)
z = a random observation from a normal distribution with mean 0 and standard deviation of 1.

Suppose a stock has an initial price (P_0) of \$80, an expected annual growth rate (v) of 15%, and a standard deviation (σ) of 25%.

a. Create a spreadsheet model to simulate this stock's price behavior for the next 13 weeks (note t=1/52 because the time period is weekly).
b. Suppose you are interested in purchasing a call option with a strike price of \$75 and an expiration date at week 13. On average, how much profit would you earn with this option? (Use 1000 replications.)

c. Assume a risk-free discount rate is 6%. How much should you be willing to pay for this option today? (*Hint:* Use Excel's NPV function.)
d. If you purchase the option, what is the probability that you will make a profit?

26. Refer to the previous question. Another type of option is the Asian option. Its payoff is not based on the price of the stock on the expiration date but, instead, on the average price of the stock over the lifetime of the option. Suppose a stock has an initial price (P_0) of $80, an expected annual growth rate (v) of 15%, and a standard deviation (σ) of 25%.
    a. Create a spreadsheet model to simulate this stock's price behavior for the next 13 weeks (note t=1/52 because the time period is weekly).
    b. Suppose you are interested in purchasing a call option with a strike price of $75 and an expiration date at week 13. On average, how much profit would you earn with this option? (Use 1000 replications.)
    c. Assume a risk-free discount rate is 6%. How much should you be willing to pay for this option today? (*Hint:* Use Excel's NPV function.)
    d. If you purchase the option, what is the probability that you will make a profit?

27. Martin manufacturing company utilizes a piece of machinery that has three different bushings that periodically fail in service. The probability distribution of the life of each bushing is identical and is summarized by the following table.

	Bushing Life (operating hours)									
	1000	**1100**	**1200**	**1300**	**1400**	**1500**	**1600**	**1700**	**1800**	**1900**
Probability	0.08	0.13	0.25	0.15	0.12	0.09	0.07	0.05	0.04	0.02

When a bushing fails, the machine stops, a repair person is called, and a new bushing is installed. Each bushing costs $35. Downtime for the machine costs the company an estimated $15 per minute. The direct on-site costs for the repair person is $50 per hour. The amount of time required for the repair person to arrive after a bushing fails is approximately normally distributed with a mean of 10 minutes and standard deviation of 2 minutes. The amount of time required to change a bushing follows a triangular distribution with minimum, most likely, and maximum values of 15, 20, and 30 minutes, respectively.
    a. On average, what is the total bushing-related costs Martin incurs to operate this machine for 20,000 hours?
    b. Martin is considering implementing another repair policy: If any of the bushings fail, all three are replaced. What is the total bushing-related costs Martin incurs to operate this machine for 20,000 hours under this policy?
    c. Should Martin implement the new policy?

28. Michael Abrams runs a specialty clothing store that sells collegiate sports apparel. One of his primary business opportunities involves selling custom screenprinted sweatshirts for college football bowl games. He is trying to determine how many sweatshirts to produce for the upcoming Tangerine Bowl game. During the month before the game, Michael plans to sell his sweatshirts for $25 a piece. At this price, he believes the demand for sweatshirts will be triangularly distributed with a minimum demand of 10,000, maximum demand of 30,000, and a most likely demand of 18,000. During the month after the game, Michael plans to sell any remaining sweatshirts for

$12 a piece. At this price, he believes the demand for sweatshirts will be triangularly distributed with a minimum demand of 2,000, maximum demand of 7,000, and a most likely demand of 5,000. Two months after the game, Michael plans to sell any remaining sweatshirts to a surplus store that has agreed to buy up to 2,000 sweatshirts for a price of $3 per shirt. Michael can order custom screenprinted sweatshirts for $8 a piece in lot sizes of 3,000.

a. On average, how much profit would Michael earn if he orders 18,000 sweatshirts? Use 1000 replications.
b. How many sweatshirts should he order if he wants to maximize his expected profit? Again use 1000 replications in each simulation you perform.

29. The Major Motors Corporation is trying to decide whether to introduce a new midsize car. The directors of the company only want to produce the car if it has at least an 80% chance of generating a positive net present value over the next ten years. If the company decides to produce the car, it will have to pay an uncertain initial start-up cost that is estimated to follow a triangular distribution with a minimum value of $2 billion, maximum value of $2.4 billion, and a most likely value of $2.1 billion. In the first year, the company would produce 100,000 units. Demand during the first year is uncertain but expected to be normally distributed with a mean of 95,000 and standard deviation of 7,000. For any year in which the demand exceeds production, production will be increased by 5% in the following year. For any year in which the production exceeds demand, production will be decreased by 5% in the next year, and the excess cars will be sold to a rental car company at a 20% discount. After the first year, the demand in any year will be modeled as a normally distributed random variable with a mean equal to the actual demand in the previous year and standard deviation of 7,000. In the first year, the sales price of the car will be $13,000 and the total variable cost per car is expected to be $9,500. Both the selling price and variable cost is expected to increase each year at the rate of inflation, which is assumed to be uniformly distributed between 2% and 7%. The company uses a discount rate of 9% to discount future cash flows.
    a. Create a spreadsheet model for this problem and replicate it 1000 times. What is the minimum, average, and maximum NPV Major Motors can expect if they decide to produce this car? (*Hint:* Consider using the NPV( ) function to discount the profits Major Motors would earn each year.)
    b. What is the probability of Major Motors earning a positive NPV over the next ten years?
    c. Should they produce this car?
30. Each year, the Schriber Corporation must determine how much to contribute to the company's pension plan. The company uses a ten-year planning horizon to determine the contribution which, if made annually in each of the next ten years, would allow for only a 10% chance of the fund running short of money. The company then makes that contribution in the current year and repeats this process in each subsequent year to determine the specific amount to contribute each year. (Last year, the company contributed $23 million to the plan.) The pension plan covers two types of employees: hourly and salaried. In the current year, there will be 6,000 former hourly employees and 3,000 former salaried employees receiving benefits from the plan. The change in the number of retired hourly employees from one year to the next is expected to vary according to a normal distribution with a mean of 4% and standard

deviation of 1%. The change in the number of retired salaried employees from one year to the next is expected to vary between 1% and 4% according to a truncated normal distribution with a mean of 2% and standard deviation of 1%. Currently, hourly retirees receive an average benefit of $15,000 per year, whereas salaried retirees receive an average annual benefit of $40,000. Both of these averages are expected to increase annually with the rate of inflation, which is assumed to vary between 2% and 7% according to a triangular distribution with a most likely value of 3.5%. The current balance in the company's pension fund is $1.5 billion. Investments in this fund earn an annual return that is assumed to be normally distributed with a mean of 12% and standard deviation of 2%. Create a spreadsheet model for this problem and use simulation to determine the pension fund contribution the company should make in the current year. What is your recommendation?

CASE 12.1: DEATH AND TAXES

Benjamin Franklin once said, "In this world nothing is certain but death and taxes." Although that may be true, there is often great uncertainty involved in when one will encounter death and how much one must pay in taxes before arriving there. Another Benjamin made a very significant contribution toward assessing the uncertainty associated with both death and taxes. Benjamin Gompertz (1779–1865) was a British mathematician who, by studying Mediterranean fruit flies, theorized that mortality rates increase at an exponential rate as age increases (*i.e.*, as an organism gets older, its chance of dying per unit of time increases exponentially). Gompertz's Law of Mortality has since become a cornerstone of actuarial and financial planning activities.

In a group of people of a given age (for example, 65), some proportion of those people will not live another year. Let q_x represent the proportion of people of age x who will die before reaching age x+1. The value q_x is sometimes referred to as the ***mortality rate*** at age x. The following formula, based on Gompertz's Law, is sometimes used to model mortality rates.

$$q_x = 1 - \text{EXP}\left(\frac{(\text{LN}(1 - q_{x-1}))^2}{\text{LN}(1 - q_{x-2})}\right)$$

Mortality rates play an important role in numerous financial planning and retirement decisions. For instance, most individuals do not want to retire unless they are reasonably certain they have enough assets to sustain themselves financially for the rest of their life. The uncertainties associated with this sort of decision create a perfect application for spreadsheet simulation.

The following questions give you the opportunity to explore several issues that actuaries and financial planners face on a daily basis. Assume the mortality rates for males at ages 63 and 64 are $q_{63} = 0.0235$ and $q_{64} = 0.0262$, respectively, and those of females are $q_{63} = 0.0208$ and $q_{64} = 0.0225$.

1. On average, to what age should a 65-year-old male expect to live?
2. What is the probability of a 65-year-old male living to at least age 80?
3. What is the probability of a 65-year-old male living to exactly age 80?
4. On average, to what age should a 70-year-old male expect to live?

5. What is the probability of a 70-year-old male living to at least age 80?
6. What is the probability of a 70-year-old male living to exactly age 80?
7. Suppose a 65-year-old male has $1,200,000 in retirement investments earning an 8% interest rate. Assume he intends to withdraw $100,000 in his first year of retirement and 3% more in subsequent years to adjust for inflation. Annual interest earnings are credited on the beginning balance less one half the amount withdrawn. For example, in the first year interest earnings would be 0.08 × ($1,200,000 – $100,000/2) = $92,000. What is the probability that this individual would outlive his retirement assets (assuming he spends all he withdraws each year)?
8. Refer to the previous question. Suppose the interest rate each year can be modeled as a normally distributed random variable with a mean of 8% and standard deviation of 1.5%. Further suppose the rate of inflation each year can be described as a random variable following a triangular distribution with minimum, most likely, and maximum values of 2%, 3%, and 5%, respectively. Under these conditions, what is the probability that this individual would outlive his retirement assets (assuming he spends all he withdraws each year)?
9. Suppose the person described in the previous question has a 65-year-old wife who is joint owner of the retirement assets described earlier. What is the probability that the retirement assets would be depleted before both spouses die (assuming they spend all they withdraw each year)?
10. Refer to the previous question. How much money should this couple plan on withdrawing in the first year if they want there to be a maximum of a 5% chance of depleting their retirement assets before they both die?

CASE 12.2: THE SOUND'S ALIVE COMPANY

Contributed by Jack Yurkiewicz. Lubin School of Business, Pace University.

Marissa Jones is the president and CEO of Sound's Alive, a company that manufactures and sells a line of speakers, CD players, receivers, high-definition televisions, and other items geared for the home entertainment market. Respected throughout the industry for bringing many high-quality, innovative products to market, Marissa is considering adding a speaker system to her product line.

The speaker market has changed dramatically during the last several years. Originally, high-fidelity aficionados knew that to reproduce sound covering the fullest range of frequencies—from the lowest kettle drum to the highest violin—a speaker system had to be large and heavy. The speaker had various drivers: a woofer to reproduce the low notes, a tweeter for the high notes, and a mid-range driver for the broad spectrum of frequencies in between. Many speaker systems had a minimum of three drivers, but some had even more. The trouble was that such a system was too large for anything but the biggest rooms, and consumers were reluctant to spend thousands of dollars and give up valuable wall space to get the excellent sound these speakers could reproduce.

The trend has changed during the past several years. Consumers still want good sound, but they want it from smaller boxes. Therefore, the satellite system became popular. Consisting of two small boxes that house either one driver (to cover the mid-range and high frequencies) or two (a mid-range and tweeter), a satellite system can easily be mounted on walls or shelves. To reproduce the low notes, a separate subwoofer that is approximately the size of a cube 18 inches on a side is also needed. This subwoofer can be placed anywhere in the room. Taking up less space than a typical large speaker system and sounding almost as good, yet costing hundreds of dollars less, these satellite systems are hot items in the high-fidelity market.

Recently, the separate wings of home entertainment—high fidelity (receivers, speakers, CD players, CDs, cassettes, and so on), television (large screen monitors, video cassette recorders, laser players), and computers (games with sounds, virtual reality software, and so on)—have merged into the home theater concept. To simulate the movie environment, a home theater system requires the traditional stereo speaker system plus additional speakers placed in the rear of the room so that viewers are literally surrounded with sound. Although the rear speakers do not have to match the high quality of the front speakers and, therefore, can be less expensive, most consumers choose a system in which the front and rear speakers are of equal quality, reproducing the full range of frequencies with equal fidelity.

It is this speaker market that Marissa wants to enter. She is considering having Sound's Alive manufacture and sell a home theater system that consists of seven speakers. Three small speakers—each with one dome tweeter that could reproduce the frequency range of 200 Hertz to 20,000 Hertz (upper-low frequencies to the highest frequencies)—would be placed in front, and three similar speakers would be placed strategically around the sides and back of the room. To reproduce the lowest frequencies (from 35 Hertz to 200 Hertz), a single subwoofer would also be part of the system. This subwoofer is revolutionary because it is smaller than the ordinary subwoofer, only 10 inches per side, and it has a built-in amplifier to power it. Consumers and critics are thrilled with the music from early prototype systems, claiming that these speakers have the best balance of sound and size. Marissa is extremely encouraged by these early reviews, and although her company has never produced a product with its house label on it (having always sold systems from established high-fidelity companies), she believes that Sound's Alive should enter the home theater market with this product.

Phase One: Projecting Profits

Marissa decides to create a spreadsheet that will project profits over the next several years. After consulting with economists, market analysts, employees in her own company, and employees from other companies that sell house brand components, Marissa is confident that the gross revenues for these speakers in 2004 would be around $6 million. She must also figure that a small percentage of speakers will be damaged in transit, or some will be returned by dissatisfied customers shortly after the sales. These returns and allowances (R&As) are usually calculated as 2% of the gross revenues. Hence, the net revenues are simply the gross revenues minus the R&As. Marissa believes that the 2004 labor costs for these speakers will be $995,100. The cost of materials (including boxes to ship the speakers) should be $915,350 for 2004. Finally, her overhead costs (rent, lighting, heating in winter, air conditioning in summer, security, and so on) for 2004 should be $1,536,120. Thus, the cost of goods sold is the sum of labor, material, and overhead costs. Marissa figures the gross profit as the difference between the gross revenues and the cost of goods sold. In addition, she must consider the selling, general, and administrative (SG&A) expenses. These expenses are more difficult to estimate, but the standard industry practice is to use 18% of the net revenues as the nominal percentage value for these expenses. Therefore, Marissa's profit *before taxes* is the gross profit minus the SG&A value. To calculate taxes, Marissa multiplies her profits before taxes times the tax rate, currently 30%. If her company is operating at a loss, however, no taxes would have to be paid. Finally, Marissa's net (or after tax) profit is simply the difference between the profit before taxes and the actual taxes paid.

To determine the numbers for 2005 through 2007, Marissa assumes that gross revenues, labor costs, material costs, and overhead costs will increase over the years. Although the rates of increase for these items are difficult to estimate, Marissa figures that gross revenues will increase by 9% per year, labor costs will increase by 4% per year, material costs will increase by 6% per year, and overhead costs will increase by 3% per year. She figures that the tax rate will not change from the 30% mark, and she assumes that the SG&A value will remain at 18%.

The basic layout of the spreadsheet that Marissa creates is shown in Figure 12.44 (and in the file Fig12-44.xls on your data disk). (Ignore the Competitive Assumptions section for now; we will consider it later.) Construct the spreadsheet, determine the values for the years 2004 through 2007, and then determine the totals for the four years.

Marissa not only wants to determine her net profits for 2004 through 2007, she also must justify her decisions to the company's Board of Trustees. Should she even consider entering this market, from a financial point of view? One way to answer this question is to find the net present value (NPV) of the net profits for 2004 through 2007. Use Excel's NPV capability to find the NPV, at the current interest rate of 5%, of the profit values for 2004 through 2007.

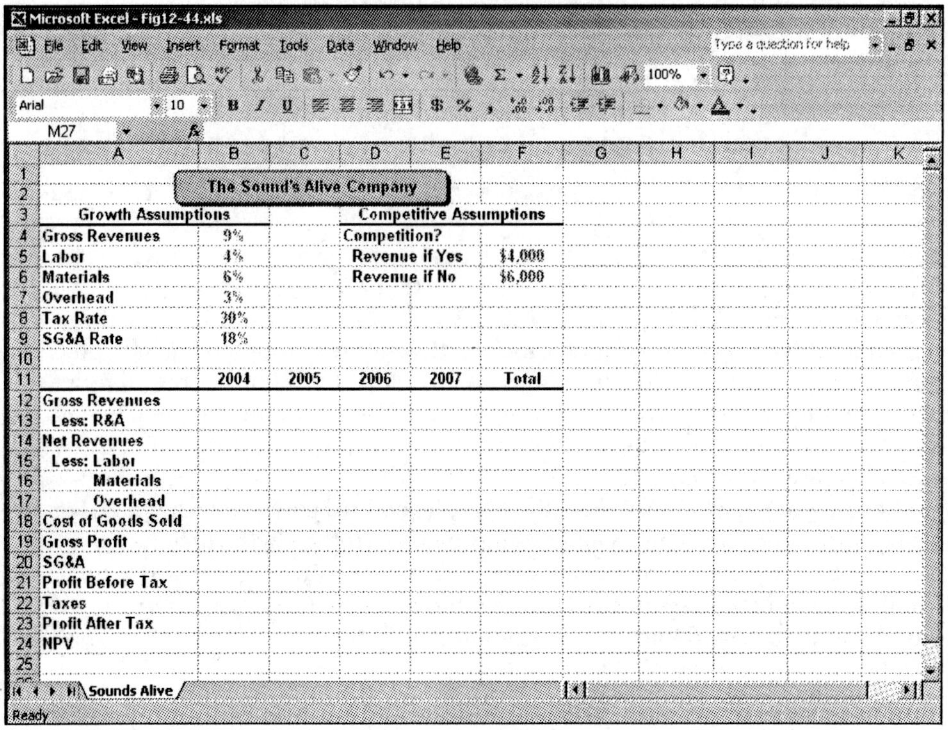

FIGURE 12.44
Spreadsheet template for the Sound's Alive case

To avoid large values in the spreadsheet, enter all dollar calculations in thousands. For example, enter labor costs as 995.10 and overhead costs as 1536.12.

Phase Two: Bringing Competition into the Model

With her spreadsheet complete, Marissa is confident that entering the home theater speaker market would be lucrative for Sound's Alive. However, she has not considered one factor in her calculations—competition. The current market leader and company she is most concerned about is the Bose Corporation. Bose pioneered the concept of a satellite speaker system, and its AMT series is very successful. Marissa is concerned that Bose will enter the home market, cutting into her gross revenues. If Bose does enter the market, Marissa believes that Sound's Alive would still make money; however, she would have to revise her gross revenues estimate from $6 million to $4 million for 2004.

To account for the competition factor, Marissa revises her spreadsheet by adding a Competitive Assumptions section. Cell F4 will contain either a 0 (no competition) or a 1 (if Bose enters the market). Cells F5 and F6 provide the gross revenue estimates (in thousands of dollars) for the two possibilities. Modify your spreadsheet to take these options into account. Use the IF( ) function for the gross revenues for 2004 (cell B12). If Bose does enter the market, not only would Marissa's gross revenues be lower, but the labor, materials, and overhead costs would also be lower because Sound's Alive would be making and selling fewer speakers. Marissa thinks that if Bose enters the market, her 2004 labor costs would be $859,170; 2004 material costs would be $702,950; and 2004 overhead costs would be $1,288,750. She believes that her growth rate assumptions would stay the same whether or not Bose enters the market. Add these possible values to your spreadsheet using the IF( ) function in the appropriate cells.

Look at the net profits for 2004 through 2007. In particular, examine the NPV for the two scenarios: Bose does or does not enter the home theater speaker market.

Phase Three: Bringing Uncertainty into the Model

Jim Allison, the chief of operations at Sound's Alive and a quantitative methods specialist, plays a key role in providing Marissa with estimates for the various revenues and costs. He is uneasy about the basic estimates for the growth rates. For example, although market research indicates that a 9% gross revenue increase per year is reasonable, Jim knows that if this value is 7%, for example, the profit values and the NPV would be quite different. Even more troublesome is a potential tax increase, which would hit Sound's Alive hard. Jim believes that the tax rate could vary around the expected 30% figure. Finally, Jim is uncomfortable with the industry's standard estimate of 18% for the SG&A rate. Jim thinks that this value could be higher or even lower.

The Sound's Alive problem is too complicated for solving with what-if analysis because seven assumed values could change: the growth rates for gross revenues, labor, materials, overhead costs, tax rate, SG&A percent, and whether or not Bose enters the market. Jim believes that a Monte Carlo simulation would be a better approach. Jim thinks that the behavior of these variables can be modeled as follows:

Gross Revenues (%): normally distributed, mean = 9.9, std dev = 1.4

Labor Growth (%): normally distributed, mean = 3.45, std dev = 1.0

Materials (%)	Probability
4	0.10
5	0.15
6	0.15
7	0.25
8	0.25
9	0.10

Overhead (%)	Probability
2	0.20
3	0.35
4	0.25
5	0.20

Tax Rate (%)	Probability
30	0.15
32	0.30
34	0.30
36	0.25

SG&A (%)	Probability
15	0.05
16	0.10
17	0.20
18	0.25
19	0.20
20	0.20

Finally, Jim and Marissa agree that there is a 50/50 chance that Bose will enter the market.

1. Use simulation to analyze the Sound's Alive problem. Based on your results, what is the expected net profit for the years 2004 through 2007, and what is the expected NPV for this business venture?
2. The Board of Trustees told Marissa that the stockholders would feel comfortable with this business venture if its NPV is at least $5 million. What are the chances that Sound's Alive home theater venture will result in an NPV of $5 million or more?

CASE 12.3: THE FOXRIDGE INVESTMENT GROUP

Inspired by a case written by MBA students Fred Hirsch and Ray Rogers for Professor Larry Weatherford at the University of Wyoming.

The Foxridge Investment Group buys and sells rental income properties in Southwest Virginia. Bill Hunter, president of Foxridge, has asked for your assistance in analyzing a small apartment building the group is interested in purchasing.

The property in question is a small two-story structure with three rental units on each floor. The purchase price of the property is $170,000 representing $30,000 in land value and $140,000 in buildings and improvements. Foxridge will depreciate the buildings and improvements value on a straight-line basis over 27.5 years. The Foxridge Group will make a down payment of $40,000 to acquire the property and finance the remainder of the purchase price over 20 years with an 11% fixed-rate loan with payments due annually. Figure 12.45 (and the file Fig12-45.xls on your data disk) summarizes this and other pertinent information.

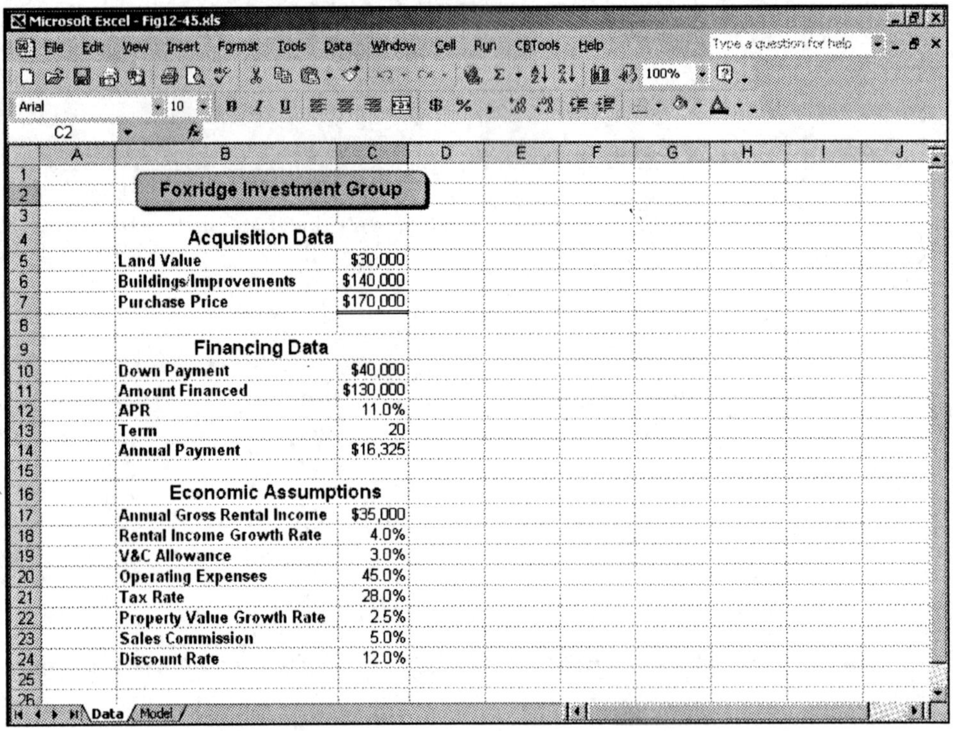

Foxridge Investment Group	
Acquisition Data	
Land Value	$30,000
Buildings/Improvements	$140,000
Purchase Price	$170,000
Financing Data	
Down Payment	$40,000
Amount Financed	$130,000
APR	11.0%
Term	20
Annual Payment	$16,325
Economic Assumptions	
Annual Gross Rental Income	$35,000
Rental Income Growth Rate	4.0%
V&C Allowance	3.0%
Operating Expenses	45.0%
Tax Rate	28.0%
Property Value Growth Rate	2.5%
Sales Commission	5.0%
Discount Rate	12.0%

FIGURE 12.45

Assumptions for the Foxridge Investment Group case

If all units are fully occupied, Mr. Hunter expects the property to generate rental income of $35,000 in the first year and expects to increase the rent at the rate of inflation (currently 4%). Because vacancies occur and some residents may not always be able to pay their rent, Mr. Hunter factors in a 3% vacancy & collection (V&C) allowance against rental income. Operating expenses are expected to be approximately 45% of rental income. The group's marginal tax rate is 28%.

If the group decides to purchase this property, their plan is to hold it for five years and then sell it to another investor. Presently, property values in this area are increasing at a rate of approximately 2.5% per year. The group will have to pay a sales commission of 5% of the gross selling price when they sell the property.

Figure 12.46 shows a spreadsheet model Mr. Hunter developed to analyze this problem. This model first uses the data and assumptions given in Figure 12.45 to generate the expected net cash flows in each of the next five years. It then provides a final summary of the proceeds expected from selling the property at the end of five years. The total net present value (NPV) of the project is then calculated in cell I18 using the discount rate of 12% in cell C24 of Figure 12.45. Thus, after discounting all the future cash flows associated with this investment by 12% per year, the investment still generates an NPV of $2,007.

Although the group has been using this type of analysis for many years to make investment decisions, one of Mr. Hunter's investment partners recently read an article in the *Wall Street Journal* about risk analysis and simulation using spreadsheets. As a result, the partner realizes there is quite a bit of uncertainty associated with many of the economic assumptions shown in Figure 12.45. After explaining the potential problem to Mr. Hunter, the two have decided to apply

Microsoft Excel - Fig12-45.xls

	Cash Flows in Year				
	1	2	3	4	5
Gross Income	$35,000	$36,400	$37,856	$39,370	$40,945
Less:					
V&C Allowance	$1,050	$1,092	$1,136	$1,181	$1,228
Operating Exp.	$15,750	$16,380	$17,035	$17,717	$18,425
Net Operating Income	$18,200	$18,928	$19,685	$20,473	$21,291
Less:					
Depreciation	$5,091	$5,091	$5,091	$5,091	$5,091
Interest	$14,300	$14,077	$13,830	$13,556	$13,251
Taxable Income	($1,191)	($240)	$764	$1,826	$2,950
Taxes Paid (Saved)	($333)	($67)	$214	$511	$826
Principal Paid	$2,025	$2,248	$2,495	$2,769	$3,074
Net Cash Flow	$2,209	$2,670	$3,146	$3,636	$4,141

Financial Summary	
Sales price @ year 5	$192,339
Less:	
Selling expense	$9,617
Tax basis	$144,545
Taxable gain	$38,177
Proceeds from sale	$182,722
Less:	
Taxes	$10,690
Loan payoff	$117,390
Net cash from sale	$54,643
PV of sale proceeds	$31,006
PV of cash flows	$11,001
Less: Original Equity	$40,000
Total NPV	$2,007

Data | Model

FIGURE 12.46
Cash flow and financial summary for the Foxridge Investment Group case

simulation to this model before making a decision. Because neither of them know how to do simulation, they have asked for your assistance.

To model the uncertainty in this decision problem, Mr. Hunter and his partner have decided that the growth in rental income from one year to the next could vary uniformly from 2% to 6% in years 2 through 5. Similarly, they believe the V&C allowance in any year could be as low as 1% and as high as 5%, with 3% being the most likely outcome. They think the operating expenses in each year should be normally distributed with a mean of 45% and standard deviation of 2% but should never be less than 40% and never greater than 50% of gross income. Finally, they believe the property value growth rate could be as small as 1% or as large as 5%, with 2.5% being the most likely outcome.

1. Revise the spreadsheets shown in Figures 12.45 and 12.46 to reflect the uncertainties outlined.
2. Construct a 95% confidence interval for the average total NPV the Foxridge Investment Group can expect if they undertake this project. (Use 500 replications.) Interpret this confidence interval.
3. Based on your analysis, what is the probability of this project generating a positive total NPV if the group uses a 12% discount rate?
4. Suppose the investors are willing to buy the property if the expected total NPV is greater than zero. Based on your analysis, should they buy this property?
5. Assume the investors decide to increase the discount rate to 14% and repeat questions 2, 3, and 4.
6. What discount rate results in a 90% chance of the project generating a positive total NPV?